The
International Development Directory

Sarah Harland
Dave Griffiths

and
Louise Walker

DIRECTORY OF SOCIAL CHANGE

Published by
The Directory of Social Change
24 Stephenson Way
London NW1 2DP
tel: 020 7209 5151, fax: 020 7209 5049
e-mail: info@dsc.org.uk
from whom further copies and a full publications list are available.

The Directory of Social Change is a registered charity no. 800517

Copyright © Directory of Social Change 2001

All rights reserved. **No part of this book may be stored in a retrieval system or reproduced in any form whatsoever without prior permission in writing from the publisher.** This book is sold subject to the condition that it shall not, by way of trade or otherwise, be lent, re-sold, hired out or otherwise circulated without the publisher's prior permission in any form of binding or cover other than that in which it is published, and without a similar condition including this condition being imposed on the subsequent purchaser.

ISBN 1 900360 85 3

British Library Cataloguing in Publication Data
A catalogue record for this book is available from the British Library

Cover design by Gabriele Kern
Text design by Linda Parker
Typeset by Directory of Social Change, Liverpool
Printed and bound by Antony Rowe, Chippenham

Other Directory of Social Change departments in London:
Courses and conferences tel: 020 7209 4949
Charity Centre tel: 020 7209 1015
Research tel: 020 7209 4422
Finance and administration tel: 020 7209 0902

Directory of Social Change Northern Office:
Federation House, Hope Street, Liverpool L1 9BW
Courses and conferences tel: 0151 708 0117
Research tel: 0151 708 0136

CONTENTS

Introduction		**5**
Part 1	**ORGANISATIONS WORKING IN DEVELOPING COUNTRIES**	**11**
	Geographical index	17
	Subject index	28
	Alphabetical listing	37
Part 2	**SOURCES OF FUNDING**	**243**
	1 Community Fund	247
	2 European Union	251
	3 Overseas Aid Committees	265
	4 UK Government Departments	273
	5 Grant-making Trusts	287
	Alphabetical listing	291
Index		**431**
Further reading and information		**441**

INTRODUCTION

Welcome to *The International Development Directory*. This guide, which replaces *The Third World Directory* published by DSC in the 1990s, is split into two main sections. The first provides information on organisations working in developing countries and the second covers sources of funding for such organisations.

Part 1 Organisations working in developing countries

This section contains details of 250 UK organisations working in developing countries. It is a general reference tool for anyone who works in the voluntary sector and for members of the public, including people looking to donate money or volunteer. There are geographic and subject indexes to help find organisations of particular interest and advice on how to use the information given.

The introduction to the section contains information for people wishing to volunteer or to find paid work with a charity. This includes a list of organisations that provide advice for potential volunteers, and details of job bulletins available online.

Charitable expenditure on work in developing countries

The total expenditure of the organisations in this guide on work in developing countries is about £1 billion a year. Taking into account the numerous smaller charities not included, it is probably reasonable to assume that about 10% of total UK charitable expenditure is on international development work. Where this money comes from is covered below – see *Part 2 Sources of funding* (page 6).

The organisations in this section that have the largest expenditure on work in developing countries are as follows.

Organisation	Year organisation started work	Expenditure on causes in developing countries
1. Oxfam	1942	£118 million (1999/2000)
2. Save the Children (UK)	1919	£80 million (1998/99)
3. British Red Cross	1870	£54 million (1999)
4. Christian Aid	1945	£53 million (1999/2000)
5. ActionAid	1971	£48 million (1999)
6. IPPF	1952	Estimate £38 million (1999)
7. CARE International UK	1946	£37 million (1999/2000)
8. Tearfund	1970	£34 million (1999/2000)
9. Marie Stopes International	1921	£34 million (1999)
10. Concern Worldwide	1968	£24 million (1998)

These organisations are recognised as major players internationally and are among the most well-known charities in the UK. According to figures published by the Charities Aid Foundation, Oxfam has been among the top five fundraising charities in the UK for several years, and others consistently appear towards the top of CAF's listing (*Dimensions 2000 Volume 2: CAF's Top 500 Fundraising Charities*, 1997/98 supplement published 2001).

Furthermore our top ten are all well established charities, having started work between 30 and 130 years ago. Most of them work across several countries in areas of relief, development and campaigning, although some concentrate on one area more than another. In general these organisations, which may initially have been set up in response to a particular crisis, have moved over the years towards a greater emphasis on sustainable development rather than short-term relief work. And it is interesting to note that, although this field of activity is not widely represented in the guide as a whole, two out of the top ten organisations listed, IPPF and Marie Stopes International, focus very specifically on reproductive healthcare.

Many of the main development organisations are now also active supporters of campaigns focusing on issues of fair trade and world debt. It is worth noting that despite the success of the Jubilee 2000 campaign, the international millennium movement to cancel the unpayable debts of the world's poorest countries, 22 of the poorest countries still spend more on servicing their debt than they spend on health services.

Seven of the ten charities provided a breakdown of expenditure according to region in their annual reports. About half of their combined work took place in Africa, with about a third in Asia and the Middle East (including CIS). Work in Latin America accounted for about 15%, with the remainder in Eastern Europe.

Smaller organisations, including many which were not large enough to be included in this guide, are often more specialised in their areas of work and geographical focus.

Part 2 Sources of funding

This section contains information on funding for UK organisations working in developing countries. The main sources covered in this guide, and the annual amount given for work in developing countries, are as follows:

Community Fund *(formerly NLCB)*	£19 million
Overseas Aid Committees	£5.8 million
UK government departments	about £180 million
215 grant-making trusts	£50 million

However, these totals pale into insignificance alongside the massive sums available from the European Union. The budget lines listed in this guide provide funds amounting to some £4.4 billion (or €7 billion) – although only a relatively small proportion of this will go to UK agencies.

The £1 billion expenditure by charities in this guide therefore cannot be accounted for by adding up the sources of funding listed. So where is the rest of the money coming from? Charity shops and other trading are very important for organisations such as Oxfam. However, very large amounts of money are also given by members of the public, through legacies and donations of goods to charity shops as well as cash gifts. CAF research indicates that international agencies are the most popular charities with the general public, to judge by the amount of voluntary income received in recent years (*Dimensions 2000 Volume 2: CAF's Top 500 Fundraising Charities*, 1997/98 supplement). The *Further reading and information* section at the end of this guide lists publications that may be useful to fundraisers aiming to raise money from individual donors.

The aim in this guide has been to include sources of funding that are accessible to most UK organisations (rather than just the larger ones). For each funding source, where possible, the guide provides criteria on who is eligible to apply for a grant, examples of previous beneficiaries, how to apply and contact details.

Some other sources of funding are also outlined in the introduction to the section. Our standard advice is that in any fundraising strategy organisations should look to have a spread of funders and should not be dependent on just one or two.

Unfortunately it was beyond the focus of this guide to provide information specifically geared towards local fundraisers in developing countries. However, this area is covered in some detail in *The Worldwide Fundraiser's Handbook* (also published by DSC).

The availability of information

Since the publication of *The Third World Directory*, the development of the internet has made research for this directory a lot easier. Most of the organisations listed in the first section of this guide have a website address and provide many services such as online donation forms and application forms for volunteers, listings of job vacancies, online books and newsletters, and links to related websites.

Of the sources of funding, only the Community Fund, the European Union and government departments make good use of the internet. The Overseas Aid Committees do not have websites, neither do most grant-making trusts.

We aimed to include as much relevant up-to-date information as possible about the bodies included in both sections of the guide. In the course of research, most of the organisations contacted were extremely helpful and efficient in providing us with information. Several actually came to us asking to be included. In carrying out our research, however, we occasionally came across organisations which refused to provide us with accounts or other information. However, we strongly take the view that it is public information, and so have included as many relevant organisations as we could find.

And finally

The research for this book has been carried out as fully and carefully as possible. We are grateful to the many officers, trustees and others who have helped us in this. Although drafts of all the entries were, where possible, sent to the organisations concerned and any comments noted, the text and any mistakes within it remain ours rather than theirs.

We would also like to thank the staff of BOND and Zoë Mars at the Institute of Development Studies for their wealth of specialist knowledge, and the many officers at the Charity Commission for their help in ordering files.

We are aware that the information in this guide is incomplete or will become out of date. We are equally sure that we have missed some relevant bodies. We regret such imperfections. If any reader comes across omissions or mistakes in this guide, please let us know so that they can be rectified in the future. A telephone call or e-mail to the Liverpool Office Research Department of the Directory of Social Change is all that is needed (tel: 0151 708 0136; e-mail: north@dsc.org.uk).

Glossary

Please note, in the entries we have generally used the terms provided in each charity's own literature.

Caucasus is a region and mountain system situated between the Black and Azor seas (west) and the Caspian sea (east), and includes parts of Armenia, Azerbaijan, Georgia and Russia.

CIS countries (the Commonwealth of International States): Armenia, Azerbaijan, Belarus, Georgia, Kazakhstan, Krygyzstan, Moldova, Russia, Tajikistan, Turkmenistan, Ukraine and Uzbekistan.

Developing countries In this guide we tend to use this term in our general text. In entries we usually adopt the equivalent term used by the organisations being discussed which may be one of the following: the third world, less/least/under-developed countries, poor/poorer/poorest countries, and the South. There is no universally accepted term, or any such accepted definition of what constitutes a developing country. There is wide variation in the level of poverty in the countries covered in this book.

Development organisations refers to organisations carrying out long-term work in a country, rather than short-term emergency relief work

Eastern European countries are for the purposes of this guide: Albania, Bosnia-Herzegovina, Bulgaria, Croatia, Czech Republic, Estonia, Hungary, Federal Republic of Yugoslavia (this is the union of the two related republics of Montenegro and Serbia), Latvia, Lithuania, Poland, Republic of Macedonia, Romania, Slovakia and Slovenia.

FYROM, Former Yugoslav Republic of Macedonia, is an alternative name used for Republic of Macedonia.

International, worldwide, overseas are terms sometimes used instead of 'developing countries'.

Local is used in this book to mean 'local' in the developing country of work (i.e. indigenous) – not local in the UK.

Ngo is an acronym for non-governmental organisation. We use it to refer to voluntary organisations which work internationally and are independent from the government in the country of operation.

Paid staff are those who receive a regular income, comparable to the income of other paid charity workers in the UK (i.e. the term does not include those who receive £100 a month, for example, and who have to raise the rest of the income themselves).

Volunteers are unwaged; they donate their time and skills. They may receive some finance (for example, grants, living expenses, travel costs) and have free accommodation, but will not receive a salary or payment for their work.

Other useful contacts

Civicus is an international alliance of citizens and their organisations that works towards strengthening citizen action and civil society worldwide. *(e-mail: info@civicus.org; website: www.civicus.org).* UK contact: *NCVO, Regent's Wharf, 8 All Saints Street, London N1 9RL (tel: 020 7713 6161; fax: 020 7713 6300; Minicom: 020 7278 1289; e-mail: ncvo@ncvo-vol.org.uk; website: www.ncvo-vol.org.uk).*

Coalition of Aid & Development Agencies in Northern Ireland (CADA ni) is a network of aid and development agencies, working to enhance awareness of development issues in Northern Ireland and influence policy at local, national and international governmental level. *5th Floor, Howard House, 1 Brunswick Street, Belfast BT2 7GE (tel: 028 9032 4202: fax: 028 9032 4133; e-mail: cadani@dialstart.net).*

The Commonwealth Secretariat is the main inter-governmental agency of the Commonwealth, facilitating consultation and cooperation between member governments and countries. *Marlborough House, Pall Mall, London SW1Y 5HX (tel: 020 7839 3411; fax: 020 7930 6128; e-mail: info@commonwealth.int; website: www.commonwealth.org).*

International Monetary Fund (IMF) works to facilitate international monetary cooperation and financial stability and provides a permanent forum for consultation, advice and assistance on financial issues. *700 19th Street, N.W., Washington DC 20431 USA (tel: +202 623 7000; fax: +202 623 4661; e-mail: publicaffairs@imf.org; website: www.imf.org).*

Open Society Institute (OSI) is a charity that develops and implements a range of programmes in civil society, education, media, public health and human and women's rights as well as social, legal and economic reform. OSI is based in New York, and operates network-wide programmes and grant-making activities. It provides support and assistance to Soros foundations in Central and Eastern Europe and the former Soviet Union, Guatemala, Haiti, Mongolia and Southern and West Africa. *400 West 59th Street, New York, New York 10019 USA (tel: +212 757 2323; fax: +212 548 4679/4600; website: www.soros.org).*

Organisation for Economic Co-operation and Development (OECD) provides governments in 29 countries with a setting in which to discuss, develop and perfect economic and social policy. *2 Rue André Pascal, F–75775 Paris Cedex 16, France (tel: +33 1 45 24 82 00; website: www.oecd.org).*

People in Aid is a UK organisation that promotes best practice in the management and support of aid personnel, and has drawn up a Code of Best Practice. *9 Grosvenor Crescent, London SW1X 7EJ (tel & fax: 020 7235 0895; e-mail: aidpeople@aol.com; website: www.peopleinaid.org).*

PART 1

ORGANISATIONS WORKING IN DEVELOPING COUNTRIES

CONTENTS	
Introduction, containing information for volunteers and jobseekers	11
Typical entry	16
Geographical index, and how to use it	17
Subject index, and how to use it	28
Alphabetical listing of organisations	37

INTRODUCTION

This section includes organisations (both registered and non-registered charities):
- working in developing countries, including Eastern Europe, the Commonwealth of International States (CIS) and poorer countries in the Middle East
- working in development, emergency relief, campaigning and development education
- with an expenditure of £150,000 or over a year, recorded in UK-based accounts.

It does not include:
- environment or conservation charities unless they work towards providing immediate economic relief to local people
- organisations which do not have a UK-office
- commercial organisations, e.g. those which take people on expeditions
- organisations which work for peace and reconciliation only
- organisations with an expenditure of under £150,000 a year
- organisations that work with refugees only in the UK.

Who should use this section?

This section is a useful reference tool for those who want general information on UK organisations working in developing countries, including people who work for development organisations, potential donors and potential volunteers/jobseekers.

The indexes provide a good starting point, and will help you to locate those organisations that work in the geographical or subject areas of interest to you.

The intention is that each entry gives you a feel for the organisation: what kinds of values it upholds, what types of causes and work it is most interested in, and its size. In addition to this, some practical information is provided such as contact details and how many members the organisation has. We also include a website address where available, and a description of the website's contents. In most instances, the entries in this section will serve only as a starting point for your research, and the websites provide an invaluable second port of call.

Volunteering overseas

Of the organisations listed in this guide, over 100 welcome volunteers for work overseas. People interested in such opportunities should use the indexes to find organisations in their areas of interest, and then read the *Volunteers/jobseekers* section of the entry for each organisation carefully, finding those which suit your preferences.

Organisations vary in what they require of volunteers. For instance: the level of previous experience required, costs which need to be covered by the volunteers themselves, how long the placements can last, what training is offered and what types of work they can be involved in. BESO, for example, requires people with expert skills, who are usually retired or near retirement age since they must be flexible in terms of availability for assignments. These volunteers have all their expenses paid. This can be compared with The Project Trust, which offers one-year voluntary work placements abroad to school leavers, at a cost of £280 a month.

Volunteering in the UK

Again, opportunities for volunteers in the UK vary from charity to charity. Some organisations actively welcome volunteers – ActionAid, for example, recognises the value of utilising the skills and time of volunteers, and at the same time acknowledges that it can offer training and experience, as well as other benefits to the volunteers themselves. Other organisations run internship programmes, where volunteers are mentored and closely trained. Some bodies, unfortunately, do not have the organisational capacity for volunteers.

Volunteers in the UK are most commonly required to help with routine office administration tasks and with fundraising activities and events. The former type of work usually requires some sort of regular commitment, such as one afternoon a week. Help with fundraising may be required on a one-off basis, for instance staffing the telephones during a charity's fundraising week.

Approaching organisations for paid work

This is a highly competitive field. Often the best way in is by acquiring experience through voluntary positions in the area of work you are interested in, or by getting related work experience in another sector or type of voluntary organisation.

Many of the organisations in this book, particularly the bigger and most well-known ones, receive hundreds of applications from hopeful individuals looking for work. These organisations often post up-to-date lists of job vacancies on their websites and some have compiled packs of very comprehensive information about their recruitment processes, also available from the website. You should be careful to carry out as much research about the charity and its recruitment processes as possible before approaching them – making full use of website services saves the charity time and money, while also giving you the latest information available.

Additional information for volunteers and jobseekers

Volunteering organisations

The following organisations' main area of work is to offer short-term opportunities overseas to volunteers. They all have entries in this section of the guide. These organisations are well-organised in terms of providing support and structured placements. Please note, many other organisations also have well-run volunteering programmes, as shown in their entries.

- AFS – International Youth Development
- Commonwealth Youth Exchange
- GAP Activity Projects
- i to i international projects
- International Voluntary Services
- The Project Trust
- Raleigh International
- Voluntary Service Overseas
- WORLDwrite

Volunteering opportunities with smaller organisations

Organisations too small to be given an entry in this guide and which have volunteering and paid work opportunities are listed below, with a brief description of their work.

Africa Book Case Positions for teachers in Africa and for young people to give talks to schools in the UK *(www.africabookcase.com)*.

The Daneford Trust Provides overseas placements for young people from inner-city London *(e-mail: dfdtrust@aol.com)*.

Emmanuel Hospital Association There are opportunities for: medical and nursing staff e.g. ophthalmologists, ENT surgeons, neonatal nurses; community health and development workers e.g. HIV/AIDS researchers and development workers skilled in micro enterprise; and other people e.g. videographers and production managers *(www.eha.org.uk)*.

The Friends of the Gambia Association (FoTGA) Voluntary positions for administration in the UK and project work in The Gambia *(www.fotga.org.uk)*.

Habitat for Humanity – Global Village Programme Runs short-term mission programmes and has long-term placements, for people to work on housing projects *(www.hfhgb.org)*.

HCJB–UK Opportunities for Christian professionals in Ecuador *(www.hcjb.org)*.

The India Development Group (UK) Limited (IDG) Opportunities to work in India, in the areas of appropriate technology and rural development *(e-mail: idguk@clata.co.uk)*.

International China Concern UK (ICC) Short-term opportunities to work in orphanages in Hong Kong. Also long-term opportunities for people with a medical qualification. Christians only *(www.icc-uk.org.uk)*.

Joint Cooperation Trust Opportunities for teachers in Tanzania for one-year placements and fundraisers in the UK *(e-mail: tice@btinternet.com)*.

Kings World Trust for Children Administration tasks in Haslemere, Surrey and for doctors, nurses and teachers (especially TEFL) in India *(www.haslemere.com/kwtc)*.

Medical Missionary Association Healthserve Helps Christian healthcare professionals to get out into the mission field *(www.mmahealthserve.org.uk)*.

Operation Sunshine Its principal need is for volunteers to sort and pack donated goods for shipment to developing countries *(e-mail: christinelewis@zoom.co.uk)*.

Peace Brigades International Volunteers take on roles in providing international observation in conflict areas to human rights defenders and peace activists threatened as a result of their work for social justice *(www.igc.apc.org/pbi/index.html)*.

The Right Hand Trust Sends Christians aged 18–30 to developing countries for eight-month placements, to be involved in teaching, administrative work, leading sports and other work in the parish *(http://ourworld.compuserve.com/homepages/righthandtrust)*.

Sudan Volunteer Programme Opportunities to teach English in Sudan for at least 12 weeks *(www.svp-uk.com)*.

Teaching & Projects Abroad Each year this organisation has 1,000 places available for people from around the world to teach English and work in other practical ways *(www.teaching-abroad.co.uk)*.

Organisations providing services and information

Organisations providing academic and vocational training for work in developing countries are listed under *Places of study & training* in the index (see p. 31). The following organisations provide other services and information for people looking to volunteer and work with a charity – additional information is provided where the organisation does not already appear in the guide.

BVALG – British Volunteer Agencies' Liaison Group Run by International Service – see their entry in this guide. BVALG coordinates volunteers to work for four development organisations.

Christian Medical Fellowship

Christians Abroad/World Service Enquiries

ICA:UK

International Health Exchange

National Centre for Volunteering Works to increase awareness of the opportunities and benefits for volunteers *(Regent's Wharf, 8 All Saints Street, London N1 9RL, tel: 020 7520 8900).*

RedR International

Returned Volunteer Action RVA publishes a range of booklets and information on volunteering issues including an introductory pack comprising the two publications *Volunteering and Overseas Development: A Guide to Opportunities* and *Thinking About Volunteering (1 Amwell Street, London EC1R 1TH, tel: 020 7278 0804, e-mail:retvolact@lineone.net).*

Working for a Charity Provides information and training for people wishing to transfer their skills to the voluntary sector *(The Peel Centre, Percy Circus, London WC1X 8EY, tel: 020 7833 8220, fax: 020 7833 1820, e-mail: enquiries@wfac.org.uk).*

Job bulletins advertising voluntary or paid positions

These are available at the following website addresses.

AlertNet: www.alertnet.org
BOND: www.bond.org.uk
Charity Job: www.charityjob.co.uk
ELDIS: Jobs & Job Hunting: http://nt1.ids.ac.uk/eldis/jobs/job_lele.htm
Idealist Jobsearch: www.idealist.org
OneWorld Jobs: www.oneworld.org
ReliefWeb: www.reliefweb.int
Returned Volunteers Action: retvolact@lineone.net (e-mail address only)
Voluntary Work Information Service and Working Abroad:
   www.workingabroad.com
World Service Enquiry: www.wse.org.uk

The Fictitious International Charity

Supports rural medical and women's development projects

Geographical focus: Ethiopia, Rwanda, Sierra Leone, Uganda

One World Building, Main Street
Western Town ZX48 2QQ
Tel: 040 1000 0000; **Fax:** 040 1000 0001
e-mail: fia@freeserve.org.uk
Website: www.fia.freeserve.org.uk
Correspondent: Jack North, Secretary

Expenditure: £300,000 (1999/2000)

Staffing: 14 full-time, salaried staff, of which 3 are based in the UK and 11 in Africa (indigenous where possible).

Website information: A breakdown of programmes by country; newsletters; how to get involved.

General: FIA was formed in 1974, by Jack North and Liz West out of their concern for village primary healthcare and women's development.

FIA never initiates projects but responds to needs expressed at community level. …During 2001 FIA will be piloting a small number of projects in Eritrea.

Membership: No formal scheme, donors and supporters are sent the newsletter.

Publications: Quarterly newsletter and occasional reports.

Trading: Catalogue only, available from the address above.

Volunteers/jobseekers: No opportunities for volunteers overseas. Occasional opportunities to help out in the UK office with administrative tasks and special events.

Name of the charity/ngo

Summary of work

Where the charity works

Contact address, telephone and fax numbers; e-mail, website addresses if available

Contact person

Total expenditure in the most recent financial year

Staffing – including numbers, where based, full or part-time, and salaried or volunteers

Charity's website: a summary of information available there

General information about the charity, describing its aims and different areas of work, giving examples of current projects

Membership – information about membership for individuals or organisations, such as number of members, subscription costs and what the members receive

Publications – details of newsletters, journals and books available from the organisation

Trading – description of items for sale; how to obtain a catalogue; where shops are located etc.

Volunteers/jobseekers: opportunities in the UK and overseas; how to get involved

GEOGRAPHICAL INDEX

This index lists organisations under the countries in which they work. However, there are various regions seeking greater or total independence from their current government. We have listed these under the internationally recognised country (at the time of publication of this guide). For example, Chechnya is listed under Russia, East Timor under Indonesia, Kosovo and Montenegro under the Federal Republic of Yugoslavia, Palestine under Israel, and Tibet under China. Serbia is also listed under the Federal Republic of Yugoslavia.

Sometimes the names of countries have changed or more than one name exists; occasionally we use simplified versions of fuller names. Examples include Myanmar, which is used for Burma; Republic of Congo, which is used for Congo Brazzaville; and North Korea, which is used for the Democratic People's Republic of Korea (DPR Korea). Zaire is not used, because it is the former name of the Democratic Republic of Congo.

Countries covered in this index

The countries listed are those which the organisations in this section have identified as their geographical focus. Please note that we have excluded wealthier countries from this list. Organisations are not listed in this index if they either stated that they had a worldwide focus, or if we were not able to identify what their geographical focus was.

For the purposes of this index, there are six main headings: Africa, America, Asia, Australasia & The Pacific, Commonwealth of Independent States and Eastern Europe. The first three of these are broken down into regions; for example, Africa is split into North Africa, Eastern Africa etc. The countries covered by each region are listed on page 18.

Organisations working in three or more countries in a region appear under the region heading. Similarly, organisations working in three or more regions in Africa, Asia and America appear under the continent heading. Those countries marked with an ★ on page 18 do not appear separately in the index. This is because any organisations working there also work in other countries and are therefore included under the approriate region or continent heading.

The index is a rough guide. Use it to locate organisations working in countries of interest. If a charity is listed under a broader region or continent, you will usually find more detailed information about the area where the charity works under *Geographical focus* in the charity's entry.

The categories for the index follow.

Africa p19

North Africa p19
Algeria; Egypt; Libya★; Morocco; Tunisia★

Eastern Africa p19
Burundi; Djibouti★; Eritrea; Ethiopia; Kenya; Rwanda; Somalia; Sudan; Tanzania; Uganda

Central Africa p20
Central African Republic; Democratic Republic of Congo; Republic of Congo; Gabon

Western Africa p20
Benin★; Burkina Faso; Cameroon; Chad; Equatorial Guinea★; Gambia★; Ghana; Guinea★; Guinea Bissau★; Ivory Coast; Liberia; Mali; Mauritania; Niger; Nigeria; Republic of Cape Verde; Sao Tome & Principe★; Senegal; Sierra Leone; Togo★

Southern Africa p21
Angola; Botswana★; Comoros Islands; Lesotho★; Madagascar; Malawi; Mauritius; Mozambique; Namibia; Réunion★; Seychelles; South Africa; Swaziland; Tristan da Cunha★; Zambia; Zimbabwe

America p22

Central America p22
Belize; Costa Rica; El Salvador; Guatemala; Honduras; Mexico; Nicaragua; Panama★

Caribbean p22
Anguilla★; Antigua &; Barbuda★; Aruba★; Bahamas★; Barbados★; Bermuda★; British Virgin Islands★; Cayman Islands★; Cuba; Curacao★; Dominica; Dominican Republic; Grenada★; Guadeloupe★; Haiti; Jamaica; Martinique★; Montserrat★; Puerto Rico★; St Helen & dependencies★; St Kitts & Nevis★; St Lucia★; St Maarten★; St Vincent & The Grenadines★; Trinidad & Tobago

South America p23
Argentina★; Bolivia; Brazil; Chile; Colombia; Ecuador; French Guiana★; Guyana; Paraguay★; Peru; Suriname★; Uruguay★; Venezuela

Asia p25

Middle East p24
Bahrain★; Iran; Iraq; Israel; Jordan; Kuwait★; Lebanon; Qatar★; Oman★; Syria★; Turkey; Yemen

North & East Asia p24
China; Macau; Mongolia; North Korea

Southern Asia p24
Afghanistan; Bangladesh; Bhutan★; India; Maldives; Nepal; Pakistan; Sri Lanka

South East Asia p25
Brunei; Cambodia; Indonesia; Laos; Malaysia; Myanmar★; Philippines; Thailand; Vietnam

Australasia & The Pacific p26
American Samoa★; Cook Islands★; Fiji; French Polynesia★; Kiribati; Nauru★; Palau★; Papua New Guinea; Solomon Islands; Tonga★; Tuvalu★; Vanuatu★; Western Samoa★

Commonwealth of Independent States p26
Armenia; Azerbaijan; Belarus; Georgia; Kazakhstan★; Krygyzstan★; Moldova; Russia; Tajikistan; Turkmenistan★; Ukraine; Uzbekistan

Eastern Europe p27
Albania; Bosnia-Herzegovina; Bulgaria; Croatia★; Czech Republic★; Estonia★; Hungary; Latvia; Lithuania; Macedonia; Poland; Romania; Slovakia★; Slovenia★; Federal Republic of Yugoslavia

Africa

ACORD
Action International Ministries
Africa Centre
African Medical and Research Foundation UK
Aid to the Church in Need
BESO
BMS World Mission
Book Aid International
CAFOD
CARE International UK
Church Mission Society
Commonwealth Society for the Deaf
Commonwealth Youth Exchange Council
Duke of Edinburgh's Award International Association
Gaia Foundation
HelpAge International
Human Rights Watch
International Planned Parenthood Federation
International Records Management Trust
Leonard Cheshire International
Leprosy Mission
Médecins Sans Frontières
Muslim Aid
Oxfam
PLAN International UK
Sight Savers International
SIM International
Tearfund
Voluntary Service Overseas
Wycliffe Bible Translators

North Africa

International Voluntary Service
Operation Mobilisation

Algeria

Motivation

Egypt

Action Partners Ministries
Donkey Sanctuary
Education for Development
Opportunity International
PLAN International UK
Project Trust
St Francis Leprosy Guild

WOMANKIND Worldwide
World University Service

Morocco

International HIV/AIDS Alliance
St Francis Leprosy Guild

Eastern Africa

Action Against Hunger UK
Action on Disability and Development
ActionAid
Africa Educational Trust
Africa Inland Mission
APT Enterprise Development
Christian Outreach – Relief and Development
CONCERN Worldwide
Crosslinks
Emmanuel International
Evergreen Trust
FARM Africa
GOAL (UK)
Homeless International
ITDG
Mission Aviation Fellowship
Oasis Trust – Global Action Initiative
Population Concern
St Francis Leprosy Guild
Scottish Catholic International Aid Fund
Send a Cow (& StockAid)
Sense International
SOS Sahel International (UK)
Marie Stopes International
WaterAid
WOMANKIND Worldwide
World University Service
World Vision UK

Burundi

Children's Aid Direct
International Alert
World Emergency Relief

Eritrea

Mercy Corps Scotland

Ethiopia

ChildHope UK

Christian Children's Fund of Great Britain
Department of Development Studies
Donkey Sanctuary
Ethiopiaid
LEPRA
ORBIS
Tropical Health and Education Trust

Kenya

ABANTU for Development
Action Partners Ministries
AFRICA NOW
Associated Country Women of the World
ChildHope UK
Christians Abroad
Church of Scotland Board of World Mission
Concern Universal
Donkey Sanctuary
Education for Development
Grace and Compassion Benedictines
Healthlink Worldwide
HelpAge International
IMPACT Foundation
International Care and Relief
International Childcare Trust
Merlin
New Frontiers International
Traidcraft Exchange
World Emergency Relief

Rwanda

Health Unlimited
International Alert

Somalia

Catholic Institute for International Relations
Health Unlimited

Sudan

Action Partners Ministries
BibleLands
Islamic Relief Worldwide
ITDG
Ockenden International
Operation Mobilisation

Tanzania
Action Health
ATD Fourth World
Christians Abroad
Concern Universal
GAP Activity Projects
Healthlink Worldwide
IMPACT Foundation
Motivation
Tools for Self Reliance
Traidcraft Exchange
Twin

Uganda
Action Health
Alzheimers Disease International
Associated Country Women of the World
Busoga Trust
Christian Children's Fund of Great Britain
Hunger Project Trust
i to i international projects
International Care and Relief
International Connections Trust
Link Community Development
Ockenden International
Opportunity International
Project Trust
Spurgeon's Child Care
Tools for Self Reliance
Tropical Health and Education Trust
Twin
Uganda Society for Disabled Children

Central Africa
Central African Republic
Africa Inland Mission
Mission Aviation Fellowship

Democratic Republic of Congo
Action Against Hunger UK
Action Partners Ministries
Africa Inland Mission
Children's Aid Direct
CONCERN Worldwide
Food for the Hungry UK
Help International
Merlin
Mission Aviation Fellowship
St Francis Leprosy Guild
World Emergency Relief

Republic of Congo
Action Against Hunger UK

Gabon
Holy Ghost Fathers

Western Africa
Action Against Hunger UK
Action on Disability and Development
Action Partners Ministries
ActionAid
Associated Country Women of the World
Concern Universal
Healthlink Worldwide
Hunger Project Trust
Mercy Ships UK
New Frontiers International
St Francis Leprosy Guild
Village AiD

Burkina Faso
ATD Fourth World
Evergreen Trust
International HIV/AIDS Alliance
International Service

Cameroon
Christians Abroad
Twin

Chad
Africa Inland Mission
Mission Aviation Fellowship

Ghana
ABANTU for Development
AFS – International Youth Development
APT Enterprise Development
CamFed
Evergreen Trust
i to i international projects
International Needs Network
Link Community Development
Opportunity International
Population Concern
Raleigh International
Tools for Self Reliance
Tropical Health and Education Trust
Twin
WaterAid
WOMANKIND Worldwide
World Vision UK
WORLDwrite

Ivory Coast
ATD Fourth World

Liberia
Children's Aid Direct
CONCERN Worldwide
International Alert
Merlin
World Emergency Relief

Mali
International Service
Islamic Relief Worldwide
Mission Aviation Fellowship
SOS Sahel International

Mauritania
Operation Mobilisation

Niger
SOS Sahel International

Nigeria
ABANTU for Development
Alzheimers Disease International
Christians Abroad
Education for Development
Holy Ghost Fathers
International Connections Trust
KINGSCARE
Population Concern
Tropical Health and Education Trust
WaterAid

Republic of Cape Verde
One World Action

Senegal
ATD Fourth World
International HIV/AIDS Alliance
World Vision UK

Sierra Leone
APT Enterprise Development
Children in Crisis
Children's Aid Direct
CONCERN Worldwide
GOAL (UK)
Holy Ghost Fathers
LEPRA
Merlin
Marie Stopes International
Tools for Self Reliance
World Emergency Relief

Southern Africa
Action for Southern Africa
Africa Educational Trust
Africa Inland Mission
Associated Country Women of the World
Catholic Institute for International Relations
Church of Scotland Board of World Mission
CODA International Training
Canon Collins Educational Trust for Southern Africa
Find Your Feet
GAP Activity Projects
Healthlink Worldwide
Help International
Homeless International
Mercy Ships UK
Mission Aviation Fellowship
New Frontiers International
Oasis Trust – Global Action Initiative
One World Action
Operation Mobilisation
Opportunity International Project Trust
SIM International (UK)
Skillshare Africa
Marie Stopes International
Traidcraft Exchange
WaterAid

WOMANKIND Worldwide
World Vision UK

Angola
Action Against Hunger UK
CONCERN Worldwide
GOAL (UK)
Holy Ghost Fathers
St Francis Leprosy Guild

Comoros Islands
Mission Aviation Fellowship

Madagascar
African Medical and Research Foundation UK
ATD Fourth World
LEPRA
Mission Aviation Fellowship
Population Concern
St Francis Leprosy Guild
Marie Stopes International
WaterAid

Malawi
Christian Children's Fund of Great Britain
Concern Universal
Edinburgh Medical Missionary Society
Emmanuel International
Harvest Help
Hunger Project Trust
LEPRA
Tropical Health and Education Trust

Mauritius
ATD Fourth World
Healthlink Worldwide
Commonwealth Youth Exchange Council

Mozambique
Action Against Hunger UK
ActionAid
Christian Outreach – Relief and Development
Concern Universal
CONCERN Worldwide
Food for the Hungry UK
GOAL (UK)
Hunger Project Trust
LEPRA

POWER – The International Limb Project
Tools for Self Reliance

Namibia
Health Unlimited
Raleigh International

Seychelles
Commonwealth Society for the Deaf
Commonwealth Youth Exchange Council

South Africa
AFS – International Youth Development
Alzheimers Disease International
ChildHope UK
Crosslinks
FARM Africa
Holy Ghost Fathers
ITDG
Link Community Development
Scottish Catholic International Aid Fund
World Emergency Relief

Swaziland
World University Service

Zambia
Action on Disability and Development
Child Advocacy International
Christian Outreach – Relief and Development
Evergreen Trust
Harvest Help
International Care and Relief
International Children's Trust
International HIV/AIDS Alliance
International Needs Network
Kaloko Trust
Pestalozzi Children's Village Trust
POWER – The International Limb Project

St Francis Leprosy Guild
World Emergency Relief

Zimbabwe
Action on Disability and Development
AFRICA NOW
APT Enterprise Development
CamFed
Crosslinks
Pestalozzi Children's Village Trust
RFI for Community Mental Health
St Francis Leprosy Guild
Tools for Self Reliance

America
Alzheimers Disease International
Duke of Edinburgh's Award International Association
Oxfam

Central America
Action Against Hunger UK
ActionAid
AFS – International Youth Development
BMS World Mission
CAFOD
Catholic Institute for International Relations
CODA International Training
Food for the Hungry UK
HelpAge International
ITDG
Médecins Sans Frontières
Mercy Ships UK
One World Action
Operation Mobilisation
Opportunity International
PLAN International UK
Scottish Catholic International Aid Fund
Sense International
Tearfund

Belize
Commonwealth Society for the Deaf
Commonwealth Youth Exchange Council

Raleigh International
Sight Savers International
Voluntary Service Overseas

Costa Rica
i to i international projects
Latin Link
Raleigh International
RFI for Community Mental Health
Twin

El Salvador
Elimnu
GOAL (UK)
Health Unlimited
Motivation
World Vision UK

Guatemala
ATD Fourth World
Health Unlimited
Human Rights Watch
Jospice International
Just World Partners
Mission Aviation Fellowship
World Emergency Relief

Honduras
CONCERN Worldwide
GOAL (UK)
Jospice International
Leonard Cheshire International
Mercy Corps Scotland
Merlin
Mission Aviation Fellowship
Project Trust
Marie Stopes International
World Emergency Relief
World Vision UK

Mexico
Action International Ministries
ChildHope UK
Donkey Sanctuary
Healthlink Worldwide
Human Rights Watch
Hunger Project Trust
International Children's Trust
International HIV/AIDS Alliance

International Planned Parenthood Federation
Jospice International
Mission Aviation Fellowship
New Frontiers International
Spurgeon's Child Care
Twin
World Emergency Relief
World Vision UK

Nicaragua
Leonard Cheshire International
Mercy Corps Scotland
Motivation
Tools for Self Reliance
Twin

Caribbean
Associated Country Women of the World
Church of Scotland Board of World Mission
Commonwealth Society for the Deaf
Commonwealth Youth Exchange Council
HelpAge International
Human Rights Watch
International Records Management Trust
Leonard Cheshire International
Mercy Ships UK
RFI for Community Mental Health
Traidcraft Exchange

Cuba
Médecins Sans Frontières
Project Trust

Dominica
CAFOD
Catholic Institute for International Relations

Dominican Republic
ActionAid
AFS – International Youth Development
Food for the Hungry UK
Opportunity International
PLAN International UK

Project Trust
Scottish Education and
  Action for Development
Tearfund
Twin
World Emergency Relief

Haiti
Action Against Hunger UK
ActionAid
ATD Fourth World
CAFOD
Catholic Institute for
  International Relations
Children's Aid Direct
CONCERN Worldwide
Emmanuel International
Médecins Sans Frontières
Mission Aviation
  Fellowship
PLAN International UK
Sight Savers International
Marie Stopes International
Tearfund
Twin

Jamaica
HelpAge International
St Francis Leprosy Guild
Sight Savers International

Trinidad & Tobago
International Connections
  Trust

South America
Action International
  Ministries
ActionAid
AFS – International Youth
  Development
Aid to the Church in Need
BMS World Mission
CAFOD
CARE International UK
Catholic Institute for
  International Relations
Christian Children's Fund
  of Great Britain
Food for the Hungry UK
Gaia Foundation
GAP Activity Projects
Healthlink Worldwide
HelpAge International
Homeless International
Human Rights Watch

International Connections
  Trust
ITDG
Jospice International
Latin Link
Leonard Cheshire
  International
Médecins Sans Frontières
Mission Aviation
  Fellowship
Operation Mobilisation
PLAN International UK
Project Trust
Sense International
SIM International (UK)
Survival
Tearfund
World ORT
World Vision UK

Bolivia
ATD Fourth World
HelpAge International
Hunger Project Trust
i to i international projects
International Service
Population Concern
St Francis Leprosy Guild
Marie Stopes International

Brazil
ChildHope UK
Concern Universal
Emmanuel International
Health Unlimited
Holy Ghost Fathers
International HIV/AIDS
  Alliance
International Service
LEPRA
Oasis Trust – Global Action
  Initiative
St Francis Leprosy
  GuildScottish Catholic
  International Aid Fund
Spurgeon's Child Care
WORLDwrite

Chile
Raleigh International

Colombia
Action Against Hunger UK
Associated Country Women
  of the World
Children of the Andes

Concern Universal
Opportunity International
Scottish Catholic
  International Aid Fund

Ecuador
i to i international projects
International Children's
  Trust
International HIV/AIDS
  Alliance
Just World Partners

Guyana
Associated Country Women
  of the World
Commonwealth Society for
  the Deaf
Commonwealth Youth
  Exchange Council
Sight Savers International
Voluntary Service Overseas

Peru
ATD Fourth World
ChildHope UK
Cusichaca Trust
Anita Goulden Trust
Health Unlimited
Hunger Project Trust
Oasis Trust – Global Action
  Initiative
Opportunity International
Population Concern
RFI for Community
  Mental Health
Marie Stopes International
Twin
World University Service

Venezuela
World Emergency Relief

Asia
ActionAid
Aid to the Church in Need
Alzheimers Disease
  International
Article 19 (Global
  Campaign for Free
  Expression)
Associated Country Women
  of the World
BESO
BMS World Mission
CAFOD
Church Mission Society

Duke of Edinburgh's Award
  International Association
Food for the Hungry UK
Gaia Foundation
HelpAge International
Human Rights Watch
International Planned
  Parenthood Federation
Leonard Cheshire
  International
LEPRA
Médecins Sans Frontières
Muslim Aid
Oxfam
Sense International
Tearfund
Wycliffe Bible Translators

Middle East
BibleLands
Church Mission Society
New Frontiers
  International
Operation Mobilisation

Iran
Ockenden International

Iraq
CARE International UK

Israel
Church of Scotland Board
  of World Mission
Edinburgh Medical
  Missionary Society
GAP Activity Projects
Healthlink Worldwide
International Service
Islamic Relief Worldwide
Medical Aid for Palestinians
RFI for Community
  Mental Health
World ORT
World University Service
  UK

Jordan
Project Trust

Lebanon
Church of Scotland Board
  of World Mission
HMD Response
Medical Aid for Palestinians
Mercy Corps Scotland
Population Concern

Turkey
Mercy Corps Scotland

Yemen
Arid Lands Initiative
Catholic Institute for
  International Relations
Marie Stopes International

North & East Asia
OMF International (UK)
Operation Mobilisation

China
Children in Crisis
Christians Abroad
Food for the Hungry UK
GAP Activity Projects
Health Unlimited
Healthlink Worldwide
Leprosy Mission
PLAN International UK
Project Trust
Rokpa Trust
SIM International (UK)
Marie Stopes International
Tibet Foundation
Tibet Relief Fund of the
  UK
Voluntary Service Overseas
World Emergency Relief

Macau
RFI for Community
  Mental Health

Mongolia
Food for the Hungry UK
International HIV/AIDS
  Alliance
Mercy Corps Scotland
Mission Aviation
  Fellowship
Raleigh International
SIM International (UK)
Marie Stopes International
Tibet Foundation
Voluntary Service Overseas
World Vision UK

North Korea
Action Against Hunger UK
Children's Aid Direct
CONCERN Worldwide
Mercy Corps Scotland

Southern Asia
CARE International UK
Child Advocacy
  International
Church of Scotland Board
  of World Mission
Commonwealth Youth
  Exchange Council
i to i international projects
IMPACT Foundation
Institute for War and Peace
  Reporting
Islamic Relief Worldwide
ITDG
Leprosy Mission
Motivation
PLAN International UK
Population Concern
RFI for Community
  Mental Health
St Francis Leprosy Guild
Sight Savers International
SIM International (UK)
Marie Stopes International
Traidcraft Exchange
Voluntary Service Overseas
WaterAid
World Vision UK

Afghanistan
Action Against Hunger UK
Afghanaid
Children in Crisis
Christian Outreach –
  Relief and Development
CONCERN Worldwide
Mercy Corps Scotland
Merlin
Ockenden International

Bangladesh
Action on Disability and
  Development
Commonwealth Society for
  the Deaf
Concern Universal
Healthlink Worldwide
Hunger Project Trust
International HIV/AIDS
  Alliance
One World Action
Oxford Mission

India
Action Health
Action International Ministries
Action on Disability and Development
Alternative for India Development
ApTibeT
Christian Children's Fund of Great Britain
Christian Outreach – Relief and Development
Commonwealth Society for the Deaf
Donkey Sanctuary
Edinburgh Medical Missionary Society
Find Your Feet
GAP Activity Projects
GOAL (UK)
Grace and Compassion Benedictines
Dr Graham's Homes, Kalimpong, India
Healthlink Worldwide
Help International
Joe Homan Charitable Trust
Homeless International
Hunger Project Trust
International Childcare Trust
International Children's Trust
International Connections Trust
International HIV/AIDS Alliance
Jospice International
Karuna Trust/Aid for India
KINGSCARE
Learning for Life
New Frontiers International
Oasis Trust – Global Action Initiative
Opportunity International
Oxford Mission
Pestalozzi Children's Village Trust
Rokpa Trust
Ryder-Cheshire
Scottish Catholic International Aid Fund
Tibet Foundation
Tibet Relief Fund of the UK
Tropical Health and Education Trust
WOMANKIND Worldwide
World ORT
WORLDwrite

Maldives
Commonwealth Society for the Deaf
Commonwealth Youth Exchange Council
Voluntary Service Overseas

Nepal
ApTibeT
Britain-Nepal Medical Trust
Edinburgh Medical Missionary Society
Education for Development
GAP Activity Projects
International Nepal Fellowship
Just World Partners
Nepal Leprosy Trust (UK)
Operation Mobilisation
Pestalozzi Children's Village Trust
Rokpa Trust
Ryder-Cheshire
Tibet Foundation
United Mission to Nepal

Pakistan
Education for Development
Jospice International
Learning for Life
Mercy Corps Scotland
New Frontiers International
Ockenden International
Project Trust

Sri Lanka
Action Against Hunger UK
Grace and Compassion Benedictines
Help International
International Alert
International Childcare Trust
International Children's Trust
KINGSCARE
Opportunity International
Project Trust

South East Asia
Action Against Hunger UK
AFS – International Youth Development
Catholic Institute for International Relations
Christian Outreach – Relief and Development
Food for the Hungry UK
Health Unlimited
Leprosy Mission
Motivation
OMF International (UK)
Operation Mobilisation
Opportunity International
PLAN International UK
Project Trust
St Francis Leprosy Guild
Scottish Catholic International Aid Fund
Marie Stopes International
Voluntary Service Overseas
World Vision UK

Brunei
Commonwealth Youth Exchange Council

Cambodia
Action on Disability and Development
Cambodia Trust
Christian Children's Fund of Great Britain
CONCERN Worldwide
Homeless International
International HIV/AIDS Alliance
Mission Aviation Fellowship
Ockenden International

Indonesia
CARE International UK
GOAL (UK)
Mercy Corps Scotland
Merlin
Mission Aviation Fellowship
Ryder-Cheshire

Laos
CONCERN Worldwide
POWER – The International Limb Project

Malaysia
Commonwealth Youth Exchange Council
GAP Activity Projects

Philippines
Action International Ministries
ATD Fourth World
ChildHope UK
Emmanuel International
GOAL (UK)
Healthlink Worldwide
IMPACT Foundation
International Care and Relief
International Connections Trust
International Family Health
International HIV/AIDS Alliance
Just World Partners
Mercy Corps Scotland
One World Action
SIM International (UK)
Traidcraft Exchange
World Emergency Relief

Thailand
ATD Fourth World
Christian Children's Fund of Great Britain
Church of Scotland Board of World Mission
HelpAge International
i to i international projects
IMPACT Foundation
International Care and Relief
Pattaya Orphanage Trust
World Emergency Relief

Vietnam
ActionAid
GAP Activity Projects
Just World Partners
POWER – The International Limb Project

Australasia & The Pacific
Associated Country Women of the World
BESO
Commonwealth Society for the Deaf
Commonwealth Youth Exchange Council
Duke of Edinburgh's Award International Association
GAP Activity Projects
HelpAge International
International Planned Parenthood Federation
Just World Partners
Mercy Ships UK
Operation Mobilisation
Ryder-Cheshire
Voluntary Service Overseas

Fiji
Article 19 (Global Campaign for Free Expression)

Kiribati
Christians Abroad

Papua New Guinea
CAFOD
Leprosy Mission
Médecins Sans Frontières
Mission Aviation Fellowship

Solomon Islands
CAFOD

Commonwealth of Independent States
Action Against Hunger UK
Aid to Russia and the Republics
AIRE Centre
BEARR Trust
BESO
HealthProm
Institute for War and Peace Reporting
International Aid Trust
International Voluntary Service
Mercy Corps Scotland
Mercy Ships UK
Operation Mobilisation
Oxfam
Russian European Trust

Armenia
European Children's Trust

Azerbaijan
Children's Aid Direct
Islamic Relief Worldwide

Belarus
Children in Crisis
Children in Distress

Georgia
International Alert

Moldova
Spurgeon's Child Care

Russia
Care & Relief for the Young
Children in Crisis
Christian Children's Fund of Great Britain
GAP Activity Projects
i to i international projects
International Alert
Islamic Relief Worldwide
KINGSCARE
Merlin
Motivation
Multi International Aid
New Frontiers International
Opportunity International
Voluntary Service Overseas
World Emergency Relief
World ORT

Tajikstan
Children's Aid Direct
Merlin

Ukraine
Care & Relief for the Young
Child Advocacy International
International HIV/AIDS Alliance
Spurgeon's Child Care

Uzbekistan
Leprosy Mission

Organisations working in developing countries – geographical index 27

Eastern Europe

AFS – International Youth Development
Aid to Russia and the Republics
Aid to the Church in Need
AIRE Centre
Alzheimers Disease International
Article 19 (Global Campaign for Free Expression)
Associated Country Women of the World
BESO
CAFOD
CARE International UK
Child Advocacy International
ChildHope UK
Children in Distress
Children's Aid Direct
Church Mission Society
Donkey Sanctuary
Duke of Edinburgh's Award International Association
European Children's Trust
GAP Activity Projects
HelpAge International
Institute for War and Peace Reporting
International Aid Trust
International Planned Parenthood Federation
International Voluntary Service
Médecins Sans Frontières
Mercy Corps Scotland
Mercy Ships UK
Muslim Aid
Operation Mobilisation
Opportunity International
Oxfam
Sense International
Tearfund
Voluntary Service Overseas
World Emergency Relief

Albania

Christian Outreach – Relief and Development
Islamic Relief Worldwide
KINGSCARE
Merlin
Partnership for Growth
PLAN International UK
Marie Stopes International
WOMANKIND Worldwide

Bosnia-Herzegovina

GOAL (UK)
HMD Response
Islamic Relief Worldwide
Novi Most International
World Vision UK

Bulgaria

Christian Children's Fund of Great Britain

Hungary

Church of Scotland Board of World Mission

Latvia

AFS – International Youth Development

Lithunia

Motivation

Macedonia

Action Against Hunger UK

Poland

Children in Crisis
Motivation

Romania

Care & Relief for the Young
Christian Children's Fund of Great Britain
Church of Scotland Board of World Mission
Food for the Hungry UK
Motivation
Oasis Trust – Global Action Initiative
Partnership for Growth
Relief Fund for Romania
Romanian Challenge Appeal
Spurgeon's Child Care
Marie Stopes International
World Vision UK

F R of Yugoslavia

Action Against Hunger UK
GOAL (UK)
HMD Response
Partnership for Growth

SUBJECT INDEX

The subject index begins with a list of the categories used. This is followed by the index itself, with organisations indexed according to relevant subject areas if they provide a service in that area and have (a) clearly stated this in their literature, and/or (b) clearly done this in practice.

UK-based work

Campaigning/advocacy p31
With the aim of benefiting people living in developing countries. Includes campaigning for debt cancellation, and organisations that provide information/ disseminate knowledge/raise awareness. (See also *Development issues (UK)* and *Trade with developing countries*.)

Development issues p31
UK development education, including publication of books about development and running librairies of such books. (See also *Campaigning/ advocacy* and *Places of study & training*.)

Networking p31
Organisations that facilitate charities working together in discussion groups, networks, coalitions and alliances.

Places of study & training p31
For people who are working in overseas development etc. – primarily for UK residents.

Research p31
Organisations that carry out research for the benefit of people who live in developing countries.

Overseas work

Disaster & emergency relief p32
Includes disaster preparedness and the provision of supplies e.g. Red Cross parcels.

Displacement/refugees p32
Organisations working exclusively with people who have been displaced or refugees worldwide. Does not cover refugees in the UK.

Landmines p32
Organisations helping to clear landmines, and raising awareness of them amongst local people. (For victims of landmine explosions, see *Rehabilitation/disability*.)

Economy & community p32

Capacity building p32
Giving organisations the means to develop, enabling them to be more effective and improve services; includes capacity building for health organisations, governments, small community groups etc. Also includes donating money and expertise/making loans.

Credit & savings p32
Helping to develop these schemes; includes micro finance schemes.

Rural community p32
Particular focus on rural community schemes (also see *Agriculture*).

Small business p33
Helping with the establishment and development of small enterprise schemes and cooperatives, including income and employment generation. Includes organisations providing microloans and tools for the establishment of small business.

Social/community work p33
Organisations that state they provide this work generally (also see *Rural community* and *Urban community*).

Trade with developing countries p33
Fair trade links and promotion, and supporting workers e.g. through establishing trade unions.

Urban community p33
Working in urban communities, including work with street children.

Education
This section refers to standard education at primary, secondary and higher education level. It does not cover education in particular vocational or lifestyle skills (except training teachers/trainers).

Education general p33
Organisations which work in education generally, or in three or more of the areas below. Does not include teaching in IT (see under *Technology*).

Child education p33
Working in child education, including young adult and personal development for people in the developing world (for British children see *Development issues* under UK-based work). Covers futher and higher education at standard age – not mature students.

Language education p33
Organisations that teach English.

Literacy p33

Training teachers p33

Health p33
Organisations that state they work in health generally, and those working in three or more of the areas below. Includes palliative care and respite care.

AIDS/HIV p34
Helping AIDS/HIV sufferers, and AIDS/HIV prevention work.

Child health p34
Includes immunisation programmes, teaching breastfeeding. (See also *Nutrition* and *Reproductive healthcare*.)

Clinical health p34
Working in clinics, hospitals, hospices, surgeries; the specific administration of drug therapy and surgical intervention, except if the work falls within the other categories. (For mobile clinics see *Community health*.)

Communicable disease p34
Working with people who have TB, leprosy, typhoid, cholera (not AIDS/HIV; see above). Covers preventative and rehabilitation work.

Community health p34
Where doctors/nurses etc. visit patients in the community. Includes general health programmes benefiting the community, mobile clinics and drug schemes.

Nutrition p34
Helping with diets for specific illnesses, e.g. diabetes/support of the general nutritional values for wellbeing and reducing the likelihood of future health problems.

Primary healthcare – see under Community health and Clinical health

Rehabilitation/disability p34
Working with people with physical and mental disabilities, enabling rehabilitation. Also preventative work. Includes blind schools, eye care, deaf schools, child disability, and the provision of prosthetic limbs. Does not include disabilities that have arisen from communicable diseases (see above).

Reproductive healthcare p35
Helping with family planning and investigating problems relating to fertility.

Natural resources/ environment p35
Working generally in this area, or in three or more areas below. Also includes organisations working to promote veganism/vegetarianism.

Agriculture p35
Helping with farming, including organic, crop farming, animal husbandry and livestock management, and veterinary care. (Also see *Rural community*.)

Biodiversity/conservation p35
Promoting the diversity of life and conservation of anything including animal protection (not trees).

Energy – energy conservation schemes see *Appropriate technology*

Forestry p35
Promoting reafforestation/protection of trees.

Housing/construction p35
Helping with constructing roads, buildings etc. Includes charities which focus on providing civil engineering work. (See also *Irrigation/water supply*.)

Irrigation/water supply p35
For crops/people. (For civil engineering see under *Housing/ construction*.)

Technology

Appropriate technology p35
Promoting technology which is alternative to mainstream technology, but appropriate to the host country.

IT p35
Providing/teaching computer and communication skills, including use of the internet and telephone etc.

Other categories

People
Charities which show a preference for these demographic groups:

Children/young people p35
including child sponsorship programmes and adoption programmes. (See also: *Urban community* in respect of work with street children; *Disaster & emergency relief* for counselling for children; *Child health*; *Child education*.)

Older people p36

Women p36

Religion
The staff or beneficiaries are followers of the religion, or the organisation has some connection with the religion.

Buddhist p36
Christian p36
Jewish p36
Muslim p36

UK-based work

Campaigning/advocacy
Action for Southern Africa
ActionAid
AIRE Centre
Alzheimers Disease International
Amnesty International
Anti-Slavery International
Article 19 (Global Campaign for Free Expression)
Associated Country Women of the World
ATD Fourth World
Baby Milk Action
BEARR Trust
BOND
CAFOD
Catholic Institute for International Relations
Child Advocacy International
Christian Aid
Christian Solidarity Worldwide
Disability Awareness in Action
Gaia Foundation
HelpAge International
Human Rights Watch
Hunger Project Trust
Institute for War and Peace Reporting
INTERIGHTS
International Alert
International Community of Women Living with HIV/AIDS
International Service
Leonard Cheshire International
Medact
Medical Foundation for the Care of Victims of Torture
Minority Rights Group
New Economics Foundation
One World Action
One World Week
OneWorld International Ltd
Overseas Development Institute
Oxfam
Panos Institute London
Population Concern
Russian European Trust
Saferworld
Save the Children
Scottish Catholic International Aid Fund
Sense International
Skillshare Africa
Marie Stopes International
Survival
UNICEF UK
War on Want
WOMANKIND Worldwide
World Development Movement
World Vision UK

Development issues
Africa Centre
Book Aid International
CAFOD
Church Mission Society
Concern Universal
Council for Education in World Citizenship
Development Education Association
Find Your Feet
Food for the Hungry UK
International Broadcasting Trust
INTRAC
Just World Partners
Manchester Development Education Project
One World Week
Peace Child International
Scottish Catholic International Aid Fund
Scottish Education and Action for Development
Tearfund
Tibet Foundation
World Development Movement
Worldaware

Networking
ACORD
BOND
Council for World Mission
Development Education Association
Disasters Emergency Committee
Ethical Trading Initiative
HelpAge International
International Institute for Environment and Development
Landmine Action
OneWorld International Ltd
Overseas Development Institute
Resource Alliance
UK Food Group
WOMANKIND Worldwide

Places of study & training
Centre for International Briefing
Crosslinks
Department of Development Studies
Development and Project Planning Centre
ICA:UK
Institute of Development Studies
INTRAC
Liverpool School of Tropical Medicine
RedR International

Research
ACORD
African Medical and Research Foundation UK
Alzheimers Disease International
Department of Development Studies
Hunger Project Trust
Institute of Development Studies
International Alert
International Institute for Environment and Development
International Records Management Trust
INTRAC
New Economics Foundation
Overseas Development Institute
Panos Institute London
Sight Savers International
World ORT

Overseas work

Disaster & emergency relief
ACORD
Action Against Hunger UK
Action International Ministries
Action Partners Ministries
ActionAid
British Red Cross
CAFOD
CARE International UK
Children in Crisis
Children of the Andes
Children's Aid Direct
Christian Aid
Christian Solidarity Worldwide
CONCERN Worldwide
Disasters Emergency Committee
Emmanuel International
GOAL (UK)
Health Unlimited
HMD Response
International Aid Trust
International Childcare Trust
International Connections Trust
Islamic Relief Worldwide
Just World Partners
Médecins Sans Frontières
Mercy Corps Scotland
Merlin
Multi International Aid
Muslim Aid
Muslim Hands
Novi Most International
OMF International (UK)
Operation Mobilisation
Oxfam
Partnership for Growth
RedR International
Save the Children (UK)
Scottish Catholic International Aid Fund
SIM International (UK)
Tearfund
United Kingdom Jewish Aid and International Development
World Emergency Relief
World Vision UK
WorldShare

Displacement/refugees
ActionAid
Aid to Russia and the Republics
Aid to the Church in Need
AIRE Centre
ApTibeT
BibleLands
Christian Outreach – Relief and Development
Church Mission Society
Medical Aid for Palestinians
Medical Foundation for the Care of Victims of Torture
Ockenden International
OMF International (UK)
Partnership for Growth
Tibet Relief Fund of the UK
World University Service

Landmines
Landmine Action
POWER – The International Limb Project

Economy & community
Action Against Hunger UK
British Red Cross
CONCERN Worldwide

Capacity building
ABANTU for Development
ACORD
BEARR Trust
BESO
CAFOD
CamFed
CARE International UK
Catholic Institute for International Relations
Charities Aid Foundation
ChildHope UK
Church of Scotland Board of World Mission
CODA International Training
Canon Collins Educational Trust for Southern Africa
Concern Universal
Council for World Mission
Echo International Health Services Ltd
Education for Development
HealthProm
HelpAge International
International Family Health
International HIV/AIDS Alliance
International Records Management Trust
Just World Partners
Leonard Cheshire International
Mercy Corps Scotland
New Frontiers International
Plunkett Foundation
Russian European Trust
Skillshare Africa
Traidcraft Exchange
TRANSAID Worldwide

Credit & savings
ActionAid
Associated Country Women of the World
CARE International UK
International Service
Mercy Corps Scotland
Opportunity International

Rural community
Action Partners Ministries
ActionAid
AFRICA NOW
Alternative for India Development
APT Enterprise Development
Arid Lands Initiative
Associated Country Women of the World
ATD Fourth World
Busoga Trust
CamFed
Church Mission Society
Find Your Feet
Harvest Help
Kaloko Trust
Plunkett Foundation
SOS Sahel International
United Mission to Nepal
Village AiD

Small business

Action International Ministries
AFRICA NOW
CamFed
Christian Outreach – Relief and Development
Edinburgh Medical Missionary Society
Grace and Compassion Benedictines
Help International
Homeless International
International Childcare Trust
Islamic Relief Worldwide
Just World Partners
KINGSCARE
Opportunity International
Partnership for Growth
PLAN International UK
Project HOPE UK
Scottish Catholic International Aid Fund
Skillshare Africa
Tools for Self Reliance
Uganda Society for Disabled Children
World Vision UK

Social/community work

Care & Relief for the Young
Children's Aid Direct
CONCERN Worldwide
European Children's Trust
GAP Activity Projects
Leprosy Mission
Voluntary Service Overseas
World Vision UK

Trade with developing countries

Ethical Trading Initiative
Fairtrade Foundation
Tibet Foundation
Traidcraft Exchange
Twin
War on Want
World Development Movement

Urban community

Action International Ministries
ActionAid
AFS – International Youth Development
Aid to Russia and the Republics
ATD Fourth World
CARE International UK
ChildHope UK
Children in Crisis
Children of the Andes
Church Mission Society
World Vision UK

Education

Action Partners Ministries
ActionAid
Africa Educational Trust
Africa Inland Mission
BESO
BMS World Mission
Book Aid International
Busoga Trust
CARE International UK
Canon Collins Educational Trust for Southern Africa
CONCERN Worldwide
Council for World Mission
Education for Development
Help International
International Care and Relief
International Records Management Trust
Karuna Trust/Aid for India
Link Community Development
Muslim Aid
Muslim Hands
Pestalozzi Children's Village Trust
PLAN International UK
Rokpa Trust
Tibet Foundation
United Mission to Nepal
Voluntary Service Overseas
World Emergency Relief
World ORT
World University Service
World Vision UK
Wycliffe Bible Translators

Child education

BibleLands
Children of the Andes
Dr Graham's Homes
Joe Homan Charitable Trust
International Childcare Trust
International Children's Trust
International Nepal Fellowship
Latin Link
Learning for Life
Nepal Leprosy Trust
Oxford Mission
Pattaya Orphanage Trust
Romanian Challenge Appeal
SOS Children's Villages UK

Language education

Aid to Russia and the Republics
Christians Abroad
GAP Activity Projects
i to i international projects
OMF International (UK)
Project Trust
Rokpa Trust
Voluntary Service Overseas

Literacy

Africa Inland Mission
Alternative for India Development
Book Aid International
Mission Aviation Fellowship
SIL UK
WorldShare
Wycliffe Bible Translators

Training teachers

ABANTU for Development
Learning for Life
SIL UK

Health

Action Against Hunger UK
Action Partners Ministries
ActionAid
Afghanaid
Africa Inland Mission

African Medical and Research Foundation UK
Alternative for India Development
BESO
BibleLands
BMS World Mission
Britain-Nepal Medical Trust
British Red Cross
Busoga Trust
CARE International UK
Catholic Institute for International Relations
Children in Distress
Christian Medical Fellowship
Christian Outreach – Relief and Development
Church Mission Society
CONCERN Worldwide
Council for World Mission
Echo International Health Services Ltd
Edinburgh Medical Missionary Society
GAP Activity Projects
GOAL (UK)
Grace and Compassion Benedictines
Health Unlimited
Healthlink Worldwide
HealthProm
Help International
International Aid Trust
International Childcare Trust
International Health Exchange
International Nepal Fellowship
International Planned Parenthood Federation
Islamic Relief Worldwide
Jospice International
Just World Partners
Karuna Trust/Aid for India
KINGSCARE
Latin Link
Liverpool School of Tropical Medicine
Medact
Médecins Sans Frontières
Medical Aid for Palestinians
Medical Foundation for the Care of Victims of Torture
Merlin
Muslim Aid
OMF International (UK)
Project HOPE UK
Relief Fund for Romania
Rokpa Trust
Romanian Challenge Appeal
Ryder-Cheshire
SIM International (UK)
Skillshare Africa
Teaching Aids at Low Cost
Tibet Foundation
Tropical Health and Education Trust
United Mission to Nepal
Voluntary Service Overseas
World Emergency Relief
WorldVision UK

AIDS/HIV
AFS – International Youth Development
International Community of Women Living with HIV/AIDS
International HIV/AIDS Alliance
Scottish Catholic International Aid Fund
Skillshare Africa

Child health
Baby Milk Action
Care & Relief for the Young
Child Advocacy International
Children of the Andes
Children's Aid Direct
International Children's Trust
PLAN International UK
Project HOPE UK

Clinical health
Child Advocacy International
HMD Response
International Care and Relief
International Connections Trust
Mercy Ships UK
Operation Mobilisation

Communicable disease
International Nepal Fellowship
LEPRA
Leprosy Mission
Nepal Leprosy Trust (UK)
Ryder-Cheshire
St Francis Leprosy Guild

Community health
Action Health
Aid to Russia and the Republics
Emmanuel International
Health Unlimited
HMD Response
International Care and Relief
Mercy Ships UK

Nutrition
Action Against Hunger UK
Children of the Andes
Emmanuel International

Rehabilitation/disability
Action Health
Action on Disability and Development
Aid to Russia and the Republics
Alzheimers Disease International
Associated Country Women of the World
BibleLands
Cambodia Trust
Christian Outreach – Relief and Development
Commonwealth Society for the Deaf
Disability Awareness in Action
Anita Goulden Trust
IMPACT Foundation
Leonard Cheshire International
Mission Aviation Fellowship
Motivation
ORBIS
Pattaya Orphanage Trust

POWER – The
  International Limb
  Project
RFI for Community
  Mental Health
Ryder-Cheshire
Sense International
Sight Savers International
Uganda Society for
  Disabled Children

Reproductive healthcare
International Family Health
International Service
PLAN International UK
Population Concern
Marie Stopes International

Natural resources/environment
AFRICA NOW
Arid Lands Initiative
Associated Country Women
  of the World
BESO
Busoga Trust
Catholic Institute for
  International Relations
CONCERN Worldwide
Find Your Feet
GAP Activity Projects
International Care and
  Relief
International Childcare
  Trust
International Institute for
  Environment and
  Development
Just World Partners
PLAN International UK
Skillshare Africa
SOS Sahel International
Voluntary Service Overseas

Agriculture
Action Against Hunger UK
ActionAid
Afghanaid
Africa Inland Mission
APT Enterprise
  Development
BMS World Mission
CARE International UK
Cusichaca Trust
Donkey Sanctuary

Emmanuel International
Evergreen Trust
FARM Africa
Harvest Help
Help International
International Service
Mission Aviation
  Fellowship
OMF International (UK)
Operation Mobilisation
Plunkett Foundation
Send a Cow (& StockAid)
World Vision UK

Biodiversity/conservation
Gaia Foundation

Forestry
Alternative for India
  Development
Evergreen Trust

Housing/construction
Afghanaid
Africa Inland Mission
Aid to Russia and the
  Republics
Children's Aid Direct
Christian Outreach –
  Relief and Development
CONCERN Worldwide
GOAL (UK)
Homeless International
Médecins Sans Frontières
OMF International (UK)
RedR International
United Mission to Nepal
Voluntary Service Overseas
World Vision UK

Irrigation/water supply
Action Against Hunger UK
ActionAid
AFRICA NOW
British Red Cross
Busoga Trust
CARE International UK
Christian Outreach –
  Relief and Development
Help International
International Service
Islamic Relief Worldwide
Médecins Sans Frontières
Mission Aviation
  Fellowship

Muslim Aid
Voluntary Service Overseas
WaterAid
World Vision UK

Technology

Appropriate technology
AFRICA NOW
Alternative for India
  Development
APT Enterprise
  Development
ApTibeT
Arid Lands Initiative
Catholic Institute for
  International Relations
Cusichaca Trust
Homeless International
ITDG
Partnership for Growth

IT
CamFed
Edinburgh Medical
  Missionary Society
International Records
  Management Trust
OMF International (UK)
OneWorld International
  Ltd
Voluntary Service Overseas

People

Children/young people
Action International
  Ministries
Africa Inland Mission
Aid to Russia and the
  Republics
BEARR Trust
BibleLands
Busoga Trust
Care & Relief for the
  Young
Children in Distress
Children of the Andes
Children's Aid Direct
Christian Children's Fund
  of Great Britain
Christian Outreach –
  Relief and Development
Commonwealth Youth
  Exchange Council

Duke of Edinburgh's Award International Association
European Children's Trust
Evergreen Trust
Anita Goulden Trust
Dr Graham's Homes
Joe Homan Charitable Trust
International Aid Trust
International Care and Relief
International Childcare Trust
International Connections Trust
International Voluntary Service
Islamic Relief Worldwide
Jospice International
KINGSCARE
Latin Link
Novi Most International
Operation Mobilisation
Oxford Mission
Pattaya Orphanage Trust
Peace Child International
PLAN International UK
Prince's Trust
Relief Fund for Romania
Romanian Challenge Appeal
Ryder-Cheshire
Save the Children (UK)
SOS Children's Villages UK
Spurgeon's Child Care
UNICEF UK
Voluntary Service Overseas
World Emergency Relief
WorldShare
WORLDwrite
Y Care International

Older people
Grace and Compassion Benedictines
HelpAge International

Women
ActionAid
AFRICA NOW
Associated Country Women of the World
CamFed
Catholic Institute for International Relations
Hunger Project Trust
International Community of Women Living with HIV/AIDS
Learning for Life
Project HOPE UK
WOMANKIND Worldwide

Religion

Buddhist
ApTibeT
Karuna Trust/Aid for India
Rokpa Trust
Tibet Foundation

Christian
Action International Ministries
Action Partners Ministries
Africa Inland Mission
Aid to Russia and the Republics
Aid to the Church in Need
BibleLands
BMS World Mission
Busoga Trust
CAFOD
Care & Relief for the Young
Catholic Institute for International Relations
Christian Aid
Christian Children's Fund of Great Britain
Christian Medical Fellowship
Christian Outreach – Relief and Development
Christian Solidarity Worldwide
Christians Abroad
Church Mission Society
Church of Scotland Board of World Mission
Concern Universal
Council for World Mission
Crosslinks
Edinburgh Medical Missionary Society
Emmanuel International
Food for the Hungry UK
Grace and Compassion Benedictines
Dr Graham's Homes, Kalimpong, India
Harvest Help
Help International
Holy Ghost Fathers
International Aid Trust
International Connections Trust
International Nepal Fellowship
Jospice International
KINGSCARE
Latin Link
Leprosy Mission
Mercy Ships UK
Mission Aviation Fellowship
Nepal Leprosy Trust (UK)
New Frontiers International
Novi Most International
Oasis Trust – Global Action Initiative
OMF International (UK)
Operation Mobilisation
Oxford Mission
St Francis Leprosy Guild
Scottish Catholic International Aid Fund
Send a Cow (& StockAid)
SIL UK
SIM International (UK)
Spurgeon's Child Care
Tearfund
United Mission to Nepal
World Emergency Relief
World Vision UK
WorldShare
Wycliffe Bible Translators
Y Care International

Jewish
United Kingdom Jewish Aid and International Development
World ORT

Muslim
Islamic Relief Worldwide
Muslim Aid
Muslim Hands

ABANTU for Development

Training and resourcing for sustainable development

Geographical focus: *Ghana, Kenya, Nigeria*

1 Winchester House, 11 Cranmer Road, London SW9 6EJ
Tel: 020 7820 0066; **Fax:** 020 7820 0088
e-mail: people@abantu.org
Website: www.abantu.org
Correspondent: Mrs Wanjiru Kihoro, Director

Expenditure: £526,000 (1997/98)

Staffing: 33 paid staff in the UK and overseas; 2 volunteers.

Website information: The website was being developed as at November 2000, and only contained information about the charity's programmes and events.

General: The following information was taken from the charity's website. 'ABANTU for Development was founded in 1991, for the purpose of harnessing resources to the benefit of African people. Abantu means 'people' in many languages, and symbolises our people-centred philosophy. The main focus of our work is on training and providing information and advice on mobilising resources towards sustainable development in Africa.

'Our aims are to:
- increase the participation of Africans, especially women in the political and economic structures of African countries;
- eradicate the cultural, legal and political obstacles to women attaining economic independence and equality before the law;
- ensure that the advancement of women's interests benefits the entire community.

'We aim to achieve these by:
- supporting African people to empower themselves though a participatory and people-centered method of training to develop skills in the areas of policy analysis, economics, healthcare, the media and the environment;
- developing and supporting trainers and non-governmental organisations (ngos);
- providing both support and networking opportunities for trainers and consultants to create an increased pool of competent Africans skilled in participatory training, gender and policy analysis;
- capitalising on the resources available in the North and other supporters living in Europe and North America.'

ACORD (Agency for Cooperation and Research in Development)

Establishing or strengthening local, non-governmental structures, and acting in emergency situations

Geographical focus: *Angola, Botswana, Burundi, Burkina Faso, Chad, Democratic Republic of Congo, Eritrea, Ethiopia, Guinea, Kenya, Mali, Mauritania, Mozambique, Namibia, Rwanda, Somalia, Sudan, Tanzania, Uganda*

Dean Bradley House, 52 Horseferry Road, London SW1P 2AF
Tel: 020 7227 8600; **Fax:** 020 7799 1868
e-mail: acord@gn.apc.org
Correspondent: The Information and Marketing Department

Expenditure: £8.4 million (1999)

Staffing: 28 to 30 paid staff, plus volunteers, all in London.

General: ACORD is an international consortium of ngos. It works under the trusteeship of its member agencies (see

Membership below) in partnership with its field teams and with local communities in Africa.

The following information was included in the trust's annual report. 'ACORD's main role is to help establish or strengthen local, non-governmental structures with a view to promoting self-reliant, participatory development. At the same time, ACORD also acts in emergency situations which seem likely to give rise to new development needs.

'The Consortium provides a platform for its members, field teams and partners to discuss development problems. ACORD's work is complementary to that of its members. Its mandate also calls on ACORD to conduct research and to elaborate specific development strategies, as well as planning and implementing medium and long-term programmes to promote self-reliance in the communities themselves. For this purpose, ACORD has to obtain the technical and financial means required from member agencies and outside sources. Local resources, skills and expertise are used to the maximum wherever they are available.'

Membership: ACORD has 11 member agencies, all based in different countries, the UK representative is Oxfam GB.

Action Against Hunger UK (AAH)

Working in crisis situations, in the fields of nutrition, food security, health and water

Geographical focus: Over 40 countries including: Afghanistan, Albania, Angola, Armenia, Bosnia, Burundi, Cambodia, Cameroon, Chad, Colombia, Democratic Republic of Congo, Republic of Congo, Ethiopia, Georgia, Guatemala, Guinea, Haiti, Honduras, Indonesia, Kenya, Kosovo, Laos, Liberia, Macedonia, Mali, Mozambique, Myanmar, Nicaragua, Niger, Russia, Sierra Leone, Somalia, Sri Lanka, Sudan, Tajikistan, Uganda, Venezuela, Yugoslavia

1 Catton Street, Holborn,
London WC1R 4AB
Tel: 020 7831 5858; **Fax:** 020 7831 4259
e-mail: aahuk@aah-uk.demon.co.uk
Website: www.aah-uk.org
Correspondent: The Administrator

Expenditure: £4.6 million (1999)

Staffing: 9 full-time salaried staff based in the UK, plus 35 overseas field workers.

Website information: Information on programmes by country including: general information about the country; activities by sector; how to get involved; job vacancies; events; questions/discussion on hunger; how to make a donation.

General: Action Against Hunger UK is part of an international network. This network provides humanitarian relief in the fields of nutrition, health, water and food security. Worldwide the network employs 400 expatriate fieldworkers and 4,000 national staff.

Action Against Hunger UK opened its London office in 1995, and became operational in 1998 and now has responsibility for five missions, in Cambodia, Cameroon, Kenya, Kosovo and Tajikistan.

Publications: A newsletter is produced three times a year, and is available on request. Also published is *The Hunger Report: Geopolitics of Hunger*.

Volunteers/jobseekers: UK salaried positions are advertised in the UK press. Skilled, fully qualified overseas fieldworkers are recruited on an ongoing basis for a register (nurses, nutritionists, agronomists, water engineers, logisticians, accountants, socio-economists). Interviews are held in London throughout the year. Send a large sae for the information pack or send a cv directly to Cathy Lennox-Cook, Human Resources Manager, either by e-mail: clc@acf.imaginet.fr or in writing to the address above.

Volunteers are welcomed in the UK office in the Fundraising and Communications Department, with occasional administration positions in other departments. Contact Sophie Noonan, Head of Communications, by e-mail: sn@acf.imaginet.fr or in writing to the address above.

Action on Disability and Development (ADD)

Empowering people who are disabled

Geographical focus: Bangladesh, Burkina Faso, Cambodia, Cote D'Ivoire, Ghana, India, Mali, Sudan, Tanzania, Uganda, Zambia, Zimbabwe

57 Vallis Road, Frome,
Somerset BA11 4QZ
Tel: 01373 473064; **Fax:** 01373 452075
Minicom: 01373 463932
e-mail: add@gn.apc.org
Website: www.add.org.uk
Correspondent: Emma Bowden

Expenditure: £1.9 million (1999)

Staffing: 109 staff including 17 in the UK, the rest being mostly local people overseas. 10 volunteers in the UK Somerset office.

Website information: Job vacancies; how to take part in the fundraising event Andes Challenge; how to make online donations.

General: The charity's vision 'is a world where disabled people can:
- participate in society as fully as they choose
- meet basic human needs such as food, education and healthcare'.

Its aim is 'to support disabled people's self-help groups in building better lives for themselves and other disabled people'.

The charity provided the following information.

'ADD works with organisations set up and run by disabled people themselves, as they strive to find their own answers to the problems they face. We may support them with training, with equipment, or with seed money, to help them set up a loan fund for their members.

'Most of ADD's workers overseas are nationals of the country where they work. Many of them are disabled themselves. They understand the challenges facing the disabled people they work with. They know how to listen to them, how to build up their confidence after a lifetime of rejection.'

Volunteers/jobseekers: There are opportunities for volunteers to work in the Somerset office. No opportunities overseas.

Action Health

Sending health professionals to provide training in developing countries

Geographical focus: India, Uganda, Tanzania

The Gate House, 25 Gwydir Street, Cambridge CB1 2LG
Tel: 01223 460853; **Fax:** 01223 461787
e-mail: actionhealth@skillshare.org
Website: www.skillshare.org
Correspondent: Robin Greenwood, Director of Action Health Programme

Expenditure: £244,000 (1998/99)

Staffing: 3 based in the UK, 16 health professionals overseas.

Website information: This charity shares a website with Skillshare Africa, please see website information in that entry (page 214).

General: Set up in 1984, Action Health responds to requests for assistance from governmental and non-governmental organisations overseas by recruiting health professionals to train their staff in healthcare and management skills. It works in long-term partnerships with these organisations.

Action Health merged with Skillshare Africa in July 2000, but continues to operate separately. Training in the host countries takes place in one of two fields:

Community health
Giving community members the knowledge, skills and support they need to recognise, prevent and treat diseases.

Community-based rehabilitation
Enabling ordinary men and women to help their own or their neighbours' children to overcome common diseases and disabilities such as cerebral palsy and polio and to reach their full potential in life.

Volunteers/jobseekers: Since it was established Action Health has sent more than 400 trainers overseas. It requires full qualified health professionals who have a minimum of two years post-qualification experience, for postings from 12 to 24 months.

Applications are considered throughout the year from physiotherapists, occupational therapists, speech and language therapists, health promotion specialists, midwives and health visitors, GPs, public health doctors and HIV/STD health educators.

Action Health considers applications from individuals, couples, families, mature people and from those with no previous experience of working overseas (although experience of travelling overseas would be a great advantage).

Most trainers take up 'The £1,000 Challenge' before being posted. This generates between £10,000 and £15,000 each year, which is used to support trainers in post.

Further information and how to apply to be a trainer is set out in full detail in a booklet available from the correspondent, '*Action Health … take up the challenge of a lifetime*'.

Action International Ministries

Helping urban people who live in poverty

Geographical focus: *Africa, Brazil, Colombia, Ecuador, India, Mexico, Philippines*

PO Box 193, Bewdley,
Worcestershire DY12 2GZ
Tel: 01299 401511; **Fax:** 01299 405273
e-mail: actionuk@btinternet.com
Website: www.actionintl.org
Correspondent: Ingo Abraham

Expenditure: £158,000 (1998/99)

Staffing: Over 130 volunteers overseas – including expats from other countries and local workers.

Website information: Summary of its work in each country; opportunities for volunteering – current vacancies according to region and short-term opportunities; reports on its own work and articles about Christian causes including development issues; news; links to other sites.

General: The following information was taken from the charity's website. 'Action International Ministries (ACTION) is a non-denominational Christian mission with over 130 missionaries in 6 countries. Its work focuses on the urban poor –

often overlooked but desperately needy street kids, orphaned and abandoned babies, squatters, prostitutes, and prisoners in places like Metro Manila (Philippines), Mexico City, São Paulo (Brazil), and Bogotá (Colombia).

'ACTION works in cooperation with local churches and other national organisations to reach people for Christ (evangelism), train them in Christian living (discipleship), and assist them in their physical and economic needs (development).

'It seeks to meet physical needs through development work such as:
- vocational/discipleship training school
- foster home and adoption programme
- rescue centres
- children's homes
- micro loans for the establishment of small businesses
- feeding programmes
- disaster relief work.'

Volunteers/jobseekers: 'Opportunities for service abound on each of ACTION's fields of ministry, and more workers are urgently needed. While ACTION's greatest need is for career missionaries, other opportunities for a cross-cultural mission experience are offered through Vision Trips, Summer of Service and Short-term Internships.'

This entry was compiled using information available on the website; it was not confirmed by the charity.

Action Partners Ministries

Relief, development work, other Christian work

Geographical focus: *Cameroon, Chad, Democratic Republic of Congo, Egypt, Ghana, Kenya, Nigeria, Sudan, UK*

Bawtry Hall, Bawtry,
Doncaster DN10 6JH

Tel: 01302 710750
e-mail: web@actionpartners.org.uk
Website: www.actionpartners.org.uk
Correspondent: The Clerk

Expenditure: £704,000 (1999)

Staffing: 19 paid staff and 4 volunteers in the UK. 40 paid staff overseas who are UK or European residents.

Website information: News archive; how to make an online donation; information for volunteers, including summer work opportunities; links to related sites.

General: The charity was formed in 1904 as the Sudan United Mission (SUM). The following information was taken from the charity's website. 'Today, the name has changed but the vision remains the same – to see the Sahel region of Africa and the peoples of that region transformed by the good news of Jesus Christ, wherever they may be living.

'In 1998 a fresh dimension was added [to the vision] – to move into working in partnership with African indigenous groups and churches. With the slight change in emphasis, came a change in name and SUM became Action Partners.

'The work undertaken in the field is varied and dynamic in nature. There are workers in medical, educational, church and rural spheres with relief work also going on in war-torn and needy areas.'

Volunteers/jobseekers: Long-term vacancies are available for volunteer teachers, administrators, medical, development and other Christian workers. Contact the correspondent or see the website for further information.

Short-term positions are also available, and in 2000, for example, a team went to help in a hospital in Cameroon from November to December, for the cost of £1,400 per person.

Please note, the charity says: 'All of our workers share a common faith in the uniqueness of Jesus Christ, the Son of God, and His power to save. No matter what the work, we are committed to seeing African people come into a dynamic relationship with the Living God.' UK-staff have to raise a proportion of their income. Overseas staff are responsible for raising their own financial support.

Action for Southern Africa
(formerly the Anti-Apartheid Movement)
Campaigning
Geographical focus: Southern Africa

28 Penton Street, London N1 9SA
Tel: 020 7833 3133; **Fax:** 020 7837 3001
e-mail: actsa@actsa.org
Website: www.actsa.org
Correspondent: Liz Dodd

Expenditure: £331,000 (1998)

General: ACTSA campaigns for peace, democracy and development 'to ensure that the people of Southern Africa are not forgotten by the decision-makers in Westminster and Brussels. They work to keep the region in the public and political spotlight and to strengthen the bonds between the peoples of Britain and Southern Africa'.

In 2000, for example, ACTSA campaigned on behalf of over 3,000 claimants in South Africa suffering from the effects of asbestos-related diseases. A case for compensation is now being heard in English courts against Cape PLC, a UK-based company responsible for mining in South Africa in the 1970s and 1980s.

Membership: Friends of ACTSA offer £5 or more a month by standing order. Friends receive a free t-shirt, an annual invitation to a Friends of ACTSA event, a special yearly report on how the money is used, membership of ACTSA and the quarterly newsletter.

ActionAid
Relief, development and campaigning
Geographical focus: Bangladesh, Bolivia, Brazil, Burundi, Dominican Republic, Ecuador, El Salvador, Ethiopia, Gambia, Ghana, Guatemala, Haiti, India, Kenya, Liberia, Malawi, Mozambique, Nepal, Nicaragua, Nigeria, Pakistan, Peru, Rwanda, Sierra Leone, Somaliland, Tanzania, Vietnam, Uganda

Hamlyn House, Macdonald Road, Archway, London N19 5PG
Tel: 020 7561 7561; **Fax:** 022 7272 0899
e-mail: mail@actionaid.org.uk
Website: www.actionaid.org
Correspondent: Suzanna Cox, Press Officer

Expenditure: £48 million (1999)

Website information: Breakdown of work into countries; information about its campaigns, how to sponsor a child, lottoaid, national recycling unit and recruitment; annual report; press releases; a list of publications.

General: ActionAid was set up in 1971. The organisation exists to help children, families and communities in the world's poorest countries to overcome poverty and secure lasting improvements in the quality of their lives.

It outlines its vision in a factsheet about its work under the following four headings:

Supporting basic rights

'By offering skills training, sharing knowledge and supplying materials, ActionAid helps poor people to gain access to the services they need.'

These services include the provision of food, water, healthcare, education and security. ActionAid helps individuals to influence governments, so that statutory services are relevant to poor people's own priorities.

Working in partnership

It encourages groups and individuals working on similar issues, within rich and poor countries, to share their knowledge and skills.

Promoting global change

ActionAid works to influence institutions such as the World Trade Organisation and World Bank, as well as national governments and donor agencies such as the European Union, within the countries where it operates and at an international level. Key issues include tied aid, trade, debt, conflict and humanitarianism and financial services.

Improving gender equity

Particularly working in the areas of literacy and savings and credit schemes which help women build confidence and develop new skills.

Its key areas of work are listed as follows:
- education (primary education and adult literacy);
- water (supply, and education about sanitation and hygiene);
- health (child and maternal health, immunisation programmes, mobile health clinics);
- urban work (healthcare, education, support for homeless children);
- food and farming (supplying farmers with seed, tools and loans for livestock and fertilisers, agricultural training, campaigning for reform of the international trade rules);
- emergency relief (including preventative work, resettling displaced people, rebuilding schools and health centres and water systems);
- HIV/AIDS (provide information, raise awareness, encourage people living with the virus to take part in its preventative and care work);
- financial services (savings and credit schemes).

Membership: Ways to get involved:
- Sponsor a child – costs 50p a day. You receive a photo and messages from your sponsored child and regular updates from ActionAid workers; e-mail: lyndaf@actionaid.org.uk or telephone: 01460 238080.
- Basics – scheme helps 'some of the world's poorest people to secure basic rights to food, healthcare, education and ways of making a living'. You will receive three postcards and an annual report about the area you support each year.

Other ways to get involved include campaigning, involving your employer, teaching children in the UK about other countries, leaving a legacy, recycling your toner cartridges, taking part in ActionAid's fundraising week or making a donation.

Publications: Publications and educational resource catalogues are available from the address above, or at the website.

Trading: A catalogue *Gifts to Go*, is available, contact Mike Pain at the telephone number above.

Volunteers/jobseekers: 'ActionAid recognises that it is in the interests of the organisation to recruit and utilise volunteers in order to maximise its efficiency, to achieve its aims and to bring new skills, experience and perspectives to our work. At the same time ActionAid believes that it can offer valuable training and work experience to volunteers together with a chance to directly contribute to our work.

'We believe that people wish to volunteer their time and labour to ActionAid for a variety of reasons. Many wish to support ActionAid in a non-financial way whilst others wish to gain valuable work experience or new skills. Others may wish to meet new people with similar interests or to readjust to the world of work following an absence.'

Volunteers could be asked to assist with a number of areas of work and the charity tries to balance its needs with volunteers' interests and skills. ActionAid is based in three offices and the relevant staff member to contact for each office is listed below:
- Chard – Volunteer Coordinator
- London – Personnel Officer
- Bristol – Office Administrator.

Also see information under Membership, above.

Afghanaid

Rural community development and engineering projects

Geographical focus: Afghanistan

2nd Floor, 16 Mortimer Street,
London W1N 7RD
Tel: 020 7255 3355; **Fax:** 020 7255 3344
e-mail: info@afghanaid.org.uk or yvonne@afghanaid.org.uk
Website: www.afghanaid.org.uk
Correspondent: Yvonne Lane, Supporter Relations Manager

Expenditure: £1.1 million (1998/99)

Staffing: UK – 2 full-time, 1 part-time. Pakistan/Afghanistan – 182 full-time, 2 part-time (over 95% are locals).

Website information: Details of current projects; history of Afghanaid; fundraising pages; on-line highlights of the newsletter; photo gallery; job and volunteering opportunities; information on Afghanistan; links to other sites; an on-line bookshop selling books about Afghanistan.

General: Afghanaid was established in 1983 to provide humanitarian relief to Afghans in hardship and distress and to assist with the rehabilitation and development of Afghanistan. Initially it worked with Afghan refugees in Pakistan, but then carried out relief work in Afghanistan. It has since shifted its focus from relief to rehabilitation, concentrating on rebuilding roads and bridges and re-establishing food supply within the country. More recently it has started to carry out longer term community development work. This involves meetings with villagers to discuss priorities and possible solutions to their problems and the formation of village organisations which take an active role in project implementation.

In 2000, its work was based mainly in the far north of Afghanistan. Work here included food production programmes, repairing roads to improve access and reducing transportation costs, which brings down the costs of food. It also worked with farmers to establish fruit nurseries and trained them in improved vegetable growing techniques. Other projects included bee-keeping to generate income and health education for women.

Afghanaid is committed to working with Afghan communities regardless of the political and military situation. Because of its neutral stance it has been able to carry out its work under a number of governments.

Publications: *Jahrchi* – bi-annual newsletter, and see bookshop on website.

Volunteers/jobseekers: UK salaried jobs are advertised in *The Guardian* and *The Guardian Weekly* (overseas). Most paid staff in Afghanistan are Afghan and are recruited locally. Where people with particular skills are needed there are very occasionally placements for professionals in Afghanistan; if you are interested e-mail/post your cv to the correspondent. See website for further information.

Opportunities for volunteering in the UK only, helping with office tasks such as large mailings, or staffing stalls at events etc. Contact the correspondent.

The Africa Centre
Promoting initiatives in Europe which assist in the development of Africa
Geographical focus: Africa

38 King Street, Covent Garden, London WC2E 8JT
Tel: 020 7836 1973; **Fax:** 020 7836 1975
e-mail: africacentre@gn.apc.org
Website: www.africacentre.org.uk
Correspondent: Dr Adotey Bing, Director

Expenditure: £356,000 (1998/99)

Staffing: 10 paid staff and 39 volunteers, all based in the Centre in London.

Website information: Archives; events (talks, discussions and conferences); links; resources; how to become a member.

General: In its 1998/99 annual report, The Africa Centre said its mission is: 'To be a flagship for Africa in Europe promoting the aspirations of Africa and its Diaspora. In particular to promote cultural, economic and socio-political initiatives in Britain and the rest of Europe to assist in the development of Africa.

'In fulfilment of which the Africa Centre will:
- promote positive awareness about Africa
- support African economies
- champion social inclusion
- support Africa's international aspirations
- promote the aspirations of the African Diaspora
- provide information on society and culture in Africa, and the Diaspora.

'Highlights of the year's programmes included the lecture by President Yoweri Museveni of Uganda on Good Governance in April 1998, a conference on African Diplomacy, and Africa Xchange, a performing arts workshop which brought South African and Nigerian performing artists to spend two weeks in the UK working with other artists and adults.'

Weekly, the Centre runs a craft market, drumming classes and a radio programme. It has a resource room holding a number of books and periodicals. It also puts on a number events (discussions and lectures) throughout the year.

Membership: Membership costs £20 for an individual (£10 student or unemployed; £35 a family). Members receive free entry to talks, quarterly mailings of events sheet, discounts on hall hire etc.

Volunteers/jobseekers: There are opportunities to volunteer at the Centre. Prospective volunteers should send a cv and letter specifying which area they would like to work in (the arts, politics & social issues, marketing or administration).

Africa Educational Trust (AET)

Education, research and dissemination of information

Geographical focus: Botswana, Kenya, Somalia, South Africa, Sudan, Swaziland, Uganda

38 King Street, London WC2E 8JS
Tel: 020 7836 5075/7940;
Fax: 020 7379 0090
e-mail: aet@mcmail.com
Website: www.africaeducationaltrust.mcmail.com
Correspondent: Dr M Brophy, Director

Expenditure: £564,000 (1998/99)

Staffing: UK – 5 full-time, 2 part-time. Africa – 6 staff and 3 representatives.

Website information: Brief information about: work in Africa and the UK; main donors; memorial scholarship funds.

General: AET was founded in 1958 by Michael Scott, an early supporter of the anti-apartheid struggle and independence movements in Africa. The charity supports:
- education in Africa
- African students studying outside of Africa
- research and dissemination of information about Africa.

The main focus of its work is on supporting education and training for people from areas where there is civil war or conflict.

The main beneficiaries are:
- girls and young women who have been denied access to education;
- children in primary schools in areas where there is ongoing civil war or conflict;
- young ex-militia men who have had no education or vocational training;
- young men and women working with local organisations and ngos in conflict situations.

In Somalia, for instance, the trust has four major programmes. These provide literacy, numeracy and vocational training for young women and ex-militia men and help to improve basic education for children in primary schools, via helping parents to become involved in the management of primary schools and training head teachers.

On a smaller scale, the trust makes grants and scholarships to students from Africa who encounter unexpected financial difficulty.

The trust also carries out research studies into education, training and employment both in Africa and for refugees in the UK.

Africa Inland Mission (AIM)

Church-planting and general development work

Geographical focus: Angola, Central African Republic, Chad, Comoros Islands, Democratic Republic of Congo, Kenya, Lesotho, Madagascar, Mozambique, Namibia, Seychelles, Sudan, Tanzania, Uganda

(UK office) 2 Vorley Road, Archway, London N19 5HE
Tel: 020 7281 1184; **Fax:** 020 7281 4479
e-mail: uk@aim-eur.org
Website: www.aim-eur.org
Correspondent: Revd John Brand, UK Director

Expenditure: £1.8 million – European Council (1999)

Staffing: 800 AIM missionaries worldwide, 200 from Europe.

Website information: List of publications – books and videos, brochures – including ones about development work; volunteering opportunities – long-term, year and summer holiday teams; donor information; a list of the charity's contacts worldwide.

General: Africa Inland Mission International is an interdenominational mission organisation serving in 15 countries in Africa and in various urban centres in the United States. AIM's primary goal is to establish and develop maturing churches through the evangelisation of 'unreached people groups' and the effective preparation of church leaders.

Since 1895, Africa Inland Mission has expanded from the first team of 7 men and women to a team of over 850 missionaries. A wide variety of ministries are used to accomplish its primary goal, including church planting, theological education, medical work, aviation, construction, literature production and printing, radio work, accounting, secretarial work and teaching. AIM is not a donor organisation.

Membership: The charity's quarterly magazine and other information on the work of AIM is available on request from the charity at the address above.

Publications: The charity produces a number of books, brochures and videos; for a list please see the website, or contact the Media Director at the address above.

Volunteers/jobseekers: Volunteering opportunities, as at November 2000, included those in the fields of: agriculture; art; church work; construction; maintenance; medicine; office work; teaching; and youth work.

AFRICA NOW

Helping rural communities to develop sustainable income generation activities

Geographical focus: Kenya, Zimbabwe

4 Rickett Street, London SW6 1RU
Tel: 020 7386 5200; **Fax:** 020 7386 5910
e-mail: africanow@compuserve.com
Correspondent: Ms Michéle Morland, Administrator

Expenditure: £602,000 (1999/2000)

Staffing: 20 salaried staff, of which 5 are based in the UK office and 15 work in Africa (2 British and 13 local staff).

General: Formed in 1981, AFRICA NOW focuses on facilitating the rural poor to generate disposable income. It especially helps women, who it identifies as the main agricultural producers in rural Africa.

Projects are initiated by local communities and implemented by AFRICA NOW's local staff or through local partners. It favours project proposals which encourage local self-sufficiency and which may be replicated elsewhere. It provides a package of financial support in the form of small loans and training in appropriate skills and technologies.

Examples of major programmes include: assisting and training local people to build rain water tanks and spring protections which ensure reliable supplies of clean water; setting up small enterprises leading to value added food processing such as cultured milk production which has a longer shelf life and thus reduces wastage; the promotion of rural technology; and natural resources management. There are also several initiatives to support women's economic activities.

In addition, the charity is involved in the provision of basic services where these are inadequate and where participatory approaches can be taken to improve services and contribute to income generation at the same time.

Membership: The charity has 3,000 members.

Volunteers/jobseekers: No overseas opportunities and few in the UK office for volunteers. Paid positions are widely advertised when available.

African Medical and Research Foundation UK (AMREF UK)

Researching information and helping to alleviate health problems

Geographical focus: *Sub-Saharan Africa, particularly Ethiopia, Kenya, Mozambique, Somalia, South Africa, Tanzania, Uganda. Also works in Botswana, Burundi, Eritrea, Gambia, Ghana, Madagascar, Namibia, Nigeria, Rwanda, Sierra Leone, Sudan, Zambia, Zimbabwe*

4 Grosvenor Place, London SW1X 7HJ
Tel: 020 7201 6070; **Fax:** 020 7201 6170
e-mail: amref.uk@amref.org
Website: www.amref.org
Correspondent: Alexander Héroys, Director

Expenditure: £1.4 million (1998/99)

Staffing: 4 full-time salaried staff, 2 part-time staff and volunteers who organise fundraising events based in the UK; 500 staff in Africa, 97% of whom are Africans.

Website information: Information on all AMREF programmes, the Flying Doctor Service and all the offices. Newsletters, publications and bibliography are available on request via the site. There are links to other useful sites.

General: AMREF is Africa's largest indigenous health charity. It was founded in 1957 in Kenya, which is where it is based. AMREF UK is one of 11 international offices in Europe and North America that raise funds to support the charity's work in Africa. Almost 70% of AMREF UK's income in 1998/99 was transferred to fund its projects in Africa. AMREF does not make grants to other organisations.

AMREF has worked with local communities and governments in sub-Saharan Africa to research and alleviate the region's health problems. It also incorporates the Flying Doctor Service. It is a field-oriented organisation that implements programmes through service delivery, training and research.

Activities are structured into five programme areas:
- sexual and reproductive health
- child and adolescent health and development
- environmental health
- health policy and systems reform
- clinical services and emergency response.

Primary healthcare is the basis for most of these activities with special emphasis given to community participation and gender equality.

Publications: It publishes health books and has a library in Kenya where research material is available.

Volunteers/jobseekers: Employment opportunities for non-African residents are advertised in the media. Unsolicited requests for employment are not accepted.

AFS – International Youth Development

Sending young people to volunteer overseas, and bringing young people from overseas to volunteer in the UK

Geographical focus: Argentina, Brazil, Canada, Colombia, Costa Rica, Czech Republic, Dominican Republic, Ecuador, Finland, France, Germany, Ghana, Guatemala, Honduras, Hungary, Indonesia, Italy, Japan, Latvia, Malaysia, Norway, Panama, Paraguay, Peru, Slovak Republic, South Africa, Thailand, UK, USA, Venezuela

National Office, Leeming House, Vicar Lane, Leeds, West Yorkshire LS2 7JF
Tel: 0845 458 2101; **Fax:** 0845 458 2102
e-mail: info-unitedkingdom@afs.org
Website: www.afsuk.org
Correspondent: The Development Director

Expenditure: £490,000 (2000)

Staffing: Worldwide staff: 800; volunteers: 120,000; participants: 10,000.

Website information: Sending programmes; hosting programmes; country information guides; volunteering opportunities in the UK; fundraising events e.g. trekking in Peru; a chat room.

General: Founded in 1947, AFS is a non-profit volunteer-based organisation offering volunteering and exchange opportunities among a network of over 50 countries around the world. AFS UK has its national office in Leeds, and is supported by volunteers throughout the UK and the Channel Islands.

'AFS working throughout the UK: There are many ways of getting involved with AFS; young people between the ages of 15 and 35 (depending on the country) can participate on one of our sending programmes and spend time living overseas with a local family getting to know another culture. Families throughout the UK can open their home to host a young person of similar age coming to the UK on one of our hosting programmes. (See under Volunteering below.) We are also looking for people to become a volunteer to help prepare our participants going overseas or support our hosted partners or simply take part in one of our events.

'AFS at a glance:
- over 10,000 participants annually
- supported by 120,000 volunteers
- present in over 50 countries
- a registered charity in the UK
- volunteer-funded
- one of the largest community-based volunteer organisations in the world.'

Membership: Free membership – members receive regular newsletters and information about the charity's work and are entitled to attend the AGM in April.

Trading: Christmas catalogue available from July each year, telephone the charity at the number above.

Volunteers/jobseekers:
Sending programmes
School Programme: This gives 16 to 18 year olds the opportunity to live in another country for a year with a local family, and attend school. Apply the autumn before departure.

International Volunteer Programme: Volunteer to work on community projects overseas. Participants must be aged between 18 and 35 (depending on country). Volunteer for six months from January or July in Brazil, Costa Rica, Ecuador, Guatemala, Honduras, Panama or Peru. Participants are asked to fundraise/contribute £2,950 towards the costs of the entire six month programme. Participants receive a fundraising presentation and strategies/plans and an information pack to help with their fundraising.

South Africa and Ghana: The charity is looking for volunteers to work on community projects dealing with HIV/AIDS and other issues such as human rights and street children, in South Africa and Ghana for six months. You must be aged between 20 and 35, able to fundraise towards the costs, flexible and adaptable with a commitment to learning from other cultures. Participants live with a host family for six months sharing in day-to-day activities, exchanging ideas and extending friendships. From being a human rights monitor to an assistant teacher, placements with AFS projects emphasise participation and learning rather than leadership. Participants are asked to fundraise/contribute £2,950 towards the costs of the entire six month programme. Participants receive a fundraising presentation and receive strategies/plans and an information pack to help with their fundraising.

Hosting programmes

International Volunteer Programme: Young participants come from various countries and are hosted in the UK while they volunteer for six months on local community projects. Placements can involve working: with people with learning disabilities; with youth workers; on conservation projects; in development education; or with disadvantaged kids etc.

School Programme: The AFS school-based programme offers high school students the chance to live with a family in a community overseas while attending school and learning a language for one year. Students come from Latin America, Indonesia, the United States and Scandinavia. They will go to the local school for the year to study A-levels or Highers etc.

Conservation Programme: Participants (17 to 20 years old) travel around the UK in the summer working on conservation camps and staying with families between camps. Participants stay with families from two to eight days. These volunteers will spend six weeks in the UK during the summer months and are mainly from Japan, USA, Hong Kong, Italy and Canada.

Christmas Programme: Young people between 15 and 18 come from countries such as Argentina, Brazil and Malaysia to live with families in the UK for six weeks over Christmas and the New Year period.

For all these programmes AFS offers the opportunity to: families to share their homes, schools to add a new dimension to their classes and communities to learn about other communities. AFS families come in all shapes and sizes – children or no children, one or two parents, young or old. AFS families are volunteer families – the AFSer will become a member of your family.

Aid to Russia and the Republics (ARRC)
(incorporating The Ladybird Orphanage Project)

Fundraising and supporting overseas projects

Geographical focus: Armenia, Azerbaijan, Belarus, Estonia, Georgia, Kazakhstan, Kyrgyzstan, Latvia, Lithuania, Moldova, Russia, Tajikistan, Turkmenistan, Ukraine, Uzbekistan

PO Box 200, Bromley, Kent BR1 1QF
Tel: 020 8460 6046; **Fax:** 020 8466 1244
e-mail: info@arrc.org.uk
Website: www.arrc.org.uk
Correspondent: Anna Littler, Charity Manager

Expenditure: £202,000 (1999/2000)

Staffing: 4 full-time and 2 part-time salaried staff, also volunteers.

Website information: How to donate online; information about sponsoring a child; prayer points; events; news; a description of its projects in different locations; opportunities for volunteering; details of its Russian crafts for sale; information about Christianity and religious freedom in Russia and central Asia.

General: ARRC (formerly Aid to Russian Christians) was established in 1973 and supports church and humanitarian initiatives (of Christian organisations and individuals) serving the communities of the Commonwealth of Independent States (CIS) and Eastern Europe.

It is a partnership organisation and relies heavily on its contacts 'on the ground'. In 1998/99 it worked closely with Ichthus Christian Fellowship, Project Kyrgyzstan, Salvation Army, Radstock Ministries and a number of individual missionaries and indigenous pastors.

Ladybird Orphanage Project helps street children, Chernobyl victims, and disabled and needy children. It focuses on raising support for children's institutions and other child-related initiatives in the former Soviet Union.

In 1999/2000 projects supported by ARRC included:
- a drop-in centre for homeless pensioners in Kyrgyzstan
- a day centre for children with disabilities in Moldova
- a night shelter for street children in Siberia, Russia
- aid to internally displaced persons from Chechnya, following the outbreak of hostilities in that area once again
- a mobile clinic for the poor in Kazakhstan
- help for babies abandoned in hospital in Siberia, Russia
- a drug rehabilitation centre in Russia.

Membership: Membership is free, and members receive a bi-monthly newsletter. For £15 a month you can sponsor a child. For further information contact the charity at the address above.

Publications: Newsletter and resource packs are available on request.

Trading: Russian gifts and crafts are for sale, contact Gillian Mahers, ARRC, PO Box 6280, Basingstoke RG22 0YG; tel: 01256 320275.

Volunteers/jobseekers: ARRC relies on a team of volunteers, including students on vacation, for various aspects of its work:

Office-based
- bi-monthly newsletter mailing
- administrative duties
- database work
- finance.

Publicity and fundraising
- ARRC exhibition stands
- Christmas card and craft fairs
- fundraising events.

Aid work
- placements in CIS and Eastern Europe (people with the following skills are particularly needed: doctors, nurses, physiotherapists, special needs teachers, school teachers, TEFL teachers, nursery nurses and decorators; a month's placement costs between £650 and £890 and applicants must raise the funds themselves).

Volunteers overseas must respect the Christian faith of their hosts, but need not be Christians themselves.

Aid to the Church in Need (UK)

Assisting the Catholic Church overseas

Geographical focus: *Worldwide (over 130 countries in Eastern Europe, Latin America, Asia and Africa)*

1 Times Square, Sutton, Surrey SM1 1LF
Tel: 020 8642 8668; **Fax:** 020 8661 6293
e-mail: acn@acnuk.org
Website: www.kirche-in-not.org
Correspondent: Neville Kyrke Smith, National Director

Expenditure: £2.4 million (1999)

Staffing: 20 in the UK.

Website information: News; descriptions of its individual projects; how to help.

General: Founded in 1947, Aid to the Church in Need assists Catholic bishops, priests, sisters, missionaries and lay people in their work overseas, primarily through promoting pastoral care. Work includes providing vehicles for priests, financing the construction of churches and training of seminarians and catechists. Aid is also given to eligible people who are refugees and people who are repressed and persecuted and prevented from living according to their Catholic faith.

Requests for support must have the recommendation of the local bishop, a full description of the project and the circumstances surrounding it, the estimated cost and all other sources approached for aid. The charity rarely supports the full cost of the project.

Publications: Bi-monthly newsletter *Mirror*. Other publications about its own or related work.

Trading: ACN Trading Ltd offers cards and other items. It is a wholly owned subsidiary of the charity, to whom all profits are transferred.

Volunteers/jobseekers: There are occasional opportunities to volunteer at the headquarters in Germany. There are also opportunities for people to help out in the UK national office and at parish level with talks and appeals. Volunteers must be over 18.

The AIRE Centre

Providing advice on individual rights in Europe

Geographical focus: *Member countries of the European Community or the Council of Europe, or aspirant members; already works e.g. in Albania, Romania and the CIS*

74 Eurolink Business Centre, 49 Effra Road, London SW2 1BZ
Tel: 020 7924 9233; **Fax:** 020 7733 6786
e-mail: aire@beinternet.com
Correspondent: The Clerk

Expenditure: £157,000 (1999)

Staffing: 3 paid members of staff and 29 volunteers.

General: The charity provided the following information.

'The AIRE Centre is a specialist law centre which provides information and advice on international human rights law and European Union law.

'The AIRE Centre also acts as the European Commission's advisory service under the Eurojus programme.

'Its lawyers litigate before the European Court of Human Rights and have submitted applications in over 30 cases.

'All of the advice is provided free of charge so that members of the public and their legal representatives can enforce their rights effectively. The AIRE Centre is committed to providing a service that is both confidential, and free from unjustified discrimination on any grounds.

'The AIRE Centre also provides training for judges, lawyers and public officials throughout the 41 states of the Council of Europe.'

The Centre, for instance, advises a number of people who wish to move country and need to have a knowledge of their rights in the country of their proposed residence. It also helps people who want to know how to apply international agreements relating to family life, asylum and other human rights and freedoms.

Many of the requests for help come from people in the UK, but it has provided assistance in Albania, Romania and the CIS, for instance, and has a network of lawyers throughout Europe who it can call upon. 'The Centre's policy is to foster open cooperation and collaboration among European ngos working in the field of human rights and to avoid duplication of effort and competition for funds.'

The AIRE Centre does not have the facilities to see clients in person, but responds to requests for information after telephone calls or through written requests for assistance.

Alternative for India Development (AID)

Training and education in rural areas
Geographical focus: India

84 Aylesford Road, Handsworth, Birmingham B21 8DW
Tel: 0121 241 0793; **Fax:** 0121 554 5854
e-mail: ravi.kumar@btinternet.com
Website: www.aidindia.net
Correspondent: Ravi Kumar

Expenditure: £331,000 (1998/99)
Staffing: 3 full-time, 3 part-time paid staff; 15 volunteers.

Website information: Projects; events; publications; links; how to make a donation.

General: AID was founded in 1982 by young people in India and the UK. It runs a wide variety of training programmes including technical, vocational and health training for people who live in rural areas. It also runs literacy centres. By providing adult education for women it seeks to liberate them from prostitution, the child marriage dowry system, untouchability and caste distinctions. Its environmental projects prevent deforestation and encourage planting new trees. It also encourages people from India who are settled abroad to involve themselves in its development activities and provides information to Europeans about rural life in India.

Membership: Organisations (£10) and individuals (£5) can become members.

Publications: Quarterly journal.

Volunteers/jobseekers: AID sends volunteers on youth exchanges to carry out development work in rural parts of India. Medical and agricultural skills are particularly needed. In most cases volunteers must be totally self-financing. The minimum period overseas is three months.

In the UK volunteers can be involved in development education fundraising and in a social and legal awareness programme.

Contact the correspondent for further information.

Alzheimer's Disease International (ADI)

Strengthening the work of its members, so that they in turn are able to improve quality of life of people with dementia and their carers

Geographical focus: *Countries where there are full members: Argentina, Australia, Austria, Belgium, Brazil, Canada, Chile, Colombia, Cuba, Czech Republic, Denmark, Dominican Republic, Finland, France, Germany, Greece, Guatemala, Hong Kong, India, Ireland, Israel, Italy, Japan, Korea, Luxembourg, Mexico, Netherlands, New Zealand, Poland, Puerto Rico, Romania, Scotland, Singapore, South Africa, Spain, Sweden, Switzerland, Turkey, UK, United States, Uruguay, Venezuela. Provisional members: Cyprus, Costa Rica, Ecuador, El Salvador, Iceland, Malaysia, Pakistan, Peru, Russia, Slovakia, Thailand, Trinidad and Tobago, Uganda, Ukraine*

45–46 Lower Marsh, London SE1 7RG
Tel: 020 7620 3011; **Fax:** 020 7401 7351
e-mail: s.frade@alz.co.uk
Website: www.alz.co.uk
Correspondent: Susan Frade, Membership and Information Officer

Expenditure: US$356,000 (1998) (About £237,000)

Staffing: 4 members of staff.

Website information: World prevalence of people with dementia (facts and figures); factsheets; list of member organisations; information about Alzheimer's disease; events; publications; details about Alzheimer University; links to related sites.

General: ADI was established in 1984, when six countries with small Alzheimer's Associations began to work together. By 2000 ADI had become an umbrella organisation for 57 organisations throughout the world. Its main purpose is to build and strengthen the work of Alzheimer's Associations so they in turn are able to meet the needs of people with dementia and their carers. ADI works towards this aim through epidemiological research, disseminating information and running workshops covering organisational issues.

Most people with dementia live in developing countries and ADI estimates that this will increase to over 70% by 2025. ADI stated in its annual report 1998/99: 'in developing countries government health budgets are constrained and money for mental health is often almost non-existent. Inevitably countries have now started to look to non-governmental organisations to fill the care vacuum.

'ADI has an important role to play in supporting its members and, in particular, facilitating the development of new member associations, most of which will come from economically disadvantaged countries.'

In 1998/99 work towards this end included:
- annual international conference in India;
- running an Alzheimer University course, inviting representatives from Malaysia, Thailand, Lebanon, Egypt, Trinidad and Tobago, Russia and Slovakia;
- organised World Alzheimer's Day – promoting awareness of the disease.

Membership: 57 Alzheimer's disease organisations are members. Only one organisation per country can be a member and they are entitled to have a seat on the ADI Council.

Publications: Quarterly newsletter *Global Perspective* and other Alzheimer's disease-related publications and factsheets including *Help for carers*, *Starting a self-help group* and *Influencing public policy*.

Volunteers/jobseekers: There are opportunities to volunteer in the charity's UK office.

Amnesty International (UK section and international section)

Human rights campaigning
Geographical focus: Worldwide

99–119 Rosebery Avenue,
London EC1R 4RE
Tel: 020 7814 6200; **Fax:** 020 7833 1510
e-mail: info@amnesty.org.uk
Website: www.amnesty.org.uk
Correspondent: Allan Hogarth, Information and Publicity Officer

Expenditure: £7.1 million (1998)

Staffing: About 100 staff, all based in the UK.

Website information: Campaigns; news; how to take action yourself e.g. get involved in campaigns or become a member; library containing books, reports, educational materials; links to other sites.

General: The organisation provided the following summary. 'Amnesty International is a worldwide movement of people who campaign for human rights. Our appeals for victims of human rights violations are based on accurate research and on international law. We are independent of any government, political ideology, economic interest or religion.'

Its mandate is to:
- seek the release of all prisoners of conscience as long as they have not used or encouraged violence;
- work for fair and prompt trials for all political prisoners;
- campaign to abolish the death penalty, torture and other forms of cruel, inhuman or degrading treatment;
- end extrajudicial executions and 'disappearances';
- oppose abuses by opposition groups;
- provide relief to needy victims of human rights violations.

In 1999, Amnesty International campaigned, for example, in relation to: the Pinochet case; the recruitment of children into armed action; the use of electro-shock weapons and the disregard for international standards on torture and the treatment of children in the USA; and human rights violations in the Kosovo crisis.

Membership: The organisation has 'more than 1 million members and supporters'. Membership subscription fees are £30 for a family and £24 for an individual, or £7.50 for a student, young person, claimant, or senior citizen. Members receive a magazine.

Publications: Books include: *In the firing line: War and children's rights* (£9.99); *Human Rights Audit 1999* (£9.99); *Most vulnerable of all: The treatment of unaccompanied refugee children in the UK* (£9.99); *Made in Britain: How the UK makes torture and death its business* (£6.99); *Dare to be different: A celebration of freedom - a children's book* (£14.99); and *A map of hope: Women's writings on human rights* (£12.99).

Also available are an educational CD ROM and teacher's workbook, reports and videos.

Publications are available from bookshops or directly from the charity: Amnesty International UK, PO Box 4, Warwickshire CV21 1RU (tel: 01788 545553; fax: 01788 579244). There is a charge of £2 per order for postage and packaging.

Volunteers/jobseekers: Permanent salaried positions are advertised in the national press, mainly *The Guardian* and ethnic papers. Most voluntary work in the UK office is of a clerical and administrative nature, assisting teams mainly in campaigning, fundraising, information and press, membership and in the post room. Office skills can be particularly helpful. The organisation says that help which volunteers provide is highly valued by the staff and is an integral part to Amnesty International's success. However, as the work is of a routine nature you should think clearly about whether voluntary work is suitable for you. The minimum period for voluntary work is three months, full-time or part-time. However, preference will be given to people who feel that they will be able to work on a long-term basis. Your application is more likely to be successful if you give advance notice of your availability.

Anti-Slavery International

Works towards eliminating all forms of slavery

Geographical focus: *Worldwide*

Thomas Clarkson House, The Stableyard, Broomgrove Road, London SW9 9TL
Tel: 020 7501 8920; **Fax:** 020 7738 4110
e-mail: r.dasani@antislavery.org
Website: www.antislavery.org
Correspondent: Raj Dasani, Supporter Services

Expenditure: £554,000 (estimated 1999/2000)

Staffing: 16 full-time, salaried staff based in the UK.

Website information: Latest news; campaigns; resources; archives; information about how to get involved; links to related sites.

General: Founded in 1839, Anti-Slavery International is the world's oldest human rights organisation and it has consultative status with the United National Economic and Social Council.

It supports 'today's fight for tomorrow's freedom' by exposing current cases of slavery and campaigning for their eradication, supporting the initiatives of local organisations to release people and pressing for more effective implementation of international laws against slavery.

It focuses on all forms of slavery including exploitative child labour, bonded labour, forced labour, trafficking of children and women, cultural practices such as early or forced marriage and traditional or 'chattel' slavery. In all areas, it sees its partnerships with local organisations and groups around the world as vital to bringing about sustainable change.

Membership: Subscription rates are £25 waged (US$40), £8 unwaged or £300 life membership (US$480). Members receive the quarterly newsletter, free loan of videos and special offers on new publications.

Publications: A quarterly newsletter is produced, as well as a number of publications.

Volunteers/jobseekers: At any one time, it often has 10 to 15 volunteers or interns and can also offer work experience placements. Volunteer placements involve practical office-based work experience and are flexible. Previously, for example, volunteers have worked from four hours a week, up to four days a week. A commitment of three months is normal. Lunch and travel expenses are provided within the London area only. Volunteers work within the library team, admin team and campaigns and programme team.

Internships tend to be more academic and project-led in content. Overseas applicants who are registered with a validated Student Exchange Scheme are invited to apply (minimum of three months). Most interns will have been or are currently in the process of achieving a Bachelors or Masters degree in a related subject, i.e. International Relations or Human Rights. London-based students studying for a Masters degree may complete an internship to compliement their coursework.

Work experience applicants normally apply through their schools or colleges and are not graduates. People aged 15–19 may apply for work experience on a full-time basis for a maximum of two weeks.

Anyone interested in applying for a position should send a cv and covering letter to Rebecca Smaga at the address above, outlining the kind of work for which they would like to be considered.

APT Enterprise Development

Skills training and specialist support for the development of small enterprises

Geographical focus: *As at 2000: Ghana, Kenya, Sierra Leone, Tanzania, Uganda, Zimbabwe*

29 Northwick Business Centre,
Blockley, Moreton-in-Marsh,
Gloucestershire GL56 9RF
Tel: 01386 700130; **Fax:** 01386 701010
e-mail: apt.enterprise@dial.pipex.com
Website: www.go.to/apt_enterprise.com
Correspondent: Michael Walsby, Chief Executive

Expenditure: £989,000 (1999)
Staffing: 5 staff members.

Website information: Information on the geographical locations of where APT works; how to make a donation; financial information; a description and examples of appropriate technology and product development.

General: Its annual review says 'APT is a UK-based charity dedicated to reducing poverty in developing countries by working with local organisations to provide skills training and specialist support for the development of small enterprises. In this way, men and women are enabled to generate their own income and thus provide for their families' survival'.

APT was established as APT Design and Development in 1984 and began by providing technical expertise and appropriate technology, but soon widened its services.

Recent projects have included:
- adapting a solar dryer for fruit and vegetables in Tanzania, to reduce wastage on food which is in excess of that which can be consumed;
- helping rural communities in Sierra Leone to increase their capability in viable farming and non-farming;
- training of trainers in Zimbabwe;
- support for potters and beadmakers in Ghana.

ApTibeT

Promoting the use of appropriate technology

Geographical focus: *India, Nepal*

Unit 4 & F5, 1st Floor, London Fashion Centre, 89–93 Fonthill Road,
London N4 3JH
Tel: 020 7281 8180; **Fax:** 020 7281 8280
e-mail: info@aptibet.org
Website: www.aptibet.org
Correspondent: Ms Lola Kehinde

Expenditure: £803,000 (1999)
Staffing: 5 paid staff; 1 volunteer.

Website information: Story of Tibet; story of ApTibeT; map of Tibet settlements; interactive form for completion by people involved with Tibetans and information about 'momos'; information about the Tibetan Environmental Network. Information about ApTibeT's: partners; technologies – facts and figures; environment projects; training programmes; educational publications.

General: ApTibeT was set up in 1984 with the aim of improving the quality of life of Tibetan people living in exile in India. It now also works with Tibetans in Nepal, as well as with ethnic Tibetan people and their host communities in South Asia.

Projects previously completed include:
- the five-year Integrated Energy Programme. The charity designed and tested nine energy efficient technologies for use in nomadic tents and homes in Ladakh. This resulted in the production of almost 1,000 pieces of equipment including passive and active solar technologies for cooking and room heating, and improved (fuel efficient) smokeless cooking stoves;
- establishing the Computer Input Centre, which provided training and employment for 20 young unemployed women;
- running the Training Programme on Project Management and Needs Analysis Workshop in five Tibetan settlements;
- the drilling of a new borewell and installation of a windmill for domestic water pumping;
- carrying out an emergency relief programme for nomads living in the Changthang region of Ladakh, North West India.

Membership: There is no membership, but names can be placed on a mailing list to receive publications, e.g. newsletter.

Publications: Newsletter.

Volunteers/jobseekers: The charity recruits people to volunteer in the UK who are able to offer time and commitment, to assist in routine office activities, fundraising, marketing and media activities, research work, and general support of field programmes. Volunteers should be interested in the sector, have numeracy skills and some IT knowledge.

A limited number of volunteers have been placed overseas in the past, but only those with relevant and previous experience, such as in appropriate building technologies, solar architecture, low technology water and sanitation provision and agricultural science.

Please contact Pete Crawford at the above address for further information.

Arid Lands Initiative

Helping communities to achieve self-sufficiency in food, water and energy

Geographical focus: Yemen, other dry land rural regions and inner-city sites (including in the UK)

Machpelah Works, Burnley Road,
Hebden Bridge,
West Yorkshire HX7 8AZ
Tel: 01422 843807; **Fax:** 01422 842241
e-mail: oasis@aridlands.freeserve.co.uk
Correspondent: The Director

Expenditure: £158,000 (1999/2000)

Staffing: 2 full-time, 2 part-time members of staff.

General: Arid Lands Initiative was registered with the Charity Commission in 1989, and works in the UK and overseas to enable poor communities to tackle their urban and rural environmental problems through their own practical action. Its overall aim is to initiate local group action so that schools, tenants associations and parish networks in the UK and indigenous groups of farmer associations and tribal networks overseas can tackle their shared common problems, in this way creating and/or reinforcing cohesion and organisational strengths within that local community.

Many of the techniques that it has pioneered overseas, in the arid zone, have been successfully transferred and applied to mobilise schools and communities to regenerate derelict land in deprived inner-city areas of the UK. As an ngo, it primarily works alongside 'common interest' groups, strengthening their capacity to identify, develop and demonstrate environmental 'best practices' that sustainably improve local self-sufficiency in food, water and renewable energy, using both traditional and innovative techniques to conserve natural resources. By stimulating practical action in carefully selected pilot schemes which typify examples of broader networks facing similar problems, its aim is to act as a catalyst for wider practical action regionally and nationally.

By documenting successful practical initiatives on broadcast quality video it aims to produce audio visual material to raise awareness, both locally through training programmes with community organisations, farmer groups, schools, tenants associations, scouts, guides etc. and through wider national and international television networks. Its work primarily focuses on the arid zone rural sector overseas and deprived inner cities, both in developed and developing economies.

Volunteers/jobseekers: There are no opportunities for volunteering overseas.

Article 19 (Global Campaign for Free Expression)

Campaigning for freedom of expression

Geographical focus: *Algeria, Azerbaijan, Bangladesh, Bosnia-Herzegovina, Bulgaria, Burkina Faso, Burma, Cameroon, China, Czech Republic, Democratic Republic of Congo, Egypt, Estonia, Ethiopia, Fiji, Hong Kong, Indonesia, Jordan, Kenya, Kosovo, Lithuania, Malawi, Malaysia, Namibia, Nigeria, Pakistan, Palestine, Russia, Sierra Leone, Slovakia, South Africa, Sri Lanka, Swaziland, Syria, Tanzania, Turkey, Ukraine, Zanzibar, Zimbabwe*

Lancaster House, 33 Islington High Street, London N1 9LH
Tel: 020 7278 9292; **Fax:** 020 7713 1356
e-mail: info@article19.org
Website: www.article19.org
Correspondent: The Information Officer

Expenditure: £1.2 million (1999)

Staffing: 15 members of staff (salaried) and 10 interns and volunteers, all based in the UK.

Website information: Recent activities; news including press releases; programmes by continent; information on freedom of expression issues; publications; how to take action e.g. get involved in campaigns; links; virtual Freedom of Expression Handbook; job vacancies.

General: Article 19 of the Universal Declaration of Human Rights states: 'Everyone has the right to freedom of opinion and expression; this right includes freedom to hold opinions without interference and to seek, receive and impart information and ideas through any media and regardless of frontiers.'

The charity, named after this declaration, works to combat censorship by promoting freedom of expression and access to official information. It works with partners in different countries to strenghthen local capacity and monitor and protest about institutional and informal censorship.

In Asia, for instance, it has focused on Burma, China, Indonesia and Sri Lanka, and has tracked the freedom of expression situation – both in law and in practice – for a decade. It monitors the wider region and campaigns on issues such as national security in Pakistan and freedom for writers in Bangladesh. In November 2000, the charity's website said: 'Recently, we have been very involved with assisting on media law reform in Indonesia, and with transitional regulations for the media in East Timor. We report annually on Hong Kong with the Hong Kong Journalists' Association. We are involved in a series of workshops in Sri Lanka, looking at particular threats to freedom of expression, such as criminal defamation penalties and the use of national security to enhance official censorship.'

Publications: Publications are available online and include: analyses of country situations; regional overviews and thematic reports; analyses of laws; briefings to courts; and submissions to international bodies. There is an annual subscription, discounts are available.

Volunteers/jobseekers: Voluntary posts and internships are available in the UK. If you are interested please send your cv/resume and a letter stating the particular areas which interest you, to Susan Johnson by email: sue@article19.org or in writing to the address above. She will reply if there are any vacancies.

Associated Country Women of the World (ACCW)

Supporting rural women and families through education, training and advocacy

Geographical focus: Australia, Austria, Bangladesh, Belarus, Belgium, Botswana, Brunei, Bulgaria, Cameroon, Canada, China, Christmas Island, Colombia, Czech Republic, Denmark, Egypt, Estonia, Fiji, Finland, Gambia, Germany, Ghana, Greece, Grenada, Guyana, Iceland, India, Indonesia, Jamaica, Kenya, Kiribati, Korea, Latvia, Lesotho, Lithuania, Madagascar, Malaysia, Mali, Mauritius, Namibia, Nepal, Netherlands, New Zealand, Nigeria, Niue Island, Norway, Pakistan, Papua New Guinea, Philippines, Poland, Republic of Ireland, Romania, Russia, St Vincent & Grenadines, Slovenia, Solomon Islands, South Africa, Spain, Sri Lanka, Swaziland, Sweden, Switzerland, Thailand, Tonga, Trinidad & Tobago, Tuvalu, Uganda, UK, USA, Western Samoa, Zambia, Zimbabwe

Mary Sumner House, 24 Tufton Street, London SW1P 3RB
Tel: 020 7799 3875; **Fax:** 020 7340 9950
e-mail: info@acww.org.uk
Website: www.accw.org.uk
Correspondent: Anna Frost, General Secretary

Expenditure: £506,000 (1999)
Staffing: 10 members of staff.
Website information: Membership form for individuals; information about conferences; how to contact the charity.
General: ACWW's objectives are:
- to raise the standard of living of rural women and families through education, training and community development programmes;

- to provide practical support to its member societies and help them set up income-generating schemes;
- to give rural women a voice at international level through its links with UN agencies.

The priorities for 1998–2001 were:
- status of women and education – human rights, children, the girl child;
- health and nutrition – the family, older persons, safer childbirth, population, AIDS, female genital mutilation, sexual and reproductive rights, drug abuse;
- environment and sustainable development – agriculture, food security, water, habitat, plant genetics;
- labour and income generation – employment, micro-credit, economic rights.

Most of the charity's work appears to be the provision of funds to its member societies. In 1999, 25 new development projects were funded. These included water projects, agricultural projects, nutrition education programmes, food processing equipment, children's homes and female circumcision awareness campaigns.

The charity also ran six area conferences in 1999, providing members with, for example, the opportunity to share their experiences and develop strategies for enabling and empowering women. Other information sharing, training and advocacy work is also carried out by the charity.

Membership: Individual membership costs £15 a year; members receive magazine *The Countrywoman* quarterly.

Trading: Limited merchandise such as pens and brooches are available from the charity.

Volunteers/jobseekers: There are no opportunities for volunteering in the UK.

ATD Fourth World

Empowering families living in poverty

Geographical focus: Belgium, Bolivia, Burkina Faso, Canada, France, Germany, Guatemala, Haiti, Ireland, Italy, Ivory Coast, Luxembourg, Madagascar, Mauritius, Netherlands, Peru, Philippines, Portugal, Senegal, Spain, Switzerland, Tanzania, Thailand, UK, USA

48 Addington Square, London SE5 7LB
Tel: 020 7703 3231; **Fax:** 020 7252 4276
e-mail: atd.uk@ukonline.co.uk
Website: web.ukonline.co.uk/atd.uk
Correspondent: The Clerk

Expenditure: £330,000 for the UK branch (1998/99)

Staffing: 380 core-workers within the international organisation worldwide.

Website information: Volunteering; journal and other publications; campaigns; breakdown of its work; greetings card sales.

General: The charity provided the following information: 'ATD Fourth World (All together for dignity) was founded in 1957 by Joseph Wresinski, together with poor families who were living in an emergency housing camp in Noisy Le Grand near Paris. Having been raised in poverty himself, he introduced the name "Fourth World" in recognition of the collective identity of the poorest and their refusal to accept poverty.

'Guided by the families at the camp, Wresinski's first actions were to replace the soup kitchen with a centre where adults could meet and to create a children's library. He said "They were as hungry for dignity as they were for running water; they were thirsty for learning".

'From the mud and terrible poverty of the camp, Wresinski called on people from all walks of life, nationalities and faiths: "We went in to that camp with empty hands and only ourselves to offer. This made it possible for us to be accepted by the most disadvantaged families".

'Today, ATD Fourth World is an international voluntary organisation that works in 25 countries on 5 continents (North and South America, Europe, Africa and Asia). There are established projects in inner city slums and deprived rural areas throughout the developed and developing worlds.

'ATD Fourth World regards the existence of extreme poverty as a denial of basic human rights. Our approach towards the alleviation of poverty is twofold:

- helping people who live in poverty to learn new skills, to regain their confidence and hope, and to encourage them to discuss and develop their efforts to overcome poverty and their struggle for dignity;
- raising public awareness of poverty through publications which tell the story of the excluded from their own perspective and share the experience and knowledge gained by the core-workers.

'Alongside the people experiencing long-term poverty, there are two other groups of people who are committed to the eradication of poverty:

- The core-workers live and work full-time alongside very poor families. At the end of 1999 there were 380 core workers, 220 having worked for more than five years and 45 having worked for at least 20 years. Both couples and single volunteers are welcomed into the organisation. They receive continuous training and support and agree to work for a minimal wage that symbolises solidarity with the poorest, but also provides them with basic security. Their aim is to assist the efforts of the poor to live in dignity and to take an active part in the running of their community.
- The Friends of ATD Fourth World are people who offer their time and skills to the organisation on a voluntary basis. They support the poorest through their involvement with ATD Fourth World and encourage their friends, relatives and associates, as well as the general public, to see the very poor as important and useful members of society.'

Publications: *The Fourth World Journal*, is produced quarterly. Other books: *Emergence from Extreme Poverty* which describes the philosophy of ATD Fourth World and of the work of full-time core workers (£5); *Artisans of Democracy* £8.50); *Participation Works* (£6); *Education: Opportunities* (£6). Publications are available from the correspondent.

Trading: The charity sells Christmas cards.

Volunteers/jobseekers: 'ATD Fourth World is based on the commitment of men and women who have been chosen to share their skills with the very poor. If you are interested in joining us either as a friend or as a full-time core-worker there are no requirements regarding age, experience, or qualifications. The main requirement is a genuine concern for those families who are exluded from society and live in perpetual poverty. You should demonstrate a willingness to work as part of a team.

'If you are interested in making a commitment, we would like you to participate in an introductory working weekend. These monthly working weekends (and our Summer workcamps) serve as a general introduction to the organisation and enable you to work alongside the core-workers, ask questions, and share with us your experience of the poor in society and your reasons for wanting to help. Accommodation is provided but you will be asked to make a small contribution towards food costs. 'If you wish to be considered for a full-time commitment, you would then take part in a three-month induction programme in England. As a "trainee" you live and work alongside the full-time core-workers, take part in manual and office work, learn about the organisation and about the lives of the most deprived families through discussions, books and videos and assist in projects with poor families.

'There is no fee for the induction programme, accommodation is provided and for the second and third months you receive a small allowance. At the end of the programme, you can go on:
- to become a core-worker in another continent (for which a commitment of two years is required);
- to stay on as a core-worker in Great Britain, or in Europe;
- to become a Friend of ATD Fourth World.

Contact Helen Penet, Training & Recruitment Officer for further information, either by telephone or in writing, at the contact details listed above.

Baby Milk Action (BMAC)

Campaigning to protect breastfeeding and to halt the promotion of artificial infant feeding

Geographical focus: *Worldwide*

23 St Andrews Street,
Cambridge CB2 3AX
Tel: 01223 464420; **Fax:** 01223 464417
e-mail: babymilkacti@gn.apc.org
Website: www.gn.apc.org/babymilk
Correspondent: Ms Patti Randall, Policy Director

Expenditure: £173,000 (1999/2000)

Staffing: 4 full-time and 1 half-time paid staff and 4 volunteers in the UK office. 80 area contacts UK-wide.

Website information: Latest news and a virtual shop selling publications and merchandise such as videos, t-shirts and miscellaneous items advertising the Nestlé boycott.

General: The following information appears on the charity's website. 'Baby Milk Action… campaigns to protect breastfeeding and to halt the promotion of artificial infant feeding. We raise awareness of the dangers of artificial feeding and campaign for improvements to the labelling and composition of artificial feeds.

'We exist to protect mothers and their babies regardless of the feeding method used. We are not anti-baby milk, but believe its properties and the need for it are over-stated.

'Baby Milk Action works to secure an infant's right to the highest level of health, a woman's right to informed choices about infant feeding, and the right of everyone to health care facilities free from commercial pressure.

'We aim to save the lives of the 1.5 million babies who die every year because they are not breastfed.

'Baby Milk Action:
- raises awareness about the damage caused by artificial feeding. We use a range of publications, videos and display materials. We also contribute to workshops, conferences and training courses. Our network of area contacts may be able to assist in running stalls or speaking at events;
- campaigns against the irresponsible marketing of baby foods which encourages mothers and health workers to favour bottle feeding;

- helps and encourages members of the public to protest against company tactics. We coordinate the international boycott of Nestlé, the world's largest baby milk manufacturer;
- works in partnership with the World Health Organisation (WHO) and the United Nations Children's Fund (UNICEF) to protect and support breastfeeding. We helped to develop the WHO/UNICEF International Code of Marketing of Breast-milk Substitutes and subsequent Resolutions and sit on the advisory panel of UNICEF's Baby Friendly Hospital Initiative in the UK;
- lobbies the UK Government and European Union to introduce laws and regulations which protect breastfeeding and improve maternity benefits;
- monitors the promotion of baby foods around the world and challenges company practices. We produce regular reports on the baby food industry's violations of the International Code;
- publishes a regular newsletter, *Update*, with the latest information on all our work and news from around the world. We also publish papers on specific issues related to infant feeding;
- maintains a comprehensive information system on infant feeding issues.'

Membership: 'We hope you will join us or send a donation. Members of Baby Milk Action receive our regular newsletter, *Update*, three times a year and are free to contact us for information or to make an appointment for access to our information system. Members who wish to become active in the campaign will be supported with advice and materials. We also have a network of area contacts in the UK who act as a focus for activities.' The charity has about 2,000 individual members and other people join in its campaigns.

Publications: Books, videos and display materials, newsletter *Update*, papers on specific issues related to infant feeding and miscellaneous items advertising the Nestlé boycott.

Trading: Merchandise which advertises the campaign such as t-shirts, pens etc.

Volunteers/jobseekers: See under Membership, above.

The BEARR Trust
Facilitating Russian ngos
Geographical focus: *The Commonwealth of Independent States*

24 Greville Street, London EC1N 8SS
Tel: 020 7404 7081; **Fax:** 020 7404 7103
e-mail: info@bearr.org.uk
Correspondent: Kyrill Dissanayake, Programme Development Officer

Expenditure: £191,000 (1999)
Staffing: 2 full-time staff, plus volunteers.

General: This charity provided the following information. It 'enables:
- Russian ngos to help people in need
- Russian and British ngos to meet, share knowledge and learn from each other
- Russian ngos to play their part in establishing a more democratic society.

'When The BEARR Trust was formed in 1991 Russia was just starting to move from a command economy to a market economy and from communism to an open democratic society. BEARR's overall aim is to help Russia become a democratic society. An essential ingredient of such a society is an alert and caring voluntary sector supporting and speaking up for people disadvantaged by poverty, age, disability, chronic illness or other handicaps. Today BEARR works to tackle Russia's social issues in partnership with Russian ngos.'

Programmes in 1999/2000 included:
- training ngo leaders in the Greater Urals and Mid-Volga regions, e.g. helping leaders to develop contacts, diversify their funding base and broaden the scope of their work;
- training carers of abused children, e.g. helping a child protection agency in Russia to develop a distance learning pack for the benefit of other organisations;
- a public debate in Britain on the subject of future cooperation with Russia.

Membership: Individuals and organisations can subscribe to *The BEARR Trust Newsletter*, at a charge of £20 a year. Individuals can become Friends of the BEARR Trust, at a charge of £25 a year. Friends receive the newsletter, the annual review and invitations to BEARR events.

Publications: *Directory of Non-Governmental Organisations of the Sverdlovsk Oblast, Russia*; *Glossary of Social Care Terms* (English to Russian with commentary); *The BEARR Trust Newsletter*, published quarterly.

Volunteers/jobseekers: None overseas. There are opportunities to help out in the UK office with administrative tasks, fundraising and special events. For more information contact the correspondent.

BESO

Offering professional expertise to organisations

Geographical focus: Albania, Anguilla, Armenia, Azerbaijan, Bangladesh, Barbados, Belarus, Belize, Bermuda, Bolivia, Bosnia-Herzegovina, Brazil, Bulgaria, Cameroon, Cayman Islands, China, Colombia, Cook Islands, Croatia, Czech Republic, Dominican Republic, Ecuador, El Salvador, Eritrea, East Jerusalem, Estonia, Ethiopia, Fiji, Gambia, Georgia, Ghana, Grenada, Guatemala, Guyana, Hungary, India, Jamaica, Jordan, Kazakhstan, Kenya, Latvia, Lebanon, Lesotho, Lithuania, Macedonia, Madagascar, Malawi, Malaysia, Mauritius, Mexico, Mongolia, Montserrat, Mozambique, Namibia, Nepal, Nicaragua, Pakistan, Palau Republic, Papua New Guinea, Paraguay, Peru, Philippines, Poland, Romania, Russia, St Lucia, St Vincent, Slovak Republic, Slovenia, South Africa, Swaziland, Tanzania, Thailand, Trinidad, Tristan da Cunha, Tunisia, Tuvalu, Uganda, Ukraine, Uzbekistan, Vanuatu, Vietnam, Yemen, Yugoslavia, Zambia, Zimbabwe

164 Vauxhall Bridge Road,
London SW1V 2RB
Tel: 020 7630 0644; **Fax:** 020 7630 0624
e-mail: team@beso.org
Website: www.beso.org
Correspondent: Katie Donald, Information Officer

Expenditure: £2.2 million (1998/99)

Staffing: BESO has offices in London, Edinburgh, Moscow and Johannesburg.

Website information: How: to offer help as a volunteer, with up-to-date information on the types of expertise from volunteers which is most urgently needed (see below); organisations in developing countries go about asking for help from BESO; companies can offer help.

General: BESO is a development agency that offers professional expertise to private, public and voluntary sector organisations in less developed communities worldwide. It works to strengthen local economies. It gives advice and training free of charge to organisations that cannot afford commercial consultants.

It works by matching requests for specific help from organisations with the most suitably qualified volunteer from its register of over 3,500 experts. Most of its volunteers are retired or near retirement age. BESO volunteers complete around 600 assignments each year lasting between two weeks and six months in duration.

Private, public and multilateral organisations can also work with BESO, e.g. through sponsoring assignments perhaps undertaken by seconded staff, or through creating partnership programmes in sectors or regions of mutual interest.

Examples of assignments which were undertaken by volunteers in 1998/99 include:
- companies in Poland received tailored advice on sales and marketing, financial planning and technical production;
- one volunteer helped to develop the Knowledge Warehouse that brings new ideas and innovations about any aspect of community activity into the Kirovograd, Ukraine;
- a volunteer helped a biscuit company in Yemen to expand their business and create new employment opportunities.

Publications: It produces several information leaflets, e.g. information on becoming a BESO volunteer and on how to receive assistance from a BESO volunteer.

Volunteers/jobseekers: It has 3,500 people on its register of experts. Volunteers need to be flexible in terms of availability for assignments, to assist for between six and eight weeks a year. Once assignments have been arranged, BESO organises and normally pays for travel and insurance for the volunteer; the client provides suitable accommodation and pays local expenses.

BESO are oversubscribed in education and human resources skills and are looking for volunteers with technical skills, particularly: bottling/canning experts, conservationists, ecologists, environmentalists, electronic engineers, food production specialists, garment manufacturers, handicrafts and marketing experts, occupational therapists, paper production experts, paramedical trainers, physiotherapists, social workers/counsellors, textiles experts and producers of sanitary ceramics.

For further information e-mail: registrar@beso.org or visit the website at the address above.

BibleLands

Christian-led projects working mainly towards the education and health of children and young people, especially those with physical or intellectual disabilities

Geographical focus: *Egypt, Israel, Jordan, Lebanon, Palestine, Sudan*

PO Box 50, High Wycombe, Buckinghamshire HP15 7QU
Tel: 01494 897950; **Fax:** 01494 897951
e-mail: info@biblelands.co.uk
Correspondent: A Jong, Chief Executive

Expenditure: £2.7 million (1998/99)

Staffing: 27 members of staff.

General: The charity was originally founded in 1854 and was previously known as Turkish Missions Aid Society and also BIBLE Lands Society. Its object when it was established was not to originate any new missionary enterprises, but to aid existing missions in the Turkish Empire. The charity now operates the Helen Keller School for Blind Children in Jerusalem and also aids the work of about 60 local Christian groups, mainly through providing funding. The charity is non-denominational.

The charity summarises its work as follows: 'We support a wide range of Christian-led projects, selecting those which are most in need. Our prime concern is for the education and health of children and young people, especially those with physical or intellectual disabilities.'

Most of the charity's financial support to projects is towards helping them to meet their running costs and expenses. It provides funding to, for example:

- schools which offer a Christian-based education. Often the schools are residential, for children from poor families who are otherwise denied schooling 'or a real future'. The charity also supports special schools for children who are disabled;
- children's homes;
- education and health rehabilitation centres, including centres for children who are disabled;
- healthcare training programmes;
- projects for Sudanese refugees and others in immediate need of food, clothing, health care or basic training in income earning skills.

The charity also provides resources, e.g. for vocational training, including training student nurses.

Membership: Sponsors (of children, nurses, or other aspects of the charity's work) receive annual progress reports, news updates, and the magazine.

Publications: Promotional literature including *ChildSponsor* leaflet, *NurseSponsor* leaflet, *CareSharer* leaflet; *Pilgrim Partners* (Bible study and video pack) - further information available from correspondent; *The Star in the East* magazine.

Trading: The charity has a subsidiary mail order trading operation – BibleLands Trading Limited.

BMS World Mission
(formerly Baptist Missionary Society) (BMS)

Christian work including educational, social, development and agricultural work

Geographical focus: Asia, Africa, Europe and Central and South America

PO Box 49, Baptist House, 129 Broadway, Didcot OX11 8XA
Tel: 01235 517700; **Fax:** 01235 517601
e-mail: mail@bms.org.uk
Website: www.bms.org.uk
Correspondent: Mike Quantick

Expenditure: £5.8 million (1998/99)

Staffing: Over 150 workers serving overseas, they include 129 full-time missionaries and candidates, 36 volunteers and 25 Youth Action Team members.

Website information: News; publications; information for prospective salaried staff and volunteers including children.

General: William Carey founded the charity in 1793 in India. The following information was taken from the charity's website. 'Today BMS world mission has partnerships with over 30 countries on four continents, Asia, Africa, Europe and Central and South America. The work is diverse and varied with BMS world mission personnel involved in evangelism, church planting, theological education, Sunday school work as well as medical, educational, literature, development, agriculture and so on'.

Its work in the different continents is summarised below:
- Asia and Africa – evangelism linked with education, health and agricultural development;
- Latin America and the Caribbean – evangelism and church planting, social work in city slums, development and

agricultural work in poor communities and theological education;
- Europe – evangelism.

Membership: Adults can subscribe to magazine *World Mission* for the cost of £8.40 UK/£19.80 overseas a year and receive six issues. Children and youth can join the World Mission Club for the cost of £2.40 a year.

Publications: *World Mission* magazine, a small selection of books and videos and youth project packs. E-mail: resources@bms.org.uk for further information.

Volunteers/jobseekers: Salaried positions in the UK office are advertised on the charity's website.

Regarding its programmes for volunteers, the charity says 'BMS is making mission possible in exciting ways all over the world, sharing the good news of Jesus with needy people, both in word and action. We're actively looking for Christians who have a heart to obey God in using their lives and skills wherever in the world God would have them be. The only "must" is a love for Christ and a desire to make him known. Please contact Kathy Kavanagh: kkavanagh@bms.org.uk for more information'.

Short-term Youth Action Teams take part in BMS's overseas work during summer holidays. Individuals should be aged 18 to 25 years old. E-mail: sbaker@bms.org.uk for further information.

The charity stated that most skills are needed in long-term situations and interested individuals should apply. As at October 2000, the following long-term posts were advertised on the website, along with with further information about the geographical location of the jobs: men or women ministers; teachers for expatriate children; director of projects; radiologist; dentist; teachers of nursing students; and rural health post staff.

BOND (British Overseas NGOs for Development)

Networking and sharing information

Geographical focus: Worldwide

Regent's Wharf, 8 All Saints Street, London N1 9RL
Tel: 020 7837 8344; **Fax:** 020 7837 4220
e-mail: bond@bond.org.uk
Website: www.bond.org.uk
Correspondent: Richard Bennett, Coordinator

Expenditure: About £500,000

Staffing: 16 staff (equivalent to 12 full-time).

Website information: Overview of BOND activities including membership information; publications; directory of members; register of UK ngo networks; members' activities search; directory of suppliers and service providers; events; news; current non-government development organisation job vacancies and events; and information about organisations providing training in development.

General: BOND is a network of UK-based ngos, set up in June 1993, and aims to improve the extent and quality of the UK's and Europe's contribution to international development, the eradication of global poverty and the upholding of human rights. Members come together in BOND to pursue their vision and purpose through: training; sharing information, experience, ideas and best practice; collective access to services and resources; and collective representation.

BOND's activities focus on:
Facilitating networking opportunities
- between members and with other ngo networks through a series of events (including working groups, learning circles and themed days) initiating

debate on key issues and supporting organisational learning;
- with UK government and EU bodies, representing the views of the member ngos in common policy statements and advocating effectively together on a diverse range of concerns;
- between members and other UK/EU external agencies, including the private sector and academic institutions, supporting effective development of inter-organisation relationships.

Providing a comprehensive training programme that enables ngos' learning needs to be met in ways which promote best practice and a strategic approach to lesson learning within and beyond the development sector

Ensuring ngos have ready access to information which enhances their work, and raising awareness on capacity-building opportunities.

All information is freely available on the BOND website (see above), or enquiries can be made to the BOND Secretariat. Details on BOND's publications are listed below. The BOND Database of Member Activities, searchable on the website, holds information on the interests and areas of operation of member organisations and reports can be generated listing the names of agencies working in a specified region, country, sector etc. There are web links to further information on the organisations listed within these reports.

Membership: In February 2001, BOND had 234 members. Members pay an annual subscription, based on their annual expenditure, and govern BOND through an Annual General Meeting.

There are four types of membership: full membership, which is open to all UK-based voluntary organisations working in international development, including those concerned with development education; associate membership, which is open to UK-based organisations which are interested in the promotion of or research into issues concerned with international development and development education but may not meet the criteria for full membership; provisional membership, for organisations working towards being active in international development or preparing to support British development ngos; and group membership for organisations active in international development who demonstrate a particular interest or expertise in the issue covered by a BOND working group.

Publications: Most BOND publications are available free of charge on the website and include: *Directory of Members*; *Register of NGO Networks*; *Training Directory and Register of Freelance Trainers*; *Guidance Notes Series* which provide 'how-to' information on topics such as logical framework analysis, advocacy, and planning and seeing through a project; *The Networker*, a newsletter; and *Advertisement Bulletin*, circulated twice a month, advertising jobs, publications, office space, equipment, training and events.

Volunteers/jobseekers: BOND provides an *Advertisements Bulletin* in response to enquiries from volunteers and jobseekers, and provides lists of ngos on its website. BOND does not have the capacity for interns or for many volunteers.

Book Aid International

Supporting literacy, education, training and publishing by providing books and other reading materials

Geographical focus: *85% of books go to sub-Saharan Africa but the charity also receives requests from other locations including South East Asia, Palestine, Cuba and the Caribbean Islands*

39-41 Coldharbour Lane, Camberwell, London SE5 9NR
Tel: 020 7733 3577; **Fax:** 020 7978 8006
e-mail: info@bookaid.org
Website: www.bookaid.org
Correspondent: Sara Harrity, Director

Expenditure: £4.2 million (1998/99)

Staffing: 30 salaried staff and approximately 12 volunteers.

Website information: Copies of the newsletter *Interchange*; information about how you can help; details of World Book Day; criteria for organisations wishing to receive book aid.

General: The charity's mission statement follows. 'Book Aid International works in partnership with organisations in developing countries to support local initiatives in literacy, education, training and publishing. We provide relevant books and information to those in greatest need – to enable people to realise their potential and contribute to the development of their communities.'

Requests are received, for example, from public schools, libraries and colleges, which are working towards the above aims. Book Aid International gathers books and reading materials and asks professionals from organisations overseas to choose what they need for themselves.

Books are donated by publishers, schools, colleges, libraries and individuals. Income from fundraising is also used to buy books to fill 'gap' areas which are rarely donated such as up-to-date atlases and dictionaries.

A key part of the work is to buy books published in Africa to help publishers there meet the information needs of their countries. This contributes to the charity's aim to find a long-term solution to the problem of local book provision.

The charity supports professional and vocational training through providing books in a wide range of subject areas from medical and legal texts to books on carpentry, forestry, catering and needlework.

Work takes place in partnership with organisations overseas with strong in-country networks which are able to distribute the books to the people who need them the most, including public library services, non-governmental organisations and the British Council.

The charity contributes towards raising the awareness of British children to development work, through promoting fundraising schemes in schools and other organisations, e.g. Girl Guides.

Membership: Donors to the charity are sent its newsletter *Interchange* twice a year.

Publications: Newsletters *Interchange* and *Partners in African Publishing*, information for volunteers and other leaflets.

Volunteers/jobseekers: No volunteering opportunities overseas. Most of the volunteers work in the library/warehouse in Camberwell, helping to stamp and pack up the books to send overseas.

A leaflet describing the nature of the charity's voluntary work and an application form is available from the correspondent.

The Britain-Nepal Medical Trust (BNMT)

Providing health programmes e.g. TB and leprosy control, drug services, community health.

Geographical focus: Eastern Nepal

Export House, 130 Vale Road, Tonbridge, Kent TN9 1SP
Tel: 01732 360284 (9am–12noon);
Fax: 01732 363876
e-mail: bnmtuk@compuserve.com;
In Nepal: dirbnmt@mos.com.np
Correspondent: Mrs Gay Peck, Company Secretary

Expenditure: £601,000 (1999)

Staffing: 5 international experts working in Nepal, 2 part-time employees in the UK, 130 Nepalese staff.

General: The charity works towards improving the health of people in eastern Nepal through TB and leprosy control, drug schemes and community health and development programmes.

BNMT has established an internationally renowned TB control programme with the highest cure rates for any developing country. It aims to strengthen this programme and work with the government to establish quality TB/leprosy services in eastern Nepal. This also involves contributing to the development of policy and guidelines through participation on national and regional level forums.

Community efforts to improve health and development are facilitated through participatory approaches. Training is provided in vegetable growing and animal husbandry as most women's groups place a high priority on undertaking projects in these areas. Sustainable drug supplies are organised with the active participation of local people.

Membership: There is a small donor base of individuals in the UK, largely composed of ex-Gurkha personnel, trekkers, climbers or people who have worked in the region.

Publications: 30th anniversary report and a brief leaflet are available.

Volunteers/jobseekers: International level contracts with paid employees are usually for three years and all posts are advertised internationally, as well as in Nepal, as and when they fall vacant. A register of prospective employees is not maintained.

The charity does not have any opportunities for volunteers.

British Red Cross

Giving skilled and impartial care to people in need and crisis - in their own homes and in the community, at home and abroad, in peace and war

Geographical focus: Worldwide

9 Grosvenor Crescent,
London SW1X 7EJ
Tel: 020 7235 5454; **Fax:** 020 7245 6315
Minicom: 020 7235 3159
Website: www.redcross.org.uk
Correspondent: Tim Garner, Information Services

Expenditure: £54 million on international work (1999)

Staffing: Around 3,000 paid staff, although many of these work with the community in Britain; 80,000 volunteers

Website information: Recent news and reports; current job vacancies in the UK and overseas; links to the international movement; a list of publications; events; online donations facility (www.redcrossdonations.org.uk).

General: The charity is part of the International Red Cross and Red Crescent Movement, the largest independent humanitarian organisation in the world.

The movement was inspired by a Swiss businessman who had been appalled at the suffering of thousands of men, on both sides, who were left to die due to lack of care after the battle of Solferino in 1859. He proposed the setting up of national relief societies of volunteers, trained in peacetime to provide neutral and impartial help to relieve suffering in time of war.

A non-political and non-religious movement, the fundamental principles which staff and volunteers must abide by are humanity, impartiality, neutrality, independence, voluntary service, unity and universality.

About 39% of the British Red Cross' expenditure goes directly towards its work in international emergency relief and development, with the remainder spent on UK services, shops, fundraising, marketing, communications and management, and administration and restructuring costs.

Overseas, the British Red Cross, as part of the international movement, helps those affected by natural or man-made disasters, as well as local communities threatened by the 'silent emergencies' of disease or hunger. The charity also helps local people in dozens of countries prepare themselves against future emergencies like floods and hurricanes.

When a Red Cross or Red Crescent Society is faced with an international development or relief need beyond its domestic resources, it will often appeal to other societies, including the British Red Cross for support in the form of money, goods in kind, or expatriate staff (delegates).

Sometimes skilled, specialist workers – like doctors, nurses or engineers – are needed and the British Red Cross will find these people through its network of overseas delegates.

Delegates who are seconded to the International Federation of Red Cross and Red Crescent Societies (the Federation) will form part of a multinational team which works alongside the volunteers and staff of the local Red Cross or Red Crescent Society. The delegates may be heavily involved operationally, but will also work to increase the capacity of the local Society, reducing the expatriate presence over time.

More basic aid may be required, like tents, blankets, food or hygiene and medical supplies - often provided through 'Red Cross Parcels'.

The British Red Cross also provides an international tracing service through its worldwide network to reunite families separated by war or natural disasters.

Membership: No membership, only volunteers and donors.

Publications: A magazine *Lifeline* is available, as well as many other leaflets and information packs. Around 450 publications, such as first aid manuals, books about the history of the movement and youth-related books are on sale, from Rachel Dixon, Purchasing Supply Department, at the address above.

Trading: The charity has shops throughout the country.

Volunteers/jobseekers: A register is kept of potential delegates, who are employed with salaries. British Red Cross holds selection days to identify suitable candidates. Applicants should be over 25, have relevant professional qualifications and experience in their field of expertise. Previous international experience is required in most cases.

See website for job vacancies. Delegates are needed from the following professional fields: medical doctors; registered general nurses; finance professionals; relief workers and logistic experts; water/sanitation engineers; institutional development and disaster preparedness specialists; information/press officers; programme managers; tracing and dissemination officers; and telecommunications specialists.

If you are interested, please contact the International Personnel Unit at the above address.

Volunteers are not sent overseas. There are over 80,000 volunteers in the UK. For futher information see the website or contact the correspondent for an information pack.

The Busoga Trust

Providing clean drinking water to people in rural areas; providing health facilities and assistance with environmental work

Geographical focus: *Uganda*

St Margaret Pattens, Eastcheap, London EC3M 1HS
Tel & Fax: 020 7283 2304
Correspondent: Roy Giles, Trust Administrator

Expenditure: £226,000 (1998/99)

Staffing: 3 part-time paid staff in the UK, 2 full-time staff in Uganda.

General: The charity was founded in 1982 by members of the Church of St Michael's, Chester Square, London.

It supplies cash, equipment, volunteers and engineering experts to help people in Busoga and Luwero, Uganda to build wells and install pumps. Youth mission teams train people in sanitation, personal hygiene, family planning, AIDS prevention and starting small-scale environmental projects.

Publications: *The Busoga Bugle* (occasional).

Volunteers/jobseekers: *Overseas:* About three volunteers each year are taken to Uganda. Individuals must be over 18 and will be involved with the provision of water, education and youth mission. The minimum period for volunteering is three months.

All expenses are met by volunteers. Accommodation is available in a hostel at £30 a month.

UK: People over 18 are welcome to help out with fundraising, administration and leaflet production. Office and design skills are useful.

For volunteering overseas or in the UK, apply in writing to the correspondent.

CAFOD (The Catholic Fund for Overseas Development)

Development, emergency relief, analysis of the causes of underdevelopment and campaigning, education in the UK in development issues

Geographical focus: *Afghanistan, Albania, Angola, Argentina, Armenia, Bangladesh, Bolivia, Brazil, Burkina Faso, Burundi, Cambodia, Chad, Chile, Colombia, Congo (DRC), Dominican Republic, East Timor, Ecuador, El Salvador, Eritrea, Ethiopia, Ghana, Guatemala, Guyana, Haiti, Honduras, India, Indonesia, Iraq, Kenya, Laos, Lebanon, Lesotho, Mexico, Mozambique, Myanmar, Nepal, Nicaragua, Nigeria, North Korea, Pacific Region, Papua New Guinea, Paraguay, Peru, Philippines, Rwanda, Sierra Leone, Solomon Islands, Somalia, South Africa, Sri Lanka, Sudan, Swaziland, Tanzania, Thailand, Turkey, Uganda, Vietnam, West Bank, former Yugoslavia, Zambia, Zimbabwe*

Romero Close, Stockwell Road,
London SW9 9TY
Tel: 020 7733 7900; **Fax:** 020 7274 9630
e-mail: hqcafod@cafod.org.uk
Website: www.cafod.org.uk
Correspondent: Karen Brand, Personnel Officer

Expenditure: £22 million (1998/99)

Staffing: 170 UK salaried staff, including about 35 based in the 12 regional offices.

Website information: Links to UK regional offices; information and application forms for current vacancies; opportunities to join in campaigns; news about different projects worldwide.

General: CAFOD is the official aid agency of the Catholic Church in England and Wales. Set up in 1962, it is the English and Welsh arm of Caritas International, a worldwide network of Catholic relief and development organisations.

It operates through funding programmes and projects. It gives priority to projects which help people to become responsible for their own development. Its work overseas falls into the following two categories:
- development programmes and projects aimed at self-sufficiency
- disaster and short-term relief work.

In almost all cases, work overseas is planned and run by local people. CAFOD doesn't usually give money to governments, but to trusted local organisations, many of them agencies of the Catholic Church. Projects submitted to CAFOD should have the approval of the local church as a norm, irrespective of whether the project is directly church-related or not. In some areas CAFOD provides expertise and training, for example in counselling people living with HIV/AIDS.

CAFOD also:
- analyses the causes of underdevelopment and campaigns on behalf of the world's poor;
- engages in education programmes in England and Wales to enable people to understand the nature and causes of underdevelopment and the Christian response to it in the light of the Church's teaching.

Great importance is attached to ecumenical collaboration.

During the year, CAFOD responded to emergencies in 40 countries, through sending donations and/or providing food packages, medical care, shelter and other essentials to refugees.

CAFOD supporters have successfully campaigned to win an international ban on landmines, to reduce unpayable third world debt and to promote fair trade.

In 1999 CAFOD's education work included bringing a young team of footballers from Liberia, made up of child soldiers, orphans and others affected by Liberia's civil war. This team toured England and Wales, meeting thousands of young people in schools and parishes throughout Britain.

Publications: *CAFOD* magazine, bulletin, fairground (for schools) and many others. These are all advertised in the publications catalogue and may also be available from regional offices.

Trading: Gifts for sale are advertised in the publications catalogue and may also be available from regional offices.

Volunteers/jobseekers: See website information for salaried positions. For further information contact the correspondent by e-mail: jobs@cafod.org.uk or in writing.

No opportunities for volunteers overseas. There are occasional opportunities to help out in the head office in London with administrative tasks. Volunteers undertake many different tasks in the regional offices, from administration to speaking at schools or assisting with fundraising events. Contact Lis Martin by e-mail: volunteers@cafod.org.uk or in writing to the address above.

The Cambodia Trust

Providing free artifical limbs and braces to people who are disabled
Geographical focus: Cambodia

11 Friday Court, North Street, Thame, Oxfordshire OX9 3GA
Tel: 01844 214844; **Fax:** 01844 216269
e-mail: office@cambodiatrust.co.uk
Website: www.cambodiatrust.org.uk
Correspondent: Douglas Heydon, Secretary

Expenditure: £890,000 (1998/99)
Staffing: 100 employees in Cambodia, 4 in the UK, 14 volunteers worldwide.
Website information: Slide show; news; links; how to make a donation.
General: The charity was formed in Oxford in 1989, in response to the suffering of the many thousands of landmine amputees and polio victims in Cambodia. Its aim is to enable people with disability to participate in the normal life of the community. It does this through:
- three rehabilitation clinics in Cambodia, which provide free artificial limbs, braces, physiotherapy and counselling to people with a disability. The majority of patients are landmine amputees or polio victims, but there are also many people with congenital defects, diseases such as leprosy, as well as those disabled in accidents;
- outreach programmes which identify patients living in rural areas and provide the encouragement, transport and accommodation they need so they can attend one of the trust's clinics for treatment;
- outreach training programmes which help disabled children attend school and help disabled adults, particularly women, to find skills training;
- an international accredited training school (Cambodian School of Prosthetics and Orthotics), which trains people from across the region in the fitting of limbs and braces;
- participation in the Disability Action Council, which the trust helped establish. The council works to uphold the rights of people with disability in Cambodia.

As at January 2001, The Cambodia Trust had begun to replicate its rehabilitation programmes in other developing countries, and hoped to open a clinic in East Timor in 2001.

Membership: It costs nothing to become a supporter. Supporters receive regular updates on the work of the trust.
Publications: Newsletters.
Volunteers/jobseekers: Opportunities occasionally arise for volunteers with the relevant skills and experience to work in the charity's clinics in Cambodia. There are also opportunities for volunteers to get involved with fundraising activities in the UK.

CamFed

Educating girls and young women in impoverished rural districts
Geographical focus: Ghana, Zimbabwe

25 Wordsworth Grove, Cambridge CB3 9HH
Tel: 01223 362648; **Fax:** 01223 366859
e-mail: info@camfed.org
Website: www.camfed.org
Correspondent: Mrs Ann Cotton, Director

Expenditure: £365,000 (1999)

Staffing: 4 full-time staff, based in the UK office.

Website information: A breakdown of its overseas projects; a monthly news update; events listing; donate online; list of funders.

General: CamFed works with rural communities in sub-Saharan Africa to improve educational opportunities for girls disadvantaged by poverty.

Led by local committees which draw together civil, traditional and government authorities, the programme responds to particular problems which limit girls' educational opportunities, such as family poverty, distance to school and the fear of harassment. More than 3,000 girls are also directly supported, enabling them to attend their local schools, through the provision of school fees and uniform in 13 rural districts of Zimbabwe and Ghana.

CamFed aims to set in motion a 'virtuous life cycle', enabling girls not only to gain access to education but also to secure rural livelihoods through training and the provision of micro-finance.

Nearly 400 young women had 'graduated' from the programme, as at July 2000. In Zimbabwe, they have formed their own organisation, CAMA (the CamFed Association of school-leavers), to be a network of support for girls and young women in rural areas. CamFed is building the capacity of local organisations, including CAMA, and its Ghanaian partner RAINS. During 2000 and 2001 CamFed and CAMA planned to introduce a programme to Zambia.

Publications: Produces *Cutting the Gordian Knot: the Benefits of Girls' Education in sub-Saharan Africa*, which is available from the address above, costing £16.50, including post and package.

Volunteers/jobseekers: Salaried posts are advertised in the national press and on the website.

Volunteer trainers were required, as at July 2000, for IT in Ghana. There are opportunities to assist in the UK office, and volunteers are sought to set up fundraising groups in their local area.

CARE International UK

Emergency relief, recovery programmes after crises, long-term development assistance, advocacy

Geographical focus: CARE International works in 66 countries worldwide. CARE International UK works in: Afghanistan, Angola, Bangladesh, Bolivia, Bosnia-Herzegovina, Cameroon, East Timor, Ethiopia, Ghana, Guatemala, Honduras, India, Iraq, Kenya, Kosovo, Lesotho, Macedonia, Malawi, Mali, Mozambique, Nepal, Niger, Peru, Rwanda, Sierra Leone, Sri Lanka, Sudan, Togo, Uganda, Yugoslavia, Zambia, Zimbabwe

Tower House, 8–14 Southampton Street, London WC2E 7HA
Tel: 020 7379 5247; **Fax:** 020 7379 0543
e-mail: info@uk.care.org
Website: www.careinternational.org.uk
Correspondent: Jane Connolly, Press and PR Officer

Expenditure: £37 million (1999/2000)

Staffing: 50 staff, nearly all full-time; about three volunteers.

Website information: Up-to-date news; detailed information about its individual projects in each country; job vacancies; events; list of donors; how to donate online.

General: CARE International UK works closely with nine other CARE

International members from the developed world.

Its mission is to serve individuals and families in the poorest communities in the world. The charity said: 'Drawing strength from our global diversity, resources and experience, we promote innovative solutions and are advocates for global responsibility. We facilitate lasting change by:
- strengthening capacity for self-help
- providing economic opportunity
- delivering relief in emergencies
- influencing policy decisions at all levels
- addressing discrimination in all its forms.

'Guided by the aspirations of local communities, we pursue our mission with both excellence and compassion because the people whom we serve deserve nothing else.'

On its website it groups its projects in the following fields and lists the countries each project works in:
- water
- agriculture
- emergency relief
- health
- urban priorities
- micro-finance
- education.

Volunteers/jobseekers: Paid jobs are advertised in national papers and on the website with information about requirements for candidates.

Volunteering opportunities are limited to the UK office and CARE International UK usually has two or three volunteers or trainees on work experience at a time who work to defined job descriptions and on set days. Applications are welcome and should be made to the Personnel Manager at the address above.

Care & Relief for the Young (CRY)

Childcare

Geographical focus: *Romania, Ukraine, Russia*

Sovereign House, Upper Northam Close, Hedge End, Southampton SO30 4BB
Tel: 01489 788300; **Fax:** 01489 790750
e-mail: ukoffice@cry.org.uk
Website: www.cry.org.uk
Correspondent: David Farndale

Expenditure: £243,000 (1999)

Staffing: 60 members of staff.

Website information: Information about how to: sponsor a child; make a donation; and become a volunteer.

General: CRY is a Christian charity which works with orphaned or destitute children as well as with families. Its activities include: street outreach; residential care; family support; training; and fostering and adoption.

Membership: CRY child sponsorship is now available at:
- Father's House – Kiev, Ukraine
- Kiev Blind School, Ukraine
- In-Family supported children – Romania
- Casa Robin Hood – Bucharest, Romania.

Contact the correspondent or see the website for an application form.

Volunteers/jobseekers: Voluntary positions may be available for administrators, health professionals, social/community workers, vocational training professionals, residential childcare workers and other Christian outreach workers.

People undertaking medium/long-term positions are provided with a contract, local salary, insurance and flights. CRY welcomes applications from qualified people in the form of a letter and cv, to the address above.

Catholic Institute for International Relations (CIIR)

Advocacy, skillsharing

Geographical focus: ICD: Dominican Republic, Ecuador, Honduras, Namibia, Nicaragua, Peru, Somalia, Yemen. IPD: Bolivia, Colombia, Guatemala, Zimbabwe. ICD & IPD: Angola, Burma, Cambodia, East Timor, El Salvador, Haiti, Indonesia, Malaysia, Philippines, South Africa, South Korea, Thailand, Vietnam

Unit 3 Canonbury Yard, 190a New North Road, Islington, London N1 7BJ
Tel: 020 7354 0883; **Fax:** 020 7359 0017
e-mail: ciir@ciir.org
Website: www.ciir.org
Correspondent: Achilleas Georgiou, Information Officer

Expenditure: About £4.3 million

Staffing: 32 paid staff in the UK and 2 volunteers. Overseas: 100 development workers and 11 country representatives, some of whom are UK residents.

Website information: Description of work in each country; description of general job opportunities overseas; up-to-date CIIR news; publications catalogue.

General: 'CIIR works in partnership with people in the developing world to strengthen their self reliance and to secure policies that achieve a more equal distribution of power and wealth.' It does this via two programmes, described below.

International Cooperation for Development (ICD) – Skillsharing

This technical assistance programme 'recruits experienced professionals to work in development projects run by local organisations ranging from cooperatives to women's groups, peasant federations and government ministries'.

Advocacy programme

This programme 'presents radical policy options at national and international levels to challenge the causes of poverty and promote a greater understanding of people's struggles for justice and development'.

Based in London, the department carries out research and analysis, arranges meetings and provides briefings to politicians, development agencies etc. in Europe and overseas. It works closely with local networks in developing countries.

Membership: Subscription: UK £15, overseas £20 and unwaged £5. You will: receive *CIIR News* four times a year, CIIR's annual review and publications in *The Comment series*; be invited to CIIR's international conferences with major speakers from developing countries; and be offered discounts on a range of books. Contact by e-mail: membership@ciir.org or write: Membership Officer, CIIR, Freepost ND 6366, London N1 7BR.

Publications: *The Comment series* – up-to-date analysis on individual countries and development issues, and *The Report series* – key findings from CIIR's international conferences. Also see Membership above.

Volunteers/jobseekers: Recruits experienced professionals to work on two year contracts (minimum), with development projects run by local organisations in developing countries. Areas of work include: primary healthcare and health education; disability and development; environment and public health; agriculture and natural resources; vocational training; gender and women's participation; appropriate technology; cooperative/small business development; community development and training; communications and media; and information technology.

Jobs for overseas posts are advertised in professional journals and newspapers. For further information e-mail: jobs@ciir.org or contact the correspondent at the address above.

Jobs in the London office are advertised in the press and on the website.

The Centre for International Briefing

International development education
Geographical focus: *Worldwide*

Farnham Castle, Farnham,
Surrey GU9 OAG
Tel: 01252 721194; **Fax:** 01252 711283
e-mail: info@cibfarnham.com
Website: www.cibfarnham.com
Correspondent: Suzanne Weeks, Marketing Services Coordinator

Expenditure: £1.6 million (1998/99)

Staffing: About 35 to 40 staff in the UK. No volunteers.

Website information: Information about the educational programmes and the centre, and opportunities to register online.

General: The Centre offers a range of educational programmes:
- scheduled and customised briefings for every country in the world – these are for first time expatriates and those with more experience who are moving to a new location, plus accompanying partners. Briefings include country and regional profiles, the business and working environment, cultural adaptations, living conditions, communication and negotiation skills, security and health;
- a range of business briefings for overseas and home-based managers with international responsibility;
- intensive tuition in all languages at any level, including written, presentation and specialist skills vocabulary;
- general and specific cross-cultural workshops – to assist companies and their managers with global development skills;
- introduction to Britain – providing guidance on living and working with the British, often provided in conjunction with an intensive introduction or refresher programme of English language tuition;
- helping human resources – highly practical workshops and seminars to allow HR managers to enhance the wide range of skills required to more effectively manage international personnel;
- programmes for expatriates and families returning to the UK.

Prices in 2000 ranged from £3,000 for five days' language tuition for five people, to £625 for a one-day human resource seminar.

Charities Aid Foundation (CAF)

Helping donors make the most of their giving and charities make the most of their resources
Geographical focus: *UK and worldwide*

Kings Hill, West Malling, Kent ME19 4TA
Tel: 01732 520000; **Fax:** 01732 520001
e-mail: enquiries@caf.charitynet.org
Website: www.cafonline.org
Correspondent: Neil Jones, Communications Director

Expenditure: About £4 million international expenditure (including grants overseas)

Staffing: 302 staff in the UK and Brussels offices, including 15 UK-based staff working on international activities and 42 employees overseas.

Website information: Country profiles with contact information; information about its services to donors; research publications; how to apply for a grant.

General: CAF's international work is built on the belief that the non-profit sector has a key role to play in every country, working alongside the government and private sector to produce a strong and effective economic and political system. Most of CAF's work is with the non-profit sector in the UK, but it also facilitates the non-profit sector in developing countries. It states that its mission is 'to work both for donors and npos (non-profit organisations), providing a range of services designed to sustain effective non-profit sectors'.

Achieving this mission has four core features:

(1) Increasing the scale of international philanthropy

CAF helps donors in the UK and US to make tax-effective international donations, trying to increase the value of those donations, and linking donors with projects in developing countries.

To make tax-efficient donations outside the UK, donors need to provide evidence that the organisation would be recognised as charitable by the UK Inland Revenue. To help with this, CAF has also compiled a list of approved overseas organisations.

Services include:
- providing an online contributions service to international npos;
- helping companies in the West to operate matched giving schemes on a global basis;
- managing grants programmes established by a number of international foundations and companies (see under Grantmaking Programme, below).

(2) Encouraging, in all countries, institutions and systems of philanthropy and social investment

CAF's overseas work is particularly focused on Bulgaria, Ghana, India, Russia and southern Africa. CAF aims to understand a country's traditions of giving and find ways of building on them.

Work includes:
- creating community foundations as a conduit for donors to give within their own local community;
- designing and managing sponsorship programmes for businessmen and foundations;
- helping to set up a payroll giving system.

(3) Working to increase the capacity of npos and the sectors in which they operate

This includes:
- help in setting up training programmes for npos in subjects such as finance, fundraising and management issues;
- giving free legal and financial consultations to npos and government bodies, covering how to establish and register an npo, how to manage employee relations etc. Also advice on how to develop a fundraising strategy and write applications;
- establishing institutions and services which support individual npos and their staff (including organising national conferences for ngos);
- publishing books about the third sector in developing countries (also makes library facilities available);
- administering Charity Know How, which provides funds to the non-profit sector in Central and Eastern Europe (please see separate entry in the Trust section of this guide, page 317).

(4) Encouraging legislative and fiscal measures to increase the effectiveness of donor support and non-profit sector activity

CAF has been involved in debates within the non-profit sector and with government in developing countries, about the future legal and taxation systems affecting the non-profit sector.

Grantmaking Programme

As well as administering a wide range of grantmaking programmes on behalf of other donors, CAF operates its own grantmaking programme. The programme is conducted by a separate grants council. The foundation's guidelines for its main programmes describe its grantmaking as follows.

'The Charities Aid Foundation makes grants to enable charities to improve their management and effectiveness. Grants are made to assist a charity:

- to improve its effectiveness in meeting its objectives;
- to improve its use of financial resources, facilities, members, staff or volunteers;
- to improve its strength or sustainability;
- to research or move into new areas of need;
- in exceptional and unforeseen circumstances, to meet an emergency financial setback or to provide a single injection of funds to maintain the viability of the charitable organisation;
- for training needed to achieve the above objectives (not routine staff training);
- for staff funding only in fulfilling the above (not regular/core costs).

'The CAF Grants Council are particularly interested in funding applications with a wide-lasting benefit and work which will improve the capacity, strength and sustainability of a charitable organisation. For example, if the charitable organisation seeks a grant for funding a consultant (fundraising or strategic review), the council are keen to see how lasting benefit and transfer of knowledge to in-house staff or volunteers will be achieved.

'Grants are for:
- small and medium charitable organisations, with a maximum total income of £1 million (preference is given to those with limited freely available funds or insufficient reserves to meet the need themselves);
- any registered (or Inland Revenue approved) organisation anywhere in the UK;
- charitable organisations of all types of organisation and beneficiary group (bar exceptions below under exclusions);
- a maximum of £10,000 (the average in 1999/2000 was £4,400).'

In 1999/2000 CAF made grants totalling £995,000, of which £79,000 was given to 15 UK charities working internationally. These included:

Coda International and Computer Aid International £8,400 towards the fees of a consultant to provide fundraising and business planning support and towards the initial salary costs and training of a shared in-house fundraiser

Minority Rights Group (MRG) £4,200 to investigate the income generating potential of putting MRG reports on the website

Consortium for Street Children £4,000 to relieve short-term cash flow problems following the loss of commercial sponsorship

Uganda AIDS Action Fund £4,000 to cover the fees of a consultant to develop a business plan and fundraising strategy

International China Concern £3,300 to cover the design and production costs of new promotional materials

Tambopata Reserve Society £1,000 to cover the salary of the Peru coordinator for two months until longer-term funding is received.

Exclusions: Grants will not be given for: capital items, buildings, vehicles, maintenance costs; core, routine or continuation costs of running or expanding the charitable organisation and associated charitable appeals; start-up costs of a new charitable organisation; academic or scientific research projects; debt, deficit or loan funding; funding that should properly be the responsibility of statutory agencies; support or services to individuals or other beneficiaries; schools, universities or NHS trusts; work already completed or currently taking place or due to start before the application has been considered.

Applications: In writing to the correspondent. Grants are decided four times a year, in February, May, August and November. Applications should be received two months in advance.

Publications: Publications include: *Dimensions of the Indian Voluntary Sector*, *Introduction to the Non-profit Sector in China* (also available for Colombia, Ghana and Nigeria) (£15 each, plus p&p); *Working with the Non-profit Sector in India* (also available for Russia and South Africa) (£40 plus p&p); *Alliance* – a quarterly journal aimed at international npos and donors; and *Cross-Border Philanthropy* – an explanatory study of levels of international giving in the UK (£15 plus p&p).

Child Advocacy International (CAI)

Working to improve the standard of children's healthcare worldwide

Geographical focus: *Worldwide but with special emphasis on Afghanistan, Albania, Bosnia, Kosova, Nepal, Pakistan, Uganda, Ukraine, former Yugoslavia, Zambia*

79 Springfields Road, Trent Vale, Stoke on Trent ST4 6RY
Tel: 01782 712599; **Fax:** 01782 610888
e-mail: cai_uk@compuserve.com
Correspondent: Meggie Szczesny, Charity Coordinator

Expenditure: £283,000 (1998/99)

Staffing: Nine paid UK medical and clerical staff (five part-time) plus 15 overseas staff (12 medical). Also five paediatricians who undertake the voluntary positions of Country Directors within the UK.

Website information: Currently under development (as at January 2001).

General: Child Advocacy International was formed in 1996 to focus on hospital care for children and in so doing complement other organisations' work in primary healthcare. It also undertakes advocacy work in pursuance of the United Nations' Convention on the Rights of the Child. Above all, CAI works on behalf of the poorest families, as even in impoverished countries those with money have access to better health than the majority. Activity is therefore focused on developing sustainable programmes in state-run hospitals. Although essential equipment is often provided (with relevant training in its use and appropriate maintenance arrangements), education and development of local healthcare staff is a major focus.

In addition to projects overseas as listed above, another important project is a collaborative venture with UNICEF and the World Health Organisation. This is developing a set of standards for what is termed the Child Friendly Healthcare Initiative which is currently being piloted in six countries including the UK (see copy of article on website: www.childfriendlyhealthcare.org).

Membership: Membership available to paediatricians and children's nurses (currently approximately 240 people). Donations are welcome and appreciated. The charity also recycles unwanted mobile phones to raise funds. For details contact the correspondent.

Publications: Publications – *CAI News Bulletins* (three times year).

Volunteers/jobseekers: Occasional salaried opportunities (local wages) for overseas medical staff and honorary Country Director roles (UK-based).

ChildHope UK

Improving the lives and defending the rights of street and working children

Geographical focus: *Project partners: Albania, Brazil, Bulgaria, Kenya, Philippines, Romania, South Africa; Consultancy with the King Baudouin Foundation, and the Open Society: Czech Republic, Estonia, Hungary, Latvia, Lithuania, Macedonia, Peru, Poland, Slovakia; Developing partnerships in 2001 in: Ethiopia, Mexico*

Lector Court, 151 Farringdon Road, London EC1R 3AF
Tel: 020 7833 0868; **Fax:** 020 7833 2500
e-mail: chuk@gn.apc.org
Website: www.childhopeuk.org
Correspondent: Geoff Cordell, Director

Expenditure: £632,000 (1998)

Staffing: 7 paid staff, 10 volunteers.

Website information: Details of programmes by country; information about street children; resources: *Learning Exchange Programme* and *Resource Pack for Project Management* (downloadable); newsletter.

General: ChildHope provided the following information. It 'is dedicated to improving the lives and defending the rights of street children worldwide. 'This is done through the development of appropriate practice, project partnership, capacity building, support and advocacy. ChildHope builds partnerships with small, local organisations overseas and, by providing information, support, training and resources aims to enhance each partner organisation's response to addressing the needs of street children within their own community. ChildHope provides capacity building support to partner organisations in Central and Eastern Europe and aims to expand this aspect of their work to partners in Africa, Asia and Latin America, including the sharing of experiences between organisations in the South.'

In 2000, appeals included:

- Project Activation, which aims to equip socially excluded youth and communities to educate themselves, their communities and the public about social issues via street theatre.
- Feliks, in Macedonia, which is a new project and was set up to initiate street work in a socially deprived district and equip disenfranchised young people and families to help themselves through education and support and community/family development.

Publications: *Learning Exchange Programme* and *Resource Pack for Project Management*, both available for free on the website; also a newsletter.

Volunteers/jobseekers: You can be involved through organising a local event in your community. Further information is available on request.

Or you can get involved in fundraising events, from parachute jumping to abseiling to white water rafting. In 2000, for example, *Streets Ahead Corporate Challenge* was organised. It was an urban orienteering event in the Square Mile, giving corporate teams opportunities to compete to win a trip to visit a project ChildHope supports. Sponsorship needed was £10,000, team entry cost £500. For information about other events like this, contact Dean Anderson, Direct Marketing and Events Fundraiser, tel: 020 7833 0868.

Children in Crisis

Helping children living in crisis situations

Geographical focus: *Afghanistan, Belarus, China, Poland, Russia, Sierra Leone, UK*

4 Calico House, Plantation Wharf, York Road, London SW11 3UB
Tel: 020 7978 5001; **Fax:** 020 7978 5003
e-mail: cic@easynet.co.uk
Website: www.childrenincrisis.org.uk
Correspondent: Mark O McKeowen, Chief Executive

Expenditure: £1.4 million (1999/2000)

Website information: Breakdown of work in each country; news; vacancies in the UK and overseas for salaried staff and volunteers; how you can help: gala events, marathon and overseas challenges, corporate sponsorship opportunities, schools and churches involvement, fundraisers wanted; how to donate; links.

General: The charity works with children who have experienced crisis situations, offering practical help and counselling. The following information describes three of its projects and was taken from the charity's website in 2000.

'**Leeds – UK**

Children in Crisis began the Axis drugs prevention programme in Leeds in 1995 to address the growing issue of drugs misuse in the eastern part of the city. The programme takes a holistic approach to the problem including the following:

- drugs prevention education in primary schools
- drugs education through drama
- parent support groups
- Community Youth Support Programme.

'**Russian Federation**

62% of families with children under 6 years old were living in poverty in the Russian Federation in 1995. The transition from communism to capitalism is taking its toll on children in the Russian Federation.

'Our programme assists street children to overcome the trauma of physical abuse they have experienced on the streets or at home.

'By creating a partnership with Russian charity Innovations, Children in Crisis has been funding psychologists, social workers and teachers to work with street children in Tsimbalina Hospital, St Petersburg. The hospital provides medical treatment to around 650 homeless children a year and is the only hospital serving street children in the city. Our programme complements this work by providing the children with much needed trauma counselling, play therapy, legal assistance and family tracing.

'**Afghanistan**

Many children in Afghanistan have become orphaned or had to flee their homes due to a continuous war that has raged there since 1979. They live in the third worst conditions in the world according to UNICEF. CiC is one of the few agencies still assisting children in the capital, Kabul. The work includes reunifying displaced children with their families, increasing access to education and improving standards of healthcare.'

Volunteers/jobseekers: Salaried positions are advertised on the charity's website.

There are opportunities for volunteers to work for up to three months in The Mountain Haven for children with cancer and other chronic illnesses in Poland. Also opportunities in London and Leeds. Contact the charity at the address above for London and Poland, or Jenny Ormescher for Leeds (0113 222 5507).

Children in Distress

Supporting children's hospices, hospitals and orphanages

Geographical focus: *Albania, Belarus, Bulgaria, Romania*

4th Floor, 91 Mitchell Street,
Glasgow G1 3LN
Tel: 0870 8704838; **Fax:** 0141 222 5355
e-mail: info@children-in-distress.org
Website: www.children-in-distress.org
Correspondent: Revd Dr J W Walmsley, Director

Expenditure: £1.2 million (1998/99)

Website information: News; geographical focus on projects and description of individual projects and future programmes; how to help via making donations, sponsoring a child, becoming a church rep or volunteering.

General: In September 1990 Revd Dr John Walmsley along with some volunteers set out with four lorries to deliver aid to the people of Romania. What they saw shocked them deeply and led them to set up this charity. In April 1991 building work began on the St Laurence's Children's Hospice in Cernavoda, a small industrial town in Romania. Here, Children in Distress cares for abandoned children infected with the HIV virus.

The following information was taken from the charity's website. 'We aim to bring quality of life and dignity in death to children that would otherwise have neither. Children come to us as gaunt little skeletons, with shaved heads and sunken eyes: many are unable to walk as they have never been out of their cots.

'Very often, within a few short months, with the help of a little medication and a lot of TLC these children are running around laughing and giggling. We make sure that we do everything we can to fill their lives with happiness and joy.

'Sometimes, however, all we can do is hold the children as they slowly slip away. At St Laurence's no child dies without a cuddle. Every child's death is treated with the significance it deserves.'

In Albania also, Children in Distress built a children's hospital which opened in October 1996. The charity also supports an orphanage in Belarus and a hospital in Bulgaria.

Volunteers/jobseekers: 'Children in Distress would be unable to function were it not for the expert help generously given to us by the medical profession. For the past ten years, British doctors and nurses volunteered to journey out to Eastern Europe and work long hours a long way from home in order to bring care and comfort to children who would otherwise have neither.'

Contact the correspondent for information about how to get involved.

Children of the Andes

Child-focused education, health, counselling and provision of food and shelter etc.

Geographical focus: Colombia

4 Bath Place, Rivington Street,
London EC2A 3DR
Tel: 020 7739 1328; **Fax:** 020 7739 5743
e-mail: info@children-of-the-andes.org
Website: www.children-of-the-andes.org
Correspondent: Gabriela Bucher, Acting Chief Executive

Expenditure: £365,000 (1999/2000)

Staffing: 2 full-time and 3 part-time paid staff; 4 volunteers.

Website information: Information on each of the projects; information from Colombia; how to make a donation; information about fundraising events such as walks in the Andes and arts events.

General: The following information was taken from the charity's website. 'Children of the Andes ... was established in 1991 to support Colombian organisations dedicated to improving the lives of the country's most vulnerable children.

'Its work focuses on the rescue and rehabilitation of Colombia's street children. Outreach programmes providing food, medicine and clothes are a life-line for children surviving on the streets, while residential homes provide a caring, supportive environment, education and training for the future.

'Children of the Andes also funds education, recreation and nutrition programmes for children caught between poverty and violence in the shanty towns. For children in remote, rainforest areas where access to healthcare is severely limited, the charity funds a flying doctor service providing routine and emergency medical attention.

'In response to escalating guerrilla and paramilitary violence in some rural areas, Children of the Andes established a pre-school for children whose families have been forced to flee from their homes. Activities based on play therapy help the children to overcome memories of atrocities they have witnessed, while a training and employment programme for their parents enables the families as a whole to start rebuilding their lives.'

Publications: Publishes newsletter *Children of the Andes*.

Children's Aid Direct

Helping to improve the lives of children and their carers who have been affected by conflict, poverty or disaster

Geographical focus: Albania, Azerbaijan, Burundi, Democratic Republic of Congo, Haiti, Kosovo, Liberia, Macedonia, North Korea, Sierra Leone, Tajikistan

12 Portman Road, Reading RG30 1EA
Tel: 0118 958 4000; **Fax:** 0118 958 8988
e-mail: enquiries@cad.tele2.co.uk
Website: www.cad.org.uk
Correspondent: The Information and Marketing Department

Expenditure: £14 million (1998/99)

Website information: News; how to donate online; how to get involved in fundraising challenges and expeditions; schools' information; children's information; links to other sites; list of merchandise.

General: The charity's mission is as follows. 'Children's Aid Direct makes an immediate and lasting improvement to the lives of children and their carers who have been affected by conflict, poverty or disaster.

'Children's Aid Direct is committed to working with children and their communities to help support them as they move from crisis to recovery. We do this in innovative and practical ways, providing food, shelter, healthcare, education, training and advice, empowering communities and enabling our donors and volunteers to be involved in working for children.'

Examples of the charity's work as at October 2000 included:

- in Kosovo, a Youth at Risk project which works with young people to give them advice in a safe environment;
- in Burundi, food is provided to mothers and children and the charity helps to establish women's cooperatives giving advice on farming, tools and food security;
- in Haiti, wells are built and maintained;
- in Azerbaijan, provision of advice and practical support for families and health professionals in health clinics;
- in Sierra Leone, the charity provides drugs and equipment to clinics.

Publications: The charity publishes a handful of books about emergency relief issues.

Trading: As well as books, the charity sells merchandise such as pens and t-shirts bearing its logo.

Volunteers/jobseekers: If you have any of the following skills, the charity would like the opportunity of considering you for a salaried position:

- oral and written fluency in French, Russian and Serbo-Croat
- nursing, driving, engineering or logistics
- financial or staff management
- experience as a volunteer/paid volunteer working with an ngo.

Please contact the Overseas Personnel Officer, at the address above.

There are opportunities for volunteering in the UK, through: getting involved in outdoor challenge events and fundraising in your local community, church, school, club or workplace; helping with reception work etc. during normal office hours, in the Reading office; and speaking at schools etc. to promote the charity's work. Contact Gaynor Jones, at the address above, for further information.

Christian Aid

Supporting long-term development, campaigning and advocacy and provides emergency aid

Geographical focus: Over 60 countries in Africa, Asia, Eastern Europe, Middle East, UK and Ireland

Interchurch House, 35 Lower Marsh, London SE1 7RL
Tel: 020 7523 2248
Website: www.christian-aid.org.uk
Correspondent: Angela Burton, Editor

Expenditure: £53 million (1999/2000)

Staffing: 500 members of staff in total, in the UK and overseas.

Website information: News; campaigns; how to join; reports on its work and related issues; job vacancies; how to donate; FAQs; links.

General: The charity provided the following information. 'Christian Aid is the official relief and development agency of 40 church denominations in the UK and Ireland. It works where the need is greatest in over 60 countries across the world, helping communities regardless of religion. Christian Aid supports local organisations to enable people living in poverty to find their own solutions to the problems they face. It believes in challenging the root causes of poverty through education, advocacy and campaigning'.

Membership: Subscribe to Christian Aid News for free; telephone the number above.

Publications: Books, videos, tapes, games, church materials, teaching packs and posters are outlined in the Resources Catalogue. If you would like to be sent one please contact the correspondent.

Volunteers/jobseekers: Information about current vacancies for salaried positions are available on the website.

No opportunities for volunteering abroad. There are opportunities to help in the UK office, e.g. with fundraising appeals and taking part in internships.

Christian Children's Fund of Great Britain (CCFGB)

Mainly child sponsorship programmes
Geographical focus: *Brazil, Bulgaria, Cambodia, Ethiopia, Guyana, India, Malawi, Peru, Romania, Russia, Thailand, Uganda*

4 Bath Place, Rivington Street, London EC2A 3DR
Tel: 020 7729 8191; **Fax:** 020 7729 8339
e-mail: gen@ccfgb.org.uk
Website: www.ccfgb.org.uk
Correspondent: Robert Pritchett, Chief Executive

Expenditure: £4.6 million (1998/99)

Staffing: 33 staff in London office (5 part-time), 2 temporary staff, 150 local staff in field offices.

Website information: A description of its work in different countries; links to requests for information about sponsoring a child; how to make a donation; news update.

General: CCFGB works extensively but not exclusively through child sponsorship programmes to 'promote the long-term care, development, health and education of poor children, regardless of race, sex or religion, anywhere throughout the world'. Every child sponsored is enrolled in a project which cares for his or her well-being and also assists the family and community to become self-sufficient through education and income-generating schemes. CCFGB does not own projects but seeks to allow local people to exercise responsibility and initiative supported by CCFGB funding.

It operates on Christian ethical principles, but acknowledges these values are shared by people of other/no faiths and it does not engage in any evangelistic activity.

Membership: Sponsorship of a child costs £15 a month, 80% of which is guaranteed to go to the field.

Publications: Quarterly newsletter *Child World*.

Trading: Christmas cards sold annually.

Volunteers/jobseekers: An application form for salaried posts is available from the Personnel Administrator at the address above.

Monday evening is 'Volunteer night', for people wishing to help with administrative tasks. Contact Janet McKeown at the address above.

Christian Medical Fellowship (CMF)

Providing information for medics (including students) wishing to work in developing countries
Geographical focus: *Worldwide*

157 Waterloo Road, London SE1 8XN
Tel: 020 7928 4694; **Fax:** 020 7620 2453
e-mail: david.clegg@cmf.org.uk
Website: www.cmf.org.uk
Correspondent: David Clegg, Overseas Support Secretary

Expenditure: £577,000 (1999)
Staffing: 13 members of staff.

Website information: News; journals and articles; events; newsletter; overseas vacancies; student elective information and how to an elective.

General: This charity mainly works in the UK, supporting Christian medics and Christian organisations which carry out medical work. Part of its focus, however, is on Christian medical work overseas; it provides information for Christian medics who are considering working overseas. The following information was taken from the charity's website.

'Developing countries still need foreign doctors…Much of the developing world's health needs are already supplied by Christian missions: in Africa alone there are over 1,000 mission hospitals most of which are short-staffed. Long-termers who can learn language and culture provide a framework for those who are able to make a useful short-term (usually six months to two years) contribution.

'A wide variety of courses are available in the UK for specific training, and support agencies supplying appropriate drugs, equipment and advice are mushrooming.'

The charity runs a Residential Refresher Course for Christian doctors, nurses and midwives working overseas (and for others shortly leaving for overseas on their first assignment). The course aims to provide:

- professional updating – the course is recognised by UKCC for nurses' requirements for PREP (PGEA and CME approval are being sought)
- help for course members to apply this knowledge in their work situations
- spiritual fellowship and refreshment
- a forum for discussion of opportunities, problems and ideas.

To receive an application form for next year's course please write to the Overseas Support Secretary at the address above.

Membership: CMF has over 4,000 British doctors as members. Membership costs £75 a year, with concessions at £25 for recently qualified doctors and members resident overseas.

CMF directly helps members working abroad through:

- sending relevant journals
- paying for histopathological services and advice in the UK
- running micro-fiche service
- running an annual refresher course.

About 1,000 medical students are members. Membership costs £1 to first year students, £8 for other years or £20 for a three year prepaid subscription. A range of support is offered e.g. residential weekend conference and booklets giving practical advice about electives.

Publications: Quarterly magazine, quarterly newsletter, publications on advances in Christian thinking within medicine are regularly made available and students' quarterly magazine *Nucleus*. A library in the London Office is available to members, and a tape library – where conference talks are available on cassette.

Volunteers/jobseekers: Overseas vacancies for salaried posts are published on the website, on behalf of other organisations.

The charity provides information to students wishing to carry out their student elective, and for medics wishing to volunteer or work in a developing country. Careers advice is also given to GPs.

'There are over twenty UK-based mission societies currently supporting medical staff abroad. Most of the latter insist, understandably, that applicants have an active Christian faith, or are at least in sympathy with the overall aims of the mission. However, because most developing countries now have strong indigenous churches of their own, expatriate doctors are less likely to have Christian pastoral responsibilites on top of their medical work. The trends are towards greater specialisation and teamwork. Other Christians will be seeking opportunities to serve through foreign governments and secular aid agencies, alongside those of all religious backgrounds and none.

'Openings exist for virtually every specialty and level of training: in small rural hospitals, large teaching hospitals, public health, development work, tropical disease, disaster relief and palliative care. In general one needs at least two years' experience post-registration at SHO/Registrar level to be useful, preferably in a combination of obstetrics and gynaecology, paediatrics, surgery and accident and emergency. In practice much training can be done "on the job".'

Christian Outreach – Relief and Development (CORD)
(formerly Christian Outreach)
Providing healthcare, community development, construction

Geographical focus: Albania, Afghanistan, Cambodia, India, Mozambique, Philippines, Rwanda, Sudan, Tanzania, Thailand, Vietnam, Zambia

I New Street, Leamington Spa CV31 1HP
Tel: 01926 315301; **Fax:** 01926 885786
e-mail: info@cord.org.uk
Website: www.cord.org.uk
Correspondent: Martin Lee, Director

Expenditure: £2.2 million (1999/2000)

Staffing: UK: 12 full-time and 4 part-time salaried employees, 2 volunteers. Overseas: 25 expatriate volunteers, as well as several indigenous staff.

Website information: Magazine; a breakdown of its work overseas; how to make a donation; a small number of links to other sites.

General: The charity states: 'The aim of CORD is to demonstrate the love of Jesus by practical care of vulnerable and marginalised people, especially children, displaced communities and refugees, by:
- endeavouring to remain a caring organisation characterised by a Christian ethos, professionalism and concern for the underprivileged
- setting up operational work in areas where there are no local organisations
- using professional Christian staff
- giving priority to areas where there are health concerns
- encouraging self-reliance and the strengthening of local structures.

'CORD's projects, which emphasise the wellbeing of individuals and communities, aim to encourage local initiative and community involvement. They include:
- healthcare
- water and sanitation
- training for local workers
- road construction
- development of small businesses
- rehabilitation for children with disabilities.'

Membership: Newsletters are free and sent bi-monthly to supporters.

Volunteers/jobseekers: Opportunities for expatriate volunteers are mainly in Mozambique, Rwanda, Albania, Tanzania, Zambia and Cambodia. Team members need to either hold qualifications in healthcare, community development or construction, or have vehicle maintenance or financial and administrative skills to be able to support the work. Contact Mrs K Bugg, Personnel Officer by at the above address, or e-mail: kbugg@cord.org.uk for further information.

Christian Solidarity Worldwide (CSW)

Working towards the liberty of persecuted Christians

Geographical focus: *Worldwide*

PO Box 99, New Malden, Surrey KT3 3YF
Tel: 020 8942 8810; **Fax:** 020 8942 8821
e-mail: admin@csw.org.uk
Website: www.csw.org.uk
Correspondent: Revd Stuart Rodney Windsor

Expenditure: £1.4 million (1999)

Website information: CSW Magazine; country profiles; news; trip reports; testimonials; how you can help; photo gallery.

General: The organisation's mission statement is as follows. 'Christian Solidarity Worldwide works for the religious liberty of persecuted Christians, helping others suffering repression, children in need and victims of disaster throughout the world.'

The charity aims to be a voice for people who are bereft of aid and advocacy. Its objectives are:

'• to obtain evidence of violations of human rights and to present that evidence to the international community
- to show solidarity with those who are suffering
- to provide such humanitarian assistance'.

It works in the following areas of principle:

- *advocacy* – the organisation reports on violations of human rights, ensuring that information reaches decision makers in the UK Parliament, the European institutions and the United Nations. Other information is provided to institutions monitoring human rights;
- *accountability and aid* – CSW provides human aid, sending staff to accompany the aid and in this way are accountable for the aid being delivered to those in need;
- *authenticity* – CSW obtains first-hand evidence of people experiencing persecution;
- *solidarity* – built through sending teams to visit people who are undergoing persecution.

In 1999, work included discussions and a joint submission with Anti-Slavery International, to International Labour Organisations, encouraging them to take action to address slavery in Sudan. CSW visited Burma (Myanmar) researching into the threat of starvation to the Karen people on the Thai/Burma border. The findings were distributed throughout the EU. Other work included delivering medicine to people in the Nuba mountains, Sudan.

Membership: On completion of a form you can become a member and you will receive regular updates on campaigns and advice on how you can help e.g. write to your MP. Donations are appreciated.

Volunteers/jobseekers: See Membership above for how to get involved in the charity's work. You can also be a church representative.

Christians Abroad (including World Service Enquiry)

Overseas recruitment, project management and information about working for development

Geographical focus: *In 2000: Cameroon, Tanzania, China, Japan, Kenya, Kiribati, Nigeria*

Room 233, Bon Marché Centre, 241–251 Ferndale Rd, London SW9 8BJ
Tel: 020 7346 5956; **Fax:** 020 7346 5955

e-mail: projects@cabroad.org.uk
Website: www.cabroad.org.uk or www.wse.org.uk
Correspondent: The Project Manager

Expenditure: About £170,000
Staffing: 4 members of staff.

Website information: Information about the WIN programme; voluntary agencies; voluntary opportunities abroad; job seeking, cvs, interviews etc.

General: Christians Abroad's work falls into two main areas:

Recruitment programme
Recruits skilled personnel, with Christian commitment, for teaching, health, community and administration posts on behalf of overseas partners. The WIN programme provides short-term placements overseas for qualified and experienced, self-funding professionals.

World Service Enquiry
Provides information and advice on working and volunteering in the developing world to people of any faith or none. One-to-one career guidance interviews are available to anyone seeking to work abroad. See also Volunteers/Jobseekers below.

Volunteers/jobseekers: World Service Enquiry offers information on voluntary and professional placements of various lengths. Terms vary between agencies. World Service Enquiry prints a free booklet *Guide to Working Overseas* which starts to explain how and where to begin your search for job opportunities (send A5 44p sae).

Opportunities Abroad is a monthly subscription job magazine listing the latest vacancies from aid, development and mission agencies. Available in print or by e-mail.

Under the recruitment programme, Christians Abroad sends between 10 to 25 people per year to work as teachers, in healthcare and administration. Applicants need to be aged 21 to 60 although age range depends on work permit conditions. Vacancies currently concentrated in Tanzania, Cameroon, China, Japan and Kiribati. Secondary school teaching experience in English, maths and science is useful, as is Teaching English as a Foreign Language (TEFL), health qualifications, typing skills and office management experience. Occasionally there are vacancies for graduates with experience of working with young people. Speculative enquiries are welcomed.

Normally, placements are for two years. Airfare, National Insurance and travel insurance expenses are met by Christians Abroad. Volunteers receive living expenses or local salary. Some posts are sterling supplemented. Vacancies are advertised in the press and listed on the website. General enquiries about work can be made to the correspondent.

There are limited opportunities for volunteering in London office. Volunteers generally need good keyboard skills and computer literacy; please contact the Director at the address above.

Church Mission Society (CMS)

Christian work, including community development, healthcare, refugee work

Geographical focus: Africa, Asia, Europe, Middle East

Partnership House, 157 Waterloo Road, London SE1 8UU
Tel: 020 7928 8681; **Fax:** 020 7401 3215
e-mail: timothy.dakin@cms-uk.org
Website: www.cms-uk.org
Correspondent: Revd Canon Timothy Dakin, General Secretary

Expenditure: £7.5 million (1998/99)

Staffing: CMS supports 34 mission partners who work in medicine and healthcare and 8 others who carry out community development work. There are over 100 other staff.

Website information: News; opportunities to serve abroad; how to make a donation; downloadable resources; links to other Christian sites.

General: CMS works with the Anglican Church and other Christians around the world. It has six core commitments, four of which are Christian evangelism/teaching-related. The other two, relevant to this guide, are:
- to encourage holistic initiatives in community development and healthcare
- to contribute to Christian work with and among refugees and migrant peoples.

CMS places special value on strengthening the ministry of women and young people.

'CMS joins with churches around the world, other mission agencies and voluntary organisations in programmes of justice and advocacy.' In Uganda, for example, local medical workers in poor communities are trained in the healing skills of obstetrics and gynaecology. CMS supports people in war-torn Sudan. With support from CMS, a local church leader in Sri Lanka is engaged in reconciliation work across the communal divide between Tamil and Singhalese in Sri Lanka. A physiotherapist in Nigeria works with children with special physical or mental needs.

Publications: *Yes* magazine, other books about its own work.

Volunteers/jobseekers: Placements overseas are available to Christians who are 'actively involved in their local church and growing in their faith', as follows: summer teams (a few weeks), or 6 to 18 month placements, for people aged 16 to 30 years; 2 to 6 years service for long-term workers of any age. See website for further information.

The Church of Scotland Board of World Mission

Sharing resources of people and money

Geographical focus: Bahamas, Bangladesh, Belgium, Bermuda, Cayman Islands, Egypt, France, Gibraltar, Hungary, India, Israel, Italy, Jamaica, Kenya, Lebanon, Malawi, Malta, Mozambique, Nepal, Netherlands, Pakistan, Portugal, Romania, South Africa, Spain, Sri Lanka, Switzerland, Thailand, Trinidad, Zambia

121 George Street, Edinburgh EH2 4YN
Tel: 0131 225 5722; **Fax:** 0131 226 6121
e-mail: world@cofscotland.org.uk
Website: www.churchofscotland.org.uk
Correspondent: Prof. Kenneth R Ross, General Secretary

Expenditure: £3.2 million for World Mission (1999)

Staffing: 20 UK office staff. 65 overseas staff including: 26 ministers and other church/ecumenical workers; 18 teachers, lecturers and educationalists; 5 doctors; 5 nurses; 1 pharmacist; 7 community development workers; 1 engineer; and 2 administration staff. About 80% of staff work in developing countries.

Website information: Breakdown of projects; map showing the location of staff overseas; world mission update (news); description of resources (books, videos etc); how to get involved; vacancies; how your money can help.

General: Most of the Board's work overseas is in the developing world and it sees 'resource sharing' as an urgent matter 'in nations where the effects of the widening gap between rich and poor is the major issue for the Church'. It helps to meet the needs it has identified through providing personnel (see Staffing above) and grants to its partner churches in developing countries.

In Malawi, for instance, its partner church, Church of Central Africa Presbyterian (CCAP), continued to be supported in 1999 with the provision of nurses training and primary healthcare at a hospital. During the year, in Malawi, the Board employed the following expatriate staff: two sister tutors, a doctor, a midwife and a headmistress. The training of a Malawian was also funded by the Board, enabling her to take over the position of Primary Health Care Director at the hospital. In addition funding was made towards the production costs of teachers' guides and training workshops, and the Livingstonia Synod AIDS project.

Membership: Church of Scotland has about 600,000 members.

Publications: *Insight*, a quarterly publication is produced – contact Mrs Katy Laidlow, Local Involvement Secretary for further information.

Volunteers/jobseekers: 'The Board welcomes enquiries from men and women interested in serving the Church overseas (in a salaried capacity). This is usually with indigenous denominations and related organisations with which we are in partnership overseas, in Church of Scotland congregations mostly in Europe, or our work in Israel.' For current vacancies contact Ms Sheila Ballantyre, Assistant Secretary (Personnel).

For information about volunteering opportunities please contact: The Director, Scottish Churches World Exchange, St Colm's International House, 23 Inverleith Terrace, Edinburgh EH3 5NS.

CODA International Training

Helping to strengthen the capacity of community organisations

Geographical focus: Central America and Southern Africa

129 Seven Sisters Road, London N7 7QG
Tel: 020 7281 0020 ; **Fax:** 020 7272 5476
e-mail: london@cit.org.uk
Website: www.cit.org.uk
Correspondent: Tony Roberts, Development Manager

Expenditure: £323,000 (1998/99)

Staffing: 6 full-time staff and a large number of volunteers.

Website information: News and newsletter; information about individual projects; financial information; volunteer opportunities.

General: CODA stands for Community Development Action. The aims of the charity are to assist community organisations in developing countries working to bring about positive changes in their locality. The following information was taken from the charity's website.

'CODA International is a UK-based overseas development organisation which provides skills and resources to partners in southern Africa and Central America. The organisations with which we work are all involved in improving the economic and social circumstances of the poorest parts of the community, from the townships of South Africa to the barrios of Nicaragua.

'CODA was founded in 1990, and since then has become a major UK development agency. Our main focus is strengthening the organisational capacity of existing local groups providing training and other resources. This may mean helping establish a computerised health information database, teaching furniture making skills to a women's co-operative, or facilitating more long-term organisational development. We have also been instrumental in founding another agency, Computer Aid, which recycles used computers to developing countries.

'CODA's projects, staff and volunteers overseas are supported by a tiny UK staff, plus a large number of committed volunteers, many of whom have previously worked for CODA and our partners abroad.'

Publications: Newsletter.

Volunteers/jobseekers: See under General, above.

The Canon Collins Educational Trust for Southern Africa (CCETSA)

Postgraduate scholarship programme for students from southern Africa in the UK and in South Africa. Also partners and supports educational projects in southern Africa

Geographical focus: *Angola, Botswana, Lesotho, Malawi, Mozambique, Namibia, South Africa, Swaziland, Zambia, Zimbabwe*

22 The Ivories, 6 Northampton Street, London N1 2HY
Tel: 020 7354 1462; **Fax:** 020 7359 4875
e-mail: ccetsa@gn.apc.org
Website: www.canoncollins.org.uk
Correspondent: Ethel de Keyser, Director

Expenditure: £1.1 million (1999)

Staffing: 3 full-time and 3 part-time staff in the London office, 2 part-time staff in the South Africa office.

Website information: The scholarship programme; projects it works in partnership with; projects it assists; new initiatives.

General: The CCETSA was established by the British Defence and Aid Fund for Southern Africa (BDAFSA) in 1981. It was set up to assist refugee South African and Namibian students to study in independent African states and in the UK. In 1990, following the unbanning of anti-apartheid organisations, the CCETSA was able to start a programme of sponsorship for students studying in South Africa, in particular support of those studying at historically disadvantaged universities. Over the years, work has expanded in an attempt to meet the urgent need for educational assistance in the region: the new programme of postgraduate scholarships has grown in southern Africa and in the UK, and now includes students from most countries in the region. CCETSA is currently working in partnership with 20 educational projects and community groups in southern Africa.

Membership: Regular appeal mailings referring to developments are sent to CCETSA supporters.

Publications: A large collection of books on South African history are available for research and purchase from the trust.

Volunteers/jobseekers: The London office is always in need of volunteer workers and welcomes enquiries to the above address. Volunteers are preferably based in London and commit to at least one day a week. Lunch and fares are provided.

Commonwealth Society for the Deaf (Sound Seekers)

Supporting deaf children

Geographical focus: *Bangladesh, Barbados, Belize, Botswana, Ethiopia, Fiji, Gambia, Ghana, Guyana, India, Jamaica, Kenya, Lesotho, Malawi, Maldives, Malta, Nigeria, Papua New Guinea, St Lucia, Seychelles, Sierra Leone, South Africa, Tanzania, Tonga,*

Trinidad & Tobago, Uganda, Zambia, Zimbabwe

34 Buckingham Palace Road,
London SW1W 0RE
Tel: 020 7233 5700; **Fax:** 020 7233 5800
e-mail: sound.seekers@btinternet.com
Website: www.sound-seekers.org.uk
Correspondent: Brigadier John Davis, Chief Executive

Expenditure: £338,000 (1999/2000)
Staffing: 3 paid staff.

Website information: Causes of deafness; description of its major projects; stories of lives which have been changed; news; annual report; list of its sponsors and donors; useful links.

General: The following information was taken from the charity's website. 'Sound Seekers is registered as a charity in the UK as the Commonwealth Society for the Deaf, which has been supporting deaf people, particularly children, in developing countries of the Commonwealth since 1959. Many of these children live in isolated rural communities, and often have no access to hearing assessment, hearing aids or basic medicines, and clean water. Furthermore, lack of transport often prevents them from attending limited medical facilities. The first contact they might have with medical or audiological specialists is that provided by Sound Seekers, which is well served by a number of volunteer ear nose and throat surgeons, audiologists and teachers of deaf children.

'The charity:
- assesses, screens and treats children with ear disease
- screens children for hearing loss
- provides (specialist) training for staff from rural clinics
- provides diagnostic equipment and hearing aids
- informs communities about good ear care
- provides training for teachers, technicians, and audiologists
- gives support to schools for deaf children.

'One of the most significant developments of 1997 was the deployment of Sound Seekers' first HARK! (Hearing Assessment and Research Centre) mobile clinic to Uganda. Based upon a Land Rover Field Ambulance, it carries its own power generator, water supply, diagnostic equipment and refrigeration unit for medicines. It is also sound-proofed, so as to allow hearing to be screened accurately. Based at Mulago Hospital, Kampala, its work takes place in rural towns and villages many miles away from the nearest clinics.'

The provision of equipment and supplies (in addition to diagnostic audiometers, earmould kits and otoscopes) and training to partner organisations are key features of its work.

Volunteers/jobseekers: There are opportunities for volunteers in the UK office. The charity stated that there is also the possibility that volunteers could work on placements with its overseas projects. Please contact the charity at the address above for further information.

Commonwealth Youth Exchange Council (CYEC)

Promoting educational exchange visits

Geographical focus: *Anguilla, Antigua and Barbuda, Australia, Bahamas, Bangladesh, Barbados, Belize, Bermuca, Botswana, Brunei Darussalam, Cameroon, Canada, Cayman Islands, Cyprus, Dominica, Fiji Islands, Gambia, Ghana, Gibraltar, Grenada, Guyana, India, Jamaica,*

Kenya, Kiribati, Lesotho, Malawi, Malaysia, Maldives, Malta, Mauritius, Montserrat, Mozambique, Namibia, Nauru, New Zealand, Nigeria, Pakistan, Papua New Guinea, St Kitts and Nevis, St Lucia, St Vincent and the Grenadines, Samoa, Seychelles, Sierra Leone, Singapore, Solomon Islands, South Africa, Sri Lanka, Swaziland, Tanzania, Tonga, Trinidad and Tobago, Tuvalu, Uganda, United Kingdom, Vanuatu, Zambia, Zimbabwe

7 Lion Yard, Tremadoc Road,
London SW4 7NQ
Tel: 020 7498 6151; **Fax:** 020 7720 5403
e-mail: mail@cyec.demon.co.uk
Correspondent: Vic Craggs, Director

Expenditure: £306,000 (1998)

Staffing: 3 full-time, 1 part-time members of staff.

General: CYEC promotes educational exchange visits between groups of young people in the UK and their contemporaries in Commonwealth countries. Through provision of advice, training and financial support CYEC aims to enable young people aged 16–25 from all sections of the community to participate in youth exchange programmes in order to promote international awareness and contribute to both personal and community development. Each leg of the exchange lasts around three to four weeks.

Young people from the partner groups plan the exchange. CYEC's kick-start grants to British groups help young people to get the process underway – but they raise over 70% of the funds themselves. Groups exchanging with poorer countries are often responsible for raising the necessary funds to ensure the partner groups can make a return visit to the UK.

Membership: CYEC works closely with statutory and voluntary youth services and schools throughout the UK and has a membership of over 200 organisations which use its free services and contribute towards its costs.

Publications: *Contact*, a handbook for the charity; *Ready, Steady, Go ... !*, a board game; and *Journeys Outward ... Journeys Inward*, personal record of achievement toolkits.

Volunteers/jobseekers: Potential partner organisations should contact CYEC at their English or Scottish office requesting the leaflet *Guidelines for Funding of Commonwealth Youth Exchanges*.

CYEC in Scotland: 30 Wyvis Crescent, Conon Bridge, Dingwall, Ross-shire IV7 8BZ (01349 861110)

Concern Universal

Sustainable and long-term development work, emergency relief, development education

Geographical focus: Bangladesh, Brazil, Colombia, Kenya, Malawi, Mozambique, Gambia, Ghana, Guinea, Nigeria, Tanzania

21 King Street, Hereford HR4 9BX
Tel: 01432 355111; **Fax:** 01432 355086
e-mail: cu.uk@concern-universal.org
Correspondent: Ian Williams

Expenditure: £3 million (1999/2000)

Staffing: 25 full-time staff.

General: Concern Universal sends funds to partner organisations in developing countries which are carrying out sustainable and long-term development and emergency relief activities. It supports projects in the areas of adult literacy, community health, child protection and education, agricultural development, capacity building, small enterprise development, water and sanitation, emergency/food rehabilitation and organisational development.

The charity also supports programmes of development education in Northern Ireland and the west of England.

Membership: The charity has an Associate Membership scheme. Contact the charity at the address above for further information.

Volunteers/jobseekers: Opportunities for volunteering in the UK only. Contact the charity at the address above for further information.

CONCERN Worldwide

Relief and development work

Geographical focus: *Afghanistan, Angola, Bangladesh, Burundi, Cambodia, Democratic Republic of Congo, Ethiopia, Haiti, Honduras, Liberia, Laos, Mozambique, North Korea, Rwanda, Sierra Leone, Sudan, Somalia, Tanzania, Uganda*

248–250 Lavender Hill, London SW11 1LJ
Tel: 020 7738 1033; **Fax:** 020 7738 1032
e-mail: infolondon@concernworldwide.org
Website: www.concern.org.uk or www.concern.ie
Correspondent: Sarah Molloy, Organiser

Expenditure: £24 million

Staffing: 91 in Ireland and the UK, and more staff overseas.

Website information: Material on development issues; a Breaking News section (press releases etc.); how to get involved – including job vacancies.

General: The charity's mission is 'to relieve suffering among the poor and make real progress towards the complete eradication of poverty'.

In reponse to emergency relief and development situations, CONCERN's work has included the provision of:

- water, sanitation and shelter
- clothes, coal, food and funds
- seed and tool distribution to rural areas
- forestry work
- health and nutrition education
- help in upgrading a hospital's paediatric unit, schools, roads, canals etc.
- primary healthcare
- access to pharmacy supplies
- help in setting up savings and micro-credit schemes
- help building community groups and networks
- improvements in access to primary education
- adult literacy programmes
- training in setting up cottage industries, including with women
- training for trainers in a vocational training centre
- training and technical support in order to develop government disaster management and preparedness.

CONCERN also carries out advocacy work on behalf of people in their own overseas projects.

Volunteers/jobseekers: CONCERN recruits volunteer professional personnel for its UK office and for its development programmes overseas. Overseas positions are mainly for the following professions:

- field management
- health – nurses/midwives
- nutrition
- environmental health
- natural resources
- accountancy
- administration
- transport management – mechanics
- engineering
- social, rural and community development work
- logistics
- education.

A minimum of 18 months' relevant post qualification experience is usually required. An initial assessment of an applicant's qualification and skills is carried out on the submission of an up-to-date curriculum vitae. On receipt of your cv, the Human Resources Officer will make further contact with you. Send your application to the HR Officer, e-mail: hrenquiries@concern.ie, post: HR Officer, Concern, 52–55 Lower Camden Street, Dublin 2, Ireland.

If you have skills which do not fall into the above categories, contact the HR Officer to discuss your potential application.

Council for Education in World Citizenship (CEWC)

Promoting education for international understanding amongst young people

Geographical focus: Worldwide

Sir John Lyon House, 5 High Timber Street, London EC4V 3PA
Tel: 020 7329 1500; **Fax:** 020 7329 8160
e-mail: info@cewc.org.uk
Website: www.cewc.org.uk
Correspondent: Heather Brown, Administrator

Expenditure: About £150,000

Staffing: 2 full-time staff as well as volunteers in London. Separate offices in Belfast and Cardiff.

Website information: Activities and events; publications and learning resources.

General: The following information was taken from the charity's website. 'CEWC is an independent organisation which helps young people understand and confront global issues and challenges. Founded in 1939 to promote education for international understanding, CEWC prepares people for their rights and responsibilities as active citizens of our interdependent and multicultural world. Through publications, activities, information, advice and support, it works with member schools, colleges, education authorities, groups and individuals.'

Publications: The charity produces a number of publications and learning resources. For further information about these contact the correspondent by e-mail to the address above.

Council for World Mission

Sharing resources amongst overseas Christian churches and organisations (mainly of the Reformed tradition)

Geographical focus: The Caribbean, East Asia, Europe, the Indian Ocean, the Pacific, South Asia, Southern Africa

Ipalo House, 32-34 Great Peter Street, London SW1P 2DB
Tel: 020 7222 4214;
Fax: 020 7222 3510/7233 1747
e-mail: council@cwmission.org.uk
Website: www.cwmission.org.uk
Correspondent: The Clerk

Expenditure: £9.3 million (1999)

Staffing: 20 staff in the UK office, a variable number of staff in churches worldwide.

Website information: Facts about its work; highlights; newsletter; campaigns; list of resources – i.e. publications and songs; greeting cards sales information; job vacancies and training opportunties; archives.

General: The following information was taken from the charity's website. 'The Council for World Mission (CWM) is a cooperative of 31 Christian denominations worldwide. They have a common commitment to God's mission and the council exists as a forum for mutual support, an exchange of news, ideas and people, and as a pool of financial resources.

'CWM was established in 1977 in its present form. It grew out of the London Missionary Society (LMS, founded 1795), the Commonwealth (Colonial) Missionary Society (1832) and the (English) Presbyterian Board of Missions (1847). Most member churches have backgrounds in the Reformed tradition. Many are United churches.

'The council was created as an experiment in a new kind of missionary organisation. No longer were the resources to come just from Europe. The council's churches voted for a democratic structure in which everyone could contribute and receive from each other as equals.

'CWM believes that the local church has the primary responsibility for carrying forward God's mission locally. As a global body, the council exists to help resource-sharing for mission by the CWM community of churches.

'The council has four permanent programmes – financial sharing, personnel sharing, mission development and education, and communication – which give encouragement, provide training opportunities, share information and give practical help to the churches' mission programmes.'

The organisation has 31 member churches worldwide.

Publications: The newsletter *Inside Out* and a list of resources is available from the address above, and on the website. First time members can get *Inside Out* and CWM's e-mail news for one year for free.

Volunteers/jobseekers: Current vacancies for Christian workers are posted on the website, under the related country headings. As at November 2000, there were positions available for:

- ministers
- teachers and lecturers
- a fundraiser project officer
- a lawyer
- a research officer
- a mission-enabler
- business and project development officers
- medical officers
- nurses
- doctors.

'If you wish to be considered for a position write to your denominational church office in your own country and tell them of your interest. Please do not apply directly to CWM. We believe that it should be the churches' responsibility to send and receive people in mission and we act through them.' Application forms and further information is available from the charity and needs to be completed and endorsed by your own denominational church.

Please note:

- CWM is not an employer, only a facilitator. Sharing takes place between a receiving and a sending church, they being the employers
- prescribed forms to place requests of service for personnel and personnel offering for long or short-term missionary service are obtainable from CWM on request
- all correspondence must be channelled through the applicant's denominational office and addressed to The Secretary for Personnel Resources and Training, at the address above.

Crosslinks

Enabling individuals to work in development and Christian ministries

Geographical focus: Ethiopia, France, Kenya, Portugal, Republic of Ireland, South Africa, Spain, Uganda, UK, Zimbabwe

251 Lewisham Way, London SE4 1XF
Tel: 020 8691 6111; **Fax:** 020 8694 8023
e-mail: info@crosslinks.org
Website: www.crosslinks.org
Correspondent: Janet Horsman

Expenditure: £1.8 million (1999)

Website information: This website was under construction as at October 2000. It already contained contact information including regional contacts, and how your church can get involved. Further pages will include a breakdown of its projects into countries, and how you can get involved.

General: The following information was taken from the charity's website. 'Crosslinks is a mission agency working mainly within the Anglican Communion. It was founded in 1922, and formerly known as The Bible Churchmen's Missionary Society … . Crosslinks' activities today can be summarised as taking "God's Word to God's World".

'Crosslinks helps individuals and local churches to be realistically involved in world-wide mission.'

Part of its work includes 'enabling mission partners and others to work in other parts of the world church'.

Its mission partners can take on a range of activities, mostly church ministries, but also, relevant to this guide, work in the fields of environmental care and medical and community development.

The Cusichaca Trust

Encouraging rural development, in particular through the reintroduction of traditional farming methods

Geographical focus: Peru

2 Spinners Court, 55 West End, Witney, Oxfordshire OX8 6NJ
Tel & Fax: 01993 709606
e-mail: cusichaca@cusichaca.org
Website: www.cusichaca.org
Correspondent: Dr A Kendal

Expenditure: £193,000 (2000)

Staffing: UK: 3 full-time and 1 half-time paid staff, no volunteers.

Peru: 1 UK-resident paid member of staff and 15 local paid staff.

Website information: Information about Peru; a description of projects; listing of partnerships.

General: The charity provided us with the following information. 'The Cusichaca Trust is a long-established charitable trust, active in Peru since 1977. Founded to undertake archaeological, anthropological and environmental research into the ancient agricultural systems of the Peruvian Andes. The trust has since pioneered integrated rural development projects in partnership with the most vulnerable farming communities. The trust has proven that the reintroduction of selected traditional technologies can lead to the reduction of poverty and the empowerment of farming communities helping ensure that future generations can enjoy levels of past productivity and integrate into the new national economy of Peru.

'Current activities include:

The Pampachiri Project, which is an integrated rural development programme with an estimated 5,000 beneficiaries in Apurimac and Ayacucho regions. Building on earlier successes at Cusichaca and Patacancha, training and local capacity building to encourage the wider replication of appropriate solutions is a primary focus. The project includes support for restoration of ancient irrigation channels and terracing, the supply of potable water, development of a horticultural centre, kitchen gardens and tree nurseries for reforestation, and the cultivation of the ancient (and newly profitable) maca root at high altitudes. Training focuses on water management, organic soil conservation, practical workshops in blacksmithy and carpentry are held and seminars given on agroecology.

Mills and Energy Project. In conjunction with Intermediate Technology Peru this project will implement one new mill and make improvements to two old mills. The project includes feasibility studies for similar further projects and training in management and administration for these and other energy installations.

Rehabilitation and Improvement of Andean Irrigated Terrace Systems Research Project. A multidisciplinary investigation of the technology of the Huari and Chanca Agricultural Systems (circa 500-1400 AD). Geographers, paleoecologists and archaeologists will survey and research ancient land use in three main and three comparative areas. The results of this work will be complemented by socioeconomic studies which will inform local rural development projects throughout the Andes.

'Future project: *The Paras Project.* A similar rural development programme to the Pampachiri project, this will emphasise the empowerment of local people to manage their own resources.'

Membership: Cusichaca Trust does not have a formal membership scheme at present, but does produce an annual update for people who have supported the trust during that year.

Publications: Technical manuals on the restoration of ancient irrigation systems are available, terraces techniques and archaeological papers have been produced and are available but there is no catalogue.

Trading: CT does not have a trading wing.

Volunteers/jobseekers: The charity does not have a formal volunteer programme but relies on the services of volunteer archaeologists and surveyors in the field. The trust would also welcome offers of voluntary assistance for a number of administrative roles in its UK office.

Department of Development Studies (SOAS)

Teaching in development studies
Geographical focus: Worldwide; Ethiopia

University of London, Thornhaugh Street, Russell Square, London WC1H 0XG
Tel: 020 7637 2388
e-mail: devstud@soas.ac.uk
Website: www.soas.ac.uk/development/home.html
Correspondent: The Administrator

Staffing: 8 full-time members of staff.

Website information: Information about its courses and research.

General: The Department of Development Studies, formerly Centre for Development Studies, was established in 1996 and provides teaching in the field of development studies, as well as carrying out research into problems of sustainable development. It is part of the School of Oriental and African Studies at University of London.

The department offers taught postgraduate courses in development studies, research training and opportunities to pursue masters and doctorate-level research on a wide variety of topics.

Other work includes managing institutional capacity-building projects in partnership with universities in Ethiopia.

This entry was not confirmed by the department. The information was compiled using the organisation's website.

Development Education Association (DEA)

Supporting and promoting the work of all those engaged in development education in the UK

Geographical focus: Worldwide/UK

3rd Floor, 29–31 Cowper Street, London EC2A 4AT
Tel: 020 7490 8108; **Fax:** 020 7490 8123
e-mail: devedassoc@gn.apc.org
Website: www.dea.org.uk
Correspondent: Nadia Mackenzie, Information Services Team

Expenditure: £353,000 (1998/99)

Staffing: 10 full and part-time staff.

Website information: Description of its members' work; sections on development education for schools, youth, adult and community and higher education audiences.

General: The charity states: 'Development education aims to raise awareness and understanding of how the global affects the local and how individuals, communities and societies can and do influence the global'. DEA is a national umbrella organisation formed in 1993, bringing together the National Association of Development Education Centres and the Inter Agencies Group of overseas development agencies engaged in development education.

Member organisations work within schools, youth organisations, adult education, community groups and higher education to support educators and students in bringing a global perspective to their learning.

The DEA offers training and capacity building, seminars and conferences, information and publications, and advice and support to its members to increase the effectiveness of development education practice. The association aims to influence and develop public policy at all levels which impact upon development education.

The DEA works closely with the development education networks in Scotland, Wales and Northern Ireland and other partner organisations such as BOND and EC-NGDO Liaison Committee.

Membership: Over 220 member organisations including Development Education Centres (DECs), ngos, local authorities, professional associations, the media, trade unions, church and faith organisations, schools, colleges, universities, community groups and youth organisations. Membership fees are dependent on size of organisation.

Publications: Regular newsletters; specialist supplements for schools, youth, adult and community sectors, for the network of local DECs and for black and ethnic minority organisations engaged in development education; reports; briefings; guidance documents; handbooks/manuals; and *Development Education Journal*.

Volunteers/jobseekers: Volunteers are welcome to help out with information and resource work, newsletters, website and administrative support. Please note, the charity only works in the UK.

Development and Project Planning Centre (DPPC)

Degree courses, professional training and research concerned with the planning and management of development projects and associated policy issues

Geographical focus: *Africa – south of the Sahara, south and south east Asia, Eastern and Central Europe*

University of Bradford,
Bradford BD7 1DP
Tel: 01274 233980; **Fax:** 01274 235282
e-mail: l.j.knight@bradford.ac.uk
Website: www.brad.ac.uk/acad/dppc/homepage.html
Correspondent: Prof. J Weiss, Head of Centre

Expenditure: About £1.5 million

Staffing: 20 academic and 8 support staff, all based in Bradford.

Website information: Detailed information about the centre's courses and how to apply; lists of staff research interests and projects undertaken; a general capability statement and description of the centre; news and current activities.

General: DPPC was established within the University of Bradford in 1967. It offers a programme of short professional development training courses in Bradford, focusing on aspects of development project planning and management, and issues in development policy. Most twelve-week courses offer the option to proceed to a postgraduate certificate qualification by assessment, and provides accreditation towards a masters degree. The centre's postgraduate programme includes four one-year taught masters courses in development and project planning, economic policy for developing and transitional economies, project planning and management and international development studies.

The doctoral programme offers opportunities to study for higher degrees by research. The centre also offers first degrees in economics. Academic staff undertake research, advisory and consultancy assignments for development agencies and overseas governments, and participate in link programmes and collaborative work with partner institutions in many countries.

Publications: Occasional series, including discussion papers and *Bradford Development Papers*.

Disability Awareness in Action (DAA)

International disability and human rights network

Geographical focus: *Worldwide*

11 Belgrave Road, London SW1V 1RB
Tel: 020 7834 0477; **Fax:** 020 7821 9539
e-mail: info@daa.org.uk
Website: www.daa.org.uk
Correspondent: The Clerk

Expenditure: £218,000 (1999/2000)

Staffing: 3 full-time staff and 3 part-time staff in the UK. No staff overseas.

Website information: Information about its campaigns and human rights and biotechnology; description of resource kits for campaigns and fundraising; reading list; links to other websites; information for students.

General: The charity says it 'is an international human rights network providing disabled people around the world with information enabling them to take action for themselves. DAA was formed in 1991 by international disability organisations because of the lack of relevant information available to disabled people'.

DAA primarily assists individual people who are disabled, providing information and resources relevant to their self-advocacy efforts. This information comes from, or is selected by, people who are disabled. DAA:

- offers advice on how to effectively use the information which it provides
- publicises commonly experienced problems and strategies to solve them
- publishes an international monthly bulletin (see publications below)
- collects and reports on cases of human rights abuses against people who are disabled, and also examples of good practice supporting their rights
- publishes resource kits and research findings that seek to provides the practical information people need to advocate for themselves
- provides evidence, information and specialist advice to the United Nations, European Union and national governments
- listens and responds to what disabled people tell them.

DAA receive anything up to 30 requests a week for assistance with student projects. It regrets that it is unable to respond to requests other than those from people who are disabled, and would advise that people see the reading list of materials, available on its website.

Publications: *Disability Tribune*, is an international monthly bulletin which is circulated free of charge to disabled people in accessible format. Other publications include: resource kits on topics such as 'media information' and 'fundraising'; *Media and Disability Rights Training Manual*; and information kits e.g. *Information Kit on the Standard Rules for the Equalisation of Opportunities for Persons with Disabilities*. Contact the correspondent for a publications order form. One copy of each format is free. For extra copies, the charity makes a charge of £5 towards production costs.

Disasters Emergency Committee (DEC)

Fundraising for its members, facilitating cooperation in the provision of emergency relief
Geographical focus: Worldwide

52 Great Portland Street,
London W1W 7HU
Tel: 020 7580 6550; **Fax:** 020 7580 2854
e-mail: info@dec.org.uk
Website: www.dec.org.uk
Correspondent: Brendan Gormley, Chief Executive

Expenditure: £22 million (1998/99)

Staffing: 4 paid staff, fluctuating numbers of volunteers.

Website information: Latest news and appeals; how to make a donation; list of members and links to their sites.

General: DEC works on behalf of its member ngos to coordinate mass fundraising appeals in the immediate wake of a humanitarian disaster. Its appeals provide a focal point for donors and it works to raise money quickly so that a swift response can be made by the member emergency relief organisations. It works to ensure that the funds raised are used in an effective, timely and fully accountable way and facilitates cooperation between organisations.

DEC runs the fundraising appeals in partnership with bodies such as the BBC, ITV, Cooperative Bank, British Telecom, other television and radio stations, regional and national press and other banks. These partners form a network of support known as Rapid Response

Network. The BBC and ITV, for example, provide free facilities for the preparation of the appeal script together with suitable footage and prime time slots for an on air presentation by a celebrity name. BT, for example, provides the phone line network for credit/debit card donations.

Membership: DEC has 14 member organisations which have met certain criteria of size and have signed a code of conduct for ngos in disaster relief.

Volunteers/jobseekers: There are no opportunities for volunteers overseas. In the UK volunteers are recruited to work on the telephones during appeals. If you are interested in volunteering, please contact the Donations Manager.

The Donkey Sanctuary (DS)

Working to prevent the suffering of donkeys worldwide and educating the owners in donkey welfare

Geographical focus: Ethiopia, India, Kenya, Mexico, Egypt, as well as in Europe

The Donkey Sanctuary, Sidmouth, Devon EX10 0NU
Tel: 01395 578222; **Fax:** 01395 579266
e-mail: thedonkeysanctuary@compuserve.com
Website: www.thedonkeysanctuary.org.uk
Correspondent: Dr Elisabeth Svendsen, Chief Executive

Expenditure: £578,000 (overseas 1999/2000)

Staffing: 6 staff in UK working on overseas projects; 2 staff overseas.

Website information: The part of the website relevant to overseas projects was under construction in January 2001. The remainder of the website contains a wide range of information about The Donkey Sanctuary's work in the UK.

General: The International Donkey Protection Trust was incorporated into The Donkey Sanctuary on 1 October 2000. The latter organisation is a rapidly growing charity working for the protection of donkeys, with an expenditure of £9 million and employing over 230 staff.

The objects of The Donkey Sanctuary are the provision of care, protection and/or permanent security anywhere in the world for donkeys and mules which are in need of attention by reason of sickness, maltreatment, poor circumstances, ill-usage or other like causes and the prevention of cruelty and suffering among donkeys and mules.

It is estimated that most of the 59 million donkeys worldwide are working donkeys, and they play an increasingly valuable role in agriculture in developing countries. The charity's overseas projects include donkey clinics in Ethiopia and on the island of Lamu, Kenya, and mobile units in Mexico and India. All veterinary treatments on overseas projects are given free of charge. A new project was being established in Egypt in 2001.

Membership: There is no membership fee; supporters who send donations are placed on the charity's database and they receive newsletters in spring and autumn, and an update in the summer.

Trading: Although The Donkey Sanctuary is not a trading company, goods which are produced by the charity are available for sale.

Volunteers/jobseekers: Voluntary work on a short-term basis is not encouraged, as the charity feels that the donkeys prefer familiar faces on a long-term basis.

The Duke of Edinburgh's Award International Association

Self-development award scheme for young people

Geographical focus: Member countries: Australia, Bahamas, Barbados, Belgium, Benin, Bermuda, Cameroon, Canada, Cayman Islands, Central African Republic, Chad, Comores, Cote d'Ivoire, Dominica, Falkland Islands, Fiji, Gabon, Gambia, Germany, Ghana, Gibraltar, Grenada, Guinea, Hong Kong, India, Indonesia, Republic of Ireland, Israel, Jamaica, Jordan, Kenya, Lesotho, Luxembourg, Madagascar, Malawi, Malaysia, Malta, Mauritius, Montserrat, Namibia, The Netherlands, New Zealand, Nigeria, Pakistan, Portugal, St Helen and Dependencies, St Lucia, St Vincent, Senegal, Seychelles, Sierra Leone, Singapore, South Africa, Sri Lanka, Swaziland, Trinidad and Tobago, Uganda, United Kingdom, USA, Zambia

The Award is also operational in: Antigua, Argentina, Austria, Bahrain, Botswana, Brazil, British Virgin Islands, Brunei, Chile, Costa Rica, Cyprus, Czech Republic, Egypt, Finland, France, Greece, Guyana, Italy, Japan, Kuwait, Lithuania, Macau, Mexico, Monaco, Nepal, Norway, Peru, Poland, Qatar, Romania, Russia, Saudi Arabia, Slovenia, Solomon Islands, Spain, Sultanate of Oman, Switzerland, Tanzania, Thailand, Togo, Turkey, United Arab Emirates, Zimbabwe

Award House, 7–11 St Matthew Street, London SW1P 2JT
Tel: 020 7222 4242; **Fax:** 020 7222 4141
e-mail: sect@intaward.org
Website: www.intaward.org
Correspondent: The Press Office

Expenditure: £939,000 (1998/99)

Staffing: 14 staff in the UK office.

Website information: Information to get you started if you wish to be a participant, award operator or volunteer if you wish to set up an award in your country.

General: This award is a development of The Duke of Edinburgh's Award which was introduced in Britain in 1956. It is designed for people aged between 14 and 25 to be 'a balanced, non-competitive programme of voluntary, leisure-time activities which encourages personal discovery and growth, self-reliance, perseverance, responsibility and service to the community'.

The award has three attainment levels – bronze, silver and gold. It has four components at each level: service, expeditions, skills and physical recreation.

Since 1956 the award has been run in a steadily increasing number of countries and at the time of research for this guide the organisation was made up of 60 National Award Authorities (NAA) and nearly 100 independent operators (see list of countries above).

If there is not already a NAA in your country, any institution or organisation concerned with young people may apply to become an independent operator and run the programme. Please contact the International Secretariat at the address above for further information.

Publications: A bi-annual magazine *Award World*.

Volunteers/jobseekers: The awards are run with the help of volunteers, described below. You 'don't need to be professionally qualified – just have a desire to share your experience with younger people'.

Administrators/committee members
Many NAAs 'would appreciate additional help with administration, keeping records,

finding instructors and assessors and setting up courses etc.'

Instructors/assessors
These volunteers are required to help the participants with a specific activity and must have some specialist knowledge of the activity. Training to help you apply your skills to this scheme will be provided.

Fundraisers and award leaders are also needed.

If you are interested, please contact your national office or the independent operator in your country for further information. Overseas addresses are available in the annual report, in *Annual World* and from its website.

Echo International Health Services Ltd (ECHO)

Providing medicines and equipment, training and other support for health services

Geographical focus: *ECHO's customers are based in over 130 countries*

Ullswater Crescent, Coulsdon,
Surrey CR5 2HR
Tel: 020 8660 2220; **Fax:** 020 8668 0751
e-mail: cs@echohealth.org.uk
Website: www.echohealth.org.uk
Correspondent: Mark Radford, Chief Executive

Expenditure: £5.6 million (1999)
Staffing: About 45 paid staff and 1 volunteer, all UK-based.
Website information: Case studies of particular projects supported; list of products – equipment, pharmaceuticals etc. available from the charity.
General: The charity provided the following information.

'ECHO operates on a not-for-profit principle, to assist providers of free or low-cost healthcare and those responding to emergency needs.

'Our primary objective is to offer a reliable, effective and affordable procurement service to meet all of your healthcare and medical supply requirements.

'We also believe in assisting the work of both health practitioners and their supporters through a range of advisory, training, back-up and information activities.'

Supplies and services available for purchase, or free of charge, include: pharmaceuticals and raw materials; medical consumables; instrument sets and equipment kits; new medical equipment; reconditioned equipment; spare parts; test equipment/tools; laboratory/diagnostic equipment; public health supplies; training and consultancy services; teaching aids; and logistics freighting.

Publications: Newsletter *Echo Around the World* and medical texts and practice books are available.

Trading: The supplies and services listed under General above are advertised in the *Medical Supply Catalogue*, which is available from the address above.

Edinburgh Medical Missionary Society (EMMS)

Working in the areas of health, hospitals and provision of medical supplies

Geographical focus: *India, Israel, Malawi, Nepal*

7 Washington Lane,
Edinburgh EH11 2HA
Tel: 0131 313 3829; **Fax:** 0131 313 4662
e-mail: emms@btinternet.com
Website: www.emms.org
Correspondent: Robin G K Arnott, Executive Director

Expenditure: £436,000 (1999)

Staffing: 4 in the UK; 1 overseas.

Website information: How to help including how to: make a donation, donate supplies, volunteer overseas or in the UK, and save stamps. Information about: its grant-making towards student electives; fundraising events e.g. bike rides; and how to order the magazine.

General: Founded in 1841, the charity says it is the oldest medical missionary society in the western hemisphere.

Internationally its work includes:

- providing grants to medical and dental students studying at Scottish or Northern Irish universities for their electives
- running the Nazareth Hospital
- being involved in primary healthcare initiatives in India
- working in partnership with other mission hospitals in Nepal and elsewhere
- sending medicines to mission hospitals.

For instance, it works with Emmanuel Hospital Association in a community healthcare programme in the Indra slum colony in New Delhi. It also helps International Nepal Fellowship to expand the work of its TB and leprosy clinic at Surkhet in Nepal.

The charity will consider making grants to the following applicants:

- Christian medical and dental students studying at Scottish or Northern Irish universities wishing to undertake their electives at a mission hospital overseas. Bursaries are awarded up to a maximum of £200, and may be less;
- people in need living in Edinburgh who are in need of a convalescent holiday;
- overseas students undertaking postgraduate studies at a UK university or hospital.

EMMS does not give grants to UK students for educational studies or degree courses at universities or colleges, other than electives.

Membership: EMMS is not a subscription membership organisation. Supporters on the mailing list receive a magazine.

Publications: Magazine *Healing Hand*, and prayer diary *Prayer Times*, published three times a year.

Volunteers/jobseekers: There are opportunities for volunteering, either in the EMMS offices for regular activities or special events, or overseas.

Volunteers can help at the charity's Edinburgh office with sorting medical supplies and equipment.

The EMMS runs a small number of events which you can get involved in, mainly sponsored bike rides and treks in Israel, India and Nepal. You could also organise carol parties in your local area in support of the Christmas Appeal.

Overseas opportunities include those for medical and dental students undertaking their electives. The Nazareth Hospital (Israel), Emmanuel Hospital Association and Lok Hospital (both in India) and Ekwendeni Hospital (Malawi) are always keen to hear from volunteers and students. People with medical, dental and nursing skills can apply, and volunteers may also be required with skills in the following areas: gardening, business management, IT, public relations, diy skills, laboratory etc. See the website for further information.

For full details of current volunteer and elective vacancies and an application form please contact:

- for Nazereth Hospital: Mrs Nana Hamati, Administration Department, Nazareth Hospital EMMS, PO Box 11, 16100 Nazareth, Israel; tel: +972 6 602 8817; fax: +972 6 657 5912

- for Emmanuel Hospital Association: Paul East, Executive Director, Emmanuel Hospital Association (UK), PO Box 43, Sutton, Surrey SM2 5WL; tel: 020 8770 0717; fax: 020 8770 9747; e-mail: info@eha.org.uk
- for Lok Hospital: Dr Stephen Alfred, 1104/84 Kalpavruksha, Vasant Vihar, Pokhran No 2, Thane 400601, Maharashtra, India; tel: +91 22 543 7799; fax: +91 22 534 1863; e-mail: alfred@bom4.vsnl.in
- for Ekwendeni Hospital: Dr Colin Dick, CCAP, Synod of Livingstonia, Ekwendeni Hospital, PO Box 19, Ekwendeni, Malawi; e-mail: ekwehealth@sdnp.org.mw
- for Nepal: Dr Rod MacRorie, Medical Director, TB and Leprosy Project, INF, PO Box 1230, Kathmandu, Nepal; e-mail: tlp@inf.org.np.

Education for Development

Training, research and consultancy in the area of adult learning

Geographical focus: *Egypt, Kenya, Nepal, Pakistan, Nigeria, Sardinia, UK (refugees)*

Block 33, University of Reading, London Road, Reading RG1 5AQ
Tel: 0118 931 6317; **Fax:** 0118 931 6318
e-mail: eddev@reading.ac.uk
Website: www.eddev.org
Correspondent: Dr Roy Williams, Director

Expenditure: £194,000 (1998/99)
Staffing: 10 UK-based members of staff.

Website information: Newsletter; project information; publications and events; its main donors. The website is also a forum for discussion and networking.

General: At the request of partner organisations Education for Development has worked in Africa, Asia and Europe. It offers training, research and consultancy in education and training for adults in literacy, agriculture, multimedia, organisation and small business development.

Central to its work is the dissemination and sharing of good practice from its experience as a northern ngo, (see under Publications and Website information).

Its core areas of work 'are within non-formal education and training, providing flexible and context-sensitive services at the request of partner organisations, firmly rooted in community participation and ownership'. It serves to strengthen the community's capacity to deliver services and does not directly deliver services.

In 1999 new initiatives underway included:
- research into how information and communication technology can be used to support the under-resourced educator and learner
- developing a literacy and conflict resolution programme with Sierra Leonean refugees in a camp in Guinea
- developing language skills with refugees in the UK.

Publications: A newsletter; a series of interactive training manuals for education and training programmes in developing countries (cost £3-£5 each); books about literacy and learning through extension (£2.50-£30); and other publications, all advertised in a small leaflet.

Volunteers/jobseekers: No longer opportunities for volunteers overseas, but UK volunteers are welcome to help out with administrative support, producing the newsletter etc.

Emmanuel International

Evangelism, community development and disaster and emergency relief

Geographical focus: Brazil, Haiti, Malawi, Philippines, Sudan, Tanzania, Uganda

PO Box 58, Chichester,
West Sussex PO19 2UD
Tel & Fax: 01243 537040
e-mail: emm.int@argonet.co.uk
Website: www.argonet.co.uk/users/emm.int
Correspondent: Derek James, UK Manager

Expenditure: £3.1 million (1998/99)

Staffing: 45 members of staff and 24 vacancies.

Website information: Information about volunteering and a shortened version of the monthly newssheet, containing information about the missionaries rather than the projects.

General: Founded in 1975, Emmanuel International encourages, strengthens and assists churches worldwide, giving practical help and meeting spiritual need. Its work includes evangelism, community development and disaster and emergency relief.

Projects in Uganda, for instance, include community development in displaced persons camps and health and nutrition work. Other projects include a community health project in Haiti and a seed and fertilizer distribution programme in Malawi.

Publications: Produces a monthly newsletter, four-monthly newssheets, a list of international personnel needs and other leaflets.

Volunteers/jobseekers: There are opportunities to volunteer in any of its locations with a commitment of a minimum of 15 months (including 2 months in cross-cultural training). Applicants should be Christians, active in their local church and aged between 18 and 65. People who are single, couples and families are welcome.

Positions available include teachers, development workers, health workers, support workers, business managers, leadership trainers, project coordinators, agriculture and food for work advisers, accountants and nutritionists.

Applications can be made at any time. For futher information about current personnel needs and requirements for applicants, contact the correspondent.

Ethical Trading Initiative (ETI)

Encouraging a cooperative approach to improving labour conditions in the supply trade

Geographical focus: Worldwide

2nd Floor, Cromwell House, 14 Fulwood Place, London WC1V 6HZ
Tel: 020 7404 1463; **Fax:** 020 7831 7852
e-mail: carol@eti.org.uk
Website: www.ethicaltrade.org
Correspondent: Carol Sheldon, Office Administration Manager

Expenditure: £260,000 (2000)

Staffing: 4 full-time staff members.

Website information: ETI Base Code; activities; events; members; reports and background papers; job vacancies.

General: ETI is an alliance of UK companies, ngos and trade unions, whose aim is to improve labour conditions in the global supply chains which produce goods for the UK market. It intends to offer a cooperative approach, as an alternative to campaigns and boycotts on one side, and company resistance on the other.

The ETI Base Code reflects the core labour standards of the International Labour Organisation and UN Universal Declaration of Human Rights. The code requires: no forced labour; freedom of association and the right to collective bargaining; safe and hygienic working conditions; no use of child labour; living wages; limits to working hours; no discrimination; regularity of employment; and no harsh or inhumane treatment.

As a condition of membership, ETI member companies have undertaken to apply the code to their international supply chains. This means identifying supplies, carrying out audits etc.

ETI organises seminars on issues relating to international labour standards and the techniques of monitoring and verification.

Membership: ETI has three categories of members and in 2000 its membership was comprised of 17 companies, 18 ngos and 4 unions.

Publications: ETI seminar and conference reports.

Volunteers/jobseekers: People interested in volunteering should contact the correspondent for further information.

Ethiopiaid

Funding indigenous, long-term development projects

Geographical focus: *Ethiopia*

Bedford House, Madeira Walk, Windsor, Berkshire SL4 1EU
Tel: 01753 868277; **Fax:** 01753 841688
e-mail: info@ethiopiaid.org
Website: www.ethiopiaid.org.uk
Correspondent: The Manager

Expenditure: £1.3 million (1999)
Staffing: 1 member of staff.

Website information: Information on funded projects; how to donate; links to relevant websites.

General: Ethiopiaid fundraises in the UK in order to provide funds that are channelled through well-established Ethiopian charities which are run by Ethiopians.

The charity prioritises indigenous longer-term development work, and in 1999 supported a wide range of projects, including: Addis Ababa Fistula Hospital towards its work in treating women who experienced injuries during childbirth; small cooperative workshops that offer people who are disabled a means to generate income and learn skills; a home for children who are disabled; a hospice; an agency which provides assistance to refugees; and a micro-credit scheme for women.

Volunteers/jobseekers: No opportunities for volunteering.

European Children's Trust (ECT) (formerly Romanian Orphanage Trust)

Promoting reformed childcare systems

Geographical focus: *Albania, Bulgaria, Georgia, Kosovo, Kyrgyzstan, Macedonia, Moldova, Romania, Russia, Ukraine*

64 Queen Street, London EC4R 1HA
Tel: 020 7248 2424; **Fax:** 020 7248 5417
e-mail: ect@eur-child-trust.org.uk
Website: www.everychild.org.uk
Correspondent: The Chief Executive

Expenditure: £4.9 million (1999/2000)
Staffing: 15 volunteers; 37 paid staff in the UK; 21 staff overseas, employed from London; 70 locally employed staff overseas.

Website information: Newsletters; press releases; news briefings; current vacancies; work carried out by region and by country; how to make a donation; how you can help.

General: This charity was formed in 1989 in response to the conditions in children's institutions in Romania. It works on the following three operational principles:

- the belief that family-based care is better than institutional care for most children;
- the belief that the responsibility for the welfare of children should be taken by national bodies using local resources;
- to only undertake improvements to existing institutions in an emergency situation. As early as possible it aims to see children moved into families or family-style provision.

Work includes:

- building local capacity and providing UK technical advisers to work alongside the in-country staff;
- developing relationships with local and central governments to lobby and support the ultimate objective of locally provided professional services supporting families and children;
- humanitarian aid in emergency situations.

ECT says that its ultimate goal is to keep children with their families. Strategies to prevent family breakdown are being developed, and families are supported for example through foster care services, counselling and advice.

In Bulgaria, for instance, ECT has supported the government's work in developing childcare reform policies. It is also working in two municipalities to develop a range of alternative services to institutional care and to prevent abandonment. Work has been done to have foster parents approved and place children with them. The charity also submitted a report to the Bulgarian government recommending projects for institutional closure.

Publications: Newsletters and articles about relevant subjects are published.

Trading: Christmas cards are available from the trust.

Volunteers/jobseekers: Volunteers are welcomed in the London office and are trained to help with various tasks. The charity sees volunteers as playing an important part in the work. Contact Heather Stephenson at the telephone number above. People with computer skills are particularly needed.

The charity has a technical assistance programme, which exists to provide advisers for assignments in the countries in which it works. The work helps to lay the foundations for child and family support services. The majority of posts require qualified social workers with relevant work experience. Workers (known as Technical Advisers) receive a local salary, accommodation expenses and a modest UK monthly allowance. New posts arise on a regular basis. For further information e-mail: lori.edington@eur-child-trust.org.uk or contact Lori Edington at the address above.

The Evergreen Trust

Running agroforestry projects and orphanages

Geographical focus: Burkina Faso, Ghana, Tanzania, Uganda, Zambia, Zanzibar

Unit 1, 126–128 Brixton Hill,
London SW2 1RS
Tel: 020 8674 3065; **Fax:** 020 8674 3310
e-mail: evergreentrust@psilink.co.uk
Website: www.evergreentrust.org.uk
Correspondent: Grant McHattie

Expenditure: About £150,000

Staffing: About 18 staff in the UK and 2 overseas.

Website information: Details of individual projects; newsletter; how to join, volunteer, become a member, fundraise, and make a donation.

General: The charity works with people in Africa for the relief of poverty mainly through the promotion of planting trees combined with agriculture. This promotes self-reliance and provides long-term benefits for communities and the environment. As well as agroforestry projects, the charity runs orphanages in Tanzania and Uganda.

Membership: Costs £17 a year and members receive a quarterly newsletter.

Volunteers/jobseekers: Volunteers are recruited to work on projects in Africa, using their expertise and enthusiasm.

1. Long-term volunteers are needed to work for at least a year. The airfare is paid and upkeep and accommodation provided.

2. Short-term volunteers are needed for placements of between two and three months. They need to raise a minimum of £2,000 for their airfare and upkeep and to put towards the project.

Volunteers can be:

- qualified in specific relevant areas, e.g. arborologist, conservationist, forester, geologist, hydro-engineer, soil scientist;
- skilled, e.g. builder, carpenter, fundraiser, secretary, teacher;
- general workers, e.g. carrying out tasks such as collecting suitable soil, preparing and applying pesticides, planting seeds, weeding;
- general workers with additional skills which could be utilised to a limited extent, e.g. artist or graphic designer, photographer;
- qualified/skilled in non-Evergreen Trust related subjects, e.g. nurse, teacher, nutitionist (the charity will try to organise opportunities for you to use your skills).

The Fairtrade Foundation

Encouraging industry and consumers to support fairer trade

Geographical focus: *Worldwide*

Suite 204, 16 Baldwins Gardens, London EC1N 7RJ
Tel: 020 7405 5942; **Fax:** 020 7405 5943
e-mail: mail@fairtrade.org.uk
Website: www.fairtrade.org.uk
Correspondent: Julia Powell, Communications Manager

Expenditure: £460,000 (1998/99)

Staffing: 10 paid members of staff and 25 volunteers.

Website information: Newsletter; annual report; products and resources list; job vacancies; information about producers; links.

General: In the 1998/99 annual report the charity provided the following information. 'The Fairtrade Foundation exists to improve the position of poor and marginalised producers in the developing world, by encouraging industry and consumers to support fairer trade.

'The Foundation does this by:

- awarding the independent consumer guarantee – the Fairtrade Mark – to products that give a better deal to third world producers. Through regular inspection and audit, we check that Marked products continue to meet Fairtrade standards
- developing procedures by which companies can monitor and improve working conditions among their third world suppliers

- promoting research into and education about the causes and effects of poverty, particularly in relation to the conduct of trade and conditions of employment for poor people throughout the world.'

Publications: *fair comment* is a newsletter available three times a year with the recommended donation of £10 a year. This provides up-to-date information about the latest fairtrade products and gives ideas for action and news of fairtrade producers.

Trading: The Fairtrade Foundation provides a guide to current fairtrade product range and supermarket availability, including the following mail order numbers:
Equal Exchange, tel: 0131 220 3484;
Oxfam FairTrade Co., tel: 01392 429428;
Traidcraft, tel: 0191 491 0855.

FARM Africa (Food and Agricultural Research Management)

Raising agricultural production
Geographical focus: *Ethiopia, Kenya, South Africa, Tanzania (soon Uganda)*

9–10 Southampton Place, Bloomsbury, London WC1A 2EA
Tel: 020 7430 0440; **Fax:** 020 7430 0460
e-mail: farmafrica@farmafrica.org.uk
Website: www.farmafrica.org.uk
Correspondent: Dr Christie Peacock, Chief Executive

Expenditure: £3.5 million (1999)

Staffing: About 300 staff overseas and 15 in the London office.

General: FARM Africa's principal activity is the development of projects in Africa to raise agricultural production and thus alleviate hunger and poverty. It seeks to achieve this by working in the following manner:
- innovative challenging and risk-taking
- specialised
- practical and operational
- catalytic, not merely providing services
- independent
- acting as a bridge between researchers and farmers
- building the capacity of people and local institutions in Africa rather than developing parallel structures
- disseminating practical experiences.

In Ethiopia in 2000 its work included:
- running an emergency employment generation scheme in an area experiencing famine
- starting to develop an initiative to investigate whether pour-on insecticides that are applied primarily to reduce tsetse fly challenge in livestock also reduce the malarial mosquito population.

Membership: Regular donors receive newsletter, annual review and membership pack.

Publications: *Improving Goat Production in the Tropics: A manual for development workers* by Dr Christie Peacock. Also limited copies available of reports resulting from grass-roots work/research overseas. Apply to address above.

Trading: Christmas cards and t-shirts for sale from address above.

Volunteers/jobseekers: Salaried vacancies are advertised on the BOND website and sometimes in *The Guardian*. Unsolicited applications for jobs are not welcomed.

Very limited opportunities for volunteers overseas. Opportunities for voluntary work in the London office, particularly in the fundraising department.

Find Your Feet (FYF)

Developing income-generating opportunities and sustainable livelihoods for people in rural areas

Geographical focus: India, Lesotho, South Africa, Swaziland, Zambia, Zimbabwe

Unit 316, Bon Marche Centre, 241–251 Ferndale Road, London SW9 8BT
e-mail: fyf@fyf.org.uk
Website: www.fyf.org.uk
Correspondent: Anthony Burnett, Communications Coordinator

Expenditure: £346,000 (1999)

Staffing: UK: 3 full-time and 2 part-time paid staff; 1 volunteer. Overseas: 3 full-time staff.

Website information: Information broken down according to individual project; brief FYF news and events; UK campaigns and activities; newsletter; annual reviews; leaflets. The website was being developed as at January 2001 and the charity said it would also include interactive facilities that enable communication to take place between users in the UK and its project partners and participants overseas.

General: This charity works in partnership with ngos, looking for solutions to rural poverty that take into consideration the needs of poor, disadvantaged and marginalised people living in rural areas and provide long-term security and sustainability.

Through its programmes, FYF enables families to utilise their natural resources and their own resourcefulness in developing long-term food security and income-generation opportunities. As at January 2001, FYF was supporting 18 programmes. With respect to its partners, FYF's role is:

- to identify, develop and provide funding for specific programmes
- to work with partners on programme planning and design
- to provide information, training and education where necessary
- to link its partners to others working on similar initiatives.

In the UK it undertakes awareness raising, development education and advocacy work, in order to share its experience and expertise in grassroots development; and to create interest in issues that have an impact on the developing world.

Projects supported by FYF in 2000 included:

- AVANI's income generation project in India, which helps tribal communities to develop their traditional wool-weaving skills into sustainable livelihoods
- The KFU, which is an umbrella organisation working in Kwazulu-Natal, South Africa, representing poor farmers. It identifies viable agricultural projects that can create sustainable opportunities for farmers
- GRASSROOTS microenterprise project in Uttah Pradesh, India, which provides poor and marginalised communities with opportunities to develop sustainable enterprises, based upon local products.

Publications: *Find Your Feet* newsletter, published twice a year; leaflets; project profiles.

Volunteers/jobseekers: In the UK the charity occasionally requires volunteers to be Overseas Programme Assistants and UK Communications/Fundraising Assistants. Please contact the charity for further information.

Food for the Hungry UK

Raising support for international development and relief work

Geographical focus: Bangladesh, Bolivia, Brazil, Burma (Myanmar), Cambodia, China, Congo, Dominican Republic, Ethiopia, Guatemala, Honduras, India, Kenya, Laos, Mongolia, Mozambique, Nepal, Nicaragua, Peru, Philippines, Romania, Rwanda, Tajikistan, Thailand, Uganda, Uzbekistan, Vietnam

44 Copperfield Road,
Southampton SO16 3NX
Tel & Fax: 023 8090 2327
e-mail: uk@fhi.net
Website: www.uk.fhi.net
Correspondent: Doug Wakeling, Executive Officer

Expenditure: £223,000 (1998)

Staffing: 1 full-time UK employee. About 1,300 staff worldwide, mainly locally employed. Currently 5 UK staff serving overseas, with their families.

Website information: Information on child sponsorship, summer work-teams and a complete listing of current vacancies worldwide. The site also provides links to FHI's overseas partners as well as to its International Relief Network, at www.relief.fhi.net.

General: 'Food for the Hungry UK (FH/UK) is working to build support (for the work of Food for the Hungry International) in UK churches and amongst the Christian community, whilst also providing an important link with major UK funding bodies.

'Food for the Hungry International is working in over 25 of the poorest nations with a variety of sustainable development projects and is also ready to respond quickly in the event of humanitarian catastrophe to bring emergency relief with Christian love and care.'

Publications: A newsletter, published three times a year and an introductory leaflet are available.

Volunteers/jobseekers: A few senior positions exist which offer a professional salary (see website for vacancies).

FH/UK organises summer work-team expeditions for volunteers to Uganda, in partnership with the Winchester Diocese. Enquiries should be addressed to the correspondent no later than February.

Self-funded overseas positions are advertised on the website, usually requiring a minimum commitment of two to three years.

The Gaia Foundation

Supporting local and national initiatives which protect and maintain cultural and biological diversity and democracy

Geographical focus: Africa, Asia, Latin America

18 Well Walk, Hampstead,
London NW3 1LD
Tel: 020 7435 5000; **Fax:** 020 7431 0551
e-mail: gaia@gaianet.org
Correspondent: Helena Paul, Projects Coordinator

Expenditure: £1.3 million (1998/99)

Staffing: 10 members of staff in the UK; 12 Associates in developing countries.

Website information: A website was under development at the beginning of 2001.

General: The charity's name, Gaia, is the ancient Greek name for the goddess of earth, and the charity says it 'embodies an understanding that humanity is part of a finite living planet which it shares with other species'. In its Annual Review 1997, the charity says that: 'Cultural diversity, biological diversity and democracy are of central concern.

'Gaia works at many different levels:
- creating greater awareness among UK and European citizens on global environmental and social justice issues and the realities facing local communities in the South, through lobbying and advocacy;
- keeping Southern ngos and grassroots movements informed about international policies which affect them, through information exchange, the preparation of briefing materials, and enabling their participation at biodiversity and trade-related fora;
- support and funding for local and national initiatives in the South which protect and maintain cultural and biological diversity.'

In practice there are a core group of Gaia Associates, who are often nationals of the countries in which they work. They include scientists, other specialists and grassroots fieldworkers, and help to orientate the work, encouraging networking, information exchange and providing support to regional, national and local initiatives in Africa, Asia and Latin America.

Priority issues in 1997 were:
- tropical rainforests: indigenous models for conservation
- agricultural biodiversity and community rights
- africa network
- genetic engineering and life patents
- the globalisation of corporate monopoly over biodiversity
- oilwatch.

In Colombia, for example, the COAMA Programme worked to demonstrate how tropical forest conservation over an area of forest the size of the UK can be achieved through the promotion of indigenous rights. Other work in Colombia included compiling information on the largely nomadic Nukak Maku Indians, for programmes to help secure territorial rights and provide access to health or education.

Publications: The trust's own publications can be ordered from the address above, as can other, related publications. They include: *Raiding the Future: patent truths or patent lies*, which is a compilation of evidence about the ethical, environmental and other impacts of patents on living materials; *The Forest Within*, writings on the ecological worldview of the Tukano Indians of the North West Amazon; and *The Movement for Collective Intellectual Rights*, which is a collection of essays on intellectual property rights and collective rights.

GAP Activity Projects (GAP)

Arranging voluntary work overseas for UK school leavers, and in the UK for volunteers from overseas on an exchange basis

Geographical focus: Argentina, Australia, Brazil, Canada, Chile, China, Ecuador, Falkland Islands, Germany, Hong Kong, Hungary, India, Israel, Japan, Lesotho, Malaysia, Mexico, Nepal, New Zealand, Paraguay, Poland, Romania, Russia, Slovakia, South Africa, South Pacific, Swaziland, Tanzania, USA, Vietnam, Zambia

Applications, 44 Queens Road, Reading, Berkshire RG1 4BB
Tel: 0118 959 4914; **Fax:** 0118 957 6634
e-mail: volunteer@gap.org.uk
Website: www.gap.org.uk

Expenditure: £1.1 million (1998/99)

Staffing: 16 full-time and 3 part-time employees.

Website information: Application process and a downloadable application form; information for teachers and parents; business partnerships; projects listed by country.

General: The charity's mission statement is as follows 'GAP Activity Projects Ltd is an educational charity which aims to promote international understanding by arranging voluntary work overseas for (18 year old) UK school leavers in the year before they enter Higher Education, training or employment and in the UK for volunteers from overseas on an exchange basis'.

Types of activity which volunteers can be involved in include Teaching English as a Foreign Language, schools work, caring work, outdoor activities, conservation and hospital work.

Volunteers/jobseekers: Contact the charity at the address above requesting an application form, or call the hotline on 0118 956 2902. All applicants need to undertake an informal interview, following submission of the form. Volunteers have to pay a basic cost of £550 (administration and support costs), plus variable costs for their air fares, insurance, medical and visa costs and, where relevant, the teaching skills course.

GOAL (UK)

Emergency relief and development

Geographical focus: Angola, Bosnia, East Timor, El Salvador, Ethiopia, Honduras, India, Kenya, Kosova, Mozambique, Philippines, Sierra Leone, Sudan, Uganda

7 Hanson Street, London W1W 6TE
Tel: 020 7631 3196; **Fax:** 020 7631 3197
e-mail: goaluk@lineone.net
Website: www.goal.ie
Correspondent: Cathy Kataria

Expenditure: IR£10 million (international total – 1999)

Staffing: 14 staff at Head Office in Ireland; 71 expatriate staff overseas; 1,006 local staff overseas; 154 local volunteers overseas.

Website information: Up-to-date news on its current overseas projects; description of projects in each country; links; how to make a donation; job vacancies; how to take part in fundraising events.

General: GOAL was founded in 1977 by sports journalist John O'Shea and four of his friends. Its work is based on the belief that every human being has a right to the fundamentals of life, i.e. food, water, shelter, literacy and medical attention. Its resources are targeted at people in the developing world who are the most vulnerable. GOAL responds to major natural and man-made disasters and also provides financial support to a range of indigenous groups and missionaries who share its philosophy. In addition, GOAL has a strong focus on helping street children.

In 2000 work included:

- supporting a number of street children projects in Calcutta, India
- providing rehabilitation programmes for disabled people living in rural villages in the Philippines
- providing health care facilities for Angolans displaced by civil war and famine
- building homes for people in Honduras who were left homeless by Hurricane Mitch
- implementing housing, sanitation and school rehabilitation projects for people in Bosnia-Herzegovina.

Volunteers/jobseekers: GOAL has ongoing overseas volunteer requirements for doctors, midwives, nurses, engineers, mechanics and support staff including

project accountants and adminstrators. Candidates must be:
- 23 years of age or older
- have relevant qualification
- have two years' work experience.

Previous overseas experience is preferable but not essential. Qualified volunteers are required to sign a contract of a minimum of one year, with a view to extending the term. In emergency situations contracts of lesser duration may be agreed. GOAL will provide a package including return airfares, suitable accommodation, modest in-country allowance, full insurance and a resettlement grant. Appropriate pre-departure training is also provided.

Please send a full cv and covering letter detailing how your experience enables you to make a worthwhile contribution to a developing country. For further information, contact GOAL at: Personnel Department, 8 Northumberland Avenue, Dun Loaghaire, Co. Dublin, Ireland.

The Anita Goulden Trust

Running a home for children who are disabled and disadvantaged
Geographical focus: *Peru*

144 Bronsart Road, London SW6 6AB
Tel: 020 7385 1483; **Fax:** 020 7610 1623
e-mail: annaubuchan@aol.com
Website: www.agtrust.org
Correspondent: Ms Annabel Buchan, Administrator

Expenditure: £187,000 (1998/99)

Staffing: No paid staff and 1 volunteer in the UK.

Website information: Newsletter; ways to make a donation.

General: In 1958, on a visit to Piura, Peru, Anita Goulden came across several abandoned and disabled children. She resolved to help them and has stayed in Piura ever since, dedicating her life to supporting such children.

The work developed and the founder and other staff now run a family home for 40 children, many of whom are severely disabled, and also a school for 250 children who are disabled or whose families cannot afford to send them to school. Other work has included helping people who live in rural areas with community projects such as building houses and roads, and improving irrigation systems.

In 1991 The Anita Goulden Trust was set up to channel donations from the UK to support the work in Peru.

Volunteers/jobseekers: No opportunities for volunteers as at January 2001.

Grace and Compassion Benedictines

Hospitality, the elderly and destitute, sick of all ages; care for young people; medical help
Geographical focus: *India, Kenya, Sri Lanka, UK*

St Joseph's, Albert Road, Bognor Regis, West Sussex PO21 1NJ
Tel: 01243 864051; **Fax:** 01243 841954
e-mail: Stjoesbognor@aol.com
Website: www.dabnet.org/gcb.htm
Correspondent: Sr Mary, Mission Coordinator

Expenditure: £256,000 overseas (1998/99)

Staffing: 199 sisters, unsalaried (114 overseas, 85 UK); 23 full-time and 62 part-time salaried staff (UK), and 39 full-time and 2 part-time salaried staff overseas.

Website information: A description of the development, life and work of the religious community with its lay partners.

General: The Community provided us with the following information: 'Founded in 1954 for the care of the old, sick and frail, we run 26 homes throughout England – sheltered flats, residential homes, geriatric nursing unit and holiday care. Each person is valued as one of a loving family whose independence and dignity is respected. In India, Sri Lanka and Kenya, in the same spirit, we run a social welfare complex, village clinics, hospitals, old people's homes, farms, craft training centres and a crèche. Our international family consists of sisters, their lay helpers and the aged, sick and poor of all religious denominations – or none. The criterion is need.

'The need for medical care is immense. We are: completing a hospital extension in Tiruvannamalai, South India, with a new upper floor giving children's ward and isolation rooms; and buying an ambulance and bringing mobile clinics to villages around Makkiyad, Kerala, where we hope shortly to build additional wards for our hospital, and X-ray facilities. In Bangalore we have opened a new craft training centre for young (mainly Muslim) village people.'

Publications: Quarterly newsletter – subscription £5 a year.

Volunteers/jobseekers: Salaried posts are advertised locally. The Community would welcome your voluntary help in one of their four houses in India, if you are going to study medicine or nursing or have already qualified in these disciplines. In England, volunteers work on central administration or on administration of individual houses, contribute to residents' care and support, fundraise and pray. Volunteers 'are of any religious faith or none and their participation is vital and enriching'. Contact the correspondent for further information.

Dr Graham's Homes, Kalimpong, India

Providing funding for Dr Graham's Homes

Geographical focus: *India*

Kintail, The Causer, Nethy Bridge, Invernessshire PH25 3DS
Tel & Fax: 01479 821222
e-mail: dghukctsec@vcassie.fsnet.co.uk
Website: www.drgrahamshomes.co.uk
Correspondent: Miss V W Cassie, Secretary

Expenditure: About £150,000 remitted to the homes a year

Staffing: 140 teachers, houseparents and office staff in India; 2 staff in the UK.

Website information: Fundraising events; child sponsorship; how to become a volunteer.

General: The UK Committee of Dr Graham's Homes raises funds in support of disadvantaged Anglo-Indian children through the Child Sponsorship Scheme and for the upkeep of the homes. The charity was founded in 1900 by Revd John Anderson Graham, a Church of Scotland Missionary, with one rented cottage and six children. One hundred years later there were over 1,000 children, half of whom were financially supported. The homes care for children from a few months old, until they complete their education at 18. The boarders live in families of about 40 children, under the care of houseparents. The most able students are prepared for college or university, and other students are trained in technical, commercial and nursing qualifications.

Membership: 'Friends of Kalimpong' and sponsors receive a copy of the UK Committee's Annual Report and the autumn newsletters. The children respond regularly with their sponsors.

Publications: *Graham of Kalimpong*, by Dr J R Minto, costs £7 including p&p, available on order from the correspondent. The charity also publishes a newsletter in the autumn.

Volunteers/jobseekers: Individuals, churches, companies and other groups can get involved in fundraising events. Occasional opportunities are available for post A-level and postgraduate students to help as an assistant teacher in the homes in India for six months between March and September. Applicants are selected by a volunteer committee and should have one of the following four skills: Duke of Edinburgh Award Scheme Leader; music; sport/rugby, swimming, cricket, tennis, basketball, netball, athletics; or maths/science. If you are interested you should send a cv to the correspondent.

Harvest Help

Rural community development, farming, clean water, primary schools
Geographical focus: *Malawi, Zambia*

3–4 Old Bakery Row, Wellington, Telford TF1 1PS
Tel: 01952 260699; **Fax:** 01952 247158
e-mail: info@harvesthelp.org
Website: www.harvesthelp.org
Correspondent: Andrew Jowett, Director

Expenditure: £368,000 (1999/2000)
Staffing: 7 staff including 3 overseas; 20 volunteers

Website information: News; how to make a donation; details of individual projects; information and materials on how schools and churches can get involved.

General: Mission statement: 'Harvest Help provides practical support to rural communities, helping them to improve their livelihoods through sustainable farming and increased self-reliance'.

Harvest Help works in partnership with independent Zambian organisations (ngos) to give practical support to rural communities. Its main focus is farming and food production but it also aims to improve the provision of clean water and education. It intended to set up a programme in Malawi in 2001.

Much of its work involves establishing farmer groups at community level and working with them to improve farming techniques, soil fertility, grain storage, access to seeds and access to training. The aim of this is not only to improve food security but also incomes, which enables the farmer's family to pay for clothes and school fees. In this way, it says, communities can work towards benefits that will last long after the life of the projects.

A small part of Harvest Help's work is development education and awareness raising in the UK. As well as keeping its supporters informed about relevant issues, it arranges speaking engagements and provides materials for school and church use.

Health Unlimited

Providing medical aid
Geographical focus: *Brazil, Burma, Cambodia, China, El Salvador, Guatemala, Laos, Namibia, Nicaragua, Peru, Rwanda, Somaliland*

Prince Consort House, 27–29 Albert Embankment, London SE1 7TS
Tel: 020 7582 5999; **Fax:** 020 7582 5900
e-mail: general@healthunlimited.org
Website: www.healthunlimited.org
Correspondent: Eve MacFarlane, Fundraising and Administrative Assistant

Expenditure: £2.3 million (1998/99)
Staffing: London – 12, South East Asia – 49, East Asia – 42, Africa – 27, Latin America – 51, all paid staff.

Website information: Details of events; how to make a donation; current vacancies with downloadable application form; opportunities to volunteer in the UK.

General: Health Unlimited was founded in 1984 by a group of British aid workers to meet the gap in the provision of medical aid to people affected by prolonged and complex conflicts. Its development approach to working in war-torn areas demonstrates that even in emergencies people can benefit from long-term initiatives which develop their skills as health workers, trainers and managers. It claims to be the only British charity specialising in such work.

Health Unlimited supports poor people in their efforts to achieve better health and wellbeing. It gives priority to the most excluded and vulnerable, in particular indigenous people and communities affected by conflict and political instability. It says it works with communities on long-term programmes that will build the skills that will enable them to improve their own health and gain lasting access to effective services and information.

Volunteers/jobseekers: The charity does not keep a register of applicants for salaried posts and are unable to respond to speculative enquiries.

The small London office is the base for project management and funding, as well as fundraising and publicity events. Posts are advertised in *The Guardian* on Monday and Wednesday. Administrative posts are also advertised in the local London press.

The majority of overseas staff are local to the area or country in which they work. Recruitment of non-local staff only takes place when the necessary skills are not otherwise available. In that instance, staff must have experience of working overseas in a development context. Employees tend to come from a background in either community health, health training, community development or development management.

Volunteers are not sent overseas. A variety of volunteer positions are available at the London office. These can include fundraising, publicity and organising events. People with writing skills and organising ability are needed, who can offer one or two days a week for three to six months. Only two or three volunteers are supported at a time, so if you are interested, please send a cv and a covering letter to the address above.

Healthlink Worldwide
(formerly AHRTAG)
Providing health information to poor communities

Geographical focus: Bangladesh, Bolivia, Brazil, Cameroon, China, Egypt, Ghana, India, Israel, Kenya, Mauritius, Mexico, Mozambique, Namibia, Nigeria, Peru, Philippines, Senegal, South Africa, Tanzania, USA, Zambia, Zimbabwe – Worldwide

Cityside, 40 Alder Street, London E1 1EE
Tel: 020 7539 1570; **Fax:** 020 7539 1580
e-mail: info@healthlink.org.uk
Website: www.healthlink.org.uk
Correspondent: Roger Drew, Executive Director

Expenditure: £2 million (1999/2000)
Staffing: 23 staff.

Website information: The charity sees its website as a key arena for its work in providing information. The *Healthlink bibliographic database* provides access to more than 17,000 records of materials focusing on the management and practice of primary healthcare, disability and rehabilitation in developing countries.

Materials include books, journals, manuals, reports, videos and CD ROMs. The *Free international newsletter database* gives details of over 150 newsletters and journals on health and disability-related issues which are available free or at low-cost to readers in developing countries. It also lists around 20 recommended journals available on subscription.

The website also includes the annual review and information about specialist programmes and partner organisations listed according to region of the world.

General: Healthlink Worldwide's mission is to improve the health of the poor and vulnerable communities by strengthening the provision, use and impact of information.

Healthlink Worldwide recognises organisations in the South as the key players in communicating effectively about health, disability and development in those countries and regions. Healthlink Worldwide seeks to play a supporting role as such organisations identify and respond to needs, and seek to assess the impact of this response.

In 1999/2000 Healthlink Worldwide restructured to focus resources on support to its partner organisations, of which there are about 30 in Africa, Asia, Latin America and the Middle East. This restructuring included the development of a Partner Support Team that seeks to work with partner organisations in developing countries to increase capacity to communicate effectively about issues relating to the health and wellbeing of poor and vulnerable people. Healthlink has kept a thematic focus. Current themes (as at 2001) are child health, HIV/AIDS, disability, poverty and health. Activities with partners in 1999/2000 included Middle East Resource and Information Training (MERIT) for participants from Egypt, Jordan, Lebanon and Palestine. This workshop included extensive use of the Arabic edition of Healthlink's Resource Centre Manual.

In addition to its work with partners, in 1999/2000 Healthlink Worldwide continued to produce a range of print and electronic publications, please see under Publications below.

The charity has also created a Consultancy Unit which carries out work that is in accordance with its mission, on a fee-paying basis. Consultancies in 1999/2000 included hosting Department for International Development's Exchange Programme (www.healthcomms.org) and its Knowledge and Research Programme on disability and healthcare technologies with GIC Limited (www.kar-dht.org).

Publications: In 1999/2000 publications included a briefing paper on HIV and Safe Motherhood and international editions of the newsletters *AIDS Action, Child Health Dialogue, Disability Dialogue* (formerly *CBR News*) and *Health Action*. It was decided to stop printing the international editions of these newsletters in 2001. However, full text for four newsletters, which are integrated versions of the above newsletters, were scheduled for 2001 and would be available from Healthlink Worldwide's website – which was also being updated from May 2001. Partner organisations would continue to produce regional editions of all the newsletters except *Health Action*, which was being replaced by an electronic bulletin and one-off publications of relevance to policy makers, including district level health managers.

HealthProm (The Association for the Promotion of Healthcare in the former Soviet Union)

Promotion of healthcare

Geographical focus: *Former Soviet Union*

Star House, 104–108 Grafton Road, London NW5 4BD
Tel: 020 7284 1620; **Fax:** 020 7284 1881
e-mail: healthprom@healthprom.org
Website: www.healthprom.org
Correspondent: Mr Chris May, Director

Expenditure: £327,000 (1998/99)

Staffing: 3 full-time salaried staff located in London, over 20 professional consultants engaged in the projects and programmes on a contract basis, and many regular volunteers.

Website information: Description of the individual programmes and publications; application forms – for membership and making donations.

General: HealthProm provided the following information. It was 'formed in 1984, and works to enhance the standard of healthcare provision in the former Soviet Union. Since 1992, the emphasis of HealthProm's work has been in developing partnership projects with reforming city and regional health departments, medical institutes and hospitals. Its work is sharply focused for greatest cost-effectiveness, primarily in mother and child health, with its 'flagship' project being Safe Motherhood. HealthProm is recognised for its pioneering role in setting standards of good practice and cultural sensitivity in its partnership projects.'

It provides:
- continuing professional education and training
- information dissemination
- advocacy.

Its healthcare specialisms are:
- maternal and child health
- child mental health (child psychiatry, social work)
- infection control (hospital and community infectious diseases)
- sexual and reproductive health
- breast cancer, hospice and palliative care.

HealthProm's programme includes local and regional activities focusing on partnerships in the Middle Volga, north west Russia, St Petersburg, the Urals, western Siberia, and the Republics of Azerbaijan, Kazakhstan, Uzbekistan and Ukraine. HealthProm is able to 'maximise its effectiveness' as a small charity by linking together the public sector, industry and ngos in a coordinated approach to local and regional activities and drawing on its 'extensive network' of health professionals who collaborate with HealthProm on the provision of services.

The charity says that it has previously:
- '• established children's day centres for providing outpatient services for children with mental health problems, working with families and developing methods of rehabilitation;
- provided training programmes for social work trainers as part of a multi-disciplinary approach to improved child mental healthcare;
- influenced government policy on infection control in obstetric and maternity hospitals in Russia resulting in the abandonment of unnecessary routine testing (e.g. costly monthly screening of hospital personnel for HIV) and substantial savings of resources;
- realised significant reductions in neonatal infections'.

Membership: Members receive issues of the newsletter, and have free access to

HealthProm's database and library, containing information on healthcare and related activities in the FSU. Membership is available for individuals, at the price of £25, or £15 with concessions. Affiliate membership is also available, at the cost of £250 – which provides potential for involvement in HealthProm programmes. Corporate membership is welcomed at £500.

Publications: Newsletter; *Safe Motherhood Manual*; *Cancer and Palliative Care Handbook*; *The Forum* – a biannual publication which aims to highlight models of good practice of healthcare partnership projects between the West and the former Soviet Union.

Volunteers/jobseekers: Vacancies for salaried posts are advertised through local and national newspapers and on its website.

HealthProm is always able to utilise volunteers, especially those who are Russian speakers. A variety of opportunities exist for volunteers including health professionals, administrative work, desktop publishing, IT and translation. For further information contact the Business Manager.

Help International

Long-term development and emergency relief

Geographical focus: Democratic Republic of Congo, India, Namibia, South Africa, Sri Lanka, Zambia

Nettle Hill, Brinklow Road, Ansty, Coventry CV7 9JL
Tel: 024 7660 2777; **Fax:** 024 7660 2992
e-mail: helpinternational@covenantministries.freeserve.co.uk
Correspondent: George Jarvis, UK Coordinating Director

Expenditure: £307,000 (1998)

Staffing: 3 paid staff; 60 voluntary representatives and 2 field directors (one voluntary).

General: Help International was founded in 1985 as Help Africa in response to a local medical need in north west Zambia. It gradually extended its work to other parts of the world. Help International is a Christian relief and development agency and all its aid is provided through a network of people across the world. Development work concentrates on providing clinics, schools, trade schools, safe water and farming aid.

In Zambia and Namibia two community centres are established which have a variety of functions: storage for medicines, clothing and food; a base for income-generating projects such as trade schools; housing for needy families; literacy training and other forms of education; and to serve as an aid distribution centre for the surrounding villages in need. Help International has also helped to establish a trade and distribution centre in Livingstone, Zambia.

Publications: Newsletter.

Volunteers/jobseekers: There are limited opportunities for overseas volunteers in Africa. People must be 18 years old or above. They can take part in care work, medical support and building and other kinds of practical aid. The period for a placement overseas would generally be four weeks but consideration can be given to longer periods. Volunteers usually meet their own flight expenses. Apply in writing with a cv. Applicants are interviewed if there is a suitable project need.

There are no opportunities for volunteering in the UK.

HelpAge International (HAI)

Working with disadvantaged older people worldwide, to achieve a lasting improvement in the quality of their lives

Geographical focus: Programmes in over 70 countries in Asia, Africa, the Caribbean, East and Central Europe and Latin America, with regional development centres in Bolivia, Jamaica, Kenya and Thailand

PO Box 32832, London N1 9UZ
Tel: 020 7278 7778
e-mail: hai@helpage.org
Website: www.helpage.org
Correspondent: Mark Gorman, Director of Development

Expenditure: £11 million (1999/2000)

Staffing: 250 staff worldwide.

Website information: Facts about ageing and useful links; details of member organisations; news about programme, research and advocacy activities; publications details and orders service; downloadable publications; information on how to join and support the charity.

General: Founded in 1983, HelpAge International is a global network of not-for-profit organisations with a mission to work with and for disadvantaged older people worldwide to achieve a lasting improvement in the quality of their lives. It works with and for older people practically through projects, at a policy level through local and international advocacy work, by capacity building with members and partners, and in emergencies, in some 70 countries worldwide.

Membership: The HelpAge International membership network consists of over 60 member organisations, including national, regional and local organisations with a wide range of skills in the field of ageing and agecare, the majority based in the South. Full, associate and institutional memberships are available.

Publications: *Ageways*, a journal of practical information on ageing and agecare issues, particularly good practice developed within the HelpAge International network, is free to carers, health workers, members of older people's groups and project staff working with and for older people in developing countries and East and Central Europe (three times a year).

Ageing and Development, a regular newsletter which aims to raise awareness of the contribution, needs and rights of older people and to promote the development of laws and policies that will bring a lasting improvement to the quality of life of disadvantaged older people, is free to policy makers, programme planners and researchers concerned with development and poverty eradication (three times a year). Also briefing papers, a series of policy papers on core issues relating to ageing; an annually updated directory of member organisations; and *Adopt a Granny News* (quarterly).

Contact 'Publications orders' by e-mail: cdobbing@helpage.org or in writing to the address above.

Volunteers/jobseekers: People who are interested in applying for a paid or voluntary position, should contact Sangeeta Patel, Personnel Manager, at the address above.

HMD Response (Humanitarian Aid, Medical Development)

Relief work in situations of war and conflict

Geographical focus: Bosnia, Kosovo, Lebanon

23 Pembridge Square, London W2 4DR
Tel: 020 7229 7447
e-mail: hmd@hmdresponse.org.uk
Website: www.hmdresponse.org.uk
Correspondent: Ashika Thanki, Programme Manager

Expenditure: £632,000 (1999/2000)

Staffing: Approximately 80 paid staff/volunteers, of which 4 are based in the UK office, the rest overseas.

Website information: A breakdown of its work in the different countries; reports; learned papers; how to get involved in its fundraising activities. As at October 2000, the website was being updated.

General: HMD Response is a British-based charity working for victims of conflict in Bosnia-Herzegovina, Kosovo and Lebanon. Established in 1992 in response to the atrocities of the Balkan war, it provides humanitarian aid – community and hospital-based healthcare projects, landmine awareness education and landmine clearance – to people in need. It says: 'All our programmes take care to place a strong emphasis on training local staff aiming to bridge the gap between emergency relief and long-term'.

During 2000 work included:
- in Bosnia-Herzegovina, medical assistance and psychosocial support for internally displaced people;
- in Kosovo, mine awareness education and training for people in the Gora region;
- in Lebanon, a mobile primary healthcare clinic and community nursing scheme.

Volunteers/jobseekers: Opportunities exist for overseas volunteering, and to help out in the UK office with adminstrative tasks and fundraising. Please contact the correspondent.

Holy Ghost Fathers

General development, advancement of the Roman Catholic faith

Geographical focus: Angola, Brazil, Gabon, Nigeria, Sierra Leone, South Africa

Congregation of the Holy Ghost,
26 Eastbury Avenue, Northwood, Middlesex HA6 3LN
Tel: 01923 829655; **Fax:** 01923 836975
e-mail: spiritans.uk@virgin.net
Correspondent: Mark Connolly

Expenditure: £547,000 (1999)

Staffing: 15 paid staff and 7 volunteers in the UK, 15 UK-based people volunteering overseas.

General: The charity provided the following information. 'A religious society with over 3,000 members, the Holy Ghost Fathers work worldwide to promote the Roman Catholic faith. By choice we go to the places for which the Church finds the greatest difficulty in providing workers. This has meant working in the slums and remote rural areas to provide the basics of life as well as bringing the Good News of the Gospel. The Good News in Brazil means the establishment of basic Christian communities and cooperatives. The Good News in Angola means the re-establishment of life, the re-starting of schools and the re-roofing of churches in a war-torn country. The Good News in the Philippines means training local church leaders and catechists.'

Joe Homan Charitable Trust

Running children's communities
Geographical focus: India

PO Box 54, Peterborough PE4 6JP
Tel: 01733 574886;
Fax/answerphone: 01733 578161
e-mail: jhct@btinternet.com
Correspondent: M Tottenham, Overseas Director

Expenditure: £212,000 (1998/99)

Staffing: 2/3 UK paid staff and 6 volunteers overseas.

General: This charity was set up by Joe Homan in 1965, in response to the need he saw in the lives of children living in poverty in South India. He borrowed half an acre of wasteland and invited some young people living at the railway station to help him build a poultry farm. The farm thrived and soon he was able to buy 32 acres of wasteland, where he started his first 'boys' town'. Since then, six other boys' towns, one girls' town and three children's villages have been built.

Each town provides a home for 85 children aged between 11 and 16 years. The children attend local schools and complete their secondary education. After that some children attend the apprenticeship scheme, working towards employment. The young people then return to help their family and community.

The towns are run by the children as much as possible, with guidance from an adult director, many of whom are ex-students.

The girls' towns concentrate on academic life, aiming to educate the girls so that they can get a job.

The children's villages are for boys and girls up to 11 years old.

Another scheme has also been set up to prevent child labour amongst girls still living at home. Parents are offered financial compensation if their children go to school.

Membership: Sponsor a child with a donation of £120, which will keep them in a town/village for a year. Sponsors receive regular reports about the children. Other grants of between £30 and £65 can be made to sponsor other aspects of the charities work.

Publications: The newsletter *Nandri* is sent to donors.

Volunteers/jobseekers: The charity requires about six volunteers to work overseas each year. They normally work for between three and six weeks each.

Homeless International

Supporting community-led housing and infrastructure-related development

Geographical focus: Argentina, Bolivia, Brazil, Cambodia, India, Kenya, Namibia, South Africa, Tanzania, Uganda, UK, Zimbabwe

Queen's House, 16 Queen's Road, Coventry CV1 3DF
Tel: 024 7663 2802; **Fax:** 024 7663 2911
e-mail: info@homeless-international
Website: www.homeless-international.org
Correspondent: John Walton, Company Secretary

Expenditure: £937,000 (1999/2000)

Staffing: 8 full-time paid staff, all UK-based. No volunteers in the UK or overseas.

Website information: News; annual review; directory of overseas partners and a description of their work; how to become a member and an online membership form; information for schools; sharing information page; resource centre.

General: The charity describes itself as follows: 'Homeless International is a UK-based charity that supports community-led housing and infrastructure-related development in partnership with local partner organisations in Asia, Africa and Latin America.

'The initiatives are all led, developed and managed by the local community groups themselves. We support partners through long-term development initiatives. We are advocates through sharing information and influencing policy. We provide financial services by scaling up access to credit for the poor through loans and guarantees. We organise technical assistance by providing practical forms of specialist help. We carry out research aiming to explore long-term solutions to poverty.

'We do not send field workers abroad to manage and administer the projects we fund. All the work that Homeless International supports is implemented at the local level by local community organisations. The projects are prepared by them and submitted to Homeless International for financial assistance. Once an organisation begins working with Homeless International it becomes a partner and the plan is to work with partners on a long-term basis.

'By supporting local organisations, rather than implementing projects directly, project costs are kept quite low. A lot of emphasis is placed on the support of local documentation so that lessons learnt by partners can be shared in a wider network.'

Membership: Individual membership is £20 a year.

Publications: *Dialogue, Why Housing and Poverty, Children and Shelter.*

Volunteers/jobseekers: There are no opportunities for volunteering in the UK and overseas.

Human Rights Watch

Protecting the human rights of people around the world mainly through campaigning, via collecting and disseminating information

Geographical focus: Afghanistan, Albania, Algeria, Angola, Argentina, Armenia, Azerbaijan, Bahrain, Belarus, Bosnia-Herzegovina, Brazil, Bulgaria, Burundi, Cambodia, Chile, China, Colombia, Croatia, Cuba, Czech Republic, Democratic Republic of Congo, Egypt, Ethiopia, Gaza, Georgia, Greece, Guatemala, Haiti, Hungary, India, Indonesia and East Timor, Iran, Iraq and Iraqi Kurdistan, Israel, Jamaica, Kazakhstan, Kenya, Kyrgyzstan, Lebanon, Liberia, Macedonia, Malaysia, Mexico, Mozambique, Myanmar, Nigeria, Pakistan, Peru, Romania, Russia, Rwanda, Saudi Arabia, Sierra Leone, Slovakia, South Africa, Sri Lanka, Sudan, Syria, Tajikistan, Tanzania, Thailand, Tunisia, Turkey, Turkmenistan, Uganda, UK, USA, Uzbekistan, Venezuela, Vietnam, West Bank, Yemen, F. R. of Yugoslavia, Zambia

33 Islington High Street, London N1 9LH
Tel: 020 7713 1995; **Fax:** 020 7713 1800
e-mail: hrwuk@hrw.org
Website: www.hrw.org
Correspondent: Rachael Noronha, Office Manager

Expenditure: $14 million (1998/99)

Staffing: There are over 200 staff worldwide, mostly full-time. A US organisation, it has offices in New York, Los Angeles, Washington D.C., London, Brussels, Sarajevo (Bosnia-Herzegovina), Moscow, Tbilisi (Georgia), Tashkent (Uzbekistan), Dushanbe (Tajikistan) and Rio de Janeiro (Brazil). The charity also has a board of directors, eight advisory committees and a council.

Website information: The organisation believes its website has a crucial role in its work. It posts its findings about human rights crises there, offering an alternative perspective from an 'indifferent press or controlling government'. Reports and publications can be ordered and donations made.

General: This organisation says 'Human Rights Watch is dedicated to protecting the human rights of people around the world. We stand with victims and activists to bring offenders to justice, to prevent discrimination, to uphold political freedom and to protect people from inhumane conduct in wartime. We investigate and expose human rights violations and hold abusers accountable. We challenge governments and those holding power to end abusive practices and respect international human rights law. We enlist the public and the international community to support the cause of human rights for all'.

Recent action has, for instance, included filing legal briefs in the case against General Pinochet where Human Rights Watch showed 'that Pinochet had erected insurmountable obstacles to his prosecution in Chile and helped convince the House of Lords that international law imposed a duty on Britain to prosecute Pinochet or extradite him to Spain'. The organisation has also been 'intimately involved in the effort to establish an International Criminal Court, a global tribunal capable of prosecuting anyone who commits genocide, war crimes or crimes against humanity'.

Membership: Donate at least $50 to the charity and you will be enrolled as a member. As well as the satisfaction of contributing to its work, you will receive a free subscription to *Human Rights Watch Update* and notice of its upcoming events such as the International Film Festival.

Publications: A number of reports and books are available. A quarterly newsletter is also produced, *Human Rights Watch Update*, which provides regular reports about the charity's efforts.

Volunteers/jobseekers: There are no opportunities for volunteering overseas but people can help out, mainly with administrative work, in the UK office. Longer-term volunteers can become involved with basic research work. Volunteers are required to work during office hours. This can be for just for one morning or for a few days a week. They receive travel and lunch expenses.

The Hunger Project Trust

Empowering people to achieve lasting society-wide solutions to overcome hunger

Geographical focus: Bangladesh, Benin, Bolivia, Burkina Faso, Ghana, India, Malawi, Mexico, Mozambique, Nigeria, Peru, Senegal, Uganda

c/o Walker Gibb, Regal House,
61 Rodney Road, Cheltenham,
Gloucestershire GL50 1HX
Tel: 01494 723693
Website: www.thp.org
Correspondent: The Administrator

Expenditure: £182,000 (1998)

Staffing: In 'the developed world' there are about 21 paid staff, although there are no paid staff in Japan, Netherlands, New Zealand or the UK (there are volunteers in this country). There are 2 paid staff in Mexico, about 24 paid staff in Africa, and other staff in India and Bangladesh (figures not available). The charity stated that there are thousands of local volunteers overseas.

Website information: News and newsletter; work in different areas; online briefing programme; how to make a donation.

General: In 1998 the charity's programmes were all focused on achieving three priorities:

- confronting and transforming the subjugation of women as central to ending hunger;
- achieving a breakthrough in its ability to measure and document the qualitative improvement to people's lives achieved through its work;
- extending its strategic processes, to reach more and more people.

It works to empower women through programmes in the areas of health, nutrition, literacy, education and income generation. In all its programmes it encourages self-reliance. Other areas of work include mobilising local leadership, village banking and evolving loans, and introducing new crops.

The charity also works as a campaigning movement of individuals and organisations who are committed to work towards a sustainable future, free from hunger.

Volunteers/jobseekers: The charity is always looking for people to donate money, and welcomes telephone enquiries from people who wish to become involved in working with the charity.

i to i international projects

Offering volunteer placements

Geographical focus: *Australia, Bolivia, Costa Rica, Ecuador, Ghana, India, Nepal, Russia, Sri Lanka, Thailand, Uganda*

1 Cottage Road, Headingley,
Leeds LS6 4DD
Tel: 0870 333 2332; **Fax:** 0113 274 6923
e-mail: info@i-to-i.com
Website: www.i-to-i.com
Correspondent: Dierdre Bounds, Director

Expenditure: £500,000 (2000)

Staffing: 9 full-time salaried staff, paid coordinators in all destination countries.

Website information: Details of latest projects; country briefings; newsletter.

General: i to i was formed in 1994, initially as an avenue for people in the UK to teach spoken English in India and Russia. It was set up in response to the need the founder saw whilst travelling and teaching and the great urge of those in the UK who wanted to work and travel abroad with a focus on self-development.

Since then, i to i has grown to offer placements in 12 countries. Each placement is checked by a UK member of staff before i to i decides to operate. Possible placements are:

- teaching English abroad – all volunteers are trained; 20-hour TEFL courses are offered at venues nationwide, they cost £195 or £175 concession; an optional extra 20-hour course is also offered;
- conserve abroad – from feeding elephants and tagging fledgling sea turtles, to forest preservation work. Applicants should have a high degree of self reliance and a real interest in the project. Related past experience or qualifications is useful but not essential;
- earn abroad – earn 'good' money in language schools using i to i's TEFL training;
- intern abroad – practise your skills or develop new ones in journalism, film, television, IT, graphic design and medical placements.

Volunteers/jobseekers: See above, and the website for further information.

ICA:UK/The Institute of Cultural Affairs Development Trust

Orientation, training and placement of international volunteers; facilitation and facilitator training; financial and capacity-building support of overseas partners

Geographical focus: Worldwide

PO Box 171, Manchester M15 5BE
e-mail: ica@ica-uk.org.uk
Website: www.ica-uk.org.uk
Correspondent: Martin Gilbraith

Expenditure: About £150,000

Staffing: 3 full and part-time staff based in Manchester, London and Exeter.

Website information: Details of all ICA's programmes including online course bookings.

General: ICA states its objective as follows.'Our mission is to build a sustainable organisation which will facilitate a social network fostering personal growth and in-depth dialogue amongst its members and contribute to the strengthening of global civil society by: offering our facilitation skills, training and supporting volunteers, mobilising support for local initiatives and sharing experience with other change agents.'

ICA's activities are divided between ICA:UK (a non-profit company no. 3970365) and ICA Development Trust (charity no. 293086).

Activities include:

- a series of open two-day training courses presenting ICA's Technology of Participation, a practical system of methods enabling a facilitator to actively involve all members of a group;
- customised facilitation and facilitator training with clients in the public, private and voluntary sectors;
- short courses for the orientation and training of people interested in volunteering overseas;
- a small number of placements with participatory local development organisations worldwide;
- Village Volunteers, a sponsorship scheme linking individual UK donors with participatory community development workers in Kenya;
- international project partnerships in Kenya, Tanzania and Ghana and a regional capacity building initiative with partners across Africa.

Membership: ICA has a membership of over 100 individuals and families worldwide.

Publications: The organisation publishes the magazine *ICA:UK Network News*.

Volunteers/jobseekers: Please visit the organisation's website, or send an sae for volunteers' or job seekers' information.

IMPACT Foundation

Eliminating avoidable disability and alleviating its effects

Geographical focus: Bangladesh, Denmark, Eastern Mediterranean, Hong Kong, India, Ireland, Kenya, Nepal, Norway, Pakistan, Philippines, Sri Lanka, Switzerland, Tanzania, Thailand, UK, USA

151 Western Road, Haywards Heath, West Sussex RH16 3LH
Tel: 01444 457080; **Fax:** 01444 457877
e-mail: impact@pavilion.co.uk
Website: www.impact.org.uk
Correspondent: Mrs Claire Hicks, Chief Executive

Expenditure: £941,000 (1999)

Staffing: 3 full-time and 4 part-time salaried members of staff based in the UK office. Offices in 10 other countries staffed by nationals.

Website information: A description of priority areas of work, and how to make a donation.

General: The foundation was founded in 1983 as the UK's link with the United Nations initiative against avoidable disability. It works in partnership with UN agencies, governments, non-governmental organisations, professional organisations, the private sector and IMPACT Foundations around the world.

IMPACT's aim is that no-one should become disabled through lack of access to medical resources, knowledge or technology. As such, projects are designed to tackle both the underlying causes of avoidable disability and treat the effects.

Its work can be divided into six priorities: ageing successfully; accessible surgery; ending hidden hunger; early identification and treatment; safer motherhood and child survival; and universal immunisation.

Projects are varied, for example, from the Lifeline Express hospital train in India and Riverboat Hospital in Bangladesh, to home gardening schemes which provide food security in the Philippines.

Publications: Newsletters are produced in May and November.

Volunteers/jobseekers: The foundation relies on the support of volunteers. This may include administrative tasks in the UK office, the organisation of fundraising events or promoting IMPACT to clubs and societies. Opportunities for volunteers overseas are very limited since there is a preference for using the skills of local people, but occasionally there is a need for doctors, anaesthetists and nurses to undertake specific missions. Contact the correspondent for further details.

Institute of Development Studies

Researching and teaching in development

Geographical focus: Worldwide

University of Sussex, Brighton BN1 9RE
Tel: 01273 606261;
Fax: 01273 621202/691647
e-mail: ids@ids.ac.uk
Website: www.ids.ac.uk
Correspondent: Zoë Mars, Academic Secretary

Expenditure: £7.7 million (1999/2000)
Staffing: 160 UK-based staff.

Website information: News; bookshop; job vacancies; information about research, broken down into categories; teaching and training courses; information services.

General: IDS is a centre for research and teaching on development. It also hosts information and knowledge management services for UK ngos and carries out advisory services in developing countries, to local charities, institutions and governments.

IDS aims to contribute to the reduction of poverty and the creation of secure livelihoods by influencing development policy and how it is applied. It works in the areas of: health and social change; environment; globalisation; poverty and social policy; governance; and participation.

Volunteers/jobseekers: Visit the website for details of job vacancies.

Institute for War and Peace Reporting (IWPR)

Supporting independent media in regions in transition; informing the international debate on conflict

Geographical focus: Offices in: Armenia, Azerbaijan, Georgia, Kazakhstan, Kosovo, Kyrgyzstan, Serbia; journalists work throughout the Balkans, the Caucasus and the Central Asian states, with additional projects elsewhere in Eastern Europe and the former Soviet Union

Lancaster House, 33 Islington High Street, London N1 9LH
Tel: 020 7713 7130; **Fax:** 020 7713 7140
e-mail: tony@ieepr.org.uk
Website: www.iwpr.net
Correspondent: Anthony Borden, Executive Director

Expenditure: £596,000 (1999)

Staffing: 14 staff based in the UK; 12 mostly indigenous staff overseas.

Website information: Publications; media programmes; opportunities for getting involved including job vacancy information and how to get involved in reporting; news and reports categorised by region of conflict; subscribe to free e-mail news service.

General: IWPR is an education and development charity, working to inform the international debate on conflict and to support the independent media in regions in transition. It aims to contribute to 'the resolution of conflict and the strengthening of civil society, democracy and the rule of law'.

The charity describes its work in practice as follows: 'IWPR supports media development through collaborative journalistic projects and other forms of practical assistance. Founded in 1991, it has pioneered cross-community editorial projects - linking contributors from different regions and diverse communities - and helped to establish ties between regional and international media.

'Long-time publisher of *WarReport*, IWPR produces several electronic reporting and monitoring services, all available at its website or via e-mail... and operates a range of training, local publications and other development programmes. IWPR consultants also assist DFID in assessing media programmes in transition countries.'

It supports media development through:
- reporting – collaborative reporting and editing projects to support the production of quality reporting published internationally and locally
- training journalists
- analysing and monitoring the regional media to assess professional performance and political influence
- project assessment and other assistance for regional media and international agencies.

Publications: The charity sees its publications as a very important aspect of its work. It publishes books, reports, the magazine *WarReport*, and several electronic publications. Many of these are available in local languages.

INTERIGHTS (International Centre for the Legal Protection of Human Rights)

Developing legal protection for human rights and freedoms

Geographical focus: Worldwide

Lancaster House, 33 Islington High Street, London N1 9LH
Tel: 020 7278 3230; **Fax:** 020 7278 4334
e-mail: ir@interights.org
Website: www.interights.org
Correspondent: Ms Emma Playfair, Executive Director

Expenditure: £667,000 (1998/99)

Staffing: 13 full-time paid staff, 20 volunteers, 15 associates/temporary staff, 15 visiting lawyers/interns.

Website information: Up-to-date news including commentaries about recent decisions of international and regional tribunals; *Commonwealth Human Rights Law Database*.

General: INTERIGHTS' literature says it provides 'leadership in the development of legal protection for human rights and freedoms worldwide through the effective use of international and comparative human rights law'.

It 'assists lawyers, judges, non-governmental organisations and victims in the preparation of cases before national, regional and international tribunals; submits amicus curiae briefs in cases raising important issues concerning the interpretation of fundamental rights; offers representation before regional and international tribunals; conducts workshops and seminars on the techniques associated with the use and interpretation of human rights law; and publishes materials to ensure that developments in human rights law are widely known'.

In 1998/99 it was involved, for instance, in linking different human rights endeavours which were taking place in countries in Africa and Central and Eastern Europe. In the Caribbean it gave its attention in its casework and training programmes to the issue of the withdrawal of several states from international mechanisms, and to the capital punishment issue.

Publications: It publishes a *Bulletin* and *Commonwealth Human Rights Law Digest*, which provide information to lawyers, judges and ngos around the world on developments in law and practice relating to international human rights. It also publishes papers and a handbook.

Volunteers/jobseekers: INTERIGHTS welcomes volunteers who have knowledge of international human rights law and are able to commit at least two days' work a week. It also has limited openings for volunteers in its library and for assisting with administration.

International Aid Trust

Development work, including supplying aid

Geographical focus: CIS, Eastern Europe

Lower Bank Forge, Derry Lane, Withnell, Chorley PR6 8RY
Tel: 01254 832333; **Fax:** 01254 831081
e-mail: logos@internationalaidtrust.org.uk
Website: www.internationalaidtrust.org.uk
Correspondent: Derrick Leach, Office Manager

Expenditure: £258,000 (1999)

Staffing: Paid staff in the UK and Eastern Europe: 1 full-time, 15 part-time. 120 volunteers in the UK and 250 volunteers in Eastern Europe, mainly local people.

Website information: News; press releases; description of projects; vacancies; how to donate; links to other sites.

General: This charity began in 1990 by taking Bibles and small amounts of humanitarian aid into Russia, Belarus, Albania and Ukraine. Its work has since expanded and has included:
- delivering aid
- giving holidays to children, creating jobs in recuperation centres in Eastern Europe
- appointing managers to oversee the work

- establishing self-help groups such as bakeries and other cottage industries
- starting a music school for partially sighted children
- funding surgical and medical treatment for people who are poor
- supplying orphanages and hospitals with medicines and equipment.

Children's camps for instance are run in southern Ukraine, where the children receive good food, new clothing, trips out, medical and dental treatment and love and care.

Volunteers/jobseekers: Get involved by: organising a collection of shoe boxes in your local area; being a local coordinator or fundraiser in other ways; or helping sort and pack in the warehouse. If you are interested, please submit a resumé to the correspondent.

International Alert

Advancing human rights, peace-building and conflict-resolution

Geographical focus: *Burundi, Liberia, Rwanda, Sri Lanka, the Caucasus (Georgia and the Caucasus part of Russia)*

1 Glyn Street, London SE11 5HT
Tel: 020 7793 8383; **Fax:** 020 7793 7975
e-mail: general@international-alert.org
Website: www.international-alert.org
Correspondent: The Press Office

Expenditure: £2.5 million (1998)

Staffing: 45 full-time staff (including volunteers and interns) running peace programmes in the geographical areas above, and advocacy programmes in the UK.

Website information: A description of its programmes; library containing reports, papers and speeches; and jobs – current vacancies and volunteering opportunities.

General: The charity's mission is stated in its annual report as follows. 'International Alert is … committed to the just and peaceful transformation of violent conflicts. As part of the international human rights and humanitarian community, Alert seeks to advance individual and collective human rights … by helping to identify and address the root causes of the violence and contributing to the transformation of the conflicts. Moreover, Alert recognises the capacity of people to resolve their own conflicts and believes that they must be the primary actors in building sustainable peace.'

The charity works with individuals and organisations, including non-governmental and grassroots organisations, and political, economic, social/cultural, research/academic, military and religious institutions and the private sector.

In 1998/99 work included:

- supporting a group of religious leaders working to diffuse tensions between antagonistic communities within Liberia
- carrying out research examining the cost of the war in Sri Lanka
- in Burundi examining questions about economic and social security
- supporting women parliamentarians in order to help them take on leadership roles, promote conflict prevention at a national level and ensure that women's concerns and welfare are addressed
- developing a way of assessing peace-building and conflict-resolution work.

Volunteers/jobseekers: The charity recruits volunteers and interns. For further information e-mail: recruitment@international-alert.org or contact the Personnel Officer at the address above.

International Broadcasting Trust (IBT)

Providing development education, and education about the environment and human rights
Geographical focus: *Worldwide*

3–4 Euston Centre, London NW1 3JG
Tel: 020 7874 7650; **Fax:** 020 7874 7644
e-mail: mail@ibt.org.uk
Website: www.ibt.org.uk
Correspondent: Paddy Coulter, Director

Expenditure: £547,000 (1999)
Staffing: 4 salaried staff.

Website information: Details of: tv productions; tv research; educational resources e.g. for schools and adults; links to other sites.

General: IBT's annual report for 1999, says: 'IBT is an independent television production company specialising in making programmes on development, environment and human rights issues. The trust's aim is to promote a wider understanding of these issues through the use of the media.

'IBT is also an educational charity. A consortium of over 50 aid and development agencies, educational bodies, churches and trade unions set up the trust in 1982, as a unique partnership between non-governmental organisations and broadcasters, educationalists and film makers. Programme guides and study materials are produced to accompany the television productions so as to maximise their educational potential and extend their shelf life.

'IBT has also adapted its mainstream adult programmes for subsequent video use in the classroom, as well as tailoring materials for youth, adult learning and community groups. Materials to accompany programmes range from action packs, study guides and posters, to textbook and magazine co-production with commercial publishers.'

Membership: IBT has over 50 member organisations (see above). It organises seminars and workshops for member organisations and publishes a range of literature.

Publications: *Fast Forward* newsletter. IBT's resource catalogue *Views of the World*, gives details of the best IBT films and print materials for school and adult educational use (also see General above).

International Care and Relief (ICR)

General relief and development work, with particular regard to the needs of young people, whether directly, or through family or community support (see below)
Geographical focus: *Kenya, Philippines, Thailand, Uganda, Zambia*

27 Church Road, Tunbridge Wells, Kent TN1 1HT
Tel: 01892 519619; **Fax:** 01892 529029
e-mail: hq@icrcharity.com
Website: www.icrcharity.org.uk
Correspondent: Mrs Terri Lewis, Assistant to Chief Executive

Expenditure: £1.9 million (1999/2000)
Staffing: 12, of whom 1 is part-time.

Website information: Sponsor a child online; news; a description of its development and emergency projects in each location.

General: ICR's vision is: 'A world where everyone has the opportunity to maximise their potential and to influence decisions that affect them'.

Its policies are 'to foster self reliance and a sustainable quality of life in the developing world and open opportunities for self improvement. To be alert to needs arising from disasters or emergencies, and where possible and appropriate to provide relief facilities. In all activities, to have particular regard to the needs of young people, whether directly, or through family or community support'.

Activities concentrate on: education, which mainly includes school rehabilitation, construction, school agricultural and income generating projects and provision of scholastic materials; primary healthcare; water development and sanitation; agriculture; micro-enterprise development; appropriate community development; and child sponsorship, by which named children are helped through their early education by individual sponsors.

International Childcare Trust (ICT)

Caring for children in need
Geographical focus: *India, Kenya, Sri Lanka*

Unit 3L, Leroy House, 436 Essex Road, London N1 3QP
Tel: 020 7354 5700; **Fax:** 020 7354 5808
e-mail: dlamont@ict-uk.org
Website: www.ict-uk.org
Correspondent: Roger Beanlands, Administrator

Expenditure: £304,000 (1998/99)

Staffing: 2 paid part-time staff and 1 full-time volunteer in the UK office, numerous local staff and volunteers overseas.

Website information: Details of individual projects in each country.

General: The charity's annual report says 'The International Childcare Trust exists for the purpose of relieving poverty and sickness and advancing the education of children and young people anywhere in the world who are in a condition of need, hardship or distress'.

ICT works to raise funds for overseas partners and then helps them to design, implement and manage projects. 'Projects are developed in conjunction with local people according to their needs and within the culture of the country of operation, and are managed and staffed by local people.'

The charity works mainly with children who are homeless or in other dangerous situations. Its programmes are as follows:

Child safety centres – these provide secure refuge and care to children who are distressed or in danger, while the charity finds their original family, or finds sponsorship or a foster family

Relief, reconstruction and development – includes providing emergency relief of shelter, food, water and medical care to displaced people, also helping to resettle them on new lands. Longer term programmes have been established for homeless street children in the form of residential care and training.

Education and vocational training – includes offering children basic education, enabling them to gain re-entry into state schools where possible. Vocational training and a modest weekly subsistence payment is available to young jobless men and women from poor backgrounds. Community projects provide literacy classes for working children and help with school fees, uniforms and equipment. After school clubs help with exam study and homework.

Family health programmes – includes ICT clinics, mobile outreach workers and dispensaries serving almost every project area. Treatment and medication are at a minimum cost and free to children and people who are poor. In shanty towns and slums ICT researches sanitation and unsafe water problems, working with residents to find the most effective solutions.

Environmental regeneration – ICT has tree nurseries, trained personnel, advice and facilities, for example, which enable small holders of eroded lands to grow plantations of mixed indigenous trees for fruit, timber and firewood which still provide them and their families with a secure income for the future.

Training in self-help income schemes – community workers build the self-help capacity of local family welfare systems and ICT lends micro-investment capital. Single parents, especially women, are encouraged and trained in smallscale income generation and savings schemes so they can purchase basic foods and pay for their children's schooling and medical costs in emergencies.

Membership: Donors receive information about the projects they support.

Publications: A newsletter, *News*.

Volunteers/jobseekers: Occasional opportunities for people to work for the charity in the UK or abroad.

International Children's Trust (ICT)

Providing education for children, and family welfare and healthcare

Geographical focus: Ecuador, India, Mexico, Sri Lanka, Zambia

1020 Lincoln Road, Walton, Peterborough PE4 6AL
Tel: 01733 576597; **Fax:** 01733 571236
e-mail: david.ict@dial.pipex.com
Website: www.childrens-trust.org
Correspondent: David R Kerr, Chief Executive

Expenditure: £409,000 (1998/99)

Staffing: 5 full-time salaried staff, of which 4 are based in the UK office and 1 works in India.

General: ICT was formed originally as International Boys' Town Trust in 1967 and renamed as International Children's Trust in 1991, to reflect the much wider involvement of work with both boys and girls and in more countries where there is the need to improve the quality of life.

The trust's mission statement is 'to alleviate poverty in the developing world by providing a sustainable future for children through education and vocational training, supported by health and family welfare for the community'.

ICT believes that providing children with education and vocational training is better than providing a purely financial handout. 'Poverty, hunger and poor health can be overcome to a great extent by education, but ICT also understands the environment and economic situation in which many people live and helps them to break out of the poverty group by creating new work opportunities.'

ICT works closely with local ngos in the project countries to ensure the projects are effectively managed. Examples of projects are:

- a programme in Mexico which, over 10 years up until 1999, helped boys and girls who lived or worked on the streets to move into a normal lifestyle
- a programme of education which in 1999 was being provided to children in rural communities in Sri Lanka. Despite the long running civil war in the area, nearly 50% of the children had been receiving educational support for more than five years and many were studying for O and A-levels.

Publications: Newsletter.

Volunteers/jobseekers: Volunteers are required to assist in the UK offices with administration tasks, also for fundraising activities/special events.

Limited opportunities for overseas volunteers with ICT's ngo partners.

International Community of Women Living with HIV/AIDS (ICW)

Working to promote the voices and improve the situation of HIV positive women throughout the world
Geographical focus: Worldwide

2C Leroy House, 436 Essex Road, London N1 3QP
Tel: 020 7704 0606; **Fax:** 020 7704 8070
e-mail: info@icw.org
Website: www.icw.org
Correspondent: The Chair of Trustees

Expenditure: £315,000 (1999/2000)

Staffing: 3 full-time; 2 part-time.

Website information: Information about its projects, events and services.

General: ICW was formed at the International AIDS Conference in Amsterdam in 1992 in response to the desperate lack of support and information available to HIV positive women worldwide. ICW aims to:

- raise awareness of HIV positive women's issues and promote effective action to address them
- reduce the isolation of HIV positive women and overcome the stigma of HIV/AIDS
- promote the human rights of HIV positive women globally
- empower HIV positive women to address and promote change in issues of importance to HIV positive women's lives.

The charity's work in the period April 1998 to May 2000 included: providing a volunteer to speak at the United Nations' headquarters on World AIDS Day; facilitating the formation of Peruvian Network of Positive Women; providing representatives to European AIDS Treatment Group, European Network of People Living with HIV and European Community Advisory Board; and running a workshop in Zimbabwe teaching self-advocacy skills to women who are HIV positive.

Membership: All HIV positive women are welcome to become members of ICW. Contact the charity by phone, fax, letter or e-mail and you will be sent an application form. You will receive a free quarterly newsletter and our information pack *A Positive Woman's Survival Kit*. We also send newsletters to related organisations and individuals. Those in the developed world pay a subscription; membership is free of charge for people from developing countries. The charity's publications are available in English, French and Spanish.

Publications: See above.

Volunteers/jobseekers: Salaried job opportunities are advertised in national and international press, specialist publications and on the internet.

Occasional opportunities arise in the UK office for volunteers to help with specific projects and special events.

International Connections Trust

Supporting local students and churches, carries out feeding programmes and medical work
Geographical focus: *Guyana, India, Nigeria, Philippines, Surinam, Trinidad, Uganda, Venezuela*

93 Acre Lane, Brixton, London SW2 5TU
Tel: 020 7924 9700; **Fax:** 020 7924 9800
e-mail: connuk@aol.com
Correspondent: A J Horswood

Expenditure: £150,000 (1999/2000)

Staffing: 2 paid staff, 3 volunteers in the UK. About 40 volunteers each year are involved in short and long-term missions overseas.

General: The charity's objects are to advance the Christian religion, and support missions projects and workers in developing countries. Its work includes: building churches and training centres; running feeding programmes; developing and improving an orphanage; providing income for students and pastors; and taking teams of medics overseas to hold dental and medical clinics.

The charity is part of International Christian Leadership Connections, which is a network of organisations in about 70 countries, which pool resources and help to facilitate each other.

Another related organisation in the UK is Connections, which is a network of churches of various denominations. It runs seminars, leadership training courses, a Bible school etc.

Publications: *Connectscope* magazine, produced twice a year. *Update* magazine, produced three or four times a year.

Volunteers/jobseekers: The charity recruits teams of volunteer doctors, dentists, nurses and support staff to carry out short-term projects in Guyana and the Philippines. Contact the correspondent for further information.

International Family Health

Promoting sexual and reproductive healthcare

Geographical focus: *IFH has previously worked in: Bangladesh, Brazil, Burkina Faso, Cambodia, China, Côte d'Ivoire, Egypt, Ethiopia*, Gambia*, Ghana, Guinea, India*, Kenya*, Malawi, Mexico, Nepal*, Nigeria*, Pakistan, Peru, Philippines, Russian Federation*, South Africa*, Sri Lanka*, Tanzania*, Turkey, Uganda*, West Bank/Gaza, Zambia*, Zimbabwe*.*

* Countries where it had partners in 2001. In 2001 it was also considering working in Bangladesh, Malawi, Namibia, Pakistan, Ukraine and Sudan

First Floor, Cityside House, 40 Adler Street, London EC1 1EE
Tel: 020 7247 9944; **Fax:** 020 7247 9224
e-mail: info@ifh.org.uk
Website: www.ifh.org.uk
Correspondent: Susan F Crane, Executive Director

Expenditure: £1.3 million (1998/99)
Staffing: 14 employees.
Website information: News and description of IFH project work and consultancy services.

General: IFH aims to improve the sexual and reproductive health of disadvantaged people in resource-poor settings, based on the principles of:

- empowering women and men to make informed choices about their sexual and reproductive health
- meeting unmet needs
- increasing access to integrated and high quality services
- gender equity.

IFH's objectives are:

- to promote an integrated approach to sexual and reproductive health
- to support the provision of comprehensive sexual and reproductive health programmes
- to develop and encourage replication of innovative methods.

IFH works to achieve its aims and objectives through promoting policy change, encouraging dialogue on sensitive issues, strengthening the capacity of local partner organisations for service provision, developing and replicating innovative methods and approaches, and providing accurate and appropriate technical assistance and information to governments, donor agencies, non-government organisations and communities.

IFH implements HIV/AIDS/STD prevention and care and women's reproductive health programmes in Africa, Asia and the former Soviet Union that focus on meeting the needs of vulnerable groups. In particular it focuses on low income and under-serviced rural and urban communities, young people, migrant workers, sex workers and injecting drug users.

Membership: IFH is not a membership organisation. Anyone interested in its work can access the website or contact the office for the latest literature about its work.

Publications: Three DFID books and the Microbicides case statement.

Volunteers/jobseekers: There are occasionally opportunities for internships.

International Health Exchange (IHE)

Recruiting, training and supporting health personnel working in relief and development programmes

Geographical focus: Worldwide

1st Floor, 134 Lower Marsh,
London SE1 7AE
Tel: 020 7620 3333; **Fax:** 020 7620 2277
e-mail: info@ihe.org.uk
Website: www.ihe.org.uk
Correspondent: The Chair of Trustees

Expenditure: £300,000 (1999/2000)

Staffing: 8 staff and 2 volunteers, all in the UK.

Website information: What the IHE does; its core functions; a register of health staff for aid work; publications programme; training programme; advocacy; contact and subscription details.

General: IHE describes its work as follows. It 'is a charity which supports the work of international aid agencies by helping to recruit, train, retain and support health personnel working in relief and development programmes. IHE provides the essential link between health workers and organisations needing their skills. We do this by:

- identifying health workers for posts in developing countries from our international register and networks
- providing individuals with career guidance and information about available job opportunities
- providing training for health workers involved in aid work
- promoting understanding of global health issues
- promoting good practice in the management and support of aid workers.'

Its services are:

Register
IHE manages this database of health specialists. It contains information about their skills, how to contact them and their availability. IHE provides these details to organisations that are recruiting for posts at short notice or who need quick access to experienced health personnel.

Health Exchange magazine and job supplement
These monthly publications contain job advertisements, news, views, features and debates on issues in the international health and development sector.

IHE Training Programmes
IHE offers a modular certificate programme and a series of short courses, workshops and seminars that aim to prepare individuals for work. Most courses are run over three or five days and are residential.

Information and advice

Booklets, factsheets and research papers designed to help aid workers, aid agencies and the health sector to recognise and understand their respective roles in the delivery of aid. (See under Publications below.) The charity also runs events and talks.

IHE advocacy and campaigns

The advocacy work aims to facilitate an exchange of knowledge between the aid and health sectors and promotes standards and best practice in human resource management.

Information for health workers not based in Europe

IHE encourages agencies which are based in western Europe and North America to broaden the geographical scope of their recruitment and selection, aiming to bring about more job opportunities for people living in developing countries.

Membership: Subscription to the magazine and job supplement: £27 (£20 for students/people who are not currently working and £23 for people living in a developing country – includes postage).

Publications: Magazine and job supplement (see under General above). Booklets, e.g. *Rights and Wrongs: A Guide to Employment Issues for UK-based Aid Workers* (£2) and *The IHE Long and Short Courses Calendars* (Free). Please add £1.50 to cover p&p. Also publishes research papers covering different issues surrounding working in aid.

Volunteers/jobseekers: The charity does not recruit people itself. To join the register, which is accessed by other charities, you need to be professionally qualified in your field, and have at least two years' post-qualification experience. The register is free to all subscribing members of IHE (see under Membership above). To join the register you need to subscribe to the magazine and job supplement. Contact the charity for an application form and subscription form and return them with an up-to-date cv.

International HIV/AIDS Alliance

Supporting community action on HIV and AIDS

Geographical focus: Bangladesh, Brazil, Burkina Faso, Cambodia, Ecuador, India, Mexico, Mongolia, Morocco, Philippines, Senegal, Ukraine, Zambia

2 Pentonville Road, London N1 9HF
Tel: 020 7841 3500; **Fax:** 020 7841 3501
e-mail: main@aidsalliance.org
Website: www.aidsalliance.org
Correspondent: James Togut

Expenditure: US$5.4 million (1999) (About £3.6 million)

Staffing: 32 members of staff (including 10 overseas).

Website information: The website was under construction in January 2001.

General: The charity says: 'The Alliance is an international non-governmental organisation established in December 1993 to support community action on HIV and AIDS in developing countries. To achieve this, the Alliance:

- mobilises and supports community action to prevent HIV infection, to care for and support those infected and affected by HIV/AIDS and to cope with the consequences of the epidemic;
- builds capacity in each country where it works so that local ngos and community-based organisations have access to ongoing technical support, training, information and other assistance, in local languages, from local experts;

- identifies and promotes more effective responses to AIDS through international activities including operations research, development of training tools and influencing the policy environment.'

In the 1997/98 biennial report the charity stated that it provides financial and technical support to 'linking organisations' in eight developing countries, they in turn support organisations at the local level. The charity's strategies include:

- helping groups document and share the lessons they have learned with others working in HIV/AIDS;
- encouraging action on both the prevention of HIV and the care of those living with HIV/AIDS;
- working to integrate HIV-related activities into more general community development initiatives;
- promoting partnerships and dialogue among the non-governmental, governmental and private sectors.

Work in the period 1997/99 included working via local partner organisations to help: a detoxification centre in Bangladesh to develop a more community-oriented approach; a self-help organisation of HIV positive men through providing technical and financial support; and by providing a skills-building workshop for another self-help organisation in the Philippines.

Publications: The following publications are all available free of charge, on request: *Newsletter Alliance News*, published three times a year; *Pathways to Partnerships*, a practical toolkit for use by ngos involved in building partnerships, in English, French and Spanish; *Building Partnerships: sustaining and expanding community action on HIV/AIDS*; *Care, Involvement and Action*; and *Mobilising and supporting community responses to HIV/AIDS care and support in developing countries*.

Volunteers/jobseekers: There were no opportunities for volunteering with the alliance either in the UK or overseas as at January 2001.

International Institute for Environment and Development (IIED)

Promoting sustainable development through research, policy studies, networking and knowledge dissemination

Geographical focus: Worldwide

Information Office, 3 Endsleigh Street, London WC1H 0DD
Tel: 020 7388 2117; **Fax:** 020 7388 2826
e-mail: information.office@iied.org
Website: www.iied.org
Correspondent: Stephen Lloyd, Secretary

Expenditure: £4.2 million (1998/99)

Staffing: 52 members of staff in the UK

Website information: Notes: new developments in the field; research findings; a list of publications in its bookshop.

General: 'IIED's mission is to make the management of the world's natural resources more efficient and equitable, tackle poverty and environmental damage in the world's urban areas, make markets responsible for the social and environmental impacts and put in place the local, national and international framework of policies and plans to make this happen'.

IIED 'conducts collaborative research and project work on natural resource management, urban development, sustainable markets and trade, environmental economics and governance issues'. It works mainly in the third world, but also works 'on northern agendas which have an impact on global environment and development problems'.

The Resource Centre for Participatory Learning and Action is a reference library located at the address above, open to the public by appointment only, from 10am–1pm and 2pm–5pm.

Publications: It has a bookshop containing 721 books and reports – including those published by IIED itself containing findings from IIED research; e-mail: bookshop@iied.org for further information.

International Nepal Fellowship (INF)

Improving health and developing health services

Geographical focus: *Western and mid-western regions of Nepal*

69 Wentworth Road, Harborne, Birmingham B17 9SS
Tel: 0121 427 8833; **Fax:** 0121 428 3110
e-mail: jmackay@inf.org.uk
Website: www.inf.org.uk
Correspondent: Judith Mackay, Recruitment Officer INF

Expenditure: £820,000 (1998/99)
Staffing: About 150 personnel in Nepal. 4 full-time and 2 part-time based in the UK.
Website information: Description of its five-year vision and information about vacancies in Nepal.
General: INF is an international and interdenominational Christian mission and describes itself as 'a bridge-builder working with individuals, communities and the government of Nepal to improve the health and develop the health services of the people of western Nepal'. Its objects are to uphold the Church and to serve the people of Nepal through medical, development and training support and other activities.

INF acts as the government counterpart for comprehensive leprosy control, treatment and rehabilitation services throughout the western and mid-western regions of Nepal. Other projects include a community health and development programme and an education project.

Publications: *Newsletter Today in Nepal*, published three times a year and prayer diaries and letters. All are available free of charge on request.

Volunteers/jobseekers: 'INF is looking for key people who are committed Christians called and equipped by God to work overseas. We have short and long-term opportunities (minimum three months and minimum age 21 years). All our personnel raise their own financial support.'

Personnel needs have included finance director, primary teachers, doctors (especially women), nurses, project and programme managers and administrators, technical director and physiotherapists. Please contact the correspondent for further information.

International Planned Parenthood Federation (IPPF)

Supporting sexual and reproductive health programmes

Geographical focus: *Afghanistan, Albania, Algeria, American Samoa, Angola, Anguilla, Antigua & Barbuda, Argentina, Armenia, Aruba, Australia, Austria, Bahamas, Bahrain, Bangladesh, Barbados, Belgium, Belize, Benin, Bermuda, Bolivia, Bosnia, Botswana, Brazil, British Virgin Islands, Brunei Darussalam, Bulgaria, Burkina Faso, Burundi, Cambodia, Cameroon, Canada, Cape Verde, Central African Republic, Chad, Chile,*

China, Colombia, Comoros Islands, Cook Islands, Costa Rica, Cote d'Ivoire, Cuba, Curacao, Cyprus, Czech Republic, Democratic Republic of Congo, Djibouti, Dominica, Dominican Republic, Ecuador, Egypt, El Salvador, Eritrea, Estonia, Ethiopia, Fiji, Finland, France, French Polynesia, Gabon, Gambia, Georgia, Germany, Ghana, Greece, Grenada, Guatemala, Guinea, Haiti, Honduras, Hong Kong, Hungary, India, Indonesia & East Timor, Iran, Iraq & Iraqi Kurdistan, Israel, Italy, Jamaica, Japan, Jordan, Kazakhstan, Kenya, Kiribati, Kyrygzstan, Latvia, Lebanon, Lesotho, Liberia, Lithuania, Luxembourg, Madagascar, Malawi, Malaysia, Maldives, Mali, Martinique, Mauritania, Mauritius, Mexico, Moldova, Mongolia, Montserrat, Morocco, Mozambique, Myanmar, Namibia, Nepal, Netherlands, New Zealand, Nicaragua, Niger, Nigeria, North Korea, Norway, Panama, Pakistan, Papua New Guinea, Paraguay, Peru, Philippines, Poland, Portugal, Puerto Rico, Republic of Ireland, Romania, Russia, Rwanda, St Kitts & Nevis, St Lucia, St Maarten, St Vincent & The Grenadines, São Tomé Príncipe, Senegal, Seychelles, Sierra Leone, Singapore, Slovakia, Solomon Islands, Somalia, South Africa, South Korea, Spain, Sri Lanka, Sudan, Swaziland, Switzerland, Syria, Taiwan, Tajikistan, Tanzania, Thailand, Togo, Trinidad & Tobago, Tunisia, Turkey, Turkmenistan, Tuvalu, Uganda, Ukraine, United Kingdom, United States, Uruguay, Uzbekistan, Vanuatu, Venezuela, Vietnam, Western Samoa, Yemen, Zambia, Zimbabwe

Regent's College, Inner Circle, Regent's Park, London NW1 4NS
Tel: 020 7487 7900; **Fax:** 020 7487 7950
e-mail: info@ippf.org
Website: www.ippf.org
Correspondent: Kathy Siddle, Communications Officer

Expenditure: £49 million (1999)

Staffing: 223 staff worldwide, plus volunteers.

Website information: 175 country profiles which provide data on the countries' sexual and reproductive health as well as the general socio-demographic situation; news; subscribe to mailing list; how you can support IPPF; newsletter for donors; annual report; job vacancies; online journals, bulletins and videos; list of resources including publications and sexwise radio series; links.

General: IPPF supports sexual and reproductive health programmes – including family planning – through more than 150 National Family Planning Associations (FPAs) in at least 100 countries worldwide. Founded in Mumbai, India in 1952, it is the world's leading voluntary organisation in this field.

The annual report for 1999 states 'IPPF and its member associations:

- promote and defend the human rights of women, men and young people to decide freely the number and spacing of their children, and the right to the highest possible level of sexual and reproductive health;
- emphasise maternal and child health, and work to promote safe motherhood;
- recognise male needs and responsibilities and actively encourage male participation in family planning and other sexual and reproductive health issues;
- promote and support equal rights and empowerment for women;
- recognise that young people have the right to sexual and reproductive information, education, health, choice, and confidentiality;

- achieve balanced population as part of development, serve the poor and contribute to poverty alleviation;
- identify and serve marginalised groups, including refugees and migrants;
- regularly monitor the standard of services they provide in order to maintain high quality of care;
- believe that skills, staff commitment, community development and the access to timely and accurate information are as important as achieving financial sustainability;
- involve committed, competent and skilled volunteers and staff;
- respect the autonomy of member associations, but require adherence to the federation's mission standards.'

Publications: *IPPF Charter on Sexual and Reproductive Rights; Real Lives*, a magazine available to FPA staff and volunteers, and others who are interested, in South Asia; publications about IPPF's work; publications on sexual and reproductive health issues; teaching and training materials; reports; and youth resources. See website for further information.

Volunteers/jobseekers: Posts are advertised in the press and on the website.

International Records Management Trust (IRMT)

Supporting developing country requirements for managing official government records

Geographical focus: *Worldwide, particularly Africa and the Caribbean*

12 John Street, London WC1N 2EB
Tel: 020 7831 4101;
Fax: 020 7831 6303/7404
e-mail: info@irmt.org
Website: www.irmt.org

Expenditure: £1.3 million (1999/2000)

Staffing: 16 UK staff.

Website information: Information — about: the Consultancy Management Group, and Rights and Records Institute; education programme; research programme; online resources; links to other sites.

General: The following information was provided at the charity's website. 'The trust was established in 1989 in order to support developing country requirements for managing official government records. By that time, its founder, Anne Thurston, had already been working for over a decade to study developing country needs in this area and the educational strategies required.'

The charity works in the following two project areas:

Consultancy Management Group

This was introduced 'to support local officials and professionals in managing official records. This includes defining legal and regulatory frameworks; developing organisational structures, including strengthening the national archives' capacity to regulate the continuum of records management functions and developing and introducing new systems and procedures for managing records; and developing professional capacity'

The Rights and Records Institute

This was conceived for two purposes. Firstly as 'a vehicle for introducing greater awareness of the importance of records and for developing educational modules and materials which could be shared between English speaking countries. It was intended that where desirable, these materials could be adapted to meet the requirements of developing countries with different administrative traditions. The aim in all cases was to ensure that the material was in line with global theory and best practice but relevant to local realities where there were severe constraints on funding and a limited technical and institutional infrastructure'.

Secondly, research projects were introduced 'to study the requirements for well-managed records in key areas, such as financial and personnel management, particularly in an environment of rapid technological change. The trust's research projects have focused on real problems and the practical solutions required to solve them.

'The range and complexity of the trust's programme areas and project work has expanded in parallel with the growth and spread of technological applications and with global development concerns, such as good governance, accountability, human rights, economic reform, transparency and accountability and cultural heritage for sustainable development. Its work has demonstrated repeatedly that neither technology nor global development agendas can be successfully addressed in the absence of effective control of official records.

'The trust recognises that the requirements for managing evidence in an electronic environment are escalating rapidly and that the solutions presently available are inadequate to meet this need; it is uniquely positioned to contribute. The time is right to develop a global strategic approach to raising awareness of the issues involved and creating greatly enhanced professional and institutional capacity. The trust is therefore committed to providing an expanded level of services and support for developing countries as they make the transition to the electronic age.'

Publications: Press releases, reports and other publications.

Volunteers/jobseekers: The charity did not have a defined volunteer programme at the time of going to print. Those who are interested in offering their services should contact the charity at the e-mail address above.

International Service (IS)

Recruiting professionals

Geographical focus: Bolivia, Brazilian Amazon, Burkina Faso, Gaza, Mali, West Bank

Hunter House, 57 Goodramgate, York YO1 7FX
Tel: 01904 647799; **Fax:** 01904 652353
e-mail: unais-uk@geo2.poptel.org.uk
Website: www.oneworld.org/is
Correspondent: The Clerk

Expenditure: £1.5 million (1999/2000)

Staffing: 14 staff in the UK, 5 field coordinators, about 80 other fieldworkers – half of whom are British.

Website information: Latest news; details of the placements with application forms; links to other websites; online publications; fundraising appeals; picture gallery.

General: IS was founded in 1953 as United Nations Association (UNA) Trust's response to the Dutch floods of that year. IS has gone on to initiate international development programmes in some of the world's poorest countries and coordinates BVALG – British Volunteer Agencies Liaison Group. Although an independent charity since 1998, International Service still maintains links with the UNA and recognises its contribution to its development and ethos.

IS never initiates projects but works in partnership with grassroots organisations to respond to the needs expressed at community level.

Publications: *Vista* newsletter (tri-annually).

Volunteers/jobseekers: There are opportunities for skilled professionals aged between 25 and 60 to work overseas. IS generally has 80 workers in the field, approximately 35 are recruited each year. It needs midwives, agriculturalists, soil and water engineers, credit and savings advisers, capacity builders and human rights lawyers. Posts are available for a minimum of two years and extensions may be possible.

The charity provides the following:
- living allowance in relation to local costs
- pre-departure and resettlement grants
- accommodation costs
- medical and personal insurance
- travel costs
- language training
- national insurance contributions
- 20-days annual leave, plus all local public holidays.

Vacancies and the application procedures are advertised in the press and on IS's website.

International Voluntary Service (IVS)

Organising international work camps

Geographical focus: *Britain, Europe, North Africa, Russia and the CIS, USA*

Old Hall, East Bergholt,
Colchester CO7 6TQ
Tel: 01206 298215; **Fax:** 01206 299043
e-mail: steve@ivsgbsouth.demon.co.uk
Website: www.ivsgbn.demon.co.uk
Correspondent: Steve Davies, Company Secretary (& Southern Regional Coordinator)

Expenditure: £149,000 (1999)

Staffing: 38 staff including 5 volunteers.

Website information: Information about workcamps including a programme of planned workcamps; details on application and placement procedures; information on other ways to get involved; events diary; link to Service Civil International.

General: IVS 'aims to promote peace, justice and understanding between people and nations through voluntary work'. It is the UK branch of an international organisation, Service Civil International (SCI), founded in 1920 by a Swiss pacifist to promote international cooperation and understanding after the First World War.

IVS's main activity is to organise a programme of short-term voluntary work projects, called international workcamps, which take place in Britain, Europe, ex-Soviet Union, USA and North Africa. The workcamps carry out activities which are useful to the community and do not replace paid labour; the workcamp 'provides opportunities to break down barriers, challenge stereotypes, learn new skills and make new friends'. A group is usually made up of six to twenty volunteers from almost as many countries, including the host country. The volunteers live and work together, sharing responsibility for the organisation of work and domestic arrangements such as cooking and cleaning. See Volunteers/jobseekers below for how to get involved.

Membership: Members receive the quarterly IVS newsletter *Interaction* which costs: £25 waged; £15 low-waged/student/unwaged; £35 family membership.

Volunteers/jobseekers: The full summer listing for international workcamps is available from the beginning of April each year (free for members, £4 non-members).

In 2000 membership and workcamp registration ranged from £40 to £120, depending on country or camp. Other information:

- workcamps take place mainly in summer – June to September – with a few in the winter and spring (please send an sae in autumn/winter for these lists)
- particular skills are not required
- groups of people of different nationalities live and work together for two to four weeks on a community-based work project e.g. projects involved with conservation or with inner city children or people with special needs
- some workcamps also contain a study theme
- volunteers make their own way to the workcamp where food and accommodation are provided
- few workcamps are possible for volunteers with children
- people with physical disabilities are encouraged to participate.

People looking for long placements to fill all of 'gap years' or long-term volunteering in developing countries should investigate other organisations.

In addition to workcamps, IVS arranges a few medium-term placements in Europe for members after workcamp participation. In the UK there are opportunities to participate in the work of IVS according to interest, locally and regionally.

Details of weekend events and working groups are publicised in regular member mailings.

The correspondent for the south of England is Steve Davies (address above).

For the North contact: Col Collier, Northern Regional Coordinator, IVS North, Castle Hill House, 21 Otley Road, Headingley, Leeds LS6 3AA; tel: 0113 230 4600; fax: 0113 230 4610; e-mail: ivsgbn@ivsgbn.demon.co.uk

For Scotland contact: Neil Harrower, IVS Scotland, 7 Upper Bow, Edinburgh EH1 2JN; tel: 0131 226 6722; fax: 0131 226 6723; e-mail: neil@ivsgbscot.demon.co.uk

For IVS Northern Ireland (a separate organisation) the address is: 122 Great Victoria Street, Belfast BT2 7BG tel: 028 9023 8147.

INTRAC (International Training and NGO Research Centre)

Training, consultancy and research services to organisations involved in international development

Geographical focus: Worldwide

PO Box 563, Oxford OX2 6RZ
Tel: 01865 201851; **Fax:** 01865 201852
e-mail: intrac@gn.apc.org
Website: www.intrac.org
Correspondent: The Administrator

Expenditure: £983,000 (1999/2000)

Staffing: 18 members of staff.

Website information: News; publications list including information on new publications; details of published research; a library; information about other work such as training, consultancy, institutional development programmes and workshops; latest job vacancies (paid and unpaid).

General: INTRAC's mission statement is as follows:

'INTRAC was set up in 1991 to provide specially designed training, consultancy and research services to organisations involved in international development and relief. Our goal is to improve ngo performance by exploring ngo policy issues and by strengthening ngo management and organisational effectiveness.

'INTRAC believes in the importance of ngos as alternative and independent actors working for sustainable development in a just and civil society. INTRAC also believes that ngo values of social justice, empowerment and participation of the poorest and most marginalised groups need to be protected and extended within wider society. INTRAC contributes to this objective by strengthening the organisational and management capacity of ngos, analysing global ngo trends and supporting the institutional development of the sector as a whole.'

Its activities are:

- short training workshops (one to five days) in areas of: civil society strengthening and institutional development, capacity building, ngo managment and developing appropriate strategies in a changing world;
- consultancy services are provided to ngos, ngo support organisations, bi- and multi-lateral agencies, and national governments on strategic ngo policy, organisational and management issues;
- research into issues of direct relevance to the ngo community. Current (as in 2001) areas of research include: ngos and the Private Sector; The ngo in the Urban Context; Developments in Civil Society in Eastern Europe and the former Soviet Union; and funding trends and North/South Partnerships.

Publications: Newsletter *ONTRAC* is available free of charge in e-mail or printed form; a series of books and occasional papers related to its work are produced, please contact the correspondent for a full list of INTRAC's latest publications.

Volunteers/jobseekers: Details of paid and voluntary positions are posted on the website.

Islamic Relief Worldwide

Relief, education, children, water and sanitation, income generation, health

Geographical focus: Albania, Azerbaijan, Bangladesh, Bosnia-Herzegovina, Chechnya, Gaza Strip, India, Mali, Pakistan, Sudan

19 Rea Street South, Digbeth, Birmingham B5 6LB
Tel: 0121 605 5555; **Fax:** 0121 622 5003
e-mail: queries@mail.islamic-relief.com
Website: www.islamic-relief.com
Correspondent: Dr Adel Sabir

Staffing: 60 full- and part-time, salaried members of staff.

Website information: Breakdown of its work by project and country; information for schools; how to donate; how to sponsor a child.

General: The following information was taken from the charity's website. 'In February 1984, two students, Dr Hany El Banna and Dr Ihsan Shbib of Birmingham University were shocked by the famines of Africa. They decided to build a charity organisation to help the needy around the world. Their first donation was just a 20 pence coin given by a 12 year old boy.

'Now Islamic Relief is an international ngo. It seeks to promote sustainable economic and social development by working with local communities through relief and development programmes.'

The programmes are:
- relief, e.g. the charity has recently helped refugees in Chechnya;
- water and sanitation provision, e.g. recently provided clean water supplies to a village in Pakistan;
- health, e.g. runs a centre in Sudan providing essential health support for women and children; activities cover nutrition, diarrhoea control,

immunisation, vitamin A distribution, health education and maternal care;
- income generation, e.g. in Bosnia, distributed cows to help locals generate income from the sale of milk;
- sponsor an orphan scheme, see under Membership below.

Membership: 'You can use either or both of the available schemes – Sponsor an Orphan Scheme and the Orphans General Fund.

'For the SOS we encourage a minimum period of one year with three months advance notice if the sponsor wishes to terminate the sponsorship. We also encourage the use of monthly bank transfers.

'Individuals or groups can contribute to the OGF at any time that they wish, although regular payment through a bank is encouraged to cut down on administration costs.

'Alternatively, if you are unable to join the programme, you can make a one-off donation by cheque or postal order.

'We are currently [as in 2001] working towards online sponsorship but until the service is available please contact either Islamic Relief's UK office, your local Islamic Relief office or e-mail us for further details.'

ITDG

Helping communities in the use of appropriate technology

Geographical focus: *Bangladesh, East Africa, Latin America, Nepal, South Africa, South Asia, Sudan, UK*

The Schumacher Centre for Technology and Development, Bourton Hall, Bourton-on-Dunsmore, Rugby CV23 9QZ
Tel: 01788 661100; **Fax:** 01788 661101
e-mail: itdg@itdg.org.uk

Website: www.itdg.org
Correspondent: Margaret Gardener, Marketing Director

Expenditure: £12 million (1998/99)
Staffing: About 400 staff worldwide.

Website information: The group site contains details of ITDG's work across the world, including project examples, technology strategies, research, case studies and advocacy themes. It also details how to support ITDG and offers a free technical enquiry service. ITDG has other websites: www.itdgpublishing.org.uk for ITDG Publishing – development publishing; www.itcltd.com for ITC – consulting organisation; and www.stepin.org for STEP – development education.

General: ITDG's mission 'is to build the technical skills of poor people in developing countries enabling them to improve the quality of their lives and that of future generations'. ITDG supports the efforts of poor communities to improve their livelihoods, and aims to develop innovative and practical approaches which can be widely replicated.

It carries out research to demonstrate what works and why and its work is designed to incorporate local knowledge and skills. It concentrates its work in the areas of:

- energy
- agro-processing
- manufacturing
- building materials and shelter
- food production
- disaster mitigation
- mining
- transport.

'With technology experience and knowledge gained, ITDG strives to inform and influence decision-makers and members of the public worldwide.' This ranges from the provision of education materials and specialist publications to advising policy-makers.

Examples of ITDG's work are: helping women in Bangladesh to establish and run a small-scale fish farming business; working with Maasai women to develop an improved traditional house with more air, light and space; and helping to design a solar lantern for household lighting.

Publications: ITDG publishes a number of books and a newsletter. See website for further details. ITDG has a publishing subsidiary, ITDG Publishing, which has a separate website.

Volunteers/jobseekers: Please contact the Personnel Department for information on recruitment.

Jospice International (St Joseph's Hospice Association)

Running 11 hospices overseas

Geographical focus: *Colombia, Ecuador, Guatemala, Honduras, India, Mexico, Pakistan, Peru*

Ince Road, Thornton, Liverpool L23 4UE
Tel: 0151 924 3812/7871;
Fax: 0151 931 5727
Website: www.jospice.org.uk
Correspondent: The Chair/Trustees/ Management Committee

Expenditure: £1.7 million (1999)

Staffing: About 80 workers.

Website information: Facts about AIDS in Guatemala; general information about its work and beliefs, including history and up-to-date information on the Jospice Imprint.

General: This charity primarily provides hospice care for people who can no longer/do not live at home. Work includes:

- 24 hour palliative care for patients whose condition is not curative and whose family is not able to look after them
- helping people with HIV/AIDS
- teaching healthcare and hygiene
- providing soup kitchens for the most badly nourished children in outlying villages
- helping other medical work to be carried out among poor people.

Three hospices are also run in Merseyside.

Publications: The charity publishes a monthly newsletter.

Volunteers/jobseekers: Volunteers are encouraged to get involved in all aspects of the charity's work in the UK, e.g. help in nursing homes, or with running fêtes. Opportunities also arise from time to time for registered nurses to volunteer for overseas placements. This would also include paediatric nurses, especially for the Guatemalan project. Applications should be made in writing to the Chair at the above address.

Just World Partners (formerly UK Foundation for the South Pacific)

Supporting local partners 'on a multi-sectorial basis'

Geographical focus: *Ecuador, Fiji, Guatemala, Kiribati, Nepal, Papua New Guinea, Philippines, Samoa, Solomon Islands, Tonga, Tuvalu, Vanuatu, Vietnam*

4a Newmills Road, Dalkeith, Midlothian EH22 1DU
Tel: 0131 663 7428; **Fax:** 0131 663 7433
e-mail: jw@justworld.org.uk
Website: www.justworld.org.uk
Correspondent: Dorothy McIntosh, Executive Director

Expenditure: £830,000 (1999/2000)

Staffing: 4 full-time and 4 part-time salaried staff.

Website information: Information about its partner organisations and information about their individual projects; contact information; links to related websites.

General: Founded in 1981, Just World Partners responds to the needs identified by in-country partner organisations. It currently (as at 2001) supports a wide range of projects throughout the Pacific and South East Asia. Concentrating primarily on health, environment, informal education and income generation, JWP also supports relief and rehabilitation programmes in addition to disaster preparedness.

Support includes: funding, training, technical assistance and the provision of resources etc. Capacity building of local partners is an integral part of its approach.

In 1997 a 'not for profit' trading arm, 'Just World Trading', was established, to promote fair trade in certified timber and a range of non-timber forest products. This reflected Just World Partners' continued involvement and support for sustainable forestry.

In the UK, Just World Partners' work is based primarily on development awareness programmes highlighting global interconnectedness, particularly on environmental issues.

Membership: Individual and corporate subscribers are welcome. Supporters receive regular updates on JWP's work through a newsletter and an annual review.

Trading: A variety of non-timber fairtrade products are available. Details available on the Just World Trading website.

Kaloko Trust
Alleviating poverty in rural areas
Geographical focus: *Zambia*

1a Waterlow Road, London N19 3NJ
Tel: 020 7281 9565; **Fax:** 020 7263 2375
e-mail: kalokotrust@btinternet.com
Website: www.kalokotrust.org
Correspondent: Andrew Brown, Administrator

Expenditure: £180,000 (1999)

Staffing: UK, 1 full-time; overseas, 1 full-time.

Website information: Basic information about the trust's work; newsletters; donate securely online.

General: Kaloko Trust was established in Zambia in 1989 by Phil Wedell, with the aim of alleviating poverty in rural areas. There are three broad components:

- *Training and resource centre*, which acts as a training and demonstration centre for improved utilisation of local natural resources. The centre also provides the nucleus of commercial production units that provide the economic basis for long-term, sustainable development.
- *Community development programmes* aimed at raising the level of community participation in development issues and establishing basic social services such as health and education.
- *Extension and resettlement programmes* aimed at building on the work of the training centre by identifying and supporting opportunities for the local population to establish secure living standards.

Membership: There is no formal membership but all donors, supporters and interested parties receive two newsletters and the annual report each year. There is a sponsorship scheme aimed at supporting children through school.

Volunteers/jobseekers: UK – occasional opportunities to support fundraising and specific projects. Overseas – a small number of opportunities for people who can offer appropriate skills.

The Karuna Trust/Aid for India

Funding of educational, medical, skills-training and cultural projects in impoverished communities

Geographical focus: India

St Mark's Studios, Chillingworth Road, London N7 8QJ
Tel: 020 7700 3434; **Fax:** 020 7700 3535
e-mail: info@karuna.org
Website: www.karuna.org
Correspondent: Peter Joseph, Director

Expenditure: £712,000 (1999)

Staffing: 8 full-time staff in the UK and 1 in India.

Website information: Newsletters; a breakdown of its projects; annual reports; how to make a donation.

General: The Karuna Trust is a Buddhist inspired charity supporting long-term development work in India, particularly amongst the Dalit (or Scheduled Caste) communities. Karuna works primarily through its Indian ngo partners, collectively known as Bahujan Hitay (which means 'for the welfare of the many'). Projects are run in areas of education, health, skill-training and indigenous culture. Although Bahujan Hitay is run mainly by Dalits who have converted to Buddhism, the projects reach out to all communities affected by poverty and discrimination. Karuna also supports a school for Tibetan refugees in Kalimpong, north eastern India, whose aim is to help preserve the language, culture and religion of Tibet. Numerous other short-term projects are funded in other Indian states. The Karuna Trust was established in 1987 and continues the work of Aid for India which was founded in 1980 by members of the Western Buddhist Order.

The charity's work includes, for example, supporting primary healthcare projects in Pune and Nagpur serving people living in slums, and running a clinic in Pune which treats about 3,000 patients a year. The Karuna Trust is the sole funder of a school for 200 Tibetan children in the Himalayas close to the border between India and Tibet. Most of the children are from refugee families who fled to India to escape the Chinese occupation. The charity also supports, for example, kindergartens, after school study classes, adult literacy classes and educational hostels.

Membership: There are about 5,000 regular supporters.

Volunteers/jobseekers: The charity does not encourage overseas volunteers apart from in exceptional circumstances. A Buddhist commitment is necessary to work with the mainly Buddhist community, and most of the project work is undertaken by people from the local community. There are very limited opportunities for volunteers in the UK.

KINGSCARE

Carries out medical and educational work, trains in self-help and vocational skills, runs children's homes

Geographical focus: Albania, Caucasus, India, Nigeria, Sri Lanka

The King's Centre, High Street, Aldershot, Hampshire GU11 1DJ
Tel: 01252 333233; **Fax:** 01252 310814
e-mail: office@kingscare.org
Website: www.kingscare.org
Correspondent: George Dowdell, Director

Expenditure: About £250,000

Staffing: 2 paid staff, 3 volunteers.

Website information: Annual report; latest newsletters and prayer letters; latest appeals.

General: The charity describes itself as a Christian poverty relief charity, aiming to 'put the love of God into action through self-help, medical and educational projects in developing countries'. It works overseas in partnership with those local churches or Christian projects with which it has built a relationship.

The charity has set up self-help projects, for instance, and works to help people improve their income so that they are not continually in need of aid. In Sri Lanka it helps families by donating a cow, which can double a family's income through the sale of milk. The charity also, for example, provides money to help people set up chicken-raising projects.

KINGSCARE also:

- runs a number of clinics based in churches in Sri Lanka and Nigeria, and a mobile clinic in the tea plantation area of Sri Lanka
- teaches young men carpentry skills, enabling them to find work
- supports children's homes in Albania
- runs a 'sponsor a child' scheme
- has set up a trauma counselling centre in Caucasus
- occasionally gets involved in emergency relief work.

Membership: Sponsor a child (£10 a month) or contribute towards another aspect of the charity's work.

Publications: Quarterly newsletter.

Volunteers/jobseekers: Occasional opportunities for volunteers with nursing or teaching skills.

Landmine Action (formerly UK Working Group on Landmines)

Running a coalition of organisations concerned with banning landmines

Geographical focus: Worldwide

First Floor, 89 Albert Embankment, London SE1 7TP
Tel: 020 7820 0222; **Fax:** 020 7820 0057
e-mail: info@landmineaction.org
Website: www.landmineaction.org
Correspondent: Gary Purkiss, Office Administrator

Expenditure: About £250,000

Staffing: 3 salaried full-time staff in London.

Website information: Contains links to member organisations' websites.

General: Landmine Action is the UK arm of the International Campaign to Ban Landmines (ICBL), which was awarded the Nobel Peace Prize in December 1997. Established in 1992, Landmine Action is a coalition of 53 UK-based charities and agencies concerned with landmines and their impact on civilians.

Many of these member agencies, such as UNICEF, Save the Children, Christian Aid and Mines Advisory Group, are either directly carrying out humanitarian mine action projects or providing support to partner agencies in carrying out humanitarian mine clearance, mines awareness, medical aid and long-term victim assistance.

Landmine Action is engaged in research and policy development, including providing research for the ICBL's Landmine Monitor Report.

It also provides secretariat support for the Paliamentary All-Party Landmine Eradication Group.

Working with its partners in the ICBL, Landmine Action has helped bring about the Ottawa Convention, which bans the use, stockpiling, production and sale of anti-personnel mines. Landmine Action continues to work for the improvement, universalisation and full implementation of international legislation banning landmines.

Membership: Only open to organisations which can show that the problem of anti-personnel mines impacts on their work. Individuals can register (free of charge) as supporters.

Publications: *Cluster Bombs* by Rae McGrath and *Turning Words into Action?* by Richard Lloyd.

Volunteers/jobseekers: Volunteers are always welcome to assist with office-based work in London and as part of the Speaker Programme worldwide.

Latin Link

Advancing Christianity and providing relief to people who are poor

Geographical focus: *Argentina, Bolivia, Brazil, Colombia, Costa Rica, Ecuador, Peru*

175 Tower Bridge Road, London SE1 2AB
Tel: 020 7939 9000/STEP: 020 7939 9014;
Fax: 020 7939 9015
e-mail: ukoffice@latinlink.org
Website: www.latinlink.org
Correspondent: Michael Masters

Expenditure: £1.7 million (1998/99)

Staffing: UK: 16 paid staff, plus occasional volunteers to help with one-off tasks such as mailing; 2 Latin American volunteers working on placements in the UK. Overseas: 90 UK long-term volunteers and 90 UK short-term volunteers.

Website information: Information on placements overseas.

General: Latin Link has two principal objects. The first is 'to advance the mission of Christ' and the second is 'to provide relief to the poor and those who are suffering hardship as a result of natural disaster, sickness, old age or disease by reason of their social and economic conditions'. It focuses on Latin American and Spanish and Portuguese-speaking people elsewhere in the world.

Areas of work include preventative medicine, community development, primary and secondary education, prison work and work with children, young people and students

Volunteers/jobseekers: Latin Link runs a number of short and long-term programmes for volunteers who raise their own financial support from churches etc. Applicants must be committed Christians and will be placed to work alongside Christian communities in Latin America. Latin Link also offers programmes to students taking medical electives, university electives (especially linguists) and Bible college electives.

Learning for Life (LFL)

Increasing the provision of education for vulnerable communities, and especially for girls, refugees and disabled people

Geographical focus: *India, Pakistan*

St George's Centre, Aubrey Walk, London W8 7JG
Tel: 020 7221 4285; **Fax:** 020 7221 4514
e-mail: learnforlife@gn.apc.org
Website: www.learningforlifeuk.org
Correspondent: Felicity Hill, Director

Expenditure: £200,000 (1999/2000)

Staffing: 2 full-time, 1 part-time salaried staff based in the UK. Three international consultants, one of whom is based in Pakistan.

Website information: Case studies; how to donate online.

General: LFL provided the following information. It 'was founded in 1993 by Charlotte Bannister-Parker and Sophia Swire as a result of their experiences in India and Pakistan.

'LFL works with local South Asian partners to increase the quality and provision of education to the most marginalised communities – in particular girls, refugees and disabled people. In 1999/2000 our work benefited over 13,000 children through the various education programmes we support. Amongst our work we have been able to support almost 3,000 Afghan refugee children in Peshawar, north west Pakistan and over 7,000 children in community initiated and managed schools around Pakistan. In addition, we have enabled further training of over 100 teachers - with a particular emphasis on the recruitment of local women. Some schools have even seen past pupils return as qualified teachers.

'LFL never initiates projects but responds to the needs expressed at a local level. We encourage innovative and flexible projects, which respond directly to the specific needs of each community or targeted group. This allows us to pilot new approaches and ideas. Furthermore, this approach allows us to enter into and contribute to an international development and educational dialogue sharing our experiences with others. For example, a whole chapter was dedicated to one of our Indian projects in the recent DFID and SCF publication – *Towards responsive schools: supporting better schooling for disadvantaged children*, DFID 2000.

'The development and capacity building of our local staff and partners is an important part of LFL's work. We work with our local partners to strengthen and encourage organisational development and sustainability, as well as that of each project. In addition, LFL is able to monitor and evaluate every project regularly through annual visits to the field.'

Volunteers/jobseekers: Salaried posts are advertised in the national press and through BOND.

No opportunities for volunteering overseas. There are occasional opportunities to help out in the UK office with administrative and special fundraising events.

Leonard Cheshire International

Supporting people with disabilities

Geographical focus: Argentina, Bahamas, Bangladesh, Barbados, Botswana, Brazil, Canada, Chile, China, Cyprus, Ethiopia, France, Ghana, Grenada, Guernsey, Guyana, Honduras, Hong Kong, India, Indonesia, Ireland, Jamaica, Japan, Jersey, Kenya, Lesotho, Liberia, Malawi, Malaysia, Mauritius, Morocco, Namibia, Nicaragua, Nigeria, Pakistan, Philippines, Portugal, Russia, Sierra Leone, Singapore, South Africa, Spain, Sri Lanka, Sudan, Swaziland, Tanzania, Thailand, Trinidad, Uganda, USA, Zambia, Zimbabwe

30 Millbank, London SW1P 4QD
Tel: 020 7802 8200; **Fax:** 020 7802 8275
e-mail: international@london.leonard-cheshire.org.uk
Website: www.leonard-cheshire.org
Correspondent: Rupert Ridge, International Director

Expenditure: £1.3 million (1998/99)

Staffing: 8 full-time members of staff in the UK.

Website information: Mainly a breakdown of UK-focused work.

General: The charity provides the following information in its *Directory of Leonard Cheshire International Services 1999/2000*.

'Leonard Cheshire International supports over 240 services for disabled people and their families in 50 countries outside the UK. In the UK, Leonard Cheshire provides a further 140 support services. The first Cheshire Service was founded in 1948 by Group Captain Leonard Cheshire, who believed that all disabled people should have the maximum opportunity to determine every aspect of their own lives.

'The services are all autonomous and have been set up, and are managed, by local people. Originally they provided mainly residential care, and this is still a major area of work, but approaches have diversified over the years and the emphasis has shifted towards more community orientated provision. Cheshire Services now include rehabilitation centres, skills training centres, support for employment and education programmes, independent living programmes and community-based support services.

'Based in London [the charity] offers support and guidance to the services around the world. Together we are creating a network of training and development programmes to:
- empower disabled people, building confidence and developing skills that will enable them to live and work independently;
- strengthen the organisational capacity of the services to meet the increasing demand;
- train staff and community workers in care and rehabilitation skills.

'We also work in partnership with local services to obtain grants for new developments.

'The International Self Reliance Programme also aims to provide disabled people with the skills and opportunities they need to find work and become more independent. We are supporting low-cost income generation schemes and small businesses by providing training and equipment.'

LEPRA (The British Leprosy Relief Association)

Carrying out related research to prevent and treat leprosy

Geographical focus: Bangladesh, Brazil, Ethiopia, India, Madagascar, Malawi, Mozambique, Nepal, Sierra Leone

Fairfax House, Causton Road, Colchester, Essex CO1 1PU
Tel: 01206 562286; **Fax:** 01206 762151
e-mail: lepra@lepra.org.uk
Website: www.lepra.org.uk
Correspondent: Terry Vasey, Director

Expenditure: £3 million (1999)

Staffing: 29 full-time salaried staff, 36 part-time salaried staff.

Website information: Newsletter; downloadable annual review; events; news; job vacancies; information about leprosy and other communicable diseases; description of projects by country; how to make a donation; how to get involved in fundraising; information for schools and young people.

General: LEPRA's aim is to eradicate leprosy worldwide by the provision of multidrug therapy (MDT), which it says is the proven cure for leprosy. It also funds research into improving the quality and effectiveness of treatment, prevention of disability and rehabilitation programmes.

In addition it runs or supports Leprosy Control Programmes or Research Programmes, contributing additional elements to those programmes such as eye care, income generation programmes, social aspects of leprosy, TB control and HIV awareness and education.

Publications: LEPRA has a newsletter, published three times a year, and a journal *Leprosy Review*. For more information contact Irene Allen at the address above.

Volunteers/jobseekers: Opportunities for salaried posts are advertised in the national press, local press and on its website.

There are occasional opportunities for volunteers to help out in the Head Office with administrative tasks and special events. Contact the correspondent for more information.

The Leprosy Mission (TLM)

Works towards leprosy control, care and education

Geographical focus: *Bangladesh, Bhutan, Botswana, Chad, China, Democratic Republic of Congo, Ethiopia, Guinea, India, Indonesia, Laos, Lesotho, Mozambique, Myanmar, Nepal, Niger, Nigeria, Papua New Guinea, South Africa, Sri Lanka, Sudan, Swaziland, Thailand, Uganda, Uzbekistan, Zambia, Zimbabwe*

Goldhay Way, Orton Goldhay, Peterborough PE2 5GZ
Tel: 01733 370505; **Fax:** 01733 404880
e-mail: post@tlmew.org.uk
Website: www.leprosymission.org
Correspondent: The Personnel Officer

Expenditure: £10 million – internationally (2000)

Staffing: Around 50 staff in the UK offices and more than 50 missionaries overseas. Over 2,300 local staff are also employed in the countries shown above.

Website information: 'Hot news'; details of its field programmes; your local office address; 'What is leprosy?'; current vacancies; development education resources for children.

General: TLM is an international Christian charity founded in 1874 and is now working in nearly 30 countries (as at January 2001). Its field staff work to meet the needs of people affected by leprosy both directly through its own hospitals and programmes, as well as in partnership with churches, voluntary agencies, patient organisations, governments and international organisations.

TLM's mission is 'to minister in the name of Jesus Christ to the physical, mental, social and spiritual needs of individuals and communities disadvantaged by leprosy, working with them to uphold human dignity and eradicate leprosy'.

TLM realises its mission through:

- '• leprosy care programmes, moving into areas of greatest need
- working to change attitudes in society which have been the root causes of stigma against people affected by leprosy
- training leprosy workers in programmes run by government and other ngos
- listening to the needs of people in communities affected by leprosy
- developing partnerships with churches and other mission groups in funding countries and in field areas
- strengthening its Christian ministry and being alive in its witness through word and deed'.

Publications: *New Day* (bi-annual magazine), prayer guides, children's leaflets, resources guide, posters.

Trading: TLM trading catalogue is available from the above address and advertises goods which include those made by people affected by leprosy. The profits go towards TLM's work.

Volunteers/jobseekers:

Skilled long-term workers

Expatriates with the right skills are needed to work overseas, but are not sent to do jobs that local people can do. Most workers take on a socio-medical teaching role, especially in places like Indonesia and Papua New Guinea. In Bangladesh, Nepal, Thailand and some of the African countries they would be doing leprosy control work and general medicine. Typical roles/skills needed are:

- doctors/surgeons
- nurse/health facilitators
- physio and occupational therapists
- social/development workers
- adminstrators
- chiropodists
- community health specialists
- rehabilitation specialists
- also a growing number of opportunities in rehabilitation.

All expatriate staff need to be:

- professionally qualified with at least two years' post qualification experience
- able to cope with loneliness, absence of Christian fellowship and a lack of Western amenities
- prepared to work alongside people who may have completely different ideas from their's
- adaptable, resourceful and persevering.

Placements are for four years after initial training in leprosy and language. Contact the office at the address above for further information.

Electives for medical students

TLM offers opportunities for electives for medical students, usually in their fourth year of training. Most of the placements are in India and last about two months.

Stamps and collectables

Get involved by saving stamps and other collectables, e.g. postcards, coins, phonecards. Send them to The Leprosy Mission Stamps and Collectables, c/o 26 Drift Road, Clanfield, Waterlooville, Hampshire PO8 0JL; tel: 023 9259 8115.

Link Community Development
(formerly Link Africa)

Planning and developing effective teacher and school development projects

Geographical focus: Ghana, South Africa, Uganda

Orwell House, Cowley Road, Cambridge CB4 0PP
Tel: 01223 506665; **Fax:** 01223 578665
e-mail: link@lcd.org.uk
Website: www.lcd.org.uk
Correspondent: Laura Garforth, Projects Officer

Expenditure: £428,000 (1998/99)

Staffing: 9 – UK plus 6 trustees, 17 – South Africa, 3 Ghana, 1 Uganda.

Website information: Education programmes in South Africa, Ghana and Uganda; how to become a member; how to make a donation; information on the hitch to Morocco (fundraising venture), Global Teachers Awards and the link schools programme.

General: Link Community Development (LCD) has three sister organisations – LCD South Africa, LCD Ghana and LCD Uganda. They work in partnership with national and decentralised departments of education and local organisations to plan and develop effective teacher and school development projects. Its programmes are focused on improving standards of education in rural and township areas. The role of the UK office is fundraising, development education and raising the charity's profile in the UK. It is not a grantmaking organisation.

Membership: £24 a year (£6 unwaged); members receive regular newsletters, an annual report and invitations to events. Application forms available at website.

Publications: *Link News* (newsletter).

Volunteers/jobseekers: Teams of development workers (generally students) work on Link Africa's projects in Africa during their summer holidays. Apply to Awards for Global Teachers for involvement in short-term work overseas and development education work in the UK. All placements last from four to six weeks. Latest information is on the website.

The Liverpool School of Tropical Medicine

Promoting improved health
Geographical focus: Worldwide

Pembroke Place, Liverpool L3 5QA
Tel: 0151 708 9393; **Fax:** 0151 709 8545
e-mail: imr@liv.ac.uk
Website: www.liv.ac.uk/lstm/lstm.html
Correspondent: Mrs Irene Reece, Fundraising Office

Expenditure: £7.5 million (1998/99)

Staffing: 159 staff.

Website information: Breakdown of all the work of the school including information about different departments.

General: 'As a centre of excellence, The Liverpool School of Tropical Medicine, through the creation of effective links with governments, organisations and institutions and by responding to the health needs of communities, aims to promote improved health, particularly for people of less developed countries in the tropics and sub-tropics by:

- providing and promoting education and training
- conducting research and disseminating the results
- developing systems and technologies for healthcare and assisting in their transfer and management
- providing consultancy services.'

Manchester Development Education Project (DEP)

Providing resources and training on development issues
Geographical focus: Worldwide

c/o Manchester Metropolitan University,
801 Wilmslow Road,
Manchester M20 2QR
Tel: 0161 445 2495; **Fax:** 0161 445 2360
e-mail: depman@gn.apc.org
Website: www.dep.org.uk
Correspondent: David Cooke/Jane Angel

Expenditure: £161,000 (1999/2000)

Staffing: 7 paid staff and 1 volunteer, all in the UK.

Website information: Newsletter; resources; publications; links to other development education organisations' websites.

General: The charity is based on the Didsbury campus of Manchester Metropolitan University. It is part of a network of educational centres and says: 'The aim of DEP is to develop and support educational practice that will:

- enable people to recognise in their own lives the links between North and South, and to acknowledge how much we can learn from one another;
- increase understanding of the economic, social, cultural, political, environmental and spiritual forces which shape the relationship between North and South, and which affect all our lives;

- enable people to achieve a more just and sustainable world, in their schools and communities as well as more widely, in which power and resources are more fairly shared by all'.

The charity provides resources and training, in subjects such as education for sustainable development, citizenship, anti-racism and cultural diversity.

The resource centre and bookshop contains educational resources such as teachers' handbooks, photopacks, simulation games and a parachute. They are selected to relate closely to National Curriculum subjects. The bookshop stocks the charity's own books. The items are all available for sale or hire. Resource lists are available on important issues, curriculum areas and topics at all key stages. The resource centre and bookshop is open Tuesday, Wednesday and Thursday each week (except during August), between 12.00 noon and 5.30 pm.

The charity also runs in-service training, e.g. 'Teaching about a locality in a developing country', or 'Education for sustainable development in primary schools'. The courses can be run in school.

Publications: Teaching resources produced by DEP include: *Global Express*, a series for Key Stage 2 and 3 teachers on development issues in the news; *Our Street – Our World: Exploring environment and development issues with 4–7 year olds –* a resource pack, produced for World Wildlife Fund; *Take Part! Speak Out!* a handbook of practical suggestions and activities to support a programme of education for citizenship in a primary school; *Values and Visions: A handbook for spiritual development and global awareness; The Southern Perspectives on Development series*, a five-book series at Key Stage 3 and 4 for geography and history teachers on a wide range of development issues.

Medact

Raising awareness of threats to health such as violent conflict, poverty and environmental degradation

Geographical focus: Worldwide

601 Holloway Road, London N19 4DJ
Tel: 020 7272 2020; **Fax:** 020 7281 5717
e-mail: info@medact.org
Website: www.medact.org
Correspondent: The Office Manager

Expenditure: £170,000 (2000/01)
Staffing: 3 paid staff in the UK.

Website information: How debt affects health; campaigns and appeals; events; news; students' information; how to join; links.

General: Medact's strapline says it is 'the health professionals' voice on the major global health issues of today'. Medact is an organisation comprised of doctors, nurses and other health professionals who are concerned about major threats to health such as violent conflict, poverty and environmental degradation.

Medact raises awareness of these issues, showing that they are of both global and local concern, educating policy-makers and the public on measures needed for the prevention of the threats.

Recent work has included:
- drawing attention to the ongoing impact on health of nuclear weapons and call for their abolition;
- working with UNICEF in former Yugoslavia by sending small teams of mental health professionals to support those working with war-traumatised children and their families;
- working with student groups at medical schools on projects such as refugee health, expanding medical curriculum and book aid schemes;

- highlighting debt relief and how this is the best medicine for people who are poor worldwide.

Membership: All health professionals and students are invited to become members of Medact. Others are welcome to join us as supporters.

The website information for students said: 'All students studying health-related topics are welcome to join, whether from podiatry to paediatrics, from nursing to nutrition, and all those in between'.

You can get involved in addressing issues 'such as:

- does the international debt burden negate all medical advances of the past 200 years? What can be done about it?
- what is the real threat to health of the nuclear race? Are the decision makers truly aware of the potential consequences for health, and how can this information alter their policy making?'

Ways of getting involved include:

- attending Medact conferences
- geting other students at your university involved, by arranging speakers, debates, local projects, international meetings etc.
- if you are a medical student you can join MedSIN (contact Medact or view the website for further information)
- come down to the Medact office and meet those involved, and see if there is anything they need help with around the office e.g. the web pages, the diary, keeping the news file updated etc.

Volunteers/jobseekers: There are opportunities for volunteers to work in Medact's UK office.

Médecins Sans Frontières (UK)

Providing emergency medical relief

Geographical focus: *Afghanistan, Albania, Algeria, Angola, Armenia, Azerbaijan, Bangladesh, Belgium, Benin, Bolivia, Bosnia-Herzegovina, Brazil, Bulgaria, Burkina Faso, Burundi, Cambodia, Central African Republic, Chad, China, Colombia, Congo (Brazzaville), Costa Rica, Côte d'Ivoire, Cuba, Democratic Republic of Congo, Ecuador, Egypt, El Salvador, Equatorial Guinea, Ethiopia, France, Georgia, Guatemala, Guinea, Guinea Bissau, Haiti, Honduras, India, Indonesia, Iran, Italy, Kazakhstan, Kenya, Kyrgyzstan, Kosovo, Laos, Lebanon, Liberia, Luxembourg, Macedonia, Madagascar, Malawi, Mali, Mauritania, Mexico, Mongolia, Montenegro, Mozambique, Myanmar, Nicaragua, Nigeria, North Korea, Palestinian Authority, Panama, Papua New Guinea, Peru, Philippines, Romania, Russia, Rwanda, Sierra Leone, Somalia, Spain, Sri Lanka, Sudan, Tajikistan, Tanzania, Thailand, Turkmenistan, Uganda, Ukraine, Uzbekistan, Vietnam, Yemen, Zambia*

124–132 Clerkenwell Road,
London EC1R 5DJ
Tel: 020 7713 5600; **Fax:** 020 7713 5004
e-mail: office@london.msf.org
Website: www.msf.org
Correspondent: Juno Wenlock

Expenditure: £5 million (1999)

Staffing: 13 salaried staff in the UK office.

Website information: This is the international website. It contains press releases; news; information about its activities by country; information for volunteers; fundraising information; how to make a donation; contact information for its offices around the world.

General: Médicins Sans Frontières says it is 'the world's largest independent organisation for emergency medical relief'. It provides relief to victims of war, natural disasters and epidemics. It is an international organisation, with support offices in the UK. MSF UK, which serves the UK and the Republic of Ireland, was set up in 1993 to recruit volunteers, provide information and raise funds.

MSF internationally, for instance:

- works on 24-hour alert, mobilising teams of medical and logistical personnel and equipment to crisis situations;
- has developed a unique logistical support system of pre-packaged and standardised kits allowing for easy and speedy deployment in the field;
- works to ensure local hospitals remain open, even in the most difficult circumstances;
- provides basic curative and preventative health services, delivering health education and aiming to rebuild basic healthcare services that have been disrupted;
- assesses children's malnutrition, entering children into supplementary or therapeutic feeding programmes where necessary;
- treats individual patients with infectious diseases to help prevent the spread of the infection to others, and carries out other work on disease control.

Activities in the 1990s included:

- targeting the infectious disease Buruli-ulcer (BU) in Benin, training nurses in its early diagnosis;
- running dispensaries in Azerbaijan, and providing technical assistance and medical material to government referral health structures;
- launching an emergency programme following Hurricane Mitch in Honduras in 1998, donating medical supplies, carrying out water and sanitation activities and strengthening the epidemiological early warning system and the system for nutritional surveillance;
- working alongside health workers in Laos to provide basic curative and preventative care in health centres, medical training and the preparation of treatment protocols. It also carried out rice distribution due to alarming levels of malnutrition.

Publications: *Dispatches*, a quarterly magazine.

Volunteers/jobseekers: MSF is always looking to recruit qualified staff for voluntary work overseas. It has a policy of sending expatriates out only if they have expertise which cannot be found locally. Two-thirds of the volunteers who work with MSF are medical professionals, although skilled support staff are also needed. It is looking to recruit people with the following professional background: medical doctors, surgeons, anaesthetists; nurses; midwives; nutritionists; epidemiologists; lab technicians; mental health professionals; water and sanitation engineers; construction engineers; logisticians with proven working knowledge of pumps, generators, vehicle mechanics, radio/communication equipment, simple water and sanitation systems, construction and basic bookkeeping; and financial controllers with proven financial experience.

Volunteers must be over 25 years old and have some experience living or travelling in developing countries. Most people are on a volunteer contract covering between 9 and 12 months. Volunteers receive a small monthly allowance of about £450 and MSF covers accommodation and

Medical Aid for Palestinians (MAP)

Providing medical and humanitarian aid

Geographical focus: Lebanon, Palestine

33a Islington Park, London N1 1QB
Tel: 020 7226 4114; **Fax:** 020 7226 0880
e-mail: info@map-uk.org
Website: www.map-uk.org
Correspondent: Saida Nusseibeh

Expenditure: £1.4 million (1998/99)

Staffing: 7 full-time staff in the London office; 4 full-time staff overseas.

Website information: Emergency appeals and how to make a donation; a breakdown of information on its activities.

General: MAP works to deliver healthcare to Palestinian refugees who have been displaced from their homes, and other disadvantaged Palestinians. Services include:

- providing training for health personnel
- undertaking renovation projects of hospitals and government clinics
- providing funding support to local organisations.

It works, for example, with Palestinian Ministry of Health, Palestinian Red Crescent Society and UK Royal College of General Practitioners to develop training programmes for GPs in the West Bank and Lebanon.

Funding support has been given, for instance, to: Atfaluna Society for Deaf Children in Gaza to provide training for deaf children and their families; Land Resource Centre, Jerusalem, to provide first aid facilities for the Bedouins in the West Bank; and The Imam Sadr Foundation, Beirut, towards supporting a primary healthcare nurse, the donation of one mobile medical unit and the procurement of essential medicines.

Medical Foundation for the Care of Victims of Torture

Helping survivors of torture and organised violence

Geographical focus: Worldwide

96-98 Grafton Road, London NW5 3EJ
Tel: 020 7813 7777; **Fax:** 020 7813 0011
Website: www.torturecare.org.uk
Correspondent: Ms Helen Bamber, Director

Expenditure: £3.5 million (1999)

Staffing: 44 full-time and 63 part-time members of staff, and 114 volunteers, all based in the UK.

Website information: News; how to make a donation; publications and briefings list and archive; information about fundraising and other events; jobs and vacancies; links to other websites.

General: Founded in 1986, the charity's mission statement is as follows. 'The Medical Foundation exists to enable survivors of torture and organised violence to engage in a healing process to assert their own human dignity and worth. We advocate respect for human rights and are concerned for the health and well-being of survivors of torture and their families. We provide medical and social care, practical assistance and psychological and physical therapy.' The Medical Foundation has premises in London where people can receive medical treatment and other care.

[preceding paragraph, top of left column:]

living expenses, and the cost of travelling to and from your home country.

Contact the Human Resources Department for further information, at the address above.

The charity also documents evidence of torture, provides training for health professionals working with other torture survivors, educates the public and decision-makers about torture and its consequences, and works to ensure that the UK government honours its international obligations towards survivors of torture, asylum seekers and refugees.

In 1999/2000 its activities included:
- working with Refugee Council initiating the Breathing Space project, with the aim of raising awareness of torture survivors' and asylum seekers' needs in communities which have been asked to take in refugees;
- giving advice to health authorities in the UK on how to deliver appropriate health services for Kosovan refugees;
- campaigning against 1999 Immigration Asylum Act's decision to provide vouchers rather than cash to asylum seekers;
- producing a medical report which examined the forensic medical reports of 78 Turkish clients, all of whom were Kurds, documenting scars and other signs which supported their stories of torture;
- training teachers in the worst affected villages of western Kosovo in how to identify and help particularly disturbed children.

Publications: The charity has published over 90 papers, relevant to its work, e.g. *In Limbo Movement Psychotherapy with Refugees and Asylum Seekers, Doctors and Torture, Caught in the Middle: A study of Tamil torture survivors coming to the UK* and *A Way Forward: A Group for Refugee Women.*

Volunteers/jobseekers: The charity employs volunteers as follows:
- professional medical staff are recruited to treat people who are victims of torture working in its London premises. E-mail: alex@torture.com or contact Alex Sklan, Director Clinical Services on the telephone number above.
- to carry out administrative work during office hours in its London office, e-mail: brede@torturecare.org.uk or telephone: 020 7813 9999
- people to help to run fundraising events, contact Jan Woolf, e-mail: janw@torturecare.org.uk or telephone: 020 7813 9999.

Mercy Corps Scotland
(formerly Mercy Corps Europe/ Scottish European Aid)

Helping people to build secure, productive and just communities

Geographical focus: Field offices in: Afghanistan, Albania, Azerbaijan, Bosnia, Eritrea, Honduras, Indonesia, Kazakhstan, Kosovo, Kyrgyzstan, Lebanon, Macedonia, Mongolia, Montenegro, Nicaragua, North Korea, Pakistan, Philippines, Russia, Tajikistan, Turkey, Turkmenistan, Uzbekistan

10 Beaverhall Road, Edinburgh EH7 4JE
Tel: 0131 477 3677; **Fax:** 0131 477 3678
e-mail: admin@mercycorps-scotland.org
Website: www.mercycorps.org
Correspondent: Cathy Ratcliff, Senior Programme Officer

Expenditure: £11 million (1999)

Staffing: Over 100 full-time staff worldwide, of which 8 are based in the Edinburgh office.

Website information: News; how to give online. The charity told us that information on job vacancies was going to be added to the website.

General: Mercy Corps Scotland works in countries in transition from civil conflict, economic collapse or natural disaster. Its largest programmes are in former

Yugoslavia, Central Asia and Turkey. Programmes include emergency relief, microcredit, economic development, conflict resolution and physical rehabilitation of infrastructure. Development of civil society is an integral part of all programmes.

Publications: Newsletters and leaflets about MCS's work are available from the above address.

Volunteers/jobseekers: Opportunities in the Edinburgh office for administrative tasks and special events. Contact the correspondent for further information. No volunteering opportunities overseas.

Mercy Ships UK

Christian organisation providing hospital ships and community health treatment, relief, development

Geographical focus: *Coastal, developing countries, see below*

The Lighthouse, 12 Meadway Court, Stevenage, Hertfordshire SG1 2EF
Tel: 01438 727800; **Fax:** 01438 721900
e-mail: info@mercyships.org.uk
Website: www.mercyships.org.uk
Correspondent: The Information Services

Expenditure: £4.8 million (1999)

Staffing: Over 700 volunteering staff from at least 30 different nations.

Website information: Virtual tours of the ships; newsletters; 'lifechanging stories'; audio and video clips about its work; make a donation online; volunteering information.

General: Mercy Ships is an international Christian humanitarian organisation which utilises ocean-going vessels as hospitals and relief and development vehicles.

During 2000 it owned and operated three ships, with a fourth ship being adapted for service:

- *Anastasis* was acquired in 1978. She contains three fully equipped operating theatres, a dental clinic, laboratory and an x-ray unit. Teams use portable medical and dental equipment to take healthcare to remote areas. Over 50 children of crew members live and attend school on board
- *Caribbean Mercy* focuses on the Caribbean basin and Central America. She has one operating theatre, used mainly to help people who are blind to see, through removal of cataracts
- *Island Mercy* is based almost permanently around the islands of the South Pacific. Her shallow draft allows her to bring on-board eye operations and mobile medical dental and optical teams into remote villages
- *Africa Mercy* was purchased in 1999. The former Danish railway ferry is currently undergoing a major conversion and refit in the UK. The 16,000 tonne vessel will eventually sail for West Africa equipped as a non-governmental hospital ship with 6 operating theatres and ward space for over 60 beds.

Volunteers/jobseekers: Opportunities are available in the UK office, other land-based offices, or on one of the ships, for people over the age of 18. There are openings for a wide variety of positions, both skilled and non-skilled, such as administration, accounting, human resouces, medical, IT, welding, carpentry, deck, engineering/technical, construction, hospitality, housekeeping, laundry, dining-room and kitchen/galley (cooking or baking).

You can work short-term, from a period of two weeks to three months. Those who would like to be appointed for more than a year must successfully complete a Discipleship Training School or Gateway Programmes (Christian training courses). Some of this training can take place aboard the ships. Accommodation is not provided for the children of short-term workers.

Each crew member pays a monthly fee to cover living expenses on board, whilst land-based office staff are responsible for their own living expenses.

For further information about working with Mercy Ships, visit the website above, or call the enquiry line on 0870 870 7447. You can also send an e-mail requesting information to the address above.

Merlin

Providing healthcare in crises

Geographical focus: *Afghanistan, Albania, Democratic Republic of Congo, East Timor, Honduras, Kenya, Liberia, Russia, Sierra Leone, Tajikistan*

5–13 Trinity Street, Borough, London SE1 1DB
Tel: 020 7378 4888; **Fax:** 020 7378 4899
e-mail: lyoung@merlin.org.uk
Website: www.merlin.org.uk
Correspondent: Lena Young, Head of Development

Expenditure: £7.5 million (1999)

Staffing: 40 London-based staff, over 700 staff based overseas.

Website information: Contains information about employment opportunities; application forms; breakdown of its programmes; medical overview; achievements; how to donate; press releases; a bibliography of articles written by Merlin personnel.

General: Merlin 'was established in 1993 as the only British humanitarian aid charity to specialise in the specific field of medical relief. Working around the world, Merlin provides medical assistance to help people caught up in natural disasters, war or epidemic disease.

'Merlin has established a reputation in the humanitarian sector for the excellence of its medical work. This has been developed in partnership with international medical institutes, including the World Health Organisation and the London School of Hygiene and Tropical Medicine, and the Ministries of Health in-country from the onset, to establish the most effective and lasting expertise and infrastructure.'

Volunteers/jobseekers: For information on voluntary positions available both in the UK and overseas, contact Human Resources, at the address above. Salaried positions are advertises in the national and specialist media and on the website.

Minority Rights Group (MRG)

Promoting human rights of ethnic, religious and linguistic minorities

Geographical focus: *Worldwide*

International Secretariat, 379 Brixton Road, London SW9 7DE
Tel: 020 7978 9498; **Fax:** 020 7738 6265
e-mail: minority.rights@mrgmail.org
Website: www.minorityrights.org
Correspondent: The Director

Expenditure: £1.3 million (1999)

Staffing: 28 full-time paid staff and 1 volunteer.

Website information: Up-to-date news and progress on its regional programmes; advocacy and training; list of publications with an ordering facility; the full text of recent reports; profiles and editions of its newsletter *Outsider*; vacancies; links to related websites.

General: 'Minority Rights Group works to secure rights for ethnic, religious and linguistic minorities worldwide, and to promote cooperation and understanding between communities.'

It summarises its activities as follows:
- advocacy – raising awareness and stimulating action on issues that affect minorities;
- training – organising courses and seminars on minority rights issues and advocacy skills which increase the capacity of minorities to effectively represent themselves in their own countries and internationally;
- publishing – disseminating research and raising awareness of the importance of treating minority and indigenous communities fairly, and of promoting cooperation between communities;
- facilitating – helping to create opportunities for members of minority and majority communities to meet and engage in constructive dialogue;
- outreach – raising awareness of minorities and minority rights issues via the media, its website and contact with governmental representatives, other ngos, universities and activists.

Membership: Yearly subscription fees (individual) are £30, you receive six reports, profiles, *Outsider* and annual report. Organisations can subscribe for £45 a year.

Publications: This charity produces a number of publications including: *World Directory of Minorities*; reports such as *Minority Rights in Yugoslavia*; *Burundi*, *Muslim Women in India*, and *Afro-Brazilians*; and books such as *Cutting the Rose – Female Genital Mutilation*, *Polar Peoples* and *Armenia and Karabagh*. For a full list of publications contact the charity at the address above, or see the website. MRG's publications are frequently distributed free of charge to organisations in the South who can use them to support their work. They are also often translated into local languages.

Volunteers/jobseekers: Job vacancies are advertised on the website. Due to a shortage of office space, there are no opportunities for volunteers or interns.

Mission Aviation Fellowship (MAF)

Providing aviation, communications and logistics services

Geographical focus: *The international partnership of MAF has bases in or flies into: Angola, Australia, Botswana, Burundi, Cambodia, Central African Republic, Chad, Comoros Islands, Democratic Republic of Congo, Ecuador, Guatemala, Haiti, Honduras, Indonesia, Kenya, Lesotho, Madagascar, Mali, Mexico, Mongolia, Mozambique, Papua New Guinea, Rwanda, Somalia, South Africa, Sudan, Suriname, Tanzania, Uganda, Venezuela, Zambia, Zimbabwe*

Castle House, Castle Hill Avenue, Folkstone, Kent CT20 2TN
Tel: 01303 850950; **Fax:** 01303 852800
e-mail: maf@maf-uk.org
Website: www.maf-uk.org
Correspondent: David Longley, Head of Development

Expenditure: £7.5 million (15 months 1998/1999)

Staffing: 94 UK-based staff, including those seconded abroad.

Website information: Latest news from abroad; events in the UK; current job opportunities; how 15-21 year olds can get involved; ways to give.

General: MAF provided the following information: It 'was formed in 1945 mainly by ex-servicemen concerned to use aviation for positive purposes in developing countries.

'A Christian-based organisation, the worldwide partnership operates over 180 aircraft in 30 countries. MAF carries staff from relief, development and medical agencies, refugee organisations, missions and national churches, into isolated locations, along with essential supplies.

'Often flying across inhospitable terrain such as deserts and mountains, MAF aircraft support far-flung communities which could take days or weeks to reach by land. Water supply projects, veterinary care, eye surgery and literacy work are among the first lines of response.

'Expanding e-mail networks provide rapid communications for agencies in many lands. MAF's professional staff team includes pilots, engineers, avionics technicians, computer specialists, builders and administrators.'

Publications: *MAF News* can be received regularly on request, with an optional donation.

Volunteers/jobseekers: Salaried positions are advertised in the appropriate technical journals.

Three-week voluntary placements are available, giving people aged 15 to 21 the opportunity to be involved with evangelism and practical work in Africa. No long-term opportunities.

Motivation

Initiating self-sustaining projects to enhance the quality of life of wheelchair users

Geographical focus: Afghanistan, Albania, Bangladesh, Cambodia, El Salvador, Indonesia, Lithuania, Malaysia, Nicaragua, Poland, Romania, Russia, Sri Lanka, Tanzania

Brockley Academy, Brockley Lane, Backwell, Bristol BS48 4AQ
Tel: 01275 464012; **Fax:** 01275 464019
e-mail: motivation@motivation.org.uk
Website: www.motivation.org.uk
Correspondent: The Administrator

Expenditure: £913,000 (1999/2000)
Staffing: 2 volunteers; 25 full-time staff.
Website information: Wheelchair designs; projects listed according to country; stories about service users; how to make a donation.
General: Motivation is a UK-registered charity working primarily in developing countries to improve the quality of life of wheelchair users.

Its work is all about trying to change the culture of disability. By working with local partner organisations it helps to establish self-sustaining wheelchair workshops which produce and distribute appropriately designed low-cost wheelchairs.

Local staff are also trained in rehabilitation and education programmes for wheelchair users, to ensure that each individual can remain healthy and achieve their maximum degree of independence. Many of the local staff trained to work in the production and distribution of wheelchairs are wheelchair users themselves.

Motivation has worked as consultants in the field of sustainable wheelchair design and production, to organisations such as International Committee of the Red Cross and Oxfam.

Publications: Quarterly newsletter *Motif*, is sent to about 2,000 people.

Trading: The charity sells its own Christmas cards.

Volunteers/jobseekers: There is the opportunity to help fundraise for the organisation by climbing Kilimanjaro. The charity occasionally recruits volunteers' if they have the skills its overseas projects or UK office need.

Staff are normally paid professionals, e.g. designers, therapists.

Multi International Aid (MIA)

Providing emergency relief including the distribution of aid

Geographical focus: Dagestan

Birchgrove House, PO Box 182, Newport NP20 6YL
Tel: 01633 854732
Correspondent: Mrs Margery Pryce-Jones

Expenditure: About £150,000 (1998/99)

General: This charity's objects are to:
- relieve poverty, distress and suffering, whether arising from war, conflict or tempest
- relieve poverty and sickness, and improve the welfare of people who live in the third world
- distribute food, medicines, clothing, shelter and funds; to carry out aid projects designed to improve health, living conditions and to support further education in third world situations.

In 1997/98, for example, the charity worked in partnership with another organisation to set up a tuberculosis screening and treatment project in Dagestan. Over a 19-month period, the two organisations screened and treated 35,000 Chechen refugees and also set up a TB clinic in a hospital. MIA supported the team financially, medically, with clothing, bedding, medicines and household goods.

Please note, this entry has not been confirmed by the charity. The entry is correct according to information on file at the Charity Commission.

Muslim Aid

Providing education, healthcare, skills training, safe clean water, emergency relief, welfare, funding projects

Geographical focus: Field offices in: Bangladesh, Somalia, Sudan.
The charity also funds projects in: Afghanistan, Albania, Australia, Azerbaijan, Bosnia, Bulgaria, Burma, Chad, Chechnya, Djibouti, Eritrea, Ethiopia, Gambia, Germany, Ghana, India, Indonesia, Iran, Iraq, Jordan, Kashmir, Kenya, Kosovo, Lebanon, Liberia, Malawi, Mozambique, Nepal, Nigeria, Pakistan, Palestine, Philippines, Rwanda, Senegal, Sierra Leone, Sri Lanka, Tanzania, Togo, Turkey, Uganda, UK, Ukraine, Yemen, Zimbabwe

PO Box 3, London N7 8LR
Tel: 020 7387 7171; **Fax:** 020 7609 4943
e-mail: mail@muslimaid.org.uk
Website: www.muslimaid.org.uk
Correspondent: Mahmood Hassan, Director

Expenditure: £2.1 million (1999)

Staffing: All paid staff: 10 in the UK; 27 in Somalia; 20 in Bangladesh; 10 in Sudan. Changing numbers of volunteers.

Website information: Case studies; information on how it spends its money and the annual report; a description of what Zakah is; how to leave a contribution to Muslim Aid in your will; and FAQ.

General: This charity was founded in 1985, and its most famous founding trustee was Cat Stevens. Supporting this charity is one of the ways in which Muslims in Britain channel their charitable giving, known as Zakah, to people in need overseas. Zakah is a donation to people who are in need, which is compulsory for Muslims who have a certain minimum wealth.

The charity states: 'We help the poor overcome the suffering they endure because they lack life's basic necessities. We provide:

- education
- healthcare
- skills training
- safe clean water
- emergency relief
- welfare for the most vulnerable'.

Muslim Aid uses the expertise of its local field staff in offices in Bangladesh, Sudan and Somalia. It funds projects run by over 250 local partner organisations in 44 countries.

In its first five years of operation, Muslim Aid focused primarily on emergency relief work. As it grew it started running long-term development projects.

In 1999 its work included:

- running a training initiative in a refugee camp in Khartoum, Sudan
- holding mobile medical missions in the Philippines
- provided aid towards students' residential needs at a college and orphanage
- flying relief supplies out to Albania.

Membership: Supporters receive the newsletter *In Focus*.

Volunteers/jobseekers: Volunteering could include: running fundraising events e.g. a bazaar; distributing leaflets promoting Muslim Aid's work among your neighbours; undertaking voluntary work at the London office '... we can always use people with skills in IT, accounting, administration, marketing, fundraising, project management, photography and desktop publishing'.

Muslim Hands
Emergency aid and education
Geographical focus: *Worldwide*

48–164 Gregory Boulevard,
Nottingham NG7 5JE
Tel: 0115 711 7222; **Fax:** 0115 711 7220
e-mail: contact@muslimhands.org.uk
Website: www.muslimhands.org.uk
Correspondent: T M Nasir, Fundraising Development Manager

Expenditure: £2.1 million (1999)
Staffing: 10 full-time staff; 50 volunteers.
Website information: Breakdown of work according to country and activity; newsletter; how to make a donation; urgent appeals.

General: The charity aims to be at the forefront in delivering relief from poverty, sickness and the provision of education worldwide, and to provide an ethical service for the collection and distribution of funds in an effective, efficient, transparent and wholly accountable manner.

'We specialise in emergency aid and education. We currently have short and long-term projects in nearly forty countries. Some of our projects are related to provision of clean water, helping the aged, medical care and shelter.'

Publications: A newsletter, *Feedback*.

Nepal Leprosy Trust (UK)
Providing holistic support for people affected by leprosy
Geographical focus: *Nepal*

15 Duncan Road, Richmond,
Surrey TW9 2JD
Tel: 020 8332 9023; **Fax:** 020 8948 2703
e-mail: NLT@dial.pipex.com
Correspondent: James Lowther, General Administrator

Expenditure: £270,000 (1999)

Staffing: 6 ex-patriate staff; 150 Nepalis.

General: The charity provided the following information. NLT 'is a Christian initiative that works with people directly or indirectly affected by leprosy by offering holistic support without any discrimination. It works in partnership with the government of Nepal and other organisations to eliminate leprosy in Nepal through information, education and communication (IEC) and leprosy control. NLT serves and empowers people affected by leprosy and other marginalised people with love in order to restore dignity.

'NLT was founded in 1972 to demonstrate that people affected by leprosy (who are among the poorest of the poor in Nepal) could be empowered to become active participants in their society. Its early work concentrated on providing new opportunities (in agriculture, animal husbandry etc.) to families previously living in a government leprosy colony in Kathmandu.

'Permission was given in 1991 to build and operate a Leprosy Hospital and Services Centre at Lalgadh, in Dhanusha district, south Nepal. This is now a very busy centre, with 23,600 visitors in 1999, registering a quarter of all new leprosy cases in the country.

'The work of NLT has grown considerably in recent years and NLT now runs a broad range of programmes in the medical, social and economic development fields. NLT emphasises empowerment for life in the community, prevention of impairment and disability and community education and development. In Kathmandu, NLT also operates a number of handicraft industries for income generation.'

NLT (UK) recruits and sends ex-patriate personnel to Nepal, to work mainly in developmental and advisory functions (see Volunteers/jobseekers' below). It also carries out communications and administration. NLT Nepal is an indigenous organisation, governed by Nepali professionals/managers and employing about 150 Nepalis. It is committed to the active involvement of those affected by leprosy.

Volunteers/jobseekers: NLT recruits and sends only a very small number of specialised ex-patriate workers to fulfil particular salaried roles. The charity stated, as at December 2000, that a full-time doctor was urgently required. As well as doctors, the charity recruits people with skills including: experience in rehabilitation or empowerment programme implementation in a developing country; prevention of impairment and disability specialists (chiropodist, occupational therapist, physiotherapist etc.); and teachers (to teach children of ex-patriate workers, provide education for Nepali staff and assist in a village school).

NLT allows a small number of student doctors, chiropodists, occupational therapists, physiotherapists etc. to carry out medical electives or short-term voluntary service. Also, others with appropriate skills might be able to volunteer to fulfil a particular need at certain times.

The New Economics Foundation (NEF)

Working to put people and the environment at the centre of economic thinking

Geographical focus: *Mainly in the UK, but some projects overseas*

Cinnamon House, 6–8 Cole Street, London SE1 4YH
Tel: 020 7407 7447; **Fax:** 020 7407 6473
e-mail: info@neweconomics.org
Website: www.neweconomics.org
Correspondent: Sue Carter, Administrator

Expenditure: £862,000 (1998/99)

Staffing: About 30 staff, associates and volunteers.

Website information: A breakdown of NEF's work into areas including a description of tools it has developed e.g. alternative currencies, social accounting and auditing; downloadable copies of recent publications *Communities Count!* and *Prove it!*; list of other publications; how to become a member; recent news and news archive.

General: NEF provided the following information, it 'grew out of the Other Economic Summit and was formed in 1986. It is now one of the UK's most creative and effective independent think tanks, combining research, policy, training and practical action. Current main areas of work are corporate accountability, the global economy, community finance, and community participation'.

Working mainly in the UK and sometimes overseas, work has included, for example:

'• advising a government task force on social exclusion
- helping a housing estate set new 'indicators' of what it wants to change
- auditing a major company's social and ethical performance
- researching new ways to fund small businesses in run-down areas
- campaigning for new legislation on banking responsibility
- writing a report on the economy and the global environment
- supporting the work of a partner organisation in India, Africa or Europe
- piloting a method to get excluded people taking part in the decisions affecting them
- developing a new technique which could build the new economy.'

Membership: Supporters subscribe to the monthly newspaper *News from the New Economy* for £20 (£10 low/unwaged, £25 overseas) or the Publications Pack for £75 (£100 overseas) and receive most of the books and reports as well.

Publications: Publications include a CD ROM entitled *Brave New Economy*. This 'charts and celebrates the diverse activities within the new economy. From corporate accountability to community enterprise and from green taxes to fair trade, it gives users a wealth of argument, real life examples, facts, figures, ideas for action and links to hundreds of key organistions'. This CD ROM and other publications are available by e-mailing: mo@centralbooks.com or from Central Books, 99 Wallis Road, London E9 5LN; tel: 020 8986 5488; fax: 020 8533 5821.

Volunteers/jobseekers: Researcher posts are salaried and are advertised in the UK national *Guardian* newspaper.

New Frontiers International

Christian organisation working towards poverty relief, through community development and empowerment programmes

Geographical focus: Cyprus, Denmark, France, Germany, Ghana, India, Kenya, Kuwait, Lesotho, Mexico, Netherlands, Pakistan, Qatar, Republic of Guinea, Russia, Sierra Leone, South Africa, Switzerland, United Arab Emirates, United Kingdom, United States of America, Zimbabwe

17 Clarendon Villas, Hove,
East Sussex BN3 4JH
Tel: 01273 234555; **Fax:** 01273 234556
e-mail: nfi@n-f-i.org
Website: www.n-f-i.org
Correspondent: Nigel Ring, Trust Administrator

Expenditure: £500,000 (2000)

Staffing: 2 full-time salaried staff based in the UK work with NFI churches worldwide to implement and monitor community development programmes.

Website information: A description of the different programmes, as well as texts of introductory guides related to various aspects of poverty relief.

General: NFI was formed in September 1981 under the leadership of Terry Virgo. The mission is to take an holistic gospel, helping body, mind and spirit, to other nations. The strategy is to assist local churches to be effective in their communities by training leaders, running conferences, and providing support through training, literature, finance etc. as needed.

Examples of community development projects include:
- assisting street children in Mexico
- empowering farmers in Sierra Leone through the provision of seed, tools and training
- distributing food in the famine areas of Kenya
- providing basic medical care, literacy training and advice to slum dwellers in Bombay
- empowering black South Africans through training and micro-enterprise
- training in improved agricultural methods in Zimbabwe.

Capacity building is a high priority in all projects, in order to encourage indigenous peoples to be independent.

Publications: NF magazine is published five times per year to give teaching and reports on different aspects of the Christian gospel and its application.

Novi Most International

Helping young people in areas of acute conflict

Geographical focus: Bosnia-Herzegovina

Bushell House, 118–120 Broad Street, Chesham, Buckinghamshire HP5 3ED
Tel: 01494 793242; **Fax:** 01494 793771
e-mail: chesham@novimost.org
Website: www.novimost.org
Correspondent: Tom Riley, Deputy Director

Expenditure: £373,000 (1998/99)

Staffing: UK: 3 full-time and 4 part-time employees. Bosnia: about 15 mission members.

Website information: Breakdown of projects and services in Bosnia; how to get involved as a short or long-term volunteer, or as a school or other donor; schools' pack; facts about Bosnia; Night 'n' Day continuous prayer chain information and updates.

General: Novi Most International is a Christian charitable organisation which works with young people in areas of acute conflict:

- to help them overcome the effects of trauma
- to equip them to enter their futures with hope and confidence
- to empower them to become the instruments of reconciliation and positive change in their community.

It works to develop projects which facilitate Christian youth workers across Bosnia, (both indigenous people and people from other countries) to take the following 'three vital steps':

1. *'Entering into their lives'*
The charity has a number of initiatives where youth workers can come into contact with young people, including the development of drop-in centres with recreational and advice services, sports ministry, skills workshops and visitation of families - including refugee centres.

2. *'Shouting their corner'*
A chief aim of a youth worker is to champion the cause of individual young people, doing everything to ensure that individual needs are met. Work includes: relief and development work - offering food and shelter etc.; psychological counselling; relational youth work; running youth camps.

3. *'Building their platform'*
The charity gives the young people 'positive opportunities to develop their own voice and make a contribution to their family, community and the Kingdom of God'. This may involve them acquiring skills in areas such as teaching, preaching, journalism and the media, sports, music and creative arts, youth work, computing or running their own business.

Membership: Partners in Aid are regular donors, who can pay e.g. £3 a month (10p a day). Prayer Partners can receive regular prayer updates or join a round-the-clock continuous prayer chain.

Volunteers/jobseekers: The charity invites people to take part in its mission work for a month, a year or a lifetime. Individuals must share the charity's Christian faith.

Oasis Trust – Global Action Initiative

Wide range of development work

Geographical focus: Brazil, France, Germany, India, Kenya, Mozambique, Peru, Romania, South Africa, Tanzania, Uganda, Zimbabwe

115 Southwark Bridge Road,
London SE1 0AX
Tel: 020 7450 9000; **Fax:** 020 7450 9001
e-mail: globalaction@oasistrust.org
Website: www.oasistrust.org
Correspondent: Karen Bridle, Supporter Development Officer

Expenditure: About £2.4 million (spent on all initiatives)

Staffing: More than 70 staff and 300 students.

Website information: Information on the four action initiatives (see below).

General: Oasis works to deliver 'Global', 'Community', 'Youth' and 'Church' action initiatives. It operates regardless of race, religion or creed.

The Global Action Initiative is relevant to this guide. Oasis works on a range of projects in developing countries, working with local churches, communities and gap year teams. It aims to help people who are poor and marginalised by meeting their basic needs and facilitating them in developing sustainable livelihoods.

Volunteers/jobseekers: Oasis has programmes running in a number of countries which last from a few weeks to a year. Applicants must be: aged between 18 and 40 who are committed Christians; prepared to be changed and challenged;

willing to get their hands dirty; and keen to learn from other cultures. Activities include teaching, working with street children, schools work and helping with vocational training projects. Programmes cost between £950 and £3,500.

Ockenden International

Promoting self-reliance for refugees and displaced people

Geographical focus: *Afghanistan, Cambodia, Iran, Pakistan, Sudan, Uganda*

Constitution Hill, Woking,
Surrey GU22 7UU
Tel: 01483 772012; **Fax:** 01483 750774
e-mail: oi@ockenden.org.uk
Website: www.ockenden.org.uk
Correspondent: Rosalyn Taylor, Fundraising

Expenditure: £2.1 million (1999/2000)

Staffing: 160 staff, plus volunteers.

Website information: Country focus; news on its projects; information for volunteers.

General: Ockenden aims to help refugees, displaced people and returnees to break out of the long-term cycle of dependency that can develop as a result of a crisis. In practice it says it 'spends considerable time researching the potential for a new programme and looking for ways to make it have the longest-lasting benefits possible. Usually this will be through the development of partnerships in which Ockenden might provide expertise, funding and training whilst the partner, whether it is the village community leaders or local community organisation, will commit to providing the labour and a long-term commitment required to develop and run the initiative originally developed in conjunction with Ockenden'.

Volunteers/jobseekers: The charity is looking to build a network of UK-based volunteers to help with fundraising and awareness building. Telephone or e-mail the correspondent, to request a volunteer pack.

OMF International (UK)

Starting new churches, general development and emergency relief work

Geographical focus: *Brunei, Cambodia, China, Hong Kong, Indonesia, Japan, Laos, Malaysia, Mongolia, Myanmar, North Korea, The Philippines, Singapore, South Korea, Taiwan, Thailand, Vietnam*

British Isles Headquarters, Station Approach, Borough Green, Sevenoaks, Kent TN15 8BG
Tel: 01732 887299; **Fax:** 01732 887224
e-mail: omf@omf.org.uk
Website: www.omf.org.uk
Correspondent: Karen Adams

Expenditure: £4.9 million (1999)

Website information: Information on its work in different countries; mission issues to think through; stories; news; information about Asia; how to volunteer; resources.

General: OMF International (UK)'s overriding goal is to see groups of indigenous people in East Asia reaching other people in their country with the Christian gospel. In addition to Christian evangelism and training, it carries out other work caring for disadvantaged people, irrespective of their religion. It works in a variety of areas of development work such as teaching English, medical and health promotion, emergency relief and research.

Volunteers/jobseekers: The charity recruits people who are committed Christians to be involved in evangelism and starting new churches and also people to use their professional skills who are: accountants; administrators; agriculturalists; architects; business people; computer experts; development workers; doctors; economists; engineers; lecturers and research workers; medics and healthcare workers; musicians; project managers; relief workers; scientists; teachers, especially in English; and vets.

One World Action

Promoting democracy and respect for human rights, and working to defeat poverty

Geographical focus: *Angola, Bangladesh, Cape Verde, El Salvador, Guatemala, Honduras, Namibia, Nicaragua, Philippines, South Africa*

Bradley's Close, White Lion Street, London N1 9PF
Tel: 020 7833 4075; **Fax:** 020 7833 4102
e-mail: owa@oneworldaction.org
Website: www.oneworldaction.org
Correspondent: Ronit Dassa, Administrator

Expenditure: £1.5 million (1998/99)

Staffing: 15 paid staff, 3 voluntary staff.

Website information: News; breakdown of its programmes by country; publications information and an order form e.g. newsletters and briefings; job vacancies; links to other sites.

General: The charity's ideal is 'a world free from poverty and oppression in which strong democracies safeguard the rights of all people'.

To this end it provides 'money, expertise and practical help to organisations committed to strengthening the democratic process and improving people's lives in poor and developing countries'.

The charity also represents these people in Europe, 'putting forward their views in debates on policy towards poorer countries and helping them to forge closer links with decision makers in Britain and the European Union'.

In 1999, for example, its work included:
- water and sanitation provision in Angola
- basic healthcare for people in shanty towns in Bangladesh
- healthcare, education and small business support for four communities in Cape Verde
- support for 17 disabled women's self-help groups, and farming for 48 rural communities in Nicaragua.

The charity works in partnership with other voluntary organisations, community and cooperative movements, women's organisations and trade unions.

Membership: One World Action calls on trade unions and trade union branches to be affiliated to its work, supporting it in helping workers to organise and gain freedom from exploitation and forced labour.

Publications: Newsletter *A Partnership for Change* and briefings.

Volunteers/jobseekers: Opportunities are available for volunteers to gain work experience and support within the organisation. Tasks available for volunteers are usually administrative. There are also opportunities to work on specialist tasks e.g. database recording, research, project administration and the production of literature. Committed volunteers may be offered out-of-house training where appropriate.

One World Week (OWW)

Campaigning on global issues
Geographical focus: Worldwide

PO Box 2555, Reading RG1 4XW
Tel: 0118 939 4933; **Fax:** 0118 939 4936
e-mail: enquiries@oneworldweek.org
Website: www.oneworldweek.org
Correspondent: The Administrator

Expenditure: £153,000 (1999)

Staffing: 5 staff, mostly part-time.

Website information: One-page site, providing general information. The charity stated in 2001 that more pages were under construction.

General: OWW is a national and increasingly international week operated under the auspices of World Development Movement (see entry on page 234). It is dedicated to development awareness and action. In 2000, over 800 towns, villages and cities used the Week to put global concerns on the map. It aims to:

- build a movement of globally aware and active citizens
- make an impact on decision makers locally, nationally and internationally
- encourage local action on global issues

OWW provides action materials, which cover issues such as: access to land; land rights for indigenous people; positive alternatives in development; sustainable agriculture; integrated development; peace and reconciliation; celebrating our multicultural landscape; globalisation; tourism; debt; poverty; and racism.

OWW distributes resources to local organisers in the 'action kit'. There is also a schools supplement (games and exercises for secondary school aged children). Local papers feature articles on OWW activities, and there are interviews on local radio stations. Events in the past have included a study day on reconciliation and communication, a pilgrimage of remembrance on African slavery and displacement, public talks and discussions and children's workshops.

Other support provided for OWW includes:

- OWW training events for local organisers
- maintaining a list of OWW events
- involvement in Reaching Out and Reaching South – a chance to enhance the southern perspectives in your development education activities.

Volunteers/jobseekers: There are lots of opportunities for getting involved in the week's events. Contact the office for details of your local group.

OneWorld International Ltd

Runing a global network of organisations, using the internet to promote human rights and sustainable development
Geographical focus: Worldwide

9 White Lion Street, London NW1 9DB
Tel: 020 7239 7635; **Fax:** 020 7278 0345
e-mail: uk@oneworld.net
Website: www.oneworld.org
Correspondent: Joanna John

Website information: News; campaigns; special reports; information about partners and centres; job vacancies for work with various development organisations; ethical commerce shop selling books and cards etc.; links to other sites.

General: OneWorld is 'an internet community of 724 internet communities, leading the way for human rights and sustainable development worldwide'. The following information was derived from its website.

'OneWorld was first launched in 1995, named OneWorld Online, under the aegis of a small British charity, the OneWorld Broadcasting Trust (OWBT).

'OneWorld Online expanded rapidly, quickly outgrowing the parent body, both in size and scope. By early 1999, the trustees and directors felt that the organisation was becoming genuinely global, and was not longer a British organisation. Following research and discussion, the organisation separated from OWBT, no longer regarding OWBT as its mothership but as a sister organisation.'

'OneWorld International has two aspects:
i) OneWorld International Foundation (a not-for profit company)
ii) OneWorld International Ltd (a not-for-profit charitable company under UK law, which covenants back to the Foundation any balance it makes).

'These charitable companies have no shares: they are controlled by "members" rather than by shareholders, and are governed in accordance with a Constitution.'

Partner organisations and centres are part of 'an ever-growing global network of organisations that share a common aim of using the internet to promote human rights and sustainable development and a shared vision and values.

'The OneWorld network currently (as in 2000) consists of eight OneWorld centres. Each of the centres have one trustee who are members of a democratic board of trustees. The centres are in Austria, Costa Rica, Finland, India, Italy, the Netherlands, the UK, the USA and Zambia.

'One of OneWorld International's major tasks is to ensure this global interchange, both at the practical level of technology, and through teamwork and knowledge sharing.

'Who can be a OneWorld partner?
- organisations working in the fields of sustainable development or human rights. This may include publicising, campaigning, researching, debating or implementing work in these areas.
- branches, departments or projects that work in the fields of sustainable development or human rights as part of larger organisations with wider aims. However, where the wider organisation is seen to significantly contravene the aims of the OneWorld community, the application will be refused.
- OneWorld gives special priority to partnership applications from ngos based in the South.

'Centres are autonomous, non-profit organisations which share the values and vision of OneWorld and want to make use of its name, technology and worldwide audience to build on the potential of the net in their own area and languages.

'If your organisation shares our values and you are planning to run a portal site aggregating material for global justice organisations in your region, then you might like to consider applying to become a OneWorld centre. In this way you will pick up the immediate advantage of the spidering, databasing and page authoring software that OneWorld has developed over the past five years, as well as working with editorial partners around the world devoted to sharing information and expertise on the same issues.

'OneWorld centres are owned and governed by not-for-profit entities in their own countries. For example: OneWorld UK is owned by the Panos Institute, and OneWorld Italy (Unimondo) is owned by the Fondazione Fontana.

'OneWorld International welcomes approaches from organisations interested in potentially becoming a OneWorld centre.

'Each centre contributes to the work of the whole, especially in two ways:

(a) Partnership

A partnership manager in each centre administers the OneWorld partners in its locality. As OneWorld particularly values the 'bottom up' knowledge of people living unheard, struggling to free themselves from poverty or marginalisation, each local centre will also identify groups, especially grassroots groups, who might become partners.

'At present the OneWorld partnership is an online community of over 700 partner organisations covering a spectrum of development, environmental and human rights activities. All these partners share their information and ideas freely through OneWorld's public interest portal dedicated to issues of global justice.

(b) Editorial

Each centre also has an editor or team of editors who organise OneWorld's pages. These pages include documents in many languages – in Spanish, French, Italian, Portugese, Arabic, English, Dutch, German, Finnish, Swedish, among many others.

'The editors produce editions in languages spoken in their locality. Some of the centres are also beginning to produce global channels where all of OneWorld's material on a given theme can easily be found.'

Membership: The organisation has 724 partners and there are 8 centres, as at November 2000.

Operation Mobilisation

Development work, provision of aid

Geographical focus: Albania, Algeria, Argentina, Australia, Austria, Azerbaijan, Bahrain, Bosnia, Brazil, Canada, Chile, Costa Rica, Czech Republic, Denmark, Ecuador, Egypt, El Salvador, Estonia, Finland, France, Germany, Guatemala, Hong Kong, Hungary, Indonesia, Iraq, Israel, Italy, Japan, Jordan, Kazakhstan, Kuwait, Lebanon, Libya, Malaysia, Mauritania, Mexico, Morocco, Mozambique, Myanmar, Nepal, Netherlands, New Zealand, Norway, Oman, Pakistan, Panama, Papua New Guinea, Paraguay, Philippines, Poland, Portugal, Qatar, Romania, Russia, Saudi Arabia, Singapore, Slovakia, South Africa, South Korea, Spain, Sweden, Switzerland, Syria, Sudan, Taiwan, Tunisia, Turkey, Ukraine, UK, United Arab Emirates, Uruguay, USA, Uzbekistan, Yemen, Zimbabwe

The Quinta, Weston Rhyn, Oswestry, Shropshire SY10 7LT
Tel: 01691 773388
Website: www.om.org
Correspondent: The Communications Manager

Expenditure: £6.2 million (1999)

Website information: Information on work in each country and contact information; how to make a donation; information for volunteers.

General: This charity's objects are to help motivate, develop and equip local churches in the developing world to communicate the Christian message to local people. Most of its work is therefore comprised of supporting churches in carrying out evangelism, Christian teaching and in setting up new churches. It does, however, also participate in development work. This includes the provision of food and clothes, setting up an orphanage, renovating clinics and helping with agricultural projects.

The charity also maintains and runs ships which have multinational crews, including up to 500 volunteers in total each year. Activities on the ships revolve around a cultural exchange programme, and include several community service initiatives and a floating book fair.

Opportunity International

Supporting micro-enterprise and community development programmes through providing loans and business training

Geographical focus: Albania, Bulgaria, Colombia, Costa Rica, Croatia, Dominican Republic, Egypt, El Salvador, Ghana, Guatemala, Honduras, India, Indonesia, Macedonia, Malaysia, Montenegro, Nicaragua, Peru, Philippines, Poland, Romania, Russia, Sri Lanka, South Africa, Thailand, Uganda, Zambia, Zimbabwe

Angel Court, 81 St Clements,
Oxford OX4 1AW
Tel: 01865 725304; **Fax:** 01865 295161
e-mail: impact@opportunity.org.uk
Website: www.opportunity.org.uk
Correspondent: The Marketing Manager

Expenditure: £1.6 million (1999)

Staffing: 8 staff in the UK, 2 overseas.

Website information: Breakdown of its work by country; highlights of the year; press releases.

General: 'Opportunity International UK exists to empower people and communities in the world's poorest countries to overcome poverty and to secure sustainable improvements in the quality of their lives.'

It is the UK branch of the Opportunity International Network.

In practice, it supports micro-enterprise and community development programmes through providing loans and business training to poor people, giving the support they need to build viable businesses.

Trust Bank
Trust Bank programmes are the group lending and saving method used by Opportunity International. Each Trust Bank has a membership of between 6 and 40 people, who receive loans typically between £15 and £200. Members of the group have to guarantee each others' loans, formulate a trust constitution and savings plan. The aim is that these groups provide solidarity and empowerment to group members, becoming a catalyst for wider change in the community.

Individual lending
Clients who have graduated through the Trust Bank programme, and new clients with established businesses, can apply for individual loans.

Publications: *Opportunity International* newsletter, mailed to supporters bimonthly.

Volunteers/jobseekers: It does not have many opportunities to send people overseas but recruits people to work in the UK office in salaried posts who have experience of fundraising from technical donors such as DFID and the EU.

The charity welcomes applications from those interested in volunteering to help in the UK office. Tasks include research for funding proposals, managing a photo library, assisting with organising special events etc. For further information e-mail: kate@opportunity.org.uk or contact Kate Hood, tel: 01865 725304.

ORBIS

Running an eye teaching hospital on an aeroplane

Geographical focus: *Worldwide, with one permanent office in Ethiopia*

Second Floor, 17 Islington High Street, London N1 9LQ
Tel: 020 7278 5528; **Fax:** 020 7278 5231
e-mail: info@ukorbis.org
Website: www.orbis.org
Correspondent: Peter Flynn, Director

Expenditure: £1.2 million (1998/99)

Staffing: Flying Eye Hospital: 24 medical and administrative staff, most of which are from the UK; the charity has a pool of nearly 250 ophthalmologists and medical experts who regularly volunteer to take part in ORBIS missions.

Website information: Tour of the plane; destinations for the year; news and information; eye care links; job vacancies internationally; how to make a donation.

General: The charity describes its work as follows. 'ORBIS is an international charity dedicated to eliminating avoidable blindness by training local doctors, nurses and other healthcare workers in the developing world in vital sight-saving techniques.

'The ORBIS team is joined by hundreds of volunteer eye surgeons and medical professionals who donate their time to share their skills.

'Programmes are held on board the ORBIS plane, the world's only flying eye hospital, and in local hospitals and clinics in the developing world.'

The flying eye teaching hospital is equipped with an examination and laser treatment room, operating room, recovery room, 52-seat classroom and library. During a training programme, surgery is broadcast live to monitors located in the plane's classroom. Host doctors watching the surgery can communicate with the operating surgeon via a two-way audio visual system.

In each country ORBIS aims to work with local partners to:
- improve the quality of ophthalmic services, through indepth training programmes
- increase access to ophthalmic services (e.g. by training community health workers in eye care)
- increase public awareness of primary eye care
- support the eye care infrastructure (e.g. establish Eye Banks and provide essential equipment)
- support the introduction and reform of appropriate national and global policies.

In Ethiopia it has set up a permanent office to help build the nation's eyecare infrastructure. It aims to develop a programme of eye care in one region of Ethiopia which can be replicated in other regions. One of the key elements of the programme as at 1999/2000 was to train 520 local community health agents in primary healthcare.

The charity is working with the World Health Organisation and other blindness organisations to develop a coordinated programme of activity to eradicate avoidable blindness by the year 2020.

Volunteers/jobseekers: The charity has opportunities for expert ophthamologists and medical professionals to volunteer on its missions in developing countries. Please contact the charity for further information.

Overseas Development Institute (ODI)

Think-tank on international development and humanitarian issues
Geographical focus: *Worldwide*

11 Westminster Bridge Road,
London SE1 7JD
Tel: 020 7922 0300; **Fax:** 020 7922 0399
e-mail: odi@odi.org.uk
Website: www.odi.org.uk
Expenditure: £5.6 million (1999/2000)
Staffing: 78 staff in the UK.

Website information: Details of: research projects; publications; library; networks; talks; fellowship scheme.

General: ODI is a think-tank on international development and humanitarian issues. The following information was taken from its website. Its mission is 'to inspire and inform policy and practice which leads to the reduction of poverty, the alleviation of suffering and the achievement of sustainable livelihoods in developing countries. We do this by locking together high-quality applied research, practical policy advice, and policy-focused dissemination and debate.

'We work with partners in the public and private sectors, in both developing and developed countries.

'***Advisory work***
The institute regularly provides advice on development issues to a wide range of organisations including governments, international agencies, and non-governmental bodies.

'***Parliament***
ODI provides research support and advice to Parliamentary Select Committees, MPs and Peers. Since 1984 the institute has provided research and administrative support to the All Party Parliamentary Group on Overseas Development. The group's recent activities have covered aid, debt, Southern Africa, EU development policy and the workings of the UN/Bretton Woods system in development.'

Its research policy programmes are:
- rural policy and environment
- poverty and public policy including centre for aid and public expenditure
- forest policy and environment
- international economic development
- humanitarian policy.

ODI also organises several specialist networks:
- *Agricultural Research and Extension Network* links over 1,400 policy-makers, practitioners and researchers in more than 100 countries.
- *Rural Development Forestry Network* disseminates research information on key issues in tropical forestry to 2,300 members in 130 countries, aiming to influence policy and decision-makers in governments and international aid agencies.
- *Humanitarian Practice Network* exists to stimulate critical analysis, advance the professional learning and development of those engaged in and around humanitarian action, and improve practice.
- *Active Learning Network* on Accountability and Performance in Humanitarian Assistance works to improve the quality and accountability of humanitarian assistance programmes by providing a forum for the identification and dissemination of best practice and the building of consensus on common approaches.

Publications: ODI's publications programme includes an extensive range of titles:
- special reports
- development policy studies
- research studies

- working papers, which present preliminary research findings on current ODI projects.

Available on its website are ODI briefing papers on contemporary development issues, ODI Natural Resource Perspectives Papers and DFID Key Sheets for sustainable livelihoods.

ODI has two journals (published quarterly): *Development Policy Review* and *Disasters: The Journal of Disaster Studies, Policy and Management*. Books can be ordered from the postal, e-mail and website addresses above.

Volunteers/jobseekers: There are no opportunities for volunteers in the UK or overseas.

Oxfam

Development, relief and campaigning

Geographical focus: *Afghanistan, Albania, Algeria, Angola, Armenia, Azerbaijan, Bangladesh, Bolivia, Bosnia-Herzegovina, Brazil, Burkina Faso, Burundi, Cambodia, Chad, Chile, China, Colombia, Dominican Republic, DR Congo, Ecuador, Egypt, El Salvador, Eritrea, Ethiopia, Georgia, Ghana, Guatemala, Guinea Bissau, Haiti, Honduras, India, Indonesia, Iran, Iraq, Israel, Jamaica, Jordan, Kenya, Kosovo, Laos, Lesotho, Liberia, Lithuania, Macedonia, Malawi, Mali, Mauritania, Mauritius, Mexico, Morocco, Mozambique, Nepal, Nicaragua, Nigeria, North Korea, Pakistan, Papua New Guinea, Peru, Philippines, Rwanda, St Lucia, St Vincent, Senegal, Serbia, Sierra Leone, Somaliland, South Africa, Sri Lanka, Sudan, Swaziland, Syria, Tanzania, Thailand, Togo, Tunisia, Uganda, Vietnam, West Bank/Palestinian Territories, Yemen, Zambia, Zimbabwe*

274 Banbury Road, Oxford OX2 7DZ
Tel: 01865 311311
e-mail: oxfam@oxfam.org.uk
Website: www.oxfam.org.uk
Correspondent: Barbara Stocking, Director

Expenditure: £118 million (1999/2000)

Staffing: Over 2,000 staff are employed on standard contracts of varying terms (most in the UK). About 1,500 staff are employed on local contracts overseas.

Website information: Up-to-date information on its development and relief programmes, the latest on Oxfam's campaigns and a range of ways you can get involved: making an online donation, taking part in campaigns, supporting Oxfam shops, volunteering, purchasing fair trade products, considering job opportunities; information on the organisation's history and policies; educational materials for children; publications; links to associated Oxfam websites.

General: Oxfam GB provided the following information, it 'is a development, relief and campaigning charity dedicated to finding lasting solutions to poverty and suffering around the world. It believes that every human being is entitled to a life of dignity and opportunity and works with poor communities, local partner organisations, supporters and world leaders to help this become a reality.

'Oxfam was founded in 1942 as the Oxford Committee for Famine Relief. It changed its name to Oxfam in the 1950s and operates today as Oxfam GB to distinguish itself from Oxfams around the world. It is a member of Oxfam International, a successful family of organisations sharing common values and committed to working together to provide a coordinated response to help overcome poverty.

'Oxfam GB works with and through other organisations to provide and support emergency relief work, community development and advocacy and campaigning initiatives. It has a high profile in the GB high street where its network of over 800 shops raises millions of pounds for its work. It has developed a supporter base of hundreds of thousands of individual donors and is also funded by governments and inter-governmental agencies.'

Oxfam's direct charitable expenditure in 1999/2000, was divided as follows:

Grants to partners	£20 million
Other grants	£514,000
Operational programmes	£49 million
Gifts in kind	£2.4 million
Programme development and support	£21 million
Information, campaigning and education	£7.7 million

Grants to partners

'Much of Oxfam's development programme is carried out through grants to local organisations which support long-term, sustainable benefits for the community. Grants are also made to fund immediate emergency relief provision in times of crisis, catastrophe or natural disaster.'

In 1998/99 the largest ten grants were listed in the annual report as shown in the table below.

The top 50 grants were listed in the annual report and ranged upwards from £37,000. Beneficiaries included: Near East Foundation – West Africa (£61,000), Early Childhood Resource Centre – Middle East/Eastern Europe and former Soviet Union (£60,000), Netherlands Organisation for International

Oxfam – Top 10 grants 1999/2000

Name of institution	Amount	Project Base
On the Line Trust	£710,000	Greenwich Meridian Line
Acord	£202,000	Horn, East and Central Africa
Relief Society of Tigrai	£157,000	Horn, East and Central Africa
Ogaden Welfare Society	£132,000	Horn, East and Central Africa
Caribbean Policy Development Centre	£119,000	Greater Caribbean
Service Formation Action Pour Le Développement Economique et Social	£118,000	Greater Caribbean
Association Nationale de Formation des Adultes	£117,000	West Africa
North East Affected Area Development Society	£95,000	South Asia
Centro Para La Accion Legal de Derechos Humanos	£83,000	Greater Caribbean
Micro-Region Costa Atlantica	£80,000	South America

Development Cooperation – East Asia (£48,000), FINCA Malawi (£38,000).

Other grants

Comprised:

Grants to Irish Oxfams	£180,000
Grants to Oxfam in Germany	£334,000

Operational programmes

'Oxfam's own staff overseas are also involved in delivery of the programme through the provision of specialist services (e.g. to address the water and sanitation needs of refugees) and also through training and networking for local organisations.'

Gifts in kind

Included the distribution of blankets and clothing, and Food Aid.

Programme development and support

This 'represents the cost of Oxfam's core field offices and the costs incurred by GB-based staff, directly providing support for Oxfam's international programme, including management, policy and advocacy work, supervision and technical support for Oxfam's emergency programmes and the running costs of the Oxfam emergency warehouse, purchasing and logistics operations'.

Information, campaigning and education

This programme 'has several key objectives. One is to contribute the experience which comes from the International Programme to the curricula and methods of school teaching and youth work in Great Britain. Another is to inform our supporters and the wider British public about our international experience of work with poor people. We also carry out research and analysis of the issues raised by our work as a contribution to public debate and policy-making in Britain and the European Union, in the interests of alleviating poverty and suffering worldwide'.

Publications: Information on a wide range of books, leaflets and policy briefing papers Oxfam publishes (about its own work and on social, economic and political issues linked to global poverty) is available on its website or from the address above.

Trading: Oxfam GB is a member of european and international fair trade bodies and supports the development of fair trade initiatives. Through its own programme, it supports the development of community-based small businesses. Fair trade products produced by these groups are available from select Oxfam shops, by mail order or via the website.

Volunteers/jobseekers: Information on how to volunteer or work for Oxfam is available on the website.

Oxford Mission

Running orphanages, schools
Geographical focus: Bangladesh, India

PO Box 86, Romsey,
Hampshire SO51 8YD
Tel & Fax: 01794 515004
Correspondent: Mrs Mary Marsh, General Secretary

Expenditure: £269,000 (1999)

Staffing: 1 part-time member of staff.

General: 'In 1879, the Bishop of Calcutta, acutely aware of the work to be done among the educated people of the city, appealed to the University of Oxford … . It was decided to form a brotherhood of the Epiphany.'

Work began in Calcutta, spread to a village east of the city where the brothers cared for a group of 'neglected Christians'. They were joined by sisters from a newly formed sisterhood and the work spread further afield. In 1947 the partition of India resulted in the separation of the work in Calcutta from that in Bangladesh.

In India the brotherhood has come to an end but the work continues under an administrator and spiritual director. Oxford Mission runs a boys' orphanage and three types of school: St Joseph's Primary School, Industrial School and Pinn School for less academic boys.

In Bangladesh, the mission runs boarding schools, a Christian students' hostel, St Anne's Medical Centre, an orphanage and a primary school. In 1970 a Bangladeshi sisterhood was founded and sisters supervise boys' and girls' hostels and a playcentre for small children, help in a school and supervise a home.

Membership: The charity has about 1,600 members.

Publications: Half-yearly journal *The Oxford Mission News*, £4 a year.

Panos Institute London

Working towards improving international understanding of regional and global development issues

Geographical focus: *Worldwide*

9 White Lion Street, London N1 9PD
Tel: 020 7278 1111; **Fax:** 020 7278 0345
e-mail: panos@panoslondon.org.uk
Website: www.oneworld.org/panos
Correspondent: Duncan Miller

Expenditure: £1.8 million (1999)

Staffing: 18 staff in London; 10 UK-staff working overseas.

Website information: The website is a source of news, opinions and perspectives from developing countries. It contains information on a range of topics about the developing world in the form of news; media briefings; oral testimonies etc; links to relevant websites.

General: Panos Institute London describes its work as follows. 'Founded in 1986 the Panos Institute raises awareness of neglected or poorly understood issues, and communicates the concerns of marginalised sectors of society. Panos promotes the plurality and diversity of the media, by working with community and information organisations worldwide, and supporting their communication activities [including]: newspapers, local-language features services, radio programmes, investigative studies and oral testimony collection.

'Panos supports journalists in the developing world in their reporting of local environment, health, gender, media and development concerns, through commissioning, workshops, seminars and other initiatives. This can mean supporting pastoralist communities in Kenya to make their own radio programmes or commissioning Bangladeshi journalists to investigate grassroots attitudes towards a large-scale flood control project. The process of gathering and sharing information can be as important as the outcome; people learn from the experience and attitudes can change along the way.

'As well as catalysing debate on a national and regional level, Panos works to ensure that perspectives from developing countries reach the Northern public through the media, so increasing the exchange of ideas and experience between developing countries and the industrialised world.'

Publications: *Panos features service* provides articles on environment, health and development by journalists in developing countries, for publication around the world; *Panos media briefings* provide information such as facts and debates on a range of topical sustainable development issues; *Panos books and reports* are generated by Panos programmes and distributed free to groups and policymakers in the developing world; and *Panos Aids Information Sheets* provide facts on HIV/AIDS to journalists and ngos, for their own use.

Partnership for Growth
(formerly Link Romania)

Providing emergency aid, technical know-how and financial support

Geographical focus: Albania, Kosova, Romania

Link House, 59–61 Lyndhurst Road, Worthing, West Sussex BN11 2DB
Tel: 01903 529333; **Fax:** 01903 529007
e-mail: info@pfg-charity.org
Website: www.p4g.org
Correspondent: Mark Shipperlee, Coordinator

Expenditure: £1.8 million (1998/99)
Staffing: 100 locals in Central and Eastern Europe; 45 paid staff and volunteers in the UK.

Website information: Country focus; information about aid transport; newsletter and press releases; fundraising appeals.

General: The charity describes its work in Romania as follows. 'After ten years operating in Romania, our work is now concentrated in three geographical areas, and includes income generation programmes as well as development projects. We still respond to emergency situations where we can, although these are few now - incidents like floods or landslides.

'We now have over 20 Romanians working as project managers – working towards our goal of encouraging Romanians to help themselves and their poor. We have several western staff overseeing operations, and new development projects are still being introduced.

'Much of our work is based around hands-on care programmes; such as soup kitchens, homeless projects, street children work, and development programmes; also our well-established agricultural project in the north east of the country. We will send trucks of aid but these are mainly focused on specific appeals – Harvest, Shoebox and Clothes Appeals.'

It describes its work in Kosova as follows. 'Since our establishment of an office and team in Kosova in July 1999, Partnership for Growth has been active in a range of humanitarian activities in the province. Our team includes Kosovars and western support workers, as we seek to establish longer term projects for the regeneration of the region.

'We have been sending 38 tonne trucks of aid into the region, a gruelling four-day journey and four-day wait at the border. Whilst we continue to send a limited amount of humanitarian aid by truck, it has become costly and therefore only specific donated items are sought. More of our work is based around hands-on care programmes, such as child trauma counselling, and development programmes such as our proposed agricultural project.'

The charity also carried out emergency relief work amongst the Kosovar refugees in Albania.

Publications: *Newslink* is a newsletter published three times a year. It is for free distribution to anyone interested in the work of the charity.

Volunteers/jobseekers: Get involved through providing a shoebox full of gifts, which is provided to families in Romania. For further information contact the charity at the address above.

Pattaya Orphanage Trust

Putting children's homes and other projects, including work with disabled children

Geographical focus: Thailand

124 North End House, Fitzjames Avenue, London W14 0RZ
Tel: 020 7602 6203; **Fax:** 020 7603 6468
e-mail: info@pattayaorphanage.org.uk
Website: www.pattayaorphanage.org.uk
Correspondent: The Chief Executive

Expenditure: £670,000 (1999)

Staffing: 8 paid members of staff.

Website information: Virtual tour of projects; breakdown of projects; downloadable newsletter; opportunities for sponsoring a child and visiting the site either as a sponsor or volunteer; events.

General: The Pattaya Orphanage is dedicated to giving a loving home and a secure future to children who are orphaned, abandoned or disabled in Pattaya City and throughout Thailand.

It has five projects in Pattaya:

- an orphanage
- a school for deaf children
- a school for blind children
- a vocational school for disabled young people
- street children's project.

The vocational school, for instance, provides training in sought-after skills – computer operation and programming, electrical hardware repair. The school places disabled youngsters into the job market with an equal chance of obtaining a job, with a record of 100% graduate employment. In 2000 the school was seeking to double the capacity of the school from 200 places to 400.

Membership: No members. Supporters receive quarterly newsletters. Child sponsorship fees are £15.12 a month or £181.44 a year. Sponsors receive occasional updates on their child's progress plus other correspondence. Application forms are available from the address above.

Volunteers/jobseekers: Opportunities exist for volunteering in Thailand. For further information contact the charity.

Peace Child International

Promoting youth empowerment

Geographical focus: Worldwide

The White House, The High Street, Buntingford, Hertfordshire SG9 9AH
Tel: 01763 274459; **Fax:** 01763 274460
e-mail: contact@peacechild.org
Website: www.peacechild.org
Correspondent: David Woollcombe, President

Expenditure: About £500,000

Staffing: 3 paid staff; 10 international volunteers.

Website information: Information about interns and its projects; newsletters; publications; weekly updates.

General: The charity's name was derived from a practice conducted by warring tribes in Papua New Guinea. When the tribes made peace they would exchange a child and that child would grow up with the other's tribe. If, in the future, conflict threatened, he or she would be sent to their people to resolve it. Such a child was called a Peace Child.

The charity's mission is to give 'today's young people the confidence and the skills to create a better tomorrow'.

Founded in 1981, Peace Child has built up a network of about 500 schools, youth groups and youth networks in 120 countries, representing millions of young people aged 12 to 25 years. Its programmes are as follows:

Be the Change!
The charity raises money in order to fund youth-led development projects. These projects have included child-to-child literacy projects in Vietnam, park restoration in Ukraine and water tanks in Nepal. This project is the charity's main work.

Student-teacher partnerships in human rights education
A programme to enable young people and their teachers to develop country-specific human rights educational materials including a resource book, teacher guide, posters, lesson plans etc.

Education for sustainable development
The charity is developing programmes of education for use at primary and secondary school level.

Student-created books on key global issues
(See under Publications).

Peace Child 2000 musical play
The charity brings young people together to produce a play which explores bridging the gap between North and South.

Membership: £10 ($15) a year for individuals, and £25 ($40) for groups. Members receive regular mailings, a copy of the half-yearly newsletter and other information.

Publications: The charity is developing a series of books and work includes: a children's edition of Agenda 21 – *Rescue Mission*; a youth edition of the Universal Declaration of Human Rights – *Stand up for your rights*; and a youth edition of the UN Environment Programmes' Global Environment Outlook – *Pachamama: Our Earth, Our Future*. All these books cost £7.99 plus £2 p&p and can be ordered from the charity at the address above. A books list giving information on other publications is also available from the charity.

Action Times is the charity's newsletter.

Volunteers/jobseekers: If you want to set up a Be the Change! project, contact the charity for a list of the criteria which you will have to meet. The charity also encourages schools and youth groups in Europe and North America to 'Adopt Projects'.

The UK office is run by people under the age of 25 and these interns are from all over the world. They must be able to pay their own way to the UK but once here all board and lodging is provided and they get weekly pocket money. Everyone lives together in a converted barn in two single sex dormitories and there is a cooking and cleaning rota and communal kitchen, dining room and lounge.

Pestalozzi Children's Village Trust

Bringing students from developing countries to study for the International Baccalaureate, at Hastings College of Arts and Technology

Geographical focus: India, Nepal, Zambia, Zimbabwe and Tibetan communities in India

Sedlescombe, Battle,
East Sussex TN33 0RR
Tel: 01424 870444; **Fax:** 01424 870655
e-mail: office@pestalozzi.org.uk
Website: www.pestalozzi.org.uk
Correspondent: Val Winslade, Director

Expenditure: £760,000 (1998/99)

Staffing: 32 staff and 6 volunteers in the UK, none overseas.

General: Since 1959 the trust has provided educational opportunities in the UK for underprivileged young people. It sponsors young people from disadvantaged backgrounds in developing countries to be educated in the UK, in accordance with the 'head, heart and hands' educational philosophy of Johan Pestalozzi.

While in the UK, the students:

- live within unique multicultural international community;
- study and work alongside each other and with people from the UK;
- share their skills and encourage international understanding;
- promote development awareness as equal partners in creating a fairer world and a more sustainable future.

The charity's programme in 2001 was to run the International Baccalaureate, in partnership with Hastings College of Arts and Technology. Between 10 and 20 new students enrol for the two-year course each year. The students must have high academic ability and come from low income families. Fee-paying European students can also take the course.

Volunteers/jobseekers: Each August/September volunteers are taken on, for periods of around 10 months, who live on site and help with educational, recreational or administrative duties.

PLAN International UK

Development, with a focus on children, and child sponsorship

Geographical focus: Albania, Bangladesh, Benin, Bolivia, Brazil, Burkina Faso, Cameroon, China, Colombia, Dominican Republic, Ecuador, Egypt, El Salvador, Ethiopia, Ghana, Guatemala, Guinea, Guinea Bissau, Haiti, Honduras, India, Indonesia, Kenya, Malawi, Mali, Nepal, Nicaragua, Niger, Pakistan, Paraguay, Peru, Philippines, Senegal, Sierra Leone, Sri Lanka, Sudan, Tanzania, Thailand, Togo, Uganda, Vietnam, Zambia, Zimbabwe

5–6 Underhill Street, London NW1 7HL
Tel: 020 7485 6612; **Fax:** 020 7485 2107
e-mail: mail@plan-international.org.uk
Website: www.plan-international.org.uk
Correspondent: Marie Staunton, Chief Executive

Expenditure: £19 million (1999/2000)
Staffing: 36 full-time staff in the UK; 5,000 overseas.

Website information: Breakdown of work by country; how individuals and schools can sponsor a child and a description of the services they receive; news; feature articles about PLAN's work.

General: In its 1999 annual review, PLAN International states: 'PLAN's goal is to build a secure future for the children in our programme countries.

'PLAN's experience shows us that the most effective way to achieve this is to implement development programmes which benefit the child's entire community.

'PLAN's belief is in working together with communities to identify their needs and meet them in the most appropriate, long-term and sustainable ways.'

Its key work areas are:

Growing up healthy
'… seeks to ensure the survival protection and healthy development of children, and the reproductive health of adolescents and adults, especially women of childbearing age'. For example, in Sudan PLAN has trained midwives to work with mothers during pregnancy, delivery and after the birth.

Learning
'… seeks to ensure that children, young people and adults acquire basic learning and life skills in order to help them realise their full potential and contribute to the development of their societies'. For example, in Paraguay it is working to

provide books, desks, and other facilities for learning and healthcare in a primary school.

Livelihood
'... seeks to increase food security and disposable family income, which will enable families to improve their children's welfare'. For example, in Madras it is teaching women how to drive rickshaws and become tailors and photographers.

Habitat
'... seeks to ensure that children live in secure, safe and healthy habitats'. For example, in the Philippines PLAN worked with the fishing communities to rehabilitate the mangrove forests.

Building relationships
'... aims to create a worldwide community of sponsors and children sharing a common agenda for child-centred development'.

Volunteers/jobseekers: No opportunities for volunteers overseas. There are opportunities within the UK offices.

Plunkett Foundation

Furthering rural cooperation
Geographical focus: Worldwide

23 Hanborough Business Park,
Long Hanborough, Oxford OX8 8LH
Tel: 01993 883636; **Fax:** 01993 883576
e-mail: info@plunkett.co.uk
Correspondent: The Clerk

Expenditure: £200,000 (2000)

Staffing: 7 full-time and 1 part-time core staff at head office; about 250 people on the register of consultants, who are called on to provide their skills at different times.

General: The charity runs rural development projects including 'proper agricultural' and 'agrotourism' projects. It provides training to other ngos, with a focus on user-benefits. It teaches knowledge and skills relevant to the constitution, structure, governance and management culture in user-benefit businesses.

It delivers seminars, workshops, conferences and one-to-one briefings on topics that include enterprise initiation and formation, organisation/management, director roles and responsibilities, strategic and business planning, and performance criteria and measurement, as well as conventional aspects of successful operation.

The foundation's library and information centre, which supports Plunkett consultants, is open, by appointment, to the public. It houses 20,000 documents.

Membership: Membership costs £45 for individuals, £176.25 for UK-based organisations and £175 for overseas organisations. A discount of 50% is available for organisations and individuals from developing countries, students and retired people. Members receive: a free copy of the annual *The World of Co-operative Enterprise*; access to co-operative and development materials via the library and information centre; newsletters detailing the current work of the foundation; 10% discount on Plunkett Foundation publications; and 10% discount on seminars and conferences.

Publications: A number of publications are available to buy. For a list please contact the charity.

Volunteers/jobseekers: There are no opportunities for volunteering.

Population Concern

Supporting the development of sexual and reproductive health services

Geographical focus: Overseas partners in: Bangladesh, Bolivia, Ethiopia, Ghana, India, Lebanon, Madagascar, Nepal, Nigeria, Pakistan, Peru, Tanzania, Trinidad, Uganda. Organisations in the following countries/territories received funding: Antigua, Gaza, Mexico, Vietnam

Studio 325, Highgate Studios,
53–79 Highgate Road, London NW5 1TL
Tel: 020 7241 8500; **Fax:** 020 7267 6788
e-mail: info@populationconcern.org.uk
Website: www.populationconcern.org.uk
Correspondent: Wendy Thomas

Expenditure: £3.1 million (1998/99)

Staffing: 21 staff, all based in the UK.

Website information: List of overseas projects; how to get an education officer to visit your school; small number of items to shop for online; links to related sites; how to donate.

General: Population Concern was set up in the early 1970s as the international wing of the UK's Family Planning Association (FPA). Its aim was to raise money for family planning programmes in less developed countries. By 1977 it became Population Concern, becoming fully independent in 1991.

Population Concern has always worked with partner organisations overseas and its overseas work expanded to include all aspects of sexual and reproductive health, with a particular focus on young people. In addition, Population Concern increasingly began to provide technical assistance and to help build the capacity of its partner organisations.

Its mission statement includes the following aims: to work 'advancing the right of all people to exercise free and informed reproductive health choice and to have access to confidential sexual and reproductive health services including family planning; particularly we promote the right of women and young people to have effective access to those services and the right of women of all ages to an education which enhances their economic and social standing'.

Population Concern works in about 19 countries worldwide and manages about 50 programmes (as at July 2000). In the UK, awareness-raising of the organisation and the issues takes place among parliamentarians, academics, educationalists, journalists, health professionals, other ngos and the general public. Population Concern also holds awareness-raising campaigns in different locations in the UK. It holds annual Youth Conferences for up to 1,000 A-level students every year.

Membership: Supporters receive a copy of the annual review in January and an update in July, as well as the catalogues (see Trading below).

Trading: A fair trade catalogue is available in spring and there is a Christmas catalogue.

POWER – The International Limb Project

Suppling artificial limbs and support devices to victims of conflict

Geographical focus: Laos, Mozambique, Vietnam, Zambia

4 Church Road, Lewknor,
Oxfordshire OX9 5TP
Tel: & Fax: 01844 353001
e-mail: power@patrol.i-way.co.uk
Website: www.power4limbs.org
Correspondent: Michael Boddington, Chief Executive Officer

Expenditure: £940,000 (1999/2000)

Staffing: UK: 2 full-time and 2 part-time paid staff and 7 volunteers. Overseas: 17 full-time paid staff and 1 volunteer.

Website information: Information on its programmes in Laos and Mozambique; how to make a donation.

General: Set up in 1994, this charity works to help people who are victims of landmines and other people who have lost a limb, through supplying, free of charge, artificial limbs and support devices.

POWER aims to:
- provide services which will continue to run efficiently in the long-term;
- restore the person's self-respect and enable them to become re-established within their local communities;
- improve the quality of artificial limbs by introducing or reinforcing appropriate technology.

The charity's work involves travelling to rural areas to persuade amputees to come to its clinics for treatment.

Work in Laos, for example, has included refurbishing and re-equipping The National Rehabilitation Centre and four provincial rehabilitation centres, and setting up a training programme to train people to be able to make and fit artificial limbs to amputees.

POWER also holds technical workshops designed to improve knowledge and practice of specific issues in the provision of prosthetic and orthotic services in low-income countries.

Membership: POWER has no membership system as such. It maintains a register of Friends who make regular financial contributions, according to their means/preferences. The Friends get a twice-yearly newsletter and occasional other literature.

Publications: *Newsletter*.

Trading: POWER is related to a wholly-owned trading subsidiary named Power4Biz Ltd. Its chief activity is owning the www.power4biz.net internet portal and virtual ISP.

Volunteers/jobseekers: The main employment opportunities with POWER are in the countries where it is operating, where it employs both expatriates and local people. In 2001 about one third of the overseas employees and 80% of the expatriate employees were qualified prosthetists or prosthetists/orthotics. It also employs expatriate administrative and financial officers on its programmes. POWER is moving increasingly to support southern ngos, especially those which provide services to disabled people. There are opportunities for those who specialise in capacity building.

POWER takes on one or two volunteers every year to help overseas. It prefers volunteers who will work for three months or longer.

The Prince's Trust

Supporting disadvantaged young people

Geographical focus: *UK (predominantly) and the Commonwealth*

18 Park Square East, London NW1 4LH
Tel: 020 7543 1234; **Fax:** 020 7543 1368
e-mail: info@princes-trust.org.uk
Website: www.princes-trust.org.uk
Correspondent: Sophie Hobbs, Projects Manager – Policy and Development

Expenditure: £40 million (planned for 2001/02)

Staffing: UK: 800 paid staff (including secondees) and 100,000 volunteers (UK-wide).

Website information: Information about how to get involved in each of its programmes; how to make a donation; opportunities for employees; bulletin board; links; latest news and press releases; listing of publications of latest research into issues affecting young people.

General: The Prince's Trust works quite specifically with disadvantaged young people aged 14 to 30 in the UK. It offers a range of opportunities, including training, personal development, business start up and support and mentoring and advice. The Prince's Trust programmes are targeted at people who have fewer opportunities than others, such as those who are unemployed, young offenders, those in and leaving care, people with disabilities and those from a minority ethnic community.

The Prince's Trust has reviewed its work in the Commonwealth to see how it can give greatest value given the funds it has available. The Prince's Trust does not now give grants to individuals or organisations from outside the UK but has rather developed its work in the Commonwealth in two ways:

- supporting and fostering links with youth business trusts in commonwealth countries in partnership with the Prince of Wales Business Leaders Forum;
- promoting opportunities for young people to participate in a commonwealth volunteer exchange programme in partnership with VSO.

For more information about the work with youth business trusts, please contact: Youth Business International, 15–16 Cornwall Terrace, Regent's Park, London NW1 4QP; tel & fax: 020 7467 3660; website: www.youth-business.org.

For more information about the volunteer exchange programme, please contact: World Youth Millennium Awards, VSO, 317 Putney Bridge Road, London SW15 2PN; tel: 020 8780 7500; e-mail: enquiry@vso.org.uk.

Volunteers/jobseekers: Please see under General above.

Project HOPE UK

Running sustainable health programmes
Geographical focus: Worldwide

Wilson Building, Stockley Park West, Uxbridge, Middlesex UB11 1BT
Tel: 020 8990 2246; **Fax:** 020 8990 4383
Website: www.projhope.org
Correspondent: Eleanor Higgins, Special Projects Manager

Expenditure: £5.2 million (1998/99)

Staffing: A small number of staff based in Uxbridge, North West London, works with over 250 Project HOPE staff all over the world.

Website information: News and events; breakdown of work into programmes; breakdown of programmes into countries; how to make a donation.

General: The charity provided the following information. 'Project HOPE is one of the world's largest international health charities. Project HOPE UK is one of a number of autonomous national Project HOPE organisations. It is currently running a wide range of long-term health programmes with local partners including a major substance abuse education programme in Russian schools, a nationwide programme of paediatric rehabilitation in Bosnia and a programme to help mothers identify the first signs of killer diseases in their children.

'It has developed a unique micro-credit programme in a number of countries which combines the economic benefits with health education – designed to ensure that the women members of the "Village Health Banks" spend a higher proportion of an increased family income on health enhancing costs.

'A major part of its work is to help in the capacity building of local organisations and success is judged on the sustainability of projects when totally in the hands of local people.

'Project HOPE UK also works closely with the British pharmaceutical industry receiving large quantities of Gift in Kind medical supplies which are distributed, respecting WHO guidelines, in emergency situations worldwide.'

Volunteers/jobseekers: If you are interested in working or volunteering for this charity, please make enquiries by phone (telephone number above).

The Project Trust

Offering gap-year opportunities

Geographical focus: Botswana, Brazil, Chile, China, Cuba, Dominican Republic, Egypt, Guyana, Hong Kong, Honduras, Japan, Jordan, Malawi, Malaysia, Namibia, Pakistan, Peru, South Africa, South Korea, Sri Lanka, Thailand, Uganda, Vietnam, Zimbabwe

The Hebridean Centre, Isle of Coll, Argyll PA78 6TE
Tel: 01879 230444; **Fax:** 01879 230357
e-mail: discover@projecttrust.org.uk
Website: www.projecttrust.org.uk
Correspondent: The Director

Expenditure: £711,000 (1999/2000)

Staffing: 16 full-time members of staff in the UK.

Website information: Focus on projects in different countries; apply to volunteer online; news; competitions; photos; links; bulletin board.

General: The charity says: 'Our aim is to educate a new generation in Britain through service in partnership with peoples overseas. We offer young school leavers the chance to spend twelve months doing voluntary work abroad'.

The projects last for 12 months overseas and cost £280 a month. Volunteers receive: full training; air fares and medical insurance; paid holidays of at least eight weeks; living allowance, board and accommodation; an opportunity to learn a new language; and help with raising sponsorship.

Each project offers work in at least one of the following areas: teaching including teaching music or English; care work; wildlife project; practical work; marketing crafts; outdoor pursuits; journalism and hospital work.

Each year about 200 volunteers are sent overseas, from the UK, the Netherlands and Eire. Six-day training courses are held at the charity's headquarters before departure. These include briefing on the customs and culture of the country, the project itself and how to have a successful year there. Volunteers are also trained in appropriate skills.

Volunteers/jobseekers: See under General above.

Raleigh International

Inspiring people from all backgrounds, ages and nationalities to discover their full potential by working together on challenging environmental and community projects around the world

Geographical focus: Belize, Chile, Costa Rica, Ghana, Mongolia, Namibia

Raleigh House, 27 Parsons Green, London SW6 4HZ
Tel: 020 7371 8585; **Fax:** 020 7371 5118
e-mail: info@raleigh.org.uk
Website: www.raleighinternational.org
Correspondent: The Clerk

Expenditure: £4.3 million (1998/99)

Staffing: Approximately 70 full-time paid staff. Each year over 1,300 volunteers participate in projects.

Website information: Information on expedition countries and projects; how to apply for an expedition; corporate training; alumni; case studies; support groups; youth 'at risk' programmes.

General: The charity runs three-month expeditions as follows:

- volunteers aged 17–25 receive training in the UK and one week's orientation and training in the expedition country before spending 10 weeks working on 3 projects – environmental, community and adventure;
- volunteer staff, aged 25 or over, receive training in the UK, plus 2 weeks in the expedition country before the 10-week expedition begins. Staff roles vary from project managers and accountants to doctors and nurses, mountain leaders and builders.

Each project team consists of around 12 volunteers and 3 staff. In 1999/2000 over 1,300 volunteers went on expedition.

Community projects

Volunteers work alongside a qualified builder, engineer or carpenter and local community members, who provide training in relevant skills. Projects have included building schools and medical centres and working in eye clinics.

Environmental projects

Volunteers work alongside scientists, e.g. conducting a biodiversity inventory, undertaking a survey of threatened species and working to improve facilities in national parks and protected areas.

Adventure projects

These projects are designed to challenge individuals through physically and mentally demanding adventurous activity. The projects may include canoeing, sea-kayaking, climbing and trekking.

Volunteers/jobseekers: See above for opportunities for volunteers. People wishing to become volunteers should download a form from the website or request one from the charity at the address above. The form should be submitted with a cheque for £30 for the cost of the induction weekend. People wishing to become staff volunteers should contact the staff office in writing or by telephone to the address above or by e-mail: staff@raleigh.org.uk to request an application form.

RedR International

Recruiting and training personnel to work for humanitarian relief agencies

Geographical focus: Worldwide

1 Great George Street,
London SW1P 3AA
Tel: 020 7233 3116; **Fax:** 020 7222 0977
e-mail: info@redr.demon.co.uk
Website: www.redr.org
Correspondent: The Clerk

Expenditure: £654,000 (1999/2000)

Staffing: UK: 18 staff; 4 volunteers helping with administrative work; and the charity has a database of 2,000 members who are called on to help with training, interviewing and debriefing.

Website information: Newsletters; events; training programmes; resources – useful publications and where to buy them; how to apply to join the register of relief workers; FAQ; search RedR library; information about the needs assessment service; annual reviews; information about RedR members in the field; RedR in the news; links to other relevant sites; list of other organisations providing jobsearch information.

General: The following information was provided on the charity's website. 'RedR relieves suffering in disasters by selecting, training and providing competent and effective personnel to humanitarian aid agencies worldwide.

RedR's register of relief workers

'The members of RedR's register form a unique body of highly motivated and competent individuals who can be called upon at very short notice to strengthen the response of front-line humanitarian agencies.

'Since its establishment in 1979, RedR members have undertaken over 700 assignments with more than 80 agencies in over 70 countries.

'Members of RedR's register are carefully interviewed and selected for their personal and professional qualities. While engineering and related technical skills lie at the heart of RedR, the range of professions represented on the register continues to grow. The ability to work effectively in a team without taking unnecessary risks under stressful and often dangerous conditions is considered to be of utmost importance.

'RedR seeks to find the best match between the requirements of any assignment and the profile of available members. RedR's membership includes those with many years' experience in disaster work as well as those just starting in the sector. Programme managers/coordinators and highly specialised technical experts as well as those with practical hands-on skills are all represented on the register and a growing number of members have experience in assessing needs and establishing programmes in the critical first few weeks of an emergency.'

The charity recruits people who have several years' relevant professional experience and who are fit and healthy to join its register of professionals. Applicants should have proven competencies in one or more of the following areas: accountancy/finance; administration/office management; advocacy; agronomy; civil engineering/construction/building; community mobilisation; electrical sources and supply; environmental management; information/PR/media; information technology; institutional development; mechanical engineering; mine clearance; needs and impact assessment; personnel management; programme management; project management; radio telecommunications; roads and bridges; sanitation; security; technical supervision; training and development; vehicle and mechanical plant; water sources; and water supply and distribution.

For further details of the application procedure, see the charity's website. Applicants receive high quality training and if work is available undertake short-term assignments (three to six months) with frontline humanitarian agencies.

Effective training for relief workers

'Extensive training programmes have been developed by RedR to broaden the range and depth of register members' skills. Subjects covered in these courses include both "hard" technical subjects (water supply, power generation etc.) and "soft" subjects (personal effectiveness, community mobilisation, managing people etc.). For a number of years these courses have also been open to non-members and more recently RedR has collaborated with individual agencies to adapt RedR courses to that particular agency's needs.

'Evaluations at the end of each course and debriefing after every assignment ensure that important lessons are learned and built into future training courses.

RedR working internationally
'Accredited RedR offices are currently established in the United Kingdom, Australia and New Zealand. All RedR offices undertake to respect the Fundamental and Operating Principles of RedR and seek to work closely together as members of RedR International. With the support of individuals and organisations in other countries, RedR seeks to recruit new register members and run training courses throughout the world. RedR's International Secretariat is based in Geneva.'

Trading: RedR has a shop at its office selling RedR t-shirts and the manual *Engineers in Emergencies*.

Volunteers/jobseekers: There are opportunities for volunteers in London to help with administrative support. Volunteers must commit to work for at least two months, for one to two days a week, Monday to Friday. Contact Chantal McIIeveen-Wright at the e-mail address above.

Also see the information about RedR's register of relief workers, under General above.

RefAid (UK for UNHCR)

Helping meet the needs of refugees, by funding UNHCR projects and raising awareness

Geographical focus: *Worldwide*

21st Floor, Millbank Tower, 21–24 Millbank, London SW1P 4QP
Tel: 020 7932 1019; **Fax:** 020 7233 5768
e-mail: gbrloref@unhcr.ch
Website: www.refaid.org.uk
Correspondent: The Administrator

Expenditure: £637,000 including UNHCR projects overseas and public awareness activities (1998/99)

Staffing: 4 paid staff and 1 volunteer in the UK.

Website information: Emergency appeals; corporate partnerships; upcoming events (such as Refugee Week); annual review; educational resources; refugee paintings; refugee definitions; volunteering and internships; how to donate.

General: RefAid's objectives are to support the work of UNHCR (United Nations High Commissioner for Refugees) by raising project funds from the private sector and by raising awareness in the UK of the issues faced by refugees worldwide. The charity started actively operating in 1996.

UNHCR is one of the largest humanitarian agencies in the world operating through 290 offices in 124 countries. UNHCR was set up by the UN General Assembly in 1951 to protect people from physical harm, to defend their human rights, and to make sure that they are not forcibly returned to countries where they could face imprisonment, torture and even death. The agency is funded almost entirely by voluntary contributions from governments and the private sector.

RefAid encourages private sector partnership and raises funds for a number of UNHCR overseas programmes across the globe. Recently these have included projects in Pakistan, Ethiopia, Armenia, Bosnia, Kosovo and Timor. The focus of RefAid's awareness raising activities has been the enablement of an annual Refugee Week.

Membership: Individuals or organisations receive the quarterly magazine free of charge. Contact the charity for further information.

Publications: Refugees magazine is available quarterly, free of charge.

Volunteers/jobseekers: Internships in the London office legal protection and public information departments are available to graduates of law, political science, economic and social relations, international relations, public policy and administration. Internships last for six months. For an application form contact the Personnel Officer at the address above.

Volunteers wishing to work with refugees in the UK should contact the Volunteer Coordinator at Refugee Council, (tel: 020 7820 3000, e-mail: gabriella.fox@refugeecouncil.org.uk).

Volunteers wishing to work with refugees overseas, should see the website for UNHCR volunteering programmes (www.unhcr.ch). UNHCR runs a scheme, Camp Sadako, which provides volunteers with a six week placement in a refugee camp. On return volunteers are expected to organise activities in order to share their experience and raise awareness about refugee issues. Candidates must be aged 21 or above.

Relief Fund for Romania

Providing support for various projects helping children, people who are sick or elderly, and other groups in need

Geographical focus: Romania

PO Box 2122, London W1A 2ZX
Tel: 020 7437 6978; **Fax:** 020 7494 1740
Correspondent: Edward Parry

Expenditure: £234,000 (1998/99)
Staffing: Varies.

General: The charity provided the following information. 'The Relief Fund for Romania was formed by prominent Romanian exiles in December 1989 and was instrumental in publicising the appalling plight of children in institutions and others in need in Romania. We then played a significant part in coordinating the aid response, transporting huge quantities of emergency supplies and networking independent aid efforts.'

The charity provides financial and material aid, promotes awareness and training campaigns e.g. training for nurses/awareness of tuberculosis, and funds the training of Romanian professionals.

It funds specific projects, which it effectively manages, including:

- mobile play and arts therapy for orphans
- street children's refuge and day centre
- mobile primary healthcare programme
- national nurse training support
- arts and music therapy for people who are institutionalised
- care of the elderly infirm at home
- national TB treatment and training programme
- rehabilitation programme for orphans
- health promotion and education
- standards of nursing care pilot project
- core funding for emerging Romanian charities
- medical staff travel and training sponsorship.'

The charity also directly funds other aid groups, e.g. it pays for an administrative assistant and office materials for Romanian Hospital Association, and funds a UK charity, Music as Therapy, which provides rehabilitation and therapy for institutionally damaged children by direct services and also through Romanian carers and professionals.

Volunteers/jobseekers: Opportunities to volunteer in the UK, in charity shops and with fundraising events.

The Resource Alliance
(formerly The International Fundraising Group)
Facilitating international fundraising for the voluntary sector
Geographical focus: Worldwide

International Support Office,
295 Kennington Road, London SE11 4QE
Tel: 020 7587 0287; **Fax:** 020 7582 4335
e-mail: contact@resource-alliance.org.uk
Website: www.resource-alliance.org
Correspondent: Stewart Crocker, Chief Executive

Expenditure: £4.2 million (1997)
Staffing: 11 full-time staff, all UK-based.
Website information: Details on its workshops, conferences and other training materials; a description of its worldwide network; a website questionnaire.
General: 'The Resource Alliance seeks to enable people working in the voluntary sector throughout the world to mobilise support for their causes by sharing and developing their skills, knowledge and experience.

'This is pursued through the following strategic aims:
- to develop a worldwide network that is both inclusive and diverse, and that encourages people involved in raising income, resources and other support for voluntary organisations to share and develop their skills, knowledge and experience
- to enable people in the voluntary sector to be more effective, by providing and increasing access to training and education in fundraising and other resource strategies
- to be an effective advocate for the growth of philanthropy and other means to enable voluntary sector organisations to achieve greater financial sustainability.'

The current programme (as in 2000) includes:
- international conferences and workshops
- fundraising workshops run in every region of the developing world
- four training courses
- *The Worldwide Fundraiser's Handbook*, published by the Directory of Social Change in association with the former IFRG.

Volunteers/jobseekers: Opportunities for salaried work are advertised in national, and depending on the position, international press.

RFI for Community Mental Health
Providing mental health and drug rehabilitation services
Geographical focus: Australia, Austria, Barbados, Costa Rica, Grenada, Hong Kong, India, Israel, Jamaica, Macau, Malta, Nepal, New Zealand, Peru, Sri Lanka, Zimbabwe

Europoint, 5–11 Lavington Street,
London SE1 0NZ
Tel: 020 7945 6187; **Fax:** 020 7945 6190
e-mail: rfi.uk@virgin.net
Website: http://business.virgin.net/rfi.uk
Correspondent: Archie McCarron, Chief Executive Officer

Expenditure: £161,000 (1999/2000)
Staffing: 5 full-time salaried staff, 1 part-time salaried staff member.
Website information: Brief details of its work.
General: The charity provided the following information, 'RFI (Richmond Fellowship International) for Community Mental Health has a worldwide commitment to the rehabilitation and social integration of those who suffer by reason of mental ill-health or addiction

and, in the case of children, deprivation and emotional, physical and sexual abuse. All Richmond Fellowship organisations exist to build a better life for people suffering from mental health or addiction problems, particularly through the provision of services involving local communities

'Founded in 1981, it works mainly in developing countries. It is the largest international voluntary organisation working in the field of mental health. There are now over 20 national affiliates of RFI, implementing mental health programmes, using the fellowship's models. In addition to halfway houses and day centres aimed at psychiatric rehabilitation, there are projects for drug addicts, adolescents and street children. RFI also advocates the rights of the mentally ill.'

Membership: Become a Friend of RFI for a year by donating £5 or more.

Rokpa Trust (Rokpa UK Overseas Projects)

Funding education, health and other development projects

Geographical focus: India, Nepal, Tibet

Rokpa UK Overseas Projects, Samye Ling, Eskdalemuir, Langholm, Dumfriesshire DG13 0QL
Tel: 013873 73232; **Fax:** 013873 73223
e-mail: charity@RokpaUK.org
Website: www.RokpaUK.org
Correspondent: Victoria Long

Expenditure: £267,000 for overseas projects (1999)

Staffing: Volunteers at the office and fundraising groups around the country.

Website information: Information about its projects in Tibet and Nepal; a link to Rokpa International's website;

how to make a donation; opportunities for volunteers.

General: Rokpa Trust runs a number of Tibetan Buddhist centres in the UK, operates three therapy centres, and runs projects to feed homeless and poor people in London, Glasgow and Birmingham. Rokpa UK overseas projects programme is relevant to this guide and raises money on behalf of Rokpa International, a charity based in Switzerland. Its main focus is on financially supporting projects supplying education, health and other developmental assistance in remote rural areas of Tibetan parts of China, the provision of emergency and long-term help to poor people in Nepal and Tibetan refugees in India. It also supports the education in the UK of Tibetans who will then return to benefit their homeland.

Volunteers/jobseekers: Volunteers are needed in the UK to help with fundraising. Other opportunities for volunteering are advertised on the website. Previous opportunities have included placements in Tibet for TEFL teachers.

Romanian Challenge Appeal

Funding a charity which helps run a care home and halfway house

Geographical focus: Romania

Unit B5, The Garrison Centre, Garrison Lane, Bordesley, Birmingham B9 4BS
Tel: 0121 766 8582; **Fax:** 0121 766 8513
Website: www.romanianchallenge-uk.org.uk
Correspondent: Dawne Haye

Expenditure: About £350,000 (1999/2000)

Staffing: UK: 2 paid staff and about 120 volunteers; Romania: 3 paid staff, and others are employed by the Romanian charity.

Website information: The website was being developed at the time of publication of this guide.

General: The Romanian Challenge Appeal funds a Romanian charity called O Noua Viata ('Our New Life' in English). This charity runs a care home and halfway house for young people and children. In 2000 it was building two new homes.

O Noua Viata aims to:

- find employment for young people on leaving education
- provide training for children in skills which benefit the community
- employ local carers
- employ trainers from the UK to help educate young Romanian workers in fields of care and life skills
- provide teaching and therapy
- develop a drop-in programme
- increase its medical work
- develop the adoption programme, whereby Romanian children are adopted by people from the United States.

Volunteers/jobseekers: There are opportunities for volunteers from the UK and other countries to work in Romania for a minimum of three weeks. The charity especially looks for professional people to help in its homes, such as physiotherapists, psychologists, people with building trade skills, nurses, doctors and teachers.

The Russian European Trust

Reforming welfare provision and social services

Geographical focus: Russia and the republics of the former Soviet Union

5 Tavistock Place, London WC1H 9SN
Tel: 020 7813 0244
e-mail: ruseurotrust@dial.pipex.com
Website: www.ruseurotrust.co.uk
Correspondent: Mark Hughes, Administrator

Expenditure: £190,000 (1999/2000)

Staffing: 2 Staff in London, 5 in Moscow.

Website information: Information about past projects; how to make donations; links to previous sites.

General: The aim of the trust is to assist with the reform of welfare provision and social services through the exchange of information and experience, and by providing advice and help for the training of social workers, departmental personnel and the management of social services.

The principal aims of the trust are set out at more length on its website and are to:

- provide technical advice and assistance on practice, training, structure and management of social services;
- help with training or re-training of civil servants and social workers and to help create training courses at all levels;
- provide examples of different models of social services delivery;
- help promotion of working partnerships between the state and ngos;
- assist with translation and adaptation of social work teaching materials;
- provide a variety of forums for the exchange of ideas between Russia and the Republics and Western Europe, and to help prevent the duplication of activity;

- raise awareness in the UK of social welfare problems facing Russia and the former Soviet Union, and of the reform programmes currently underway.

Examples of past projects include:

Russian, Social Democracy
The aims of this project were to assist the Ministry of Labour and Social Development in Russia with possible amendments to social services legislation, and to raise awareness amongst members of the Russian parliament to the importance of having realistic legislation.

Occupational Therapy, Russia and Kyrgystan
This project's aims included training up to 40 people from Kyrgyzstan in occupational therapy and to set up a centre for training in the profession.

Support for the development of services
– for older people in Kemerovo and Kemerovo Oblast.

Volunteers/jobseekers: Volunteers are not used.

Ryder-Cheshire

Providing children's homes, combatting TB, disability, rehabilitation, health
Geographical focus: Australia, East Timor, India, Nepal, New Zealand, Papua New Guinea

82 Queens Road, Brighton BN1 3XE
Tel: 01273 821056; **Fax:** 01273 821059
e-mail: info@rydercheshire.org.uk
Website: www.rydercheshire.org.uk
Correspondent: The Director

Expenditure: £520,000 (1999/2000)
Staffing: 20 in the UK, 230 overseas.
Website information: Information about overseas projects by country; opportunities for staff and volunteers in the UK.

General: Ryder-Cheshire was founded by Sue Ryder and Leonard Cheshire at the time of their marriage in 1959 and since then it has developed disability and health projects in developing countries. From 2000 it will concentrate on developing initiatives to combat TB while continuing to support existing services overseas. There are Ryder-Cheshire organisations in Australia and New Zealand which support work in developing countries as well as running domestic health and disability services. Ryder-Cheshire also works in the UK where it runs the Ryder-Cheshire Volunteers schemes.

Volunteers/jobseekers: Volunteering opportunities exist for help within the charity's work in the UK and in North India. Please contact the charity for further information.

Saferworld

Working towards the prevention of armed conflicts, through raising awareness and developing effective approaches
Geographical focus: Worldwide

46 Grosvenor Gardens,
London SW1W 0EB
Tel: 020 7881 9290; **Fax:** 020 7881 9291
e-mail: general@saferworld.demon.co.uk
Website: www.saferworld.co.uk
Correspondent: Jane Brading, Administration Assistant

Expenditure: £850,000 (1999/2000)
Staffing: 14 full and part-time paid staff; 5 volunteers and interns; 1 part-time paid adviser.

Website information: Information on projects; publications; press releases and articles; how to become a member online; recent saferworld activities; useful links;

job vacancies, including information about internship.

General: The charity says 'Saferworld is an independent foreign affairs think-tank working to identify, develop and publicise more effective approaches to tackling and preventing armed conflicts'.

Part of its initial mission was 'to press for closer policy dialogue between ngos and governments on ways to tackle new post-Cold War security challenges'. It says that 'ministers and civil servants are increasingly turning to Saferworld for fresh thinking and analysis'.

In its 1999/2000 annual report, the charity described its two other programmes as follows.

Arms Programme

Saferworld works to:
- strengthen the EU Code of Conduct on Arms Exports;
- develop effective controls on arms transfers from Central and Eastern Europe;
- promote coordinated restraint with other suppliers, particularly the US and Canada;
- introduce controls on illicit arms trafficking at national, regional and global level;
- develop and implement new regional action programmes to tackle the proliferation of small arms in southern and eastern Africa, south-east Europe and the Caucasus;
- build networks of ngos in Europe and internationally to push for tougher controls.

Conflict Prevention Programme

Saferworld works to:
- research how the EU can put peace-building initiatives at the heart of its development policy and help officials to analyse conflict risks;
- assess the impact of EU policies on the risks of violence in the Horn of Africa and make practical proposals as to how these policies could be better targeted;
- produce reports on how the EU can help manage crises and resolve current conflicts;
- work to encourage the reform of the security sector in developing countries.

Membership: £18 a year (waged), £10 a year (unwaged) and £20 (overseas); members receive the newsletter *UPDATE* three times a year.

Publications: Newsletter *UPDATE* and reports and articles on arms and security and conflict prevention are produced.

Volunteers/jobseekers: Internships are available in the research and communications department. Details are available on the website.

St Francis Leprosy Guild

Treating and helping rehabilitate people who have leprosy

Geographical focus: Angola, Bangladesh, Bolivia, Brazil, Cameroon, Democratic Republic of Congo, Egypt, Ethiopia, Ghana, India, Indonesia, Jamaica, Kenya, Madagascar, Morocco, Myanmar, Nigeria, Pakistan, Philippines, South Korea, Sri Lanka, Sudan, Tanzania, Thailand, Uganda, Vietnam, Zambia, Zimbabwe

73 St Charles Square, London W10 6EJ
Tel: 020 8969 1345; ; **Fax:** 020 8969 3272
e-mail: enquiries@StFrancisLeprosy.org
Website: www.StFrancisLeprosy.org
Correspondent: The General Secretary

Expenditure: £374,000 (2000)

Staffing: One part-time paid general secretary from 27 March 2001, plus three part-time volunteer secretaries.

General: St Francis Leprosy Guild works to cure people who have leprosy, rehabilitate into the commuinity those who have been cured, and give residential support to those whose physical disability requires it.

Most of the charity's expenditure is spent in funding to hospitals, missions and other places where treatment and help is given to people who have leprosy. Most of the institutions are staffed by Catholic missionaries, usually Sisters. The charity also contributes towards the cost of specific items of the work, such as vehicles and water pumps.

Volunteers/jobseekers: The charity occasionally helps medical students to travel to leprosy stations in developing countries, for short periods in furtherance of their studies. In 2000 the charity spent £1,824 in support to such students.

Save the Children (UK)
Child-focused campaigning, development and relief work
Geographical focus: *Worldwide*

17 Grove Lane, London SE5 8RD
Tel: 020 7703 5400; **Fax:** 020 7703 2278
e-mail: enquiries@scfuk.org.uk
Website: www.savethechildren.org.uk
Correspondent: The Public Enquiry Unit

Expenditure: £85 million (1998/99)
Staffing: UK, including HQ about 872 staff; overseas local staff, about 2,120.

Website information: How to get involved – who to contact, how to help in a shop and with local fundraising, local events information and job vacancies according to geographical regions; links to related sites; details of projects and campaigns; information for schools; factsheets of latest news; make donations (one-off or regular); gift catalogue; subscribe to the newsletter by e-mail; and list of other publications.

General: The charity provided the following information: 'Save the Children is the UK's leading international children's charity, working to create a better future for children. In a world where children are denied basic human rights, we champion the right of all children to childhood. We put the reality of children's lives at the heart of everything we do. Together with children, we can help build a better world for present and future generations.

'Save the Children works in the UK and across the world. Emergency relief runs alongside long-term development and prevention work to help children, their families and communities to be self-sufficient. We learn from the reality of children's lives and campaign for solutions to the problems they face. We gain expertise through our projects round the world and use that knowledge to educate and advise others.

'All our work is underpinned by our commitment to making a reality of the rights of children, first spelt out by our founders and now enshrined in the UN Convention on the Rights of the Child.'

Publications: Save the Children produces a range of publications, both free and priced. These include a quarterly magazine, a youth magazine and educational materials. Catalogues advertising books include: *Children's Rights, Children and Violence, Child Labour, Resources for Working with under 8s,* and *Resources for Working with Young People Aged 8–18.*

Details are available on request from the Public Enquiry Unit at Save the Children, tel: 020 7716 2268; e-mail: publications@scfuk.org.uk.

Volunteers/jobseekers: Positions are advertised on the website and in the national press.

Scottish Catholic International Aid Fund (SCIAF)

Development, relief and campaigning generally, representing the Catholic Church in Scotland

Geographical focus: Brazil, Cambodia, Colombia, El Salvador, Eritrea, Ethiopia, Guatemala, Honduras, India, Kenya, Laos, Myanmar, Nicaragua, Philippines, Rwanda, South Africa, Sudan, Tanzania, Uganda, Vietnam

19 Park Circus, Glasgow G3 6BE
Tel: 0141 354 5555; **Fax:** 0141 354 5533
e-mail: sciaf@sciaf.org.uk
Website: www.sciaf.org.uk
Correspondent: Paul Chitnis, Chief Executive

Expenditure: £2.6 million (1999/2000)

Staffing: 20 staff, all based at the Glasgow headquarters.

Website information: Latest updates; news and campaigns.

General: The charity provided the following information, 'SCIAF is the official aid and development agency of the Catholic Church in Scotland. It supports development projects in its priority third world countries and emergency, relief and rehabilitation projects anywhere overseas and also has an established development education programme in Scotland. It is a member of the Catholic Development Network CIDSE and acts as a distinct Scottish development voice on many national consortia.

SCIAF supports projects which aim for long-term change which enable poor people to gain control of their lives. The priority sectors are:

- active citizenship (human rights, strengthening civil society)
- security sustainable livelihoods
- HIV/AIDS.

Membership: SCIAF supporters receive regular mailings about the organisation's work.

Volunteers/jobseekers: Opportunities for salaried posts are advertised in the national press. There are opportunities for volunteers within the Glasgow office.

Scottish Education and Action for Development (SEAD)

Development education in Scotland, supporting projects overseas

Geographical focus: Dominican Republic

167–171 Dundee Street, Edinburgh EH11 1BY
Tel: 0131 477 2780; **Fax:** 0131 477 2781
e-mail: sead@gn.apc.org
Correspondent: Liz Ferguson, Information and Membership Development Officer

Expenditure: £314,000 (1999/2000)

Staffing: 3 full-time; 2 part-time; 1 volunteer: all in the UK.

General: SEAD works with communities in Scotland to promote knowledge and understanding of global causes and effects of poverty. It raises awareness of issues which concern people in Scotland and draws parallels with the experience of people in developing countries.

Membership: £15 a year (£4 unwaged).

Publications: Conference Report *Stealing from the Poor: People, Poverty and Globalisation* (2000), free. *Sead News* is a free quarterly newsletter.

Volunteers/jobseekers: No opportunities for volunteers overseas. There are opportunities for volunteers in Scotland.

Send a Cow (& StockAid)

Promoting the sustainable development of livestock farming systems and local self-reliant groups
Geographical focus: Ethiopia, Kenya, Sudan, Uganda

Unit 4, Priston Mill, Priston,
Bath BA2 9EQ
Tel: 01225 447041; **Fax:** 01225 317627
e-mail: sacuk@sendacow-stockaid.org.uk
Website: www.sendacow-stockaid.org.uk
Correspondent: Pat Simmons, Communications

Expenditure: £362,000 (1998/99)
Staffing: 2 full-time and 5 part-time staff in the UK; 9 staff overseas.

Website information: News; *Lifeline* newsletter; how to get involved as ambassadors in the UK; how to make a donation.

General: The charity's mission statement is 'to work with the people of East Africa to overcome poverty and malnutrition through the sustainable development of livestock farming systems and local self-reliant groups'.

The charity was set up in 1988 when a Ugandan bishop appealed to British farmers for help. Most of Uganda's quality dairy cows had died, while Britain had milk surpluses. Between 1988 and 1996, over 300 cows were flown from the UK. All animals are now bought within Africa. Most are given to women, particularly widows, single mothers and those bringing up dependants orphaned by AIDS. The cows provide milk for the family and for sale, and manure which greatly improves crop yield. In 1998, the charity launched StockAid, which supplies small stock such as goats, to people who have suffered most from war, drought, cattle raiding and AIDS. All recipients guarantee to pass on their animal's first female offspring to another poor household, who do the same in their turn.

In 1998/99, over 400 households were provided with cows, goats or pigs. Other work included: running the Village Bull Scheme and supporting farmers' groups in Ethiopia, Kenya and Sudan.

Publications: *Lifeline*, a quarterly newsletter, which is sent to supporters and is also available on the website.

Volunteers/jobseekers: The charity does not send volunteers overseas, but welcomes enquiries for people interested in becoming a local ambassador in the UK – giving talks to schools, churches etc.

Sense International

Supporting the development of services for deafblind people worldwide
Geographical focus: Asia, Latin America, Central and Eastern Europe, East Africa

11–13 Clifton Terrace, Finsbury Park,
London N4 3SR
Tel: 020 7272 7774/020 7281 4373;
Fax: 020 7272 6012
e-mail: si@sense.org.uk
Website: www.sense.org.uk/international
Correspondent: The Director

Expenditure: About £450,000 (budget 2000/01)
Staffing: 14 full-time staff (5 in the UK, 5 in India, 2 in Romania, 1 in Latin America, 1 in East Africa), 3 volunteers.

Website information: Breakdown of its projects by country and information about how to get involved in fundraising events.

General: Sense International supports the development of services throughout the world for deafblind people (individuals who are both deaf and blind).

It has offices in the UK, India and Romania. It does not provide its own services, but works with local partner organisations and supports their ability to develop sustainable deafblind programmes. It offers its partners technical support, training and expertise, helping them to develop their capacity to run deafblind programmes independently. Sense International concentrates on building sustainable infrastructures in the countries where it works and this involves in-country support, training and investment in areas such as domestic income generation, communications and public education. It was voted UK International ngo of the Year in 2000.

In India, Sense International has contributed to an increase from 1 to 15 deafblind programmes in the last three years (as at December 2000). The government has officially recognised deafblindness as a unique disability and Asia's first teacher training programme in this field started in 2000.

Sense International began work in Romania in 1998 and says: 'Progress has since been phenomenal. The Romanian government now recognises deafblindness and in September 1999 opened two new deafblind units in partnership with Sense International. A new Parents Association has been established and our Patron, Princess Anne, recently visited to meet parents and children. However, more work is needed as hundreds of deafblind children still live in orphanages and hospitals'.

Sense International supports other partner organisations throughout Latin America and Central and Eastern Europe and in 2000 started an East Africa programme.

Sense International runs a professional development programme for individuals working in the deafblind field and has been the transnational coordinator for a number of European Union funded programmes, mainly concerned with employment issues for deafblind people.

The organisation also supports the work of two international deafblind networks: Deafblind International and the European Deafblind Network. Please e-mail: si@sense.org.uk or visit the websites: www.deafblindinternational.org and www.edben.org for further information.

Membership: Sense International is not a membership organisation, but it does produce a free regular newsletter which is available on request from the e-mail address above.

Publications: *Sense International News* is the charity's newsletter.

Volunteers/jobseekers: Sense International is always keen to involve volunteers in its work and is happy to consider applications for work in the UK and overseas. Please e-mail the address above for futher information.

Sight Savers International (Royal Commonwealth Society for the Blind)

Developing sustainable, accessible, affordable eye care services

Geographical focus: Bangladesh, Belize, Cameroon, Gambia, Ghana, Guinea, Guyana, Haiti, India, Jamaica, Kenya, Liberia, Malawi, Mali, Nigeria, Pakistan, Sierra Leone, Sri Lanka, Tanzania, Togo, Uganda, Zambia, Zimbabwe

Grosvenor Hall, Bolnore Road, Haywards Heath, West Sussex RH16 4BX
Tel: 01444 446600; **Fax:** 01444 446688
e-mail: information@sightsaversint.org.uk
Website: www.sightsavers.org.uk
Correspondent: Maddy Flynn, Information Centre

Expenditure: £12 million (1999)

Staffing: 78 UK-based staff, 10 overseas.

Website information: News and events; breakdown of work by country and within country by project; case studies of people who have been helped; information about blindness; how to help e.g. with donations and fundraising; regional contact people; gallery.

General: 'Sight Savers' vision is of a world in which no one is needlessly blind and where everyone who is irreversibly blind or severely visually impaired has the resources they deserve to lead a life of dignity.'

The charity states it 'works with partner organisations in poor and the least served communities to help establish and support permanent activities that prevent and cure blindness, restore sight and provide services to blind people.

'Sight Savers acts as a catalyst, offering expertise as well as some financial backing. Its projects are time limited and plan for the phased withdrawal of Sight Savers' support as the partner's capacity grows.'

In Ghana, for instance, its early work included surveys into the extent and transmission of river blindness, and the charity also introduced rehabilitation for incurably blind people. In 2000, there were projects to help promote eye care, prevent river blindness, expand educational opportunities for blind children and develop community-based rehabiliation programmes.

Membership: Donors receive leaflets and *Sight Savers News*.

Publications: *Sight Savers News*, a thrice yearly newsletter.

SIL UK

Language development, focus on literacy and translation in minority languages

Geographical focus: Worldwide

Horsleys Green, High Wycombe,
Buckinghamshire HP14 3XL
Tel: 01494 682206; **Fax:** 01494 682220
e-mail: ip_uk@sil.org
Website: www.sil.org.uk
Correspondent: Ian Mowatt, International Programmes Department

Expenditure: £753,000 (1998/99)

Staffing: About 420 people

Website information: Information about literacy; training courses in the UK; how to get involved.

General: SIL UK works to promote the written development of minority languages. SIL literacy workers, trained in England and elsewhere, work in over 70 countries. The SIL worker is 'a facilitator who empowers local communities to develop a literate environment for themselves'. This involves training teachers, developing books for teachers to use and an alphabet and writing system with which to write them. Support must be established from community leaders and government. The literacy work depends on a team approach and close working relationships with local people.

Membership: SIL UK does not maintain a mailing list.

Volunteers/jobseekers: Opportunities for getting involved in literacy work, long-term and short-term, are available for people from all types of fields. Initial training for literacy work is given by SIL, with further in-service training in the field and during subsequent periods of leave.

All volunteers are committed Christians. Recruitment is via Wycliffe Bible Translators (see entry on page 241).

SIM International (UK)

Christian outreach including relief and development work, healthcare

Geographical focus: Angola, Bangladesh, Benin, Bolivia, Botswana, Burkina Faso, Central African Republic, Chile, China, Côte d'Ivoire, Ecuador, Ethiopia, Eritrea, Gabon, Ghana, Guinea, India, Kenya, Liberia, Madagascar, Malawi, Mauritius, Mongolia, Mozambique, Namibia, Nepal, Niger, Nigeria, Pakistan, Paraguay, Peru, Philippines, Réunion, Senegal, South Africa, Sudan, Swaziland, Tanzania, Togo, Uruguay, Zambia, Zimbabwe

Wetheringsett Manor, Wetheringsett, Stowmarket, Suffolk IP14 5QX
Tel: 01449 766464; **Fax:** 01449 767148
e-mail: info@sim.co.uk
Website: www.sim.co.uk
Correspondent: Brian N Freed

Expenditure: £4.1 million (1998/99)

Staffing: 34 members of staff in the UK, including 7 part-time employees; 16 UK staff working overseas; over 1,800 other missionaries overseas.

Website information: How to get involved; links to other SIM sites; a brief summary about each country; news; list of resources e.g. videos, free literature, magazine; children's books and videos.

General: This charity primarily works to promote the Christian faith. Its outreach includes relief, development and healthcare work. It describes these areas of its work in its literature as follows: 'For SIM, development means meeting the needs of suffering or disadvantaged people in the name of Christ. In times of emergency, SIM missionaries are at the forefront of relief efforts with food, shelter and emergency aid.

'And when the crisis has passed, SIM missionaries provide agriculture, livestock, as well as small business training and assistance for communities working toward long-term stability.

'SIM is involved with several general hospitals and clinics. As primary care and preventative measures become more critical, doctors, nurses, and other healthcare professionals train village workers in community-based healthcare – including awareness and prevention of HIV/AIDS.'

Membership: Donors and any person interested in the work who have requested information, receive the quarterly magazine, free of charge.

Publications: Quarterly magazine *Mission Together.*

Volunteers/jobseekers: Pace Teams are short-term teams for Christians to get involved in outreach in developing countries. Teams last for up to six weeks and costs between £900 and £1,500. Other short-term programmes run for between 2 and 24 weeks.

There are also opportunities to become a long-term volunteer overseas. Contact the charity for more information.

Skillshare Africa

Sharing and developing skills, assisting organisational development and growth

Geographical focus: Botswana, Lesotho, Mozambique, Namibia, South Africa, Swaziland

126 New Walk, Leicester LE1 7JA
Tel: 0116 254 1862; **Fax:** 0116 254 2614
e-mail: info@skillshare.org
Website: www.skillshare.org
Correspondent: Rebecca Watson, Public Relations Officer

Expenditure: £2 million (1999/2000)

Staffing: 41 salaried staff; 16 in the UK and 25 in southern Africa (all local staff).

Website information: Information on overseas recruitment opportunities including online application forms; news.

General: Skillshare Africa was formed in 1990 and formerly part of International Voluntary Service (see page 150). It works for sustainable development by sharing and developing skills, assisting organisational effectiveness and supporting organisational growth. It provided the following information: 'We are a needs driven charity and work in partnership with the people and communities of southern Africa (our partnership organisations). We recruit development workers to share their skills in the region and also locate financial support from other bodies for organisations wishing to raise project funding.

'Our main areas of work are education and vocational training, healthcare, engineering and planning, income generation, agriculture and environmental conservation, HIV and AIDS and empowering disadvantaged groups.

'We also work with partner organisations to improve their organisational effectiveness and efficiency using a quality model.'

Publications: Newsletter, published every four months; individual country plans for each of the countries in which it works.

Volunteers/jobseekers: Salaried posts in the UK are advertised in the national press, trade press and on its website.

Development workers are recruited to share their skills in southern Africa, usually for around two years. The range of skills being looked for is varied, but whatever your field of work, you need to have a combination of relevant professional qualification and relevant work experience. Applications from couples where both have relevant skills are welcomed. Some placements will accept accompanying partners, and in certain cases, accompanying children are accepted. Applicants receive pre-departure training. You will be paid either a local salary or an allowance. A full information pack and application form is available from the correspondent, or the website.

There are also volunteering opportunities in the UK through its supporters' association, Friends of Skillshare Africa.

SOS Children's Villages UK

Promoting and supporting, within the UK, the worldwide work of SOS Children's Villages in caring for destitute children and young people

Geographical focus: Worldwide

32a Bridge Street, Cambridge CB2 1UJ
Tel: 01223 356589; **Fax:** 01223 322613
e-mail: info@sos-uk.org.uk
Website: www.sos-uk.org.uk
Correspondent: Daniel Fox, Chief Executive

Expenditure: £790,000 (1999)

Staffing: 4 full-time, 2 part-time staff.

Website information: An interactive map showing the work that the charity supports; ways in which the donor can contribute including how to sponsor an SOS Children's Village (£20 a month); FAQ.

General: The charity provided the following information. 'SOS Children's Villages UK was established in 1968 to support the worldwide work of SOS Children's Villages in caring for children and young people who have no one else to care for them, regardless of race, creed, gender or politics. The first SOS Children's Village was opened in Austria in 1949. Today [as at July 2000] there are 131 autonomous SOS Children's Villages national associations, running over 400

SOS Children's Villages and more than 1,100 associated projects, caring for over 200,000 children. SOS Children's Villages UK is not directly involved in project management.

'The primary focus of all SOS Children's Village projects is to provide family-sized homes for orphaned and abandoned children caring for them until they achieve independence. This includes giving them the education and training they need. Associated projects include kindergartens, schools, vocational training centres and medical and social centres. These associated projects also support the local communities.'

Membership: Individuals and groups are able to sponsor a specific village, project or child and will receive a progress report from 'their' village at least once a year. In addition, all supporters receive the quarterly newsletter *SOS Children's World*. See the website for further information.

Publications: *SOS Children's World* is published quarterly and is available free.

Trading: Christmas cards are sold in support of the charity's work.

Volunteers/jobseekers: The charity's policy is to employ local personnel. There are exceptions to meet a particular skill shortage. Decisions relating to human resources are taken by the SOS Children's Village association in the country in which the charity's facilities are located.

SOS Sahel International (UK)

Supporting conservation and management of natural resources and food security projects in the rural areas of the Sahel region

Geographical focus: Eritrea, Ethiopia, Kenya, Mali, Niger, Sudan

1 Tolpuddle Street, London N1 0XT
Tel: 020 7837 9129; **Fax:** 020 7837 0856
e-mail: mail@sahel.org.uk
Correspondent: Duncan Fulton, Director

Expenditure: £2.1 million (1999/2000)

Staffing: 9 full-time, salaried staff in the UK, about 200 full-time salaried overseas staff, of whom 8 are expatriates.

General: The charity provided the following information, 'SOS Sahel International (UK) has been working with village and nomadic communities across the Sahel region since 1985, combining local knowledge with technical expertise to conserve woodlands, manage natural resources, combat poverty and increase self-reliance.

'Changing national policies on land tenure and the natural environment over the last decade have created a favourable climate for increased local participation and ownership. The Natural Forest Management Project in Sudan and the Takieta Joint Forest Management Project in Niger have piloted strategies for involving all forest-users in drawing up management plans for local woodlands.

'SOS Sahel also has a research programme which has looked at issues raised by its field experience, such as the role of women heads of household in environmental managment. A current programme is exploring ways of resolving conflict over resources between farmers and pastoralists.'

Membership: Supporters receive a copy of the annual review.

Publications: Occasional publications (list available from the London office) include technical manuals and outputs from research programmes.

Volunteers/jobseekers: None overseas. There are opportunities in the London office, mainly for administrative tasks. Contact the correspondent for further information.

Spurgeon's Child Care

Promoting childcare and family support services.

Geographical focus: *Brazil, Latvia, Mexico, Moldova, Romania, Uganda, Ukraine*

74 Wellingborough Road, Rushden, Northamptonshire NN10 9TY
Tel: 01933 412412; **Fax:** 01933 412010
e-mail: scc@spurgeons.org or mwillis@spurgeons.org
Website: www.spurgeonschildcare.org
Correspondent: Marilyn Willis, Public Relations Manager

Expenditure: £3 million (1999/2000)

Staffing: 350 paid staff; 400 volunteers.

Website information: Latest news; information on its work in different countries; how to sponsor a child and a sponsorship form.

General: This charity provides childcare facilities and family support. The charity's aim is to help 'children and young people to take their place in a very different society from their parents'. It does this in Romania, for example, by offering support to parents to maintain children in the family and has developed 13 centres. It employs Romanian staff only. Each centre offers community-based services including education, play, family support, counselling, healthcare, after school and practical assistance. It works in partnership with Romanian churches and is supported by UK churches.

The charity has set up similar family centres for education and support in most of the other countries in which it operates and has also helped with building projects, holiday clubs, school work and through the provision of playground equipment.

Membership: No membership. Child sponsorship costs £15 a month, and sponsors receive an information pack. Regular donors receive three magazines a year.

Volunteers/jobseekers: There are opportunities for volunteering; contact the charity at the above address for details and availability at different locations.

Marie Stopes International (MSI)

Providing of reproductive healthcare and family planning services

Geographical focus: *Albania, Angola, Australia, Bangladesh, Bolivia, Cambodia, China, Ethiopia, Haiti, Honduras, India, Kenya, Madagascar, Malawi, Mongolia, Mozambique, Myanmar, Nepal, Pakistan, Peru, Philippines, Romania, Sierra Leone, South Africa, Sri Lanka, Tanzania, Uganda, UK, Vietnam, Yemen, Zimbabwe*

153–157 Cleveland Street, London W1 6QW
Tel: 020 7574 7400; **Fax:** 020 7574 7418
Website: www.mariestopes.org.uk
Correspondent: Dr Tim Black, Chief Executive

Expenditure: £30 million (1999)

Staffing: 548 staff, including UK, head office and overseas.

Website information: Breakdown of work by country including contact information; information about level of reproductive healthcare provision in each country; breakdown of its services; press centre; campaigns; resources for members of the public, schools and medical centres in the UK; links; recruitment information.

General: The charity's mission is to ensure the fundamental human right of all people to have children by choice, not chance. MSI runs a wide number of programmes and services in the UK and also works in 38 countries offering the full range of reproductive services. In developing countries it works through local partners which manage the work and tailor the services to meet the specific needs of each country. Services include contraception, male and female sterilisation, abortion, health screening, obstetric and primary healthcare.

In Vietnam, for example, MSI works with the Ministry of Health to provide family planning and reproductive health services through its network of Marie Stopes centres. It has established six centres and also delivers services through mobile health centres.

MSI press teams can facilitate journalists' enquiries on reproductive and population issues in a variety of ways: arrange field trips where journalists can visit MSI centres; arrange interviews with experts on reproductive health issues in the UK and overseas; and provide press releases, for instance, on contraception, abortion, female sterilisation and so on.

Publications: MSI Newsletter *First People*; *MSI Country factsheets* and *Reproductive Health for Refugees*, a series of factsheets.

Volunteers/jobseekers: No volunteers are required at head office.

Survival
Advocacy and campaigning for human rights on behalf of tribal peoples

Geographical focus: *Argentina, Australia, Bangladesh, Bolivia, Botswana, Brazil, Canada, Central African Republic, Chile, Colombia, Ecuador, Ethiopia, French Guinea, Guyana, India, Indonesia, Kenya, Malaysia, Mexico, Namibia, New Zealand, Panama, Paraguay, Peru, Philippines, Russia, Rwanda, Sudan, Tanzania, USA, Venezuela*

11–15 Emerald Street,
London WC1N 3QL
Tel: 020 7242 1441; **Fax:** 020 7242 1771
e-mail: info@survival-international.org
Website: www.survival-international.org
Correspondent: Stephen Corry

Expenditure: £729,000 (1999)

Staffing: 16 full-time staff and about 12 volunteers in the UK. About 5 full-time staff in other European countries. No staff in developing countries.

Website information: Online catalogue and shop online; bookshop online; campaigns - latest and archives; information about tribes; how to join online; events; links.

General: Survival supports tribal people, advocating their right to decide their own future and helping them protect their lives, lands and human rights. Its work includes:

Campaigning
Campaigns are directed at 'governments, companies, banks, extremist missionaries, guerrilla armies, museums, narrow-minded conservationists and anyone else who violates tribal peoples' rights'. It promotes mass letter-writing and carries out, for example, vigils at embassies and direct lobbying of people in power.
A mass letter writing campaign was conducted in 2000/01, protesting to the Brazilian government, a mining company and World Bank about their failure to demarcate the land of the Awá Indians in Brazil. As a consequence of this failure many Awá Indians were killed and their land invaded.

Educational programmes
Programmes aimed at people in the North 'set out to demolish the myth that tribal peoples are relics, destined to perish through "progress". We promote respect for their cultures and explain the contemporary relevance of their ways of

life. The charity publishes materials for schools and the general public about tribal peoples – who they are, how they live and the problems they face and educates the public about the dangers of tourism in tribal areas.

Survival also provides a platform for tribal representatives to talk directly to the companies which are invading their land. It disseminates information to tribal peoples, using community radio and literature, giving them the information they need to make their voices heard.

Funding

The charity aims to ensure that development organisations working with tribal peoples receive proper funding.

Membership: Regular donors of between £2 and £20 a month, receive free information about tribal peoples.

Publications: Survival stocks a wide selection of books of interest, this includes a selection of documents produced by Survival for its supporters, as well as educational and more specialised magazines and books. Many materials are available in French, Italian and Spanish as well as English. Titles include *Disinherited Indians in Brazil* (£5); *Maasai rights in Ngorongoro, Tanzania* (£10) and *Tourism and human rights* (£5). Back copies of Survival newsletters are available (£1.50). Children's publications are: *We, the world* – Survival's full-colour activity pack for 8-12 year olds (£1); *Tribes of the rainforest: don't just save the trees, save the people* (£0.50); *Rainforests for tomorrow* (£3). Background sheets cost £4 for a pack of five including a ring binder folder, a full set costs £9. They cover topics such as: Dayaks in Sarawak, Malaysia; Twa in Rwanda; and Jummas in Bangladesh.

Trading: The charity shop sells basket work, wood carvings, Inuit knives, tribal jewellery and a CD of tribal music.

Teaching Aids at Low Cost (TALC)

Suppling teaching aids and materials
Geographical focus: Worldwide

PO Box 49, St Albans,
Hertfordshire AL1 5TX
Tel: 01727 853569; **Fax:** 01727 846852
e-mail: info@talcuk.org
Website: www.talcuk.org
Correspondent: David Chandler, General Manager

Expenditure: £336,000 (1998/99)

Staffing: 11 staff and 11 volunteers.

Website information: Full list of materials available including information about delivery and postal costs; job advertisements.

General: The charity provided the following information. 'TALC was founded in 1965 by Professor David Morley when he was a lecturer at the Institute of Child Health in response to many requests from overseas students for teaching-aids and equipment to use in their own countries.

'Prof. Morley spent five years in a Nigerian village where, when he started, 373 out-of-every 1,000 babies born died before their first birthday.

'He found that he could cut this mortality rate by 80% by promoting breast feeding and introducing the concept of under five's clinic for healthy children as well as sick.

'After starting out in a small way by sending out transparencies, demand grew and the charity expanded into books and teaching aids. Since then TALC has continued to grow and has distributed over 10 million books, slides and accessories relating to health and community issues to thousands of health workers throughout the developing world.

'Use of this has enabled doctors and health workers to make the right diagnosis and provide the right treament resulting in the saving of many lives and the alleviation of an enormous amount of pain and suffering.

'Ill-health leads to poverty and poverty breeds ill-health. TALC provides self-help materials to disadvantaged areas to combat poverty and believes that low-cost teaching materials it provides will continue to raise standards of healthcare throughout the world.'

Publications: TALC has a small sales area within the Resource Centre at the Institute of Child Health, 30 Guildford Street, London WC1N 1EH, where books can be bought. This activity is managed by volunteers.

Volunteers/jobseekers: Salaried posts are advertised in the press only. Opportunities are available for volunteers (see information about the sales area under Publications). Contact the correspondent for further information.

Tearfund

Relief and development; Christian education and evangelism

Geographical focus: *Grants and gifts were given to organisations in the following countries/territories in 1999/2000: Afghanistan, Albania, Angola, Argentina, Armenia, Bangladesh, Bolivia, Botswana, Brazil, Bulgaria, Burkina Faso, Burundi, Cambodia, Chad, Chile, China, Colombia, Costa Rica, Democratic Republic of Congo, Dominican Republic, Egypt, El Salvador, Eritrea, Ethiopia, Georgia, Ghana, Guinea, Guinea Bissau, Haiti, Honduras, India, Iraq, Jordan, Kazakhstan, Kenya, Kosovo, Laos, Lebanon, Liberia, Macedonia, Malawi, Mali, Mauritania, Mexico, Morocco, Mozambique, Myanmar, Nepal, Nicaragua, Niger, Nigeria, Pakistan, Peru, Philippines, Russia, Rwanda, Senegal, Serbia, Sierra Leone, Somalia, South Africa, Sri Lanka, Sudan, Syria, Tajikistan, Tanzania, Thailand, Turkey, Turkmenistan, Uganda, Venezuela, Vietnam, Yemen, Zambia, Zimbabwe*

100 Church Road, Teddington, Middlesex TW11 8QE
Tel: 0845 355 8355
Website: www.tearfund.org
Correspondent: Graham Fairbairn

Expenditure: £34 million (1999/2000)
Staffing: 248 staff in the UK and 69 overseas.

Website information: News; current job vacancies in the UK and overseas; Tearcraft shop and opportunities to shop online; site for children and young people.

General: The charity's objectives are: 'to relieve poverty, suffering and distress and prevent disease and ill health among the peoples of the world; and to promote Christian education and evangelism'. It works to proclaim and demonstrate the Christian faith through relief and development work; and supporting partners in their work with the poor and vulnerable communities throughout the world.

In 1999/2000, it was involved with 566 projects worldwide, with 418 partners in 89 countries. Work included:

- disaster response operations in Liberia, Burundi, Sudan, Kosovo, Albania and Mozambique
- carrying out major church promotions, educating people about development issues and raising funds
- launching a new initiative which focuses on meeting the needs of children living in unstable and vulnerable situations

- ongoing development work.

Publications: *TearTimes*, a magazine is sent to supporters.

Trading: Tearfund sells fairly-traded crafts; for a catalogue please contact the charity.

Volunteers/jobseekers: Tearfund uses volunteers in a wide variety of ways in promoting its work, particularly through churches. There are also opportunities for volunteer involvement through the sale of craft goods traded by Tearcraft.

Vacancies are advertised on the charity's website and in the national press. Applicants have to hold Christian values in line with the charity.

Tibet Foundation

Promoting Tibetan Buddhism and culture; providing aid for education and healthcare and the relief of poverty amongst Tibetan communities

Geographical focus: *Tibetans and their culture in India, Mongolia, Nepal and Tibet*

1 St James's Market, London SW1Y 4SB
Tel: 020 7930 6001; **Fax:** 020 7930 6002
e-mail: enquiries@tibet-foundation.org
Website: www.tibet-foundation.org
Correspondent: Phuntsog Wangyal, Director

Expenditure: £402,000 (1999/2000)

Staffing: All working from London or home-based offices in the UK: 1 full-time unpaid director and 2 full-time and 4 part-time paid members of staff and 6 unpaid volunteers.

Website information: A breakdown of its activities and aid programmes; information about its cultural events; how to become a member and a downloadable application form; how to make a donation.

General: The charity aims to help people of Tibetan origin, promoting their religion and culture, improving standards of education and healthcare, providing facilities for training and job creation and relief of poverty among the Tibetan communities.

To further these aims the charity organises a variety of aid programmes and cultural events in the UK and Europe, and provides a trading outlet for Tibetan handicrafts and general information on Buddhism, the Dalai Lama, Tibet and its people and culture. It also arranges tours of Tibetan monks and artists performing traditional dance and music, and visits of Tibetan physicians giving consultation and lectures on Tibetan medicine.

Membership: The cost is £15 (£20 overseas). Members receive a quarterly newsletter, priority booking and members prices on events, special promotions from the shop and discount from various companies using the membership card.

Publications: The charity publishes a quarterly newsletter containing feature articles on Buddhism, the Dalai Lama and the Tibetan culture, reports and updates on its aid programmes and coming events.

Trading: A shop is run from the address above, which provides an outlet for Tibetan artisans to sell their works. For further information tel: 020 7930 6005 or e-mail: shop@tibet-foundation.org.

Volunteers/jobseekers: No positions for volunteers overseas at January 2001. Volunteers are welcome in the UK. For further information contact the manager at the address above.

Tibet Relief Fund of the UK

Supporting Tibetan refugees
Geographical focus: India, Tibet

Tower House, Unit 4, 139 Fonthill Road, London N4 3HF
Tel: 020 7272 1414; **Fax:** 020 7272 1410
e-mail: members@tibet-society.org.uk
Website: www.tibet-society.org.uk
Correspondent: Angela Lewis

Expenditure: £277,000 (1999/2000)

Website information: News and events; details of programmes; how to make a donation and how to sponsor a child's education.

General: The charity supports Tibetan refugees, mainly those in India, and seeks to create a sustainable life in exile in India and Nepal through improving their health, developing their education and providing suitable training and skills. It:

- supports Tibetan refugees efforts to build their communities in exile by working with them and supporting their own initiative to ensure access to vital services such as primary healthcare, clean water, housing and education;
- encourages development of skills, expertise and employment by providing access to vocational and specialised training leading to long-term employment;
- helps to maintain the Tibetan way of life by supporting the Tibetan people's effort to preserve, maintain and develop their unique culture, which is in danger of being eroded;
- sustains new postive initiatives for Tibetans remianing in Tibet by aiding where possible projects which support people who poor and disadvantaged and provide education and healthcare.

The charity's work in refugee settlements in India and Nepal has included:

- new medical equipment for two hospitals
- construction of a home for older people
- medical grants for people who are destitute
- construction of homes for people who are disadvantaged
- books for school libraries
- equipment for schools
- solar water heating for a home for older people
- school campus for new refugees
- vocational training schemes
- safe water systems
- income generation schemes.

Within Tibet, the charity is focusing on providing schools and medical care in areas where there are few or no facilities.

The charity's Sponsorship in Exile programme provides vital support for over 1,200 Tibetan children.

Volunteers/jobseekers: The charity does not have an overseas programme for volunteers. The London office has openings for volunteers who are computer literate and interested in gaining work experience in the charity sector.

Tools for Self Reliance (TFSR)

Working with tradesmen and women, to improve their working situation
Geographical focus: Ghana, Mozambique, Nicaragua, Sierra Leone, Tanzania, Uganda, Zimbabwe

Netley Marsh, Southampton SO40 7GY
Tel: 023 8086 9697; **Fax:** 023 8086 8544
e-mail: techsupport@tfsr.org
Website: www.tfsr.org
Correspondent: Bob White, Group Support Worker

Expenditure: £832,000 – including value of donated tools (1997/98)

Staffing: 7 staff located at Southampton who oversee the work; 50 people who act as tool collectors only; in addition there are about 70 groups in the UK who collect and refurbish tools.

Website information: Information about artisans and the tools which are needed; country focus; how the charity works; how you can help; links.

General: TFSR aims to help artisans in the third world by supplying them with refurbished hand tools. There are networks of voluntary groups throughout Britain who collect and refurbish tools. The charity works with indigenous organisations which are already assisting such artisans, in order to ensure that the tools which are sent are part of a bigger programme of training etc.

Other work includes: running an educational programme in Britain which reflects the concerns of its partners and examines the causes of poverty; and campaigning to persuade larger agencies and governments to recognise the vital role that hand tools play in development.

Membership: Free membership; the management committee is drawn from that membership. All members receive a regular newsletter and invitations to events and meetings.

Publications: *Forging Links* newsletter, published three times a year.

Volunteers/jobseekers: Volunteers work in the UK, in tool-refurbishing, assisting other volunteers, collecting tools from donors, helping at special events with publicity and awareness raising, and helping in the office at Netley Marsh.

Traidcraft Exchange

Working the charitable arm of Traidcraft, the UK's largest independent fair trade organisation

Geographical focus: Bangladesh, Caribbean, India, Kenya, Malawi, Pakistan, The Philippines, Tanzania, South Africa, UK, Zambia, Zimbabwe

Kingsway, Gateshead NE11 0NE
Tel: 0191 491 0591; **Fax:** 0191 482 2690
e-mail: comms@traidcraft.co.uk
Website: www.traidcraft.co.uk
Correspondent: Andy Redfern, International Director

Expenditure: £2 million (1999/2000)

Staffing: UK: 36 full-time and 9 part-time. Overseas: 1 full-time post in Africa.

Website information: Details of Traidcraft's work; annual review; social accounts; news; producer information; fact sheets; some online ordering.

General: The charity provided the following information. 'Founded in 1986, Traidcraft Exchange is a charitable company, limited by guarantee. It has three main areas of activity:

- capacity building through small and medium-sized enterprise development in the South;
- promoting an ethical approach to trade among the international business community;
- raising awareness among UK consumers of international trade issues and encouraging them to use their purchasing power in support of fair trade.

'Among the major achievements of Traidcraft Exchange in recent years has been the establishment of partner organisations, in South Africa, Zambia, Tanzania, India, Bangladesh and The Philippines, to provide effective in-country services to strengthen and support small and medium-sized enterprises, and promote market development. During 2000/2001 this network was to be extended with a £2.5 million partner development project in Malawi. A new three-year capacity-building project had also been initiated in Kenya. The strength of this overseas work was recognised with a Worldaware Business Award in 2000.

'In the UK, Traidcraft Exchange's pioneering work on social accounting earned one of the first UK Social Reporting Awards in 2000. It contributes to the government's Ethical Trading Initiative and has been part of the company law review body.'

It is not a grant-making charity.

Trading: Traidcraft Exchange works closely with its sister organisation Traidcraft plc, to maximise the fair trade benefit to producers. For a copy of the current Traidcraft catalogue telephone 0191 491 1001.

Volunteers/jobseekers: Vacancies for salaried positions are advertised in the national and sector press and the website.

Some opportunities for volunteering exist in the UK. Contact the correspondent for details.

TRANSAID Worldwide

Working to ensure transport and logistics have maximum positive impact on the effects of poverty and equality

Geographical focus: Worldwide including sub-Saharan Africa, India

East Side Offices, King's Cross Station, London N1 9AP
Tel: 020 7922 4939; **Fax:** 020 7922 9090
e-mail: info@transaid.org
Website: www.transaid.org
Correspondent: Sarah Nancolias

Expenditure: Over £200,000

Staffing: 4 paid staff; varying number of UK volunteers.

Website information: Examples of programmes and case studies; information on how the organisation works in practice - systems and procedures; volunteering opportunities; information on its members and supporters; how to become a corporate member; how to make a donation; links to other sites.

General: TRANSAID Worldwide is an independent UK based charity which draws support from the transport/ distribution sector. It is committed to improving the contribution of transport and logistics to the development of poorer countries. it seeks to achieve appropriate transport solutions that improve livelihoods by working in partnership to develop systems and build local capacity. The emphasis is on working with local people helping them to help themselves.

Membership: Corporate membership is open to companies and organisations, particularly in the transport and logistics sector. For further details please contact the organisation at the address above.

Publications: *Transport management manual; Newsletter; Hub & Spoke*, e-mail newsletter.

Volunteers/jobseekers: There are opportunities for industry secondees who have appropriate transport/logistics experience to take part in short term projects overseas. Priority is usually given to employees from member companies.

In the UK, there are often volunteer opportunities at the TRANSAID office (above). Please write or e-mail, stating interests and enclosing a cv if possible.

The Tropical Health and Education Trust (THET)

Training for healthcare, promotion of health through collaboration in teaching and research

Geographical focus: Ethiopia, Ghana, India, Malawi, Nigeria, Uganda

24 Eversholt Street, London NW1 1AD
Tel: 020 7611 8705; **Fax:** 020 7611 0683
e-mail: vpthet1@aol.com
Website: www.thet.org
Correspondent: Victoria Parry, Programme Manager

Expenditure: £300,000 (1999)

Staffing: 4 staff (full-time and part-time) in the UK, 2 overseas.

Website information: The website was still being developed as at March 2001, and contained brief news and a short description of the charity's work.

General: The charity provided the following information. 'THET was established in 1988 to assist those who are responsible for training healthcare workers in the poorer countries of the world to reach their goals, so that they are able to prepare those who are being trained in the most appropriate and effective way for the tasks they will be called on to do, relevant to the needs of the local community.

'THET responds to requests from hospitals/medical schools in Africa: the dean or director is asked to define the goals of the institution for training a range of health workers so that they are competent to deal with common local health problems. THET then identifies a group in the UK, with whom they may collaborate to enable the overseas partner to reach its goals in training and service.

'THET is, for example, assisting staff at the Gondar College of Medical Sciences, north west Ethiopia, to train rural health centre nurses in the care of patients with chronic diseases. The patients no longer need to walk for up to 100 miles for treatment in Gondar, but can receive treatment close to home.'

Volunteers/jobseekers: Vacancies for salaried posts are advertised in the national press. Qualified health professionals based at a UK hospital who can commit to long-term links with hospitals in Africa, are required in a voluntary capacity.

Twin

Enabling smallscale producers to sell their products to international markets

Geographical focus: Cameroon, Costa Rica, Dominican Republic, Ghana, Haiti, Mexico, Nicaragua, Peru, Tanzania, Uganda

Third Floor, 1 Curtain Road, London EC2A 3LT
Tel: 020 7375 1221; **Fax:** 020 7375 1337
e-mail: info@twin.org.uk
Website: www.twin.org.uk
Correspondent: The Clerk

Expenditure: £377,000 (1998/99)

Staffing: 13 employees.

Website information: This website was under development as at March 2001.

General: The charity says in its 1998/99 annual report: 'Twin seeks to use trade to positively redress the imbalance between North and South, to build better livelihoods for the poorest and the most marginalised in the trading chain and to promote development and longer term shifts in the political and economic environment'.

It undertakes development projects which enable smallscale producers to improve the quality of their products, process and package them, and sell them to international markets. They also enable them to retain more of the benefits of production and implement social and economic development programmes from the extra income earned. They produce a quarterly newsletter, *The Network*, and provide a free information service, both of which inform producers in the South about markets and technology in the North. Consultancy is given in trade and technology to international ngos. Areas of expertise include sources of finance, joint development projects and exporting. Fairer trading practices are promoted through conferences and seminars.

Twin assists the Small Farmers' Cooperative Society made up of coffee producers in Africa, and Central and South America, gives support to pecan and Brazil nut producers in Peru and works with cocoa producers in Ghana.

Publications: *The Network* is a quarterly bulletin sent to organisations and individuals worldwide. *The Commodity Directory* lists hundreds of tropical commodities, their uses and markets. *Coffee Bulletin* comes out fortnightly and is faxed to subscribers.

Trading: Twin trades in the UK under the auspices of Twin Trading with coffee, chocolate, nuts and other products.

Volunteers/jobseekers: No opportunities for volunteers overseas. In the UK, volunteers are only used for specific projects. For further information, contact the charity at the address above.

Uganda Society for Disabled Children (USDC)

Helping to ensure better provision for children with disabilities

Geographical focus: *Uganda*

68 Adrian Road, Abbots Langley, Hertfordshire WD5 0AQ
Tel: 01923 263102; **Fax:** 01923 270002
e-mail: ugandasoc@aol.com
Website: www.charitynet.org/~usdc
Correspondent: Stuart Craig, UK Representative

Expenditure: £496,000 (1999/2000)
Staffing: 1 member of staff in the UK office, who acts as a support to the main office in Kampala. In Uganda, 25 staff, mostly in 6 field offices covering 11 districts.

Website information: Map and key statistics about Uganda; information about disability in general; case study of a child, parent and facilitator involved in the work of the organisation; accounts; how to make a donation.

General: The charity's mission is to help disabled children to reach their full potential and lead fulfilling lives.

USDC was started in 1985 as a UK ngo, directed and managed from London, with representatives in Uganda. In April 2000, USDC Uganda became a fully independent, locally managed ngo. The role of the UK office has therefore changed to one of fundraising and general support.

USDC's work in Uganda centres mainly on 'community-based rehabilitation', a programme of visits by specialist staff to children and their families in their own homes, coupled with an education and awareness-raising programme. USDC works closely with government, and regularly makes referrals to key services (such as physiotherapy, corrective surgery).

USDC works with local education services, teachers and community leaders to help ensure better provision for children with disabilities, particularly improved access to schools.

In some districts, USDC is pioneering residential 'Vocational Training Centres', where disabled young people can enrol on one-year courses, studying computer skills, carpentry, metalwork and screen-printing, with the aim of helping them to establish their own businesses. The trainees can be sponsored by UK supporters for £12 a month.

USDC does not give grants, whether to individuals or other organisations, under any circumstances.

Volunteers/jobseekers: Occasionally, self-funded volunteers with relevant skills are utilised in the Kampala office. Volunteering opportunities in the UK are limited to researching potential sources of funds, and to volunteers working from home. Enquiries in both instances to the correspondent.

UNICEF UK

Raising awareness and funds in support of UNICEF's global programmes; promotes children's rights in the UK

Geographical focus: Works in over 160 countries worldwide

Africa House, 64–78 Kingsway, London WC2B 6NB
Tel: 020 7405 5592; **Fax:** 020 7405 2332
e-mail: info@unicef.org.uk
Website: www.unicef.org.uk
Correspondent: Jo Bailey

Expenditure: £28 million (1998/99)

Staffing: 90, including staff based in Chelmsford and across the UK.

Website information: Latest news; campaigns; education provision – teaching schools about development; events; how to get involved in fundraising; how to make a donation; advertising for cards and gifts.

General: The charity provided the following information. 'UNICEF – The United Nations Children's Fund – is the only global organisation working specifically for children and children's rights. It works with local communities and governments in over 160 countries to help every child reach their full potential through long-term and emergency work on healthcare, education and protection for children at risk.

'UNICEF UK was established in 1956 and is one of 37 national committees for UNICEF based in industrialised countries. As UNICEF's representative in this country, UNICEF UK raises awareness and funds in support of global UNICEF programmes, as well as supporting children's rights in the UK.

'UNICEF is unique within the United Nations family in that it receives no statutory UN funding, and so both UNICEF and UNICEF UK are dependent on voluntary donations from governments and individuals for their income.'

Membership: There are 50 UNICEF groups, branches and committees around the UK with nearly 500 voluntary members who are responsible for raising money for UNICEF. There are another 100 committed voluntary fundraisers around the UK.

Volunteers/jobseekers: 'UNICEF groups, individual volunteers and community organisations around the UK all help UNICEF to raise over £1.5 million each year. There are seven regional officers in England, and officers for Scotland, Wales and Northern Ireland who are on hand to offer support with your fundraising efforts. They can provide you with a range of promotional materials including posters, badges and collection tins. Your regional officer can also offer fundraising advice and help you to get local press coverage.'

To get involved, please contact your regional officer; contact the charity at the above address first to find out who that is.

United Kingdom Jewish Aid and International Development (UKJAID)

Jewish-led humanitarian organisation, working in relief and development

Geographical focus: Worldwide

33 Seymour Place, London W1H 6AT
Tel: 020 7723 3442; **Fax:** 020 7723 3445
e-mail: ukjaid@talk21.com
Correspondent: Daniel Casson, Chief Executive

Expenditure: £304,000 (1999)

Staffing: 1 full-time and 1 part-time paid member of staff; 20 volunteers.

General: The charity provided the following information. 'UKJAID is unique in the British Jewish community in that it is a Jewish-led humanitarian organisation which responds to international manmade and natural disasters and aims to create programmes of sustainable development.'

In 1999 its charitable allocations totalled £261,000 and were mainly in response to the Kosovo crisis. The bulk of the funds were used for a schools' rebuilding programme and trauma treatment and training programmes. Additionally it made allocations in response to Hurricane Mitch survivors and continued its Home Care project in Sarajevo and support for a home for abandoned children in Rwanda.

Other smallscale programmes started in 2000 and included a sunflower seed oil production project in Zambia, a youth leader training programme for Tibetan refugees in India and a scheme to encourage hosts of celebrations (e.g. weddings) to accept a voluntary tax, the proceeds to combat hunger.

The charity's aim is to mobilise Jewish resources to where they can make the most impact.

Publications: *UKJAID Newsletter.*

Volunteers/jobseekers: Volunteers are encouraged both for work in the UK and within the overseas projects.

United Mission to Nepal (UMN)

Education, engineering/industrial development, health and rural development

Geographical focus: Nepal

Communications Office, PO Box 126, Kathmandu, Nepal
Tel: 977 1 228118; **Fax:** 977 1 225559
e-mail: com@umn.org.np
Website: www.umn.org.np
Correspondent: KhemRaj Shrestha

Expenditure: US$6 million (1998/99)

Staffing: Over 1,000 Nepali nationals, and about 140 expatriate volunteers.

Website information: Facts about Nepal; a map showing the different activities it carries out in different places in Nepal; a description of the activities and different localities; stories of people who have benefited from the work; and current vacancies and details on the application procedure.

General: The charity provided us with the following information. 'UMN is an international, inter-denominational Christian mission, and has been working in Nepal since 1954. Its areas of involvement include education, health, engineering/industrial development and rural development. There are currently [as at January 2001] 40 projects or related organisations through which it works, located in Kathmandu and throughout the rest of Nepal.

'As the largest international non-government organisation in the country, UMN has been privileged to support His Majesty's Government and the people of Nepal in a number of crucial areas. By addressing the needs of the poor and marginalised in developing human resources, in focusing on organisational development and capacity building, and in building up physical infrastructure, UMN has proved itself to be an important and trusted player in the broad picture of Nepal's efforts to promote sustainable economic and social development.'

Volunteers/jobseekers: 'UMN acts as an "umbrella" organisation to a number of Christian mission bodies and agencies from around the world which recruit personnel in their own countries and second these people to work with the UMN. The UMN does not provide a stipend or salary of any kind as financial support is provided by the "sending" Christian mission body/agency. Support is required for all offers of service with UMN. All expatriate "volunteers" who work with the UMN are sent to UMN by one of these member mission groups; UMN does not recruit expatriates directly.'

Village AiD

Rural development

Geographical focus: *Cameroon, Gambia, Ghana, Sierra Leone*

Lumford Mill, Riverside Works, Buxton Road, Bakewell, Derbyshire DE45 1GJ
Tel: 01629 814434; **Fax:** 01629 812272
e-mail: villageaid@gn.apc.org
Correspondent: The Executive Coordinator

Expenditure: £393,000 (1999)

Staffing: 3 full-time staff in the UK and Africa, 6 volunteers.

General: The charity provided the following information. 'Village AiD works in some of the poorest and most marginalised communities, fostering sustainable development by helping people to acquire skills, confidence, and a coherent system of human rights, enabling them to plan their own development and decide their own priorities. Women, who play the major role in agriculture, need small business skills and credit to generate extra income to pay for their children's education and healthcare; young people, excluded from traditional power structures, need skills and integration in their own communities. Most recent programmes address these issues. Village AiD works with indigenous partner organisations in each country.'

Membership: Around 900.

Publications: Two bulletins each year, distributed to members. A limited number of extra copies are available, please enquire.

Volunteers/jobseekers: There are no openings abroad for volunteers. Locally-based volunteers are always welcome.

Voluntary Service Overseas (VSO)

International development, working through volunteers

Geographical focus: *Albania, Bangladesh, Belize, Bhutan, Bulgaria, Cambodia, Cameroon, Canada, China, Czech Republic, Eritrea, Ethiopia, Fiji, Gambia, Ghana, Guinea Bissau, Guyana, Hungary, India, Indonesia, Kenya, Kiribati, Laos, Latvia, Lithuania, Macedonia, Malawi, Maldives, Mongolia, Mozambique, Namibia, Nepal, Netherlands, Nigeria, Pakistan, Papua New Guinea, Philippines, Romania, Russia, Rwanda, Slovakia, Solomon Islands, South Africa, Sri Lanka, Tanzania, Thailand, Tonga, Tuvalu, Uganda, UK, Vanuatu, Vietnam, Zambia, Zimbabwe*

317 Putney Bridge Road,
London SW15 2PN
Tel: 020 8780 7200; **Fax:** 020 8780 7300
Website: www.oneworld.org/vso
Correspondent: Kate Cunningham, Communications Division Coordinator

Expenditure: £27 million (1998/99)

Staffing: 250 paid staff in the UK head office and possibly a futher 150 in Kent and offices overseas. In the UK a network of local groups support overseas members; there are nearly 1,000 members of local groups. About 2,000 volunteers are taking part in overseas placements each year.

Website information: Information for prospective volunteers; country snapshot profiles; list of publications such as books and working papers – with opportunities to order online; UK job vacancies; description of merchandise; information about events and local groups.

General: VSO's objects are 'to advance education and to aid in the relief of poverty anywhere in the world. To fulfil these objects, VSO:

- sends volunteers to other countries to share and develop their skills and understanding and to share their experience with others on their return;
- undertakes or assists in works and projects of all kinds;
- educates the public concerning the nature, causes and effects of poverty and limited education in other countries;
- conducts and pursues research concerning these matters and publishes or otherwise makes the results of such research available to the public.

In 1999, for instance, over 1,900 volunteers were working overseas. A list of the types of work undertaken appears under Volunteers/jobseekers below.

Its work in educating the public in 1998/99 included:

- a campaign to promote fairer tourism
- artists residences in UK schools, and support to teachers
- raising awareness of the impact of HIV/AIDS.

Publications: Books and papers about development work and what it is like to work overseas are available to order directly from the charity or the website.

Volunteers/jobseekers: Opportunities in the UK for volunteers to be involved with fundraising and campaigning.

Overseas volunteers usually need recognised qualifications and relevant work experience. They need to be aged 20 to 70. Volunteers aged 18–25 and without qualifications can, however, apply to the Youth Programme.

VSO matches volunteers' skills with those requested from overseas employers, so that they can help where they are most needed. The types of skills requested are listed below. The list is not exhaustive, and if you have a different skill to offer, please contact the charity.

Accountants, administrators, agriculturists, art/craft educators, audio-visual specialists, scientists/biomedical scientists, bricklayers/masons, builders, business and credit advisors, carpenters/joiners, civil/structural/mechanical/electronic engineers, community workers, computing, curriculum development, IT trainers, dentists, doctors, DTP operators, editors, electricians, environmentalists, farm managers, financial managers, fisheries advisors, food technologists, foresters, graduates BScMaths/Science or BA with TEFL for secondary school teaching, graphic designers, health educators, horticulturists, hospital administrators, hotel and catering managers, human resource manager, journalists, lawyers, librarians, livestock specialists, management trainers, marketing advisors, mechanics, metal workers, midwives, nurses, nutritionists, occupational therapists, pharmacists, physiotherapists, plumbers/pipefitters, primary teachers, probation officers, publishing trainers, radiographers, social workers, special education teachers, speech therapists, sports coaches, teachers, teacher trainers, tourism development advisors, town planners, vets, water engineers and youth workers.

Most volunteers need to spend a minimum of two years overseas, working in one place. Volunteers do not need to provide their own funding as VSO offers a comprehensive package appropriate to each programme. In most cases, this includes return airfares, social security contributions, training to prepare you before going overseas, language and orientation courses when you arrive, grants where appropriate, medical insurance, endowment contributions or NHS pension. The overseas employer provides a modest living allowance and accommodation.

Contact the charity at the address above for an application form and further information.

War on Want

Campaigning against world poverty, project funding

Geographical focus: Worldwide

Fenner Brockway House, 37–39 Great Guildford Street, London SE1 0ES
Tel: 020 7620 1111
e-mail: mailroom@waronwant.org
Website: www.waronwant.org
Correspondent: The Director

Expenditure: £1.1 million (1999/2000)
Staffing: 3 staff and 5 volunteers.

Website information: Details on its campaigns and overseas projects; opportunities for volunteering; list of current job vacancies; journal *Up Front*.

General: War on Want was set up in 1951 by Harold Wilson and Victor Gollancz. Its Vice President is Roy Hattersley [as in 2000] who is quoted in the charity's literature as saying 'War on Wants exists because in the developing world there is a need. The need is for solidarity not charity. For a hand-up not a hand-out. For an end to poverty not just its symptoms'.

War on Want has two main programmes, project funding and campaigning.

Projects
It funds over 20 projects in 11 countries each year. The work that these partner organisations do is 'about equipping people to bring an end to oppression and poverty themselves'. Project expenditure in 1998/99 totalled £483,000.

Funded projects include: Indonesia Garment Workers Association, which is a 'trade union that helps prevent the exploitation of workers through legal aid'; and Tanzania Women's Legal Aid Programme, which 'gives assistance to women and girls allowing them to fight for their own rights'.

War on Want says 'We don't preach or send experts to tell people how things should be done. We do provide much needed support and listen to what they want'.

Campaigns
It campaigns 'against world poverty and works in partnership and solidarity with people across the globe'. It says about its campaigns:

'• we're proud of our past successes. Support for legitimate independence struggles and progressive social movements remains a central plank in our work. We will always speak out for those on the margins and the exploited;

- we don't use racist imagery in our campaigns. We prefer to show the politics behind the poverty;
- in the global economy workers are linked as never before. When workers organise they become powerful and can help end poverty and oppression. That's why we campaign internationally to ensure that workers are free to organise;
- workers' rights are human rights – everyone should be protected by international minimum standards at work. Our links with workers' groups around the world helps us to identify practical ways to combat poverty.'

Membership: Costs £15 (waged), £2 (unwaged) and £20 (household). You receive information on current campaigns and how to contribute to the campaigns yourself.

Publications: Journal *Up Front* is produced.

Volunteers/jobseekers: The charity provided the following information: 'Are you interested in volunteering for a non-governmental organisation, either as part of the work experience module or for general experience?

'We are currently [as at July 2000] looking for volunteers to work in our headquarters in London. We require people who can work at least one day a week, but preferably for two or three days a week. War on Want also seeks volunteers to help run stalls at conferences and events on a more casual basis. All travel and lunch costs will be paid for by War on Want.

'Some experience of working in the charity sector would be useful, as well as a strong understanding of third world issues. If you would like to help, please send your cv to David Rudkin at the office or e-mail address above.'

WaterAid

Providing safe water, adequate sanitation and hygiene prevention

Geographical focus: Bangladesh, Ethiopia, Ghana, India, Madagascar, Malawi, Mozambique, Nepal, Nigeria, Pakistan, Tanzania, Uganda, Zambia

Prince Consort House, 27–29 Albert Embankment, London SE1 7UB
Tel: 020 7793 4500; **Fax:** 020 7793 4545
e-mail: wateraid@wateraid.org.uk
Website: www.wateraid.org.uk
Correspondent: The Information and Publicity Officer

Expenditure: £9.6 million (1999/2000)

Staffing: 62 members of staff in the UK; 17 UK-staff working overseas, plus many other locally appointed staff;
25 volunteers in the London office and 200 volunteers working through UK local committee structures.

Website information: Section for teachers and schoolchildren; research papers and information sheets; gallery of images; latest news; how to help – events, job vacancies and how to donate.

General: WaterAid, with its partners, uses practical solutions, and all the resources available to it, to provide safe water to the world's poorest people. So that health benefits are maximised, it does this through projects which integrate domestic water provision, sanitation and hygiene promotion. It works with individuals and families in their communities, paying special attention to the role of women, to enable them to take ownership of these projects and to maintain a lasting supply of safe water.

Publications: Available free: *Oasis*, a journal which covers news and stories from WaterAid's work overseas – issues in spring and autumn; *On Tap*, providing ideas for fundraisers; *Country Information Sheets*; *Development Issue Sheets*, which cover a range of issues; *Special Reports*; resources for fundraisers are also available. Other resources include educational materials, ranging from between £2.50 to £5, videos, slides and posters.

Trading: WaterAid provides an annual Christmas catalogue. For more information please contact WaterAid Trading at the above address.

WOMANKIND Worldwide

Networking and providing resources including funding, towards women's rights and development

Geographical focus: *Albania, Egypt, Ethiopia, Ghana, India, Kenya, Malawi, Nicaragua, Peru, Somalia, South Africa, Sudan, Zimbabwe*

Viking House, 3rd Floor, 5–11 Worship Street, London EC2A 2BH
Tel: 020 7588 6096; **Fax:** 020 7588 6101
e-mail: info@womankind.org.uk
Website: www.womankind.org.uk
Correspondent: Maggie Baxter, Executive Director

Expenditure: £830,000 (1998/99)

Staffing: 15 full-time salaried staff.

Website information: Facts and figures about the gender gap and other issues; map linking to the work the charity does and where; two or three publications.

General: The charity provided the following information. 'WOMANKIND Worldwide was launched on International Women's Day 1989. The trustees determined that the charity should concentrate on supporting women's organisations in the belief that just as a group of women has greater strength than one woman alone, women can best bring about significant change through organising collectively. They also determined that the charity should focus on development rather than on welfare.

'Since its inception WOMANKIND has provided over £3 million to over 80 organisations in Latin America, South Asia and sub-Saharan Africa. In addition, WOMANKIND staff and consultants in the field provide groups with training, networking contacts and international linkages.

'In the last two years [i.e. 1998/1999 and 1999/2000] WOMANKIND has moved from supporting "projects" in the above regions to the development of "programmes". The intention is a more strategic approach to development and to offer increased learning between programmes. This leads to having a pool of experience on which to call to strengthen our advocacy role. Our support has extended to several new countries in Africa as well as the Balkans region.

'We are an ngo in special consultative status with the Economic and Social Council of the United Nations.'

In the UK, the charity focuses on advocacy and awareness raising. Each November it runs a White Ribbon Day campaign highlighting issues relating to violence against women from an international perspective.

Membership: It is not a membership organisation. However, individuals can become supporters by giving a standing order donation. In return they receive the twice-yearly newsletter plus the annual review.

Volunteers/jobseekers: Salaried positions are advertised in the national press.

There are no opportunities for volunteering overseas. Vacancies do arise, in all departments in the London office. Contact personnel for details at the address above.

World Development Movement (WDM)

Campaiging to tackle the root causes of poverty

Geographical focus: Worldwide

25 Beehive Place, London SW9 7QR
Tel: 020 7737 6215; **Fax:** 020 7274 8232
e-mail: wdm@wdm.org.uk
Website: www.wdm.org.uk
Correspondent: The Head of Personnel and Administration

Expenditure: £797,000 (1999)

Staffing: 21 staff based in London and one person in WDM Scotland.

Website information: Recent press releases; information about campaigns and resources; a form to request further information; vacancies for paid and volunteer posts; information about the work of local groups in the UK including contacts; how to order publications; links to WDM Scotland's site, which contains its newsletter; information on its campaigns and e-mail networks.

General: WDM, launched in 1970, campaigns in the UK and with other groups within the European Union and worldwide for policy changes that tackle the root causes of poverty. It focuses on: trade systems which discriminate against poor countries; multinationals that exploit the poor; third world debt; the arms trade; and aid. WDM provided the following examples of its work:

- '• in 1994, WDM exposed the damage done by British arms exports and how these exports are backed by the government and the banks
- in 1997, it campaigned to end the Aid and Trade Provision – so more aid now goes directly to the poorest people
- in 2000, WDM helped to secure UK support for the Biosafety Protocol – protecting poor farmers from GM companies.

'For 2000 and beyond, WDM will continue to campaign for global rules on trade, investment, finance and debt that provide real opportunities for the world's poor.

'WDM's non-charitable status enables it to campaign without restrictions. It operates through its 100 local groups and 12,000 supporters, and campaigns in unison with other non-governmental organisations throughout the EU and worldwide. To publicise its message in the UK, WDM informs the public with educational and campaigning materials, lobbies parliament and holds demonstrations. The World Development Movement Trust is a charity which funds the research and educational aspects of WDM's work. Gift Aid donations and CAF vouchers can be given to this trust (CC No. 1064066).

Membership: £16 a year (waged), £8 (unwaged), £30 (affiliate) and £22 overseas.

Publications: *WDM in Action* magazine (published quarterly).

Volunteers/jobseekers: There are no opportunities for volunteering overseas, but a wide range of opportunities for volunteers in campaigning, supporter development and fundraising in its London office and with 100 local groups across the UK. Contact the correspondent for an application form.

World Emergency Relief (WER)

Relief and development, with a focus on helping children

Geographical focus: Albania, Burundi, China, DR Congo, Dominican Republic, Guatemala, Honduras, Kenya, Kosovo, Liberia, Mexico, Philippines, Romania, Russia, Sierra Leone, South Africa, Thailand, Venezuela, Zambia

Barley Mow Centre, Barley Mow Passage, Chiswick, London W4 4PH
Tel: 020 8742 1223; **Fax:** 020 8742 3405
e-mail: info@wer-uk.org
Website: www.wer-uk.org
Correspondent: Alex D Haxton, Director of Operations

Expenditure: £8.9 million (1999/2000)

Staffing: UK Office: 2 full-time and 3 part-time. Offices also in USA, Hong Kong, Netherlands.

Website information: Photo gallery; annual report; FAQ; information for volunteers; how to donate to the charity.

General: World Emergency Relief is an international charity working in the area of humanitarian relief and development with a strong focus on 'giving children a chance'. It is a non-denominational fellowship of Christians around the world, working together and with other groups to help people in need.

Although committed to respond to meet urgent need WER seeks to develop projects in conjunction with local partners which will benefit and enhance the social position of individuals as well as the nation.

Founded in the USA in 1985 and established in the UK in 1995, WER seeks to release funding to local indigenous organisations or groups. All projects are closely evaluated.

In addition WER has developed an effective Gift in Kind partnership with companies enabling many goods including food, medicines, clothing and educational material to be donated and then distributed to the WER partners throughout the world. Over £6 million at market value was donated in 2000.

Projects supported in 2000 included: orphanages in Burundi, Romania and Russia; medical care in Russia, Burundi and Uganda; street children projects in Philippines, Burundi, Congo and Dominican Republic; AIDS projects in Africa; dental clinics in Uganda; and specific women's issues projects in various regions.

Volunteers/jobseekers: WER is looking for volunteers to work in London in administrative roles, as well as in various outreaches worldwide. Overseas positions are available for people with teaching or administration experience, or with professional skills, especially in medicine or dental medicine. It is helpful if applicants can speak French or Spanish. People can apply via the website, or telephone Alex or Safija for further information, at the number above.

World ORT (ORT)

Providing technical and vocational training

Geographical focus: *Argentina, Brazil, Canada, Chile, France, Germany, India, Israel, Mexico, Netherlands, Peru, Russia, Switzerland, UK, Uruguay, USA*

Press & Publicity, 126 Albert Street, London NW1 7NE
Tel: 020 7446 8500; **Fax:** 020 7446 8507
Website: www.ort.org
Correspondent: Jennifer Rubenstein

Expenditure: £2.4 million (1999)

Website information: *Frontline News*; updates; reports; bi-monthly newsletter; press releases; training programmes; breakdown of activities.

General: Founded in 1880 in St Petersburg, World ORT works to provide technical and vocational training. ORT was originally a Russian acronym for Obshestwo Propostranienia Truda, meaning The Society for Handicrafts and Agricultural Work. Now the charity has reassigned the acronym to stand for Organisation for Rehabilitation and Training. It was first founded as a private organisation for Jewish people who are in need, but now extends its services to other people in need worldwide.

ORT: builds schools; develops curricula; sets up laboratories; develops high-tech educational systems; and produces hardware, software and course information, and other teaching aids and training publications. It:

- conducts its own educational research and acts as consultant to many other institutions including government bodies;
- runs schools and colleges for 7 to 18 year olds and offers higher education such as practical engineering degrees and BScs for technical teachers within its teacher training institutions;
- cooperates with many governmental and international aid agencies to assist and operate programmes at the request of countries in the developing world;
- aims to establish self-sustaining projects which can be operated by a local trained workforce.

Publications: Bi-monthly newsletter.

World University Service UK (WUS)

Bringing education to refugees and communities living through conflict

Geographical focus: Egypt, Israeli occupied territories, Kenya, Peru, Sudan, Swaziland, Uganda

14 Dufferin Street, London EC1Y 8PD
Tel: 020 7426 5820; **Fax:** 020 7251 1315
e-mail: overseas@wusuk.org
Website: www.wusuk.org
Correspondent: The International Director

Expenditure: £1.7 million overseas (1999/2000)

Staffing: 11 people working on the overseas education programmes; 16 providing advice and support for refugees in the UK; 1 fundraiser; 1 management/administration staff.

Website information: Latest news; how to make a donation online.

General: WUS (UK) is part of a network of WUS committees throughout the world. It is committed to the importance of education and training especially for refugees. It works in the following three ways:

Bringing refugee students to the UK
– To complete their education at UK universities before their eventual return.

The scheme works with South African, Sudanese and Ugandan students, helping to bring them to study in the UK

Supporting other bodies
– Supporting and backing the work of other voluntary organisations, education institutions and emerging governments in developing education facilities both formal and non-formal.

The projects team supports partners in their work, to prepare funding applications to statutory donors and to monitor and report on progress. Training is delivered on a range of organisational and educational topics. The charity also makes grants to these projects. In 1999/ 2000, the charity supported, for example:

- learner centred adult literacy work in Africa and the Middle East
- resource centres for refugees and forums for pluralistic debate on education in the Occupied Territories
- curriculum development in Peru.

'The two main groups with which WUS worked were Palestinians (in West Bank, Gaza and Lebanon) and southern Sudanese (as refugees in surrounding countries and displaced in north Sudan). This led to involvement with the diaspora of both groups in the UK and some involvement in lobbying and awareness raising work about their situation.'

Grants made in the year totalled £2 million, of which £1.4 million was given to overseas projects. The largest grants were £204,000 to Arab Resource Collective: publishing, networking and training in the Middle East; £202,000 to Association of Educational Publications: materials production and teacher training in Peru; £167,000 to Literacy and Adult Basic Education; £121,000 to Early Childhood Resource Centre on the West Bank; and £117,000 to African Network for the Prevention and Protection against Child Abuse and Neglect in Kenya.

Remaining grants ranged from below £1,000 to £111,000 and included: £107,000 to Palestine Education Network: training, networking and information in the West Bank and Gaza, £69,000 to Training of Khartoum Literacy Teachers and Teacher Trainers, £18,000 to Tamer Publishing Institute in the West Bank and £3,000 to Displaced Community Education Centre in Sudan.

Providing direct service and advice to individuals

– To enable them to gain access to appropriate education and training in the UK and elsewhere.

The charity works with refugees and asylum seekers in the UK through the Refugee Education and Training Advisory Service (RETAS), and made grants totalling £680,000 in 1999/2000 in support of this work. This service provides advice on education issues, training in job search skills and help in gaining recognition of qualifications gained in other countries. For more information telephone 020 74265800, or write to the address above.

Membership: Members receive three editions of *WUS magazine* each year and invitations to conferences and talks. They have a say in WUS's work and can be a voting member at the AGM. Contact the charity for more information.

Publications: *WUS magazine*.

Volunteers/jobseekers: Limited opportunities arise for volunteers to work in the UK offices.

World Vision UK

Education, street children, health, agriculture, water supply, income generation, emergency relief, campaigning

Geographical focus: Please note the following may not be a complete list of the countries in which the organisation works. Bangladesh, Bolivia, Bosnia, Brazil, Cambodia, Chile, El Salvador, Ethiopia, Ghana, Honduras, India, Indonesia, Kenya, Laos, Malawi, Mexico, Mongolia, Mozambique, Philippines, Romania, Rwanda, Senegal, Sri Lanka, Sudan, Thailand, Vietnam, Zimbabwe

599 Avebury Boulevard,
Milton Keynes MK9 3PG
Tel: 01908 841010; **Fax:** 01908 841001
e-mail: info@worldvision.org.uk
Website: www.worldvision.org.uk
Correspondent: Vicky Joynson

Expenditure: £22 million (1998/99)

Staffing: 82 full-time paid staff and equivalent of 4 full-time volunteers in the UK, plus overseas staff.

Website information: Recent news and fundraising appeals; publications index; examples of work around the world; project areas; selection of country factfiles; how to sponsor a child; job vacancies in the UK and overseas; opportunities for students to volunteer.

General: The charity says that 'the heart of World Vision's mission is to enable families and communities to transform their condition and gain self-reliance in a sustainable manner'.

World Vision helps communities in developing countries through running education, street children, health, agriculture, water supply and income generation programmes, for example:

- in Uganda it helps people who are HIV positive by providing medicine supplies, education and rehabilitative care. It also carries out educational preventative work;
- in Brazil it runs a house which helps 250 street children a month, providing them with shelter, food, medical help and social and educational activities;
- it runs primary health classes, teaching about immunisation, antenatal and postnatal care, how to prevent diarrhoea in infants and how to avoid illness and preventable disease e.g. through boiling water or having mosquito nets;
- in Rwanda it provides for children who survived the genocide, through supplying: items such as bedding, cooking pots and school books; visits by community workers – providing friendship and support; skills training so that child can earn money and recover their dignity and hope; seed, tools, small livestock and advice on farming and animal breeding; and education in income generation schemes.

The charity responds to emergencies, for example in January 2001 it provided emergency medical assistance to people in El Salvador following an earthquake. It also ran a fundraising appeal.

World Vision also works at international level to change the conditions that create poverty in the first place. Work includes:

- supporting the Jubilee 2000 campaign;
- working with corporations operating in developing countries to ensure they make a positive contribution to local communities;
- raising their concerns to governments through meetings, briefing papers, the discussion papers series and special reports.

Campaigns have included lobbying for an international agreement that would stop countries using children to fight in wars; helping raise awareness of the plight of Palestinian children; and highlighting the role of the international community in conflict countries like Sudan and Angola.

Publications: Discussion papers are available without cost, although a donation of £2.50 is welcomed. The charity also publishes special reports and technical reports. Titles include *Buy in or Sell out: Understanding Business – NGO Partnerships*; *Globalisation and development*; *African Voices on Advocacy*; *Palestine – Peace Process*; and *A Draft Framework for Emergency Sanitation Intervention*.

Volunteers/jobseekers: Job vacancies in the Milton Keynes office are advertised on the website.

Opportunities for salaried work overseas, usually at least one year contracts, are available to people who are fully sympathetic with World Vision's values, and who have: experience of working in a developing country for a minimum of six months; language skills, such as French, Portuguese and Spanish; and qualifications appropriate to the project, e.g. in agriculture, construction, finance, health, human resource management, information technology, logistics, project management skills training, social work, transport management and water engineering. Contact Cliff Eaton (tel: 01908 841045, fax: 01908 841014, e-mail: cliff.eaton@worldvision.org.uk) with a copy of your cv, requesting more information on how to apply, an application form and a full job description. See website for current vacancies.

Student Challenge is a five week volunteering programme for people aged 19–26 who are still studying or have recently graduated. It costs £1,400, which covers flights, accommodation, food, internal travel and insurance. See the website for locations in the year you wish to apply. For further information tel: 01908 841007 or e-mail: studentchallenge@worldvision.org.uk.

Worldaware (formerly called Centre for World Development Education)

Education in development issues and the concept of the interdependent nature of the world

Geographical focus: Worldwide

31–35 Kirby Street, London EC1N 8TE
Tel: 020 7831 3844; **Fax:** 020 7831 1746
e-mail: info@worldaware.org.uk
Website: www.worldaware.org.uk
Correspondent: Tony Boardman, Director

Expenditure: £601,000 (1999/2000)

Staffing: 8 full-time and 5 part-time staff, and volunteers.

Website information: Details of its different areas of work; publications list; development news digest – search for recent news headlines which are related to development. Also see other websites, outlined under General below.

General: Supported by business and government, Worldaware aims to promote the widest understanding of the formal education sector of global development issues, their importance and the interdependence of the modern world. It works mainly with teachers and young people, but also has strong links with the business community and politicians.

Worldaware's principal outputs are:

Education
- it promotes a range of teaching materials for UK schools at both primary and secondary level, offering advice to teachers on a request basis;
- it publishes *Global Eye* (on behalf of DFID), a termly development magazine geared to the National Curriculum, for use as a teaching and classroom resource. Every secondary school receives a copy, and it is also available with additional interactive features on the web in both secondary and primary versions (www.globaleye.org.uk);
- Worldaware Teacher Resource Centre contains a range of teaching materials available to buy by direct mail-order.

Business
- the website: www.business-worldaware.org.uk gives information about its work with the business community, providing the opportunity for feedback and exchange of ideas;
- Worldaware Business Group has members from a range of companies, large and small, who wish to engage with each other and representatives of government, international agencies, ngos, academia and the media on global development issues;
- *Business Worldaware* is a bi-monthly publication bringing news on development issues to business managers;
- the annual Worldaware Business Awards recognise the achievements of British and Commonwealth companies who through their commercial activities have helped to promote sustainable development in developing countries.

Membership: Membership of the Worldaware Business Group is open to any commercial organisation, ngo or individual. Annual rates are graduated depending on size and status from £25 to

£100. Members receive regular mailings and are entitled to attend all meetings and other events organised by the group.

Individuals and companies are also invited to support Worldaware's wider educational activities through donations and/or the provision of services.

Publications: Catalogues (covering primary and secondary teaching resources) are available from the address above, or via the website. Also see other publications under General above.

Volunteers/jobseekers: There are occasionally opportunities for volunteers, especially those with development education or teaching experience, to assist in education work. There are also opportunities for administrative work. Opportunities are UK-based, usually at the Worldaware offices.

WorldShare
Supporting the indigenous church in developing countries
Geographical focus: *Worldwide*

Bawtry Hall, Bawtry,
Doncaster DN10 6JH
Tel: 01302 710273; **Fax:** 01302 710027
e-mail: 100657.147@compuserve.com
Website: www.worldshare.org.uk
Correspondent: John Rose, Chief Executive

Expenditure: £700,000 (1999/2000)

Staffing: 5 office staff, 2 area managers.

Website information: Brief information, including how to sponsor a child (£12 a month).

General: The charity provided the following information. 'WorldShare was founded in 1947 by a group of businessmen anxious to support the Chinese Church when all missionaries were forced to leave China. Today [July 2000] councils in the UK, USA, Canada, Australia and Singapore raise money and prayer support for Christian ministries in Latin America, Africa, Eastern Europe, Middle East and elsewhere in Asia.

'We do not initiate... projects, but respond to the requests of the indigenous church. Projects range from Bible College student and child sponsorship schemes, to evangelism amongst remote Brazilian fishing villages, and literacy programmes in northern India.

'Recently our partners already working in Guatemala, Macedonia and South Africa, have found themselves bringing humanitarian aid and rebuilding programmes to those affected by Hurricane Mitch in Guatemala, war in the Balkans and floods in Mozambique.'

Volunteers/jobseekers: 'We seldom have vacancies for salaried positions. When they do occur, they are advertised in the local press and national Christian newspapers.

'Because the purpose of our work is to enable those in developing countries to carry out their own programmes we do not send workers overseas. For the same reason we do not sponsor British students, nor do we sponsor overseas students to study in the West.'

WORLDwrite
Youth exchanges; promoting international understanding
Geographical focus: *Brazil, Ghana, India*

The WORLDwrite Centre, Millfields Lodge, Millfields Road, London E5 0AR
Tel & Fax: 020 8983 5435
e-mail: worldwrite@easynet.co.uk
Website: www.worldwrite.org.uk
Correspondent: The Director

Expenditure: £222,000 (1998/99)

Staffing: No paid staff; 70 volunteers.

Website information: International exchange report packs; briefing documents; workshop enrolment information; celebrity appeal; archives; information for schools (request a presentation e.g. about sustainable development for the cost of £30); how to become a volunteer or make a donation.

General: WORLDwrite is an international voluntary youth project and educational charity, encouraging links between young people across the globe. The charity provided the following information. 'WORLDwrite won enormous public support and celebrity backing for an exchange visit to Hiroshima in August 1995 on the fiftieth anniversary of the atomic bombings of Hiroshima and Nagasaki. In 1996 we coordinated a Europe-wide anti-racist exchange and tour, linking up with German school students, Algerian youth groups and holocaust survivors.

'In 1997 WORLDwrite arranged the first leg of a youth exchange and internet link up with Ghana in West Africa. British school students successfully challenged the notion that young people in Africa cannot cope with computers.

'In 1998 a trip was undertaken to the Brazilian Rainforest to investigate sustainable development programmes in the rainforest. In 1999 the charity hosted a return visit of school students from Brazil.

'In 1999 the charity began forming links with India. Visits to Delhi, Bombay, Calcutta and the Narmada valley gave participants a unique insight into the Indian perspective on development.

'In 2000 The Millennium Relay linked young people from Ireland, Germany, and the UK, with others in Ghana, Brazil and India, bringing them face to face with the challenges confronting their peers in the South and the chance to relay to the world what they have learned on the other side of the globe.

'WORLDwrite is led by volunteers and school students. Participants and volunteers attend action committees across the UK to develop and implement programmes.'

Volunteers/jobseekers: There are several opportunities for volunteering, in the UK e.g. help with fundraising, and overseas on youth exchanges.

Wycliffe Bible Translators (WBT)

Bible translation into minority languages, community literacy development programmes

Geographical focus: *Operate in over 70 countries; focus on Africa, Asia, CIS*

Horsleys Green, High Wycombe, Buckinghamshire HP14 3XL
Tel: 01494 682268
e-mail: askus@wycliffe.org
Website: www.wycliffe.org.uk
Correspondent: The Response Centre

Expenditure: About £1.5 million (1999/2000)

Staffing: Over 300 international full-time and part-time volunteers (i.e. unsalaried but self-supporting), of which 30 are UK-based.

Website information: Information on opportunities for volunteering; downloadable resources for churches and other groups wanting to get involved; press releases; newsletter; FAQ; how to make a donation; links e.g. to information about different people groups.

General: The charity says: 'WBT was founded in the 1930s, 17 years after Cameron Townsend tried to sell Spanish Bibles to Cakchiquel Indians in Guatemala but found that none could read them. He was envisioned to provide

Mother Tongue Translations for all peoples of the world that they might know and understand the Bible in their own language. WBT UK was set up 20 years later.

'It also seeks to facilitate nationals, by means of partnership, in the translation and use of the Bible in field training programmes that includes literacy translation principles and Bible-use workshops.

'There are numerous language projects worldwide, especially in Africa and Eurasia (former Soviet Union).'

Membership: People who make voluntary contributions receive the quarterly newsletter as well as the intercom and branch newsletters.

Publications: *Words for Life* (quarterly newsletter).

Volunteers/jobseekers:

Long-term volunteers

There is a need for support staff in the UK. In field branches the following are needed: support staff including IT and administration staff; centre management staff; teachers; and member care staff. Other jobs can include: building/maintenance; finance staff; literacy workers; surveyors; and translators.

Short-term volunteering programmes

These range from three weeks to two years and include language work and facilitation, training and using your existing skills.

Short-term voluntary helpers can work at the UK centre (especially foreign nationals improving their English); they work for free board and lodging and receive £25 a week as well as free membership. Contact correspondent, or write to the other addresses below.

Other addresses

2 Oxgangs Path, Edinburgh EH13 9LX; tel: 0131 445 2000

5 Glenkeen Avenue, Newtownabbey BY37 0PH; tel: 01232 866649.

Y Care International

Funding projects which work with young people (usually projects which local YMCAs overseas help to run)

Geographical focus: Worldwide

3–9 Southampton Road,
London WC1B 5HY
Tel: 020 7421 3022; **Fax:** 020 7421 3017
e-mail: enq@ycare.ymca.org.uk
Website: www.ycare.ymca.org.uk
Correspondent: Dr Christopher Beer, Director

Expenditure: £2.2 million (1998/99)

Staffing: 12 paid staff and 1 volunteer in the UK.

Website information: This site was under construction as at November 2000.

General: Y Care International is the international development agency of the YMCA movement. It focuses 'on the needs and contributions of young people in the developing world who face the severest of economic and social conditions'. It seeks to 'support young people and their communities by providing financial support for projects which aim to promote self sufficiency'. It works in the following areas:

- street children
- working children and child labour
- education and vocational training
- girls and young women
- HIV/AIDS awareness
- drugs awareness and rehabilitation
- disability
- refugees/human and natural disaster.

Funds are normally channelled through local YMCAs which develop projects with their local communities. It runs educational workshops on its programmes.

PART 2
SOURCES OF FUNDING

CONTENTS

Introduction, containing information on other sources of funding	243
1 Community Fund (formerly National Lottery Charities Board)	247
2 European Union	251
3 Overseas Aid Committees	265
4 UK Government Departments	273
5 Grant-making trusts	287

INTRODUCTION

Each chapter has an introduction with advice on how to use it, except for the chapter on Overseas Aid Committees, where the entries are self-explanatory.

Please note: all these sources of funding are relevant to organisations only. This guide does not cover grants to individuals.

Other sources of funding

There are many sources of funding relevant to organisations working internationally which were beyond the scope of this book. Some of these are listed below. Further information, including details on how to apply to these funders, is available in *The WorldWide Fundraiser's Handbook* (also published by DSC). Another useful point of contact is The Resource Alliance (see entry on page 204). The *Further reading and information* section (page 441) lists other publications which may be useful to fundraisers.

Other UK-based sources of funding

National charities: Useful sources of funding may be found in Part 1 of this book – *Organisations working in developing countries*. Many of the larger agencies fulfil their mission by working in 'partnership' with smaller, specialist organisations, often with a preference for local organisations. The larger agency may offer expertise and advice as well as funds, and have a long-term interest and influence in how the money is used.

Individuals: Members of the public are another invaluable source of funds (accounting for 35% of all charitable giving in the UK). There are a range of publications available to assist you in raising money from the general public.

UK companies: *The Guide to UK Company Giving* (also published by DSC) provides information on the charitable support of over 500 UK companies. Of those listed in the third edition, only a couple of dozen companies stated that some sort of priority is given to supporting organisations working in developing countries. This indicates that direct support from companies in the UK is rare. To increase your chances of success, we recommend that in the first instance you should approach multinational companies via the local branch in the country where the development work is being carried out.

Other non UK-based sources of funding
Local companies
Larger local companies in your country of operation may also support charities.

Overseas government aid programmes
Grants are given by the governments of developed countries, often under the banner of 'helping the world's poorest'. The suggested norm is 0.7% of the gross national product (as advised by the UN). Grants given by the British government and the governments of Jersey, Guernsey and the Isle of Man come under this heading – see pages 265 to 285. Government grants generally tie in with the country's foreign policy interests.

Multilateral aid
This aid, channelled through large United Nations agencies, is called multilateral because many governments contribute to the costs of the programmes of these agencies. Usually multilateral aid is allocated to government programmes in the country of work, but increasingly these international agencies are looking to cooperate with ngos. It is more common for UN agencies to fund large international charities such as the International Red Cross and Oxfam than smaller organisations.

Charities should apply to the specialist UN agency working in their field of interest (e.g. WHO for health matters, FAO for agricultural matters). Relevant UN agencies are:

- FAO – Food and Agriculture Organisation (webmaster@fao.org)
- ILO – International Labour Organisation (www.ilo.org)
- IFAD – International Fund for Agricultural Development (www.ifad.org)
- UNICEF – United Nations Children's Fund (www.unicef.org)
- UNDP – United Nations Development Programme (www.undp.org)

- UNESCO – United Nations Educational and Scientific Cooperation Organisation (www.unesco.org)
- UNHCR – United Nations High Commissioner for Refugees (www.unhcr.ch)
- UNFPA – United Nations Population Fund (www.infpa.org)
- World Bank (www.worldbank.org)
- World Food Programme (www.wfp.org)
- WHO – World Health Organisation (who-www.who.int/)

Trusts based in other developed countries

The USA is home to a large number of grant-making trusts. Most of these trusts are focused on supporting USA-based causes, but many of them support ngos, including non USA-based organisations.

The Foundation Center in the USA is a useful source of information on US grant-making trusts (www.foundationcenter.org). The following publications by Chapel & York are also available from DSC: *Directory of American Grantmakers* and *Fundraising from America*.

The European Foundation Centre offers a similar service in Europe, promoting and supporting the work of foundations and corporate funders active in and with Europe (www.efc.be/).

1 COMMUNITY FUND
(formerly National Lottery Charities Board)

> **Grant total:** £350 million (estimated for 2001/2002)
> **Address:** St Vincent House, 16 Suffolk Street, London SW1Y 4NL
> **Tel:** 020 7747 5300; **Fax:** 020 7747 5220 (enquiries)
> **E-mail:** enquiries@community-fund.org.uk
> **Website:** www.community-fund.org.uk
> **Minicom number:** 020 7747 5347

Formerly the National Lottery Charities Board, the Community Fund is not an independent charity, but a government appointed body responsible for distributing 4.7% of the National Lottery's profits. (This, together with distributions by the other boards – sport, arts, heritage and New Opportunities Fund – makes up the 28.5% going to good causes.) In many ways it functions like a grant-making trust. Its overriding aim is to 'help to meet the needs of those at greatest disadvantage in society and to improve the quality of life in the community'.

It was anticipated that in 2001/2002 the Community Fund would experience a rapid fall in the amount of money available for grantmaking (by about £100 million). This can be partly attributed to the Community Fund having caught up with earlier underspends and also to funds being channelled to the government's New Opportunities Fund.

Community Fund programmes

The Community Fund has six funding programmes from spring 2001, of which only one, the international grants programme, can be approached for funding for projects overseas. The others are: main grants programme; grants for less than £60,000; research grants; small grants scheme (Wales); and Awards for All (England, Scotland and Northern Ireland).

International grants programme

This programme is aimed at voluntary organisations based in the UK that work with partner organisations abroad. It will also fund UK organisations working with partners on development education in the UK.

Deadlines have been set each year for applications. For the 2001 international grants programme, the application phone line opened on 30 October 2000, and closed on 26 January 2001. Around 420 applications were received and announcements of grant awards were to be made in autumn 2001 (about £19 million). However, please note that the Community Fund stated it was likely that the international grants programme would operate on a continuous basis, following a review in 2001 and starting in April 2002.

Organisations do not need to be registered charities to receive grants. However, they must be set up for charitable, benevolent or philanthropic purposes, and have a constitution, or a set of rules, which defines their aims, objectives and operational procedures.

Under the international programme projects can be supported which:
- reduce poverty and economic insecurity
- assist disadvantaged people to manage their environment in sustainable ways
- improve access to housing, education, healthcare and water
- promote and protect human rights
- enable marginalised people to influence public opinion, policy and practice
- improve understanding of development work
- strengthen the relative social, economic and political position of women and/or girls.

The programme continues to focus on projects benefiting people in need in Africa, Asia, the Middle East, Central and South America, the Caribbean and Central and Eastern Europe.

The International grants office was set up in early 1996 to operate this programme and manage and monitor grants awarded. Between 1996 and 2000, four programmes were run, with a total of £107.5 million awarded.

In 2000/2001 the fifth programme was being administered and its budget for grant allocations was about £19 million, down from £24 million in the previous year. In 1999/2000, 102 grants were made and about one in five applications were successful.

The top ten grants in 2000/01 were:
£1 million to Health Unlimited, towards a project working to improve access to health information and services for people in the African Great Lakes area by broadcasting a radio and magazine programme throughout the region.

£881,000 to Agency for Cooperation and Research in Development. The project aimed to establish a network of village banks in the south of Eritrea, managed by and accountable to its clients, thereby improving the livelihoods of communities, and also raising awareness of gender issues.

£844,000 to WaterAid, for a project working towards the improvement of the portable water supply and addressing the sanitation needs of 250,000 people in poor rural communities in south India.

£722,000 to *Catholic Institute for International Relations (CIIR)*, for a project working with the Ministry of Health and Labour to improve primary health services for people in north west Somalia.

£712,000 to *Oxfam*, for improving access to education in the Zambezia Province, Mozambique, working with the Ministry of Education.

£568,000 to *VSO*, working to support 40 partner organisations tackling AIDS / HIV in Malawi, Mozambique, Namibia, South Africa, Zambia and Zimbabwe.

£527,000 to *Amnesty International (UK) Section*, towards research missions which document and publicise instances of torture or cruel, inhuman or degrading treatment or punishment, particularly against women, children and sexual and racial miniorities.

£505,000 to *HelpAge International*, to support community level income generation projects, to provide training to organisations working with older people and research poverty faced by older people. This project is focused on helping older people in Grenada, Haiti, Jamaica and St Vincent and the Grenadines.

£504,000 to *TRAX Programme Support*, for increasing crop output and income among poor farmers in rural areas of Ghana and Togo which have suffered environmental degradation and consequent rural poverty.

£500,000 to *WWF-UK*, towards ensuring long-term sustainability of conservancies in Namibia.

Other grants were all for less than £500,000 and were made as follows:

£400,000–£499,000	6
£300,000–£399,000	13
£200,000–£299,000	17
£100,000–£199,000	19
£0–£99,000	37

Grants can be for capital and/or project funding, for up to five years. There is no requirement for match funding.

Applications

Applications can only be made on the appropriate form, available by telephoning 0845 791 9191 (Minicom: 0845 755 6656) or by visiting the website.

For the international grants programme, 12 staff 'work closely with the voluntary sector and hold regular consultations in all four countries of the UK to share information about the programme and to hear feedback on all aspects of the application, assessment and grant management processes. The team is supported during the application-processing period by 50+ development professionals who assess applications against the criteria published in the application pack.'

Grant decisions are made by the fund's UK committee, which considers recommendations made by an advisory panel.

Once grants have been awarded, beneficiaries are assigned to a grants officer who acts as the main contact between the Community Fund and the grant recipient organisation. Project progress is reported annually and the grant officer may undertake a monitoring visit to the project at some time during the life of the grant.

2 EUROPEAN UNION

The European Union (EU) funds a range of work outside of its member states, mostly through the annual budget of the European Community (EC). This funding is categorised into a series of numbered 'budget lines'. The budget lines currently established for external aid are listed in this chapter. Support began as 'overseas development' work in the former colonies in Africa, the Caribbean and the Pacific region (ACP states). It has now expanded to include countries all over the world, in Asia and Latin America and more recently in the Mediterranean area and in Central and Eastern Europe. It has also developed in terms of the areas of work, for example adding budget lines specifically for human rights and democracy.

The EC's external aid is managed by the departments outlined below. To access the websites for all these departments go to http://europa.eu.int/comm/dgs_en.htm.

The External Relations Directorate General aims to provide a clear identity and coherent approach for all external activities. In particular, and relevant to this guide, it deals with: the European states which are not members of the EU or which are applying to be members; Caucasus and the Central Asian republics; the Middle East and south Mediterranean countries; Latin America and Asia.

The Development Directorate General works in close cooperation with the External Relations Directorate General, EuropeAid and ECHO. Its task is to formulate the development cooperation policy. Its aim is to eradicate poverty in developing countries by bringing about sustainable development. In achieving this aim it will promote democracy, the rule of law, good governance and respect for human rights. Priority is given to the most disadvantaged countries and the poorest groups of people in more developed countries.

The EuropeAid Co-operation Office, a new department established in January 2001, is responsible for implementing the programmes developed by the directorate generals above. It is responsible for all phases of the project cycle: identification and appraisal of projects and programmes, preparation of financing decisions, implementation, monitoring and evaluation. Funding for the programmes comes from the EC and from the European Development Fund (see page 252).

When a budget line is open for grant applications, it issues a 'call for proposals'. Many of these budget lines are the responsibility of EuropeAid. Calls for proposals are published on the website: http:europa.eu.int/comm/europeaid/index.htm.

By clicking on 'Tenders and Grants' or 'Quick Tender Search' you can then select the programme you are interested in, and the relevant country or countries etc. It will list any 'calls' which are open; information on those which are recently closed or will be open in future is also available.

European Community Humanitarian Office (ECHO) manages several budget lines relevant to emergency relief work and has been described in a separate entry on page 256.

The Enlargement Directorate General is responsible for the Commission's policy on the expansion of the EU, including the preparation of the 13 countries applying to become member states – the 'pre-accession strategy'. There are many budget lines dedicated to this purpose. The Commission states that enlargement is 'one of the most important opportunities for the European Union [in the] ... 21st Century'. The main programmes, Phare and ISPA, have entries in this chapter. These programmes are administered by this directorate and not by EuropeAid.

Applying to Europe

The best advice for getting to grips with European funding is to get to know your way around the website. By doing this you can keep up-to-date with the budget lines (revised every year) and with the Commission, which has recently undergone much reorganisation. Addresses of departments seem to remain more constant. All the calls for proposals are published on the Commission's website, along with detailed guidelines and budgets. The website is enormous and at first seems to be an unfathomable maze. In this chapter we have given details of many webpage addresses to help you get started. The main website address is: http://europa.eu.int.

It is also important that you contact the relevant departments (everyone will speak English). For detailed information see *A Guide to European Union Funding for NGOs: Your Way Through the Labyrinth* by ECAS – Euro Citizen Action Service. The 7th edition (available from the Directory of Social Change) will include up-to-date information on the Commission and the new EuropeAid Co-operation Office.

European Development Fund (EDF)

The European Development Fund is not part of the Community's budget lines. The income from the fund comes directly from the member states. It was created by the Lomé Convention and is the major development cooperation between the EU and the ACP (Africa, Caribbean and Pacific) countries. The main principle of the successive Lomé Conventions is the desire for cooperation and effective partnership in terms of the economic, cultural and social development of the ACP countries, from which the EU and the ACP countries will mutually benefit. The new Cotonou Agreement has built on the model of the Conventions, focusing on a combination of politics, trade and development. The five interdependent areas of the agreement are: a comprehensive political dimension, taking into account peace-building, conflict resolution, respect for human rights and good governance; participatory approaches ensuring the involvement of civil society and social and economic players; a strengthened focus on poverty reduction; a new framework for economic and trade cooperation; and a reform of financial cooperation.

Funding cycles last for five years. From 1995 to 2000 €13 million was given through the fund. Unfortunately information for the next funding cycle was not available at the time of going to press.

There are two strands to EDF:

- *Programming aid/the National Indicative Programme (NIP)* – this decides the level of financial aid to each individual country, based on factors such as GNP, status, economic situation, physical elements etc. Once the Development Directorate General has decided the budget for each country, the funds are distributed towards projects identified by the beneficiary government and the EC desk officer.
- *Non-programming aid* – under this strand individual projects in the ACP states can apply and they are assessed in their own right (not in connection with their host country). Support is given towards structural adjustments and for humanitarian and rehabilitation assistance.

For further information see the website:
http://europa.eu.int/comm/development/faq/explanationproject_en.htm

Programming is the responsibility of the Development Directorate General. Postal address: 200 Rue de la Loi, B-1049 Brussels.

Headquarters: 12 Rue de Genève, B-1140 Brussels.

Contact: Jacobus Richelle, tel: +32 2 296 3638.

Projects operating under both programmes are implemented by EuropeAid; see the website: http://europa.eu.int/comm/europeaid/tender/index_en.htm

The fund is administered from each country by desk officers. Their names and e-mail addresses can be found on the website:

http://europa.eu.int/comm/dgs/development/desk.htm

Information given in this chapter

This chapter lists the budget lines for 2001. There are also more detailed entries on some of the funding programmes. These entries try to show a cross-section of the types of funding available, concentrating on the larger programmes.

Budget lines for external aid in 2001

Budget lines are categorised under the following headings:
   Pre-accession strategy (B7-0)
   Humanitarian and food aid (B7-2)
   Cooperation with developing countries in Asia, Latin America and Southern Africa, including South Africa (B7-3)
   Cooperation with Mediterranean countries and the Middle East (B7-4)
   Cooperation with countries of Central and Eastern Europe, the Balkans, the New Independent States and Mongolia (B7-5)
   Other cooperation measures (B7-6), which include:
      Training and promotion of awareness on development issues (B7-61)
      Environment, health and the fight against drugs in the developing countries (B7-62),
      Specific measures involving third world countries (B7-66)
   European initiative for democracy and human rights (B7-7)

The budget lines are in draft form, including the titles of each budget line. Under each category one or two budget lines are described in detail. This is followed by a list of all lines in that category, showing the amount available in euros for 2001 (unless otherwise stated).

Budget lines

B7-0 Pre-accession strategy

ISPA – Instrument for Structural Policies for Pre-Accession (B7-020)

ISPA is one of the three financial instruments (with Phare and Sapard) to assist the candidate countries in the preparation for accession. Its main priorities are:

- familiarising the candidate countries with the policies and procedures of the EU
- helping them catch up with EU environmental standards
- expanding, and linking with the trans-European transport networks.

ISPA will concentrate on the most costly environmental directives, these are: dealing with drinking-water supply where this is a major problem; the treatment of waste water; solid waste management; and air pollution. Developing efficient transport systems is an essential part of the candidate countries' economic development strategies. ISPA will contribute to the development of railways, roads, ports and airports. A small part of the ISPA budget is available to fund preparatory studies and technical assistance.

Beneficial area: Bulgaria, Czech Republic, Estonia, Hungary, Latvia, Lithuania, Poland, Romania, Slovakia and Slovenia.

Eligibility: Projects should have a significant impact in the field of environmental protection or improving transport networks. They are selected and approved according to how they fit in the national programmes on the environment and transport, which form the central elements of accession partnerships.

Projects should cost a minimum of €5 million.

Further information: See website: www.inforegio.cec.eu.int/wbpro/ispa/ispa_en.htm for further details.

Application details: Applications must be sent to the Directorate General for Regional Policy, at 200 Rue de la Loi, CSM2 493, B-1049 Brussels.

Directorate F: IPSA and pre-accession measures: Marc Franco, Director
tel: (+32) 2 295 1430
fax: (+32) 2 296 1096

See: www.inforegio.cec.eu.int/wbpro/ispa/contacts_en.htm for contacts in each candidate country.

Phare (B7-030)

The Phare programme is the main channel for the EU's financial and technical cooperation with the countries of Central and Eastern Europe. It was set up to support economic and political transition and currently supports 13 partner countries (see below under Beneficial areas). Its role has evolved to keep pace with political developments and it is now particularly concerned with the future enlargement of the EU. Of the 13 partner countries, 10 have applied to become members of the EU. For the 10 applicant countries, Phare's aim is to help them prepare for EU membership. A 'pre-accession strategy' has been developed which will target the individual needs of each applicant or candidate country as it prepares for accession.

Phare activities in the candidate countries focus on institution-building and investment. The first priority is to help the countries acquire the capacity to implement the 'acquis communitaire' which is the entire body of legislation of the European Community.

Institution building

Phare will help the national and regional administrations, as well as the regulatory and supervisory and other bodies, to prepare for the implementation of the European Community objectives.

Investment

This is to bring the industries and major infrastructure of the countries up to EC standard, largely in the areas of the environment, transport, industrial plant, quality standards in products, working conditions etc. Since 2000, the focus has also been on aid for agricultural development (under the programme Sapard) and structural aid which will particularly focus on transport and the environment.

Phare has continued to support the three non-candidate countries in providing support in their transition to democracy and a market economy. Reforms in all Phare countries involve fundamental political, economic and social changes. Key areas of support are:

- public administration
- agricultural resettling
- civil society and democratisation
- education and training (human resources development)
- infrastructure (transport, energy and telecommunications)
- environment and nuclear safety
- private sector development (enterprise restructuring, privatisations, Small and Medium-sized Enterprises – SMEs, financial sector)
- social development, employment and health.

Most programmes are national; however there are some multi-beneficiary programmes which involve several partner countries at one time. Multi-beneficiary programmes have focused on the environment, telecommunications, energy, transport, nuclear safety, customs and the fight against drugs. There are also Cross-Border Cooperation (CBC) programmes recognising problems faced by border regions, they have primarily focused on financing infrastructure and environmental projects. Other programmes are 'horizontal' programmes which are initiated by the Commission, and partner countries are invited to participate.

Beneficial area: Albania*, Bosnia-Herzegovina*, Bulgaria, Czech Republic, Estonia, the former Yugoslav Republic of Macedonia (FYROM)*, Hungary, Latvia, Lithuania, Poland, Romania, Slovakia and Slovenia.

* non-candidate countries.

Eligibility: All applicants must have their central administration and/or principal place of business in either a EU Member state or a Phare country (see above).

Further information: See the website: http://europa.eu.int/enlargement/pas/phare.htm for further information.

Application details: For information contact: Phare and Tacis Information Centre, 19 Rue Montoyer, B-1000 Brussels
tel: +32 2 545 90 10
fax: +32 2 545 90 11
e-mail: phare-tacis@cec.eu.int

Phare is managed under the Enlargement directorate, see website: http://europa.eu.int/comm/dgs/enlargement/index_en.htm.

There is an Enlargement address book, downloadable from the website: http://europa.eu.int/comm/enlargement/pas/phare/work/pab.htm.

There is also a contacts page: http://europa.eu.int/comm/enlargement/contacts/index.htm.

Budget lines in this category:
B7-01 The Sapard Pre-accession instrument (€540,000,000)

B7-020 Instrument for structural policies for pre-accession (ISPA) (€1,058,400,000)

B7-030 Economic aid to the associated countries of Central and Eastern Europe – Phare (€1,365,910,000)

B7-031 Cross-border cooperation (€159,000,000)

B7-0311 Cooperation in the Baltic Sea region (€4,000,000)

B7-040 Pre-accession strategy for Malta (€7,500,000)

B7-041 Pre-accession strategy for Cyprus (€11,500,000)

B7-050 Pre-accession strategy for Turkey (Not established at the time of going to press.)

B7-2 Humanitarian and food aid

ECHO

ECHO is the European Community Humanitarian Office. Its role is to launch operations to meet immediate humanitarian needs. It manages a series of budget lines which provide funding for emergency relief and protection operations, helping victims of natural disasters or armed conflict in non-member countries. It aims to save lives, and/or ensure people's short-term survival by providing relief in the form of food, medicines, water and sanitation, temporary shelter etc. The operations are carried out by ngos and specialist organisations with which it has formed partnerships.

ECHO aims to focus on the following in 2001:

- Needs-based intervention, the main criterion for which is the vulnerability of a population. This will be measured as far as possible by indicators such as the number of refugees/internally displaced people in a given country,

how disaster prone it is, the morbidity and mortality rates, etc.
- 'Forgotten crises', that is, those no longer in the public limelight (as well as those that are).
- Post-crisis situations: ECHO will assist in the immediate aftermath of a crisis, supporting short-term rehabiliation measures (it will then hand over to other agencies and donors as soon as possible).
- It will endeavour to work with other major humanitarian players in order to achieve a common vision, provide complementary and coherent services making more effective use of resources.
- It will ensure that 'horizontal issues' (see below) are covered by operations and are actually implemented.

Horizontal issues are those that arise out of ECHO's work, these have been identified as follows:

- the security of relief workers;
- the phasing out of operations when ECHO wants to withdraw;
- specific measures to prepare for potential disasters in pre-defined disaster-prone countries;
- mainstreaming human rights considerations to avoid any negative side-effects or the undermining of the human rights of recipients of humanitarian aid;
- communication between the partners in the field, which will involve the introduction of guidelines to ensure consistency in the quality of service provided by the different partners with which ECHO works.

ECHO is also concentrating on more effective and regular evaluation.

For further details, the 'ECHO Aid Strategy 2001' is available on the web page: http://europa.eu.int/comm/echo/en/whatsnew/whatsnew_8-1.htm.

Beneficial area: Africa, Caribbean, Pacific, Eastern Europe and the Commonwealth of Independent States, Middle East, North Africa, Asia and Latin America.

Eligibility: An ngo must be an ECHO partner in order to apply for ECHO funding. A number of criteria must be fulfilled to become an ECHO partner. These are laid out in the Council of Regulations (EC) No 1257/96, available from ECHO on request. The main criteria concern the legal basis of the ngo, its administrative and financial management capacities, experience in the field of humanitarian aid, results of previous operations and impartiality. The ngo's suitability for community financing is evaluated on the basis of these criteria.

Application details: For an ngo to become an ECHO partner, it must submit a written application, backed by documentation such as the legal registration of the ngo with national authorities, act of incorporation, annual report, list of board members, letters of reference, organisation chart etc. After studying the documentation and any additional information ECHO will conduct an evaluation of the ngo's performance based on operational, administrative and financial criteria. If the evaluation is successful ECHO and the ngo will sign a formal written agreement, the Framework Partnership Agreement (FPA). The ngo will then be an ECHO partner and eligible for Community funding.

See: http://europa.eu.int/comm/echo/en/index_en.html for further information.

See: http:// europa.eu.int/comm/echo/en/present/about7.htm for who's who in ECHO. As well as contacts for the different ECHO departments, there is a list of contacts (including addresses) for the ECHO office in each country where ECHO is involved.

Echo is divided into six operational units:

Echo 1 ACP countries

Echo 2 Central and Eastern European countries; New Independent States

Echo 3 Asia, Latin America, Mediterranean countries, Middle East

Echo 4 General affairs and relations with European institutions, other donors and international organisations; disaster preparedness; support for major crises; statistics and database

Echo 5 Human resources, including training and contractual relations with ngo

Echo 6 Finances; audit.

Budget lines in this category

B7-20 Food aid (€455,000,000)

B7-210 Aid, including emergency food aid to help populations of developing countries after disasters, and other third countries hit by disasters or serious crises (€455,000,000)

B7-219 Operational support and disaster preparedness (€8,000,000)

B7-3 Cooperation with developing countries in Asia, Latin America and Southern Africa, incl. South Africa

ALA – Financial and technical cooperation with Asian developing countries and Financial and technical cooperation with Latin American countries

The European Union's cooperation with countries in Asia and Latin America has developed from a purely economic relationship to one which includes addressing issues of democracy and human rights, the environment and the fight against drugs. Decentralised cooperation is now also a focus, as well as new perspectives on economic, industrial, scientific and technical cooperation.

The EU has supported the democratic transition by supporting the strengthening of institutions and also projects which develop a genuine culture of respect and effective human rights protection. In the fields of financial and technical aid emphasis has increasingly been on programmes for the urban sector, the participation of women, respect for the cultural identity of indigenous peoples, education, training and environmental protection.

Programmes in Latin America

The EU has developed relations with each country: 'bilateral relations'. As part of this cooperation, aid is given to support initatives concerned with the issues outlined above. Overall, the biggest priority for development cooperation with Latin America is the fight against extreme poverty, marginalisation and social exclusion.

There are also several 'horizontal programmes' which have been established to benefit all Latin American countries. Examples are as follows:

- The Al-Invest Programme aims to promote better collaboration between European and Latin American businesses in commercial transactions, direct investment, joint ventures, subcontracting and economic alliances. See: www.al-invest.org for further information.

- The ALFA programme (Latin American academic training) aims to encourage cooperation between higher education establishments in Europe and Latin America. The objective is to enhance scientific and technological potential as well as the economic, social and cultural situation in participating countries through training and the transfer of knowledge. See: http://alfa-program.com for further information.

- The ALURE programme (optimal use of energy resources in Latin America) strives to promote cooperation between players in the EU and Latin American energy markets. It is working for a better response to new economic, social and environmental challenges, and improving the technical, economic and financial performance of the energy operators involved.
- The URB-AL programme focuses on decentralised cooperation, aiming to bring about real improvements in the socio-economic conditions and quality of people's lives. It targets the towns, regions and other authorities representing local communities in the EU and Latin America. See: www.urb-al.com for further information.
- ALIS is a new programme which was to start in 2002. It aims to promote the benefits of using information technologies and to try to bridge the digital divide.

Programmes in Asia

Examples of these programmes:

- The Asia Invest Programme aims to promote business cooperation between companies in the EU and Asia. It provides a range of grants and support measures to help companies to research new markets, to do business in unfamiliar cultural environments, to meet and evaluate potential partners and to identify investment opportunities. Grants are given to organisations acting on behalf of the companies, e.g. a chamber of commerce or sector or professional association whose role is to run the project for the group. See: www.asia-invest.com for further information.
- The Asia Urbs Programme is an EC-funded initiative in decentralised cooperation. It supports urban development projects that are implemented by Asian and European local governments. Public and private sector organisations can be involved but all projects must be done through a local government body. Each project should involve two partner towns. There is preference for projects which focus on minority groups (women, ethnic groups, youth, children) and poverty alleviation. See: www.asia-urbs.com for further information.

Beneficial area: Afghanistan, Argentina, Bangladesh, Burma, Bhutan, Bolivia, Brunei, Brazil, Cambodia, Chile, China, Colombia, Costa Rica, Cuba, El Salvador, Ecuador, Guatemala, Honduras, India, Indonesia, Laos, Malaysia, Maldives, Mexico, Nepal, Nicaragua, Pakistan, Panama, Paraguay, Peru, Philippines, Singapore, Sri Lanka, Thailand, Uruguay, Venezuela, Vietnam and Yemen.

Further information: See: http://europa.eu.int/comm/external–relations/la/index.htm for further information on EU and Latin America.

See: http://europa.eu.int/comm/external_relations/la/country.htm for further details about bilateral relations in each Latin America country.

Application details: Cooperation with Asia and Latin America is the responsibility of the External Relations Directorate General.

Directorate G: Latin America

Directorate H: Asia (except Japan and Korea)

Contact for both directorates: Francisco Da Camara-Gomes;
Tel: +32 2 296 92 69

Programmes are administered by EuropeAid; for calls for proposals see the website: http://europa.eu.int/comm/europeaid/tender/index_en.htm

Budget lines

B7-300 Financial and technical cooperation with Asian developing countries (€262,150,000)

B7-302 Aid to uprooted people in Asian countries (€36,000,000)

B7-303 Rehabilitation and reconstruction operations in developing countries in Asia (€15,000,000)

B7-304 Aid for the rehabilitation of East Timor (€28,380,000)

B7-310 Financial and technical cooperation with Latin American developing countries (€167,775,000)

B7-311 Economic cooperation with Latin American developing countries (€167,775,000)

B7-312 Aid to uprooted people in Latin American countries (€21,350,000 in 1999)

B7-313 Rehabilitation and reconstruction operations in developing countries in Latin America (€71,800,000)

B7-320 European programme for reconstruction and development (EPRD) (€121,100,000)

B7-4 Cooperation with Mediterranean countries and the Middle East

MEDA – Measures to accompany reforms of the economic and social structures in the Mediterranean non-member countries (B7-410)

The MEDA programme is the main financial instrument for the implementation of the Euro-Mediterranean Partnership. It is comparable to the Phare and Tacis programmes in that it makes economic transition and free trade the central issue. The overall aim of the programme is to build lasting links between the Euro-Mediterranean partners, that is, the member states of the EU and the 12 Mediterranean countries and territories (see below under Beneficial areas), in areas of common interest. MEDA II, the revised MEDA programme, will run from 2000 to 2006. It aims to create a Euro-Mediterranean Free Trade Area by 2010. It aims to focus on the wider framework of the Euro-Mediterranean Partnership which will mean that priority will be given to fewer, larger projects.

There are two strands under MEDA. The main one, accounting for about 90% of MEDA's funds, is the Bilateral Indicative Programmmes. The following nine countries/territories are eligible: Algeria, Egypt, Jordan, Lebanon, Morocco, Palestinian Authority, Syria, Tunisia and Turkey. The funding is allocated by National Indicative Programmes. The main aim is to support economic transition especially with regard to implementation of free trade and the strengthening of the socio-economic balance e.g. social policy measures. (The three countries excluded from this programme are considered to have relatively high Gross Domestic Products – GDPs.)

The other strand, the Regional Indicative Programmes (multi-lateral programmes), accounts for the remaining 10% of MEDA funds and includes all 12 countries. The funding is divided into three areas:

- political and security dimension – the aim is to create peace in the region;
- economic and financial dimension – the carrying out of regional projects which complement the bilateral measures and promoting the cooperation between ngos;
- social, cultural and human dimension – the aim is to improve people's understanding of each other. Funding

under this line covers education, youth, the media, development of civil society and dialogue between cultures and civilisations.

Under this last line, three programmes have been created, Euromed Heritage, Euromed Audiovisual and the Euro-Mediterranean Youth Action Programme.

Beneficial area: Algeria, Cyprus, Egypt, Israel, Jordan, Lebanon, Malta, Morocco, Palestinian Authority, Syria, Tunisia and Turkey.

Eligibility: Funding is open to states and regions, and also local authorities, regional organisations, public agencies, local communities, organisations which support business, private operators, co-operatives, mutual societies, associations, foundations and ngos.

Application details: MEDA is the responsibility of: External Relations Directorate.
General Head of Unit: Patrick Laurent, 10th Floor, 133 Rue de la Loi, B-1040 Brussels.

Projects are implemented by EuropeAid, for calls for proposals see the website: http://europa.eu.int/comm/europeaid/tender/index_en.htm.

Budget lines in this category

B7-410 MEDA (Measures to accompany the reforms to the economic and social structures in the Mediterranean non-member countries) (€712,770,000)

B7-420 Community operations connected with the Israel-PLO peace agreement (€47,950,000)

B7-5 Cooperation with countries of Central and Eastern Europe, the Balkans, the New Independent States and Mongolia

Tacis

Tacis aims to give grant-aided technical assistance to 13 countries in Eastern Europe and Central Asia (see below). Tacis has become a more strategic instrument in the cooperation process between EU and partner countries. In 2000, it began to focus on fewer areas of cooperation. These were:

- institutional, legal and administrative reform
- private sector and economic development
- consequences of changes in society, infrastructure networks
- environmental protection
- rural economy
- nuclear safety.

Each programme focuses on no more than three of the above areas. Programmes are national, multi-country, or cross-border (to promote cooperation and the development of links between neighbouring countries).

Beneficial area: Armenia, Azerbaijan, Belarus, Georgia, Kazakhstan, Kyrgystan, Moldova, Mongolia, Russia, Tajikistan, Turkmenistan, Ukraine and Uzbekistan.

Further information: For further details visit the following website: http://europa.eu.int/comm/external_relations/ceeca/tacis/index.htm

Application details: Once agreed by member states, technical assistance projects are put out to tender. Organisations from the EU (and also from applicant countries) are selected to implement projects, transferring their knowledge to beneficiaries in the partner countries.

For information contact: Phare and Tacis Information Centre, 19 Rue Montoyer, B-1000 Brussels;
tel: +32 2 545 90 10;
fax: +32 2 545 90 11
e-mail: phare-tacis@cec.eu.int

For contact addresses in the different partner countries go the following website: http://europa.eu.int/comm/external_relations/ceeca/tacis/contacts.htm.

Budget lines in this category
B7-51 European Bank for Reconstruction and Development Community Subscription to the Capital (n/a)

B7-52 Assistance to partner countries in Eastern Europe and Central Asia (n/a)

B7-521 Cross-border cooperation (€23,000,000)

B7-522 Rehabilitiation and reconstruction operations in the partner countries of Eastern Europe and central Asia (€10,000,000 in 1999)

B7-541 Assistance for the countries of the Western Balkans (€304,000,000)

B7-542 Assistance for the reconstruction and democracy in the Republic of Serbia (€240,000,000)

B7-546 Aid for the reconstruction of Kosovo (€175,000,000)

B7-6 Other cooperation measures

Support for ngos (B7-6000)
The Commission has recognised the ability of ngos to identify and react quickly to needs and emergencies in the developing world. The EC offers financial support to ngos from member states for work in the developing world. The Commission saw several advantages in replacing traditional government to government cooperation with support to ngos. Importantly, ngos are better placed to work with local communities and to identify and address grass root needs. They are more economical. They are driven by local initiatives rather than donors and they can mobilise resources quickly in emergencies. Ngos are often working in the most hazardous circumstances, and they are already there when emergency aid is needed. Since 1975, ngos have become an important and highly respected part of the Commission's commitment towards external cooperation.

There are two strands of support offered:
- activities in developing countries (80% of the available funds);
- awareness-raising and education within Europe (20%).

Further information: See: http://europa.eu.int/comm/development/sector/ngo/index.htm for further information.

There are several 'key documents' on this website under the heading ngo which may be helpful.

Applications details: Details on the annual applications procedure can be found on the website: http://europa.eu.int/comm/development/sector/ngo/cofinancing_en.htm.

Budget lines in this category
B7-6000 Community contribution towards schemes concerning developing countries by non-governmental organisations (ngos) (€199,400,000)

B7-6002 Decentralised cooperation in the developing countries (€3,230,000)

B7-610 Training and promotion of awareness on development issues including periods of training at the

Commission for nationals of third world countries (€3,730,000)

B7-62 Environment in the developing countries (€16,000,000)

B7-6200 Environment in the developing countries and tropical forests (€40,830,000)

B7-6210 North-South cooperation schemes in the context of the campaign against drug abuse (€5,176,000)

B7-6211 Aid for poverty related diseases (malaria, tuberculosis) in developing countries (Not known)

B7-6212 Aid for population and reproductive healthcare, including HIV/AIDS (€20,704,000)

B7-622 Integrating gender issues in development cooperation (€2,020,000)

B7-624 Grants to egos which combat child discrimination in developing countries (Not known)

B7-626 Campaigns against sex tourism in third countries (€1,000,000)

B7-63 Social infrastructure and services (Not known)

B7-6313 Aid for basic education in developing countries (Not known)

B7-641 Rehabilitation and reconstruction measures for the developing countries, particularly ACP states (€15,000,000 in 1999)

B7-6600 External cooperation measures (€17,500,000)

B7-661 Community participation in action concerning anti-personnel mines (€11,460,000)

B7-7 European initiative for democracy and human rights

European Initiative for Democracy and Human Rights

This initiative brings together a series of budget headings dealing with the promotion of human rights. They are Promotion and protection of human rights (B7-701), Support for democratisation (B7-702) and Prevention of conflict and dealing with conflict consequences (B7-703).

The Commission identified 10 themes as having priority in the 2001 calls for proposals. All priorities have equal status but their importance varies between geographic regions.

The priorities, divided under the three budget headings, are:

Promotion and protection of human rights

- support for education, training and awareness-raising;
- support for measures to combat racism and xenophobia and to protect minorities and indigenous peoples;
- promoting and protecting the freedom of opinion, expression and conscience, and the right to use your own language;
- promoting and protecting the rights of children;
- initiatives aimed at the abolition of the death penalty.

Democracy and governance

- contributions to promoting and strengthening the rule of law, the independence of the judiciary and a humane prison system;
- promotion of pluralism both at political and civil society level by strengthening institutions and organisations and by promoting independent and responsible media and free press;
- promoting good governance, particularly by supporting administrative accountability and the prevention and combating of corruption;
- promoting the participation of the people in the decision-making process

in particular by promoting the equal participation of men and women in civil society, in economic life and in politics.

Conflict prevention and dealing with conflict consequences
- supporting human rights and democratisation activities aiming at preventing, resolving and dealing with the consequences of conflict, including supporting measures facilitating the peaceful conciliation of group interests, and support and assistance for the victims of human rights violations during conflicts.

Beneficial area: The fund works in many countries throughout the world. A full list of eligible countries in 2001 was available on the website: http://europa.eu.int/comm/europeaid/cgi/frame12.pl.

Eligibility: Applicants must:
- be non-profitmaking (except some media organisations);
- be ngos, private or public sector operators or local authorities;
- have their headquarters within the EU or in a beneficiary country; only exceptionally can the headquarters be in another third country;
- be directly responsible for the preparation and management of the project, and not be acting as an intermediary.

The minimum grant for a project is €300,000 and there is no maximum. The EC will give up to 80% of the project costs, although local organisations can receive100% of costs.

Further information: For further information, see the website: http://europa.eu.int/comm/external_relations/human_rights/intro/index.htm

Application details: Applications must be submitted using the standard application form, attached to the Guidelines for Applicants available from the website. The format and instructions must be strictly observed. For each application, one signed original and five copies must be supplied by the applicant. The deadline in 2001 was 19 March.

The department responsible for programming is: Directorate General for External Relations: http://europa.eu.int/comm/external_relations/index.en.htm.

Projects are implemented by EuropeAid, for calls for proposals see the website: http://europa.eu.int/comm/europeaid/tender/index_en.htm.

Budget lines in this category

B7-701 Promotion and defence of human rights and fundamental freedoms (€35,200,000)

B7-702 Support for the democratisation process and strengthening the rule of law (€35,200,000)

B7-703 Promotion of the respect for human rights and democratisation by preventing conflict and restoring civil peace (€19,100,000)

B7-704 Support for the activities of international criminal tribunals and for the setting-up of the International Criminal Court (€3,000,000)

B7-709 Support for democratic transition and the supervision of electoral processes (€5,000,000)

B7-81 External Aspects of Environment Policy

B7-810 LIFE – Operations outside Community territory (€2,925,000)

B7-811 Contribution to international environmental activities, including the Global Environment Fund (€4,230,000)

B7-830 Cooperation with third countries on education and vocational training (€2,115,000)

3 OVERSEAS AID COMMITTEES

Jersey Overseas Aid (JOA)

Contact: Mr Leslie R Crapp, Hon. Executive Officer
Address: La Botellerie, La Rue de la Botellerie, St Ouen, Jersey JE3 2HL
Tel: 01534 483855; **Mobile:** 07797 711150; **Fax:** 01534 483813
e-mail: lesliecrapp-joa@jerseymail.co.uk
Other contacts: *President* Tel: 01534 720783; Fax: 01534 639277
Committee Clerk, Jersey Overseas Aid Committee, States Greffe, Morier House, St Helier, Jersey JE1 DD
Tel: 01534 502000; Fax: 01534 502098

Budget: £4.6 million (2001)
£4.2 million (2000)
£4.3 million (1999)
£2.8 million (1998)

The following information was mainly extracted from JOA's Explanatory Booklet. This booklet is sent to all beneficiaries, as well as to people making enquiries.

Background

The Island of Jersey is part of the British Isles but not the United Kingdom. It has its own government (the States of Jersey) and its own laws and in almost all respects is a self-governing community. The practical affairs of government are carried out by committees (akin to UK Ministries), each of which is accountable for aspects of community life e.g. finance, health, education etc. In 1968 the States Assembly voted to give money for overseas aid and Jersey Overseas Aid Committee was set up to administer that money.

The money donated to overseas aid has increased over the years. However, in 2000 the amount was estimated to be less than 0.2% of Jersey's Gross National Product (GNP), still far short of the target of 0.7% GNP as recommended by the United Nations. Jersey is a signatory to Agenda 21 which commits Jersey to moving to a target of overseas aid funding which is comparable with that of other nation states, but is based on taxation revenue rather than GNP.

In 2001 Jersey Overseas Aid allocated about 80% of its funds to recognised organisations working in overseas development, and 15% in response to disasters and emergencies. The remainder was spent on funding overseas community work projects made up of Jersey resident volunteers and organised by Jersey Overseas Aid, and in supporting Jersey charities working in overseas development.

Grant-making policy

Grant aid for organisations working in overseas development
(£2.6 million in 1999)

Jersey Overseas Aid supports about 60 charities on a regular basis. Its strategy is concentrated on the reduction of poverty in third world countries and to this end it supports projects in health and medical care, effective education, safe drinking water and food security, self-help schemes and in the elimination of child labour and abuse.

There is an upper limit for projects of £65,000. Both capital and certain running costs are eligible. However, salaries and running costs, including costs of monitoring, will only be considered where there is a specific project having an identifiable end or aimed at being self-supporting and independent. Projects should usually be capable of completion within 12 months of commencing.

In addition to the above applications the committee will invite 10 agencies to submit a single project for three years' funding. Applications from other organisations will not be considered. Grants for three year projects are for up to £150,000.

Agencies working in disaster and emergency relief (including DEC) (£381,000 in 1999)

The upper limit for a grant for disasters and emergencies work is £40,000. The total amount JOA will spend on any one disaster is £140,000 (in this case, grants would be made to a number of different beneficiaries).

'Applications to be funded must meet the criteria that they are for the immediate relief of human suffering, proportional and appropriate to need, non-partisan and independent of political considerations.'

Grants can be made for general use in dealing with a specified emergency or disaster, or in dealing with an identified part of the agency's needs. Should funding for long-term development work be required following a disaster relief project, an organisation would need to make an application for grant aid for development work (see above), not for emergency relief.

Community work projects (£289,000 in 1999)

JOA organises parties of volunteers from Jersey to work in developing countries on a community project for up to four weeks. Participants contribute £350 towards their own travel expenses and JOA funds any additional costs of the trip.

In 2000, JOA allocated £180,000 of its budget to community projects in developing countries such as those with which volunteers are placed. The volunteers engage in Jersey fundraising activities to finance additional support for the community projects. In 1999, they raised about £20,000 in this way.

Grants to Jersey charities working overseas (£35,000 available in 2000)

In 2000 JOA set aside £35,000 of its budget for this new programme of grantmaking to award to recognised Jersey charities working overseas. Grants are made on the basis of matching specific fundraising on a £ for £ basis, up to £3,500 per project. The project must be well structured and have monitoring systems in place for measuring how the money is spent. It must meet the same grant aid criteria as for other organisations working in overseas development.

Grants in 1999

1999 was an unusual year; in addition to the £3.3 million budget, the States of Jersey voted for an additional £1 million to fund work in Kosovo. Of this £1 million, £800,000 was spent in 1999 and the balance in 2000.

Donations were made to 57 overseas aid organisations. About two thirds of these received three or less grants each. Save the Children received 12 grants in 1999 totalling £208,000, the largest number of grants and grant total to one organisation in that year. Other organisations received grants ranging from £300 up to £192,000. The average amount given to a single organisation was £49,000. Grants included:

Save the Children – £50,000 towards the first year of a three year project for urban children at risk – Tanzania; £16,000 towards providing water and sanitation in kindergartens – Laos; and £12,000 towards the renovation of a school in Cambodia

Plan International UK – £30,000 towards a rainwater harvesting project – India; and £18,000 towards a sanitation and hygiene project in El Salvador

Marie Stopes International – £20,000 towards a vehicle and medical equipment in Uganda; and £7,500 towards ultrasound machines in Vietnam

One World Action – £21,000 towards disabled women's groups in Nicaragua

Rotary Club Jersey – £6,500 to Jaipur limb project, worldwide.

Disaster and emergency relief grants ranged between £15,000 and £30,000 and were made to 16 projects. Oxfam received five grants totalling £129,000 towards: cyclone relief in West Bengal, India; earthquake disaster, Columbia; water and sanitation, Kosovo; emergency water and sanitation, Sierra Leone; and relief from drought in Kenya. Other beneficiaries were: World Vision (three grants totalling £73,000); UNICEF (two grants totalling £48,000); Christian Aid (two grants totalling £46,000); Disasters Emergency Committee (DEC) (£30,000); and Opportunity International UK and UK Foundation for the South Pacific (both £20,000).

Kosovo disaster special funding grants were made to DEC, Mines Advisory Group, Oxfam and UNICEF, towards general costs, feeding programmes, deployment of mines advisory teams and winter shelter programmes.

Community work projects took place in Zambia, Zimbabwe and Uganda in 1999. In Zimbabwe, for example, 11 volunteers from Jersey went to work with St Pauls' Mission. The project was to fund and assist in building two staff houses and a hospital laboratory. The total cost of the trip was £54,000, of which £3,900 was covered by the volunteers. Five other community work projects received grants including Orguis schools project in Kenya (£25,000), Orphaids – Ecuador (£15,000) and provision of a borehole – Zambia (£2,000).

Exclusions

Grants are not made for projects to be administered by governments, members of governments or their officers; nor usually to individual schools, hospitals, communities or groups. JOA will, however, consider such applications where they are submitted by an established aid agency, preferably one where JOA has established connections through the agency's UK headquarters or the UK branch of an international agency.

Applications

Organisations working in overseas development

All enquiries should in the first instance be addressed to the contact above. Applicants must submit their projects in the format laid down by JOA, details of which are available from the contact. JOA distributes a substantial proportion of its grant funds to applicants from its list of 60 organisations in January of each year. The agencies are invited to submit their proposals by October/November of the preceding year, and about two thirds are required to attend a short interview in London during November/December, spread over the course of four days. A small balance is carried forward for spending later in the year to meet special situations as they arise.

In 2000, the committee received 70 enquiries from charities not already on the list. Of these only three were accepted by the committee, including Médecins Sans Frontières and Merlin. Nearly all new enquiries will be refused. The committee deals mainly with principal agencies and requests smaller ones to approach the principal agencies to see if they would support any of their projects. It would be up to the principal agency to include the project in their application to the committee and to be responsible for the monitoring of the project and controlling its funding.

Agencies working in disaster and emergency relief

JOA has administrative procedures designed for quick response. No application form is required. The request should set out the broad details of the emergency or disaster in executive summary form on no more than two pages of A4, ensuring that all matters relating to JOA's criteria are covered, and stating the amount of funding requested.

'It is important to identify the priority for the need for a specific project as against the other needs of the disaster/emergency. Where a number of ngos are involved in the disaster the committee needs to know what steps have been taken to coordinate the efforts of ngos and avoid duplication.

'The summary should be faxed to each of the president, honorary executive officer and the committee clerk, so that immediate action can be taken in the event that one or more of these persons is absent. Arrangements are then made to circulate JOA members with copies and a decision is made by telephone. Agencies are therefore advised on the decision in a matter of days after receipt of the faxed application and are promptly funded.

'An update report is required on the progress of the relief work, this should be in executive summary form and subject to circumstances would be expected within six months of the grant being made.'

Community work projects

A sub-committee is responsible for considering applications and administering grants. All enquiries should be addressed to the committee clerk.

Jersey charities working overseas

A sub-committee considers applications and makes recommendations to the main committee. The sub-committee meets quarterly to interview eligible applicants. Application forms and details can be obtained in writing in the first instance to the committee clerk. Please mark the envelope 'Local Application'.

Guernsey Overseas Aid Committee

Contact: Douglas Guilbert, Committee Secretariat
Address: Sir Charles Frossard House, PO Box 43, La Charroterie, St Peter Port, Guernsey GY1 1FH
Tel: 01481 717000; **Fax:** 01481 712520

Budget: £860,000 (2000)
£810,000 (1999)

The following information was extracted from the committee's funding criteria document. 'Assistance is directed to clearly defined projects in areas of greatest need in the third world. Priority will be given to "least developed" countries as designated by UNICEF.

'Projects given priority

- *basic needs* – priority is towards the provision of basic needs to reduce human vulnerability, with the general emphasis being on rural development;
- *self-sufficiency* – the aim is to support long-term development projects aimed at leading the community ultimately to self-sufficiency;
- *sector* – health, education, agricultural and economic projects will be considered equally, on their merits;
- *environment* – development projects should aim to reduce the vulnerability of inhabitants of underdeveloped regions to disasters;
- *disadvantaged groups* – development programmes for communities should aim to benefit all members and should not discriminate against any vulnerable groups;
- *welfare projects* – projects should contribute to ending suffering, not solely relieving it.'

The committee does not make grants to emergency relief appeals from the budget. However, in addition to the budget it administers £200,000 on behalf of the States of Guernsey, which is made available for grants in response to appeals from DEC. In 2000, £25,000 was donated towards the Mozambique floods appeal (£150,000 in 1999).

'Aid is normally distributed through well-known agencies or organisations, irrespective of race or religion. Where the agency is not a UK-registered charity, it is essential to receive references from well-known international organisations, or individuals well known to the committee.'

Grants were broken down in 1999 and 2000 as shown in the table below. The total given in 2000 was £860,000 (£810,000 in 1999). Examples of grants are shown below.

Agriculture/fisheries

£10,000 to SOS Sahel for agriculture extension and training support in Sudan; and £9,200 to Trocaire towards a community grinding mill in Mozambique. Two smaller grants were given to organisations working in Cambodia.

Education

£27,000 to Help an African School Child, towards constructing classrooms

	Africa	Indian sub-continent	Latin America & the Caribbean	Other Asia & Pacific
	2000 *(1999)*			
Agriculture/fisheries	£19,000 *(£89,000)*	- -	- *(£12,000)*	£2,500 -
Education	£144,000 *(£72,000)*	£66,000 *(£38,000)*	- *(£45,000)*	- *(£12,000)*
Health	£195,000 *(£227,000)*	£80,000 *(£84,000)*	£28,000 *(£37,000)*	£23,000 *(£21,000)*
Integrated development	£138,000 *(£96,000)*	£96,000 *(£65,000)*	£9,800 -	£59,000 *(£12,000)*
Sub-total	£496,000 *(£484,000)*	£242,000 *(£187,000)*	£37,000 *(£94,000)*	£85,000 *(£45,000)*

and other school buildings in Tanzania; £25,000 each to Oxfam towards the Zambezia Education Programme in Mozambique and World Vision UK towards the rehabilitation of schools affected by a cyclone in India; £24,000 to PLAN International UK, towards renovating and equipping a primary school in Guinea; and £13,000 to Save the Children UK, towards the construction of community early childcare and development centres in Nepal. Six other grants were given ranging between £8,600 and £25,000.

Health

£32,000 to Christian Engineers in Development, for providing clean water in Uganda; £26,000 to Arpana Charitable Trust (UK), towards hospital equipment in India; £12,000 to The Leprosy Mission, towards the costs of a Toyota jeep in Sudan; and £11,000 to Sight Savers International, towards equipment and consumables for an eye care programme in Haiti. 17 other grants were given ranging between £6,000 and £30,000.

Integrated development

£25,000 to HelpAge International, towards livelihood, health and agricultural support for older people, in Cambodia; £25,000 to Children's Aid Direct, for assistance to unaccompanied children in Burundi; £19,000 to Opportunity International UK, towards expanding credit and community development for marginalised women and men in Ghana; and £11,000 to CAFOD, towards institution building and income generation in Bangladesh.

19 other grants were given, ranging between £2,100 and £24,000.

Exclusions

UK operating costs, individuals, conferences or seminars. Funding must be specific and general requests for donations cannot be considered.

Applications

'Detailed applications are necessary for every request for aid and to some extent the information necessary will depend on the nature of the application.

'Applications should be submitted in the format of the approved Project Summary Form [see Headings for Project Summary Form below] and should be no more than three to four pages in length, with detailed budget costings provided specific to the request.'

Headings for Project Summary Form
Section A

Country, District, Name of project, Amount requested, Aims of project, Agency.

Section B

Statistics as determined by UNICEF, showing poverty level: Sector, Least developed (yes/no), Under 5's mortality rate, Life expectancy, Access to drinking water, GNP, Literacy.

Section C

Local involvement, Sustainability, Physical environment, Disadvantaged groups, Integrated, Cost effectiveness, Monitoring, Other comments.

'The objective of every request should be encapsulated within the first six to ten lines on the section "Aims of Project". This should stand out in order to make the committee aware from the outset as to exactly what is requested, where, why, and the number of direct and indirect beneficiaries.

'No more than five applications should be submitted at any one time.

'*Monitoring*

Implementing agencies are responsible for monitoring that the project has been completed satisfactorily and detailed reports are required for futher funding of the project to be justified.

'The committee should receive a progress report of each project funded within six months of the grant having been made.'

Isle of Man Overseas Aid Committee

Contact: Anne Shimmin, Secretary to the Overseas Aid Committee
Address: Chief Executive's Office, Government Office, Douglas, Isle of Man IM1 3PN

Budget: £300,000 (2001/02)
£175,000 (2000/01)
£125,000 (1999/2000)
£100,000 (1998/99)

The Overseas Aid Committee is responsible for administering the distribution of the Isle of Man Government's development aid funding and for providing donations to international emergency/disaster appeals. The amount available for the latter in 2001/02 was £25,000 and is included in the budget figure above. The committee usually makes these donations through the British Red Cross.

Useful information for applicants is contained in the committee's remit. It reads as follows.

'The committee will provide development aid grants particularly to the following areas:

- projects to assist self-sufficiency
- safe drinking water and food security
- environmental protection and sustainable development
- effective education and training
- basic healthcare and medical care.

'Projects in these areas that address the role of women and gender equality will be strongly encouraged.

'Grants will normally only be made to projects submitted by non-governmental organisations, including many well known charities. The committee will, however, occasionally consider requests from local people to support particular projects.

'The committee is strongly supportive of appropriate projects which involve a local (Isle of Man) fundraising element.'

The committee provided an annual report for 1998/99, when the majority of the grants were made towards work in Africa and Asia, although this represented the number of submissions received from those areas rather than any bias towards these areas on behalf of the committee. Healthcare, food security and training/education were the main themes of the projects that received support.

Examples of causes supported in previous years:

- a Christian Aid agricultural development project in South India, concentrating on the areas of livestock, wasteland development, housing development and leadership training;
- a HelpAge International project to construct a small income-generating bakery, increasing the availability of bread to people who attend a centre in Ethiopia and providing employment for older people and other disadvantaged people;
- the replacement of the main soak battery which charges a maize grinding bill at a rural training centre in Zimbabwe (Manx Wind Energy Services);
- the sponsorship of two people from Asia to complete childcare and

education courses at Hertford Regional College;
- a World Vision mother and child health awareness programme in Belarus.

The committee supplied information on funding allocated from the budget for 1999/2000. Larger grants allocated from the budget (not local fundraising) in 1999/2000 were £24,000 to VSO, £19,000 to HelpAge International towards three different projects, £14,000 to Christian Aid, £12,000 to CAFOD towards three different projects and £11,000 to The Leprosy Mission.

Members of the Committee in 2001

G H Waft; J R Kniveton; Mrs H Hannah; C J Foster (the first three are political, Mr Foster is a lay member).

Applications

In writing to the contact. The committee usually meets in the middle of March to allocate the majority of funding for the coming year. To be considered at this meeting, project submissions should reach the contact by the end of February. The committee states that it 'requires a project report to be submitted upon completion of each project. If the project is ongoing or incomplete an interim report should be submitted no later than twelve months after the receipt of funding from the committee.'

4 UK GOVERNMENT DEPARTMENTS

This section gives information on central government grants available to voluntary organisations working with an international scope. The information that follows is based on the international section of *A Guide to Funding from Government Departments & Agencies* (also published by DSC). Organisations based in any UK country but working overseas may be eligible to apply for a grant from these departments.

> This section covers funding from:
> **Foreign and Commonwealth Office**
> *Foreign Policy Grants*
> **Department for International Development**
> Civil Society Challenge Fund
> *Partnership Programme Agreements*
> Development Awareness Fund
> Humanitarian Assistance
>   Conflict, Human Rights and Humanitarian Policy
>   Disaster Preparedness and Mitigation
>   Refugees and Migration
> Innovations Fund for Emerging Thinking and Methodologies
> Enterprise Development Innovation Fund
> Geographical Desks
>
> The two programmes shown in italics are grants-in-aid as opposed to competitive programmes. These are grants given on a continuing basis to bodies towards their operational costs.

A new government fund is to be set up to ensure that every child in the Commonwealth receives a primary education. It is expected to be a multi-million-pound fund and will mark the Queen's jubilee year in 2002. Information on the progress of this fund will be published on the Treasury's website: www.hm-treasury.gov.uk

General tips for applicants:
- the contact names and telephone numbers given below may become out of date; personnel changes are frequent;

- closing dates for applications are usually in September/autumn, with successful applicants notified in January, so that funded programmes can start in February/March;
- find out what the current criteria, priorities, application procedures and deadlines are on the department's website, and by phoning or e-mailing the contact person for the fund; contacting previous grant beneficiaries and reading the news will also be helpful;
- when contacting staff in government departments be clear about the questions you want to have answered; civil servants reply helpfully to the questions asked, but rarely offer information;
- follow the application procedure carefully; there will usually be either a standard application form or you will be asked to write an initial letter outlining your idea (a concept note) followed by full proposal if the letter is successful;
- demonstrate clearly how your project will help the government department achieve its objectives;
- be truthful, for example, about whether you are working in a partnership arrangement (funders can recognise inconsistencies etc.);
- good applications will show: an assessment of the impact of the project in relation to the department's objectives; that the organisation has the capacity to undertake the project without affecting its core activity; that any risks, in terms of operation or funding, have been identified in advance and that thought has been given to the future funding of the project; and that the organisation has a self-evaluation system and that users, partners and stakeholders are regularly consulted. They will also show that they have been researched thoroughly and costed carefully;
- successful applicants should invest in building up a good track record with the department, for example returning reports and information asked for on time.

Foreign and Commonwealth Office

Foreign and Commonwealth Office, Whitehall, London SW1A 2AH
Tel: 020 7270 3000
website: www.fco.gov.uk

Foreign Policy Grants

Grant-in-aid: £6.6 million (1999/2000)

Grants are awarded to organisations which help further foreign policy aims and objectives. Many are annual and longstanding so there is less scope for new applications. In 1999/2000 a total of 22 grants were made to organisations in the voluntary sector. The larger grants were made to: Westminster Foundation for Democracy (£4 million); Commonwealth Foundation (£690,000); ICRC – International Committee of the Red Cross (£600,000); Anglo/German Foundation (£250,000); British Association for Central and Eastern Europe (£240,000); British Russia Centre (£230,000); Great Britain/China Centre (£214,000); Franco/British Council (£90,000); Encounter (£57,000); Canning House (£44,000); Atlantic Council of the UK (£31,000);

UN Association (£24,000); and UK/Canada Colloquia (£15,000).

Smaller grants ranging between £3,000 and £15,000 included those to the Joint Commonwealth Council, the Hague Academy of International Law, the Spanish Tertulias and the West India Committee.

Contact: Carol J Varney, Resource Budgeting Department, Room 428, 1 Palace Street, London SW1E 5HE; tel: 020 7238 4027; fax: 020 7238 4004.

Department for International Development

94 Victoria Street, London SW1E 5JL

20 Victoria Street, London SW1H 0NF

Abercrombie House, Eaglesham Road, East Kilbride, Glasgow G75 8EA

Public enquiry point: 0845 300 4100
e-mail: enquiry@dfid.gov.uk
website: www.dfid.gov.uk

Civil Society Department

Civil Society Challenge Fund

Abercrombie House, Eaglesham Road, East Kilbride, Glasgow G75 8EA
Tel: 01355 844000; **Fax:** 01355 843457
New funds available: £4.3 million (2000/01)

Ongoing funding from the former Joint Funding Scheme: £16 million (2000/01)

The Civil Society Department replaced the Non-Governmental Organisations Unit during 1999 and the first round of the new Civil Society Challenge Fund was launched in that year. The fund is open to any UK-based non-profit group, organisation or network/alliance/coalition, which shares the department's overall objective: the eradication of poverty.

The fund's overall aim is to increase the proportion of people in developing countries able to understand and demand their rights – civil, political, economic, and social – and to improve their economic and social well-being. The fund supports a broad range of initiatives which assist this process. Activities funded should be linked explicitly to the following:

- providing people who are poor and socially excluded with access to information and networking which enables them to have more influence over decision makers at all levels;
- building sustainable know-how in developing countries;
- strengthening North-South civil society links and alliances.

Priority is given to initiatives which are innovative. In all cases, the department will be seeking approaches with potential for dissemination and replication by other organisations, including the department's country-wide programmes. In addition to funding projects, other initiatives which are more short-term or are one-off will be considered.

Activities proposed for funding must:
- have clear and achievable objectives, and be able to show how these will be assessed;
- include the building of sustainable local know-how or 'capacity' (see below);
- demonstrate that learning is an integral part of the project, and how lessons learned will be disseminated;
- be complementary to/not conflict with DFID's agreed strategies for individual countries, where these exist.

'Capacity building' is defined in this context as the strengthening of groups, organisations and networks to increase their ability to contribute to the elimination of poverty. Activities can include: leadership development; programme planning and implementation; policy research and advocacy; information access, use and dissemination; building alliances, coalitions, networks, North-South partnerships and inter-sectoral partnerships; and financial sustainability.

Proposals based on operational activities on the ground should be clearly linked to strategies for strengthening the voice of poor and marginalised people. The fund will support projects with service delivery components where they:

- enable poor people to get essential and quality services to which they would otherwise not have access
- improve the equity of overall service provision
- improve cost-effectiveness and community ownership
- enhance the sustainability of services.

Examples of grants in 2000/01:

AIDS Alliance, promotion of effective and sustainable responses to HIV/AIDS in Ecuador (£1.1 million)

World University Service, to address the need for literacy and continuing education especially amongst women in Uganda (£990,000)

ADD, improving the economic and social wellbeing of poor disabled people in four areas of Bangladesh (£870,000)

Health Unlimited, developing a culturally acceptable and sustainable community-based healthcare system in Santa Lucia and San Pedro, Guatemala (£830,000)

Birdlife International, for institutional capacity building/community forest management in North West Cameroon (£830,000)

Anti-Slavery International, to establish and develop a network of ngos in six countries in western Africa committed to eradicating child domestic servitude and cross-border trafficking (£14,000).

Priority themes for 2001/02:

- initiatives to enhance the capability of poor and marginalised people to participate in public policy formulation at local, national or international levels, including budget processes. They could either be aimed at developing the skills and know-how of poor people to interact effectively with decision-makers, or seek to develop poor people's understanding of local and national policy and budget formulation processes to enable more informed debate
- initiatives which build relationships with 'non-traditional' partners in developing countries, i.e. links and closer working with, for example, trade unions, advocacy, and human rights monitoring groups.

Priority themes are not exclusive and other good initiatives will continue to be supported. Proposals may be accepted for activities in any developing country, though it is expected that the majority of activities will be in countries where DFID already has significant programmes.

Funding: Up to 50% of total costs can be provided, with the balance coming from any non UK government sources. Funding levels for smaller projects and one-off initiatives (up to £10,000) are flexible and decided on a case by case basis. Funding is limited to a maximum of five years and is not available for follow-on phases of projects.

Applications: There is a two-tier application process: concept note submission followed by a full proposal. Full proposals will be considered competitively twice a year, in early April and in early October. Full proposals must be received by 30 November for the April decision round, and not later than 31 May for the October decision round.

Applicants must also be able to demonstrate that:
- they have established links with partners in developing countries, and that their link, in terms of the activity to be funded, adds value beyond simply being a channel through which DFID funds are transferred (though they do not have to be organisations whose primary purpose is overseas development);
- they are legally constituted in the UK, although UK charitable status is not necessary;
- they share DFID's core values of mutual respect, equity and justice, openness and transparency;
- they have the capability to account for any DFID funds received.

For further information:
tel: 01355 843583; fax: 01355 843457; website: www.dfid.gov.uk.

Partnership Programme Agreements (PPAs)
Total anticipated funding:
£48 million (2001/02)

This arrangement replaces the former Block Grant Scheme for which the total funding was £48 million in 2000/01.

PPAs recognise that organisations with international influence and reach, and with established track records for managing significant human and financial resources, should qualify for strategic funding at the centre and over a useful timeframe, rather than on a case by case, or project by project, basis.

DFID seeks to maximise collaboration with such organisations in pursuit of the international development targets, through Partnership Programme Agreements (PPAs). PPAs link strategic funding to mutually-agreed strategic outcomes.

Criteria and application procedures for PPAs (2002/03)
Any non-profit organisation (or alliance/network) based in the UK will be considered for a PPA provided it has:
- demonstrated congruence between the organisation's mission and objectives, as defined in DFID's White Paper/s and Target Strategy Papers;
- been involved for at least five years in one or more of the strategic areas covered by DFID's Target Strategy Papers. Organisations which have a single issue focus, for example education or health, are eligible to apply, but they will require the endorsement of the appropriate DFID department before negotiations can start. DFID's Civil Society Department will be responsible for seeking this endorsement;
- experience of working in a range of developing and/or transition countries. Organisations which focus on particular groups of countries or regions will require endorsement by the appropriate DFID overseas office/s or country department/s. DFID's Civil Society Department will be responsible for seeking this endorsement;
- demonstrated capacity to link 'grass roots' work with wider policy/influencing/advocacy work;
- a minimum of £750,000 funding from DFID as a whole over the three-year period.

Most PPAs are likely to be with individual organisations; however, the feasibility of PPAs with alliances of smaller organisations working together at the strategic level may also be considered.

Examples of funding in 2000/01 under the former Block Grant Scheme: Oxfam (£5.6 million); Save the Children Fund (£4.8 million); Christian Aid (£3.1 million); Worldwide Fund for Nature (£2.3 million); Catholic Fund for Overseas Development (£2 million).

Grants to Volunteer Organisations (2000/01): VSO (£22 million); CIIR (£2.1 million); Skillshare Africa (£1.6 million); UNAIS (£1.1 million); BESO (£1.4 million).

For further information contact: tel: 01355 84 3583; fax: 01355 84 3457; website: www.dfid.gov.uk.

Development Awareness and Education Section

Development Awareness Fund

Abercrombie House, Eaglesham Road, East Kilbride, Glasgow G75 8EA
Tel: 01355 844000; **Fax:** 01355 843457
Grant total: £5 million (2000/01)
£3 million (1999/2000)
£1.5 million (1998/99)
Mini grant programme:
£330,000 (2000/01)
£293,000 (1999/2000)
£140,000 (1998/99)

The fund's overall aim is to support activities which promote public knowledge and understanding of development issues, of our global interdependence, of the need for international development and of the progress, both achieved and potential. DFID will consider project proposals which fall within this broad aim, and which explicitly promote the following:

- knowledge and understanding of the major challenges and prospects for development, in particular the poverty reduction agenda, but also for developing countries themselves;
- understanding of our global interdependence, and in particular understanding that failure to reduce global poverty levels will have serious consequences for us all;
- understanding of and support for international efforts to reduce poverty and promote development including the international development targets; recognition of progress made, and that further progress is both affordable and achievable;
- understanding of the role that individuals can play, enabling them to make informed choices.

DFID is particularly interested in supporting projects which engage new audiences. The fund is primarily focused on UK audiences, but may, exceptionally, support activities focused on overseas audiences.

Applicants should normally meet a proportion of project costs from their own resources or from other sources but in exceptional circumstances DFID will meet 100% of project costs. DFID will not normally provide general core funding to agencies. However, administrative costs can be included where these are integral to the delivery of a project's objectives. Funding up to a maximum of three years can be considered.

Up to £100,000 a year towards the total project costs can be awarded. In exceptional cases larger projects may be considered. A Mini Grants Programme for applications under £10,000 a year for England, Scotland, Wales and Northern Ireland is administered on DFID's behalf, see contact details below.

Exclusions: Projects involving construction works; items of equipment, other than as an integral part of a wider project; scholarships for full time study even if part of a wider project; initiatives which clearly fall within the criteria of other funding programmes operated by DFID; initiatives which involve direct lobbying of the UK government or of international organisations of which the UK is a member, or which involve lobbying for or against activities of particular companies, individuals or institutions.

Applications: New project proposals can be submitted at any time before the end of the November which precedes the financial year in which the project is due to start (for example, proposals for a project starting in May must be submitted by the end of the preceding November).
Contact: John Murray, Fund Manager; tel: 01355 843255; fax: 01355 843539.

Development Awareness Mini-grant Programme Contacts

England: Development Education Association; 3rd Floor, 29–31 Cowper Street, London EC2A 4AP; tel: 020 7490 8108.
Contact: Doug Bourn

Scotland: IDEAS, 34–36 Rose Street, North Lane, Edinburgh EH2 2NP; tel: 0131 225 7617.
Contact: Katrin Taylor

Wales: Cyfanfyd, Welsh Centre for International Affairs, Temple of Peace, Cathays Park, Cardiff CF1 3AP; tel: 029 2022 8549.
Contact: Dominic Miles

Northern Ireland: Coalition of Aid & Development Agencies (CADA), 4 Lower Crescent, Belfast BT7 1NR; tel: 028 9024 1879.
Contact: Stephen McCloskey

Conflict & Humanitarian Affairs Department

Humanitarian Assistance
94 Victoria Street, London SW1E 5JL
Total grant: £100.75 million (2000/01) comprising:

£11 million (Conflict and Humanitarian Policy)

£15 million (Emergency Response)

£15 million (Kosovo Humanitarian Policy)

£10 million (Mines Action Initiative)

£37 million (Multilateral Partnerships)

£5 million (Programmed Emergency Response)

£2.5 million (Refugees and Migration)

£5 million (World Food Programme and other food aid).

These are the department's emergency funds. Support is available to agencies for:
- rapid onset disaster relief;
- gradual onset disaster relief and other complex political emergencies; or technological or natural disasters (for which DFID's geographical departments and overseas offices are responsible);
- national and technological disaster preparedness, prevention and mitigation;
- post disaster repair and rehabilitation;
- conflict preparedness, prevention, reduction, and mitigation;
- policy and institutional development, including monitoring and evaluation, training and research.

Geographical range

The department can provide assistance in response to natural and technological disasters anywhere outside the UK. The Head of Department is Dr Mukesh Kapila.

tel: 020 7917 0778; fax: 020 7917 0502
e-mail: M-Kapila@dfid.gov.uk

The department is divided into three teams:

Team One (Global Issues and Institutions)

Humanitarian policy, Red Cross (ICRC, IFRCS), and UN agencies (OCHA, UNHCR, IOM, WFP), interests in other multinational agencies (UNDP, UNICEF, WHO), NGO relations, UN general, ECHO/ European Union.

Team Leader: Sarah Richards;
tel: 020 7917 0792; fax: 020 7917 0502.

Team Two (Humanitarian Programmes)

Rapid onset responses, prolonged emergencies (including Afghanistan, and North Korea). Response preparedness capacity building, disaster prevention, military/civil relations, de-mining.

Team Leader: Matt Baugh;
tel: 020 7917 0040; fax: 020 7917 0502;
e-mail: M-Baugh@dfid.gov.uk

Team Three (Conflict and Security)

Conflict reduction, security sector issues, sanctions and arms proliferation issues, human rights in conflict, OHCHR.

Team Leader: Sarah Beeching;
tel: 020 7917 0599; fax: 020 7917 0502;
e-mail: S-Beeching@dfid.gov.uk

The two main areas of funding are: humanitarian assistance and conflict policy, and projects including human rights and humanitarian policy. Examples of grants given in these and other areas follow below. With one exception, the examples relate to 1999/2000 and do not correspond exactly with the categories for 2000/01 shown at the beginning of this entry.

Conflict Policy and projects including human rights and humanitarian policy:

Grant total: £6.2 million (1999/2000)

Grants were committed to 33 projects in 1999/2000. They ranged from £3,000 to £416,000. Recipients included: ACCORD, Preventive Action Programme (£250,000); International Alert, business and conflict research (£165,000); International Peace Academy, to improve understanding of the political economy of civil wars (£344,000); Responding to conflict, to develop self-sustaining, practical conflict handling capacity among practitioners in areas of instability (£200,000); Institute for Security Studies, for the drafting of legislation on firearms and ammunition in South Africa (£62,000); Saferworld, to support implementation of the South African Action Programme on light weapons and illicit transfers (£81,000); Media Trust, to appraise the potential role that Radio Gulu could play in conflict resolution and peace-building (£10,000); INTRAC, for research on conflict assessment (£104,000).

Humanitarian Assistance:

Grant total: £26 million (1999/2000)

A total of 81 grants were made in 1999/2000 to 42 organisations. Examples included: International Medical Corps, support to Kosovo health sector (£5 million); HALO Trust de-mining in Kosovo (£3 million); World Vision, essential food items for cyclone victims in India (£200,000); ActionAid, emergency support to flood victims in Mozambique (£160,000); SCF, food and other essential items for victims of conflict in Kashmir (£150,000); UK Jewish Aid, trauma treatment in Kosovo (£50,000).

Disaster Preparedness & Mitigation:

Grant total: £1 million (1999/2000)

Commitments were made to 12 programmes in 1999/2000. They ranged from under £5,000 to over £300,000. Grants included: Pan American Health Organisation, to assist Latin American and Caribbean countries in adopting disaster preparedness measures (£303,000); World Bank, for research on the economic and financial impacts of disasters (£253,000); Intermediate Technology Development Group, for support to the Duryog Nivaran network in South Asia, looking at livelihood options for disaster risk reduction (£60,000); University of Cape Town, for integration of disaster mitigation practice into ongoing development programmes across southern Africa (£219,000); IDNDR UK Committee, to support their activities in the last year of the decade for natural disaster reduction (£92,000).

Refugees & Migration:

Grant total: £2.5 million (2000/2001)

In addition to the projects funded through UNHCR, four grants to four organisations were made in 1999/2000. The grants ranged from £62,000 to £195,000, and were to assist ngos working in refugee situations worldwide as well as to increase knowledge and awareness of refugee and forced migration issues.

Please note: the DFID NGO Refugee Fund and the joint DFID/UNHCR NGO Fund have both ceased to exist. Applications for funding for emergency projects to benefit refugees and internally displaced people (IDPs), as well as strategic and knowledge generation projects relating to refugee or forced migration issues, should be addressed to the Conflict and Humanitarian Affairs Department of DFID.

Applications: The booklet, Guidelines on Humanitarian Assistance, covers the areas of funding referred to above. It covers the format for making proposals, reporting, budgeting and appraisal systems, etc.

Geographical departments/desks (see page 285) with responsibility for a country or region usually deal with 'predictable emergencies' – long-running complex political emergencies or frequently recurrent natural disasters. Disaster preparedness and conflict reduction projects are also funded by geographical departments as well as from central budget.

If in any doubt as to where to send an application, contact this department for advice, tel: 020 7917 0379, or the department's public enquiry point, tel: 0845 300 4100.

Social Development Department

Innovations Fund for emerging thinking and methodologies

94 Victoria Street, London SW1E 5JL

Grant total: £380,000 (2000/01)
£380,000 (1999/2000)

The fund is designed to contribute to innovative activities with an element of risk, aimed at: developing and disseminating new ideas; generating new tools and methods for best practice, system and policy development; and building capacity in the South. The following areas of work are most likely to attract funding:

- development and testing of participative methods for information collection and use which involve the people who are poor;

- improving understanding of, and how to support, social institutions which can have a role in tackling poverty, for example, in areas such as control over land, labour and capital influenced by membership of kinship groups; common property resources; and savings and credit mechanisms;
- development of methods for promoting greater autonomy of, for example, street children, older people, people with disabilities, refugees, victims of violence or conflict;
- development of strategies for strengthening civil society in representing/advocating on behalf of people who are poor;
- development of methods to enhance poor and socially excluded people's access to information through organisations such as citizens' advice bureaux, community theatre groups, grassroots video, and local media, and by the use of electronic communications;
- development of tools to strengthen women's empowerment, through for example, gender mainstreaming, participation in decision-making and challenging violence;
- development of good practice in forming/monitoring business codes of conduct and methods to eliminate exploitative and hazardous labour conditions.

Proposals need to cover two or more countries. Most proposals are expected to fall within £5,000 to £50,000 a year and should be planned to achieve their aims within two years, although an extension to three years may be possible in exceptional circumstances.

Examples of recent grants: ITDG UK, for development of materials on mainstreaming strategy in the UN (£130,000 over 2+ years); Manchester University, to produce training and information resources in theatre-based participatory development techniques (£50,000); Womankind Worldwide, for review of ngo experience in delivering Beijing Platform for Action (£29,000); Overseas Development Institute, for handbook of good practice in Poverty Participatory Assessments (£22,000).

Applications: Full guidance for applicants is available from Helen Ireton, Fund Administrator, tel: 020 7917 0627; fax: 020 7917 0197; e-mail: sdd@dfid.gov.uk

Further information and advice are also available from Martin Elliot, Head of Policy Coordination (tel: 020 7917 0488), and John Howarth, Desk Officer (tel: 020 7917 0283).

Proposals are considered competitively twice a year in late spring and early autumn and need to be submitted by the end of May or the end of October.

Enterprise Development Department

Enterprise Development Innovation Fund

94 Victoria Street, London SW1E 5JL
Total funding: £600,000 (2000/01)
£350,000 (1999/2000)

The Enterprise Development Innovation Fund (EDIF) aims to encourage the development of new and innovative ideas for enterprise development through the funding of action research projects which offer real scope for broader lesson learning and replication.

For the period September 2000 to August 2001 EDD will be inviting applications for funding within a specific number of research themes. Additional insights into how these specific areas can be best utilised for the promotion of enterprise development are of particular interest to the department. Research themes will be revised annually to reflect new and developing innovations. Applicants should ensure that they have up-to-date application forms and guidelines before submitting projects for consideration. The research themes are:

Theme 1: Financial Services

(a) New microfinance products. Microfinance practitioners have realised the need to look at the full spectrum of financial services required by low-income households. Applications are invited which explore and provide insights into the following areas:

- Micro-insurance: this is one type of financial service that is gaining increasing attention. It is a category of products that address clients' need for risk management. Insurance mechanisms provide protection by pooling risks across many households. DFID is particularly interested by life, health and property insurance.
- Micro-pensions allow informal sector workers/low income households to save a small part of their income over a prolonged period of time, providing them with an income once they are no longer in employment.
- Micro-leasing is a contractual arrangement between two parties which allows one party (the leasee) to use an asset owned by the other (the leasor) in exchange for specified periodic payments. Micro-leasing can therefore expand the access of upper strata micro-enterprises and small businesses to medium-term financing for capital equipment and technology.

(b) Post conflict or post emergency microfinance. The experiences of microfinance in post conflict or post emergency situations are not particularly well documented. Applications would be welcomed which are able to add to the body of research on the effective delivery of microfinance in such situations and/or provide innovative insights into appropriate and effective delivery mechanisms for post conflict microfinance.

(c) Mechanisms to support microfinance for agricultural activities. For various reasons (repayment schedules, loan cycles, loan amounts), 'mainstream microfinance' is not suitable for the financing of agricultural activities. The development of financial products tailored to meet the needs of the agriculture sector is of specific interest.

(d) Innovative areas of microfinance provision. This general category invites applications in other areas of innovative provision of microfinance services.

Theme 2: Business Development Services

(a) The use of information and communication technologies in the provision of business development services. Applications which fall into the following fields are particularly welcomed:

- encouraging business access to new technologies such as the internet, either individually or in conjunction with traditional media, to improve access to market knowledge and increase business to business communication;
- exploring the possibilities and opportunities that e-commerce could offer to small producers and service providers in developing countries;
- examining the use of ICT for low cost distance and technical training for small producers;
- exploring the use of new technologies as a means of increasing access and reducing barriers to training for small scale producers.

(b) The use of entrepreneurs as trainers for micro, small and medium enterprise (MSME) development. Using existing entrepreneurs in the development and delivery of training for MSMEs offers real scope to provide cost-effective, flexible services which meet the real needs of businesses. Applications are welcomed in the following areas:

- encouraging government bodies, training institutes and ngos to join up and work very closely with private entrepreneurs in the development and provision of training for MSME development. This approach would seek to use the skills of experienced and successful entrepreneurs (as opposed to institutional trainers) to undertake key educational tasks such as training needs analysis; curriculum design; and where appropriate, the actual business-to-business training
- encouraging the use of existing entrepreneurs in training for MSME development through the development of apprenticeship based schemes which allow trainees the chance to develop practical skills in a work-based environment.

(c) Innovative approaches in the provision of business development services (BDS). This general category invites applications in other areas of provision of BDS.

Theme 3: Legal and Regulatory Environment

(a) Mechanisms for extra judicial business dispute arbitration. Formal legal mechanisms to resolve contractual disputes are often inaccessible to those in micro or small enterprises. Yet access to such services is imperative if smaller players in the market are to be given a fair deal. DFID is interested in exploring the use and development of external agencies (such as chambers of commerce or business associations) as providers of such arbitration services to those in micro and small enterprises.

(b) Engaging the public and private sectors in the development and enforcement of better policy, laws and regulation. This general category aims to examine innovative ways of developing more effective regulation mechanisms for MSMEs.

A number of the DFID's partners have used the fund in the past to facilitate the development of smaller projects which were not able to be financed via the traditional bilateral programme. In light of this need, applications from those partners wishing to fund small, innovative projects which fall outside the predetermined themes will also be considered. Three 'open' categories for projects in business development services, financial service provision and supervision and regulation have been added to the list for this purpose. Partners should note that only a small percentage of funding will be put aside for general projects of this nature. Competition is expected to be quite intense.

The EDIF welcomes applications from a range of institutions including ngos, consultancy companies, academic institutions, membership based organisations or organisations representative of business such as chambers of commerce, business associations or industry federations. In most cases, they will be seeking applications from organisations in the North with clear links to similar institutions in the South. In certain instances, however, applications direct from southern based organisations will be considered. Projects submitted should fall within a financial range of £75,000 to £200,000 (in total) and should be not more than three years in duration.

Examples of previously funded projects relevant to this guide: New Economics Foundation, research on international experience of regulating community and microfinance: lessons for the UK and developing countries; Foundation for Small and Medium Enterprise Development, University of Durham, developing the Small Business Unit with the New Economics University, Hanoi; CARE UK, capacity building of community-based organisations in Jaffna, Sri Lanka.

Applications: The above guidelines were valid for two separate bidding rounds in September 2000 and March 2001. Copies of the full guidelines can be downloaded from the DFID website: www.dfid.gov.uk

The EDIF has a two-stage bidding process. Interested organisations are initially asked to submit a brief concept note, outlining their proposed project and draft budget. If this initial application is successful, applicants will be informed of the decision within two weeks of submission and asked to forward a full project proposal. Successful applicants at the first stage will receive feedback and some limited guidance may be given on the development of the full proposal. (Guidelines for submitting concept notes and full proposals can be found in *A Guide to Funding from Government Departments & Agencies*.)

Deadlines for submission of concept notes and proposals for 2000/01 were: 22 September 2000, 3 November 2000, 30 March 2001 and 11 May 2001. Decisions were made two weeks after the deadlines for proposals.

Applications or queries should be made to Enterprise Development Department, 94 Victoria Street, London SW1E 5JL; e-mail: edd@dfid.gov.uk. Applicants are requested to forward hard copies of any applications submitted via e-mail. For further information contact: Holger Grundel, Enterprise Adviser; tel: 020 7917 0228.

Geographical Desks

20 and 94 Victoria Street and overseas

Applications can be made by ngos direct to each of the geographical desks, or sectoral departments, for funding. This also applies to the countries covered by the former Know How Fund – approaches should be made to the desks within the Central and South Eastern Europe Department (CSEED) and Eastern Europe and Central Asia Department (EECAC).

Approach the public enquiry desk to find the location of the desks: tel: 0845 300 4100; fax: 01355 843632; e-mail: enquiry@dfid.gov.uk

5 GRANT-MAKING TRUSTS

This section contains information on 215 grant-making trusts that support causes in developing countries with grants totalling over £50 million a year. Trusts are included if they regularly give grants totalling £5,000 or more to causes in developing countries. Trusts that vary in their grant-making policy from year to year and that sometimes make grants totalling that amount are not included. While many of the trusts listed also support UK causes, the entries focus only on grantmaking to causes in developing countries. Trusts which only support individuals are excluded from this guide.

Size, subject and geographical areas

The top 10 grant-making trusts, in terms of amount given to causes in developing countries, are shown in the table (please note, the table shows grant totals to causes in developing countries).

Top 10 Grant-making Trusts

Comic Relief (Charity Projects) — £10.6 million (1999/2000)
Women and girls, disability, people affected by conflict or living in towns or cities, pastoralists – in Africa

The Westminster Foundation for Democracy — £4 million (2000/2001)
Strengthening democracy worldwide

The Parthenon Trust — £3.8 million (1999)
General development and relief causes worldwide

The Ruben and Elisabeth Rausing Trust — £3.5 million (1999)
Human rights, self-reliance and sustainability, environment – worldwide

The Diana, Princess of Wales Memorial Fund — About £3.2 million (1998/99)
Communities affected by landmines, cluster bombs etc. worldwide

The Gatsby Charitable Foundation — £1.7 million (1999/2000)
General in Africa

The Rhodes Trust Public Purposes Fund — £1.3 million (1998/99)
Education in Africa and the Commonwealth

Methodist Relief and Development Fund — £1 million (1999/2000)
Community development, emergency relief and development education, in Africa, Asia, Latin America and Eastern Europe

The Rotary Foundation — About £1 million a year
General in developing countries

PPP Healthcare Medical Trust — £800,000 a year
Healthcare, public health research, training and development, in Africa and Asia

These larger grantmakers do not appear to show strong patterns of preference for supporting a certain type of work or geographical area, with the possible exception being that there is a *slight* preference for causes in Africa.

Unlike those listed above, most trusts included in this guide state simply that they support causes in the developing world. These trusts may have more specific criteria for giving in the UK, which sometimes is carried through to influence their giving overseas. Since the grant-making policies are not more specific, we decided not to list the trusts in a subject or geographical index.

Making applications

As with approaching any funder, applying to grant-making trusts needs to take place with care and forethought. Most trusts receive many more applications than they could possibly fund, so you need to make sure your application stands out above the rest.

Applications should be targeted at those trusts which are most likely to support you. Try to narrow them down to a list of no more than 20 trusts in the first instance, which you will actually apply to. Consider:

- what areas of work they are interested in supporting, including whether there are any geographical restrictions
- how much they give per year/per application
- what type of funding they prefer (e.g. start-up, revenue, capital or projects)
- how and when they want to receive applications
- if there is any special information required.

Fundraisers are increasingly being advised to take the personal approach. Wherever possible try to develop a relationship with the trust before you make your application. Does anyone you know have a contact on the board of trustees? You could also telephone the trust and ask for advice on your application and if possible arrange a meeting with them.

Each trust is different; most require you to complete their application form, or if they don't have one, to write a fundraising letter. Whatever kind of application, always enclose: a set of your most recent accounts, or a budget for the year if you are a new organisation; a budget for the particular project you are wanting support for, including estimated income and expenditure; and an annual report (if you have one). When deciding to send this and any other 'additional information', only include that which is relevant to the application and which will help the funder to make a decision in your favour.

Top tips for writing your application
- keep your letter clear and concise;
- describe clearly the cause and the needs which will be met – the people who will benefit from your work, how many and for how long – rather than offer a description of your organisation;
- show conviction about the importance of your work;
- show that there is something innovative about your work;
- state the obvious: what your organisation does, who the cheque should be made payable to, what the grant is for and the amount being requested;
- pitch the size of your grant request to suit each trust (some trusts for example will never be able to make grants of over £500);
- show that you are responsible and reliable and have thought things through: describe the relevant experience of staff who will work on the project for which you are seeking funds, state what you will do when funding runs out, talk about how you will monitor the work;
- if you want the trust to fund a piece of work that will continue after its grant has run out, try to show how the work will be funded when the grant expires;
- maintain contact with the trust during the course of an application. Inform them of any successes, invite them to functions, send newsletters etc.

For further details on making applications to trusts, please see *Writing Better Fundraising Applications* and *Fundraising from Grant-making Trusts and Foundations* (also published by DSC).

Unsolicited applications

A number of trusts did not wish to be included in this guide and several reasons have been given for this. The most common are that trusts say they receive too many irrelevant applications or that they are a 'private trust'. No registered charity is private and in our opinion trustees and administrators of trusts should not resent applications for grants, but should rather be committed to finding those charities most eligible for assistance. Some trusts support the same organisation year after year, or target organisations they have found out about through their own research, and therefore do not invite applications from elsewhere. In these cases it is understandable that the trusts would not want to advertise their grant-making. However, we continue to include all the trusts, since our research acts as a survey of all grant money available to overseas causes.

Several trusts state that they will not consider unsolicited applications. It can be the case that this is stated simply as a deterrent to applicants. We suggest therefore that otherwise eligible applicants should write to these trusts with caution, aware that they may have valid reasons for asking organisations not to apply. We advise that you state in your letter that if you are not eligible to be considered the trust should not feel obliged to respond to your application – do not even enclose a stamped addressed envelope. If they do not respond, do not chase them.

The Fictitious Trust

General

Geographical focus: Southern Africa

The Old Barn, Main Street,
New Town ZX48 2QQ
Tel: 0151 100 0000; **Fax:** 0151 101 0001
Correspondent: Ms A Grant, Appeals Secretary
Trustees: Lord Great; Lady Good; A T Home; T Rust; D Prest.

Total grants: £150,000 (2000/01)

Overseas grants: £50,000 (2000/01)

General: The trust supports welfare charities in general, with emphasis on disability, homelessness and ethnic minorities. The trustees will support both capital and revenue projects. 'Specific projects are prefered to general running costs.'

In 2000/01 the trust had assets of £2.3 million and an income of £165,000. Over 200 grants were given, totalling £150,000, including £50,000 to charities working overseas.

The largest overseas grants were £5,000 each to Action on Disability and Development, Leonard Cheshire International and Mission Aviation Fellowship. The remaining grants were of between £1,000 and £2,000 and included those to: Action for Southern Africa, AFRICA NOW, SOS Children's Villages and WOMANKIND Worldwide.

Exclusions: No support for bodies not having registered charitable status, individuals or religious organisations.

Applications: In writing to the correspondent. Trustees' meetings are held in March and September and applications should be received not later than the end of January and the end of July respectively.

- **Name of the trust**
- **Summary of main activities** – what the trust does in practice rather than what its trust deed allows it to do
- **Geographical area** of grant-giving including where the trust can legally give and where it gives in practice
- **Contact address**, telephone and fax numbers; e-mail and website addresses if available
- **Contact person**
- **Trustees**
- **Grant total** (not income) for the most recent year available, covering grants overseas and in the UK
- **Grant total overseas** for the most recent year available, covering only grants for causes in developing countries
- **General information**, including:
  • background or summary of the trust's overall activities and its policy for giving overseas
  • financial information – we note the assets and ordinary income
  • typical grants range, to indicate what a successful applicant can expect to receive
  • large grants given overseas, to indicate where the main money is going, which often gives the clearest indication of trust priorities
- **Exclusions** – listing any areas, subjects or types of grant the trust will not consider
- **Applications** including how to apply and when to submit an application

The 29th May 1961 Charitable Trust

General

Geographical focus: *UK and overseas*

c/o Macfarlanes, 10 Norwich Street, London EC4A 1BD
Tel: 020 7831 9222; **Fax:** 020 7831 9607
Correspondent: The Secretary
Trustees: V Treves; J H Cattell; P Varney; A J Mead.

Total grants: £3.5 million (1999/2000)
Grants overseas: £92,000

General: This is a large trust, named after the date on which it was established by the late Helen Martin of Kenilworth, Warwickshire. The trust supports a wide range of charitable organisations across a broad spectrum, with grants for both capital and revenue purposes. Some grants are one-off, some recurring and others spread over two or three years.

About 40% of the funds in each year goes to the Midlands, and 20% to London and the south of England. Most of the remainder is given to UK-wide charities, with a small proportion going overseas. In 1999/2000 the trust had assets of £90 million and an income of £3.5 million. Grants to 348 organisations totalled £3.5 million, including overseas grants totalling £92,000.

Beneficiaries included Amnesty International (£30,000), Prisoners Abroad (£15,000) and CARE International UK (£10,000). Smaller grants included those to DEC Mozambique Appeal (£5,000), Book Aid International (£4,000) and Sight Savers International (£2,000).

Exclusions: Grants to UK-registered charities only and not to individuals.

Applications: In writing to the correspondent, including a set of recent accounts. The trustees meet in February, May, August and November. Applications cannot be acknowledged.

The A B Charitable Trust

Promotion and defence of human dignity

Geographical focus: *UK and developing countries*

12 Addison Avenue, London W11 4QR
Correspondent: T M Denham, Secretary
Trustees: Y J M Bonavero; D Boehm; Mrs A G M-L Bonavero; Miss C Bonavero; Miss S Bonavero.

Total grants: £164,000 (1998/99)
General: The trust gives grants for the promotion and defence of human dignity.

In 1998/99 it had an income of £171,000, including £162,000 from donations received. Grants totalled £164,000 and the balance at the year end stood at just over £200,000.

Grants to 59 organisations were made, ranging from £500 to £5,000. Grants of £5,000 were given to 13 organisations including Medical Foundation for the Care of Victims of Torture and Prisoners Abroad. Most of the other grants were for £2,500 and were given to a range of organisations.

Exclusions: Applications should be from UK-registered charities only. No support for medical research, animal welfare, expeditions, scholarships or conservation and environment causes.

Applications: In writing to the correspondent, up to a maximum of four A4 pages if appropiate, plus the most recent audited accounts. The trustees meet on a quarterly basis in March, June, September and December.

The Acacia Charitable Trust

Jewish, education, general

Geographical focus: UK and overseas

5 Clarke's Mews, London W1N 5RR
Tel: 020 7486 1884; **Fax:** 020 7487 4171
Correspondent: Mrs Nora Howland, Secretary
Trustees: K D Rubens; Mrs A G Rubens; S A Rubens.

Total grants: £143,000 (1998/99)
Grants overseas: About £30,000

General: In 1998/99 the trust had assets of £1.6 million and an income of £88,000. From a total expenditure of £178,000, grants totalled £143,000, which were broken down as follows:

education	51%
overseas aid	21%
UK charities	20%
Jewish charities (other than education)	8%

Beneficiaries included World ORT Union (£25,000) and British ORT (£10,000). Most of the beneficiaries were also supported in the previous year.

Applications: In writing to the correspondent.

Access 4 Trust

Children, welfare

Geographical focus: Worldwide; mainly Bangladesh, Ghana and Uganda

Slater Maidment, 7 St James's Square, London SW1Y 4JU
Tel: 020 7930 7621
Correspondent: C Sadlow
Trustees: Miss S M Wates; J R F Lulham.

Total grants: £202,000 (1998/99)
General: The trustees' report for 1998/99 states: 'The trust has directed a major part of its resources towards women and children to assist in the relief of poverty and to overcome disadvantages; it is intended that this policy will continue'. Most grants, as in previous years, were to assist families in need and their children, with funds going overseas to developing countries, mainly to Bangladesh, Uganda and Ghana.

The assets in 1998/99 stood at £658,000. The income was £223,000, of which £152,000 was from donations (compared with only £400 in the previous year when the income was £54,000). Grants totalled £202,000.

The trust listed 30 grants of £850 and above in the accounts, of which 4 were to individuals. The largest grants included those to Womankind Worldwide (£50,000), ActionAid (£10,000), Rains Appeal Ghana (£5,400) and Wulugu Project – Ghana (£5,000). Grants ranging from £1,000 to £3,000 went to 14 organisations including Welfare Centre for Disabled – Bangladesh.

Applications: In writing to the correspondent.

The Sylvia Adams Charitable Trust

See below

Geographical focus: Africa, the Indian sub-continent and South America

24 The Common, Hatfield, Hertfordshire AL10 0NB
Tel: 01707 259259; **Fax:** 01707 259268
Correspondent: Kate Baldwin, Grants Manager
Trustees: A D Morris, Chair; R J Golland.

Total grants: £324,000 (1998/99)
General: This trust was set up using the income from the sale of works of art at Bonhams, following Sylvia Adams' death. In 1998/99 the trust had assets of

£9 million and an income of £5.4 million. Grants totalled £324,000.

The trust's aim is to improve the quality of life of people who are disadvantaged, through alleviation of disease, sickness and poverty. Both UK causes and causes in the developing world are supported; grants are divided about equally between the two. The trust divides its giving into three main areas: children and young people, people with disabilities and people living in poverty. It is particularly interested in helping to enable people to become self-supporting and in supporting self-help projects.

Overseas grants are given in 'the Indian sub-continent, Africa and South America but not Eastern Europe, the former Soviet Union or the Middle East. The trust targets children and young people, people with disabilities and people living in poverty. The trustees are interested in schemes which enable people with disabilities or other marginalised groups to participate fully in the societies of which they are a part. This may include projects which promote access to education, training or employment'.

The focus worldwide is on primary healthcare and health education, access to education, appropriate technology and community enterprise schemes. In 1998/99 grants were given to 29 organisations: 16 to charities working in the UK and 13 to those working overseas. The latter ranged from £1,800 to £25,000. The largest went to The Graham Layton Trust towards building a new eye hospital in Pakistan. Other large grants went to Uganda Society for Disabled People for a vehicle for community rehabilitation (£19,000) and Sense International for a full service for deafblind children and adults in India (£18,000). Other recipients included Womankind Worldwide for training and income generation in Peru (£11,000) and Nepal Leprosy Trust to establish a self-care training unit for people cured of leprosy learning to live with their disabilities (£8,700). Smaller grants went to supporting a literacy course in South America and to a Bradford Study Group for research in Bangladesh.

Exclusions: No support to charities only benefiting older people, UK charities benefiting people who have HIV/AIDS, medical research or animal charities. Grants are not made to projects in war zones or to emergency relief appeals. The trust makes all its grants through UK-registered charities and not directly to the country concerned.

Applications: In writing to the correspondent, up to a maximum of four A4 pages, explaining why your organisation should be supported and which piece of work or capital expenditure you wish to be funded. Applications should include a copy of the latest annual report and accounts, a half page summary of the project signed by the chief executive and any additional supporting material.

Deadlines for overseas applications are the end of February for a decision in May and the end of August for a decision in November.

The Ajahma Charitable Trust

Development, health, disability, poverty, women's issues, family planning, human rights, social need

Geographical focus: Worldwide

4 Jephtha Road, London SW18 1QH
Correspondent: Suzanne Hunt, Administrator
Trustees: Jennifer Sheridan; Elizabeth Simpson; James Sinclair Taylor; Michael Horsman.

Total grants: £315,000 (1998/99)
Grants overseas: £101,000

General: The trust generally supports established charities. It aims to balance donations between international and UK charities.

The trust considers grants in the following areas: development; health; disability; poverty; women's issues; family planning; human rights; and social need.

It has also favoured applications from new groups and those which may have difficulty finding funds from traditional sources.

In 1998/99 the trust had assets of £6.2 million and an income of £235,000. Grants totalled £315,000, of which 32% went to charities for overseas work and 68% was given for charitable work in the UK. A total of 47 grants were given, ranging from £1,000 to £25,000.

The largest grants went to Oxfam (£25,000), International Service (£20,000), Health Unlimited (£15,000) and International Agency on Tobacco and Health (£11,000).

Other beneficiaries included One World Action and Who Cares? Trust (£10,000 each), Civil Liberties Trust (£8,000), Prisoners Abroad (£7,500) and Village Aid (£3,000).

Exclusions: Grants are normally only given to medium-sized organisations with an income of between £350,000 and £4 million a year. The trust will not consider applications with any sort of religious bias or those which support animal rights/welfare, arts, medical research, buildings or equipment.

Applications: The trustees meet in May and November; the closing dates for applications are the end of March and middle of September. Information about applying should be sought first from the administrator.

The Alchemy Foundation

Health, welfare, famine relief

Geographical focus: *Worldwide, but mostly UK*

Trevereux Manor, Limpsfield Chart, Oxted, Surrey RH8 0TL
Tel: 01883 730600; **Fax:** 01883 730800
Correspondent: Richard Stilgoe, Trustee
Trustees: Richard Stilgoe; Annabel Stilgoe; Revd Donald Reeves; Esther Rantzen; Alex Armitage; Andrew Murison; Holly Stilgoe; Jack Stilgoe; Rufus Stilgoe; Joseph Stilgoe; Dr Jemima Stilgoe.

Total grants: £812,000 (1998/99)
Grants overseas: About £200,000

General: This trust was established by Richard and Annabel Stilgoe in 1985 and receives a steady income of over £1 million a year from the royalties of the musicals *Starlight Express* and *The Phantom of the Opera*. Smaller grants are given to organisations supporting people in need, including children and young adults, older people and people with an illness or a disability. About £200,000 a year is reserved for international relief agencies working in developing countries, which tend to receive larger grants. A large grant is given annually to Orpheus Trust, a sister charity which supports music projects for people with disabilities.

In 1998/99 the trust had an income of £1.2 million and gave grants to organisations totalling £812,000.

Overseas grants included £100,000 each to Oxfam and WaterAid, £11,000 to Centre for the Rehabilitation of the Paralysed (Bangladesh) and £2,000 to Cambodia Trust.

Applications: In writing to the correspondent. Due to the large demand, unsolicited applications are unlikely to be successful.

The Allachy Trust

Development projects

Geographical focus: *Developing countries*

3 Endsleigh Street, London WC1H 0DD
Correspondent: Miss E Aspden, Administrator
Trustees: A W Layton, Chair; Lord Newby; J R Sandbrook.

Total grants: Est. £50,000 (1999/2000)
Grants overseas: Est. £50,000

General: This trust makes grants towards development projects, particularly those with sustainable objectives and/or environmental emphasis, geared towards community self-sufficiency.

The trust estimated that in 1999/2000 its assets would total £1.4 million and grants would range from £3,000 to £20,000, totalling £50,000. The trust stated that it welcomes applications for funding in tranches over two or three years.

In 1997/98 grants to eight organisations totalled just under £52,000. The largest was £20,000 to SOS Sahel. Five of the other beneficiaries had not received a grant previously.

Other grants were to Indian Development Group (£9,000), Find Your Feet (£8,300), Development of Rural Sichuan and Evergreen Trust (£5,000 each), Y Care International (£2,000), Our Lady of the Rosary (£1,500) and Fairtrade Foundation (£1,000).

Exclusions: No grants for individuals, general charity funds, provision of health, veterinary or general education services to end users, or building projects.

Applications: In writing to the correspondent, submitting the project proposal, budget, annual report or brochure and accounts.

The H B Allen Charitable Trust

General, predominately UK but some grants for third world development

Geographical focus: *Unrestricted, but UK-registered charities only*

Teigncombe Barn, Chagford, Devon TQ13 8ET
Tel: 01647 433235
e-mail: hballen.charitabletrust@btinternet.com
website: members.nbci.com/hballenchtrust
Correspondent: Peter Shone, Trustee
Trustees: Heather Allen; Peter Shone.

Total grants: £838,000 (2000)

General: Grants are given for general charitable purposes in the UK, with a preference for: welfare and environmental nautical charities; child health and welfare; and hospices. A few grants for third world development are also given. Both one-off and uncommitted recurrent grants are given for revenue and capital purposes. In 2000 grants totalled £838,000 with aid and development beneficiaries including Intermediate Technology, Save the Children Fund, Silsoe Aid for Appropriate Development, Tools for Self Reliance and WaterAid.

Exclusions: No grants to non-registered charities.

Applications: In writing to the correspondent by October for consideration in December.

Ambika Paul Foundation

General, education, children, young people

Geographical focus: *UK, India*

Caparo House, 103 Baker Street, London W1M 1FD
Tel: 020 7486 1417

Correspondent: Lord and Lady Paul, Trustees
Trustees: The Lord and Lady Paul; Hon. A Punn; Hon. Ambar Paul; Hon. Akash Paul; Hon. Angad Paul.

Total grants: £27,000 (1998)
General: This trust is funded by the Paul family and makes grants for general charitable purposes. The main areas of interest are education, children and young people.

Grants and donations are made in India and the UK direct to organisations, e.g. universities, colleges, schools, societies.

In 1998 grants totalled £27,000.

Exclusions: No grants are made to individuals, including for academic fees, gap years or overseas travel.
Applications: In writing to the trustees.

The AS Charitable Trust

See below
Geographical focus: *UK and developing countries*

Bixbottom Farm,
Henley-on-Thames RG9 6BH
Tel: 01491 577745
Correspondent: The Administrator
Trustees: R St George Calvocoressi; C W Brocklebank.

Total grants: £24,000 (1998/99)
General: This trust's grants are aimed particularly at projects which combine the advancement of the Christian religion with either Christian lay leadership, third world development, peacemaking and reconciliation, or other areas of social concern.

In 1998/99 the trust had assets of £6.2 million and an income of £166,000. Grants totalled £24,000. Beneficiaries included International Films and Christian International Peace Service.

Applications: In writing to the correspondent.

The Ashden Charitable Trust

Environment, homelessness, urban rejuvenation, arts
Geographical focus: *Worldwide, but mostly UK*

9 Red Lion Court, London EC4A 3EF
Tel: 020 7410 0330; **Fax:** 020 7410 0332
Correspondent: Michael Pattison, Director
Trustees: Mrs S Butler-Sloss; R Butler-Sloss; Miss Judith Portrait.

Total grants: £730,000 (1999/2000)
Grants overseas: £216,000

General: This is one of the Sainsbury Family Charitable Trusts, which share a joint administration. Its areas of interest are:
- (in the UK) transport, pollution and energy issues
- (overseas) the application of renewable or sustainable energy to poverty reduction
- homelessness and associated support needs
- national and local work for urban rejuvenation
- grass-roots special needs or inner city arts activities, with a developing interest in environmental drama.

In 1999/2000 it had assets of £20 million and was continuing to receive further donations from the settlor. Total expenditure was £825,000 including £730,000 in grants.

The 1999/2000 accounts stated under Environmental projects overseas: 'The trust continues to support community-based renewable energy projects that aim to help people to help themselves in an environmentally sustainable way. These projects often combine some biogas and micro-hydro technologies with income generation and agricultural activities and the trust is particularly interested in the contribution that renewable energy can make to the alleviation of poverty.

'A successful seminar held in Tanzania last year, to hear directly from practitioners about the real potential for renewable energy, helped the trust to refine its criteria for support, and to develop guidelines for a new award for renewable energy. The trust has therefore joined forces with the Whitley Awards Foundation to establish The Ashden Award for Renewable Energy, which will reward past achievement and provide funding for innovative developments in the field of community-based renewable energy anywhere in the world. The website www.whitley-award.org gives further details.

'Following a field visit to East Africa earlier this year, the trust has decided to explore the potential for a major programme of small-scale credit for community-based renewable energy, with a possible focus on the education sector. If the early results look promising, this is likely to become a major focus during the coming one or two years, and will work primarily through indigenous networks and organisations.

'The trust has also continued to focus on training through support for ITDG (Intermediate Technology Development Group) in East Africa.

'The trust continues to support the enhancement of schools (through improvements to buildings, equipment and training facilities) in Tanzania and Uganda.

'Grant-making is informed by field-visits, seminars (such as the Arusha seminar) and advice from key organisations such as ITDG.'

Beneficiaries included: National Agricultural Research Organisation – Uganda to support school improvements in rural areas (£37,000 over four years); World Vision UK towards six wind pumps to provide water for both domestic and irrigation purposes in Wajir – Kenya (£25,000); Community Action for Rural Development – India for a project to install improved stoves (£15,000); Oxfam for a solar oven project in Honduras (£11,000); and Village Education Project – Tanzania towards a new teacher resource centre (£1,500).

Exclusions: No grants to individuals.

Applications: In writing to the correspondent. Unsolicited applications are unlikely to be considered for this trust.

The Ashworth Charitable Trust

Welfare

Geographical focus: *Worldwide, but mostly UK with a preference for Devon*

Foot Anstey Sargent, 4–6 Barnfield Crescent, Exeter, Devon EX1 1RF
Tel: 01392 411221; **Fax:** 01392 218554
e-mail: alexander.elphinston@foot-ansteys.co.uk
Correspondent: A Elphinston, Secretary
Trustees: C F Bennett, Chair; Miss S E Crabtree; A Elphinston; Mrs K A Gray; G D R Cockram.

Total grants: £126,000 to organisations (1998/99)

General: The trust currently supports:
- Ironbridge Gorge Museum Trust;
- people living in the areas covered by certain medical practices around Exeter.

Such grants are to be paid only for particularly acute needs;
* humanitarian projects.

In 1998/99 the trust's assets were £3.6 million and it had an income of £153,000. Grants to 49 organisations totalled £126,000 and ranged from £500 to £10,000. Generally, grants appeared to be one-off.

Development organisations to benefit included Médecins sans Frontières (£5,000) and Anti-Slavery International.

Exclusions: No grants to animal-based charities; research; or the preservation of buildings.

Applications: In writing to the correspondent.

The Richard Attenborough Charitable Trust

Actors, overseas aid, general

Geographical focus: *UK and developing countries, with a preference for South Africa*

Beaver Lodge, Richmond Green, Surrey TW9 1NQ
Tel: 020 8940 7234
Correspondent: Lady Attenborough, Trustee
Trustees: Lady Attenborough; Lord Attenborough.

Total grants: £140,000 (1998/99)
General: This trust not surprisingly focuses much of its grantmaking on acting-related organisations. It also makes a number of grants to overseas and human rights organisations.

In 1998/99 the trust's assets totalled £418,000, mostly held in Attenborough Securities Ltd (£173,000) and Henry Moore Bronze (£100,000). The trust's income was £232,000 and it made 42 grants totalling £140,000, 13 of which were recurrent. Grants ranged from £100 to £21,000.

Recipients included One World Action (£11,000), Mandela Sponsorship Fund (£8,000) and Gandhi Foundation (£5,000). Smaller grants went to Amnesty International and Human Rights Watch.

Applications: The funds of this trust are donated principally to charities with which the trustees are associated. They greatly regret, therefore, that they are unable to reply to any unsolicited applications.

The Avenue Charitable Trust

General

Geographical focus: *Worldwide, but mostly UK*

c/o Sayers Butterworth, 18 Bentinck Street, London W1U 2AR
Tel: 020 7935 8504; **Fax:** 020 7487 5621
Correspondent: Sue Brotherhood
Trustees: The Hon. F D L Astor; The Hon. Mrs B A Astor; S G Kemp.

Total grants: £425,000 (1998/99)
General: The trust supports a wide variety of charitable purposes with a preference for human rights organisations. Most grants are given in the UK.

In 1998/99 the trust's assets rose from £526,000 to £890,000 after a large donation from the settlor of £750,000. Grants ranging from £15 to £80,000 were given to 75 organisations and totalled £425,000.

Organisations to benefit included Anti-Slavery International, Asylum Aid, Kurdish Human Rights Project, Medical Aid for Palestinians and Polish Institute & Sikorski Museum.

Applications: The trust has stated that all available income is committed to existing beneficiaries.

The Scott Bader Commonwealth Ltd

Supporting people and communities in need, particularly through education
Geographical focus: UK and overseas

Wollaston, Wellingborough, Northamptonshire NN9 7RL
Tel: 01933 666755; **Fax:** 01933 665020
e-mail: commonwealth_office@scottbader.com
website: www.scottbader.com
Correspondent: Denise Sayer, Commonwealth Secretary
Board of Management: S Carter; L Brown; C Tutler; J Wojakowski; D Johnson; P G Anfield; D Muir; M Jones.

Total grants: £220,000 approved (1999)
General: This trust was 'founded on the belief that a socially responsible undertaking cannot merely exist in its own interests. It is part of the whole national and international community.'

In the developing world, preference is given to initiatives which provide support for poor rural people and their communities to enable them to become self-sufficient, and expecially to initiatives arising from the communities' own expressed needs and wishes. The trust also provides emergency aid to people in times of natural disasters. Preference is given to organisations with an administrative base in the UK.

In 1999 the trust had assets of £433,000 and an income of £205,000. Grants paid totalled £169,000, plus a further £51,000 of agreed future funding.

Previous recipients have included Harvest Help, The Joe Homan Trust, Africa Now, Book Aid, Find your Feet, International Childcare Trust and Triple Trust.

Exclusions: No grants to: general appeals; large well-known organisations; animal charities; individuals in need; travel and adventure schemes; or arts projects.

Applications: In writing to the correspondent presenting information on no more than four sides of A4. All applications are acknowledged and they are considered by the trustees in January, April, July and October after being reviewed by the correspondent.

Veta Bailey Charitable Trust

Training of medical and paramedical personnel
Geographical focus: UK and local organisations working in developing countries

The Cottage, Tiltups End, Horsley, Stroud, Gloucestershire GL6 0QE
Tel: 01453 834914; **Fax:** 01453 833399
Correspondent: B L Worth, Trustee
Trustees: Brian Worth; Dr Elizabeth McClatchey; John Humphreys.

Total grants: £67,000 to organisations (1999/2000)
General: The trust's 1998/99 annual report states that grants will be made 'in the main, [for] the training of medical personnel in third world countries and [for] projects which assist in the development of good healthcare practices throughout the world'.

In 1999/2000 the trust had assets of £328,000 and an income of £63,000, including £41,000 in donations. Grants totalled £75,000.

Most grants went to UK charities working overseas, as below (1998/99 figures in brackets when applicable):
Voluntary Service Overseas, Malawi £9,300 (£18,000)
LEPRA, Brazil £7,800
Centre for Caribbean Medicine £6,000

Africa Now, Kenya £5,100
International Nepal Fellowship, Nepal £5,000 (£7,000)
Mildmay, Uganda £5,000
UNA International Service, Brazil £5,000
Tearfund, Bangladesh £4,000
Ockenden Venture, Afganistan £4,000
Sight Savers, India £2,300 (£21,000)
Initiatives for Deaf People, various countries £1,500 (£250)

Other unspecified grants to UK charities totalled £3,000. Grants of £4,000 each were given to local organisations in Cameroon and Kenya. Travel and educational grants to individuals (see exclusions) totalled £8,500.

Exclusions: Grants directly to individuals are only given to medical electives. Other grants can be given to projects for an individual but must be through a recognised sponsoring agency.

Applications: In writing to the correspondent by June, for consideration at a trustees' meeting in August.

The Cecile Baines Charitable Trust

Medical, children and young people, maritime, environmental

Geographical focus: UK, Europe and Africa

c/o Antrak Group Limited, Marc House, 13–14 Great Saint Thomas Apostle, London EC4V 2BB
Tel: 020 7332 6010
Correspondent: Doris Sharp
Trustees: R H Baines; Mrs R C Cunynghame; Mrs D Sharp.

Total grants: £6,300 (1998/99)
General: This trust makes donations in the UK, Africa and Europe for medical research, children and youth, maritime and environmental causes.

In 1999/2000 the largest grants included £1,100 to Children in Crisis for work in Sierra Leone, and £1,000 each to DEC Mozambique Flood Appeal and Samaritans for general work.

In the previous year, the trust had assets of £107,000 and an income of £48,000, and gave grants totalling £6,300.

Applications: In writing to the correspondent.

The Balcraig Foundation

Relief of pain, hardship or distress, particularly among children

Geographical focus: Scotland, Africa

Balcraig House, Scone, Perth PH2 7PG
Tel: 01738 552303; **Fax:** 01738 552101
Correspondent: David McCleary, Secretary
Trustees: Ann Gloag; David McCleary; Jonathan Scott.

Total grants: Around £2.5 million
General: Grants are given to organisations in Scotland and Africa. The trust owns a residential property in Blantyre (Malawi) and uses the rental income to fund projects in the country in addition to its other grantmaking.

In 1995/96 the trust gave grants totalling £2.5 million. No further information is available, although it is thought this level of giving has continued.

Past recipients have included a hospital in Malawi and an orphanage in Kenya.

Exclusions: No grants to individuals.

Applications: In writing to the correspondent, setting out a brief outline of the project for which funding is sought. The trustees meet quarterly.

The Balmore Trust

General

Geographical focus: *Developing countries and UK, particularly Strathclyde*

Viewfield, Balmore, Torrance,
Glasgow G64 4AE
Fax: 01360 620742
Correspondent: The Secretary
Trustees: J Riches; Ms R Jarvis;
Ms O Beauvoisin; C Brown; Ms J Brown;
J Eldridge; Ms R Riches; B Holman.

Total grants: £25,000 (1999/2000)
General: The trust donates two-thirds of its grants to overseas projects for general purposes. The remainder is given to local projects in the UK working with women, families and teenagers in areas of greatest social need. Holiday schemes in the UK are looked on favourably, with medical and educational projects receiving a preference overseas.

Grants are one-off and generally for core, project and start-up costs. They usually range from £50 to £3,000, although applicants new to the trust rarely receive more than £500 (overseas) or £200 (UK).

In 1999/2000 the trust had assets of £80,000 and an income of £26,000. Grants totalled £25,000.

Beneficiaries included: Amajuba Education Trust – South Africa, for university fees (£4,000); Child in Need Institute – Calcutta, for medical aid and malnutrition relief (£2,800); Sophia Mission Institute – Myanmar for education (£2,700); and Wells for India, for water projects (£1,200).

Exclusions: No grants to individuals.

Applications: In writing to the correspondent. Organisations not personally known to the trust are unlikely to be successful. Please enclose an sae if a reply is needed.

The Baring Foundation

Strengthening the voluntary sector and ngos, arts, displaced peoples

Geographical focus: *England and Wales, Latin America, sub-Saharan Africa*

60 London Wall, London EC2M 5TQ
Tel: 020 7767 1348; **Fax:** 020 7767 7121
e-mail: baring.foundation@ing-barings.com
website: www.baringfoundation.org.uk
Correspondent: Toby Johns, Director
Trustees: Nicholas Baring, Chair; Tessa Baring; Lady Lloyd; Martin Findlay; Sir Crispin Tickell; Anthony Loehnis; Janet Lewis-Jones; J R Peers; Dr Ann Buchanan; R D Broadley.

Total grants: £2.8 million (2001)
Grants overseas: £650,000

General: This foundation has three separate grant programmes, each with its own eligibility, grants policy and application procedure (which are comprehensively described on the trust's website, from which much of the following information is taken). These are: Strengthening the voluntary sector (grants to organisations working throughout England and Wales and local groups in London, Merseyside, Cornwall and Devon); Arts in education and in the community; and International.

A new international grants programme started in January 2001. This policy replaces any international programmes which have operated in the past and is expected to continue for at least two or three years before being reviewed. The foundation intends to increase the impact of the international grants by increasing the size and length of the individual grants.

Grants are given to non-profit organisations in the UK which work in partnership with ngos and community-based organisations (cbos) in sub-Saharan Africa and Latin America and are seeking to benefit people disadvantaged or marginalised by long-term migration and displacement. Organisations less likely to obtain unrestricted funding from other sources are prioritised. The programme will provide two types of funding within a single grant (although applications for only one component will be considered):

- *Core funding* – to build the organisation's own capacity to support partner organisations in developing countries, especially Latin America and sub-Saharan Africa. Preference is given to organisations which can show that increasing their own capacity will also benefit ngos in the beneficial areas. Grants for core funding range from £10,000 to £30,000 a year.
- *Block grant* – to the applicant organisation which re-grants it to its partner ngos and cbos to fund capacity-building initiatives that address the needs of migrants and displaced people. Block grants range from £15,000 to £50,000 a year. (Please note that any extra costs required to provide technical support or administer these grants may be budgeted for in the core funding.)

Grants may last for up to three years and the maximum grant is £240,000 (£80,000 a year for three years), although the foundation expects most applications to be for less than this.

Priority is given to work that fulfils two or more of the following objectives:

- forms a coherent programme with clear strategic goals;
- improves coordination and collaboration between agencies;
- improves the efficiency and influence of several ngos and cbos (in a single country or more than one country);
- leads to the intended beneficiaries having more control of decision-making in the development and management of initiatives.

No exact aspects of capacity building or activity are specified. The following are all examples of what may be funded:

Capacity building
- leadership and management development
- policy research and advocacy
- the application of new thinking and practices
- field or technical skills
- information access and dissemination
- building alliances and other forms of collaboration
- administration, financial management and fundraising.

Activities
- developing networks and other partnerships
- training programmes and the design and preparation of training courses and materials
- research and dialogue with policy and decision makers about issues affecting ngos and community groups
- workshops, meetings and exchange visits to develop or share skills and experiences
- piloting new approaches
- improving information resources and upgrading capacity in information and communications technologies
- improving financial and administrative systems.

The trustees are looking for evidence of the following when assessing grants, that:

- the planned activities respond in practical and focused ways to specific problems and opportunities that have been identified by partner organisations and communities and have clearly defined objectives;

- the context of the work (e.g. the nature and significance of the issues addressed and relevant work being done by other organisations) is understood and has been taken into account during planning;
- close partnerships with ngos and/or cbos are being or will be developed and control of activities will be with and will be assumed by partner organisations or community-based groups;
- the planned activities contain strategies for ensuring that several organisations learn new skills and knowledge;
- the impact of the activities will be cost effective;
- gender issues are addressed;
- the benefits of the work are likely to last after the period of the grant.

Organisations must also demonstrate they have the management structure, staff and track record to undertake the project they are planning. They must also have a commitment to equal opportunities and working in an environmentally-friendly manner.

Exclusions: The international grants programme does not support:
- expeditions
- bursaries or scholarships
- medical research or equipment
- animal welfare or wildlife conservation
- vehicles
- purchase, conversion or refurbishment of buildings
- religious activity
- emergency relief
- general fundraising appeals
- work that has already been completed or will have started while the application is being considered
- continued funding of activity that has already taking place or will be repeated.

Applications: (For international grants only.) In writing to the correspondent, including a datasheet available from the correspondent or the website. Very helpful guidelines are available from the foundation or on its website; applicants are strongly advised to read these before applying. Applicants are also advised to contact the foundation if there is any doubt about eligibility.

The trust states: 'Applicants should note that there may be very strong competition for funding. It is possible that only two or three grants will be awarded each year.' All applications are acknowledged and decisions are sent in writing. The foundation may telephone or visit applicants for further information.

Initial outline proposals should be no longer than four pages. They should be presented under the following headings and contain the following information, covering both the core and project elements of the proposed work: applicant organisation; goals; needs; beneficiaries; approach; timetable; how the work will be assessed; budget; accounts; strategic plan; annual report; and details of the staff and volunteers (for exact details of the sub-sections under each category see information on the website). Short-listed applicants will be invited to submit a fuller proposal of no more than 10 pages to explain the work in detail. Applicants will also be asked to make a short presentation and answer questions on their work. Successful applicants are required to produce a report and evaluation of the project that is funded, which must be made public (up to 10% of the grant may be used for this purpose).

Applications are considered once a year. The following timetable for 2001 is expected to be similar each year (check the website each October for exact dates):

end of November 2000 – guidelines issued

end of February 2001 – deadline for submission of outline proposals

March – selection of applicants for second stage (full proposals and presentations)

end of May – deadline for full proposals

June – presentations and selection of proposals to be recommended to foundation's council

end of September – council makes final decisions.

The Barnabas Trust

Community welfare, education, Christian mission

Geographical focus: UK and overseas

63 Wolsey Drive, Walton-on-Thames, Surrey KT12 3BB
Tel: 01932 220622
Correspondent: Mrs Doris Edwards, Secretary
Trustees: K C Griffiths, Chair; N Brown; D S Helden.

Total grants: £426,000 to organisations (1998/99)

General: The trust gives grants to local, UK and international organisations towards community welfare, education and Christian mission. In practice, most of the grant total is given towards evangelical causes. The trust has a list of around 50 regularly supported charities. After these grants have been made there is usually around £150,000 to £200,000 available for unsolicited applications. These new grants range from £250 to £5,000 and are mostly given to 'overtly evangelical projects' rather than international aid and development.

In 1998/99 the trust had assets of £4.7 million generating an income of £208,000. Grants to 108 organisations totalled £426,000, with 8 individuals receiving a total of £11,000.

Grants to international medical institutions and welfare charities included £5,000 to Prison Fellowship and £1,000 each to AIDS Care, Education and Training (ACET), Mathare Community Outreach – Kenya and Worldshare – Guatemala.

Grants to overseas educational charities and establishments included those to Haggai Institute (£6,000), Book Aid (£3,000), Overseas College – Kenya (£2,000) and Danoka Training College – Kenya (£1,000).

Applications: In writing to the correspondent, giving as much detail as possible, and enclosing a copy of the latest audited accounts. Please note that overseas grants are only given if the applicant is personally known to the correspondent. Unsolicited overseas applications are not considered. Applicants are asked to telephone the correspondent if there is any doubt about whether to apply. The trustees usually meet quarterly in March, June, September and December.

The Batchworth Trust

Medical, social welfare, general – see below

Geographical focus: Worldwide

33–35 Bell Street, Reigate, Surrey RH2 7AW
Tel: 01737 221311
Correspondent: M R Neve, Administrative Executive
Trustees: Lockwell Trustees Ltd.

Total grants: £288,000 (1999/2000)
Grants overseas: £141,000

General: The trust mainly supports well-known charities in the following fields

(listed with the percentage of grants given under the category in 1999/2000):
social welfare 29%
foreign aid 49%
medical 12%
youth and education 10%
environment less than 1%
arts nil

In 1999/2000 it had assets of £6.6 million and an income of £232,000. It made 29 grants totalling £288,000, some of which were recurrent.

Grants to aid organisations included £5,000 each to African Medical Mission, Farm Africa, Intermediate Technology and International Red Cross.

Exclusions: No grants to individuals.

Applications: In writing to the correspondent, enclosing an sae if a reply is required.

The Berkeley Reafforestation Trust

Reafforestation projects

Geographical focus: *Worldwide*

3 Harley Gardens, London SW10 9SW
Tel: 020 7370 1965
Correspondent: R J B Portman, Trustee
Trustees: Rodney Portman; Loulou Cooke; Nicholas Foster; Rozzie Portman.

Total grants: £25,000 (1998/99)
Grants overseas: £25,000

General: The trust aims to relieve poverty by encouraging tree planting and tree management internationally to combat land erosion/degradation, rural poverty and ecological and environmental deterioration. Part of its work is to make grants to tree and forestry projects in the third world.

In 1998/99 the trust had assets of £52,000 and an income of £36,000. Grants to four organisations totalled £25,000. The largest was £10,000 to Trees for Life in India. Other grants were given to: Royal Botanic Gardens, Kew, for a project in Zimbabwe to identify species, seed provenance and harvesting methods to achieve optimum wood fuel production (£7,900); MPT in Kenya (£4,500); and CHIRAG towards establishing 1,300 acres of woodland in India (£2,200).

Applications: In writing to the correspondent, although please note the trust states it 'does not solicit applications'.

Miss Jeanne Bisgood's Charitable Trust

General, with a preference for Roman Catholic charities

Geographical focus: *Worldwide*

12 Water's Edge, Brudenell Road, Poole BH13 7NN
Tel: 01202 708460
Correspondent: Miss J M Bisgood, Trustee
Trustees: Miss J M Bisgood; P Schulte; P J K Bisgood.

Total grants: £73,000 (1999/2000)
General: The trust has general charitable purposes, with three particular areas of preference; these are:
• Roman Catholic organisations
• local organisations in Poole, Bournemouth and the county of Dorset
• UK groups caring for older people.

Other grants are given to a wide range of groups, including UK charities for projects overseas.

In 1999/2000 the trust had assets of £1.3 million and an income of £87,000. Grants ranged from £25 to £2,500 and totalled £73,000.

The main beneficiary was CAFOD, which received three grants totalling £6,500 for relief work. Other grants included £2,000 each to Intermediate Technology, Sight Savers International and Survive-Miva, and £1,300 to St Francis' Leprosy Guild.

Applications: In writing to the correspondent.

The Bishop Simeon CR Trust

Young people, education, welfare
Geographical focus: South Africa

1 Middlemead Road, Tiverton,
Devon EX16 6AZ
Tel & Fax: 01884 251933
Correspondent: Mrs B Byrom, Administrator
Trustees: Revd Canon Geoffrey Brown, Chair; Joan Antcliff; Angela Cunningham; Christopher Lintott; Nathanial Masemola, Solomon Motsiri; Peter Roberts; the Father Superior of the Community of the Resurrection; Clive Scott; Judith Scott; Patricia Sibbons; Howard Thompson; Julie Williams.

Total grants: £53,000 (1999/2000)
Grants overseas: £53,000

General: The trust seeks to help people whose lives have been affected by the inequalities and injustices of apartheid in South Africa. Support is given to education and welfare projects in deprived rural and urban areas of South Africa.

In 1999/2000 the trust had assets of £52,000 and an income of £81,000. Grants totalled £53,000.

Larger grants included those to Highveld Education Trust for educational bursaries (£7,000), Trevor Huddleston CR Memorial Centre for educational upgrading programmes (£5,800) and Nothemba Children's Centre for education and social care of street children (£4,400). Smaller grants included £3,000 each to: Ekukhanyeni Community Counselling Centre for youth work, literacy and community advice; Masakane Trust for pre-school development; and HIV Hospice in Highveld for AIDS terminal care. In addition £2,000 was given to Johannesburg College of Education for a teacher upgrading programme.

Exclusions: No direct grants to individuals.

Applications: In writing to the correspondent. The trust is currently not looking for new initiatives to support and applications are unlikely to be successful.

The Boltons Trust

Social welfare, medicine, education, international peace
Geographical focus: Worldwide

44a New Cavendish Street,
London W1M 7LG
Correspondent: Clive Marks, Trustee
Trustees: Clive Marks; Henry B Levin; Mrs C Albuquerque.

Total grants: £632,000 (1998/99)
General: The main aims of the trust are:
- the pursuit of peace and understanding throughout the world and the reduction of innocent suffering;
- to support education.

The current policy is to select and support a strictly limited number of projects and the trust does not consider any applications.

In 1998/99 the trust had an income of £104,000 and gave grants totalling £632,000. Most grants were given to religious organisations, although other beneficiaries included Power (Prosthetics and Orthotics World Education Relief) for landmine victims (£40,000) and Mine Victims Fund (£10,000).

The trust had commitments of £370,000 for 1999/2000 and £170,000 for 2000/2001, of which £100,000 and £50,000 respectively was for international peace.

Applications: In writing to the correspondent. 'Sadly, the trust can no longer respond to unsolicited applications.'

The P G & N J Boulton Trust

Disaster relief, Christian
Geographical focus: *Worldwide*

28 Burden Road, Moreton,
Wirral CH46 6BQ
e-mail: email@pgnjbt.org.uk
website: www.pgnjbt.org.uk
Correspondent: Miss N J Boulton, Chair
Trustees: Miss N J Boulton, Chair;
L J Marsh; B J Knight; A L Perry; S Perry.

Total grants: £63,000 (1998/99)
Grants overseas: £63,000

General: The aim of this trust is to assist victims of disasters and any other charitable causes. In practice, the trust gives a substantial proportion of its support to Christian missionary work, and also supports the areas of poverty relief, medical research, healthcare and disability. It gives preference to smaller charities where 'a relatively small gift can make a significant difference'. In 1998/99 the trust had assets of £1.8 million and an income of £99,000. Grants totalled £63,000. Other expenditure included property costs of £17,000 and administration costs of £7,500.

Development and relief agencies received grants of between £1,000 and £3,000 with projects funded in Bangladesh, Cambodia, Crimea, Honduras, Iran, Israel, Peru, Romania, South Africa and Uganda.

Recipients included African Enterprise, Ebenezer Emergency Fund, International Red Cross, Operation Mobilisation and Southeast Asia Outreach.

Exclusions: No grants to individuals.

Applications: In writing to the correspondent. Owing to the number of applications received the trustees cannot acknowledge all of them. Successful applicants will receive a response within two months.

The Bower Trust

General
Geographical focus: *Wales and developing countries*

New Guild House, 45 Great Charles Street, Queensway, Birmingham B3 2LX
Tel: 0121 212 2222
Correspondent: Roger Harriman, Trust Administrator
Trustees: Mrs C V E Benfield; G Benfield; R Harriman; F C Slater.

Total grants: £10,000 (1999/2000)
Grants overseas: About £6,000

General: This trust gives grants to charities working in either the third world or Wales.

In 1999/2000 the trust had assets of £579,000 and an income of £31,000. Grants ranging from £24 to £3,000 totalled £10,000.

Beneficiaries working overseas included Friends of the Gambia Association (£1,300), People for a Landmine Free World (£1,000), UNICEF (£800), Oxfam (£500), Survival International (£400), Tourism Concern (£200) and Amnesty International (£24).

In the previous year beneficiaries included: ActionAid, British Red Cross, Friends of the Gambia Association, Karuna Trust, Médecins Sans Frontières

(UK), Merlin and SOS Sahel International UK.

Applications: In writing to the correspondent.

The Broad Oak Trust

Overseas aid, people who are disadvantaged, environment

Geographical focus: UK and overseas

The Broadhurst, Brandeston, Woodbridge, Suffolk IP13 7AG
Tel & Fax: 01728 685751
Correspondent: Lord Cunliffe

Total grants: £9,400 (1997/98)
General: The trust's policy is to give recurrent grants to 15 UK-registered charities working in the fields of overseas aid, welfare in the UK and the environment.

In 1997/98 the trust had an income of £11,000. Grants totalled £9,400 and included £1,500 each to British Red Cross, Oxfam and Sight Savers International, with £300 each to Feed the Minds and Friends of the Earth.

Exclusions: Grants to UK-registered charities only. No grants to individuals.

Applications: This is a small family trust giving all its income to 15 regular beneficiaries. Unsolicited applications cannot be considered.

The Bromley Trust

Human rights, conservation

Geographical focus: Worldwide

Ashley Manor, King's Somborne, Stockbridge, Hampshire SO20 6RQ
Tel: 01794 388241; **Fax:** 01794 388264
Correspondent: Keith Bromley, Trustee
Trustees: Keith Bromley; Anna Home; Alan P Humphries; Lady Anne Prance; Lady Ann Wood; Anthony Roberts.

Total grants: £410,000 (2000/01)
Grants overseas: Over £350,000

General: The aims and objects of the trust are to make grants to charitable organisations which:

'a) combat violations of human rights, and help victims of torture, refugees from oppression and those who have been falsely imprisoned

'b) help those who have suffered severe bodily or mental hurt through no fault of their own, and if need be their dependants: try in some small way to off set man's inhumanity to man

'c) oppose the extinction of the world's fauna and flora and the destruction of the environment for wildlife and for mankind worldwide.'

The trust's objectives are narrow and it hardly ever departs from them. By far the greater part of the income goes to charities that are concerned with human rights; a comparatively small proportion is given to charities concerned with the preservation of the world's environment. In general, conservation interests are limited to the preservation of rainforests and national and international conservation issues, not local projects. One-off grants are occasionally made, but are infrequent. Grants are given to UK-registered charities only.

The trust's declared policy is to give larger amounts to fewer charities rather than spread its income over a large number of small grants. Consequently the trust is slow to add new charities to its list. The trust's mainstream charities normally receive their grants in two half-yearly payments for a period of not less than three years, barring unforeseen circumstances.

The mainstream charities (as at April 2000): Medical Foundation for the Care of Victims of Torture; The Redress Trust;

Anti-Slavery International; Survival International; Prisoners of Conscience Appeal Fund; Amnesty International (UK Section) Charitable Trust; Ockenden International; Asylum Aid; Prisoners Abroad; Prison Reform Trust; Writers & Scholars Educational Trust; Minority Rights Group; Justice Educational & Research Trust; Childhope; International Childcare Trust; Koestler Awards Trust; Institute of Psychiatry – Istanbul Human Rights Centre; Karuna Trust; Womankind Worldwide; Inside Out Trust; Kurdistan Human Rights Project; Population Concern; Marie Stopes International; Greenpeace Environmental Trust; Durrell Wildlife Conservation Trust; Reserva Ecologica de Guapi Açu (REGUA) (The Brazilian Atlantic Rainforest Trust); Birdlife International; Fauna & Flora International; British Butterfly Conservation Society; Wildfowl & Wetlands Trust; Wildlife Conservation Research Unit; Countryside Restoration Trust; Aldeburgh Productions; Manic Depression Fellowship; Orchard Vale Trust; Prisoners' Education Trust; The New Bridge; The Hardman Trust; Penrose Housing Association; Find Your Feet; Marine Conservation Society; Tree Aid; Rio Atlantic Forest Trust.

In 2000/01 the trust had an income of around £350,000 and gave grants totalling £410,000, including £270,000 in regular grants to the organisations above.

One-off grants totalled £140,000. Beneficiaries included Jubilee 2000 (£30,000 in two grants), Rainforest Concern and Survival International for a special appeal (£10,000), Fair Trials Abroad and Farm Africa (£3,000 each) and Money for Madagascar (£2,000).

Exclusions: No grants to individuals, expeditions, scholarships or non-UK-registered charities.

Applications: In writing to the correspondent, on one (or at most two) sheets outlining objectives and achievements, accounts (a summarised version will be sufficient) and any other information thought to be important. The trustees meet in April and October, although a sub-committee can convene between meetings if necessary.

Burdens Charitable Foundation

General

Geographical focus: *Mainly UK and developing countries, with a preference for sub-Saharan Africa*

St George's House, 215–219 Chester Road, Manchester M15 4JE
Tel: 0161 832 4901; **Fax:** 0161 835 3668
e-mail: pam@burdens.co.uk
Correspondent: Pam Maddocks, Secretary
Trustees: Arthur Burden; Roland Evans; Godfrey Burden; Hilary Perkins; Sally Schofield.

Total grants: £427,000 (1999/2000)
Grants overseas: £98,000

General: The foundation was created in 1977 by Mr and Mrs W T Burden, who endowed it with shares in the business Mr Burden had created in 1929, WTB Group Ltd. The foundation expects to be able to give about £400,000 a year in grants, the total being maintained in real terms over time. A very large number of small grants are made, mostly to small charities, and divided between overseas aid organisations and welfare charities in the UK. Few local charities are supported outside the Manchester area.

The present aim is to allocate about half the income to the UK and half to less privileged countries overseas. The grants are intended to be of a size and duration

sufficient to make a significant difference to the causes aided. Priority is given to:
- the relief of human suffering, impairment and economic deprivation
- small, highly focused and local community groups rather than large UK/international charities
- groups where volunteers play a key role in the service being delivered
- social outreach projects based on local churches and established faith groups
- low-cost umbrella agencies acting as monitoring conduits of similar criteria to the above.

Grants, mostly small – generally less than £1,000 in the UK – may be one-off or recurring over two or more years. They can be for core costs, salaries, capital assets, etc. without any exclusions in principle, save only that they really do make a difference. In general, large charities/projects and causes using professional fundraising costs to any substantial extent do not score particularly well.

Causes which rarely or never benefit include animal welfare (except in less developed countries), the arts and museums, political activities, most medical research, preservation etc. of historic buildings and monuments, and sport.

In 1999/2000 the trust had assets of £11 million and an income of £360,000. Grants totalled £427,000, including 27 overseas grants totalling £98,000.

The largest were £6,000 to Ockenden International for work in Afghanistan and £5,000 each to: ACET (Uganda), APT Enterprise Development (Sierra Leone), Merlin (Kosovo), Mozambique Schools Fund, National Library for the Blind (Books Around the World), Nepal Leprosy Trust, ROKPA UK for international projects, Sight Savers International and Sylvia Wright Trust.

Other beneficiaries included World Vision (Orissa – India) and Y Care International for use in Zimbabwe (£4,000 each), African Christian Teaching Service (£3,000) with £2,500 each to ApTibeT, British Red Cross for the Turkey earthquake appeal, Nairobi Hospice Charitable Trust, Tearfund and WaterAid.

Exclusions: No grants to individuals.

Applications: In writing to the correspondent, including accounts, annual reports and outline business plans.

The Clara E Burgess Charity

Children

Geographical focus: UK and worldwide

The Royal Bank of Scotland plc, Private Trust and Taxation, PO Box 356, 45 Mosley Street, Manchester M60 2BE
Tel: 0161 236 8585
Correspondent: The Senior Trust Officer

Total grants: £1 million (1999/2000)
General: The trust was established in October 1998 when assets of over £10 million were transferred from the estate of the late Douglas Burgess. It makes grants towards 'the provision of facilities and assistance to enhance the education, health and physical well-being of children, particularly (but not exclusively) those under the age of 10 years who have lost one or both parents'. Within these boundaries grants can be made to the following causes: education/training, overseas projects, disability, social welfare, hospitals/hospices, medical/health and medical research. The overwhelming majority of grants are given in the UK and they range from £500 to £45,000.

The grant total rose from £320,000 in the first year of operation to over £1 million in the second year. Overseas beneficiaries included Luweera Medical

Centre, Mildmay Mission Hospital and Relief Fund for Romania.

Exclusions: Grants are given to UK-registered charities only.

Applications: On a form available from the correspondent. The trustees meet to consider grants in February, May, August and November and applications should be received in the month before those meetings. The trust states that applications should be as brief as possible as the trustees will ask for any further information they require.

Audrey and Stanley Burton 1960 Charitable Trust

Health, arts, education, social welfare

Geographical focus: *Yorkshire, UK, Europe, Africa*

Trustee Management Ltd, 19 Cookridge Street, Leeds LS2 3AG
Correspondent: The Secretary
Trustees: Audrey Burton; Amanda Burton; Deborah Hazan; Philip Morris; David Solomon; Raymond Burton.

Total grants: £683,000 (2000)

General: The trust makes one-off and project grants towards health, the arts, education and social needs. Although the trust has a beneficial area of UK, Europe and Africa, preference is given to charities in Yorkshire.

In 2000 it had assets of £1.1 million, an income of £459,000 and grants totalled £683,000. Overseas grants in 1998/99 included £20,000 to Oxfam, £2,500 to Anti-Slavery International and £1,000 to World Vision.

Exclusions: No grants to individuals.

Applications: In writing to the correspondent. Unsuccessful applications are not acknowledged. Charities new to the trust must include detailed information and accounts. This trust has already established over many years the major charities to which it contributes and is therefore unlikely to add to its list.

The Edward Cadbury Charitable Trust

Religion, general

Geographical focus: *Worldwide, but mostly UK*

Elmfield, College Walk, Selly Oak, Birmingham B29 6LE
Tel: 0121 472 1838
Correspondent: Mrs M Walton, Secretary
Trustees: Charles E Gillett, Chair; Christopher Littleboy; Charles R Gillett; Andrew Littleboy; Nigel Cadbury.

Total grants: £1.1 million (1999/2000)

General: The trust aims to support the voluntary sector in the West Midlands in areas including education, Christian mission, ecumenical mission and inter-faith relations. There is a preference for newly established charities. A few grants are given to UK groups working overseas.

In 1999/2000 the trust had assets of £24 million and an income of £893,000. Grants to 160 organisations totalled £1.1 million, including £500,000 to Ironbridge Gorge Museum Trust.

Overseas beneficiaries of larger grants included Christian Aid (£40,000), Jubilee 2000 Coalition (£30,000) Responding to Conflict (£18,000), University of Cape Town (£7,900) and Population Concern (£5,000). Grants of £1,000 each went to Book Aid International, Medical Foundation for the Care of Victims of Torture and Prisoners of Conscience. Recipients of smaller grants included Tools for Self Reliance (£750) and Kosovo Crisis Appeal (£250).

Exclusions: Grants are given to UK-registered charities only and not to students or other individuals. The trust is unlikely to fund projects which have popular appeal or areas which are normally publicly funded.

Applications: At any time, but allow three months for a response. Applications that do not come within the trust's policy as stated above will not be considered or acknowledged.

The trust does not have an application form. Applications should be made in writing to the correspondent. They should clearly and concisely give relevant information concerning the project and its benefits, an outline budget and how the project is to be funded initially and in the future. Up-to-date accounts and the latest annual report are also required.

G W Cadbury Charitable Trust

General

Geographical focus: *Mostly UK, USA and Canada*

New Guild House, 45 Great Charles Street, Queensway, Birmingham B3 2LX
Tel: 0121 212 2222
Correspondent: Roger Harriman, Trust Administrator
Trustees: Mrs C A Woodroffe; Mrs L E Boal; P C Boal; Miss J C Boal; N B Woodroffe; Miss J L Woodroffe.

Total grants: £170,000 (2000)
General: The trust gives grants for general charitable purposes, with a preference for population control and family planning. Grants are given to organisations in the UK (70%), USA (20%) and Canada (10%), although they can be for projects outside of these countries.

In 2000 it had assets of £6.1 million and income of £267,000. Grants to 81 organisations totalled £170,000.

Past beneficiaries have included Christian Aid, Harvest Help, International Planned Parenthood Federation, Marie Stopes International, Nairobi Hospice Trust, Project Trust, Womankind Worldwide and Worldwide Fund for Nature.

Exclusions: Grants are given to registered charities only. No grants to individuals or scholarships.

Applications: In writing to the correspondent. The trust states that it does not respond to unsolicited applications.

The William Adlington Cadbury Charitable Trust

General, including UK charities working overseas on long-term development projects

Geographical focus: *Worldwide*

2 College Walk, Selly Oak, Birmingham B29 6LQ
Tel: 0121 472 1464 (am only)
e-mail: christine@stober.freeserve.co.uk
website: www.wa-cadbury.org.uk
Correspondent: Mrs Christine Stober
Trustees: Brandon Cadbury; James Taylor; Rupert Cadbury; Katherine van Hagen Cadbury; Margaret Salmon; Sarah Stafford; Adrian Thomas; John Penny.

Total grants: £513,000 (1999/2000)
General: The trust makes a large number of modest grants, with very few for more than £5,000. About half the awards are to new applicants. Only a small number of charities receive annual grants for revenue costs.

Applications are encouraged from ethnic minority groups and women-led initiatives.

The trust has grant programmes for the West Midlands, UK and Ireland, and International. The latter supports UK charities working overseas on long-term development projects.

In 1999/2000, 1,080 appeals were received with 259 grants made, giving a success rate of 24%. However, every tenth application was for individuals or expeditions, which the trust does not fund. The largest grants were £20,000 each to British Red Cross and Oxfam for its Orissa cyclone appeal. In autumn 2000 the trust was planning a visit to West Africa to identify suitable new projects for support.

Exclusions: No support for individuals (whether for research, expeditions, educational purposes, etc.), projects concerned with travel or adventure and local projects/groups outside West Midlands.

Applications: In writing to the correspondent, including the charity's registration number, a brief description of the charity's activities, details of the specific project, a budget of the proposed work, the most recent accounts, details of what funds have already been raised for the project and how any shortfall is to be met. However, many applicants prefer an initial telephone discussion before using the online application form available on the website.

The Calpe Trust

See below

Geographical focus: *Worldwide*

The Hideaway, Hatford Down, Faringdon, Oxfordshire SN7 8JH
Tel: 01367 870665; **Fax:** 01367 870500
Correspondent: R H Norton, Trustee
Trustees: R H L R Norton, Chair; B E M Norton; E R H Parks.

Total grants: £40,000 (1998/99)
Grants overseas: £40,000

General: The trust makes grants in the areas of peace, human rights, medical, refugees, homelessness, social deprivation, war and disaster relief and other charitable purposes.

In 1998/99 the trust made grants totalling £40,000, to 46 organisations. Beneficiaries of larger grants included Anti-Slavery International (£5,000), CIIR – Hurricane Mitch (two grants totalling £2,800) and Chernobyl Children's Project (£2,000). Grants of £1,000 to £1,500 included those to CAFOD, The Howard League, Society of St Peter the Apostle, 3-H Fund and UNICEF.

Exclusions: No grants for animal welfare.

Applications: In writing to the correspondent. Applications need to be received by June or December for consideration in the following month.

The Canning Trust

General

Geographical focus: *UK and developing countries*

4–6 Abingdon Road, London W8 6AF
Tel: 020 7937 3233; **Fax:** 020 7937 1458
Correspondent: P Ong, Trustee
Trustees: A J MacDonald; A W Reed; P Ong.

Total grants: £40,000 (1997/98)
General: Grants are made to smaller organisations in the UK and the third world for general charitable purposes. In 1997/98 the trust's assets totalled £196,000. It had an income of £54,000 and made 10 grants ranging between £1,000 and £6,500 totalling £40,000. Beneficiaries included Friends of

Hadhramut, Kafue Fisheries Ltd (£5,000 each) and New Life Centre – Dehva Dun (£2,000).

Applications: Unsolicited applications are not considered. The trust states that it generally only makes grants to charities which staff, ex-staff and friends are directly involved with.

The Caring and Sharing Association East Sussex

General

Geographical focus: *Developing countries*

Virginia, Whatlington Road, Battle, East Sussex TN33 0JN
Tel: 01424 773417
Correspondent: Thomas C Long, Trustee
Trustees: Mrs Susanne R Madden, Chair; Mrs L Elizabeth Gorsuch; Mrs Joyce Potter; Mrs Janet Waddams; Roy H Tucker; Mrs Jennifer Hewitson; Miss Valerie Luff; Thomas C Long; Mrs Valerie Ballard.

Total grants: £82,000 (1998/99)
General: The following information was included in the trust's 1998/99 annual report. 'In 1982 the Bishop of Lewes initiated a movement in which church members and other individuals would give up some personal expenditure previously made as part of each individual's normal day-to-day lifestyle. The monies saved would be used to support third world projects of limited and specific nature, designed to eliminate poverty and ill health.'

Local representatives in East Sussex collect money from members and forward it to the treasurer. In 1998/99 the income from members totalled £84,000. Assets in that year totalled £18,000 and grants were made totalling £82,000. A list of grant beneficiaries was not included in the trust's accounts.

Applications: In writing to the correspondent.

The Carpenter Charitable Trust

Christian, humanitarian

Geographical focus: *UK and overseas*

The Old Vicarage, Hitchin Road, Kimpton, Hitchin, Hertfordshire SG4 8EF
Correspondent: M S E Carpenter, Trustee
Trustees: M S E Carpenter; Mrs G M L Carpenter.

Total grants: £54,000 (1999/2000)
General: This trust gives grants for Christian outreach and humanitarian purposes, in the UK and overseas.

In 1999/2000 it had assets of £1.1 million and an income of £31,000. In all, 63 grants were made totalling £54,000.

The largest grants were: £2,500 each to Gospel Gifts for distribution of gospels to mark the millennium, Kosovo Crisis Appeal, and Salvation Army for work in Albania; £2,000 each to Mission Aviation Fellowship for general purposes and Salvation Army for a minibus for Hertford and Ware; £1,500 each to Crisis for general purposes, Daily Telegraph Christmas Appeal (split between The Passage, Send a Cow and UNICEF) and Save the Children Fund – Mozambique appeal; and £1,000 each to Habitat for Humanity GB for general purposes and St Albans DBF for Christ Church Nazareth library project.

Exclusions: No grants to individuals or for church repairs.

Applications: In writing to the correspondent.

The Casey Trust

Children and young people
Geographical focus: *Worldwide*

27 Arkwright Road, London NW3 6BJ
Correspondent: Ken Howard, Chair
Trustees: Kenneth Howard; Edwin Green; Judge Leonard Krikler.

Total grants: £105,000 (1999/2000)

General: This trust was established to help children and young people worldwide and supports new projects in a variety of countries. The trust tries to support new projects which would not have happened or continued without its support.

In 1999/2000 grants totalled £105,000, a sharp rise from £53,000 in the previous year. The trust continues to fund children-based projects at home and abroad. A three year grant was given to Child Psychotherapy Trust for funding psychotherapy for victims of torture and grants were made to Orbis for sight-saving equipment in Africa and UNICEF for its work in Mozambique.

Exclusions: Grants are not given to 'individual applicants requesting funds to continue studies'.

Applications: In writing to the correspondent.

The Thomas Sivewright Catto Charitable Settlement

General
Geographical focus: *UK and overseas*

Clarebell House, 5–6 Cork Street, London W1X 1PB
Correspondent: Miss Ann Uwins
Trustees: Hon. Mrs Ruth Bennett; Lord Catto; Miss Zoe Richmond-Watson.

Total grants: £200,000 (1999)

General: Grants are given for general charitable purposes, including international aid and development.

In 1998/99 the trust had assets of £6.4 million, a significant increase from £3.3 million in the previous year. This was due to the receipt of a legacy from the estate of the Honourable Isabel Ida Gordon Catto of £3.7 million. A further £149,000 was given from the legacy to the income fund and grants totalled £200,000 compared to £79,000 the year before. Grants ranged from £50 to £20,000, although 103 of the 177 beneficiaries received less than £1,000.

Grants included £1,000 each to British Red Cross, CARE International, Oxfam for the Sudan emergency appeal, Sarajevo Charter and Y Care International and £500 each to Calcutta Tercentenary Trust, The Horn of Africa Charity, Merlin, Refugee Council and VSO.

Exclusions: No support for non-UK-registered charities, expeditions, educational/travel bursaries or unsolicited applications from churches of any denomination. Grants are unlikely to be considered in the areas of community care, playschemes, and drug abuse, or for local branches of UK organisations such as scout groups.

Applications: In writing to the correspondent, enclosing an sae.

CfBT Education Services

Education
Geographical focus: *UK and overseas*

1 The Chambers, East Street, Reading, Berkshire RG1 4JF
Tel: 0118 952 3900; **Fax:** 0118 952 3926
e-mail: gen@cfbt-hq.org.uk
website: www.cfbt.com
Correspondent: The Development Fund Manager

Trustees: Andrew Stuart, Chair; Thelma Henderson; Anita Higham; Iain MacArthur; Stephen Yeo; J Webb; S Yeo.

Total grants: £977,000 to organisations (1999/2000)

General: Grants are given for educational projects in the UK and overseas. The principal object is 'to advance education for the public benefit':

- to promote and assist in the teaching of English as a foreign language;
- to promote and assist in the promotion of the teaching of other subjects and disciplines in education or training establishments throughout the world;
- to promote, carry out and commission research into and develop knowledge and materials relating to the above objects.

In 1999/2000 grants to organisations totalled £977,000. A further 21 grants to individuals towards postgraduate courses of study and for research and studentships totalled £60,000. A total of 45 donations to organisations in the range of £500 to £160,000 were made. Beneficiaries included: Educational Low-priced Sponsored Texts (ELST) to enable students in developing countries to buy key textbooks at accessible prices (£160,000); Uganda Orphans Rural Development Programme – HIV/AIDS education and counselling (£30,000); High/Scope & Grassroots – early childhood education in Africa (£21,000); Save the Children Fund – education provision for Kosovan refugees (£20,000); and flood damaged schools in Vietnam (£1,500).

Exclusions: The following are not funded: loans; general appeals; grants to replace statutory funding; buildings or capital costs; projects which have only a local focus; research of a mainly theoretical nature; running costs; the arts, religion, sports or recreation; conservation, heritage or environmental projects; animal rights or welfare; expeditions, travel, adventure/holiday projects; educational exchanges between institutions; and staff salaries.

Applications: Initially in writing to the correspondent, who will then advise applicants whether or not to make a formal application. The trustees meet in March, June, September and December.

The Charities Advisory Trust

General

Geographical focus: Worldwide

Radius Works, Back Lane,
London NW3 1HL
Tel: 020 7794 9835; **Fax:** 020 7431 3739
e-mail:
charities.advisory.trust@ukonline.co.uk
Correspondent: Hilary Blume, Director
Trustees: Dr Cornelia Navari; Dr Carolyne Dennis; Prof. Bob Holman; Ms Dawn Penso.

Total grants: Usually about £300,000

General: A principal activity of this charity is running the Card Aid operation which raises substantial sums for charities participating in its annual Christmas card operation. However, the operation also raises a surplus which is given out in the form of grants to other charites – typically about £300,000 annually.

Grantmaking is not pre-planned. As the trustees and director are active in the voluntary sector, most issues arise outside any application process, but 'we do get unsolicited applications as a result of our appearance in the directories. We probably respond to five per cent in any positive way – and often this may be a token £100.

'We give very substantial grants – say two a year at around the £100,000 level. ... Smaller amounts, say up to £20,000, may be given on a long-term or one-off basis in the categories for which we have a special interest, or have a special relationship with a charity.

'Other grants may be because we have an interest at a particular time, or want to meet a particular need.'

The trust's present areas of interest are:
- income generation projects
- homelessness
- museums
- cancer research and treatment
- peace and reconciliation.

However, grants are wide-ranging and no area of work is excluded if a sufficiently interesting or unusual project comes along. There is a special interest in the odd, unusual or unforeseeable situation that falls outside normal funding categories. For example, a recent grant was to help a small charity that had received a large but complex legacy and lacked the resources to pay for the necessary legal fees, to realise its benefaction in a tax-effective way.

Grants in 1998/99 totalled £702,000 and were dominated by an exceptionally large grant of £340,000 to enable an indigenous group in south India to buy back a tea plantation that had been created from the forests where the people concerned had previously lived. Other 1998/99 grants went to providing travel and telephone cards for refugees (£15,000, via the Refugee Council) and a local project for school books and uniforms in Grenada - West Indies (£5,000). The interest in peace and reconciliation was represented by £5,000 to KOLOT in Israel and to a Protestant/Catholic young people's football team.

Exclusions: No grants to:
- expeditions
- scholarships
- missionary activities of any religion
- private education
- healthcare where state provision exists
- individuals (except rarely when the applicant is recommended by those known to the trust).

Applications: In writing to the correspondent.

Charities Aid Foundation

This charity appears in the list of Organisations working in developing countries; see page 79.

Charity Know How

Skill-sharing partnership projects between charities or voluntary organisations in the UK and the regions below

Geographical focus: *Worldwide, but mostly Central and Eastern Europe and the former Soviet Union*

114–118 Southampton Row,
London WC1B 5AA
Tel: 020 7400 2315; **Fax:** 020 7404 1331
e-mail: ckh@caf.charitynet.org
website: www.charityknowhow.org
Correspondent: Andrew Kingman, Director
Trustees: Trustees of the Charities Aid Foundation (*see page 81*). Grants Committee: representatives from the fund's contributors.

Total grants: £389,000 (1998/99)
Grants overseas: £389,000

General: 'Charity Know How is a grant-making organisation which was established in November 1991 initially to assist the revitalisation of the voluntary sector in Central and Eastern Europe and the former Soviet Union through the funding of skill-sharing partnership projects. CKH is administered by Charities Aid Foundation (CAF) and is funded by a body of trusts and foundations.

'What do we fund?

CKH operates a range of grants programmes in Eastern Europe and former Soviet Union countries, increasingly fostering east-east partnerships, though its programmes remain open to the involvement of a UK charity.' In partnership with CAF Russia, alongside CKH, CAF also administers the DFID-funded programme partnerships in the non-profit sector. Grants of up to £500,000 are made, with the aim of strengthening the voluntary sector in Russia.

In 2000/01 CKH was exploring the possibility of offering grants as part of structured programmes in Africa and elsewhere. CKH also implements a number of longer-term capacity-building and extensive training programmes, providing micro-grants to local groups and associations in particular regions. Increasingly these programmes are focused within a particular sector, for example, disability groups in Russia, youth in the Balkans, or HIV/AIDS in East Africa. Finally, CKH also aims to serve as an information provider for ngos. Through the CKH website, the Contact Finder will provide advice and information to ngos on all aspects of relationship building.

'Where do we fund?

'General Programmes

Only UK ngos and ngos in Central and Eastern Europe and former Soviet Union countries are eligible to apply as an applicant or partner. Grants awarded must include as principle beneficiary an ngo in at least one of the countries listed below. Ngos from other countries in Central and Eastern Europe (i.e. Czech Republic, Estonia, Hungary, Latvia, Lithuania, Poland, Slovenia) may apply as part of an application involving at least one ngo from one of the following countries: Albania, Armenia, Azerbaijan, Belarus, Bosnia-Herzegovina, Bulgaria, Croatia, Federal Republic of Yugoslavia, Georgia, Kazakstan, Kyrgyzstan, Macedonia (FYROM), Moldova, Romania, Russia, Slovakia, Tajikistan, Turkmenistan, Ukraine and Uzbekistan.

'Partnership Development Grants

Ngos from any Central and Eastern Europe or former Soviet Union country or the UK can apply. Applications from partnerships of two or more non-UK ngos (east-east partnerships) are particularly encouraged.

'Global Grants

Grants awarded must include as principal beneficiary ngos from at least two countries from the following regions: any Central and Eastern Europe or former Soviet Union country; Africa; Asia; Latin America.

'Grants can be given towards the following projects:

- exploratory work aimed at further activity which includes a large element of the transfer of "know-how";
- visits to any eligible countries or to the UK to enable ngo sectoral and organisational learning and development;
- training programmes for ngo staff and volunteers, usually in areas such as financial management, strategic planning, lobbying, volunteer management, governance, fundraising, public relations etc., rather than in specific professional skills such as nursing techniques, artistic skills or journalism, although all capacity-building initiatives will be considered. Training programmes supported tend to be workshops and seminars (and very occasionally conferences) or short-term placements within organisations;

- professional advice visits from charity or ngo representatives to assist with organisational aspects of an individual ngo, coordinating bodies or the sector as a whole;
- translation and adaptation of training or information materials for ngos, although this cannot be the sole activity of the project;
- the costs of publications if this component of the project is clearly and explicitly planned as part of a broader effort to develop specific organisation(s), and not simply to provide information to a broader audience. An effort must also be made to ensure that any publication proposed does not duplicate material already available.'

In 1999/2000 grants totalled £389,000. The three grants made for work in Hungary give a feel for the kind of projects that are supported:

£9,200 to Civic College Foundation, Hungarian Association for Community Development and The Northern College to translate materials on aspects of democracy, prepare internet versions and train 12 trainers to deliver courses to people involved in community development

£5,100 to Association of Family, Children and Young People, Jasz Nagykun Szolnok Megyei Nepfoiskolai Tarsasag (JNSMNT) and WYN Fostering Services Ltd for reciprocal workshops/visits to examine foster care practice and development potential with a view to developing capacity with JNSMNT to manage such services

£2,100 to Association for Children with Life Threatening or Terminal Conditions and their Families (ACT), Bethesda Children's Hospital of the Hungarian Reformed Church Department of Oncology and Warsaw Hospice for Children to support the participation of five UK practitioners, who have extensive experience of hospice and palliative care, to lead sessions at the First Annual European Course on Palliative Care for Children.

Exclusions: The following activities cannot be funded:
- applications from individuals
- retrospective grants
- the preparation of funding proposals or applications
- any building or capital costs
- the costs of transporting humanitarian aid or medical equipment
- the costs of offices, salaries or equipment (e.g. fax machines)
- attendance at conferences where the benefit to ngo development is not clearly demonstrated
- activities considered by the committee to be for personal rather than institutional development
- youth, artistic or cultural exchanges
- the promotion of a specific religion or sectarian belief.

Applications: An application form and guidelines are available from the website or can be requested from the office by e-mail or telephone. The executive committee meets four times a year, in March, June, September and December. The deadlines in 2001 were 23 January, 24 April, 24 July and 23 October.

The Chelsea Square 1994 Trust

General

***Geographical focus:** London, the south of England and occasionally Kenya*

The Middle House, Chapel Road, Rowledge, Farnham, Surrey GU10 4AN
Tel: 01252 793337
Correspondent: John Talbot, Trustee
Trustees: John Talbot; Isabel Burlington; Jonathan Woods.

Total grants: £46,000 (1998/99)

General: In the past this trust gave grants 'to charities in England, Wales and Kenya which are known to the trustees or in response to appeals received'. The present policy, however, is to support charities based in London, the south of England and very occasionally overseas.

In 1998/99 it had assets of £1.2 million and an income of £44,000. Grants were made totalling £46,000. Overseas grants included £2,000 to Médecins Sans Frontières, £1,500 to Christian Aid Africa, and £1,000 each to Chrisco Kibera Nursery School – Kenya and Crisco Kukuma Development – Kenya.

Applications: In writing to the correspondent.

The Cheruby Trust

Welfare, education, general

Geographical focus: UK and worldwide

62 Grosvenor Street, London W1X 9DA
Tel: 020 7499 4301
Correspondent: Sheila Wecshler
Trustees: A L Corob; L E Corob; T A Corob; Mrs S P Berg.

Total grants: £34,000 (1997/98)

General: The trust makes grants towards welfare, education and for general charitable purposes. In 1997/98 its assets totalled £61,000 and it had an income of £58,000. (The income is dependent on donations from trustees.) Grants to 11 organisations totalled £34,000. The surplus of income over expenditure at the year end was £25,000, which was made available for future grantmaking.

The largest grant was £10,000 to Save the Children in two grants of £5,000 each for the Homeless fund and Third World fund. Other recipients included Amnesty International and Sight Savers International (£2,000 each) and Trees for Life (£500).

Applications: In writing to the correspondent.

Christadelphian Samaritan Fund

General, third world

Geographical focus: UK and overseas

1 Sherbourne Road, Acocks Green, Birmingham B27 6AB
Tel: 0121 706 6100
Correspondent: K H A Smith, Treasurer
Trustees: K H A Smith; R R Sirett; J Morris; M Weston Smith; J A Balchin; D P Ensell; Mrs M Howarth; N Moss.

Total grants: £90,000 (1999)

General: The trust supports aid charities in the third world and other charities registered in the UK. In 1999 it had assets of £48,000 and income of £91,000; grants totalled £90,000. No further information was available for this year.

In 1997 The Red Cross received £2,400 in response to the North Korea Appeal and £1,000 for the Iran earthquake appeal. Smaller grants included those to Oxfam for North Korea, Camphill Village Trust and Turning Point.

Exclusions: No grants to individuals.

Applications: In writing to the correspondent.

Christian Response to Eastern Europe

Christian, emergency relief

Geographical focus: In practice Romania, Albania, Moldova, Belarus

30 Westwood Hill, Cockwood, Starcross, Essex EX6 8RW
Tel: 01626 891622

Correspondent: Robert Baker
Trustees: Adrian Huxham; Hugh Scudder; Peter Corney.

Total grants: Around £65,000
General: The trust has taken over the overseas grants programme from The Huxham Trust. The new trust supports Christian work in Eastern Europe, particularly in Romania, Albania, Moldova and Belarus. Grants are given in the following categories:

- humanitarian aid and medical missions in Eastern Europe
- Christian churches in Eastern Europe
- support to individuals for education and voluntary Christian work, with a preference for missions in Eastern Europe.

In 1998 the trust had an income of £115,00 and a total expenditure of £71,000. Further information on the size and beneficiaries of grants was not available.

Applications: In writing to the correspondent.

Unfortunately this entry was not confirmed by the trust. However, it was correct according to information on file at the Charity Commission.

The J A Clark Charitable Trust

Peace, conservation, health, the arts, general

Geographical focus: *South west England and overseas*

PO Box 1704, Glastonbury, Somerset BA16 0YB
Correspondent: Mrs P Grant, Secretary
Trustees: Lancelot Pease Clark; John Cyrus Clark; Thomas Aldham Clark; Caroline Pym; Aidan J R Pelly.

Total grants: £142,000 (1999)
General: This trust was founded by J Anthony Clark, of the well-known Quaker shoe firm. It supports a wide range of organisations in the south west of England and overseas.

In 1999 the trust had assets of £6 million and an income of only £171,000. Grants totalled £142,000. Beneficiaries included Students International for scholarships in Zimbabwe (£23,000), Marie Stopes International for an outreach project in Madagascar (£10,000), Inner City Scholarship Fund (£8,000), Ashoka for an individual in Thailand (£6,000), Jubilee 2000 Coalition (£5,000) and Network Foundation for various projects (£4,900).

Exclusions: No support for independent schools (except for special needs), conservation of buildings or individuals.

Applications: In writing to the correspondent, including project details and most recent accounts. Receipt of applications will not be acknowledged. All applications are considered and applicants may be asked to provide further information. Grants are made in October/November.

The Cleaford Christian Trust

Poverty, health, schools, culture, religion, technology

Geographical focus: *Romania*

46 Hazell Road, Farnham, Surrey GU9 7BP
Tel: 01252 717166; **Fax:** 01252 717137
e-mail: cleaver@cleaford.co.uk
website: www.cleaford.co.uk
Correspondent: A R Cleaver

Total grants: £35,000 (2000)
General: This trust supports individuals and organisations in Romania. Its main areas of work are:

- helping people in need by providing food, clothing, literature and medical equipment
- health
- church and primary schools
- cultural and religious teaching
- the advancement of the Christian religion and upkeep of churches
- information technology and computer projects.

Applications: Applications are only accepted via The Hungarian Baptist Convention of Romania.

The Clothworkers' Foundation

General

Geographical focus: *UK and overseas*

Clothworkers' Hall, Dunster Court, Mincing Lane, London EC3R 7AH
Tel: 020 7623 7041
Correspondent: Michael Harris, Secretary
Trustees: 37 governors of the foundation: Peter Rawson, Chair of the Trusts and Grants Committee; Richard Jones, Deputy Chair.

Total grants: £3.5 million (1999)
Grants overseas: £257,000

General: The trust has general charitable purposes with grants ranging from £1,000 to £50,000 for capital expenditure. There is little support available for large, well-known UK organisations or their local branches.

In 1999 grants to 176 organisations totalled £3.5 million and were broken down into the categories of: relief in need/welfare; education/science; children/youth; medicine/health; overseas; arts; heritage/environment; and church. Overseas grants totalled £257,000 (7% of the total). Recipients included Motivation Charitable Trust for its wheelchair project in Africa (£40,000) and Action Health for a self-help project in the Nilgri Hills, south India (£33,000).

Exclusions: No grants to:
- relieve statutory funds;
- individuals, including sponsorship of fundraising activities for a charity;
- repairs of churches unless there is a connection to The Clothworkers' Company or it is important in relation to national heritage;
- schools or colleges (unless connected to The Clothworkers' Company);
- grant-making trusts.

Grants are only given to UK-registered charities. Successful applicants are normally barred from reapplying for five years.

Applications: All applicants must complete a data information sheet, which should accompany the written application/appeal. Applications should be made in writing on headed notepaper. Ideally, the appeal letter itself should be no longer than two and a half pages of A4 plus a detailed budget for the project, an annual report and latest audited accounts.

In the application letter, applicants should endeavour to:
- introduce the work of the applicant charity; state when the charity was established; describe its aims and objectives; and define precisely what the applicant charity does and who benefits from its activities;
- comment upon the applicant charity's track record since its inception and refer to its notable achievements and successes to date;
- describe the project requiring funding fully, clearly and concisely and comment on the charity's plans for the future;
- provide full costings or a budget for the project(s) to include a detailed breakdown of the costs involved;

- give details of all other applications which the applicant charity has made to other sources of funding, and indicate precisely what funds have already been raised from other sources for the project.

All applicants are, of course, perfectly at liberty to request a precise sum of money by way of grant. However, it can be more beneficial to concentrate on providing accurate and detailed costings of the project concerned, thereby enabling the foundation to make its own judgement as to the level of financial support to be considered.

Applicants can greatly help their cause by concentrating on clarity of presentation and by providing detailed factual information. The foundation will then do its utmost to ensure that the application receives the fullest and most careful consideration.

Trustees meet in January, March, May, July, October and November. The committee's recommendations are then placed before a subsequent meeting of the governors. Accordingly, there is a rolling programme of dealing with and processing applications and the foundation prides itself on flexibility. All unsuccessful applicants receive a written refusal letter.

Dr R J Colley Charitable Trust

Christianity, humanitarian aid
Geographical focus: Worldwide

Wrigleys Solicitors, 19 Cookridge Street, Leeds LS2 3AG
Tel: 0113 244 6100; **Fax:** 0113 244 6101
Correspondent: M P W Lee, Trustee
Trustees: Dr R J Colley; M V Carey; M P W Lee.

Total grants: £24,000 (2000)

General: The trust gives donations to Christian and humanitarian charities, both in the UK and overseas. Most of the beneficiaries are specified in the trust deed although other charities may apply.

In 2000 the trust had assets of £336,000 and an income of £16,000. Grants totalled £24,000. Recipients of grants included Action Partners, The Bible Society, Leprosy Mission and Tearfund.

Applications: In writing to the correspondent.

The George Henry Collins Charity

General

Geographical focus: *Greater Birmingham area and overseas*

St Philips House, St Philips Place, Birmingham B3 2PP
Correspondent: David L Turfrey and Lucy Chatt
Trustees: A D Martineau; H Kenrick; Mrs E A Davies; A A Waters; M S Hansell; A R Collins.

Total grants: £43,000 (1999/2000)
Grants overseas: Possibly about £4,300

General: This trust gives grants for general charitable purposes in the Greater Birmingham area, and will also consider donating one-tenth of the annual income to charities for use overseas.

In 1999/2000 it had £1.4 million in assets and an income of £91,000, all of which was available for grantmaking, although only £43,000 was actually given in grants. Grants included £1,000 to CARE International and £500 each to Marie Stopes International and Sight Savers International.

Exclusions: No grants to individuals.

Applications: In writing to the correspondent.

Comic Relief (the operating name for Charity Projects)

Women and girls, disability, people affected by conflict or living in towns or cities, pastoralists

Geographical focus: Africa (two-thirds) and UK (one-third)

5th Floor, 89 Albert Embankment, London SE1 7TP
Tel: 020 7820 5555; **Fax:** 020 7820 5500
Minicom: 020 7820 5579
e-mail: red@comicrelief.org.uk
website: www.comicrelief.org.uk
Correspondent: The Africa Grants Team
Trustees: Peter Benett-Jones, Chair; Bisi Adeleye-Fayemi; Richard Curtis; Colin Howes; Mike Harris; Emma Freud; Matthew Freud; Lenny Henry; Melinda Letts; Claudia Lloyd; Eric Nicoll; Laurence Newman; Nalini Varma.

Total grants: £15 million (1999/2000)
Grants overseas: £11 million

General: Comic Relief has two grants programmes, one for the UK and one for Africa. Both programmes operate on a two year cycle, each with five 'rounds' of applications. The total sum of money available for grantmaking during this period depends on the success of each Red Nose day. When this book went to press new guidelines were due to be published in May 2001, but precedent suggests that the general direction of grantmaking may remain substantially unchanged.

Grants are made towards core costs and, in some cases, capital costs. Grants can be for up to five years, and up to a total of £1 million. Typically, though, most grants tend to be between £150,000 and £300,000 over three to five years.

Comic Relief exists to tackle poverty and promote social justice in the UK and Africa. It does this by helping those people to help themselves and by meeting their immediate needs and tackling the root causes of their disadvantage to work towards long-term change.

For African grants, the priority areas are:
- women and girls
- disability
- people affected by conflict
- people living in towns or cities
- pastoralists.

In 1999/2000 grants in Africa totalled £11 million and grants in the UK totalled £4.6 million.

Beneficiaries in Africa included: Healthlink Worldwide, East Africa, to support a range of local organisations to develop child-centred approaches to HIV/AIDS (£325,000); Ashoka (UK), working in Burkina Faso to strengthen local women's organisations to challenge harmful traditions and practices faced by young girls (£162,000); and Homeless International to support its work in Namibia with the local Shack Dwellers Foundation (£127,000).

Applications: Please send an A4 sae (57p stamp) addressed to the Africa Grants Team for an application pack.

The Wallace Curzon Charitable Trust

Children

Geographical focus: UK, especially the south of England, and Nepal

Homanton House, Shrewton, near Salisbury, Wiltshire SP3 4ER
Tel: 01908 620441
Correspondent: Fritz Curzon, Secretary
Trustees: Peter Curzon; Fritz Curzon; Robert Spooner.

Total grants: £21,000 (1998/99)
General: The trust supports organisations working for relief in need and education

of children in the UK (particularly the south of England) and overseas, especially Nepal. The trust has a regular list of beneficiaries, although a small number of unsolicited applications are also funded. One grant each year is given to a VSO volunteer, although this is normally given to someone already known to the trust.

In 1998/99 the trust had assets of £453,000 and an income of £23,000. Grants to 21 organisations totalled £21,000. Beneficiaries included Simon Peter Ministries of Nepal children's home (£5,000), Children of the Rising Sun Home - Kenya (£1,000) and GAP Activity Projects (£500).

Applications: The trust states that only a very small percentage of applications are successful (less than 5% receive a positive response). Due to the low approval rate written applications should be kept simple. Unsuccessful applicants will only receive a reply if an sae is enclosed.

The Miriam K Dean Refugee Trust Fund

Third world development

Geographical focus: *Mainly Tanzania and India (including Tibetan refugees)*

7 Hillside, Whitchurch,
Hampshire RG28 7SN
Tel: 01256 895181; **Fax:** 01256 895060
e-mail: brian@btims.freeserve.co.uk
Correspondent: Brian Tims
Trustees: Trevor Dorey; Val Dorey; Hugh Capon; Jill Budd; Gina Livermore.

Total grants: £156,000 (1999)
Grants overseas: £156,000

General: In 1999 the trust had assets of £268,000 and an income of £153,000, including £117,000 in legacies and donations. One-off and recurrent grants totalled £156,000 and were given to:

- people in Tanzania (£26,000 – three grants including £21,000 to Diocese of Zanzibar and Tanga and £2,900 to Hospital Teule, Muheza);
- Tibetan refugees in north India (£36,000 – four grants including £19,000 to ApTibeT and £13,000 to Mussoorie, Tibetan Homes Foundation);
- people in south India (£88,000 – three grants including £47,000 to an individual, presumably for a project he was working on, and £15,000 to Centre for Disabled Children, Narasaraopet).

Exclusions: The trust states it is unable to award major block grants to organisations in the UK or Europe. No grants are given to individuals for Operation Raleigh or other overseas trips.

Applications: The trust does not wish to receive any applications. Its funds are fully committed to projects/organisations already known to the trustees.

The Diana, Princess of Wales Memorial Fund

Communities affected by landmines, cluster bombs, etc.

Geographical focus: *Worldwide, but mostly UK*

The County Hall, Westminster Bridge Road, London SE1 7PB
Tel: 020 7902 5500; **Fax:** 020 7902 5511
e-mail: memorial.fund@memfund.org.uk
website: www.theworkcontinues.org
Correspondent: Dr Andrew Purkis, Chief Executive
Trustees: Lady Sarah McCorquodale, President; Christopher Spence, Chair; Jenny Brindle; Earl Cairns; John Eversley; Michael Gibbins; Andrew Hind; Anthony Julius; Baroness Pitkeathley; Nalini Varma.

Total grants: £9.6 million (1998/99)

Grants overseas: About £3.2 million

General: This trust was set up in memory of Princess Diana, giving to causes she was particularly interested in. For UK grants, the fund prioritises the following: refugees and asylum seekers; prisoners' families; young people and mental health; young people with learning disabilities; and advocacy.

About one third of the fund's grants go to international work, focusing on assisting communities affected by landmines, cluster bombs, etc. and help with the rehabilitation and reintegration of the most disadvantaged people after conflict, particularly those who face prejudice from other communities. Applicants should work in partnership with local organisations and include an element of advocacy.

The trust has the following guidelines for international grant applications:

'Geographical location: we will consider applications for work in developing countries, and in Central and Eastern Europe. However, precedence will be given to least developed countries. In all cases, the project must address the needs of the most disadvantaged. The trustees will welcome applications for work linked thematically across national boundaries.

'Gender: applications should show how gender issues have been taken into consideration, both for planning and implementation.

'Disability: applications should show how disabled people have been taken into consideration, both in planning and implementation. For example, projects supporting general services should specify measures taken to make these as accessible as possible to disabled people.

'Charitable status: grants will only be made to UK-based and registered charities. These may include UK-registered charities run by displaced people in relation to their international work.

'Work in post-conflict communities: in areas where tension between different religious or ethnic groups has been a significant cause of conflict, applications must demonstrate that the proposed activities will at least do no damage to existing community relations. At best, the project activities should be designed to improve relations between the divided groups.

'Monitoring and evaluation: the trustees expect all applications to have appropriate monitoring and evaluation built into the project.'

In 1999 the trust had assets of £84 million and an income of £15 million. Total expenditure was £12 million including £9.6 million in grants.

Overseas beneficiaries included Sandy Gall's Afghanistan Appeal for physiotherapy assessment and provision of prosthetics and mobility aids (£300,000 over three years), HelpAge International – Rwanda for the inclusion of older people in rebuilding communities (£250,000 over three years), Village Aid – Sierra Leone for the establishment of literacy and civic education groups by and for young people (£211,000 over four years) and Save the Children Fund – Colombia (£200,000 over three years).

Recipients of smaller grants included Y Care International for vocational skills training, sexual health advice and the development of national youth radio broadcasting (£67,000 over three years), Hope for Children – Sri Lanka for prosthetics, landmine awareness and education and training for children who have been disabled in landmine accidents or from disease or birth problems (£40,000), and Agency for Co-operation and Research in Development (ACORD Rwanda) for a research project into child-headed households (£34,000).

Exclusions: For international grants, applicants must be UK-based ngos. All disability projects should be open to all disabled people, not just those disabled by landmines. Mine clearance projects must take an integrated holistic approach to mine action.

No grants are given for: individuals; services run by statutory or public authorities; fundraising bodies; promotion of religious beliefs; rapid response to emergency situations; retrospective funding; debts; or party political organisations.

Applications: On a form available from the grants department at the above address, on receipt of an sae. Application packs must be requested by May each year.

The trust has stated that its guidelines may change in future years and recommends viewing the website or contacting the correspondent before considering making an application.

The Dickon Trust

Disaster relief, general

Geographical focus: *Worldwide, but mostly UK, particularly Northumberland*

Tranwell House, Morpeth,
Northumberland NE61 6AF
Tel: 01670 513120
Correspondent: J R Barrett, Secretary to the Trustees
Trustees: J R Barrett; Mrs D L Barrett; P J Dudding; Brig. R V Brims; R R V Nicholson.

Total grants: £27,000 (1998/99)
General: The trust gives grants for general charitable purposes to well-known UK organisations and charities local to Northumberland. A small number of disaster relief grants are also made.

In 1998/99 the trust's assets totalled £1.1 million and it had an income of £81,000, roughly half of which was from investments and half from donations. Grants totalled £27,000 and after other expenditure the trust had a surplus for the year of £52,000.

Red Cross received grants towards four of its funds; Red Cross Kosovo received £2,500, and £1,000 each was given to the organisation's Central American Hurricane Appeal, Northumbria branch and Bangladesh branch. Other grants for overseas organisations were £1,000 to Sudan Crisis Appeal and £250 to UNICEF.

Applications: In writing to the correspondent. Overseas grants are only given proactively to meet national disasters.

The Dinam Charity

International understanding, general

Geographical focus: *Worldwide*

Thomas Edgar Church Adams,
5 East Pallant, Chichester,
West Sussex PO19 1TS
Tel: 01243 786111
Correspondent: The Trustees
Trustees: Hon. Mrs M M Noble; Hon. Mrs G R J Cormack; Hon. E D G Davies; J S Tyres.

Total grants: Around £115,000
Grants overseas: Around £23,000

General: Exact, up-to-date information on this trust is largely unavailable. The trust is believed to give 20% of its grant towards overseas aid and development, 20% to Welsh organisations and the remaining 60% to UK and local charities, especially those concerned with animal welfare, children and young people. The largest beneficiary appears to be David Davies Memorial Institution, which regularly receives over two-thirds of the grant total.

The most recent financial information comes from 1995/96 when the trust had an income of £178,000. Grants totalled £117,000. The most recent list of grants on file at the Charity Commission is for 1988/89 when the grant total was £131,000 and overseas organisations to benefit included Oxfam Nicaraguan Hurricane Disaster Appeal (£1,000) and WaterAid (£500).

Exclusions: Grants are only given to registered charities. No grants to individuals.

Applications: Applications can be made at any time. Unsuccessful applicants will not be notified unless an sae is enclosed with the application.

The Douglas Charitable Trust

Universities, churches, homeless, third world

Geographical focus: *Scotland and developing countries*

Turcan Connell, Princes Exchange, 1 Earl Grey Street, Edinburgh EH3 9EE
Tel: 0131 228 8111; **Fax:** 0131 228 8118
Correspondent: The Secretary
Trustees: Revd Prof. D Shaw; D Connell; E Cameron.

Total grants: £209,000 (1998/99)
General: The trust mainly supports Scottish universities and church restoration projects. Grants are also made to charities which help people who are deprived or homeless as well as third world charities.

In 1998/99 the trust had assets of £496,000 and grants totalled £209,000.

Applications: In writing to the correspondent.

The Dulverton Trust

Youth and education, general, welfare, conservation

Geographical focus: *UK and limited support in Africa*

5 St James's Place, London SW1A 1NP
Tel: 020 7629 9121; **Fax:** 020 7495 6201
e-mail: trust@dulverton.org
Correspondent: Maj. Gen. Sir Robert Corbett, Director
Trustees: The Hon Robert Wills; Lord Carrington; Lord Dulverton; Colonel D V Fanshawe; the Earl of Gowrie; Sir John Kemp-Welch; Sir Ashley Ponsonby; Lord Taylor of Gryfe; J Watson; Dr Catherine Wills; C A H Wills.

Total grants: £3.1 million (1999/2000)
Grants overseas: £158,000

General: The trust concentrates on youth and education, conservation and general welfare. Other areas of priority are religion (principally through The Farmington Trust in Oxford), peace and security, and, to a lesser extent, industrial understanding. Grants, often substantial, are made outside these specified areas of interest but probably only on the personal recommendation of a trustee. There is an extensive small grants programme for local causes, whose coverage is probably more general still. Awards are made towards capital or revenue costs, and are normally one-off payments.

Overseas assistance is generally restricted to a small number of long-standing associations in Central and East Africa.

Occasional grants are made in response to appeals from South Africa.

Grants in 1999/2000 totalled £3.1 million and were broken down into the following categories: youth and education; general welfare; conservation; religion; Africa; minor appeals; peace and security; industrial understanding; preservation; annual subscriptions; local appeals; and miscellaneous.

Under the 'Africa' section (£108,000 in total), a modest level of support continues to be provided for projects in the east and south of Africa. The largest grant was awarded to University of Cape Town Trust for the work it is conducting for the advancement of multiracial education. The Kenya Wildlife Trust was awarded a three-year grant.

Also during the year a grant of £50,000 was made to CARE International for its work in Macedonia, outside the trust's usual beneficial area.

Exclusions: The trust does not operate within the broad fields of medicine and health, including drug addiction and projects concerning mental and physical disability. Also generally excluded are projects concerning museums, churches, cathedrals and other historic buildings. Grants are not made to individuals or for expeditions.

The whole field of the arts is excluded together with projects for schools, colleges and universities. The trust very seldom operates within the Greater London area, or in Northern Ireland.

No grants to overseas charities, except for the limited activity with long-standing associations in Central and East Africa, and occasionally South Africa.

Applications: Applications should be made in writing to the correspondent. Trustee meetings are held four times a year – in January, May, July and October.

There is no set format for applications, but it is helpful if they can include the background and a clear statement of the aims of the appeal, together with the funding target and any progress made in reaching it. Applications should, if possible, be restricted to a letter with a maximum of two sheets of paper. A copy of the most recent annual report and accounts should be included.

The John Ellerman Foundation

Health, welfare, art, conservation
Geographical focus: *UK and overseas, other than Central or South America*

Aria House, 23 Craven Street,
London WC2N 5NS
Tel: 020 7930 8566; **Fax:** 020 7839 3654
e-mail:
postmaster@ellerman.prestel.co.uk
website: www.ncvo-vol.org.uk/jef.html
Correspondent: Eileen Terry, Appeals Manager
Trustees: Peter Pratt, Chair; Dennis Parry; Angela Boschi; David Martin-Jenkins; Vice-Admiral Anthony Revell; Mrs Beverley Stott.

Total grants: £4.4 million (2000/01)
Grants overseas: £374,000

General: This trust gives large grants of between £10,000 and £100,000 for core, project or capital costs for between one and three years. The trust is particularly interested in innovative projects and cooperation between charities. Grants are given to UK rather than local organisations (of any size) for projects mostly in the UK. Although overseas grants are available for projects anywhere except Central or South America, in practice these are mostly given in southern Africa and only to charities with a UK base.

In 2000/01 grants totalled £4.4 million and were broken down into the following categories: medical and disability; community and development; arts; conservation.

In 1999/2000 grants were given to 23 overseas organisations totalling £374,000, mostly for medical or welfare purposes. Most of the grants were given in Africa, including four to organisations in South Africa with which Sir John Ellerman had a connection. Larger grants included £40,000 to Commonwealth Society for the Deaf for its HARK mobile clinic in the western Cape and £30,000 to Merlin for running its Africa desk. Other grants included £10,000 each to Book Aid International (the only grant outside its normal categories), Gordon Layton Trust towards a new eye hospital in Pakistan (the only Asian grant) and Population Concern.

Exclusions: Grants are given to UK-registered charities only, for projects outside of Central or South America. Circulars will not receive a reply. No grants towards:

- medical research
- individuals
- individual hospices
- local branches of large well-known UK organisations
- 'friends of' groups
- education or educational establishments
- religious causes
- conferences and seminars
- sports and leisure facilities
- vehicle purchase (unless for aid transport)
- replacement of public funding
- deficit funding
- domestic animal welfare.

Applications: In writing to the correspondent. There is a two-stage process. Initial applications should be kept brief (no more than two pages) and include a description of the charity and the current need for funding. Successful applicants will then be asked to fill in an application form and provide further information. Initial telephone enquiries are welcomed.

The Edith M Ellis 1985 Charitable Trust

Quaker, ecumenical, education, peace and international affairs, general

Geographical focus: *UK, Ireland and overseas*

Field Fisher Waterhouse, 35 Vine Street, London EC3N 2AA
Correspondent: The Clerk
Trustees: A P Honigmann; E H Milligan.

Total grants: About £30,000
General: The trust supports organisations in the following categories:
- international
- Great Britain
- peace and international affairs and service
- Ireland
- education and social affairs and service
- miscellaneous.

It also makes grants to individuals who wish to work on development projects through organisations such as the Project Trust, Africa Inland Mission and World Society for Protection of Animals.

In 1995/96 the trust had an income of £49,000 and its total expenditure was £35,000. Further information was not available.

Applications: In writing to the correspondent. Telephone enquiries are not invited.

The Emerging Markets Charity for Children

Children

Geographical focus: UK and overseas, especially developing countries

Lazard Brothers, 21 Moorfields, London EC2P 2HT
Tel: 020 7448 2079
Correspondent: Stephanie Field, Director
Trustees: S Field; E Littlefield; H Snell; A McLeod.

Total grants: £562,000 (1998)
General: Grants are given to children's organisations in the UK and developing countries. The trust aims to relieve poverty, deprivation and distress as well as advance education and training by means of grants, including the establishment of scholarships, prizes and other awards.

In 1998 the trust had assets of £86,000 and an income of £606,000, over half of which came from donations. Grants totalled £562,000.

Applications: In writing to the correspondent.

Equine Welfare Grants Programme – Brooke Hospital for Animals

Equine welfare projects in developing countries

Geographical focus: Worldwide

Brooke Hospital for Animals, Broadmead House, 21 Panton Street, London SW1Y 4DR
Tel: 020 7930 0210; **Fax:** 020 7930 2386
e-mail: info@brooke-hospital.org.uk
website: www.brooke-hospital.org.uk/grants/home/html
Correspondent: Helen McArdle, Grants Officer

Total grants: About £500,000 a year
Grants overseas: £500,000

General: This grants programme has been set up by the Brooke Hospital for Animals (BHA), which is a charity that aims to improve the condition and well-being of working equines overseas both by providing free veterinary treatment for the working horses, donkeys and mules of poor people, and by advising and educating their owners and users.

The grant programme has been open for applications since 21 July 2000 and the charity estimated that it would have about £500,000 available to be given in grants each year. The average size for each grant is £30,000.

The following information is taken from the programme's application pack.

'Eligible organisations for grants are:
- UK and overseas universities
- UK universities working in partnership with overseas universities
- international and overseas charities and ngos
- international charities and ngos working in partnership with overseas organisations.

'Non-eligible organisations:
- local authorities
- state-run organisations and institutions
- trading/profit-making companies
- organisations aimed primarily at promoting a specific religious or political view.

'BHA will fund:
- projects to improve welfare of working equine animals by: healthcare initiatives; husbandry improvement programmes; educational/extension programmes (e.g. animal welfare awareness); equipment initiatives designs;

- applied research in, for example: equine veterinary science; extension (dissemination of information); equine husbandry; epidemiology; ethnoveterinary medicine; nutrition.

'Research:
In the case of applied research, BHA will give priority to collaborative work between UK and overseas academic institutions. BHA will provide support for applied research that demonstrates the goal of the research to be a practical solution to improve equine welfare. Protocols for experiments must not result in unnecessary suffering of animals. Procedures that are acceptable are:

- administration of substances that do not induce disease, enterally, parenterally, by external application or by variation of diet;
- withdrawal of body fluids/blood;
- minor diagnostic procedures that might be undertaken on clinical subjects and may also be used on normal animals as controls.

'Applicants should be aware that 90% of grants awarded will be no greater than £30,000 a year. There will also be a seed grant programme with a ceiling of up to £10,000. Grants (project and research) will normally be funded for periods of one, two or three years.'

Exclusions: 'BHA will not fund:
- organisations which do not believe in the practice of euthanasia for animals to relieve suffering
- individuals unless affiliated to a university or organisation
- legal action
- political action/lobbying
- advertising campaigns
- projects which result in prosecution of owners
- large building costs
- land purchase
- work that has already been done
- the preparation of funding proposals or applications
- work that results in suffering of animals e.g. animal experimentation.'

Applications: In writing to the correspondent.

The Ericson Trust

See below

Geographical focus: UK organisations working at home or abroad

Flat 2, 53 Carleton Road, London N7 0ET
Tel: 020 7607 8333
Correspondent: Ms C Cotton, Trustee
Trustees: R C Cotton; V J Barrow; Ms C Cotton.

Total grants: £30,000 (1998/99)
General: The guidelines state 'requests for core funding, running costs or particular items can be considered. Most grants are between £500 and £2,000'. The trust's priority areas are shown below, with examples of overseas beneficiaries in 1998/99 where applicable.

- prisons, prison reform, mentoring projects and research in this area (Apex, Howard League, Prison Reform Trust and Trail-Blazers);
- developing countries (DORS: Development Organisation of Rural Sichuan, International Service and Tools for Self Reliance);
- welfare of refugees (Medical Foundation for the Care of Victims of Torture and Praxis);
- community projects and local interest groups, including arts projects;
- psychiatric research and rehabilitation;
- homelessness;
- human rights (Anti-Slavery International and Prisoners of Conscience);
- older people.

In 1998/99 the trust's assets totalled £728,000, it had an income of £29,000 and grants totalling £30,000 were made to 26 charities, 16 of which had received grants in the previous year. The trust informed us in January 2001 that it has been receiving many direct requests from charities in developing countries, especially from Africa and Asia: 'Hardly any of our overseas grants go directly overseas to a project; almost all go through the kind of Britain-based charities which are able to send out experienced fieldworkers to assess or take part in the organisations needing support. The only exception will be one in 2000 where two of our trustees have direct contact with a certain Latin-American community project. It is still the case that some of the projects we favour are small scale and hardly any are direct disaster relief.'

Exclusions: No grants are made to: charities primarily concerned with children and young adults; charities concerned with medical conditions and physical disability; schools; religious organisations (except welfare administered by religious bodies); animal welfare charities; or individuals.

Applications: Applicants should first send a concise description of the project and be prepared to send accounts if requested. There is no special application form. Less well-known projects may want to include an endorsement by a relevant person. Successful applicants are asked to acknowledge receipt of the grant cheque as promptly as possible. Grants are made in March and October, although only a few applications are successful each year and explanations are not always available.

Everest Marathon Fund

Health and education in rural Nepal
Geographical focus: Nepal

3 Elim Grove, Windermere,
Cumbria LA23 2JN
Tel: 01539 445445; **Fax:** 01539 447753
e-mail: bufo@btinternet.com
website: www.everestmarathon.org.uk
Correspondent: Mrs Penny Sherpani
Trustees: The Committee of Management.

Total grants: About £60,000 every 18 months
Grants overseas: About £60,000 every 18 months

General: The trust promotes the health and education of the Nepalese people, particularly in rural areas where facilities are minimal. It does not run its own projects, but instead supports other organisations which have projects underway. Funds are raised through the Everest Marathon, which takes place every 18 months. This is organised by Bufo Ventures Ltd and raises on average about £60,000. In 2001 grants were given to Britain-Nepal Medical Trust, INF TB/Leprosy Project, Narnche Bazaar Dental Clinic, Nepal Leprosy Trust, Nepal School Projects and WaterAid.

Applications: In writing to the correspondent. The trust supports projects that it already has contact with and does not invite unsolicited applications.

Farthing Trust

Christian, general
Geographical focus: UK and overseas

48 Ten Mile Bank, Littleport, Ely, Cambridgeshire CB6 1EF
Correspondent: Heber Martin, Trustee
Trustees: C H Martin; Mrs E Martin; Miss J Martin; Mrs A White.

Total grants: £150,000 (1998/99)

General: In 1998/99 the trust had assets of £1.1 million and an income of £292,000, including £229,000 in donations. Grants totalled £150,000 and were mostly given to Christian organisations in the UK and overseas. This included £35,000 to overseas Christian missions, £14,000 to overseas Christian churches and £1,000 to overseas general charities.

Applications: Applications and enquiries should be made in writing to the correspondent. Applicants will only be notified of refusal if an sae is enclosed. Priority is given to those personally known to the trustees or recommended by those personally known to the trustees, and there would appear little point in applying unless contact has been established.

Feed the Minds

Christian literature, education, development

Geographical focus: *Developing countries including Eastern Europe*

Albany House, 67 Sydenham Road, Guildford, Surrey GU1 3RY
Tel: 01483 888580; **Fax:** 01483 888581
e-mail: headoffice@feedtheminds.org
website: www.feedtheminds.org
Correspondent: Dr Alwyn Marriage, Director
Trustees: Revd Canon John Lowe; Christopher Bayne; John Clark; Dr Pauline Webb.

Total grants: £433,000 (1999/2000)

General: The trust represents 23 mainstream UK churches and missionary societies. Grants are generally between £1,000 and £5,000 a year; some are recurrent. Grants can be given for:

- theological books in indigenous languages for colleges, correspondence courses and libraries;
- capital investment in Christian publishing houses to produce books and literature or initiate new lines (preference is given to books created, written and produced locally in the indigenous language of the people they will benefit);
- capital investment for Christian bookshops;
- cash to meet the production costs of tapes, literature, mini-libraries and resource centres;
- support for literacy and development programmes;
- funds for health-related and HIV/AIDS awareness programmes and associated literature;
- financial support for the churches' liturgical material and hymn books.

Grants usually fall into five categories:
- publishing and distribution
- libraries and theological education
- human development and aid
- communication projects such as radio, video and cassettes
- training for employees of Christian publishing houses.

In 1999/2000 the trust had assets of £585,000 and an income of £748,000. Grants totalled £433,000. Beneficiaries included Multimedia in Zambia to publish Christian textbooks (£10,000), Scripture Union in South Africa for HIV/AIDS literature and education (£6,500), Novosibirsk Christian Publishing House in Russia to set up libraries in Siberian villages (£5,000), Organismo de Desarrollo Integral Boliniano in Bolivia for its adult literacy programme (£4,000) and Kampala YMCA in Uganda (£2,000).

Exclusions: No grants to individuals.

Applications: In writing to the correspondent. The trustees meet in March and September. The trust has previously stated that applications should be submitted at least six months before the funding is required.

Allan & Nesta Ferguson Charitable Settlement

Education, poverty, peace

Geographical focus: *Worldwide*

Stanley Tee, High Street, Bishop's Stortford, Hertfordshire CM23 2LU
Tel: 01279 755200; **Fax:** 01279 758400
e-mail: jrt@stanleytee.co.uk
Correspondent: James Richard Tee

Total grants: £375,000 to organisations (2000)

General: The trust supports education, poverty and peace, giving grants to both individuals and organisations throughout the world.

In 2000 it had assets of £42 million generating an income of £575,000. Grants to organisations totalled £375,000 with a further £138,000 given to individuals. A list of beneficiaries was not available for this year.

In 1998 grants to organisations totalled £448,000 and overseas beneficiaries included Karuna (£8,600), Africa Educational Trust (£3,500), Nepal Trust and Traidcraft Exchange (£3,000 each), Student Partnerships Worldwide (£2,000), World Voices (£1,000), Headway (£500) and International Care and Relief (£150).

Applications: In writing to the correspondent.

The Donald Forrester Trust

Disability, general

Geographical focus: *Worldwide*

231 Linen Hall, 156–170 Regent Street, London W1R 5TA
Tel: 020 7434 4021
Correspondent: Brenda Ward
Trustees: Wendy Forrester, Chair; Anthony Smee; Michael Jones; H Porter.

Total grants: £709,000 (1999/2000)

General: The trust concentrates on helping people who are sick or disabled, particularly older people and children. A smaller number of beneficiaries work in other areas, such as animal welfare, heritage and conservation, the arts and overseas aid. Grants are usually made to large, well-known organisations.

The trust's assets of more than £10 million in 1999/2000 were held mainly as investments in Film and Equipment Ltd. Income, at £728,000, came mostly from dividends and Gift Aid from the same source. The trust made 130 grants totalling £740,000, ranging from £3,000 to £10,000.

Grants included £10,000 each to British Red Cross, Save the Children and UNICEF UK, and £5,000 each to Christian Aid, Send a Cow, Sight Savers International, Tearfund and UNICEF UK – Calcutta Railway Children.

Applications: In writing to the correspondent. 'Regrettably, applications for aid cannot be considered as this would place an intolerable strain on administrative resources.' The trustees meet in February and September.

The Timothy Franey Charitable Foundation

Children, health, education, arts
Geographical focus: *Mainly UK, but see below*

32 Herne Hill, London SE24 9QS
e-mail: franeyfoundation@aol.com
Correspondent: T Franey, Trustee
Trustees: T Franey; S Franey; P Morrison.

Total grants: £58,000 (1999/2000)
Grants overseas: About £17,000

General: The trust states that it supports 'charities that devote a high proportion of their work and resources to the care and help of underprivileged and sick children and also … causes in the south east London area which are concerned with health or education and the arts'.

In 1999/2000 assets totalled £500,000 and the income £48,000. Grants totalled £58,000, of which £22,000 was to local charities in south east London. About 30% of funds went on overseas support.

Exclusions: No grants to individuals. The trust states: 'We mainly support registered charities, or work with them in funding specific situations and projects.'

Applications: The trust now only accepts applications by e-mail. Further information will be requested by the trust if required. Applications in writing or by phone will not be accepted.

The Jill Franklin Trust

Overseas development, refugees, prisons, church restoration
Geographical focus: *Worldwide*

78 Lawn Road, London NW3 2XB
Tel & Fax: 020 7722 4543
e-mail: lawnroad@blueyonder.co.uk
Correspondent: Norman Franklin, Trustee
Trustees: Andrew Franklin; Norman Franklin; Sally Franklin; Sam Franklin; Tom Franklin.

Total grants: £101,000 (1999/2000)
Grants overseas: £10,000

General: The trust gives most of its support in the UK. It states it has about £10,000 a year to spend on grants to organisations working overseas, including committed funds. Grants are given in the following areas:

- special development projects in the Commonwealth with low overhead costs;
- organisations helping and supporting refugees coming to, or already in, the UK.

In 1999/2000 the trust had an income of £106,000. Only one-tenth of the grants were for £1,000 or more, although most were for at least £500.

Grants included £1,000 each to Medical Foundation for the Care of Victims of Torture and Prisoners Abroad.

Exclusions: Grants are not given to:
- encourage the 'contract culture', particularly where authorities are not funding the contract adequately;
- religious organisations set up for welfare, education etc., of whatever religion, unless the users of the service are from all denominations, and there is no attempt whatsoever to conduct any credal propaganda or religious rituals;
- students or any individuals or for overseas travel.

Applications: In writing to the correspondent, including the latest annual report, accounts and budget. The trustees tend to look more favourably on an appeal which is simply and economically prepared rather than glossy, 'prestige' and mailsorted brochures. Many worthy applications are rejected simply due to a lack of funds.

Sydney E Franklin Deceased's New Second Charity

Overseas development, endangered animals, people in need

Geographical focus: *Worldwide, with a preference for the third world*

c/o 39 Westleigh Aveue,
London SW15 6RQ
Correspondent: Dr R C G Franklin, Trustee
Trustees: A Franklin; Dr R C G Franklin; Ms T N Franklin.

Total grants: £32,000 (2000/01)

General: The trust supports smaller charities with low overheads dealing with third world self-help projects or endangered species, and also organisations working with people who are disadvantaged due to poverty, famine, war or man-made or natural disasters.

In 2000/01 it had an income of around £30,000 and grants totalled £32,000. Beneficiaries included Kerala Federation for the Blind for an Indian blind group (£4,500), Womankind Worldwide (£2,500), Future Matters Foster Care Agency and International Institute for Environment and Development (£2,000 each, both for addressing poverty in East Africa), Environmental Investigation Agency and Survival International to preserve indigenous tribes and people worldwide (£1,500 each), with £1,000 each to several other charities addressing endangered species and child health and poverty worldwide.

Exclusions: No grants to individuals or large umbrella groups.

Applications: In writing to the correspondent. Trustees meet at the end of each year and applications are not acknowledged.

The Frays Charitable Trust

Overseas development, general in the UK

Geographical focus: *UK and Africa*

21 Buckingham Gate, London SW1E 6LS
Tel: 020 7828 4091
Correspondent: E R H Perks, Trustee
Trustees: C N Withington; D B Withington; E R H Perks.

Total grants: £15,000 (1998/99)

General: This trust provides grants for organisations in the UK and Africa.

In 1998/99 the trust had assets of £458,000 and an income of £12,000. Total expenditure was £18,000 including £15,000 in grants. Kiloran Trust received £11,000, while £4,200 went to Sustrans.

In the previous year grants totalled £13,000 and beneficiaries included Iran Aid (£3,800), Kulika Charitable Trust and Tools for Self Reliance (£1,300 each), Sunseed Trust (£900), Tools for Solidarity (£800) and Frontier (£100).

Exclusions: No grants to individuals.

Applications: In writing to the correspondent.

Maurice Fry Charitable Trust

General

Geographical focus: *UK and overseas*

98 Savernake Road, London NW3 2JR
Correspondent: L Fry
Trustees: L E A Fry; A Fry; Mrs F Cooklin; Mrs L Weaks.

Total grants: £40,000 (2000)

General: This trust has general charitable purposes, although its main areas of interest are medicine and health, welfare, humanities, environmental resources and international causes. Grants range from £200 to £3,000.

In 2000 £40,000 was given in grants, however, no further information was available for this year. In 1996/97 the trust had assets of just over £1 million, an income of £41,000 and grants were made totalling £35,000.

Grants included Intermediate Technology and Marie Stopes International (£2,800 each), Tree Aid (£2,700), Anti-Slavery International and Refuge (£2,500 each), Island Trust (£2,300), NSPCC (£2,000), and Fleet Carers and Friends of the Earth (£1,500 each).

Exclusions: No grants to individuals.

Applications: In writing to the correspondent. The trust states that it does not respond to unsolicited applications.

The Fulmer Charitable Trust

International development
Geographical focus: *Worldwide*

Estate Office, Street Farm, Compton Bassett, Calne, Wiltshire SN11 8SW
Tel: 01249 760410
Correspondent: J S Reis, Chair

Total grants: £60,000 a year
Grants overseas: £45,000 a year

General: This trust donates 75% of its grant total to charities in third world countries 'where there is an immediate need'.

The remaining 25% is split between Christian charities, charities involved in education and small local projects in Wiltshire. It has about £60,000 available to be donated in grants each year.

Most beneficiaries receive two grants of £500 to £1,500 each a year. Third world charities supported have included CARE International, Sight Savers International, Tearfund, Ethiopiaid, Africa Now, Send a Cow, VSO, Save the Children and SOS Children's Village.

Applications: In writing to the correspondent.

Fund for Human Need

Relief of poverty
Geographical focus: *Worldwide, but mostly developing countries*

25 Marylebone Road, London NW1 5JR
Tel: 020 7486 5502; **Fax:** 020 7467 5233
Correspondent: Stan Platt

Total grants: £38,000 to organisations (2000)

General: The trust's main aim is to help remove hunger and relieve poverty anywhere in the world regardless of politics, race and creed. Grants of between £500 and £1,000 are given to around four or five organisations for specific items or welfare funds, with grants of around £200 each given to individuals, including refugees, asylum seekers and people who are homeless to help them get over a hurdle rather than as long-term help.

In 2000 the trust had assets of £89,000 and an income of £33,000. Grants totalled £39,000, including £1,100 to individuals. This grant total was larger than usual due to the distribution of a restricted gift received during the previous year.

Previous beneficiaries have included: Asra Hawariat School in Ethiopia; Boys Town – Kingston, Jamaica; Centre for Disabled Children – Bangladesh; Colon School – Panama; and Churches Commission on Overseas Students.

Exclusions: No scholarships or grants for projects in the UK or to large, well-known organisations.

Applications: In writing to the correspondent.

The Angela Gallagher Memorial Fund

Children and youth, Christian, humanitarian

Geographical focus: *UK and worldwide*

Church Cott, The Green, Mirey Lane, Woodbury, Exeter, Devon EX5 1LT
Tel: 01395 232097
Correspondent: Mrs D R Moss, Secretary
Trustees: N A Maxwell-Lawford; P Mostyn; P A Wolrige Gordon; A Swan.

Total grants: £46,000 (1998/99)
General: Primarily the trust makes grants to registered charities for the benefit of children and young people in the UK. It is also interested in supporting Christian, humanitarian and educational causes worldwide.

In 1998/99 the trust's assets totalled £1.2 million, generating an income of £48,000. In the past it had also received Gift Aid donations doubling the income. Management and administration costs totalled £16,000 and 69 grants were given totalling £46,000. Grants ranged from £500 to £3,000 and only a few were recurrent from the previous year.

Overseas grants included £3,000 to CAFOD, £1,000 each to Red Cross International and Uganda Society for Disabled Children, and £500 each to Africa Link and Traidcraft Exchange.

Exclusions: No grants for equipment or to individuals, animal welfare or charities for older people.

Applications: In writing to the correspondent for consideration at trustees' meetings which are held twice a year. Applications are not acknowledged without an sae. Please note that the trustees will not make grants unless they have received a full set of accounts.

The Gatsby Charitable Foundation

General

Geographical focus: *UK and Africa*

9 Red Lion Court, London EC4A 3EF
Tel: 020 7410 0330; **Fax:** 020 7410 0332
website: www.gatsby.org.uk
Correspondent: Michael Pattison, Director
Trustees: Christopher Stone; Miss Judith Portrait; Andrew Cahn.

Total grants: £22 million (1999/2000)
Grants overseas: £1.7 million

General: This trust is one of the many large Sainsbury Family Charitable Trusts, and is proactive in finding its beneficiaries, not responding to unsolicited appeals.

In 1999/2000 the trust had assets of £393 million and an income of £22 million. Grants totalled £22 million and were broken down into the following categories: technical education; mental health; disadvantaged children; plant science; developing countries (Africa); economic and social research; cognitive neuroscience; the arts; social renewal; and general.

The 1999/2000 annual reports states that grants in developing countries (which totalled £1.7 million) are given:

'To promote environmentally sustainable development and poverty alleviation through selected programmes aimed at supporting basic agriculture and other enterprise in selected African countries.'

The trustees support a range of projects in the third world in the spheres of economic research and via direct programmes to help people in poverty, concentrating on African countries with reasonable stability to support small-scale wealth creation in agriculture and manufacturing, and primary healthcare of women and small children. The trustees have also decided to work through local people to develop sustainable projects and ensure any effort is genuinely responsive to local needs.

The trust has regularly supported the establishment of local trusts in sub-Saharan Africa, directed by local trustees, which now exist in Kenya, Tanzania, Uganda and Cameroon. It has recently instituted a major programme in the Western Cape to enhance the maths, science and technical education of black South Africans, at all levels, giving £744,000 to Scientific and Industrial Leadership Initiative.

Tanzania Gatsby Trust received £540,000 to work through partner agencies to deliver support services, loans and marketing assistance. West Africa Rice Development Association in Ivory Coast received £360,000 to disseminate new conventionally bred varieties of rice in Ghana and Nigeria. National Agricultural Research Organisation in Uganda was also supported, receiving £325,000 towards its banana extension programme.

Beneficiaries of smaller grants included Kenya Gatsby Trust (£36,000), Legal Resources Centre – South Africa (£22,000) and University of Cape Town (£15,000).

The major financial overseas commitment is to a collaboration between John Innes Centre, based in Norwich, to research improvements to several subsistence crops, and the International Institute of Tropical Agriculture based in Nigeria.

Applications: Please note that unsolicited applications are discouraged and unlikely to be successful.

The Gibbs Charitable Trusts

Methodist, Christian, general

Geographical focus: *Africa, Bristol and Lambeth*

8 Victoria Square, Clifton, Bristol BS8 4ET
Correspondent: Dr James M Gibbs, Trustee
Trustees: Mrs S M N Gibbs; Dr J N Gibbs; A G Gibbs; Dr J M Gibbs; W M Gibbs; S E Gibbs; Dr J E Gibbs; Mrs C Gibbs; Mrs E Gibbs; Mrs P Gibbs.

Total grants: £91,000 (1999/2000)
Grants overseas: About £25,000

General: The 1999/2000 annual report stated the 'policy remains to support three main categories of work: innovative undertakings by Methodist churches and organisations; other Christian causes – especially of an ecumenical nature; and a wide category within the field of the creative arts, education and international concern'. Overseas, the trust only supports organisations working in Africa. Many of the trustees have worked in African countries and have numerous contacts with organisations there. They are proactive in identifying projects to support.

In 1999/2000 the grant total was £91,000, broken down as follows:

Methodist work	£31,000
other Christian causes	£24,000
other causes	£36,000

Overseas beneficiaries included Oxfam (£15,000) and Jubilee 2000 (£4,000). Oxfam is a regular beneficiary and channels funds to smaller organisations.

The trust provided a list of beneficiaries which received grants at distributions during 2000 in April, August and December, some of which would be recorded in the 2000/2001 annual report. In these distributions, grants were made to 12 organisations for overseas work, totalling £28,000, including: Jubilee Plus and Methodist Relief and Development Fund (each £5,000), Oxfam (£4,000), INASP – book distribution in Africa (£3,000), Tearfund – Ethiopia Community Project (£2,000), Hope and Homes for Children (£1,000) and Worldwrite – Ghana Link (£500).

Exclusions: Individuals and animal charities are not supported.

Applications: The trust does not provide guidelines on how to apply and does not normally notify unsuccessful applicants. It discourages telephone enquiries. Projects supported are frequently those known to the trustees.

A large number of requests are received, particularly from churches undertaking improvement, refurbishment and development projects, but only a few can be helped. Those churches selected for support, as in other areas of work, are likely to be ones about which the trustees have particular knowledge.

The Grimmitt Trust

General

Geographical focus: *UK and overseas*

Grimmitt Holdings, Woodgate Business Park, Kettles Wood Drive, Birmingham B32 3GH
Tel: 0121 421 7000; **Fax:** 0121 421 9848
Correspondent: David W Everitt, Trustee
Trustees: P W Welch; Mrs M E Welch; D W Everitt; J S Sykes; D C Davies; P B Hyland; M G Fisher; C Hughes Smith; C Humphreys; Dr C Kendrick; Dr D Owen.

Total grants: £185,000 (1999/2000)
Grants overseas: £14,000

General: Grants are given to organisations in the Birmingham area. Local branches of UK organisations are supported, but larger UK appeals are not.

In 1999/2000 the trust had assets of £606,000 and an income of £277,000, including Gift Aid payments of £156,000 from Grimmitt Holdings Limited. Grants totalled £185,000 and were broken down into the following categories: cultural and educational; disability; community; children and youth; medical and health; overseas; older people; and benevolent.

Overseas grants totalled £14,000. The only one listed in the accounts was £4,000 to WaterAid (£3,500 in the previous year). The other grants were of under £2,000.

Applications: In writing to the correspondent.

The Walter Guinness Charitable Trust

General

Geographical focus: *UK and overseas, with a preference for Wiltshire and Hampshire*

Biddesden House, Andover, Hampshire SP11 9DN
Correspondent: The Secretary
Trustees: Hon. F B Guinness; Hon. Mrs R Mulji; Hon. Catriona Guinness.

Total grants: £122,000 (1998/99)
General: The trust was established in 1961 by Bryan Walter, the second Lord Moyne, in memory of his father, the first Lord Moyne. Most grants are given to charities which the trust has been consistently supporting for many years.

The assets of the trust stood at £3.9 million in 1998/99 generating an income of £143,000. A total of £122,000 was given in 163 grants, ranging from £50 to £10,000.

Larger grants included those to UNIPAL (£9,000), Asylum Aid (two grants totalling £1,500), Find Your Feet (£1,100), and £1,000 each to Disasters Emergency Committee – Sudan Crisis, LEPRA and Ockenden Venture. Smaller beneficiaries included: Africa Venture, Intermediate Technology, Oxfam and Marie Stopes International (£500 each), American Field Service International Education Programme (£250) and Anti-Slavery International (£100).

Exclusions: Previously the trust has stated: 'We are unlikely to be able to support anything unless there is a personal connection, a local connection or unless the organisation has previously been supported by our trust.'

Applications: In writing to the correspondent, but please note the above. The trust states that it is unable to respond to unsuccessful applications.

H C D Memorial Fund

See below

Geographical focus: *Worldwide*

Reeds Farm, Sayers Common, Hassocks, West Sussex BN6 9JQ
Tel: 01273 832173; **Fax:** 01273 832146
Correspondent: Jeremy Debenham, Secretary
Trustees: Nicholas Debenham, Chair; Bill Flinn; Dr Millie Sherman; Jeremy Debenham; Catherine Debenham.

Total grants: £807,000 (1998/99)
Grants overseas: £153,000

General: The trust has previously described itself as 'a tight-knit family charity, largely dependent on annual voluntary donations from its contributors', which 'makes grants to charities of all sizes, but prefers medium and small. About half in UK/Ireland and half overseas'. Both capital and revenue grants of between £5,000 and £50,000 are available for up to three years (occasionally longer), although most grants are one-off and between £10,000 and £20,000.

The 1998/99 annual report stated that grants were given towards:
- third world development;
- food, medicine and material aid and support for volunteer workers in Africa, India, Mexico and Honduras;
- help for people who are homeless or disabled and other social, medical and educational work in the UK and Republic of Ireland;
- a hospital in Mexico.

During the year the trust had an income, mostly from donations, of £397,000. Grants totalled £807,000, including 10 for work overseas totalling £153,000.

Concern America received £30,000 for 'PISTA/volunteers' in Mexico and £20,000 for flood relief work in Honduras. Other recipients included Hopes and Homes in Ukraine (£40,000), Intermediate Technology for agricultural development in Africa (£30,000), Oxfam for flood relief in Bangladesh (£15,000), and Angels International for children's hospital equipment in Belarus (£8,000).

Exclusions: No grants to animal charities or individuals.

Applications: In writing to the correspondent. Please note that the trust has a preference for seeking out its own projects and only rarely responds to general appeals. 'Unsolicited applications are acknowledged, but very rarely accepted. The majority of projects have been found through first or second-hand contacts of a contributor.'

The Hadley Trust

Social welfare

Geographical focus: Worldwide

Grandon, Hadley Green Road, Barnet, Hertfordshire EN5 5PR
Correspondent: P Hulme, Trustee
Trustees: Mrs J Hulme; P W Hulme.

Total grants: £925,000 (1998/99)
General: This trust was formed in 1997. Its objects allow it to 'assist in creating opportunities for people who are disadvantaged as a result of environmental, educational or economic circumstances or physical or other handicap to improve their situation, either by direct financial assistance, involvement in project and support work, or research into the causes of and means to alleviate hardship'.

The trust received an initial endowment of £36 million which generated an income of £2 million. In 1998/99 61 grants were made totalling £925,000. Further information was not available.

Applications: In writing to the correspondent. The trust stated in its report that is has successfully identified and established relationships with a number of registered charities which have objectives consistent with its own.

The Alfred Haines Charitable Trust

Christian and welfare projects

Geographical focus: *Principally Birmingham and immediate Midlands areas, also overseas*

c/o Bloomer Heaven, 33 Lionel Street, Birmingham B3 1AB
Tel: 0121 323 3236; **Fax:** 0121 323 3237
e-mail: ahct@quothquan.org
Correspondent: The Trustees
Trustees: W I Jollie; A L Gilmour.

Total grants: £156,000 (1998/99)
Grants overseas: £42,000

General: The trust prefers to support specific projects and concentrates on helping smaller charities based in Birmingham and the immediate surrounding area. Most support is for local organisations helping people to improve their quality of life, although Christian social actions projects involving outreach into the community through care is also considered. The trust states: 'Projects overseas or outside the West Midlands, whether Christian or not, will only be considered where the applicants are known to a trustee or are recommended by someone known to a trustee who has first-hand knowledge of the work.'

Grants are generally one-off, although projects may be funded annually for up to three years. The trust prefers to make grants towards specific items and does not give to large appeals.

In 1998/99 the trust had assets of £2.5 million and an income of £92,000. Grants totalled £156,000, including 20 grants totalling £42,000 towards humanitarian and Christian overseas aid (including healthcare, childcare, water provision, education and literacy work). A list of beneficiaries was not available. In 1997/98 grants included £2,500 to Mission Aviation Fellowship to airlift medical supplies in Tanzania.

Exclusions: No grants for:
- activities which are primarily the responsibility of central or local government or some responsible body
- animal welfare
- church buildings – restoration, improvements, renovations or new ones
- environmental – conservation and protection of wildlife and landscape
- expeditions and overseas trips
- hospitals and health centres

- individuals, including students (unless personally known to the trustees and of long-term benefit to overseas communities)
- large UK charities, even if for local projects
- loans and business finance
- medical research projects
- purely evangelical project
- overseas appeals (unless personally known to the trustees)
- the promotion of any religion other than Christianity
- schools, universities or colleges.

Applications: In writing to the correspondent, although overseas grants are only made to organisations personally known to the trustees.

The Paul Hamlyn Foundation

Arts, education, general in India
Geographical focus: UK and India

18 Queen Anne's Gate,
London SW1H 9AA
Tel: 020 7227 3500; **Fax:** 020 7222 0601
e-mail: information@phf.org.uk
website: www.phf.org.uk
Correspondent: Patricia Lankester, Director
Trustees: Lord Hamlyn; Lady Hamlyn; Michael Hamlyn; Jane Hamlyn; Lord Gavron; Mike Fitzgerald.

Adviser, Arts: Sir Claus Moser; Adviser, Publishing: Sue Thomson; Adviser, Penal Reform: Roger Graef.

Total grants: £2.2 million (1999/2000)
Grants overseas: over £163,000

General: The Paul Hamlyn Foundation was established in 1987 and endowed with a personal gift of £50 million from the founder. The trustees' emphasis is on helping to increase the opportunities available to people.

Although the trustees may proactively give grants to other projects, applications are considered from the following areas:

- *The arts* – projects which address inequality and opportunity, particularly in relation to young people. Priority is given to schemes which raise awareness and accessibility of high-quality art to new audiences or are relevant to young people at risk, prisoners and young offenders. Specific programmes for arts in education, Awards for Artists and student bursaries are also available.
- *Education* – initiatives which address the inequalities and disadvantages faced by young people or which seek to combat disaffection and alienation among young people. Specific programmes for access to books and reading projects for young people in public care and publishing training schemes are also available.
- *Small grants programme* – one-off grants up to £5,000 to local schemes or initiatives which fall within the trust's aims to represent the major part of the funding required,
- *India* – local projects, focusing on: development schemes; programmes to strengthen ngos generally through training, information exchange and networking; and schemes which benefit disadvantaged children.

In 1999/2000 16 overseas grants totalled £163,000. The largest grant in India was £35,000 to Jaipur Foot programme, an initiative long supported by this foundation, for the supply of low-cost artificial limbs. Also, £21,000 was given to Delhi Council for Child Welfare for its orthopaedic hospital and £15,000 to Mobile Creches for the care of the children of migrant workers at construction sites.

Exclusions: No grants for:
- general appeals or endowments

- capital projects
- buying, maintaining or refurbishing property or equipment
- individuals (except where the foundation has established a special scheme)
- individual organisations such as schools, theatre companies, etc.
- educational projects concerned with particular issues such as the environment/health
- large, well-known UK charities
- retrospective funding
- organisations which do not have charitable purposes.

Applications: In writing to the correspondent on five sides of A4 plus budget and annual report and accounts. Potential applicants are strongly advised to see the detailed application guidance notes, which state: 'The best thing is to make an exploratory telephone call or write a letter describing your work before making a formal application to the foundation. We are always happy to discuss your ideas at an early stage.'

For small grants, the trustees meet each month except August and December. Applications for up to £30,000 are considered in March, June, September and November, with larger amounts considered in February, April, June and October. Applications should arrive six weeks before these dates.

Beatrice Hankey Foundation Ltd

Christianity, education

Geographical focus: *UK and overseas*

6 Arundel Place, Farnham, Surrey GU9 7HQ
Correspondent: Mrs S M Legg, Secretary
Trustees: Prof. E G Wedell; Mrs A M Dawe; Revd J Elliott; Mrs A C Lethbridge; Mrs I Mentincke-Zuiderweg; Mrs N Starosta; Mrs H Pawson; Revd Mother L Morris; Revd D Savill; Revd Canon J W D Simonson; Mrs D Sampson.

Total grants: £32,000 (1998)
General: Grants are given worldwide for the advancement of the Christian religion, especially for training missionaries, and to support study and training courses in Eastern Europe.

In 1998 the trust had assets of £795,000 and an income of £39,000. Grants ranging from £50 to £2,500 totalled £32,000.

Grants included £2,000 to Sudan Church Association, and £1,000 each to Mission to Romania, Kalko Trust and Medical Foundation for the Care of Victims of Torture.

Applications: In writing to the correspondent.

The Lennox Hannay Charitable Trust

Disability, general

Geographical focus: *UK and overseas*

Robert Fleming Trustee Co. Ltd, 25 Copthall Avenue, London EC2 7DR
Correspondent: The Trust Manager
Trustees: Robert Fleming Trustee Company Ltd; Walter L Hannay; Caroline F Wilmot-Sitwell.

Total grants: £337,000 (1998/99)
General: The trust has general charitable purposes, regularly supporting the same large, well-known UK charities each year. It also supports UK charities working overseas with people with disabilities. Grants are also available for ecology, endangered species and community development.

In 1998/99 the trust had assets of £12 million and an income of £350,000.

Grants ranged from £2,000 to £47,000 and totalled £337,000.

Beneficiaries included Health Unlimited (£47,000), Save the Children Fund (£15,000), Tibet House (£9,000), International Planned Parenthood Federation (£8,600) and Raleigh International (£2,000).

Exclusions: Grants are given to UK-registered charities only and not to individuals.

Applications: In writing to the correspondent. The trust cannot respond to unsolicited applications.

Miss K M Harbinson's Charitable Trust

General

Geographical focus: UK and developing countries

190 St Vincent Street, Glasgow G2 5SP
Tel: 0141 204 2833
Correspondent: The Secretary
Trustees: A Maguire; G L Harbinson; R Harbinson.

Total grants: £171,000 (1994)
General: The trust supports development organisations, giving grants ranging from £1,000 to £9,000, often in two instalments during the year. In 1993/94 grants included: £9,000 each to ActionAid, Intermediate Technology, Marie Stopes International and Oxfam; £8,000 each to British Red Cross and Worldwide Fund for Nature; £4,000 each to Breadline Africa, Care Britain, Ethopiaid and UNICEF; £3,000 to Romanian Orphanage Trust; and £2,000 to Sight Savers International.

Up-to-date information was unavailable.

Applications: In writing to the correspondent.

The Dorothy Hay-Bolton Charitable Trust

Work with deaf and blind people

Geographical focus: UK and overseas

F W Stephens & Co., 10 Charterhouse Square, London EC1M 6LQ
Tel: 020 7251 4434
Correspondent: Brian E Carter, Trustee
Trustees: Brian E Carter; Stephen J Gallico.

Total grants: £22,000 (1997/98)
General: The trust makes grants towards charities working with people who are deaf or blind, particularly children and young people.

In 1997/98 the trust's assets were £1 million, it had an income of £45,000 and 14 grants were made totalling £22,000. After spending £8,000 on management and administration costs, the trust had a surplus of £15,000 at the year end.

Grants to organisations were for either £1,000 or £2,000. Beneficiaries included Brainwave, Pattaya Orphanage, Tarabai Desai Eye Hospital and Research Centre, and Voluntary Service Overseas.

Applications: In writing to the correspondent.

The Charles Hayward Foundation

Welfare and health, medical research, general overseas

Geographical focus: Worldwide

Hayward House, 45 Harrington Gardens, London SW7 4JU
Tel: 020 7370 7063/7067
Correspondent: Mark Schnebli
Trustees: I F Donald, Chair; Mrs A M Chamberlain; Sir Jack Hayward; Sir Graham Hearne; Mrs S J Heath; Dr J C Houston; B D Insch; J N van Leuven; A D Owen; Miss A T Rogers; Ms J Streather.

Total grants: £2 million (1998/99)

General: The two trusts established by Sir Charles Hayward (The Hayward Foundation and The Charles Hayward Trust) were combined on 1 January 2000 to become The Charles Hayward Foundation.

The foundation runs a number of grant-making programmes, which include one for UK and regional charities, a community grants programme and an overseas funding programme.

The overseas grants programme gives between eight and ten grants of £3,000 to £15,000 a year for capital costs of buildings, extensions, adaptations, equipment and furnishings. Project funding is sometimes granted for start-up or development activities where this is not yet part of the ongoing revenue requirement of the project. Funding priority areas are:

- *Health* – clean water, basic health education, provision of basic medical facilities, HIV/AIDS prevention, etc.
- *Youth at risk* – orphans, street children, children whose parents have HIV/AIDS, child mental health.
- *Education* – capital grants for the building of schools, training of teachers, provision of books and equipment, etc.
- *Special needs* – care and rehabilitation of people with learning or physical disabilities or mental health problems.
- *Older people* – relief of older people who are in need.

Within these areas, the trust prefers projects which: address the causes of poverty and disadvantage; increase self-help and reduce economic insecurity; demonstrate, through analysis of need, extensive consultation of local people and maximum user involvement; and which are economically and environmentally sustainable.

Exclusions: Grants are only given to UK-registered charities. No grants for
- individuals
- revenue
- loan repayments
- transport or travel
- bursaries
- general repairs
- endowment funds
- replacement of government funding
- computers.

Grants are not available retrospectively, although they are only paid on evidence of expenditure such as receipts, invoices, cost-coded management accounts, etc. Grants may be withdrawn if not taken up within 12 months.

Applications: In writing to the correspondent, from whom detailed guidelines for applicants are available. Initial applications should be on no more than three sides of A4, plus annual accounts and reports, including:

- name and location of organisation
- contact details
- description of organisation including present work, priorities and size of operation (how many people are helped and how)
- description of proposed project
- details of political and economic situation of the country the project will be located
- project cost, keeping capital and revenue costs separate
- funds raised and pledged and outstanding shortfall
- timetable for the project.

All applications receive a reply, and the trust may request further information. There is often a waiting list and trustees only meet four times a year to consider applications so it may be several months before you receive an answer.

The Headley Trust

Arts, environment, health, education, overseas development
Geographical focus: Worldwide

9 Red Lion Court, London EC4A 3EF
Tel: 020 7410 0330; **Fax:** 020 7410 0332
Correspondent: Michael Pattison, Director
Trustees: Sir Timothy Sainsbury; Lady Susan Sainsbury; T J Sainsbury; J R Benson; Miss Judith Portrait.

Total grants: £6 million approved (1999)
Grants overseas: £425,000

General: This is one of the Sainsbury Family Charitable Trusts which share a joint administration. Like the others, it is primarily proactive, aiming to choose its own grantees, and it discourages unsolicited applications. The trust has a particular interest in the arts and in artistic and architectural heritage and has made big grants, especially to help match lottery funding, to museums, galleries, libraries and theatres. There are ongoing programmes for the repair of old churches and cathedrals. The trust also supports a range of social welfare issues. Its support for activities in developing countries is focused on Sub-Saharan anglophone countries and on Central and Eastern Europe. There is a small Aids for Disabled Fund (£30,000 in 1999).

In 1999, grants were categorised under: arts and environment (home); arts and environment (overseas); medical; developing countries; education; health and social welfare. Of the total of 270 approved grants totalling £6 million, 13 were given in the developing countries category totalling £425,000.

Under the 'arts and environment (overseas)' category, support is given to art conservation projects of outstanding artistic or architectural importance, particularly the restoration of buildings, statuary or paintings, primarily in the countries of Central and Eastern Europe. Grants are channelled through established reputable conservation organisations in the countries concerned. Awards in 1999 included £66,000 to Uhrovec Castle in Slovakia for restoration, £52,000 to a church in Lasi in Romania for wall paintings and £30,000 to Peggy Guggenheim Museum in Venice.

Under the 'developing countries' category, priority is given to projects in Sub-Saharan anglophone Africa, Central and Eastern Europe and the Commonwealth of Independent States. Focus areas include:

- water projects (e.g. which give disadvantaged communities access to safe water, preserve ecologically or culturally important wetland areas, improve sanitary conditions or promote better use of water);
- forestry projects (e.g. which preserve areas of natural woodland or encourage environmentally or socially sustainable methods of forestry);
- education and literacy projects (e.g. which improve quality of education and literacy standards for underprivileged people through supply of material, construction, training support, etc.);
- health projects (particularly those which support blind or partially sighted people).

The largest grants went to ActionAid for an AIDS project in Malawi (£71,000), Health Unlimited for the development of best practice in primary healthcare (£45,000), The Mid-Africa Ministry for healthcare for people who are disabled in Uganda (£39,000), and The British Council in Ethiopia for learning resources for healthcare professionals

(£37,000). A further grant under another heading was £21,000 for a new mental health resource centre in Bucharest, Romania.

Applications: In writing to the correspondent. However, the trust states: 'proposals are generally invited by the trustees or initiated at their request. Unsolicited applications are discouraged and are unlikely to be successful, even if they fall within an area in which the trustees are interested.'

Henhurst Charitable Trust

General, development

Geographical focus: *Developing countries*

Henhurst Farm, Foots Lane, Burwash Weald, Etchingham, East Sussex TN19 7LE
Tel: 01435 883239
Correspondent: Clifford John Lewis, Trustee

Total grants: About £8,000 (1998/99)
Grants overseas: £8,000

General: In 1998/99 the trust had an income of £7,600 and its total expenditure was £8,200. Further information for this year was not available at the Charity Commission.

In 1993/94, the most recent year for which accounts were available in the public files, the trust's assets totalled £106,000, it had an income of £5,700 and it gave 42 grants totalling £7,500. Grants ranged between £15 and £750.

The largest grants were £750 each to Intermediate Technology and WaterAid, £500 to World Wildlife Fund UK and £400 to VSO. Over a quarter of the smaller beneficiaries were overseas development organisations, including Bosnia Convoy, Romanian Orphanage Trust and Sight Savers International.

Applications: In writing to the correspondent.

The Hilden Charitable Fund

Homelessness, race relations, penal affairs, overseas causes

Geographical focus: *UK and overseas, but mostly London*

34 North End Road, London W14 0SH
Tel & Fax: 020 7603 1525
e-mail: hildencharity@hotmail.com
Correspondent: Rodney Hedley, Secretary to the Trustees
Trustees: Mrs M G Duncan; Mrs A M A Rampton; Dr D S Rampton; Mrs G J S Rampton; J R A Rampton; A J M Rampton; C S L R Rampton; Dr M B H Rampton; Prof. C H Rodeck; Mrs E K Rodeck; C H Younger; Ms M E Baxter.

Total grants: £503,000 (1999/2000)
Grants overseas: £136,000

General: In 1999/2000 the trust had assets of £14 million, an income of £493,000 and distributed £503,000 in the following categories: minorities; third world; penal affairs; homelessness; Scotland; Scottish Community Foundation; playschemes; other. In all, 25 grants were made in the third world category, totalling £136,000.

The charity's guidelines for applicants include the following information: 'Grants are rarely given to well established national charities or to individuals. Fund policy is directed largely at supporting work at a community level within the categories of interest stated above.' Please note, that under point (6) below, the trustees ask ngos to encourage local overseas partners to apply to the trust direct.

'Priorities given to different types of work within the main categories may change from time to time, as dictated by circumstances. It should not be assumed, therefore, that an application, even though it may generally qualify, will necessarily be considered. Grants, capital or revenue, rarely exceed £5,000 and are not often made for salaries.

'Types of applications sought by trustees:

'(1) In supporting overseas development the trustees wish to hear from projects which focus on community development, education and health.

'(2) Funds are available for capital and revenue funding. The funding programme is designed to help small and medium-size initiatives.

'(3) The trustees will consider applications from countries within the developing world. At present applications from Ghana, Ethiopia, Tanzania, South Africa and Bangladesh are particularly welcome.

'(4) In supporting community development, education and health initiatives, the trustees will particularly welcome projects which address the needs and potential of girls and women.

'(5) Where possible the trustees would like to fund a number of projects in one geographical area. In funding projects, the trustees will be interested in projects which develop the capacity of local people.

'(6) The trustees will be pleased to hear from UK ngos and hope that UK ngos will encourage their local partners, if appropriate, to apply directly to Hilden for grant aid.'

In 1999/2000 the two largest grants under the third world heading were both of £10,000; they were made to Catholic Fund for Overseas Development for the Venezuela emergency appeal in response to the landslide in December 1999, and to Mozambique Schools Fund towards building a school.

Other larger grants were £9,500 to Farm Africa for agricultural development and wells in Ethiopia, £7,500 to Womankind Worldwide for supporting women's rights in Nicaragua, £6,500 to Zenzele in Cape Town for a training and employment project, and £5,600 to St Matthew's Children's Fund also for agricultural development and wells in Ethiopia.

Of the remaining grants, 16 were of £5,000, one for £2,500 and two for £2,000. Other beneficiaries included: African Initiatives to help to provide education for Maasai people in Tanzania; CODA International towards the provision of agricultural rehabilitation to an area devastated by Hurricane Mitch; Fairtrade Foundation to fund a cocoa farming project in Belize; Legal Assistance Trust for work on land rights in South Africa; and The Community School in Ghana; and Wulugu Project in Ghana for its education programmes for girls and young women.

Exclusions: Grants are rarely given to well-established UK charities or to individuals.

Applications: All applicants are required to complete a very brief summary form outlining the request before it is considered. Otherwise all applications will be regarded as enquiries. Potential applicants should contact the office for guidelines and forms.

'Applications should include enclosures of:
- most recent financially inspected accounts
- most recent annual report
- projected income and expenditure for the current financial year
- explanation of how your reserves stand

- particular features of your costs, e.g. high transport costs in rural areas
- details of other funders approached
- any significant achievements and/or problems or difficulties
- how you approach equal opportunities
- any "matching grant" arrangements.'

Please be clear in your application about when the proposed work is to start, and give the relevant timetable.

'For projects overseas applicants should provide:
- evidence of commitment amongst local people and communities to the proposed work programme;
- a coherent plan of how the work is going to be carried out with relevant budgets. Budgets should be presented in the context of the overall budget of the applicant ngo;
- a plan of how the work is going to be maintained and developed in the future by involving relevant agencies and attracting money and resources;
- an explanation of why the local project seeks the help of a UK aid agency;
- details of local costs (e.g. salaries of state-employed teachers and medical personnel; cost of vehicles, petrol, etc.), and notes of any problems over exchange rates or inflation;
- an account of the political, economic, religious and cultural situation in the country/area;
- a comment on the extent to which the project can rely on government and local state funding in the country concerned;
- details of monitoring and evaluation.'

Trustees meet approximately every three months.

L E Hill Memorial Trust

General

Geographical focus: *Mostly Scotland, also overseas*

Turcan Connell, Princess Exchange, 1 Earl Gray Street, Edinburgh EH3 9EE
Tel: 0131 228 8111
Trustees: Turcan Connell Trustees Ltd.

Total grants: Around £16,000

General: The trustees support a wide range of activities, including the disaster appeals of international children's charities and charitable organisations promoting international cooperation between schools. Most grants range between £200 and £2,000.

Applications: In writing to the address above.

The Jane Hodge Foundation

Medicine, education, Catholic organisations

Geographical focus: *Worldwide, but mostly Wales*

Ty-Gwyn, Lisvane Road, Cardiff CF14 0SG
Tel: 029 2076 6521
Correspondent: Margaret Cason, Secretary
Trustees: Sir Julian Hodge; Lady Moira Hodge; Teresa Hodge; Robert Hodge; Joyce Harrison; Derrek Jones; Ian Davies; David Austin.

Total grants: £1.1 million (1998/99)

General: A large portion of the available funds is given in ongoing grants to local organisations in Cardiff, such as funding chairs at University of Wales and major building projects. Support is also given to charities working in developing countries.

In 1999 the foundation had future grant commitments worth over £5 million, including £3 million towards the building of a new cathedral in Cardiff.

In 1998/99 the foundation's assets stood at £27 million and its income was £1.4 million. Grants totalling £1.1 million were distributed under the following headings: medical (£351,000); educational (£256,000); religious (£223,000); and other (£240,000).

As in previous years, sympathetic consideration has been given to various charities based in developing countries, including payments to Missionary Sisters of the Holy Rosary, One World Action, Salesian Sisters of St John Bosco in India and Society of Catholic Missionaries.

Exclusions: Grants are only given to UK-registered or exempt charities. No grants to individuals.

Applications: In writing to the correspondent. In 2000 the foundation said it was receiving about 300 applications a month but despite the volume of requests received, every application is acknowledged.

The Hope Trust

Christian, addiction, rehabilitation, health

Geographical focus: *Scotland, Europe, Central and South America, Africa*

Drummond Miller, 31–32 Moray Place, Edinburgh EH3 8BZ
Tel: 0131 226 5151
Correspondent: Carole Hope
Trustees: Revd Prof. D W D Shaw; Revd Prof. A C Cheyne; Very Revd Dr W J G McDonald; Prof. G M Newlands; Prof. D A S Ferguson; Revd G R Barr.

Total grants: £87,000 (1997)
General: This trust has existed for over 100 years. It supports organisations providing education and literature to combat the misuse and effects of alcohol and drugs, and the promotion of the Reformed Churches, rehabilitation centres and health education.

In 1997 it had assets of £1 million and an income of £110,000. Grants ranged from £100 to £6,000 and totalled £87,000.

Exclusions: No grants for buildings or refurbishments.

Applications: In writing to the correspondent.

Human Relief Foundation

General

Geographical focus: *Bangladesh, Bosnia, Iraq, Lebanon, Somalia and other regions requiring urgent relief/aid*

4 Claremont, Bradford BD7 1BQ
Correspondent: Dr N S Al-Ramdhani, Chair
Trustees: Dr Nabeel Al-Ramdhani, Chair; Dr Saad Mustafa; Dr Ali Al-Quirbi; Dr Haytham Al-Kaffaf; Wael Musabbah; Anas Osam Tawfeek; Farid Sabri; Osama Abdulla; Sultan Al-Qassime.

Total grants: £412,000 (1999)
Grants overseas: £412,000

General: The trust gives grants for the relief of poverty and sickness and to protect and preserve good health and advance education of those in need from impoverished countries, in particular Bangladesh, Bosnia, Iraq, Lebanon and Somalia. Infrastructure, support and development and cultural activity are also funded.

In 1999 the trust had assets of £699,000 and an income of £1 million. Grants totalled £412,000.

Beneficiaries included Red Crescent – UAE (£139,000), Qatar Charitable Trust

(£73,000), Muslim Aid (£31,000), Islamic Relief Worldwide (£27,000), Elrahm Trust (£19,000) and Muslim World League – Saudi Arabia (£15,000).

Exclusions: No grants to individuals or for medical expenses, tutors or examination fees.

Applications: In writing to the correspondent.

The J J Charitable Trust

Environment, literacy

Geographical focus: *Worldwide, but mostly UK*

9 Red Lion Court, London EC4A 3EF
Tel: 020 7410 0330; **Fax:** 020 7410 0332
Correspondent: Michael Pattison, Director
Trustees: Julian Sainsbury; M L Sainsbury; Miss Judith Portrait.

Total grants: £600,000 (1999/2000)
General: This is one of the Sainsbury Family Charitable Trusts which share a joint administration. Like the others, it is primarily proactive, aiming to choose its own grantees, and it discourages unsolicited applications. The trust gives its major support to environmental work, both in the UK and overseas. In addition the trust shows a particular interest in dyslexia and other problems affecting literacy, particularly among young people at risk. Only a small number of grants are made. Few of them are for less than £5,000 and occasionally grants can be for more than £100,000.

In 1999/2000 it had assets of £18 million and an income of £2.8 million. Grants to 37 organisations totalled £600,000 and were broken down as follows: literacy support (15 grants totalling £67,000); environment – UK (11 grants totalling £162,000); environment – overseas (5 grants totalling £93,000); general (3 grants totalling £28,000); Merlin (£50,000).

Under 'environment – overseas', the trustees continue to support community-based agriculture projects which aim to help people to help themselves in an environmentally sustainable way. The trustees have started to look at a small number of projects in Central and Eastern Europe. Beneficiaries were SOS Sahel (£35,000), Farm Africa (£18,000), Tree Aid for its Barsologho Tree Project in Burkino Faso and Oxfam for three projects in Kenya (£15,000 each), and Intermediate Technology (£10,000).

Under the 'general' category, £9,500 was given to CARE International UK to provide drama workshops and performances with refugees and host communities in Macedonia, with £8,000 to Oxfam.

A £50,000 interest-free loan was given to Merlin for work in Mozambique, which was separate from the other grants in the accounts.

Applications: In writing to the correspondent. Please note that unsolicited applications are discouraged and unlikely to be successful.

The Jephcott Charitable Trust

Alleviation of poverty, general

Geographical focus: *UK, developing countries*

Cotley, Streatham Rise, Exeter EX4 4PE
Correspondent: Mrs Meg Harris, Secretary
Trustees: Mrs M Jephcott, Chair; Dr P Davis; Judge A North; Mrs A Morgan.

Total grants: £137,000 (1999/2000)
General: The trust's 1998/99 annual report states that it is particularly

interested in giving grants for start-up costs. Previously it has stated that its priorities are population control, education, health and the environment. Grants are usually for a specific project or part of a project. Core funding and/or salaries are rarely considered. 'Pump-priming' donations are offered – usually grants to new organisations and areas of work. As well as being reactive (responding to applications) the trust is becoming increasingly proactive.

The trustees are flexible in their approach, but take the following into account when considering a project:
- the ability to evaluate a project (with overseas projects local involvement is thought to be essential for ongoing success);
- the involvement of a third party e.g. DFID, ngos, National Heritage;
- financial: level of administration costs, reserves held within the group etc.;
- whether the project is basic or palliative and whether it is one-off or ongoing;
- to what extent the organisation has helped itself.

In 1999/2000 the trust's assets stood at £4.6 million, giving an income of £143,000. A total of £137,000 was given in 23 grants, ranging from £750 to £14,000. Seven of the beneficiaries were also supported in the previous year.

The largest grants were £14,000 to Woodside Sanctuary, and £10,000 each to ADESA, Mozambique Schools Fund and Winter Comfort. Other recipients included Archbishop Joseph Cababa Ssunga Health Centre (£7,500), World Medical Trust (£6,000), Anglo-Peruvian Child Care Mission (£2,500) and Miyana Community Centre – Uganda (£750).

Exclusions: No grants to individuals or for medical research. No response is given to general appeals from large, well-known organisations. Core funding and/or salaries are rarely considered.

Applications: Guidelines and application forms are available on request and receipt of an sae. Trustees meet in April and October and must have detailed financial information about each project before they will make a decision.

The Jerusalem Trust

Promotion of Christianity
Geographical focus: *Worldwide*

9 Red Lion Court, London EC4A 3EF
Tel: 020 7410 0330; **Fax:** 020 7410 0332
Correspondent: Michael Pattison, Director
Trustees: Sir Timothy Sainsbury; Lady Susan Sainsbury; V E Hartley Booth; Canon Gordon Bridger; Mrs Diana Wainman.

Total grants: £3.1 million (1999)
General: This is one of the Sainsbury Family Charitable Trusts which share a joint administration. Like the others, it is primarily proactive, aiming to choose its own grantees, and it discourages unsolicited applications. The trust supports a wide range of Christian evangelical and charitable activities at home and abroad. Unusually, these include Christian media activities and Christian art. Over 100 grants are made each year averaging over £20,000.

The activities of this trust are limited by its legal objects to the support of Christian activities or organisations. The regular income of the trust in 1999 was £3.2 million, but additional donations were received of £9 million for the endowment and £530,000 in unrestricted funds. Grants totalled £3.1 million with grants approved broken down as follows:

	No.	Total
Christian evangelism/ relief work overseas	27	£674,000
Christian media	11	£404,000
Christian education	21	£722,000
Christian art	4	£11,000
Christian evangelism, social responsibility (UK)	54	£1,260,000

Beneficiaries included Tearfund and World Vision UK towards relief and development work (£100,000 each), Mission Aviation Fellowship towards the cost of purchasing a small aircraft for use in Mongolia (£30,000), Covenant Home Ministries towards the construction of a new dormitory at a Christian school and orphanage in Kisumu – Kenya (£15,000), and Scripture Union Africa towards the 'Aid for Aids' programme in eastern and southern Africa (£14,000).

Exclusions: No grants towards building or repair work for churches or to individuals.

Applications: In writing to the correspondent. However, 'proposals are generally invited by the trustees or initiated at their request. Unsolicited applications are unlikely to be successful, even if they fall within an area in which the trustees are interested'.

The Jerwood Charitable Foundation and The Jerwood Foundation

General

Geographical focus: *Mostly UK, also a few grants in Nepal*

22 Fitzroy Square, London W1P 5HJ
Tel: 020 7388 6287; **Fax:** 020 7388 6289
website: www.jerwood.org.uk
Correspondent: Roanne Dods, Director
Trustees: Alan Grieve, Chair; Viscount Chilston; Lady Harlech; Dr Kerry Parton; Edward Paul; Julia Wharton; Anthony Palmer; Barbara Kalman; Tim Eyles.

Total grants: Over £5 million (2000 projection)

General: The Jerwood Charitable Foundation, as a new charity established in 1999, supports revenue projects while the associated Jerwood Foundation, established in 1977, by which it is funded and which is not a UK charity, continues to fund capital projects in its own name. The combined level of grantmaking was expected to rise to over £5 million in 2000.

The Jerwood Charitable Foundation is now responsible for revenue awards, donations and sponsorship in the UK which were previously undertaken by The Jerwood Foundation itself. It is dedicated to funding and sponsorship of the visual and performing arts, and education in the widest sense. It will continue to allocate a proportion of funding to conservation, environment, medicine, science and engineering. The charity shares with The Jerwood Foundation a dedication to imaginative and responsible funding and sponsorship in areas of human endeavour and excellence which foster and enrich the fabric of society.

The trust states: 'We aim to monitor chosen projects closely and sympathetically and are keen to seek recognition of the foundation's support. Our strategy is to support outstanding national institutions while at the same time being prepared to provide seed-corn finance and financial support at the early stages of an initiative when other grant-making bodies might not be able or willing to act. The foundation may wish to be sole sponsor (subject to financial considerations) or to provide partnership funding.

'In particular The Jerwood Charitable Foundation seeks to develop support and reward for young people who have demonstrated achievement and excellence, and who will benefit from a final lift to launch their careers. This special role is intended to open the way for young achievers and give them the opportunity to flourish.'

Although the trust normally funds UK projects, it will also consider a very small number of applications from UK organisations operating overseas, usually within Nepal. International initiatives supported by the trust include: Gurkha Welfare Trust to support the children of former Gurkha soldiers; Student Partnership Worldwide to help send young British students to study in Nepal to benefit from non-formal education and training in environmental awareness; and IMPACT in Nepal to fund an ENT camp in Dhangadi, orthopaedic camps in Nepalgunj and Dharan, an ear camp at Jankpur and an ear surgery camp at Siraha. Merlin is also regularly supported for its work in places such as Afghanistan, Siberia and Sudan.

Exclusions: The Jerwood Charitable Foundation will not consider applications on behalf of:
- individuals
- building or capital costs (including purchase of equipment)
- projects in the fields of religion or sport
- animal rights or welfare
- general fundraising appeals which are likely to have wide public appeal
- appeals to establish endowment funds for other charities
- appeals for matching funding for National Lottery applications
- grants for the running and core costs of voluntary bodies
- projects which are of mainly local appeal or identifiable with a locality
- medical research without current clinical applications and benefits
- social welfare, particularly where it may be considered a government or local authority responsibility
- retrospective awards.

The trustees may, where there are very exceptional circumstances, decide to waive an exclusion.

Applications: Applications should be by letter, outlining the aims and objectives of the organisation and the specific project for which assistance is sought. Applications should include:
- a detailed budget for the project, identifying administration, management and central costs;
- details of funding already in place for the project, including any other trusts or sources which are being or have been approached for funds. If funding is not in place, details of how the applicant plans to secure the remaining funding is required;
- details of the management and staffing structure, including trustees;
- the most recent annual report and audited accounts of the organisation, together with current management accounts if relevant to the project.

The foundation may wish to enter into discussions and/or correspondence with the applicant which may result in modification and/or development of the project or scheme. Any such discussion will in no way commit The Jerwood Charitable Foundation to funding that application.

As the foundation receives a large number of applications, it regrets that it is not possible to have preliminary meetings to discuss possible support before a written application is made. Please read the section above on funding exclusions before submitting an application.

J G Joffe Charitable Trust

Overseas development
Geographical focus: *Developing countries*

Liddington Manor, The Street, Liddington, Swindon SN4 0HD
Tel: 01793 790203; **Fax:** 01793 791144
Correspondent: Lord Joffe
Trustees: Mrs V L Joffe; Lord Joffe.

Total grants: £497,000 (1998/99)
General: Lord Joffe, the settlor of the trust, was the co-founder of what has become the Allied Dunbar insurance company. He is now Chair of Oxfam. Grants ranging from £5,000 to £50,000 are made every year to a few dozen organisations that concentrate their activities in developing countries, dealing with such issues as debt relief, human rights and development.

In 1998/99 the trust held assets of nearly £11 million which generated an income of £331,000. Grants to 32 organisations totalled £497,000.

The largest grants were £85,000 to Institute of Community Studies, £66,000 to 3WI Education Trust, and £50,000 each to New Economics Foundation and Jubilee 2000 Coalition. These four grants accounted for over half the grant total.

The remaining grants ranged from £2,000 to Sri Lanka Peace Foundation to £25,000 each to Amnesty International and Ashoka (UK) Trust. Other beneficiaries included European Palestine Israel Centre, Medical Foundation for the Care of Victims of Torture, Money Management Council, Mozambique Schools Fund, Tools for Self Reliance and War on Want.

Applications: In writing to the correspondent. However, the trust states: 'The trustees have an ongoing relationship with a number of charities and their decisions on which to support at any one time are based on their assessment of the quality of leadership and the impact that the initiatives which they support are likely to have.' The trustees go on to say that they do not consider 'applications' when making grants.

The Elton John Aids Foundation

HIV/AIDS
Geographical focus: *UK and overseas, excluding North America*

1 Blythe Road, London W14 0HG
Tel: 020 7603 9996; **Fax:** 020 7348 4848
e-mail: admin@ejafuk.com
Correspondent: Robert Key, Director
Trustees: Sir Elton John, Chair; Robert Key; John Scott; David Furnish; Lynette Jackson; Neil Tennant; Frank Presland; Colin Bell; Anne Aslett; Margaret Littman; Johnny Bergius; James Locke; Tim Cohen.

Total grants: £1.4 million (1999)
General: The trust supports projects concerned with the alleviation of the physical, mental and emotional hardship of people with HIV/AIDS and prevention programmes. Grants are given in the UK and overseas, except North America. Grants range from £250 to £150,000 and average £20,000.

In 1999 the trust had assets of £435,000 and an income of £1.6 million. Grants totalled £1.4 million.

Beneficiaries included ActionAid – Malawi to support 24 local AIDS organisations with training to help them carry out HIV/AIDS prevention and care activities (£80,000), Population Services – Mumbai, India for a HIV/AIDS prevention programme for truck drivers (£61,000), and Sihanouk Hospital – Cambodia for a volunteer corps programme.

Exclusions: No grants for research, individuals, repatriation costs, conferences or educational courses. Drug treatment costs, capital costs and retrospective funding will only be considered in exceptional circumstances.

Applications: Initially in writing in the form of a project outline. If appropriate, a funding application form, guidelines and a request for specific information (e.g. audited accounts) will be sent.

Ernest Kleinwort Charitable Trust

General

Geographical focus: *Worldwide*

PO Box 191, 10 Fenchurch Street, London EC3M 3LB
Tel: 020 7475 5478; **Fax:** 020 7475 5558
Correspondent: The Secretary
Trustees: Kleinwort Benson Trustees Ltd.

Total grants: £1.9 million (1999/2000)
General: The trust has general charitable purposes, giving half of its grant total on a recurring basis to around 20 UK and international organisations, and half in smaller grants to applicants. The 1999/2000 annual report stated: 'During the year the trustees made a total of 284 donations, principally in the fields of wildlife and environmental conservation, disability, medical research, elderly welfare and youth and welfare, and preference was given to charities in Sussex.'
A significant amount was donated to charities working in developing countries for conservation and planned parenthood.

During the year the trust had assets of £59 million generating an income of only £1.6 million. Grants totalled £1.9 million.

Recipients in developing nations included Intermediate Technology and Population Concern (£30,000 each), Merlin (£10,000) and Jamaica Family Planning Association (£8,000).

Applications: In writing to the correspondent. The trustees meet in March and October.

The Kulika Charitable Trust

Sustainable agriculture, poverty alleviation and development, environment and conservation

Geographical focus: *Uganda*

4 The Mount, Guildford, Surrey GU2 4YN
Tel: 01483 563567; **Fax:** 01483 562505
e-mail: uk@kulika.org
Correspondent: Andrew Jones
Trustees: D J Burnstone; Miss P A M Brenninkmeyer; T A Brenninkmeyer; Mrs M M E Wentworth-Stanley; A J van Amelsvoort; Dr C P Peacock; Mrs S Errington; Langersal Limited.

Total grants: £115,000 to organisations (1998/99)
General: The trust concentrates its work in the following four main areas:

- provision of educational scholarships to Ugandan students through a scholarship programme;
- provision of training of Ugandan farmers through a sustainable agricultural training programme;
- limited support for poverty alleviation and development projects in Uganda;
- limited support for environmental and conservation projects in Uganda.

The scholarship programme provides opportunities for Ugandans to study at graduate and postgraduate levels. Limited support for technical and vocational training is also provided. Scholarships are awarded by a committee based in Kampala, not the UK office. At any one time over a hundred students are sponsored by institutions within Uganda.

Very few scholarships are awarded for study outside the country, and then only for postgraduate study where there is a clear link to the development of Uganda's infrastructure or services, and where the course of study is not available locally.

The sustainable agricultural training programme takes selected Ugandan farmers to train as 'Key Trainers' who complete a ten-month course (part residential, part on-farm) in sustainable agriculture and farmer-to-farmer extension. On completion of the course, Key Trainers are equipped to teach others in their communities in sustainable agriculture techniques and practices, the adoption of which can help smallholder farmers and their families to increase production and enjoy better livlihoods.

In 1998/99 £253,000 was given to individuals in the form of educational grants and scholarships and £199,000 was spent on the sustainable agriculture training programme.

In total the trust had assets totalling £5 million. It had an income of £406,000, (the income of £2.3 million in 1997/98 was due to the unusually high level of fundraising in that period). Grants to organisations totalled £115,000 and were listed in the accounts as follows:

general charitable	£14,000
overseas project aid	£72,000
sustainable agriculture	£29,000
conservation	–

Beneficiaries of grants in excess of £1,000 were listed in the trustees' report. The Kulika Charitable Trust in Uganda received six grants totalling almost £90,000, towards e.g. project work, core costs, sustainable agriculture and training, including training for individuals. Other grants listed were: £15,000 to Bannabikira Daughters of Mary; £10,000 to World University Service (UK), towards the cost of administering its Campus Scholarship Scheme; and £3,000 to Child Welfare & Adoption Society (Uganda).

The trust's annual report stated that it wishes to continue supporting similar projects at a similar financial level to those funded in 1998/99. It also stated that because of the need to fund work in Uganda, the trust again made no grants to projects designed to improve and conserve the environment (1996/97: £5,000; 1997/98: nil).

Exclusions: Applications for sponsorship for undergraduate studies outside Uganda are not considered. The trust cannot consider applications for postgraduate study where the student has less than two years' work experience in a field relevant to the proposed course of study.

Applications: Applicants for the scholarship or training programme should write to the scholarship coordinator or the sustainable agricultural coordinator at The Kulika Charitable Trust (Uganda), PO Box 11330, Kampala, Uganda. Applications should be received by 31 December for sponsorship in the following academic year.

Acknowledgements can only be sent to candidates selected for interview in March or April.

Other general enquiries, including those by applicant organisations, can be made to either the UK or Uganda office, although it should be understood that it is the intention of the UK trustees that grant-making decisions will generally be taken in Uganda and not in the UK in the future.

The Beatrice Laing Trust

Health, welfare

Geographical focus: Worldwide, but mostly UK

Box 1, 133 Page Street, Mill Hill, London NW7 2ER
Tel: 020 8238 8890; **Fax:** 020 8238 8897
Correspondent: Miss Elizabeth Harley
Trustees: Sir Kirby Laing; Sir Maurice Laing; Sir Martin Laing; David E Laing; Christopher M Laing; John H Laing.

Total grants: £789,000 (1998/99)
Grants overseas: £100,000

General: This is the member of the Laing family group of trusts that concentrates particularly on small grants for the relief of poverty and distress. As with the other trusts in the group, many are in the form of regular annual payments to UK charities, large and small, but in this case a number of local causes are also supported, both in the UK and overseas. Grants are given to support people who are homeless, elderly, disabled or socially disadvantaged within the UK and to development agencies in the third world.

In 1999 grants totalled £789,000 and were broken down as follows:

	No.	Total
child and youth	46	£372,000
health and medicine	158	£285,000
social welfare	10	£269,000
overseas aid	31	£100,000
religion	9	£15,000

Beneficiaries of larger grants included Mariners to provide engines for a barge to create a ferry link between the island of Chinde and Mozambique (£17,000), United Nations Association International Service towards the Urban Sanitation Project in Mali (£11,000) and APT Enterprise Development towards the 'Aid to Artisans' project in Ghana (£10,000). Recipients of smaller grants included British Red Cross (£1,000) and Raleigh International (£500).

Exclusions: No grants to individuals. In almost all cases, grants to overseas projects are made through UK-registered charities.

Applications: One application only is needed to apply to this or the Kirby, Maurice and Hilda Laing trusts. Multiple applications will still only elicit a single reply; even then applicants are asked to accept non-response as a negative reply on behalf of all four trusts, unless an sae is enclosed. Applications are considered monthly.

These trusts make strenuous efforts to keep their overhead costs to a minimum. As they also make a very large number of grants each year in proportion to their income, the staff must rely almost entirely on the written applications submitted in selecting appeals to go forward to the trustees. Each application should contain all the information needed to allow such a decision to be reached, in as short and straightforward a way as possible. Specifically, each application should say:
- what the money is for
- how much is needed
- how much has already been found
- where the rest is to come from.

Unless there is reasonable assurance on the last point the grant is unlikely to be recommended. Due to the very large number of grants being made by a small staff, the plea above for simple, straightforward applications is even more appropriate than for other funders.

The Kirby Laing Foundation

Health, welfare, Christian, general

Geographical focus: *Worldwide, but mostly UK*

Box 1, 133 Page Street, Mill Hill, London NW7 2ER
Tel: 020 8238 8890; **Fax:** 020 8238 8897
Correspondent: Miss Elizabeth Harley
Trustees: Sir Kirby Laing; Lady Isobel Laing; David E Laing; Simon Webley.

Total grants: £2.9 million (1999)
Grants overseas: £75,000

General: Along with the other Laing family trusts, this is a general grantmaker with a Christian orientation and awards almost all kinds of grants. The grants are widely spread, the large ones in particular probably representing close personal interests of the trustees. Alone in the group, this foundation gives substantial grants to arts organisations. However, the foundation is keen to point out that there is no general programme of grants for the arts.

In 1999 grants totalled £2.9 million and were broken down as follows

	No.	Total
child/youth (inc. education/training)	15	£1,464,000
religion	24	*£440,000
health and medicine	25	£249,000
social welfare	10	£269,000
overseas aid	9	£75,000
cultural/environmental	12	£89,000
small grants (<£5,000)	116	£230,000

* *This figure includes an exceptional grant of £250,000 for the Faith Zone in the Millennium Dome.*

In the past overseas grants have included those to University of Cape Town and Rocklands Campsite Trust, both in South Africa. Grants have also been given in recent years to projects in Bangladesh, Kenya, Mexico, Tanzania and Zimbabwe.

Exclusions: In general grants are only given to overseas projects through UK-registered charities. No grants to individuals. The trust rarely gives to the running costs of local organisations.

Applications: See The Beatrice Laing Trust.

The Maurice Laing Foundation

General

Geographical focus: *Worldwide, but mostly UK*

Box 1, 133 Page Street, Mill HIII, London NW7 2ER
Tel: 020 8238 8890
Correspondent: Miss Elizabeth Harley
Trustees: David Edwards, Chair; Sir Maurice Laing; Thomas D Parr; John H Laing; Peter Harper; Andrea Gavazzi.

Total grants: £1.2 million (1999)
Grants overseas: £57,000

General: This foundation has become a major funder of a small number of environmental initiatives with very large grants. More grants, though not so large, are made to medical institutions, with a particular focus on a small number of university departments carrying out scientific research into the efficacy of complementary therapies. There is limited support for welfare organisations and an extensive programme of smallscale support for the core costs of a range of UK organisations.

This trust has decided to donate half its income each year to the associated Maurice and Hilda Laing Charitable Trust (see next entry). In addition, in 1999 a further £650,000 was transferred to that trust as this foundation's contribution to the joint Laing trusts' support for the Faith Zone in the Millennium Dome. (To minimise double counting, the grant total listed above does not include these transfers.)

The foundation makes about 200 grants a year. They may be one-off, spread over a period of years, or ongoing. They can be very large, up to several hundred thousand pounds. Many of the small grants, of less than £5,000 each, represent annual donations to the core funding of national organisations working in a variety of fields. There are, however, very few grants to local branches of UK organisations, or to local charities whose work is similar to that carried out elsewhere by other organisations.

Grants to unconnected organisations totalled £1.2 million and were broken down as follows:

	No.	Total
cultural/environmental	13	£790,000
health and medicine	25	£366,000
child and youth	13	£121,000
overseas aid	6	£57,000
social welfare	4	£70,000
small grants (<£5,000)	136	£260,000

The trustees continue to encourage scientific research into the efficacy of complementary health remedies and to make significant sums available to environmental and conservation organisations. Projects falling into the fields of youth development, social welfare and overseas aid also continue to be of interest. In the latter category the trust made a grant of £255,000 to IMPACT's Riverboat Hospital in 1998 towards work in Bangladesh.

Grants in 1999 included £380,000 to World Humanity Action Trust for WHAT's two-year programme looking at issues of governance in relation to the global environment, and £50,000 to Royal Commonwealth Society for the Deaf to cover the purchase of a landrover for the HARK (Hearing Assessment and Research Centre) project in South Africa.

Exclusions: In general, grants to oversea projects are only made through UK-registered charities. No grants to groups or individuals for education or travel purposes, including attendance at conferences or overseas exchange programmes. Support is rarely given to the running costs of local organisations.

Applications: See The Beatrice Laing Trust.

Maurice and Hilda Laing Charitable Trust (formerly The Hilda Laing Charitable Trust)

Christianity, relief of need

Geographical focus: *Worldwide, but mostly UK*

Box 1, 133 Page Street, Mill Hill, London NW7 2ER
Tel: 020 8238 8890
Correspondent: Miss Elizabeth Harley
Trustees: Sir Maurice Laing; Lady Hilda Laing; Peter Harper; Robert M Harley; Thomas D Parr.

Total grants: £2.7 million (1999)
Grants overseas: £82,000

General: This trust is funded primarily by transfers from the associated Maurice Laing Foundation. It is mainly concerned with the relief of poverty in the UK, largely through Christian organisations, and relief of poverty overseas, with a particular emphasis on work with children, as well as with evangelism. It has identified three main areas of giving:

Advancement of the Christian religion

Priorities are:
- evangelistic activities intended to spread the Christian gospel message, both in the UK and overseas;
- religious education, from primary school to postgraduate level;

- projects designed to promote Christian ethics/family life, especially among young people.

Relief of poverty in the UK

Support for projects in this category is usually confined to those with a Christian basis to avoid overlap with Maurice Laing Foundation, i.e. to projects where Christian faith is being manifested through practical action to help those in need. Preference will be given to projects of a practical nature rather than to research projects.

Relief of poverty overseas

Many beneficiaries will have a Christian foundation but this requirement is not exclusive in this category. Any overseas project aimed at relieving poverty is eligible but particular priorities are:

- work with children in need
- projects addressing the issue of population control through work to improve the basic education of women and the quality of reproductive and primary healthcare and education.

The 1999 grants were classified as follows:

	No.	Total
advancement of religion	25	*£2.3 million
religion, social action	11	£151,000
health and medicine	4	£95,000
overseas aid	9	£82,000
child and youth	1	£5,000

* *This figure includes a grant of £1.8 million to the Faith Zone of the Millennium Dome).*

Exclusions: In general, grants to overseas projects are only made through UK-registered charities. No grants to groups or individuals for the purpose of education, travel, attendance at conferences or participation in overseas exchange programmes.

Applications: See The Beatrice Laing Trust.

The Law Society Charity

Law and justice

Geographical focus: Worldwide, but mostly UK

113 Chancery Lane, London WC2A 1PL
Tel: 020 7320 5899
Correspondent: K M Jones
Trustees: G W Staple, Chair; Ms Howells; J N W Dodds; K P Byass; F A Smith; S Gadhia.

Total grants: £1.2 million (1999/2000)
General: The trust makes grants in support of charitable activities which are in the furtherance of law and justice. This includes:

- charitable educational purposes for lawyers and would-be lawyers
- legal research
- promotion of an increased understanding of the law
- charities concerned with the provision of: advice; counselling; mediation services connected with the law; and welfare directly/indirectly of solicitors, trainee solicitors and other legal and Law Society staff and their families.

In 1999/2000 the trust's income was £2.2 million, most of which was received under a deed of covenant from The Law Society and The Law Society Services Limited. Grants totalled £1.2 million, of which £810,000 was given to The Law Society for educational purposes.

The remaining grants were for £10,000 or less. Beneficiaries included a number of human rights organisations, such as Fair Trials Abroad (£10,000), Amnesty International (£4,800) and Asylum Aid (£2,000).

Applications: In writing to the correspondent. The trustees meet quarterly, usually in April, July, September and December.

The William Leech Charity

Health and welfare, aid and development

Geographical focus: *Worldwide, but mostly north east England*

4 St James Street,
Newcastle upon Tyne NE1 4NG
Tel: 0191 232 7940
Correspondent: Mrs Kathleen M Smith, Secretary
Trustees: R E Leech, Chair; Prof. P Baylis; C Davies; A Gifford; N Sherlock; D Stabler.

Total grants: £491,000 (1998/99)
Grants overseas: £32,000

General: The charity's mission is 'to encourage local and community spirited people to create and sustain interest in voluntary charitable work'. Supported organisations are usually in Northumberland, Tyne and Wear and Durham. (Work in Teesside and other adjacent areas is said to be no longer supported.)

Roughly one third of the income is used to support research projects at University of Newcastle, while a separate designated fund 'awards grants to charities with a local connection assisting projects in underdeveloped areas in the world with special emphasis on the third world'. The charity also makes crisis loans (often to churches) and 'challenge grants' which match other funding pound for pound.

In 1998/99 its assets were worth over £13 million generating £578,000, of which £491,000 was paid in 175 grants. Overseas grants are generally given from The Lady Leech Fund. This fund has an income of around £40,000 per annum, which is to be distributed to developing third world projects which have, if possible, a strong connection with the usually beneficial area. Grants are normally up to about £5,000 and payable to a registered charity (not individual). In suitable cases grants could be extended up to three years. The ideal arrangement would be for someone whose home is in north east England, but is actually working with a project overseas. This fund gave 10 grants totalling £32,000 to overseas causes including grants for emergency disaster relief in Bangladesh and Honduras and for assisting children and communities in Ghana, Malawi and Romania.

Organisations supported included Christian Aid and WaterAid (£5,000 each), and Action Health and VSO (£3,000 each).

Exclusions: No grants to:
- community centres (exceptionally, those in remote country areas may be supported);
- running expenses of youth clubs (as opposed to capital projects);
- repairs or running expenses of churches (churches engaged in social work, or using their buildings largely for 'outside' purposes, may be supported);
- sport;
- the arts;
- individuals;
- organisations which have been supported in the last 12 months (it would be exceptional to support an organisation in two successive years, unless promised such support in advance);
- holidays, travel, outings;
- minibuses (unless over 10,000 miles a year is expected);
- schools;
- housing associations.

Applications: A full written application is required, including an annual report. Appeals are considered bi-monthly.

The Leigh Trust

Drug and alcohol rehabilitation, criminal justice, asylum seekers/racial equality

Geographical focus: *UK and overseas*

Clive Marks and Company, 44a New Cavendish Street, London W1M 7LG
Tel: 020 7486 4663; **Fax:** 020 7224 2942
Correspondent: The Trustees
Trustees: Hon. David Bernstein; Dr R M E Stone.

Total grants: £465,000 (1999/2000)
General: This trust was established in 1976. It makes grants to a variety of registered charities concerned with drug and alcohol rehabilitation, criminal justice and asylum seekers/racial equality. It is the policy of the trustees to support those organisations which are in greatest need.

In 1999/2000 the trust had assets of £4.6 million and an income of £134,000. The current policy is to distribute investment revenue and a proportion of capital gains. Grants totalled £465,000.

The 20 largest grants were listed by the trust and totalled £289,000. These included £20,000 to Refugee Council towards asylum seekers, £15,000 to Prisoners Abroad for general funding, and £10,000 each to Penal Reform International (NACRO) to assist people facing the death sentence in the Caribbean and Charities Evaluation Service towards a refugee project.

Exclusions: No grants to individuals.

Applications: Initial applications should be made in writing to the trustees, enclosing the most recent accounts and an sae. Applications should state clearly on one side of A4 what the charity does and what it is requesting funding for and show a detailed budget and other sources of funding for the project. The charity may be requested to complete an application form. It is likely that an officer of the trust will wish to visit the project before any grant is made. Trustees' meetings are held quarterly.

Unfortunately the trustees can only respond favourably to very few applications.

The Leonard Trust

Christian, overseas aid, medical research

Geographical focus: *Overseas and UK, probably with a preference for Winchester*

Manor Farm, Bramdean, Alresford, Hampshire SO24 0JS
Tel: 01962 771344
Correspondent: Mrs Tessa Feilden, Trustee
Trustees: Tessa Feilden; Dominic Gold; Carol Gold.

Total grants: £30,000 (1997/98)
General: The trust supports Christian, medical research and overseas aid organisations.

In 1997/98 grants totalled £30,000. Donations included £5,000 to Tearfund, £3,000 each to Church Missionary Society and Lepra, and £2,000 to British Red Cross. Other beneficiaries included Botton Village Appeal Fund, CAF Bulgaria Appeal, Evangelism Explosion and UNICEF.

Exclusions: No grants to individuals.

Applications: In writing to the correspondent.

The Erica Leonard Trust

Welfare and overseas work

Geographical focus: UK and overseas, with some preference for Surrey

Old Farmhouse, Elstead, Surrey GU8 6DB
Tel: 01252 702230
Correspondent: R C E Grey, Trustee
Trustees: R C E Grey; A C Kemp; J L G Cash.

Total grants: £53,000 (1997/98)
General: The trust states that it has a preference for supporting 'smaller charities (many in the Surrey area), where donations of £1,000 would make quite a difference'. Trustees like to maintain their links with charities which they know well and where the charity has a good track record. The trust also responds to emergency needs and to applications from those charities where money is being raised for a special purpose.

In 1997/98 the trust had assets of £780,000 and an income of £55,000. Grants totalling £53,000 were made to 37 organisations.

Beneficiaries included Third World Link – wells for India (£4,000), Argentinian Homes Foundation and BRINOS Deaf Aid Programme in Nepal (£1,000 each), and Brazilian Charity and Cape Town Quaker Peace Centre (£500 each).

Applications: In writing to the correspondent. The trust states that it prefers to give to charities in which the trustees have personal involvement.

The Linbury Trust

General

Geographical focus: Worldwide

9 Red Lion Court, London EC4A 3EF
Tel: 020 7410 0330
Correspondent: Michael Pattison, Director
Trustees: Lord Sainsbury of Preston Candover; Lady Sainsbury; Miss Judith Portrait.

Total grants: £10 million (1999/2000)
General: One of the Sainsbury Family Charitable Trusts which share a joint administration, this trust was established by Lord Sainsbury of Preston Candover. Much of the trust's support has been for major capital projects in the arts and education and it has pioneered research funding of chronic fatigue syndrome. It is also concerned with some social welfare issues such as drug abuse, homelessness and the problems of young people at risk.

In 1999/2000 the trust had assets of £149 million and an income of £8.4 million. Grants to 112 organisations totalled £10 million, including £463,000 to third world education/welfare.

The trustees have continued to support both undergraduate bursaries and doctoral students at University of Cape Town (£239,000). The 20 PhD student awards provide for two years at University of Cape Town and one year in the UK at the universities of Bristol, Oxford and Sheffield. The rationale behind this programme is to attract and keep some of the ablest African students within the teaching faculties of South African universities. The trustees have also continued to support excavations at the important but relatively little known Roman site at Butrint in southern Albania (£70,000).

Other beneficiaries included Nelson Mandela Children's Fund for work with South African children (£75,000), Disasters Emergency Committee for its Kosovo appeal (£50,000) and Faultline for work following the Turkish earthquake (£15,000). Smaller beneficiaries included No Frontiers, Save the Rhino Trust and Street Symphony.

Applications: In writing to the correspondent. A single application will be considered for support by all Sainsbury Family Charitable Trusts. However, 'because of the trustees' pro-active approach, unsolicited applications are only successful occasionally, although all applications in the listed fields are considered on their merits'.

Enid Linder Foundation

Health, welfare

Geographical focus: *Worldwide*

35 Tranquil Vale, Blackheath, London SE3 0BD
Tel: 020 8297 9884
Correspondent: Brian Billingham, Secretary
Trustees: Jack Ladeveze; Audrey Ladeveze; M Butler; G Huntly; J Stubbings.

Total grants: £477,000 (1998/99)

General: The trust supports around 10 new recipients and a wide range of regularly supported groups each year, mainly in the field of health, particularly among children and people who are disabled. Local (to London and the south of England), UK and international charities are all supported.

In 1998/99 the trust had assets of £8 million and an income of £568,000. Grants to 98 organisations totalled £477,000.

Overseas beneficiaries included Médecins Sans Frontières (£25,000), Intermediate Technology (£10,000) and UNICEF (£2,500).

Applications: In writing to the correspondent.

Lloyd's Charitable Trust

General

Geographical focus: *UK and overseas*

Lloyd's of London, One Lime Street, London EC3M 7HA
Tel: 020 7327 1000 ext. 5925
Fax: 020 7327 6368
website: www.lloyds.com
Correspondent: Mrs L Harper, Secretary
Trustees: H R Robinson, Chair; A A Duguid; P Barnes; Lady Delves Broughton; A G Cooper; R Gilkes; G Morgan; M G Wade.

Total grants: £320,000 (1999)
Grants overseas: £68,000

General: The trust has general charitable purposes, including making grants to organisations working overseas. In 1999 it had assets of £2.6 million and an income of £700,000. Grants totalled £320,000.

In 1998 Lloyd's chose five charities to receive a share of £200,000. Of these, two were involved in work overseas. The first was CARE International – PAX Project in Bosnia-Herzegovina (£125,000 was committed over three years). The second was Save the Children – Rural Education Project in Brazil to help fund a 'agro-ecological' education programme designed to be relevant to children's lives and to prevent migration to the cities (£76,000 was committed over three years).

Other selected charities were British Trust for Conservation Volunteers, Crimestoppers Trust and Alzheimer's Research Trust. These five charities will be partners of Lloyd's for the next three years and no other grants will be made. In view of the change in policy the trust states that it is unable to respond positively to other ad-hoc appeals received. However, in practice, 31 out of 1,100 appeals were supported with grants totalling £120,000. These grants appeared to be given exclusively to UK causes.

Exclusions: The trustees have previously stated: 'Consideration is not given to any appeal where it is likely that the donation would be used for sectarian purposes nor to local charities or regional branches of a charity where it is possible to support the central funds. Support is not given to individuals.'

Applications: In writing to the correspondent, including recent reports and accounts. The trustees meet in March, June, September and December.

The Lyndhurst Settlement

Social problems, civil liberties, environment, conservation

Geographical focus: Usually UK. Overseas applications are considered if there is a strong civil liberty component, but these must be from UK-registered charities

15–19 Cavendish Place,
London W1M 0DD
Correspondent: Michael Isaacs, Trustee
Trustees: Michael Isaacs; Anthony Skyrme; Kenneth Plummer.

Total grants: £175,000 (1999/2000)
General: The policy of the trust is to encourage research into social problems with a specific emphasis on safeguarding civil liberties, maintaining the rights of minorities and protecting the environment, which the trustees regard as an important civil liberty. The trustees prefer to support charities (both innovatory and long-established) that seek to prevent, as well as relieve, hardship.

Beneficiaries include not only civil liberty, immigration and penal reform organisations, but also a number of birth control advisory centres, environmental and conservation groups, AIDS groups and homeless organisations. In 1999/2000 the settlement had assets of £938,000 (£1.1 million in 1998/99) and an income of £75,000. Grants to 69 organisations totalled £175,000, 22 of which were supported in the previous year. Out of about 1,000 requests received during the year it gave grants to 69 charities. It is the trustees' policy to maintain a level of distribution in excess of income. This will result in a decrease in the settlement's capital over coming years.

Grants ranged from £500 to £8,000 and recipients working overseas included Prisoners of Conscience (£4,000), Tibet Foundation (£2,500), Medical Foundation for the Care of Victims of Torture (£1,300) and Western Kurdistan Association (£1,000).

Exclusions: Grants are only given to UK-registered charities and not to individuals. The trust does not normally support medical or religious charities, although it may respond to the social needs of people with HIV/AIDS in the UK.

Applications: In writing to the correspondent at any time. Requests must include a brief description of the aims and objectives of the the charity. Unsuccessful applications will only be acknowledged if an sae is provided.

The Lyndhurst Trust

Christian

Geographical focus: UK and overseas

66 High Street, Swainby, Northallerton,
North Yorkshire DL6 3DG
Correspondent: W P Hinton, Trustee
Trustees: W P Hinton; J A L Hinton; Dr W J Hinton.

Total grants: £80,000 (1998/99)

General: The objects of the trust are 'the advancement, promotion and support of the Christian religion in any part of the world'. Charities supported are usually promoting awareness of the Christian gospel, particularly in areas where people have never had the opportunity of hearing it. In practice, the trust supports specific charities on a regular basis. The trust states: 'There is little scope for supporting additional appeals of which we already receive a large quantity'.

In relation to future grant-giving, the trust stated the following in its annual report: 'the needs of the disadvantaged in society have been increasingly recognised by the allocation of additional funds to those charities ministering to these needs, particularly those that are seeking to meet the scourge of drug abuse through the provision of Christian rehabilitation programmes.'

In 1998/99 the trust had assets of £1.9 million and an income of £51,000, mainly from investments. Grants totalled £80,000. The trust divides its grants geographically as follows:

	Total	No.	%
third world	£29,000	25	35
Europe and the rest of the world	£11,000	8	13
north east England	£20,000	21	25
UK general	£21,000	19	27

Almost all grants are recurrent and most organisations are known to the trustees who like to build up a partnership and therefore like regular updates on what is happening with the project and their money. Donations to third world organisations were in the range of £30 to £2,000. Beneficiaries included Bible Mission International (Tibet/Bhutan), Global Care (Azerbaijan), International Connection (Guyana), OMS International (Colombia), Overseas Missionary Fellowship (China) and Tearfund (Asia). The only new third world beneficiaries were Don Sumners Evangelical Association (Mexico) and Emmanuel Fellowships (Swaziland/Uganda).

Grants given in Europe were all for £1,000 and included those to Albanian Ecclesiastical Trust, Bible Society and European Christian Mission.

Exclusions: No support for individuals or building work.

Applications: In writing to the correspondent enclosing an sae if a reply is required. Requests are considered quarterly but note the comments above.

The Lyras Family Charitable Trust

Relief of need, disaster aid, religion, general

Geographical focus: UK, Greece and worldwide

Snow Hill Trustees Ltd, 1 Snow Hill, London EC1A 2EN
Tel: 020 7334 9191; **Fax:** 020 7334 7973
Correspondent: T Cripps, Secretary
Trustees: J C Lyras; J M Lyras; R H J de C Moore.

Total grants: £46,000 (1998)

General: Grants of up to £2,500 are given for:

- worldwide disaster funds
- relief of poverty
- advancement of the Greek Orthodox religion
- general charitable purposes.

In 1998 the trust had assets of £782,000 and an income of £60,000. Grants totalled £46,000.

Beneficiaries included Red Cross for its Central America emergency appeal (£2,500), Friends of the Hellenic Bobyleva Appeal (£2,000) and Save the

Children for the Sudan crisis appeal (£1,500).

Applications: In writing to the correspondent, although funds are fully committed and unsolicited applications are not requested.

M N R Charitable Trust

Christian, general

Geographical focus: *UK, overseas*

24 Bevis Marks, London EC3A 7NR
Tel: 020 7220 3398
Correspondent: Bryan K H Rogers
Trustees: John S Mellows, Chair; Andrew N Russell; David E Ryan.

Total grants: £119,000 (1999)
General: The name of the charity was changed from the N R Charitable Trust in 1999. It was established in 1983 for the main purpose of receiving contributions from the partners of Mazars Neville Russell and making donations to charitable causes, especially those concerned with the advancement of the Christian faith. The trust stated 'grants are only awarded to those organisations with whom the trustees have active involvement'.

In 1999 most of the trust's income of £105,000 came from Gift Aid donations from the participating partners in Mazars Neville Russell. Grants totalling £119,000 were made to 53 organisations. A list detailing the top 25 grants, all of over £1,000, was provided by the trust. Grants of £15,000 each were made to International Needs for the Columbia Earthquake, Tearfund for work in Yemen and World Vision for the Kosovo Appeal. In addition, £10,000 went to Medina Valley Centre.

Exclusions: No grants to individuals.

Applications: Unsolicited applications are not considered.

Mariapolis Limited

Unity, ecumenism

Geographical focus: *UK and overseas*

57 Twyford Avenue, London W3 9PZ
Tel: 020 8992 7666/020 7373 9808
Correspondent: Carlo Poggi, Secretary
Trustees: Timothy M King; Rumold Van Geffen; Bartonu Mayans.

Total grants: £28,000 (1998/99)
General: This trust promotes the international Focolare Movement in the UK, and grantmaking is only one area of its work. It works towards a united world and its activities focus on peace and cooperation. It has related interests in ecumenism and overseas development. Activities include organising conferences and courses, and publishing books and magazines.

In 1998/99 the trust had assets of £1.1 million and an income of £404,000. Total expenditure was £248,000, including £28,000 in grants.

No grants list was included in the accounts, although the 1998/99 annual report stated: 'The charity has links with several projects in the developing world, particularly in Brazil, the Philippines and the Cameroon Republic. It gives aid to these either directly or through International Centre Pia Associazione Maschile Opera di Maria (PAMOM) in Rome. On occasions it provides for the education in the UK for students from developing countries'.

Applications: In writing to the correspondent.

Marr-Munning Trust

Overseas aid

Geographical focus: *Worldwide, mainly developing countries*

9 Madeley Road, Ealing, London W5 2LA
Tel: 020 8998 9593
Correspondent: D Gleeson
Trustees: Joan Honor; W Macfarlane; Mary Herbert; J O'Brien; C A Alam; Margaret Lorde.

Total grants: £102,000 (1997/98)
General: The trust makes grants to overseas aid organisations mainly working in the third world. In 1997/98 its assets totalled £2.7 million and it had an income of £305,000, including £204,000 from rents and £38,000 from donations. Total expenditure was £267,000, including £94,000 spent on property maintenance and £102,000 given in grants.

Grants are listed in the accounts month by month, according to when they were distributed. The country where the beneficiary is based was also usually listed.

The largest grants were £10,000 each to Health Unlimited, Sense, Sound Seekers and UNICEF – North Korea followed by £7,500 was given to IMPACT – India. The remaining grants were up to £5,000.

Grants totalling £8,700 were made to a presumably connected charity, Marr-Munning Ashram, which is based in India. Other grants given in April 1997 included: £1,300 to Gram Niyojan - India; £1,000 each to Joe Homan Trust and Nilgiris Adivasi – both in India; and £500 each to Fund for Human Need – Jamaica and Village Services – India.

Grants made in February 1998 were to a number of different countries: £5,000 each to Cambodia Trust and Save the Children – Vietnam; £2,000 each to Africa Now, Aid to Romania and Almsakin Hospital – Pakistan; and £600 to Hope – Sri Lanka.

Exclusions: No grants to individuals.
Applications: In writing to the correspondent. Please note that funds are currently fully committed.

The Marsh Christian Trust

General

Geographical focus: *Worldwide, but mostly UK*

Granville House, 132–135 Sloane Street, London SW1X 9AX
Tel: 020 7730 2626; **Fax:** 020 7823 5225
Correspondent: Lorraine McMorrow, Administrator
Trustees: B P Marsh; A B Marsh; R J C Marsh; N C S Marsh.

Total grants: £114,000 (1998/99)
Grants overseas: £9,700

General: The trust makes grants in the following areas (percentage of grant fund allocation from the 1994–97 triennial report in brackets): arts and heritage (22.5%); healthcare and medical research (22.5%); social welfare (20%); environmental causes/animal welfare (15%); education/training (9%); overseas appeals (8.5%); miscellaneous (2.5%).

The trustees will normally only make grants to registered charities which are experienced within their chosen field of work. Long-term core funding of appropriate work is the trust's normal approach, taking the form of money given on a recurring annual basis subject to yearly resubmission and review.

In 1998/99 it had an income of £142,000 and assets of £3.5 million. It made 225 grants totalling £114,000; 118 of these had been supported in the previous year. The financial report showed high administration costs of £67,000, but this can be accounted for by the proactive nature of the charity and the large number of small grants made.

Past recipients have included ActionAid, Medical Aid for Poland Fund, Prisoners Abroad, Sight Savers International and Voluntary Service Overseas.

Exclusions: No grants to individuals or for building work. The trustees are not interested in single projects or sponsoring proposals.

Applications: In writing to the correspondent, including a copy of the most recent accounts. The trustees currently receive about 8,000 applications each year for UK and overseas grants, of which 7,800 are new to the trust. Decisions are made at monthly meetings.

The trustees attempt to visit each long-term recipient at least once every three years to review the work done, learn of future plans and renew acquaintance with those responsible for the charity. Advice on fundraising and other organisational problems is also offered free of charge.

The Maxco Trust

Christian

Geographical focus: *Worldwide*

57 Beacon Way, Rickmansworth, Hertfordshire WD3 2PB
Tel: 01923 350221
Correspondent: The Trustees

Total grants: £1.2 million to organisations (1999)
General: This trust aims to maximise resources for Christian outreach. It allows individuals to pool their resources and make donations of greater significance to Christian organisations around the world, especially evangelical charities.

In 1999 the trust had assets of £22 million and an income of £1.6 million, including £394,000 in donations. Grants to organisations totalled £1.2 million, with £23,000 going to individuals.

Beneficiaries included International Fellowship of Evangelical Students (£71,000), Operation Mobilisation (£45,000), Tearfund (£37,000) and Slavanka (£15,000). Recipients of smaller grants included ACET (£2,000), African Christian Press (£1,200 in two grants), Intermediate Technology (£1,000), Jubilee 2000 (£600), Romanian Aid Fund Ltd (£130) and Oxfam (£75).

Applications: Due to the nature of this trust, unsolicited applications cannot be considered. The trust states it: 'acts as a clearing house for Christians who wish to use us a channel to increase their charitable giving. All our grants are therefore made to Christian causes chosen by the original donors.'

Mercury Phoenix Trust

AIDS, HIV

Geographical focus: *Worldwide*

The Mill, Mill Lane, Cookham, Berkshire SL6 9QT
Tel: 01628 527874
Correspondent: Peter Chant
Trustees: M Austin; H J Beach; B H May; R M Taylor.

Total grants: £544,000 (1999/2000)
General: The trust was set up in memory of Freddie Mercury by the remaining members of the rock group Queen and their manager. It makes grants to 'help relieve the poverty, sickness and distress of people with AIDS and HIV and to stimulate awareness and education in connection with the disease throughout the world'.

Starting with the Freddie Mercury Tribute Concert for AIDS Awareness, the trust's fundraising activities have included a fan-initiated annual national street collection, a Queen album and a ballet which was inspired by the music of Queen and Mozart.

The trust's information leaflet states: 'Applications for grants have come in from many countries around the world and collaboration has been realised with groups as far removed as World Health Organisation, to grass-root organisations run partly by voluntary workers in Uganda, Kenya, South Africa, Zambia, Nepal and India. The trust is following the latest developments in drug therapies and adapting funding policy to the changing needs of those affected by HIV/AIDS in the UK and elsewhere'.

In 1999/2000 the trust's assets totalled £1.3 million. The total income of £544,000 was given in grants.

Further information on beneficiaries for this year was not included with the accounts. Past beneficiaries have included: ActionAid; AIDS Foundation South Africa; Love in Action, South Africa; Nepal International Consumers Union; Rajasthan Mahila Kalyan Mandal; Romanian Angel Appeal; TASO, Uganda; Uganda AIDS Action Fund; VSO; Zambia Trust; and Zamili Gallery D'Afrique.

Applications: In writing to the correspondent.

Merstham Aid Project

Welfare

Geographical focus: Developing countries

1a Bourne Road, Merstham, Surrey RH1 3HF
Tel: 020 8688 4466
e-mail: paul@mapweb.org.uk
website: www.mapweb.org.uk
Correspondent: Mrs Debbie Bell

Total grants: £6,000 (1997/98)
Grants overseas: £6,000

General: The trust involves members of the local community who seek to provide practical help to poor communities in developing countries, such as funding wells, schools, clinics, medical supplies and VSO workers. Its aims are to raise money to finance projects to help poorer people to help themselves and sponsor volunteers for work in developing countries. Most of the organisations supported are regular beneficiaries.

In 1997/98 the trust had assets of £9,700 and an income of £5,600, mostly from fundraising events. Grants to five organisations totalled £6,000.

The largest grant was £3,600 to VSO. Other beneficiaries were WaterAid (£1,000), Moyo and Sight Savers International (£500 each), and ActionAid (£360).

Applications: In writing to the correspondent. The trust maintains personal contact with recipients to ensure first-hand knowledge of how the money is being spent.

Methodist Relief and Development Fund

Community development, emergency relief, development education

Geographical focus: Africa, Asia, Latin America, Eastern Europe

25 Marylebone Road, London NW1 5JR
Tel: 020 7467 5158; **Fax:** 020 7467 5233
e-mail: mrdf@methodistchurch.org.uk
Correspondent: Kirsty Smith, Manager
Trustees: Revd D Halstead; Ms R Shackleton; Stephen Boateng; H Dalzell; Ms Karen Drayton; Luis Algorta; Mrs Fiona Bidnell; Revd H J Keys; Dr J Leitch; Revd C F Makonde; Revd F Munce; Mrs Pamela Stone; Miss Ellie O'Malley.

Total grants: £1 million (1999/2000)
Grants overseas: £1 million

General: The trust responds to the needs of small indigenous organisations without major funding from other sources. Primarily funded by Methodists in the UK and Ireland, the trust supports projects which are both religious (Christian or other) or secular.

MRDF never initiates projects, but responds to local needs where community participation is high, and where sustainability and empowerment of community members is essential. Funding can cover costs or project work. Preference is given to work in the poorest developing nations.

Grants are given towards development (48% of grants in 1998/99), humanitarian aid (44%) and education (8%). The trust gives both one-off and recurrent grants. Recurrent grants are given on a two or three year basis, with funds allocated annually, although second year grants are dependent on satisfactory reporting on the first year.

In the first quarter of 2000, 24 grants were made totalling £242,000. The largest grant was £33,000 to Methodist Church of Mozambique towards emergency flood relief. Other larger grants went to ACT Mozambique for disaster relief (£30,000), Sambidzanai in South Africa towards sewing training (£21,000), Ethiopian Environment ngo for soil and water conservation (£20,000), ACT Venezuela (£15,000), Westnell Nurseries in Peru for nursery education (£14,000), and £13,000 each to CSKS in Bangladesh for street children outreach and RefAid towards training for refugees in Ethiopia.

Other grants ranged from £440 to £11,000. Recurrent grants included £11,000 to Azafady in Madagascar to provide pit latrines, water wells and pharmacies, £3,800 to Development Education Association (DEA) to run a course in globalisation, development and sustainability for development workers and educators, and £2,800 to Christian Social and Welfare Association in India to enable women in five Andhra Pradesh villages to earn a living, read and write and understand health issues.

Beneficiaries of one-off grants included Harvest Help, Zambia for an agricultural adviser (£11,000), Obra Rural Metodista in Chile towards pig farming (£10,000), Grassroots in Zimbabwe towards a gender violence theatre (£9,800), Fambidzania Permaculture Centre in Zimbabwe towards outreach training (£7,700) and Sana Centre in Bosnia for reconciliation (£7,500).

In 1998/99 the trust had an income of £1.3 million, nearly all of which came from donations, gifts and legacies. Grants totalled around £1 million. The trust is also involved in tree planting projects in Ghana, India and Kenya.

Applications: In writing to the correspondent.

The Metropolitan Drinking Foundation and Cattle Trough Association

Water projects

Geographical focus: UK and developing countries

Oaklands, 5 Queensborough Gardens, Chislehurst, Kent BR7 6NP
Tel: 020 8467 1261
Correspondent: R P Baber, Secretary and Treasurer
Trustees: Executive committee: A E Buxton; J E Mills; I Evans; R P Baber; Mrs I De Pelet; J King; R Sheridan-White; Sir J Smith; M W Elliott; J Barrett; R E T Gurney.

Total grants: £19,000 (1999)

General: The trust supports projects to provide clean water supplies in developing countries, drinking fountains in schools and the restoration of disused drinking fountains. So far, the trust has supplied 4,100 drinking fountains, 930 cattle troughs, 3,700 water wells/storage and 24 water tanks.

In 1999 it had assets of £566,000 and an income of £39,000. Grants to UK and third world organisations totalled £19,000.

Applications: In writing to the correspondent.

The Mettyear Charitable Trust

Children, education, relief, welfare

Geographical focus: *Mostly Lewes and East Sussex, also disaster relief worldwide*

Bridges Farmhouse, Laughton, Lewes, East Sussex BN8 6BS
Correspondent: Jean-Mary Crozier, Administrator
Trustees: Susan Mettyear; Peter Mettyear; Kevin Ardagh.

Total grants: £20,000 (1998/99)

General: This trust mainly supports housing, homelessness, children and schools in Lewes. It occasionally supports victims of torture, prisoners of conscience and local civic amenities society projects working to provide water supplies worldwide, particularly in Nepal. It offers one-off grants and interest-free loans of between £300 and £5,000, although most grants are for £500 to £1,000.

In 1998/99 the trust had assets of £404,000 and an income of £14,000. Grants totalled £20,000. Beneficiaries for work overseas included ActionAid and Kosovo Crisis (£2,000 each) and Mozambique Flood Appeal (£1,000).

Exclusions: No grants for expeditions, animal welfare, scholarships or any fund of direct benefit to an individual.

Applications: In writing to the correspondent.

The Millfield Trust

Christian

Geographical focus: *UK and worldwide*

Millfield House, Bell Lane, Liddington, Swindon, Wiltshire SN4 0HE
Tel: 01793 790181
Correspondent: D Bunce, Trustee
Trustees: D Bunce; Mrs R Bunce; P W Bunce; S D Bunce; A C Bunce.

Total grants: £100,000 to organisations (1998/99)

General: This trust was set up to provide grants to Christian organisations and has supported a number of missionary societies for the last 50 years. Grants are given solely to organisations known to the trustees and new applications are not considered.

In 1998/99 the trust had assets of £145,000 and an income of £73,000 comprised of Gift Aid donations and investment income. Grants to 57 organisations totalled £100,000 and grants to individuals totalled £3,900.

The largest grant was £25,000 to Tearfund. Others ranged from £50 to £23,000 and were mostly to Christian groups, although some grants were made to development organisations including British Red Cross and Send a Cow (each £1,000) and UNICEF (£100).

Applications: No replies are given to unsolicited applications.

The Modiano Charitable Trust

Jewish, general

Geographical focus: UK and overseas

Rodwell House, 100 Middlesex Street, London E1 7HD
Tel: 020 7377 7550
Correspondent: G Modiano, Trustee
Trustees: G Modiano; Mrs B Modiano.

Total grants: £26,000 (1997/98)
General: This trust gives about half of its income to Jewish organisations and also supports a number of development organisations, mainly those working with people in need and arts organisations. Grants can be one-off or recurrent.

In 1997/98 the trust income, comprised of Gift Aid donations, was £30,000. Grants to 42 organisations totalled £26,000. Overseas grants included £3,000 to Sarajevo Children's Project and £1,800 to Bulgaria Relief.

Applications: In writing to the correspondent.

John Moores Foundation

Literacy and health in South Africa, particularly those concerned with women and children. Relief of man-made and natural disasters worldwide

Geographical focus: South Africa and worldwide

7th Floor, Gostins Building, 32–36 Hanover Street, Liverpool L1 4LN
Tel: 0151 707 6077; **Fax:** 0151 707 6066
Correspondent: Tara Parveen, Grants Director
Trustees: Mrs Jane Moores; Barnaby Moores; Ms Mary McAleese; Peter Bassey.

Total grants: £812,000 (1999/2000)
Grants overseas: £100,000

General: The trust supports (as well as social welfare purposes in Merseyside and Northern Ireland) literacy and health projects in South Africa, relief of man-made and natural disasters worldwide and one-off exceptional grants that interest the trustees.

In 1999/2000 the trust had assets of £13 million, an income of £803,000; grants totalled £812,000. Three out of every four grants were for £5,000 or less, although most were at least £1,000. While the trust's main priority is in Merseyside and Northern Ireland, it has given some substantial grants to organisations working in developing countries.

Grants are given to organisations in South Africa concerned with literacy and health, particularly those concerned with women and children. However, these grants are made to organisations with which the trust is already in contact. One-off grants are also awarded towards the relief of natural or man-made disasters such as famine, floods and earthquakes, although these are only given to the larger aid agencies. In 1999/2000 a grant of £100,000 was given to British Red Cross Mozambique Appeal. In the previous year £50,000 each was granted to British Red Cross Emergency Appeal for Central America and Christian Aid for emergency relief in Sudan.

Exclusions: No grants to individuals.

Applications: Unsolicited applications from organisations working in the developing world are not considered.

The Morel Charitable Trust

Arts, race relations, inner-city and overseas development

Geographical focus: UK and developing countries

34 Durand Gardens, London SW9 0PP
Correspondent: S E Gibbs, Trustee
Trustees: J M Gibbs; W M Gibbs; S E Gibbs; B M O Gibbs; S Gibbs; E Gibbs.

Total grants: £52,000 (1999/2000)
Grants overseas: £43,000

General: The trust's 1999/2000 annual report lists its aims as 'support of the arts, in particular drama, organisations working for improved race relations, inner city projects and third world projects'. The trust normally funds aid projects of which the trustees have a personal knowledge.

In 1999/2000 the trust had an income of £45,000. Grants totalled £52,000, of which £43,000 was given overseas, broken down as follows:

	No.	Total
general	9	£19,000
science/health	3	£4,500
publishing	2	£2,500
Ghana	4	£2,500
Zambia	2	£1,000
Bangladesh	1	£5,000
Sierra Leone	1	£5,000
Honduras	1	£1,000
Kenya	1	£300
South Pacific	1	£500

The largest grants were £7,000 to Jubilee 2000 and £5,000 each to Oxfam projects in Bangladesh and Sierra Leone. Child to Child received £3,500 for general purposes and £2,000 to reprint *Health into Mathematics*. Other grants included: £2,000 each to Fair Trade Foundation, Merlin and VSO; £1,000 each to Sight Savers International, Tree Aid and Y Care International; £500 each to APT Enterprise Development, BAI Forest, Harvest Help and Medical Missionary Society; and £200 each to Link Africa and Project Trust.

Exclusions: No grants to individuals.

Applications: In writing to the correspondent. The trustees meet in January, April and September.

The Morris Charitable Trust

Welfare, health, older people, education

Geographical focus: UK and overseas, with a preference for Islington

Management Department, Business Design Centre, 52 Upper Street, Islington Green, London N1 0QH
Tel: 020 7359 3535
Correspondent: Marcia Green, Chair's PA
Trustees: Mrs G Morris; J A Morris; P B Morris; A R Stenning.

Total grants: £121,000 (1998/99)

General: The trust was founded in 1989 by the Morris family, owners of the City Industrial Limited Group. These companies contribute a proportion of profits to fund charitable activity.

The object of the trust is to promote charitable causes, in particular to relieve people who are deprived, sick or elderly and to advance education for the public benefit. The trust supports UK and international community charitable causes; however, there is a preference for making grants locally in Islington.

In 1998/99 the income was £103,000 (mainly from donations) and its assets totalled £116,000. Grants totalled £121,000: local organisations received 57 grants (£81,000); and UK/international organisations, 183 grants (£40,000).

Exclusions: No grants to individuals.

Applications: In writing to the correspondent.

The Moss Charitable Trust

Christian, general

Geographical focus: Worldwide, with an interest in southern England

7 Church Road, Parkstone, Poole, Dorset BH14 8UF
Tel: 01202 730002
Correspondent: P D Malpas

Total grants: £166,000 to organisations (1999/2000)

General: The objects of the trust are: to benefit the community in the county borough of Bournemouth and the counties of Dorset, Hampshire and Sussex; the advancement of religion either in the UK or overseas; the advancement of education; and the relief of poverty, disease or sickness.

To meet its objects, the trust provides facilities for contributors to give under deed of covenant, Gift Aid or direct giving and redistributes such monies according to their recommendations. The trustees also make grants from the general income of the fund.

In 1999/2000 the income was £412,000, of which £387,000 came from Gift Aid and covenants and was all restricted funds. Grants to organisations totalled £166,000, while £29,000 was given to individuals.

Beneficiaries included World Outreach (£35,000), Tearfund (£9,000), Victory Outreach (£5,000), Bulgaria Support Fund (£2,000) and Connect International (£1,000).

Applications: No funds are available by direct application. Because of the way in which the trust operates they are not open to external applications for grants.

The Network Foundation

Third world debt, environment, human rights, peace, arts

Geographical focus: Worldwide

3 Churchgates, Church Lane, Berkhamsted, Hertfordshire HP4 2UB
Correspondent: Vanessa Adams, Administrator
Trustees: A Bergbaum; John Broad; Oliver Gillie; J McClelland; Dr F Mulder; M Schloessingk.

Total grants: £556,000 (1998/99)

General: This is the grant-making arm of Network for Social Change, a group formed in the 1980s to support progressive causes. It is 'a community of wealthy individuals seeking to realise their visions in ways that enable others'. Grants, for up to £15,000, typically go to campaigning organisations addressing issues such as environmental sustainability and economic and social justice.

There is an annual funding cycle, in which grants to a maximum per project of £15,000 are made, falling into five categories:
- arts for change
- education
- health and wholeness
- human rights and peace
- preservation.

The focus is on projects which are likely to effect social change, whether by example, publicity, lobbying or other legal and charitable means. The trust supports projects which redistribute wealth to those in need, promote alternative healthy living options, promote human rights, safeguard the earth's resources and promote peace and non-violence.

Smaller grants are also made four times each year on the basis of members' earmarked contributions, and to projects sponsored by members. Larger grants, usually spread over several years, can be made where a group of Network members join together to coordinate the most effective means of bringing about social change in one particular field. Jubilee 2000 coalition was established following a significant initial contribution from this trust (£92,000 in 1997/98). A further grant to Jubilee 2000 was made in 1998/99.

In 1998/99 the foundation had an income of £625,000 and grants to 50 organisations totalled £556,000.

The largest grants ranged from £13,000 to £15,000 and included those to Campaign against the Arms Trade to finance a fundraising development coordinator, The Ethiopian Gemini Trust towards a video project, Action for Conservation through Tourism for a demonstration of community-led tourism and Medical Foundation for the Care of Victims of Torture towards public affairs.

Recipients of smaller grants included The Kaloko Trust for a women's dairy project in Zambia (£11,000) and Sarajevo Drum Orchestra (£3,000).

Applications: In writing to the correspondent. Please note: 'Projects funded by the Network Foundation are all researched and sponsored by members; unsolicited applications are not considered.'

The Noel Buxton Trust

Child and family welfare, penal matters, education, development work

Geographical focus: UK, eastern and southern Africa

28 Russell Square, London WC1B 5DS
Correspondent: Margaret Beard, Secretary
Trustees: Richenda Wallace, Chair; Joyce Morton; Simon Buxton; Paul Buxton; David Birmingham; Angelica Mitchell; Jon Snow; Jo Tunnard.

Total grants: £106,000 (1999)
Grants overseas: £33,000

General: Grants are made for the following:
- The welfare of children in disadvantaged families and of children in care. This will normally cover families with children of primary school age and under, although work with children in care will be considered up to the age at which they leave care. (Grants are NOT given for anything connected with physical or mental disability or any medical condition.)
- The prevention of crime, especially work with young people at risk of offending (the welfare of prisoners' families and the rehabilitation of prisoners and housing of any kind are excluded).
- Education and development in Eastern and Southern Africa.

The trust seldom gives grants of more than £2,000 and often considerably less. Applications for recurrent funding over several years and for running costs are considered. Due to the size of grants, contributions are not normally made towards salary costs.

In 2000 the trust had assets of £2.3 million and an income of approximately £100,000 which was spent on grants spread equally across the three areas of giving.

Exclusions: The trust does not support: academic research; advice centres; animals; the arts of any kind; buildings; conferences; counselling; development education; drug and alcohol work; the environment; expeditions, exchanges, study tours, visits, etc. or anything else involving fares; housing and homelessness; human rights; anything medical or connected with illness or mental or physical disability; older people; anywhere other than the UK and Eastern and Southern Africa; peace and disarmament; race relations; youth (except for the prevention of offending); and unemployment.

Applications: There is no application form and applications may be submitted at any time. They should state the organisation's charity registration number and the name of the organisation to which grants should be paid if different from that at the head of the appeal letter. The following should be included: budget for current and following year; details of funding already received, promised or applied for from other sources; and the latest available annual report/accounts in their shortest available form.

In order to reduce administration costs the trust does not acknowledge receipt of applications or reply to unsuccessful appeals. Every effort is made to communicate a decision on successful appeals as soon as possible (normally within six months).

The Nuffield Foundation and Commonwealth Relations Trust

Education, child protection, family law, justice, mental health, ageing

Geographical focus: *The Commonwealth, UK*

28 Bedford Square, London WC1B 3JS
Tel: 020 7631 0566; **Fax:** 020 7323 4877
website: www.nuffieldfoundation.org
Correspondent: Sarah Lock, Director
Trustees: Baroness O'Neill, Chair; Prof. Sir Tony Atkinson; Rt Hon. Dame Brenda Hale; Prof. Sir Robert May; Prof. Sir Michael Rutter; Mrs Anne Sofer; Dr Peter Doyle.

Total grants: £6.3 million to organisations (1999)
Grants overseas: £649,000

General: The trust supports a wide range of causes in the UK and other Commonwealth countries. In 1999 it had assets of £247 million generating an income of £8.6 million. Grants totalled £9.3 million, of which £6.3 million went to organisations, £1.6 million in individual award schemes and £1.4 million in directly managed projects. Grants were broken down into the following categories: education and science; child protection, family law and justice; access to justice; mental health; ageing; disability (Viscount Nuffield Auxiliary Fund); rheumatism research (Oliver Bird Fund); Commonwealth (Commonwealth Relations Trust); and open door (miscellaneous).

The Nuffield Commonwealth Programme – the Commonwealth Relations Trust (£649,000 in 16 grants) supports the establishment and improvement of policy and provision in developing Commonwealth countries and promotes links between the UK and these countries. It does this by funding activities that develop the expertise and experience of practitioners and policy makers.

Applications will be considered for activities in Commonwealth countries in Southern and Eastern Africa. Proposals that are relevant to the Commonwealth as a whole may also be considered. Support will be given for: education; law; mental health; child welfare; and older people and their families. Exceptional projects outside these fields but in the foundation's wider fields of education, health and social welfare will be considered. Applicants must be non-profit UK-based organisations with strong links to partner organisations in the country of benefit.

All proposals must:
- have a clearly defined outcome – training must be linked to a planned programme of subsequent work
- involve new ideas or application of previous experience in a new area
- contribute to the long-term development of expertise within the county or region concerned
- utilise UK expertise and experience.

Beneficiaries in this category in 2000 included Department of Forensic Medicine – University of Dundee for medico-legal training and education gender and a child project in South Africa, and University College London/ Royal Free and University College Medical School for professional development programme for health professionals in Tanzania (£250,000 each), International Extension College for improving teacher education through human resource departments at ITEK – Uganda (£212,000), and Tropical Health and Education Trust to establish a sustainable training programme in trauma management in Malawi (£174,000).

Applications: Initially in writing to the correspondent. A member of staff will then advise you whether the proposal comes within the trustees' terms of reference and whether there are any particular questions or issues you should consider. The outline should describe:
- the issue or problem you wish to address
- the expected outcome(s)
- what will happen in the course of the project
- (for research projects) an outline of the methods to be employed
- an outline of the budget and the timetable.

The outline must not exceed three pages although additional supporting information is welcomed. If you are advised to proceed with a full application, the staff member dealing with your proposal may suggest a meeting or, if matters are straightforward, may advise you to proceed straight to a full application. Detailed guidelines are available on the trust's website; applicants are advised to view this before applying.

The Father O'Mahoney Memorial Trust

Medical or educational aid

Geographical focus: *Developing countries*

Our Lady of the Wayside Church, 566 Stratford Road, Shirley, Solihull, West Midlands B90 4AY
Tel & Fax: 0121 733 6998
Correspondent: P Hirons
Trustees: C Carney-Smith; Ms C A Hearn; D M Maclean; M A Moran; Fr G Murray; A H Sanford; Mrs P Hirons; Mrs M Jennings; Mrs B Carney.

Total grants: £36,000 (2000)
Grants overseas: £36,000

General: The trust makes small grants to projects in developing countries of a medical or educational nature. It also supplies medicine and medical aid 'where a secure means of reception can be established with the beneficiaries. The trust collects and stores suitable materials for this purpose'. The trust tends to favour small projects which fall outside the scope of major charities and which need funding to become established. Beneficiaries which are the exception to this rule are CAFOD and Age Concern.

The trust has a number of connections with Roman Catholicism; for example, it is based at a Roman Catholic church, was set up in memory of a priest, and two local Roman Catholic schools help with its fundraising. This is reflected in its grantmaking.

In 2000 grants were made totalling £36,000. Donations were made to organisations in East Timor, India and Mozambique, with recipients including Child in Need Institute and a TB centre in Calcutta (£5,000 each).

Applications: In writing to the correspondent. The trustees meet every two months to consider applications.

The Oakdale Trust

Social work, medical support, medical research, general

Geographical focus: *Worldwide, especially Wales*

Tansor House, Tansor, Oundle, Peterborough PE8 5HS
e-mail: oakdale@tanh.demon.co.uk
Correspondent: Rupert Cadbury
Trustees: B Cadbury; Mrs F F Cadbury; R A Cadbury; F B Cadbury; Mrs O Tatton-Brown; Dr R C Cadbury.

Total grants: £129,000 (1998/99)

General: The trust gives preference to Welsh charities engaged in social work, medical support groups and medical research. Some support is given to UK charities working overseas and to conservation projects at home and abroad. The average grant is around £500.

In 1998/99 the assets of the trust stood at £4.3 million, with a large proportion still comprised of shares in Cadbury Schweppes plc. The income was £161,000 including £61,000 in donations received. A total of 144 grants totalled £129,000. Management and administration costs were very low at just £347. Overseas grants included those to CARE International (£5,000), Marie Stopes International (£2,000), Prisoners Abroad and WaterAid (£1,000 each), Uganda Society for Disabled Children and Womankind Worldwide (£500 each), and Chernobyl Children Project Teifi Valley (£250).

Exclusions: No grants to individuals, holiday schemes, sport activities, expeditions, church restorations or UK projects which exclude Wales.

Applications: An official application form is available on request but is by no means compulsory. Applicants are free to submit requests in a preferred format although applications should be clear and concise, covering aims, achievements, plans and needs supported by a budget. Applicants applying for grants in excess of £750 are asked to submit a recent set of audited annual accounts (which can be returned on request).

The trustees meet twice a year in April and September to consider applications and award grants. No grants are awarded between meetings. Unsuccessful applicants are not normally notified and applications are not acknowledged even if accompanied by an sae.

Onaway Trust

General

Geographical focus: *UK, USA and worldwide*

275 Main Street, Shadwell, Leeds LS17 8LH
Tel: 0113 265 9611
e-mail: david.onaway@btinternet.com
Correspondent: D Watters, Trust Administrator
Trustees: J Morris; Ms B J Pilkinton; A Breslin.

Total grants: £117,000 (1998)

General: This trust's objects were stated in its 1996/97 annual report as follows: 'To relieve poverty and suffering amongst indigenous peoples by providing seed grants for (small) self-help, self sufficiency and environmentally sustainable projects.

'... These projects aim to make significant differences to the lives of the world's traditional/indigenous peoples who continue to struggle for both spiritual and physical survival in their own lands

'... These [grants] empower the recipients to flourish and affirm the quality of their lives within traditional communities; thereby preserving invaluable knowledge, which might otherwise be lost to future generations.'

Additional, secondary objects are to make grants for the benefit of the 'world environment and animal welfare'.

In 1998 the trust's assets totalled £534,000 and its income was £175,000 including a donation of £122,000 from The Joseph Trust, which was a regular supporter before it recently dissolved.

Grants totalling £117,000 were given to 38 new and ongoing projects (17 of the beneficiaries had been supported in the previous year). At least six grants were made to individuals towards, for example, travel costs and expenses, etc. A further £31,000 was spent in management and administration costs.

Grants included those to Earth Action Network (£9,000), Jeel Al Amal – Middle East (£6,000), ApTibeT and Tibet Information Network (£5,000 each), Compassion in World Farming (£4,500) and Society for Promoting Self-Reliance (£3,000).

Applications: In writing to the correspondent, enclosing an sae.

The Paget Charitable Trust
(also known as Joanna Herbert-Stepney Charitable Settlement)

General – see below

Geographical focus: *Worldwide*

The Old Village Stores, Dippenhall Street, Crondall, Farnham, Surrey GU10 5NZ
Tel: 01252 850253
Correspondent: Joanna Herbert-Stepney, Trustee
Trustees: Joanna Herbert-Stepney; Lesley Mary Blood; Mrs Joy Pollard.

Total grants: £302,000 (1999/2000)

General: Sheer need is paramount and in practice nothing else can be considered. There is a preference for the unglamorous and projects where a little money goes a long way. Priorities include organisations working in the third world, children who are deprived, older people, animal welfare and 'green' projects. In some cases, ongoing support is given, explaining the shortage of funds for new applicants. Overseas projects can only be funded via UK-registered charities.

In 1999/2000 the trust had assets of £4.1 million and an income of £163,000. The trust gave 162 grants totalling £302,000.

International aid and development beneficiaries included ApTibeT (£12,000), Ellenor Foundation Romania Appeal (£10,000), and Oxfam (£6,000), with £2,000 each to Ethiopiaid, Farm Africa and Medical Foundation for the Care of Victims of Torture, and £1,000 each to Cambodia Trust and United Aid for Azerbaijan.

Environmental beneficiaries included Traidcraft Exchange (£1,000), and Friends of the Earth Trust and Greenpeace Environmental Trust (£500 each).

Exclusions: Grants are only given to registered UK charities and the trust cannot send money directly overseas. The trust does not give grants to individuals (including students), mental disability, medical research and young people.

Applications: In writing to the correspondent, although a preliminary telephone call could save time. There is no application form. The trustees meet in spring and autumn.

Panahpur Charitable Trust

Christian, missionary, education, convalescence, relief

Geographical focus: *UK and overseas*

Jacob, Cavenagh and Skeet, 6–8 Tudor Court, Brighton Road, Sutton, Surrey SM2 5AE
Tel: 020 8643 1166
Correspondent: The Trust Department
Trustees: P East; Miss D Haile; Mrs E R M Myers; A E Perry.

Total grants: £141,000 (1998/99)

General: This trust was established in 1911 in the will of Sydney Long Jacob. It supports Christian and overseas charities as well as individuals, focusing on scripture distribution/reading encouragement, relief work, missionary work, education and retreats.

In 1998/99 the trust had assets of £4.4 million and an income of £191,000. Grants totalled £141,000.

Previous beneficiaries have included Amnesty International, Christian Outreach and Interserve.

Applications: In writing to the correspondent. Applications will not be successful or acknowledged unless the applicant is already known to the trust.

The Parthenon Trust

General

Geographical focus: *Worldwide*

Saint-Nicolas 9, 2000 Neuchâtel, Switzerland
Tel: 0041 32 724 8130
Fax: 0041 32 724 8131
Correspondent: John Whittaker, Secretary
Trustees: Geraldine Whittaker, Chair; Dr J M Darmady; Prof. C N Hales.

Total grants: £7.1 million (1999)
Grants overseas: £3.8 million

General: This is a UK-registered charity, although the secretary is based in Switzerland. The trust supports:

- children in need, refugees and people in disaster/famine areas
- disadvantaged people, particularly in the third world
- longer-term development in the third world
- medical research in areas which appear to be under-funded
- medical training and provision of medical supplies
- patient care and hospices
- people with mental and physical disabilities.

The trust's current practice is to make 50 to 60 grants each year, many of them for under £50,000, some for over £150,000 and a very few for seven figures. Many of the grants are given to organisations operating in the third world. The majority of the grant total is given to a regular list of beneficiaries, with new recipients generally accounting for around a fifth of the grant total.

In 1999 the trust had an income of slightly over £6 million, almost entirely from donations and gifts. Grants to 44 organisations totalled £7.1 million and were broken down as follows:

37% to medically-related purposes in the UK and overseas; 28% to development projects in the third world and emergency relief; 35% other (including assistance to children and people who are mentally or physically disabled).

The largest grants were £1.8 million to Médecins Sans Frontières (UK), £1.5 million to Save the Children and £1 million to International Committee of the Red Cross.

Exclusions: No grants for individuals or scientific/geographical expeditions.

Applications: Anybody proposing to submit an application should telephone the secretary. Unsolicited applications are not normally acknowledged.

The Philanthropic Trust

Homelessness, overseas development, welfare (human and animal), environment, human rights

Geographical focus: UK, Africa, Asia

Trustee Management Limited,
19 Cookridge Street, Leeds LS2 3AG
Correspondent: The Trust Administrator
Trustees: Paul H Burton; Jeremy J Burton; Amanda C Burton.

Total grants: £106,000 (1998/99)
General: The trust was created in 1995 by P H Burton. Special consideration is given to institutions relating to people who are homeless, developing countries, welfare (both human and animal), the environment and human rights.

Total income for 1998/99 was £226,000 and assets totalled £3.1 million. Grants totalled £106,000, and ranged from £100 to £5,000, though most were for £1,000. Overseas agencies to benefit included UNICEF (£3,000), and Power International Limb Project (£2,000), with £1,000 each to Bangladesh Floods, Medical Foundation for the Care of Victims of Torture, Oxfam and Y Care International.

Exclusions: No grants for the arts, education, religious organisations, expeditions or individuals. Grants are given to UK-registered charities only.

Applications: In writing to the correspondent. Unsuccessful appeals will not necessarily be acknowledged.

Hugh Pilkington Charitable Trust

Education

Geographical focus: UK, East Africa

27 Northmoor Road, Oxford OX2 6UR
Tel: 01865 56947; **Fax:** 01865 510735
Correspondent: Robin Shawyer, Executive Officer

Total grants: £1.7 million (1997/98)
General: The trust's 1997/98 annual report stated: 'The principal object of the trust continues to be to provide educational opportunities at post-secondary level to refugees and displaced students in East Africa, with counselling and support, to equip them to meet the challenges of development in Africa. The primary focus of the trust has been on the educational needs of the Southern Sudanese people, but the trust has also addressed the educational needs of other refugees in East Africa and the Horn. It is the aim of the trust not only to assist refugees and people who are displaced to study but also to provide advice, group training and work attachments so that they may gain access to relevant advice and employment. The trustees seek to provide opportunities in British universities, mainly at postgraduate level, and at universities in Africa, mainly at undergraduate level.'

Grants are given in four main areas:
- *Sponsorships* – the trust has directly sponsored study in institutions in Africa and the UK, and has cooperated with The Windle Charitable Trust, World University Service of Canada (WUSC), United World Colleges and other partners to provide study opportunities for African refugees.
- *Educational advice and language training* – the trust provides educational advice to several hundred refugees annually, refers refugees to sources of help and equips them for study through the support of students in the English language programmes of The Windle Charitable Trust both in Nairobi and in Kakuma refugee camp.
- *Managed programmes* – the trust is contracted to manage two UNHCR educational programmes in Uganda. The DAFI projects assisted 40 refugee students at tertiary level and a grant of $50,000 through the UNESCO Peace Prize Project enabled the trust to support 58 refugees of outstanding ability at secondary school. The partnership between the trust and UNHCR will ensure more effective access by refugees to university study in Uganda, particularly for women and people who are disabled.
- *Skills for southern Sudan* – This project has offered work attachments, training through workshops and employment advice to the southern Sudanese community in the UK and East Africa. A successful group training project in civil administration was held in East Africa in February 1998 and further group training seminars are planned. The project has also begun a major consultation on the development of a long-term training strategy for southern Sudan.

In 1997/98 the trust had assets of £7.8 million and an income of £1.2 million. Grants totalled £1.7 million which was broken down as follows:

organisations	£257,000
individual sponsors	£1,070,000
UNHCR programmes	£163,000
Skills for Southern Sudan	£91,000
counselling	£36,000
programme support	£68,000

The two grants given under the heading 'organisations' were to The Windle Charitable Trust (£241,000) and World University Service UK (£16,000).

Beneficiaries in the 'Skills for Southern Sudan' programme included Charity Projects (£72,000), Africa Educational Trust (£9,700) and City Parochial Fund (£5,100).

Applications: In writing to the correspondent.

The Pilkington Charities Fund

General

Geographical focus: Worldwide

14 Chapel Lane, Formby, Liverpool L37 4DU
Tel: 01704 834490
Correspondent: Roberts Legge & Co., Chartered Accountants
Trustees: Jennifer Jones; Arnold Pilkington; Neil Pilkington.

Total grants: £829,000 (1998/99)
General: The trust was originally set up for the benefit of the employees and ex-employees, as well as their dependants, of Pilkington plc, based in St Helens. A large amount is still donated each year to C & A Pilkington Trust Fund for this purpose (£97,000 in 1998/99). The trust's other grants remain mainly for social welfare in Merseyside, but substantial support is also given for

medical research and care and overseas aid. Most grants range from £1,000 to £5,000, though larger grants for up to £50,000 typically go to UK charities, including those working overseas, apparently as part of multi-year commitments.

In 1998/99 assets of £19 million generated an income of only £636,000, with 120 organisations receiving grants totalling £829,000. The British Red Cross received £60,000 for emergency relief work in Kosovo and £10,000 for its Hurricane Mitch projects. Other recipients included Intermediate Technology (£30,000), Ockenden Venture and Oxfam (£10,000 each), Cambodia Trust and UNAIS (£5,000 each), Friends Centre for Rehabilitation of the Paralysed in Bangladesh (£3,000) and Sight Savers International (£1,000).

Exclusions: No grants to individuals.

Applications: In writing to the correspondent. Applications are considered in April and November.

The Polden-Puckham Charitable Foundation

Peace and security, ecological issues, social change

Geographical focus: UK and overseas

BM PPCF, London WC1N 3XX
Correspondent: M Bevis Gillett, Secretary
Trustees: Carol Freeman; Candia Carolan; David Gillett; Harriet Gillett; Jenepher Gordon; Heather Swailes; Anthony Wilson.

Total grants: £405,000 (1999/2000)
Grants overseas: £134,000

General: 'In its work the foundation aims to support projects that change values and attitudes, that promote equity and social justice, and that develop radical alternatives to current economic and social structures.' It prefers to make grants available to small, pioneering organisations which find it difficult to attract funds from other sources. The foundation supports work in the following areas, with grants usually in the range of £1,000 to £15,000:

Peace – development of ways of resolving international and internal conflicts peacefully, and of removing the causes of conflict.

Ecological issues – work which tackles the underlying pressures and conditions leading towards global environmental breakdown, particularly initiatives which promote sustainable living.

Other areas – PPCF also provides limited support to human rights work, in particular where it is related to peace, ecological and women's issues. It has a long-standing link with the Society of Friends.

In 1999/2000 the trust had assets of £13 million generating an income of £309,000. Grants were awarded to 76 organisations totalling £405,000.

Grants to third world projects totalled around £134,000. Recipients included Charity Know-How for Eastern Europe (£9,000), Fairtrade Foundation and Jubilee 2000 Coalition (£4,000 each), and Tourism Concern (£3,000).

Many of the organisations supported have received help in previous years. Grants are often given for core funding. Grants totalling £16,000 had been approved for 2000/2001 and £99,000 for 2001/2002.

Exclusions: No grants to: ngos; individuals; travel bursaries (including overseas placements and expeditions); study; academic research; capital projects (e.g. building projects or purchase of nature reserves); community or local projects (except innovative prototypes for widespread application); general appeals; and non-UK organisations.

Applications: The trustees meet twice a year in spring and autumn; applications should be submitted by 15 February and 15 September respectively. Decisions can be made on smaller grants between these meetings. The foundation will not send replies to applications outside its area of interest. Up-to-date guidelines will be sent on receipt of an sae. *The Review of Grant-Giving 1990-2000* is also available on receipt of a 9 inch by 6 inch sae.

PPP Healthcare Medical Trust

Healthcare, public health research, training and development
Geographical focus: Mainly UK, also Africa and Asia

13 Cavendish Square, London W1G 0PQ
Tel: 020 7307 2622; **Fax:** 020 7307 2623
e-mail: ppptrust@ppptrust.org.uk
website: www.ppptrust.org.uk
Correspondent: David Carrington, Chief Executive
Trustees: Mark Sheldon, Chair; Bernard Asher; Lawrence Banks; Prof. Yvonne Carter; Prof. Richard Cooke; Ram Gidoomal; Sir Anthony Grabham; Prof. Mary Marshall; Dr Harry McNeilly; Sir Peter Morris; Prof. Brian Pentecost; Sir Keith Peters; Prof. Lord Renfrew; Michael Sayers; Dr Elizabeth Vallance; Peter Lord; Prof. John Swales.

Total grants: About £17 million
Grants overseas: About £800,000

General: PPP Healthcare Medical Trust was set up in 1983 and initially financed by a covenanted donation from Private Patients Plan 'to assist the development and expansion of private charitable hospital facilities', later adding medical education and research and the care of older people to its aims. As a result of the acquisition of the PPP healthcare group by Guardian Royal Exchange, the trust received £540 million, expected to generate around £17 million to be donated in grants each year. The trust is now completely independent of the PPP healthcare company.

The trust makes substantial grants for research, training and the development of service delivery across the whole healthcare field. It emphasises its interest in interdisciplinary work and, although many of its initial grants were for medical research or practice, its field is much wider, covering all aspects of healthcare and public health.

In July 2000 the chief executive listed seven new programmes as being prepared, all of them to be in operation by spring 2001. They included:
- a nursing research initiative
- an annual special award, for which publicity will be sought
- an international grants programme, worth about £800,000 a year.

On a smaller scale grants are made towards seminars and conferences that are intended to encourage interdisciplinary working and for the running costs of patient and service user support groups.

The trust has decided to set aside 5% of its annual distributable income to support projects which will enable poor and marginalised people in Africa and Asia to gain access to better and sustainable health, particularly in Uganda, Tanzania and northern India (i.e. Rajasthan, Bihar, Himachal Pradesh, Madya Pradesh, Uttar Pradesh and Orissa). The grants programme has as its core themes:
- maternal and child health
- water and sanitation.

The trust supports UK-based organisations working with local partners.

Grants are made for specific purposes – 'a defined, time specific and costed piece of work with tangible outcomes that are directly relevant to the aims of the programme'. The maximum grant is £200,000 a year for up to five years, although the trust expects most grants to be for much less than this.

Exclusions: No grants to individuals.

Applications: In writing to the correspondent. Unsolicited applications are not considered. The trust identifies charities and university departments and invites them to submit proposals for projects that they are developing, or plan to develop, in partnership with organisations in the regions concerned. On the basis of outline applications, the trust shortlists a smaller number of projects and asks the applicant organisations to complete a full application form, assessed by a specialist committee of the trust consulting people with expertise as appropriate.

Prairie Trust

See below

Geographical focus: *Worldwide*

83 Belsize Park Gardens,
London NW3 4NJ
Tel: 020 7722 2105; **Fax:** 020 7483 4228
Correspondent: Mrs C Nonweiler, Secretary
Trustees: Dr R F Mulder; James Sinclair Taylor.

Total grants: £41,000 (1998/99)
Grants overseas: £18,000

General: The trust supports a small number of organisations working on issues of third world development, the environment and conflict prevention, particularly to support policy and advocacy work in these areas. The trustees are interested in supporting innovative and entrepreneurial approaches to traditional problems. The trust states it is proactive in seeking organisations to support and it is unable to consider unsolicited applications. The trust prefers to support a small number of organisations for a long period of time; it supports Network for Social Change every year (nearly £12,000 in 10 grants in 1998/99).

In 1998/99 the trust had assets of £510,000 and an income of £28,000. Grants totalled £41,000 and were broken down in the accounts as follows:

	No.	Total
overseas development and advocacy	4	£18,000
corporate social responsibility	2	£10,000
conflict prevention	1	£2,500
health issues	2	£1,500
environmental issues	2	£3,300
arts for social change	1	£1,000
UK poverty advocacy	3	£5,000
other	2	£270

Five organisations received 'overseas development and advocacy' grants totalling £18,000. These were: Network Foundation (three grants totalling £5,500); Lincoln Charitable Trust (£5,000); Oxfam for matching funding and sponsorship (£3,300 in two grants); RESULTS Education for core funding, sponsorship and a sponsored walk (£2,900 in three grants); and Right to Hope Trust (£1,000).

Applications: In writing to the correspondent. Please note, the trust states: 'As we are a proactive trust with limited funds and administrative help, we are unable to considered unsolicited applications.'

The W L Pratt Charitable Trust

General

Geographical focus: UK, particularly York, and overseas

Messrs Grays, Duncombe Place, York YO1 7DY
e-mail: ccgoodway@grayssolicitors.co.uk
website: www.grayssolicitors.co.uk
Correspondent: C C Goodway, Trustee
Trustees: J L C Pratt; R E Kitching; C C Goodway.

Total grants: £53,000 (1999/2000)
Grants overseas: £11,000

General: The trust gives support to: religious and social objectives in Britain, with priority to York and district including health and community services; food production; and the relief of famine and disease in the third world.

In 1999/2000 the trust had assets of over £1 million and gave about £53,000 in grants. This included seven grants to overseas charities totalling £11,000, three of which were one-off.

Overseas beneficiaries (one-off and ongoing) included Christian Aid and Sight Savers International (£2,400 each), Save the Children (£2,000), Commonwealth Society for the Deaf (£1,300), British Red Cross and Humanitarian Aid Limited (£1,000 each), and Oxfam (£800).

Exclusions: UK and overseas grants are restricted to well-known registered charities. No grants to individuals. No grants for buildings or for the upkeep and preservation of places of worship.

Applications: In writing to the correspondent. Applications will not be acknowledged unless an sae is supplied. Telephone applications are not accepted.

The Prince of Wales's Charitable Foundation

Unknown

Geographical focus: Worldwide

The Prince of Wales Office, St James's Palace, London SW1A 1BS
Correspondent: Stephen Lamport, Trustee
Trustees: Rt Hon. Earl Peel; Sir Michael Peat; Stephen Lamport; Mrs Fiona Shackleton.

Total grants: £500,000 (1999/2000)
Grants overseas: £30,000

General: The trust principally continues to support charitable bodies and purposes in which The Prince of Wales has a particular interest.

The restricted fund is held by the foundation for the purpose of enabling United World Colleges (International) Ltd to provide scholarships to students to attend at the ten United World Colleges located around the world (£56,000 in 1999/2000).

During 1999/2000 the trust had assets of £4.7 million and income was £974,000, including £699,000 net income from subsidiary companies, £118,000 from donations received and an investment income of £157,000. The foundation has two wholly owned subsidiaries, Duchy Originals Ltd and A G Carrick Ltd, from which most of its income is derived. To ensure an even flow of income for the foundation, £500,000 was transferred to the designated fund (part of the capital) during the year. Grants totalled £500,000, including £30,000 in overseas aid. Further information was not available.

Exclusions: No grants to individuals.
Applications: In writing to the correspondent.

Purley Overseas Trust (POST)

Agricultural, health, educational projects

Geographical focus: Third world

63 Foxley Lane, Purley, Surrey CR8 3EH
Tel: 020 8660 3770
e-mail: r.strange@ucl.ac.uk
Correspondent: R Strange

Total grants: £8,000 (1999/2000)
Grants overseas: £8,000

General: POST generally gives grants ranging from £250 to £2,000 to assist development in the third world. Grants are largely given towards three areas; agricultural, educational and health projects.

Health grants in 2000/01 included those to Sight Savers International, a WaterAid project and a health worker in Ghana. Educational projects were for Street Child India and a nursery school in South Africa. Agricultural projects included a rainforest initiative and Send a Cow, which is revitalising exhausted land in Ethiopia.

In 1999/2000 the trust had an income of £8,000, all of which was given in 12 grants. The income was gained largely from donations and events run by the trust including bridge evenings, a barbecue and concerts.

Applications: In writing to the correspondent.

The Eleanor Rathbone Charitable Trust

Women-focused international projects, general in the UK

Geographical focus: Worldwide, with a preference for Merseyside

3 Sidney Avenue, Wallasey,
Wirral CH45 9JL

e-mail:
eleanor.rathbone.trust@tinyworld.co.uk
Correspondent: Lindsay Keenan
Trustees: Dr B L Rathbone; W Rathbone; Ms Jenny Rathbone; P W Rathbone; Lady Morgan.

Total grants: £233,000 (1999/2000)
Grants overseas: £41,000

General: The trust concentrates its support largely on the following:

- charities and charitable projects focused on Merseyside (over 70% of beneficiaries in 1999/2000);
- charities benefiting women and unpopular and neglected causes but avoiding those with a sectarian interest;
- special consideration is given to charities with which any of the trustees have a particular knowledge or association or in which it is thought Eleanor Rathbone or her father William Rathbone VI had a special interest.

Most grants are on a one-off basis, although requests for commitments over two or more years are considered.

In 1999/2000 the trust had assets of just over £6.3 million, producing an income of £249,000. Grants to 134 organisations totalled £233,000. Grants ranged from £100 to £12,000 and included 20 international grants totalling £41,000.

The largest grants under the 'international' section were £5,000 each to British Red Cross (Merseyside) Kosovo Appeal, Canon Collins Educational Trust for South Africa and Womankind Worldwide (for Medica Kosova). Other larger grants included those to Music as Therapy (£3,000), and Medical Foundation for the Care of Victims of Torture and Refugee Women's Legal Group (£2,000 each). Smaller grants included £1,000 each to ActionAid, Africa Now, RUSS (Rwandan

Women's University Scholarships), Tools for Self Reliance and UNIPAL, with £500 to Traidcraft Exchange.

Exclusions: Grants are not made in support of:
- any activity which relieves a statutory authority of its obligations
- individuals unless (and only exceptionally) it is made through a charity and it also fulfils at least one of the other positive objects mentioned above.

The trust does not generally favour grants for running costs, but prefers to support specific projects and services, or contribute to specific items.

Applications: No application form; the trust asks for a brief proposal for funding including costings, accompanied by the latest available accounts and any relevant supporting material. It is useful to know who else is supporting the project.

To keep administration costs to a minimum, receipt of applications is not usually acknowledged. Applicants requiring acknowledgement should enclose an sae. Trustees currently meet three times a year; dates vary.

The Ruben and Elisabeth Rausing Trust

Human rights, self-reliance and sustainability, environment

Geographical focus: *UK and Europe, USA, Africa*

39 Sloane Street, London SW1X 9LP
Tel: 020 7235 9560; **Fax:** 020 7235 9580
e-mail: rer@arcticnet.com
Correspondent: Kirsty Wood, Administrator
Trustees: Lisbet Koerner; Sigrid Rausing; Joshua Mailman; Tara Kaufman.

Total grants: £4 million (1999)

General: This trust makes a relatively small number of generally large grants. Recipient organisations are mainly but not exclusively in Britain, the USA or Europe, though their work is often international.

The trust has the following aims:
- To promote and protect human rights globally. Human rights, in this context, is defined primarily with reference to the rights which are inherent in democracies, including free expression, the right to organise and freedom from political violence, including oppression on the grounds of race, religion, gender, level of income or sexual preference. Political violence and oppression are, however, defined as individual acts as well as the systematic violence perpetrated by states, and thus includes, for example, violence against women and racist acts.
- To promote economic self-reliance and ecological sustainability. It incorporates organisations which work for the alleviation of poverty with due regard for the relationship to local environments and cultures. The projects chosen must be oriented towards creating self-reliance and sustainability, rather than creating a relationship of dependence and disempowerment. The trust appreciates careful research on the impact of aid with particular reference to gender. This category also includes projects which are primarily concerned with nature conservation and ecology.

Grants in 1999 totalled over £4 million and were categorised by the location of the recipient organisations:

UK – 26 grants totalling £2,173,000
USA – 14 grants totalling £1,520,000
Europe – 6 grants totalling £240,000
Africa – 2 grants totalling £55,000

The largest grants included £760,000 to Amnesty International, £550,000 to

Human Rights Watch, £250,000 to Oxfam, £200,000 to Global Fund for Women, £150,000 each to International Women's Health Coalition and Medical Foundation for the Care of Victims of Torture, and £100,000 each to Ashoka and UNICEF. Other recipients included Women Living Under Muslim Law, Europe (£60,000), Gaia Foundation and Mineral Policy Institute, Africa (£25,000 each), and Foundation Trust for Chinese Medicine (£7,000).

Applications: In writing to the correspondent. Unsolicited applications cannot normally be considered or acknowledged.

The Rhodes Trust Public Purposes Fund

Oxford University, overseas, general
Geographical focus: UK and overseas.

Rhodes House, Oxford OX1 3RG
Tel: 01865 270902; **Fax:** 01865 270914
Correspondent: Dr John Rowett, Secretary
Trustees: Rt Hon. William Waldegrave; Sir John Kerr; Sir Richard Southwood; Dr C R Lucas; Prof. R J O'Neill; Mrs R Deech; Miss R Hedley-Miller.

Total grants: £2.7 million (1998/99)
Grants overseas: £1.3 million

General: The primary purpose for which the trust was established, and for which it continues to be used and managed, is to provide scholarships to be allocated each year to enable students from selected countries of the Commonwealth, the USA and Germany, to spend two or three years on an undergraduate or postgraduate course at Oxford University.

The Public Purposes Fund, from which the trustees can appropriate property to the scholarship fund, can make grants for educational and other charitable purposes, in any part of the Commonwealth or the USA. The policy has been to restrict its use to educational purposes in Oxford University and Commonwealth countries in Africa and the Caribbean.

The combined income for 1998/99 was £6 million. The cost of maintaining the scholarship programme was £3.9 million and charitable donations from the Public Purposes Fund amounted to £2.7 million. In addition, £75,000 was granted from the Scholarship Capital Reserve Fund and £44,000 from the South Africa Fund. At the year end, the assets stood at about £197 million.

The grants from the Public Purposes Fund were broken down as follows:

Oxford University   £1.3 million
African & Commonwealth £1.3 million
other   £41,000

African and Commonwealth: A total of 22 grants were given. The three largest were to University of Witwatersan Foundation (£517,000), Rhodes University – Eden Grove Centre (£274,000) and University of Cape Town (£100,000). Other grants ranged from £5,000 to £61,000 and included Liverpool University's Diabetes Education (£61,000), Valley Trust (£51,000), World University Service UK – Campus Scheme (£7,000) and African Book Collection Trust (£5,000).

Exclusions: Grants to institutions only. No grants to individuals.

Applications: To the correspondent in writing. Trustees meet in June and November.

The Rhododendron Trust

Welfare, culture, overseas aid

Geographical focus: UK and overseas

BDO Stoy Hayward, 7–9 Irwell Terrace, Bacup, Lancashire OL13 9AJ
Tel: 01706 873213; **Fax:** 01706 874211
Correspondent: P E Healey, Trustee
Trustees: Peter Edward Healey; Dr Ralph Walker; Mrs Sarah Ray; Dr David Michael Smith.

Total grants: £36,000 (1999/2000)
Grants overseas: £18,500

General: The trust was established in 1974, with subsequent injections of capital in the following few years. Grants of either £500 or £1,000 are given to overseas charities and to UK welfare and cultural charities.

In 1999/2000 the income was £48,000 and grants totalled £36,000, broken down as follows:

overseas charities	£18,500
UK charities – social welfare	£14,500
cultural charities	£3,000

Overseas grants were made to 37 organisations and were all for £500. Beneficiaries included ASAP, Book Aid International, Dhaka Ahsania Mission, Help Age International, International Development Partnerships and Uganda Society for Disabled Children.

Exclusions: No grants to individuals, or for medical research.

Applications: In writing to the correspondent. Applications are not acknowledged. Donations are made in February.

The Richardson Family Charitable Trust

General

Geographical focus: UK and overseas

143 Rosendale Road, London SE21 8HE
Tel: 020 8670 3153
Correspondent: J A M Richardson, Trustee
Trustees: J A M Richardson; B E Richardson; S D Fish; P Tranter.

Total grants: £18,000 (1999)
General: In 1999 the trust had assets of £156,000 and an income of £7,500. Six grants were made in the year, totalling £18,000.

The largest grant was £5,000 to L'Arche, an organisation which works with adults with learning difficulties in India. This donation was part of a five-year commitment. Other grants included £4,000 to Apnalya, a registered Indian charity working in the slums of Bombay, to put towards its endowment for the funding of core office and administrative expenses; and £2,500 to Network Foundation which was passed on to Jubilee 2000 for raising awareness of third world debt.

Applications: In writing to the correspondent.

The Karim Rida Said Foundation

Health, disability, education, children at risk

Geographical focus: Middle East, particularly Iraq, Jordan, Lebanon, Palestine and Syria

Second Floor, 4 Bloomsbury Place, London WC1A 2QA
Tel: 020 7691 2772; **Fax:** 020 7691 2780
e-mail: admin@krsf.org

website: www.krsf.org
Correspondent: Catherine Roe, Director
Trustees: Wafic R Said, Chair;
A Rosemary Said; His Excellency Ghayth Armanazi; Dr Peter Clark; Mrs Sirine Idilby; Lord Powell.

Total grants: £948,000 (1998/99)
General: The trust has three programmes:
- *Scholarship programme:* this is its main vehicle for promoting education in the Middle East and it supports students from Egypt, Jordan, Lebanon, Palestine or Syria to study at postgraduate level in the UK, USA or the Middle East.
- *Projects programme:* funding projects in the fields of disability, health and education for children at risk, in Iraq, Jordan, Lebanon, Palestine and Syria.
- *Culture programme:* providing opportunities for people in Britain to understand the Arab culture and language better.

In 1998/99 the trust had assets of £27 million and an income of £955,000. Grants totalled £948,000. It supported 40 projects in the Middle East, accounting for 42% of the grant total. Another 52% of the grant total was donated in scholarships, with the remaining 6% given under the cultural programme. In all, 63% of project grants were for work with children and young people with disabilities.

The largest project grants in the year were: £25,000 to National Employment Fund for Disabled People – Syria; £22,000 to Medical Aid for Iraqi Children; £16,000 to Save the Children Fund – Lebanon; £15,000 each to International Service – West Bank, Quaker Peace and Service – Lebanon and St John's Opthalmic Hospital – East Jerusalem; £12,000 to Happy Home – Lebanon; and £11,000 each to Birzeit University's Community and Public Health Department and General Union of Disabled Palestinians – both West Bank.

Exclusions: No grants for general appeals, sponsorship events, conferences, newsletters or individuals (except through the scholarship programme).

Applications: On a form available from the correspondent. If the proposed project is eligible for a grant, it will be visited. Applications for scholarships can be made through the correspondent, the offices of the British Council in Damascus, Amman, Beirut, East Jerusalem or Gaza City, or the universities of Oxford and Cambridge.

Mrs L D Rope's Third Charitable Settlement

Relief of poverty, education, religion, general
Geographical focus: UK and overseas

Crag Farm, Boyton, near Woodbridge, Suffolk IP12 3LH
Fax: 01473 217182
Correspondent: Crispin M Rope
Trustees: Mrs Lucy D Rope, Jeremy P W Heal; Crispin M Rope.

Total grants: £440,000 (1998)
General: The trust gives a range of grants to both new and existing beneficiaries (although new grants are not available in every category). Grants are generally given for the relief of poverty, advancement of education and religion and other charitable purposes, including overseas aid and development.

In 1998 the trust had assets of £17 million and an income of £525,000. Grants totalled £440,000.

In the previous year beneficiaries included CAFOD for its work overseas (£40,000) and St Stephen's Hospital in

Uganda for a community healthcare project (£16,000).

Exclusions: The trust cannot support unsolicited applications for:
- new projects
- individuals working overseas
- charities considered to be 'wealthy'
- areas covered by statutory bodies
- core funding for salaries
- office running costs
- fundraising and professional fees
- capital grants
- medical research, healthcare or palliative care
- students
- fees for private education
- environmental or animal welfare appeals
- debt repayments.

Applications: In writing to the correspondent. Please note the above.

The Rotary Foundation

General

Geographical focus: *UK and developing countries.*

Kinwarton Road, Alcester, Warwickshire B49 6BP
Tel: 01789 765411; **Fax:** 01789 765570
e-mail: secretary@ribi.org
website: www.rotary-ribi.org
Correspondent: The Secretary

Total grants: About £2 million a year
General: Between 1979 and 2000, The Rotary Foundation distributed a total of £55 million. Usually about £2 million is given each year. It was started in 1917 and has two main areas of work. First there is an extensive programme of international scholarships and exchanges, instigated through local Rotary groups. This includes scholarships to students in developing countries and grants to university teachers who wish to serve them. Secondly the foundation is a major supporter of development work.

For example, the foundation is supplying the vaccine for polio eradication in the Polio plus campaign, which is part of six vaccination programmes for children, carried out with the assistance of UNICEF and WHO. This is a development of the existing programme for Health, Hunger and Humanity. Under this scheme the foundation gives grants for largescale, one to five year projects. To be eligible for consideration projects must be major international efforts of Rotary clubs or districts, involving personal participation of Rotarians. They must be designed to provide significant long-term benefits of a self-help nature, preferably to large numbers of people. Projects must have the support of Rotarians and governments in the benefiting country.

Priorities for funding are: health (primary healthcare, health education, treatment and rehabilitation); hunger (food publications, preservation and distribution with a particular emphasis on agro-forestry and aquaculture); community development (with a particular emphasis on income development); and humanity (literacy and vocational training).

Exclusions: No funding is given for works of a capital nature, e.g. buildings and construction.

Applications: In all cases, programmes to be supported and candidates for scholarships are selected by individual Rotary clubs or Rotarians. Rotary clubs make their own selection policies and choose their preferences for the type of scholarships they wish to award each year. Not all types of scholarships are available each year and may vary from district to district. For application forms, literature and further information about the availability of scholarships in your Rotary district, please contact the District Rotary

Foundation Chair in your nearest Rotary Club. The foundation cannot respond to appeals. Applications are forwarded to Rotary International in America.

The Rowan Charitable Trust

International aid, social welfare, general

Geographical focus: *Worldwide.*

c/o PricewaterhouseCoopers,
9 Greyfriars Road, Reading RG1 1JG
Tel: 0118 959 7111; **Fax:** 0118 960 7700
Correspondent: The Secretary
Trustees: C R Jones; Mrs H E Russell.

Total grants: £571,000 (1998/99)

Grants overseas: £377,000

General: The trust gives a mix of one-off and recurrent grants. It has regularly given grants to a limited number of large UK organisations and development agencies, but also gives smaller grants to much smaller organisations and locally-based projects. The trust will support advocacy and challenges to powerful economic forces, on behalf of the poor, the powerless or the left out, especially if they themselves are enabled to participate in articulating a vision of economic justice.

The trust gives two thirds of its money to overseas projects and one third to social welfare projects in the UK. Over 100 grants are made a year, rarely for more than £25,000 and most for between £1,000 and £10,000. Larger grants usually go to charities with which the trust has an existing connection, with large annual awards upwards of £15,000 tending to go to those working in developing countries. Smaller one-off grants, sometimes repeated, go to a variety of beneficiaries, including many campaigning groups. The trust is open to radical projects and organisations.

The focus of overseas grants is on projects which will benefit disadvantaged groups and communities in such spheres as:

- *Agriculture* – especially crop and livestock production and settlement schemes.
- *Community development* – especially appropriate technology and village industries.
- *Health* – especially preventative medicine, water supplies, blindness.
- *Education* – especially adult education and materials.
- *Environmental* – especially protecting and sustaining ecological systems at risk.
- *Human rights* – especially of women, children and disabled.
- *Fair trade* – especially relating to primary producers and workers.

The trust is interested in projects which:

- involve the local community in planning and implementation
- invest in people through training and enabling
- have a holistic concern for all aspects of life.

In 1998/99 the trust made 77 grants totalling £377,000 for work overseas and 40 grants worth £194,000 to UK organisations. About three-quarters of recipients in the previous year reappeared in this grants list.

In the overseas sector long-standing relationships continued with Christian Aid and Intermediate Technology (£50,000 each) and UNICEF (£30,000). Grants for £10,000 went to Church Mission Society, Leprosy Mission, Newick Park Initiative and Rurcon. The remaining grants ranged from £500 to £8,000. Recipients included Jubilee 2000 Coalition, UK Foundation for the South Pacific, Conciliation Resources, Dian Fossey Gorilla Fund, Tools for Self Reliance, Survival for Tribal Peoples and

Wales Gurkha Villages Aid Appeals Committee.

Exclusions: No grants for: individuals; buildings, building work or office equipment; and academic research.

Applications: In writing to the correspondent. No application forms are issued and the trustees meet in February and August.

Applications should include: a brief description (two sides of A4 paper) of, and a budget for, the work for which the grant is sought; the organisation's annual report and accounts; and an indication of the core costs of the organisation.

An application needs to provide the trustees with information about:
- the aims and objectives of the organisation
- its structure and organisational capacity
- what the funds are being requested for and how much is being requested
- how progress of the work will be monitored and evaluated.

'Unfortunately the volume of applications received precludes acknowledgement on receipt or notifying unsuccessful applicants. The trust is unable to make donations to applicants who are not, or do not have links with, a UK-registered charity.'

The Joseph Rowntree Charitable Trust

Conflict management and human rights

Geographical focus: UK, Republic of Ireland, South Africa and the surrounding area

The Garden House, Water End, York YO30 6WQ
Tel: 01904 627810; **Fax:** 01904 651990
e-mail: jrct@jrct.org.uk
website: www.jrct.org.uk

Correspondent: Steven Burkeman, Secretary
Trustees: Andrew Gunn, Chair; Ruth McCarthy, Vice-Chair; Margaret Bryan; Christine Davis; Beverley Meeson; Marion McNaughton; Roger Morton; Vas Shend'ge; David Shutt; Peter Stark; Emily Miles; John Guest.

Total grants: £4.2 million (1999)
Grants overseas: £393,000

General: Grants are given mostly to organisations in the UK and Republic of Ireland, although a number of grants are also given in South Africa. About 200 grants are made each year, ranging in size from a few hundred pounds to over £100,000, and from one-off to three-year grants. They cover, at present: poverty and economic justice, peace, democratic process, racial justice, corporate responsibility, religious concerns and justice and reconciliation in South Africa and in Ireland (North and South). The trust states that due to a large volume of applications generally only one in nine applications is successful.

In 1999 the trust had assets of £183 million generating an income of £5 million. Grants to 170 organisations totalled £4.2 million, including £393,000 to organisations in South Africa.

The trust supports conflict management and the building of a human rights culture in the new South Africa, in both urban and rural settings. In its conflict resolution work, the trust prioritises support to projects in Kwa-Zulu/Natal.

In recent times, grants have focused on the following issues:
- conflict management in urban and rural settings;
- the use of para-legal training and legal mechanisms to empower farm-workers and other marginalised communities;

- policy research on South Africa's security and defence arrangements;
- industrial and community mediation;
- work which focuses on the Truth and Reconciliation Commission;
- the promotion of the constitutional rights of lesbians and gay men;
- work to combat the abuse of women and sexual harassment.

The trust is an associate member of Interfund, an international donor consortium with a staffed office in Johannesburg. While grants are almost exclusively given in South Africa, on occasion it is willing to fund work elsewhere in southern Africa.

Examples of recent grants include:
- South African Centre for Public Interest Information: R406,000 over two years for core costs;
- Freedom of Expression Institute: R225,000 over three years for workshops on freedom of expression and on key legislation;
- Christian Fellowship Trust: £20,000 towards the costs of preparing a history of the organisation.

Exclusions: The trust considers applications from South Africa, but does not generally fund work in South Africa originating in the UK.

Applications: In writing to the correspondent, accompanied by a brief application form available from the correspondent. Detailed guidelines are available from the correspondent which applicants are strongly advised to read.

Trustees' meetings are usually held in March, June, September and November; applications should arrive at least 10 weeks earlier. See the trust's website for detailed information on current deadlines and policy.

The Rufford Foundation

Nature conservation, sustainable development, environment, general

Geographical focus: Worldwide

5th Floor, Babmaes House, 2 Babmaes Street, London SW1Y 6HD
Tel: 020 7925 2582; **Fax:** 020 7925 2583
e-mail: taylor@rufford.org
website: www.rufford.org
Correspondent: Siân Taylor, Trust Administrator
Trustees: J H Laing; A Gavazzi; C R F Barbour; A J Johnson; K W Scott; M I Smailes; V Lees.

Total grants: £1.9 million (1999/2000)
General: The foundation was established in 1982 by John Hedley Laing. The trustees have a strong interest in nature conservation, the environment and sustainable development, with approximately three-quarters of the foundation's funding going to these areas. The trust tends to concentrate on projects in non-first world countries.

In 1999/2000 74 grants totalled £1.9 million. The average grant rose to £26,000 from £18,000 in the previous year.

The largest grants of £100,000 or over went to conservation charities. In total over half the beneficiaries were conservation charities or others working overseas, such as Wildlife Protection Society of India (£63,000), International Society for Ecology and Culture (£15,000) and United Mission to Nepal (£13,000). Recipients of grants under £5,000 included African Initiatives, Friends of Russian Children and Sight Savers International.

In April 2000 £2.8 million had been approved in future grant commitments.

Exclusions: No grants for: building or construction projects; organisations which are not UK-registered charities; and individuals.

The trustees tend not to provide gifts to projects which seek to exclusively benefit local communities e.g. playgroups, youth clubs, luncheon clubs. The trust rarely accepts applications for funding salaries. There is a definite and conscious attempt to avoid replacing statutory funding and no loans are made.

Applications: In writing to the correspondent. Applications must include:
- a comprehensive plan outlining the project for which funding is being sought
- a full budget
- a covering letter with contact details
- a copy of the charity's most recent accounts
- a copy of the latest annual report (if available).

Applications are assessed monthly. Gifts of over £5,000 will be considered at trustees' meetings held twice a year. Each application is assessed individually and the trust strives to respond within four weeks. Any incomplete applications received, or applications which fail to meet with the trust's criteria as outlined above will immediately be rejected.

Ryklow Charitable Trust 1992
(also known as A B Williamson Charitable Trust)

Education, health and welfare
Geographical focus: *Worldwide*

Robinsons Solicitors, 83 Friar Gate, Derby DE1 1FL
Tel: 01332 291431; **Fax:** 01332 291461
e-mail: info@robinsons-solicitors.co.uk
Correspondent: Stephen F Marshall
Trustees: A B Williamson; Mrs K Williamson; J B Nickols; J V Woodward; A Williamson; E J S Cannings.

Total grants: £73,000 to organisations (1998/99)

General: The trust says that its notes for applicants 'have been compiled to help applicants understand how best it is felt the trust can be operated and the constraints of time under which the (unpaid) trustees must work. It will help enormously if you try to ensure that your application follows these guidelines if at all possible'.

Applications will only be considered for activities if they meet the following descriptions:
- medical research, especially that which benefits children
- assistance to students from overseas wishing to study in the UK or for UK students volunteering for unpaid work overseas
- projects in the developing world – especially those which are intended to be self-sustaining or concerned with education
- help for vulnerable families, minorities and the prevention of abuse or exploitation of children
- conservation of natural species, landscape and resources.

In 1998/99 the trust had assets of £1.5 million. Half the income of £101,000 was from donations, the remainder from investments. Grants totalling £73,000 were given to 61 organisations, 22 of which had been supported the previous year. Grants were in the range of £500 to £4,000. The two largest donations were £4,000 each to NSPCC and Plan International, while Gaumati (Nepal) High School Fund recieved £1,500.

The trust made 58 grants of £1,000 each. Education causes supported included Mozambique Schools Fund, Tiger Kloot Educational Institution and The African Academy for CADD Training.

The trust gave to a wide variety of organisations including a number working in the areas of conservation, welfare and development. Recipients included Coral Cay Conservation, Galapagos Conservation Trust, Farm Africa, Aboriginal Support, CARE International, Oxfam and Traidcraft. An undisclosed number of grants were made to individuals in the year totalling £6,300.

Applications: 'Applications should be brief. We are a small charity with few trustees and there is little time for all in turn to read numerous or long documents.

'A statement of your finances is a must, or better still, an audited financial report. Individual applicants unable to provide either should send details of the precise purpose for which help is required with reputable back-up evidence.

'The trustees read all applications (of which there are many) over the months of January and February because they feel that this is the only fair way of comparing the merits of one against another. To allow us to arrive at a fair distribution of available monies we ask that all applications reach us between 1 September and 31 December in any calendar year. Trustees can then devote January and February to the study of the needs before them. When decisions have been reached cheques are despatched at the end of March.

'Unfortunately we are unable to help every applicant no matter how deserving the cause may be. To keep down costs we do not write to unsuccessful applicants. Therefore if you have not heard from us before the end of April you will know that your application has been unsuccessful in that year.'

The Alan and Babette Sainsbury Charitable Fund

General

Geographical focus: Worldwide, but mostly UK

9 Red Lion Court, London EC4A 3EF
Tel: 020 7410 0330
Correspondent: Michael Pattison, Director
Trustees: Hon. Simon Sainsbury; Miss Judith Portrait.

Total grants: £974,000 (1999)
Grants overseas: £554,000

General: This trust, during the lifetime of Alan Sainsbury, was not administered as part of the Sainsbury family group of trusts. This was changed by the trustees after his death in 1998 and it is now adopting the usual policies standard for all the Sainsbury Family Trusts. In 1999 the trustees reviewed the capacity of the fund to continue to support all the charities which have been regular beneficiaries and not respond to unsolicited applications.

In 1999 the trust had an income of £468,000 and gave grants totalling £974,000, broken down as follows:

	No.	Total
education	4	£109,000
health and social welfare	30	£166,000
overseas	7	£554,000
scientific and medical research	7	£56,000
the arts	6	£29,000
religion	5	£61,000

Under the 'overseas' category, a grant of £450,000 to Pestalozzi Children's Village Trust made up much of the total. The only other grant over £6,000 was £79,000 to Canon Collins Educational Trust for Southern Africa. A grant was given to Medical Foundation for the Care of Victims of Torture under the 'scientific and medical research' category.

Applications: In writing to the correspondent. Unsolicited applications are discouraged and are unlikely to be successful.

St Mark's Overseas Aid Trust (SMOAT)

Emergency relief and development
Geographical focus: Worldwide

49 Redstone Hill, Redhill RH1 4BG
Tel: 01737 772811
Correspondent: R Salmon, Chair

Total grants: £10,000 (1998/99)
Grants overseas: £10,000

General: The trust gives grants for relief work in the third world. Most of the grants are given to regular beneficiaries.

In 1998/99 the trust had assets of £7,400 and an income of £18,000, mostly from donations and fundraising activities such as cookbooks, treasure hunts and barn dances. Grants totalled £10,000.

Beneficiaries included Send a Cow in Uganda (£4,500 in two grants), WaterAid in India (£2,600), Intercare for supply of hospital facilities in Cameroon (£1,500), with £650 each to Friends of Khasdoshir for its 'schools under the sky' programme in Bangladesh and to TOC H. A grant was also given to VSO for an individual.

Applications: In writing to the correspondent.

The Saranda Charitable Trust

General
Geographical focus: UK and overseas

8 Hillbury Road, London SW17 8JT
Tel: 0117 946 4000
Correspondent: Mrs S C Dangerfield
Trustees: David Humphreys; Sarah Dangerfield; Miranda McWhirter.

Total grants: £16,000 (1998/99)
General: Grants are given for general charitable purposes in the UK and overseas. In 1998/99 the trust's assets totalled £448,000, the income was £18,000 and grants totalled £16,000. Overseas 'annual donations' included £500 each to Africa Now, UNICEF and WWF UK. A further grant of £5,000 was made from the 'emergency fund' and went to British Red Cross.

Exclusions: Grants to UK-registered charities only; not to individuals.

Applications: In writing to the correspondent.

Schroder Charity Trust

See below
Geographical focus: UK, occasionally overseas

31 Gresham Street, London EC2V 7QA
Correspondent: B V Tew, Secretary
Trustees: B L Schroder; Mrs C B Mallinckrodt; Mrs C L Fitzalan Howard; J H R Schroder; T B Schroder; Mrs L K E Schroder-Fane.

Total grants: £104,000 (unrestricted grants 1999)
General: This trust is the vehicle through which Schroder plc and its UK subsidiaries principally undertake their UK charitable giving. It focuses on causes with a previous track record, or on areas where trustees have a special interest. Areas supported include: medicine and health; people who are older; social welfare; education; humanities; arts; heritage; environmental resources; and international relief/overseas aid.

In 1999 the trust had assets of £5.8 million and an income of £658,000, of which £534,000 was for restricted purposes and £104,000 unrestricted. During the year 62 appeals were received, plus a further 767 from staff under a matching donations scheme. Of these, 547 charities received grants, 341 from the restricted and unrestricted funds and 206 from the restricted fund for matching donations.

Grants made from the restricted and unrestricted funds were listed together in the trust's accounts (but matching donations were listed separately); by far the largest grant was £75,000 to Disasters Emergency Committee – Kosovo Crisis Appeal. Other beneficiaries included British Red Cross (£5,800), ActionAid (£2,500), BESO (£2,000), CAFOD (£1,800), Tree Aid (£1,500) and UNICEF (£1,000), with £500 each to Book Aid, Medical Supplies in Romania and VSO.

Exclusions: No grants to individuals.

Applications: In writing to the correspondent, for consideration monthly.

The Scouloudi Foundation

Medicine and health, humanities and disability

Geographical focus: *UK charities working domestically or abroad*

Hays Macintyre, Southampton House, 317 High Holborn, London WC1V 7NL
Tel: 020 7969 5500
Correspondent: The Administrators
Trustees: Miss S E Stowell; M E Demetriadi; J D Marnham; J R Sewell.

Total grants: £161,000 (1999/2000)
General: The foundation was established in 1962 by Irene Scouloudi, a historian and philanthropist, and to date has given £2.7 million in grants. In 1999/2000 the trust had an income of £250,000 and assets of £5.6 million. It made grants totalling £161,000 (£211,000 in 1998/99). The current policy of the trustees reflects the interests and intentions of the founder. The annual income is divided between three categories of grants (amount given in grants is shown in brackets):

Historical awards: An annual award is made to Institute of Historical Research at University of London to allow it to support research and publications in the field (£62,000 in 1999/2000).

Regular donations: These are made up of annual donations to a specified list of UK charities. It is the policy of the trustees to review the donees on a five-yearly cycle (£82,000). Grants included £850 each to Voluntary Service Overseas, WaterAid and Y Care International.

Special donations: These are made once a year in response to specific applications to fund capital projects and other extraordinary needs (£17,000). Extraordinary needs include natural disasters and five grants were awarded in this category, three of which went to British Red Cross projects – in India (£3,000), Turkey (£2,000) and Venezuela (£3,000). Disasters Emergency Committee – Kosovo also received £4,000. In previous years special donations have taken the form of smaller grants benefiting a wider range of organisations, including more in the UK.

Distribution across all categories during the year can be broken down as follows:

older people	£6,000
children & young people	£7,900
environment	£9,500
famine relief & overseas aid	£3,600
handicapped & disability	£13,000
humanities	£80,000
medicine & health	£16,000
social welfare	£9,400
welfare of armed forces & sailors	£3,400
natural disasters	£12,000

Exclusions: Grants are given to UK-registered or exempt organisations only. Donations are not made to individuals, and are not normally made for welfare activities of a purely local nature. The trustees do not make loans.

Applications: Applications for special donations, giving full but concise details, should be sent to the administrators at the address above by 1 March for consideration in April.

Copies of the regulations and application forms for historical awards can be obtained from: The Secretary, The Scouloudi Foundation Historical Awards Committee, c/o Institute of Historical Research, University of London, Senate House, London WC1E 7HU.

SEM Charitable Trust

Disability, general

Geographical focus: UK, Israel and South Africa

Saffery Champness, Fairfax House,
Fulwood Place, Gray's Inn,
London WC1V 6UB
Correspondent: M Cohen, Trustee
Trustees: Mrs Sarah E Radomir;
Michael Cohen.

Total grants: £37,000 (1998/99)

General: The trust makes grants mainly to disability-related organisations. In 1998/99 its assets totalled £340,000, the income was £41,000 and the 11 grants made, totalled £47,000. Seven recipients were also supported in the previous year.

Grants included £11,000 to HAFAD, £5,000 to KWA Basketball Association, £4,500 to MASADA, £1,500 to Afasic Cobra Football Club, £1,000 each to Tape Aids for the Blind and West London Synagogue, and £500 each to Habonim South Africa and Maris Stella School – adult literacy programme.

Applications: In writing to the correspondent.

Servite Sisters' Charitable Trust Fund

General

Geographical focus: Worldwide

Parkside, Coldharbour Lane, Dorking, Surrey RH4 3BN
Tel: 01306 875756; **Fax:** 01306 889339
e-mail: m@servite.demon.co.uk
Correspondent: Michael J W Ward, Secretary
Trustees: Sister Joyce Mary Fryer OSM; Sister Ruth Campbell OSM; Sister Eugenia Geraghty OSM; Sister Catherine Ryan OSM.

Total grants: £305,000 (2000)
Grants overseas: £141,000

General: This trust is run by the English province of the international religious order of The Servants of Mary (known as Servites). The province has 78 members, most of whom have given their working lives to the charitable activities of the order. When any of the members carry out any work independently of the charity, any earnings are covenanted to the charity.

The trust was set up in 1993 and makes grants principally to support organisations carrying out:

- activities intended primarily to help women who are marginalised physically, spiritually or morally;
- activities intended to alleviate the distress of refugees and other disadvantaged migrants.

The funds may also be used to help the Servite family in the third world/Eastern Europe.

Grants are one-off and average £2,500. In 2000 grants to 114 organisations totalled £305,000, of which £141,000 was given towards causes in developing countries.

Overseas grants included £5,000 for rehabilitating pregnant girls who had been abducted by guerrilla soldiers in Sierra Leone, £4,800 for manual equipment for training women and girls to earn a living in South Africa, £4,500 for a new women drug addict rehabilitation scheme in Nepal, £4,400 for clothing, medical care and furnishings for Tibetan refugees in India, and £4,000 each for helping a group of indigenous women to contribute to a more just society in Guatemala and rehabilitating rescued women and girls who had been trafficked in Bangladesh.

Smaller grants included £3,100 for fishing equipment for a women's income-generation group in Uganda, £3,000 for a comprehensive women's development programme in Nigeria, £1,600 for the running costs for a hostel for women with mental disabilities in Cameroon and £1,400 for embroidery equipment for a women's development programme in The Philippines.

Exclusions: No grants towards building projects, individuals or Indian ngos.

Applications: In writing to the correspondent with brief details of your organisation, project and needs.

The Barnett & Sylvia Shine No 1 & No 2 Charitable Trusts

General

Geographical focus: *Worldwide*

Messrs Paisner & Co., Bouverie House, 154 Fleet Street, London EC4A 2DQ
Tel: 020 7353 0299
Correspondent: M D Paisner, Trustee
Trustees: M D Paisner; Sybil Shine.

Total grants: No 1 fund: £60,000 (1998/99)

General: The No 1 Charitable Trust was established in 1975 by Sylvia Shine. In 1980 half the assets of the trust were transferred to the No 2 Charitable Trust. In 1981 the executors of the estate of the late Sylvia Shine transferred several paintings, jewellery and cash to the trusts. In 1998/99 the No 1 fund had assets totalling £2 million and an income of £67,000. It made grants totalling £60,000, in the range of £100 to £10,000.

Grants included £10,000 to Canon Collins Educational Trust for South Africa, £5,000 each to Soweto Black Women's Charitable Trust and Traidcraft Exchange, and £1,000 each to St Joseph's Hospice and Institute for Commonwealth Studies. The trust also supported four environmental/wildlife organisations.

In 1999/2000 the No 2 fund had an income of £55,000 and expenditure of £11,000.

Applications: In writing to the correspondent.

The Ernest William Slaughter Charitable Trust

Health, welfare

Geographical focus: *Worldwide*

c/o Ozannes, PO Box 186, 1 Le Marchant Street, St Peter Port, Guernsey GY1 4HP
Tel: 01481 723466
Correspondent: R A R Evans
Trustees: Mrs J Harris; Mrs M A Matthews.

Total grants: £38,000 (1997/98)

General: The trust makes grants for a range of organisations, including a number of health-related charities, especially those caring for people who are older or chronically sick. Grants range from £500 to £5,000.

In 1997/98 its income was £71,000 and grants were made to 13 organisations totalling £38,000. A list of grants was not available for that year.

In the previous year, grants totalled £39,000 and included £5,000 to Little Sisters of the Poor Foetal Medicine Foundation, £4,000 each to Médecins Sans Frontières, Medilink and Vision Aid, and £3,000 to Motivation. The smallest grant was for £500.

Applications: In writing to the correspondent.

The SMB Trust

Christian, general

Geographical focus: *UK and overseas*

15 Wilman Road, Tunbridge Wells, Kent TN4 9AJ
Tel: 01892 537321
Correspondent: Mrs B M O'Driscoll, Trustee
Trustees: Eric Donald Anstead; Philip John Stanford; Mrs B O'Driscoll.

Total grants: £131,000 (1998/99)
General: The chair's 1998/99 report stated: 'The trustees have continued to give regular support to a number of core charities covering a wide spectrum of needs.' One-off appeals are also considered. The trust appears to have a preference for Christian and welfare purposes, giving grants to local, UK and international organisations.

In 1998/99 the trust had assets of £5.2 million and an income of £169,000. It gave 120 grants totalling £131,000, of which 51 were recurrent. Grants ranged from £200 to £4,000, but were mainly for £1,000.

Grants included: £8,300 in eight grants to Leprosy Mission; £2,000 each to Dentaid and British Red Cross; £1,200 to Tearfund; and £1,000 each to CAFOD, Ethiopiaid, Health Unlimited, Impact, Interhealth and Jubilee Campaign.

Exclusions: No grants to individuals.
Applications: In writing to the correspondent for consideration quarterly.

The N Smith Charitable Trust

General

Geographical focus: *Worldwide*

Bullock Worthington & Jackson, 1 Booth Street, Manchester M2 2HA
Tel: 0161 833 9771
Correspondent: The Trustees
Trustees: J S Cochrane; T R Kendal; P R Green; J H Williams-Rigby.

Total grants: £115,000 (1998/99)
Grants overseas: £16,000

General: In 1998/99 the trust's assets had risen to £3.6 million and it had an income of £111,000. After expenses of £20,000 (£18,000 of which was in legal costs), it gave £115,000 in grants, mostly to UK organisations. In the accounts grants were broken down into: poverty and social work (£41,000); health and medical research (£35,000); overseas aid (18 grants totalling £16,000); education (£13,000); arts (£6,000); environmental work and animals (£5,000).

Grants listed under 'overseas aid' ranged from £750 to £1,500, including those to ActionAid, Homeopathic Trust, Kosovo Appeal, Oxfam and Traidcraft Exchange.

Exclusions: Grants to UK-registered charities only and not to individuals.
Applications: In writing to the correspondent. The trustees meet in March and October.

The Souter Charitable Trust

Social welfare, Christianity, third world development

Geographical focus: *Worldwide, but mostly Scotland*

PO Box 7412, Perth PH1 1WH
Tel: 01738 634745; **Fax:** 01738 440275
Correspondent: Linda Scott, Secretary
Trustees: Brian Souter; Elizabeth Souter; Linda Scott.

Total grants: £1.4 million (2000)

General: The trust was established in 2000, and in January 2001 it took over some of the grant-making activities of The Souter Foundation. The trust's policy is to assist 'projects engaged in the relief of human suffering in the UK or overseas, particularly those with a Christian emphasis'.

In 2000 grants totalled £1.4 million, of which £285,000 was given in small one-off grants of £1,000 or less. After committed funds, there was expected to be £300,000 available for small grants in 2001.

Exclusions: Only one application a year can be considered from each organisation. No grants are given towards research, capital funding, building projects, personal education and expeditions.

Applications: In writing to the correspondent, enclosing an sae. Applications should be brief (no more than two sides of A4) and include accounts (but no other promotional material). The trustees meet every two months and all applications are acknowledged.

Please note that overseas applications for The Souter Foundation will now be considered by this trust.

W F Southall Trust

(incorporating K and P Southall Charitable Trust)

Quakers, peace, education, addiction, social welfare, general

Geographical focus: *Mostly UK, also overseas*

c/o Rutters Solicitors, 2 Bimport, Shaftesbury, Dorset SP7 8AY
Tel: 01747 852377
Correspondent: S Rutter, Secretary
Trustees: Donald Southall, Chair; Daphne Maw; Christopher Southall; Annette Wallis; Mark Holtam; Joanna Engelkamp; Claire Greeves.

Total grants: £291,000 (1999/2000)

General: Grants are given towards Quaker charities, peace, education, alcohol and drug addiction, social welfare and related charities.

In November 1999 the trust incorporated the funds of K and P Southall Charitable Trust which had some common trustees and similar objects. This brought the joint assets up to £5.7 million. In 1999/2000 the combined income came to £1 million and grants to 169 charities totalled £291,000.

Grants to organisations working overseas included £2,500 each to Fourth World Action and Traidcraft Exchange, £2,000 each to Oxfam, Sight Savers International and Tools for Self Reliance, £1,500 to Karuna Trust, £1,000 each to Action for People in Conflict and Intermediate Technology, £750 to Christian Aid and £500 to Marie Stopes International.

The trust has stated its plans to continue support for charities which have benefited in the past, as well as supporting smaller organisations where the help will make a significant difference. Preference is given to charities of which trustees have detailed knowledge.

Exclusions: Grants to UK-registered charities only, and not to individuals.

Applications: In writing to the correspondent, but note the above.

The Spear Charitable Trust

General

Geographical focus: *Worldwide, with a preference for the UK*

Roughground House, Old Hall Green, Ware, Hertfordshire SG11 1HB
Tel & Fax: 01920 823071
e-mail: franzel@farmersweekly.net
Correspondent: Hazel E Spear, Secretary
Trustees: P N Harris; K B Stuart Crowhurst; F A Spear; H E Spear.

Total grants: £200,000 (1999)
General: This trust was established in 1994 with general charitable purposes and for the welfare of employees and former employees of J W Spear & Sons plc, their families and dependants.

In 1999 the assets stood at £5.3 million and the income was £199,000. Grants totalled £200,000, including £19,000 given in welfare grants and £73,000 listed as 'sundry donations' (less than £5,000 each).

International aid and development grants ranged between £2,500 and £8,500 and recipients included Children of Mukuru, Farm Africa, Guyana Diocesan Association and Kindu Trust.

Applications: In writing to the correspondent.

The Spring Harvest Charitable Trust

Christianity

Geographical focus: *UK and overseas*

14 Horsted Square, Uckfield, East Sussex TN22 1QL
Tel: 01825 769111
Correspondent: The Clerk to the Trustees
Trustees: Faith Forester; I C Coffey; J S Richardson; C A M Sinclair.

Total grants: £690,000 to organisations (1998/99)
General: The main objects of this trust are to support Christian evangelism and other welfare or 'compassion' causes. This focus is not surprising since the majority of the trust's income comes from Spring Harvest, a Bible teaching event (£650,000 in 1998/99).

In 1998/99 grants totalled £720,000, including 57 grants to organisations ranging between £3,000 and £74,000 and totalling £471,000. Other grants to organisations (not listed in accounts) totalled £219,000. Grants to individuals totalled £30,000.

Grants included £74,000 to Tearfund, £40,000 to Mercy Ships International, £20,000 to Saltmine, £19,000 to Novi Most International, £10,000 to International Care and Relief, £8,500 to Partnership for Growth, £5,000 to Batonga Water Project and £4,000 to Children in Distress.

Applications: In writing to the correspondent.

The Staples Trust

Development, environment, women's issues

Geographical focus: Worldwide, but mostly UK

9 Red Lion Court, London EC4A 3EF
Tel: 020 7410 0330; **Fax:** 020 7410 0332
Correspondent: Michael Pattison, Director
Trustees: Miss Jessica Sainsbury; Alexander J Sainsbury; T J Sainsbury; P Frankopan; Miss Judith Portrait.

Total grants: £643,000 (1999/2000)
General: This is one of the Sainsbury Family Charitable Trusts which share a joint administration. It gives most of its support to development/environmental work overseas. It also supports UK-based environmental activities. It is unusual among trusts in having women's issues as a particular concern. The three main objects are as follows.

Overseas development

The trustees are interested in supporting projects which contribute to the empowerment of women, the rights of indigenous people, improved shelter and housing, income-generation in disadvantaged communities and sustainable agriculture and forestry. They are particularly interested to support development projects which take account of environmental sustainability and, in many cases, the environmental and developmental benefits of the project are of equal importance.

Environment

Projects are supported in developing countries, Central and Eastern Europe and the UK. Grants are approved for renewable energy technology, training and skills upgrading and, occasionally, research. In Central and Eastern Europe, trustees are interested in providing training opportunities for community/business leaders and policy makers and in contributing to the process of skill-sharing and information exchange. In the UK, the trustees aim to help communities protect, maintain and improve areas of land and to support work aimed at informing rural conservation policy.

Women's issues

The trustees remain interested in domestic violence issues. Although their priority is innovative strategic programmes of support with a UK focus (particularly interagency work and work to tackle domestic violence from the male perpetrator perspective), they also provide smaller grants to assist local refuge services and women's self-help groups.

Frankopan Scholarship Fund

The trustees have also established a fund to assist exceptionally talented students primarily from Croatia to further or complete their studies (in any discipline) in the UK.

In 1999/2000 the trust had assets of £12 million generating an income of £636,000. Total expenditure was £669,000, including £643,000 in grants. Approved grants totalled £465,000 and were broken down as follows:

	No.	Total
overseas development	9	£101,000
environmental	8	£161,000
women's issues	8	£158,000
general	1	£5,000
Frankopan Scholarship Fund	4	£39,810

Grants for overseas development included those to Tibet Information Network for its news and research service in Kathmandu (£21,000), Medica for medical and social care for women in Kosovo (£20,000), Minority Rights Group (£15,000), Drukpa Kargyud Trust for continuing costs of the construction and maintenance of a new school in the village of Shey in Ladakh – northern India and Learning for Life to maintain a schools/teacher training and curriculum development programme for primary schools in 40 villages in Uttar Pradesh – Himalayas (£10,000 each). Recipients of smaller grants included Mines Advisory Group for emergency mine clearance work in Kosovo and Soapbox Expeditions for the construction of a healthcare clinic in the Kibera slum in Nairobi (£5,000 each), and Animus Association to allow its director to study at Tavistock Institute, London (£3,500).

Environmental grants included those to Intermediate Technology for a micro-hydro credit programme in Peru (£58,000), ActionAid for a micro-hydro project in Nepal (£30,000), Jaisalmer in Jeopardy for the StreetScape programme in Rajasthan (£21,000), World Vision UK to allow a Kenyan ngo to provide clean water and irrigation in Wajir (£15,000), Renewable Energy Technology Assistance Programme for a Kenyan ngo to assist public and private institutions to acquire energy-saving stoves (£11,000) and Regional Environmental Centre – Hungary towards environmental workshops (£5,400).

Applications: In writing to the correspondent. Please note, the trust says that 'proposals are generally invited by the trustees or initiated at their request' and that 'unsolicited applications are discouraged and are unlikely to be successful'. The staff, and in some cases individual trustees, already have a relationship with many established organisations in the relevant fields. These organisations feel free to approach the trust with their ideas. Those outside this circle should not be deterred from doing likewise.

The Sir Halley Stewart Trust

Medical, social and religious research

Geographical focus: *Mostly UK, but some overseas funding (currently South and West Africa is a priority)*

22 Earith Road, Willingham,
Cambridge CB4 5LS
Tel & Fax: 01954 260707
website: www.sirhalleystewart.org
Correspondent: Mrs Sue West, Administrator
Trustees: Prof. Lennard Jones, Chair; Prof. Harold C Stewart; Dr Duncan Stewart; Sir Charles Carter; William P Kirkman; Lord Stewartby; George Russell; Prof. Phyllida Parsloe; Miss Barbara Clapham; Prof. J Wyatt; Michael Ross Collins; Brian Allpress; Prof. Philip Whitfield; Prof. C Hallett.

Total grants: £834,000 (1999/2000)
General: This Christian-based trust divides its grantmaking into three areas – medical, social and educational, and religious – each with a separate grants committee. The three committees are not mutually exclusive. For example, the social trustees are anxious to fund projects which address the social aspects of the problems which the medical trustees consider to be important. There are about 50 new grants a year, typically for one or two salaries over three years, and averaging perhaps a total of £27,000 over this period. In most years, over 50% of funds has been given towards medical research. Grants are usually in the form of a salary and the trustees prefer to support innovative and imaginative people – often promising young researchers – with whom they can develop a direct relationship. Sometimes a contribution towards the expenses of a project are given. The trust prefers to fund unfashionable or unpopular causes. Grants are normally limited to two or three

years, but are sometimes extended. Small individual grants are sometimes given. In general, the trustees do not favour grant-giving to enable the completion of a project initiated by other bodies.

Income is typically about £1 million, but was nearly £2.5 million in 1999, largely due to a legacy gift of over £1.5 million. Grants were broken down as follows:

medical grants	£355,000	(47%)
social grants	£266,000	(36%)
religious grants	£126,000	(17%)
total	£747,000	

Size of grants	*No.*	*Total*
under £1,000	27	£9,000
£1,000–£4,999	23	£38,000
£5,000 and over	35	£700,000

The trustees have selected certain areas of special interest which are currently treated as priorities. Each priority may be reflected in the social, religious and medical fields.

Religious

The trust is committed to advancing Christian religion. The trustees' particular interests are:

- theological training in cases where there is special and specific need (e.g. in Africa or Eastern Europe);
- teaching in the UK about Christianity outside the formal education system;
- encouragement of specific groups of people (e.g. older people, people with disability, students in higher education, those from ethnically mixed communities) to explore their spiritual needs and strengths.

Anyone contemplating approaching the trust for support in this field is strongly advised to make a preliminary enquiry before submitting an application as the guidelines may change.

Grants in this section have included £40,000 over two years to University of Cambridge – Margaret Beaufort Institute of Theology to enable students from Zambia and Kenya to take a two-year MA course.

Social and educational

Applications are welcomed for research and development projects which will have a direct impact on the conditions of a particular group of people, as well as having wider implications. The trustees are particularly interested in:

- projects which attempt to prevent and resolve conflicts and increase understanding within families and across racial, cultural, class, religious and professional divides;
- projects which involve conflict resolution and reconciliation;
- projects which attempt to help people to 'move beyond disadvantage' – and its consequences, e.g. youth unemployment, rehabilitation of offenders, homelessness, prevention of the downward spiral of youth criminality, race relations;
- projects which address the needs of people, especially the young and older people, which are not met by statutory services but are nevertheless serious;
- small-scale projects overseas, particularly in Africa, which are aimed at community development.

Beneficiaries have included Highway Hospice Association in Natal, South Africa for the salary and costs of a nursing sister to help to start one of 27 satellite hospices in the greater Durban area (£48,000 over four years), Lifeline Network International for the 'Nehemiah Project' to promote rehabilitation of war traumatised children in Sierra Leone (£15,000), and Plan International UK's Genital Mutilation Project in Burkina Faso for the training of animators who then pass on their training to local community volunteers (£10,000).

Medical

Projects should be simple, not molecular, and capable of clinical application within 5 to 10 years; they may include a social or ethical element. Non-medical trustees should be able to understand the application and appreciate the value of the work. Projects may be of a type unlikely to receive support from research councils or large research-funding charities.

The trustees particularly welcome applications concerned with:
- problems associated with older people such as Alzheimer's disease, nutrition, osteoporosis and incontinence
- prevention of disease and disability in children
- prevention, diagnosis and treatment of tropical infectious and parasitic diseases
- innovative projects, involving any discipline, which are likely to improve healthcare
- ethical problems arising from advances in medical practice.

Grants included £51,000 over three years to Medical Research Council Laboratories in Fajara, The Gambia to employ a research assistant to work on the project 'Who Gets Tuberculosis?'.

Personal grants

'Each year the trustees are entitled to £1,000 each to donate to charitable causes of their choice.' Between 1994 and 1999 these included The Mouth & Foot Painting Artists Organisation, The Fan Museum, Rosehill Theatre Trust, Harefield Hospital Scanner Appeal and Medical & Scientific Aid for Vietnam, Laos and Cambodia.

Exclusions: No grants for:
- general appeals of any kind
- personal education, fees for courses
- educational and travel projects for young people
- the purchase, erection or conversion of buildings, or other capital costs
- running costs of established organisations
- university overhead charges.

Applications: The application should come, in the first instance, from the individual concerned, rather than the 'host' organisation. Applications can be received throughout the year. Assessment can take several weeks, so applicants should allow for this when submitting their proposals. The following is reprinted from the trust's own material:

'How to apply to us for a grant

'First make sure that your project falls within the trust's current areas of interest. If you are in doubt, a quick telephone call to the trust office is welcomed.

'There is no formal application form. Applicants should write to the administrator with a short description of the proposed work. We need to know exactly what you plan to do with the grant, where you will be doing the work, how much money you will need and approximately how long the work should take. You need to state what you believe will be the benefit of your work, within what time frame and how the findings will be disseminated. We also require a brief cv. Development projects should indicate where they hope to obtain future funding after the trust's support has ended.

'If we cannot help you we will let you know. It is worth pointing out that we receive many applications for support, and although your work may fit the objects of the trust, we may not necessarily be able to help you.

'If it is decided to take your application further, it will be seen by those trustees who are most interested in that particular field. Please note that this process may take several weeks. You may be asked for more details at this stage. These trustees may then recommend that the application be considered at a full trustees' meeting at which final decisions are made.'

Full trustees' meetings are held three times a year, in February, June and October.

The Stobart Newlands Charitable Trust

Christian causes

Geographical focus: *Worldwide*

Mill Croft, Hesket Newmarket, Wigton, Cumbria CA7 8HP
Tel: 01697 478261
Correspondent: Mrs Margaret Stobart, Trustee
Trustees: R J Stobart; Mrs M Stobart; R A Stobart; P J Stobart; Mrs L E Rigg.

Total grants: £744,000 (1998)
General: Up to 50 grants a year, nearly all made on a recurring basis to Christian religious and missionary bodies. The trust wishes to emphasise that unsolicited applications are most unlikely to succeed.

The trustees are directors and shareholders of J Stobart and Sons Ltd, which gives the trust around £500,000 a year, forming the major part of its income. The total income in 1998 was £843,000 and its assets were a little over £3 million. The grants list for that year showed 30 organisations in receipt of grants over £1,000, 25 of which were supported in the previous year. The major beneficiaries were: Operation Mobilisation (£150,000 in 1998, £101,000 in 1997); World Vision (£105,000 and £60,000); Mission Aviation Fellowship (£80,000 and £51,000); and Keswick Convention (£118,000 and £7,000).

In 1998 these made up 61% of the grant total. A further nine grants to previously supported organisations were for between £10,000 and £26,000 and accounted for another 22% of the total. The largest went to Way to Life, Tearfund, London City Mission, Open Air Mission and Every Home Crusade (each receiving £20,000 or more).

The five new beneficiaries were Manchester City Mission (£30,000), Evangelical Alliance (£10,000), Trans World Radio (£5,000), 'SASRA' (£2,500) and Leprosy Mission (£2,000). Just under £8,000 was disbursed in grants of £1,000 or less.

Exclusions: No grants to individuals.

Applications: 'The trust does not welcome applications. Unsolicited applications are most unlikely to be successful.'

The Bernard Sunley Charitable Foundation

General

Geographical focus: *UK and overseas*

53 Grosvenor Street, London W1X 9FH
Tel: 020 7409 1199; **Fax:** 020 7409 7373
Correspondent: Dr Brian Martin, Director
Trustees: John B Sunley; Mrs Joan M Tice; Mrs Bella Sunley; Sir Donald Gosling.

Total grants: £3.2 million (1998/99)
General: The grant-making pattern of the foundation has been little changed for many years. Most large grants are for buildings or their refurbishment, or for medical or research equipment. An occasional big exception has been support for university endowments.

The largest grants are mostly in one of four fields:
- schools (usually independent), colleges and universities
- medicine, for research facilities, staff accommodation and general buildings and equipment
- youth, mainly for local building projects but often through national youth organisations
- community welfare, covering most forms of disability or need, though few child welfare organisations appear to be supported.

These main areas are said to account, typically, for about 80% of the value of the grants, in approximately equal proportions over time. There is also, in most years, a substantial value of grants for art and museum projects, for churches and for wildlife and conservation. The geographical spread is narrow, with most of the money, and the grants, going for work in London, Hertfordshire, Kent or Northamptonshire. The relatively small total of grants for work overseas usually includes a few awards for specifically Spanish activities; there are no comparable grants for work in other European countries.

In 1998/99 the trust had assets of £68 million and an income of £3.4 million. Grants totalled £3.2 million and were broken down into the following categories: universities, colleges and schools; the arts, museums, etc.; community aid and recreation; youth and sport; churches and chapels; professional and public bodies, miscellaneous; hospitals, medical schools, research institutions; general medicine; provision for older people, including housing; service charities; wildlife and the environment; and overseas. Grants in the latter category totalled £88,000 in 1998/99 and £178,000 the year before.

Overseas beneficiaries included Joint Co-operation Trust in Tanzania (£40,000 in two grants), AMREF (£10,000), Book Aid International (£7,500), and Commonwealth Society for the Deaf – Sound Seekers and VSO (£2,500 each).

Exclusions: 'We would reiterate that we do not make grants to individuals; we still receive several such applications each week. This bar on individuals applies equally to those people taking part in a project sponsored by a charity such as VSO, Duke of Edinburgh Award Scheme, Trekforce, Scouts and Girl Guides, etc., or in the case of the latter two to specific units of these youth movements.'

Applications: In writing to the correspondent to be considered in January, May or October. The trust has stated: 'The foundation has only three full-time members of staff, and so cannot actively seek projects to support, having to rely on unsolicited applications or upon trustee-originated intelligence .... The accounts of organisations which send in applications are very closely examined and are viewed more favourably if they are up to date.'

The letter should include clear succinct details covering:
- what project the grant is required for
- cost, sources of expected funding and how much has been raised or pledged to date
- if it is for a building, some back-up such as costings and drawings
- the last set of audited or independently examined accounts (as the case may be) should be enclosed, plus any annual report or review prepared by the charity
- any appeal documentation.

Tadworth and Walton Overseas Aid Trust (TWOAT)

Third world development and public awareness

Geographical focus: *Developing countries*

49 Shelvers Way, Tadworth,
Surrey KT20 5QL
Tel & Fax: 01737 350452
e-mail: mike.fox@iclway.co.uk
website: members.aol.com/twoatnet
Correspondent: Mike Fox

Total grants: £8,200 (1998/99)
Grants overseas: £8,200

General: The aims of this charity are to:
- raise funds to relieve poverty in the third world
- tell people of third world problems
- sponsor visits to the third world
- be non-sectarian and enable local people to make donations towards third world needs
- be an example to communities.

In 1998/99 the trust had an income of £6,900 and its total expenditure was £8,200. The trust has now donated over £100,000 since it was formed in 1982.

Beneficiaries have included: San Andres Children's Home in Chosica – Peru towards building extra toilets and showers (£750); Hope Now to assist its House of Babies orphanage in Cherkassy – Ukraine and Motivation to train local people to manufacture wheelchairs to meet the needs of people in Honduras (£600 each); Street Child India to establish a shelter for homeless children; and St John's School for the Deaf in The Gambia to provide materials for the school's vocational training programme (£500 each), with £350 each to Eye Camps in India and St John Ophthalmic Hospital in Jerusalem. Grants are also given to both gap year students and VSO volunteers for projects in the developing world.

Exclusions: Projects must be of at least three months' duration and have longer-term benefits.

Applications: In writing to the correspondent. Please note the trust states its funds are very limited and it prefers to support projects in the third world which have links with Surrey.

The Lady Tangye Charitable Trust

Catholic, overseas aid, general

Geographical focus: *UK and worldwide, with some preference for the Midlands*

55 Warwick Crescent, Arthur Road,
Birmingham B15 2LH
Tel: 0121 454 4698
Correspondent: The Clerk

Total grants: £25,000 (1997/98)

General: In 1997/98 the trust's assets totalled £468,000; it had an income of £36,000 and made grants totalling £25,000. It appears to make grants worldwide and has some preference for the Midlands, Catholic charities and overseas aid organisations.

Of the 13 grants made, 12 were for £2,000. Beneficiaries included Amnesty International, CAFOD and UNICEF.

Applications: In writing to the correspondent.

C B & H H Taylor Trust

Quaker, development, general

Geographical focus: *Worldwide, with a preference for the West Midlands and Ireland*

c/o Home Farm, Abberton, Pershore, Worcestershire WR10 2NR
Correspondent: W J B Taylor, Trustee
Trustees: Mrs C H Norton; Mrs E J Birmingham; J A B Taylor; W J B Taylor; Mrs C M Penny; T W Penny.

Total grants: £127,000 (1999/2000)
General: The trust's geographical areas of benefit are:

- organisations serving the West Midlands
- organisations outside the West Midlands where the trust has well-established links
- organisations in Ireland
- UK-based charities working overseas.

The general areas of benefit are:

- Religious Society of Friends (Quakers) and other religious denominations (usually around 75% of the grant total)
- healthcare projects
- social welfare: community groups; children and young people; older people; people who are disadvantaged and disabled; people who are homeless; housing initiatives; and counselling and mediation agencies
- education: adult literacy schemes; employment training; and youth work
- penal affairs: work with offenders and ex-offenders; and police projects
- the environment and conservation
- the arts: museums and art galleries; and music and drama
- Ireland: cross-community health and social welfare projects
- UK charities working overseas on long-term development projects.

The trust favours specific applications. It does not usually award grants on an annual basis for revenue costs. Applications are encouraged from minority groups and woman-led initiatives. Grants, which are made only to or through registered charities, range from £500 to £3,000. Larger grants are seldom awarded.

In 1999/2000 the trust had assets of £5.7 million and an income of £132,000. Management and administration totalled only £850. Grants to 104 organisations totalled £127,000.

Grants included £2,000 each to Little Star Chechnya and Oxfam – Mozambique, and £1,000 each to Farm Africa and Sivaniria.

Exclusions: The trust does not fund: individuals (whether for research, expeditions, educational purposes, etc.); local UK projects or groups outside the West Midlands; or projects concerned with travel or adventure.

Applications: There is no formal application form. Applicants should write to the correspondent giving the charity's registration number, a brief description of the charity's activities and details of the specific project for which the grant is being sought. Applications should include a budget for the proposed work together with a copy of the charity's most recent accounts. Trustees will also wish to know what funds have already been raised for the project and how the shortfall will be met.

The trust states that it receives more applications than it can support. Therefore, even if work falls within its policy it may not be able to help, particularly if the project is outside the West Midlands.

Trustees meet twice-yearly in May and November. Applications will be acknowledged if an sae is provided.

The Three Oaks Trust

Welfare (see below)

Geographical focus: *Overseas and UK, with a preference for West Sussex*

PO Box 243, Crawley,
West Sussex RH10 6YB
Correspondent: The Trustees
Trustees: The Three Oaks Family Trust Co. Ltd.

Total grants: £186,000 to organisations (1998/99)

Grants overseas: £53,000

General: Grants are given to UK organisations for: projects which aid people with psychological or emotional difficulties; educational projects where there is a special needs element; support to individuals and families living in the community (towards families staying together); physical disability; welfare and illness; medical research; environmental issues; and overseas aid.

In 1998/99 the assets totalled £6.4 million with an income of £234,000. Grants were approved totalling £378,000, of which £186,000 was paid to organisations during the year (including £48,000 to overseas projects) and £15,000 to individuals. The remainder was reserved for future commitments; £33,000 to be paid in 2000 and £124,000 to be given during 2001–2005.

Overseas grants included those to Help the Aged towards the I-CARE sight saving project in India and Sight Savers International for sight saving projects worldwide. Also, under the 'physical disability' heading, a grant of £5,000 was given to Medical Foundation for the Care of Victims of Torture.

Applications: The trust states in its annual report that it intends to continue supporting the organisations it has supported in the past and is not planning to fund any new projects in the near future. To save administration costs it does not respond to requests unless it is considering making a donation.

The Tilda Foundation

Health, education, Asian charities, general

Geographical focus: *UK and Asia*

c/o Tilda Limited, Coldharbour Lane,
Rainham, Essex RM13 9YQ
Tel: 01708 717777; **Fax:** 01708 717700
Correspondent: Shilen Thakrar
Trustees: S Thakrar; R Thakrar; V Thakrar; R Samani.

Total grants: £38,000 (1997/98)

General: The trust makes grants towards health, education, Asian charities and for other purposes.

In 1997/98 the trust had an income of £134,000, comprised mainly of donations. Grants to 20 organisations totalled £38,000. The large surplus, £96,000, was transferred into the capital account, resulting in assets at the year end totalling £131,000.

Beneficiaries of larger grants included Raghuvanshi Charitable Trust and Self Realisation Fellowship (£10,000 each), Arpana Charity (£4,000), Vasravi Water Works (£3,000) and Bharatiya Vidya Bhavan (£2,500). Other beneficiaries included Asian Foundation for Help (£100).

Applications: In writing to the correspondent.

The Tisbury Telegraph Trust

Christian, overseas aid, general
Geographical focus: *UK and overseas*

35 Kitto Road, Telegraph Hill,
London SE14 5TW
e-mail: rogero@howzatt.demon.co.uk
Correspondent: Mrs E Orr, Trustee
Trustees: John Davidson; Alison Davidson; Eleanor Orr; Roger Orr; Sonia Phippard.

Total grants: £65,000 (1998/99)
General: The trust gives grants to Christian organisations, international aid agencies and large UK charities, supporting a mix of new and previously supported recipients.

In 1998/99 the trust's assets totalled £80,000 and its income was almost entirely comprised of Gift Aid donations of £77,000. Grants totalling £65,000 were made to 60 organisations. International aid and development organisations to benefit included Ethiopiaid (£3,000), World Vision (£2,500) and Tearfund (£2,000) with £300 each to Leprosy Mission and Traidcraft Exchange.

Exclusions: No grants to individuals towards expeditions or courses.

Applications: In writing to the correspondent. However, it is extremely rare that unsolicited applications are successful and the trust does not respond to applications unless an sae is included.

The Tory Family Foundation

General

Geographical focus: *International and Kent, principally in the locality of Folkestone*

The Estate Office, Etchinghill Golf, Folkestone, Kent CT18 8FA
Tel: 01303 862280
Correspondent: P N Tory, Trustee
Trustees: P N Tory; J N Tory; Mrs S A Rice.

Total grants: £80,000 (1998/99)
Grants overseas: £12,000

General: The trust states grants are given predominantly to organisations local to Kent, particularly Folkestone. Grants are also given to UK organisations if their work would benefit local people. A small number of grants are also given to overseas organisations.

The trust was established in 1984. By 1998/99 it had assets of £2.2 million and an income of £135,000. After expenses of £25,000 the trust gave 71 grants totalling £80,000, including £12,000 in 14 grants in the category 'overseas'. This included grants of £2,000 each to APT Enterprise Development, Churches Commission and Marie Stopes International. Smaller grants included those to Sight Savers International (£1,000), UNICEF (£500) and 'humanitarian educational and long term projects' (£100).

Exclusions: UK grants are only given in Kent. Only selected correspondence/appeals are acknowledged to keep expenses to a minimum. No grants are given for further education or to non-registered charities.

Applications: In writing to the correspondent at any time.

The Toy Trust

Children

Geographical focus: *Worldwide, but mostly UK*

British Toy & Hobby Association,
80 Camberwell Road, London SE5 0EG
Tel: 020 7701 7271
Correspondent: Mrs Karen Baxter

Trustees: The British Toy and Hobby Association; T G Willis; A Munn; J D Hunter; N Austin; D L Hawtin.

Total grants: £191,000 (1999)

General: This trust is administered by British Toy and Hobby Association (BTHA) and all the trustees are also officers of the Association. It makes grants to children's charities, including charities working in crisis situations which are connected with children.

In 1999 the trust had assets of £136,000 and an income of £146,000 was derived mainly from fundraising events such as a family fun day and a dinner dance. The BTHA also donated £16,000. Grants to 51 children's causes totalled £191,000. The trust gave a list of the top eight donations, which included UK Committee for UNICEF (£13,000), Children in Crisis (£6,250) and World Vision (£5,000).

Applications: In writing to the correspondent.

Fred & Pat Tuckman Foundation

International aid and development
Geographical focus: Worldwide

6 Cumberland Road, Barnes, London SW13 9LY
Fax: 020 8746 3918
Correspondent: Mrs P C Tuckman, Trustee

Total grants: £6,300 (1998/99)
Grants overseas: £6,300

General: The trust gives grants to students, averaging around £400. A number of small grants are given to well-established charities, such as Breadline Africa, Ethiopiaid, Intermediate Technology, MIND, Sight Savers International, UKJAID, UNICEF and World Jewish Relief.

In 1998/99 the trust had an income of £7,600 and gave grants totalling £6,300. No grant information was available since 1994/95, when grants totalled £1,600 with the organisations listed above receiving £10 to £50.

Applications: In writing to the correspondent.

The TUUT Charitable Trust

General, but with a bias towards trade union favoured causes
Geographical focus: Worldwide

Congress House, Great Russell Street, London WC1B 3LQ
Tel: 020 7637 7116; **Fax:** 020 7637 7087
Correspondent: J L Wallace, Secretary
Trustees: Lord Christopher; J Monks; J Knapp; A Tuffin; M Walsh; M Bradley.

Total grants: £108,000 (1998/99)

General: The trust was set up by the trade union movement in 1969 for the sole purpose of owning the unit trust management company. It was the intention that profits distributed by the company should go to good causes rather than individual shareholders. It is a requirement of the trust deed that all trustees must be trade unionists, the intention being to ensure that causes benefiting should broadly be those that would be supported by the movement.

In 1998/99 the trust had assets of £1.7 million and an income of £119,000. Grants totalled £108,000. Beneficiaries included: Hope and Homes for Children, providing a small family home for 10 children in Mozambique; The GAP Foundation in The Gambia, helping in its crop planting project by funding two wells; One World Action towards six community shelters which helped save the lives of over 25,000 people during the Bangladeshi floods; and War on Want to strengthen the Bangladesh Agricultural Farm Labourers' Federation by providing a literacy and numeracy programme for landless labourers and to raise awareness and the profile of trade unionism.

Applications: 'Request for Donation' forms will be supplied on request.

Bernard Van Leer Foundation (UK) Trust

Child development
Geographical focus: *Worldwide, but mostly UK*

The Royal Bank of Scotland plc, Private Trust and Taxation, 2 Festival Square, Edinburgh EH3 9SU
Tel: 0131 523 2648; **Fax:** 0131 228 9889
Correspondent: David Macdonald
Trustees: The Royal Bank of Scotland plc.

Total grants: nil (1999/2000)
General: Grants are given to governmental and non-governmental projects seeking to improve the lives and opportunities of young people. The following is taken from the trust's guidelines: 'Our mission is to enhance opportunities for children from zero to seven years, growing up in circumstances of social and economic disadvantage, with the objective of developing their innate potential to the greatest extent possible. We concentrate on children from zero to seven years because scientific findings have demonstrated that interventions in the early years of childhood are most effective in yielding lasting benefits to children and society.'

Grants are made in 40 countries aimed at advancing approaches to child development and sharing the knowledge and experience gained. Preference is given to projects in countries where the Van Leer group of companies is based.

Grants are given for a variety of projects: in both developing and industrialised countries; in urban slums, shanty towns and remote rural areas; which focus on children living in violent settings, children of ethnic and cultural minorities, children of single or teenage parents and children of refugees or migrants; which work to improve quality in daycare centres, pre-schools, health or other services; which may develop community-based services; or which may improve the quality of home environment by working with parents, family members or caregivers.

No grants were made from 1998 to 2000, although this was not due to any policy change; the trust is expected to return to its former levels of giving in the near future. In 1996/97 grants totalled £395,000.

Exclusions: Grants are not given to individuals, nor for the general support of organisations. The trust does not provide study, research or travel grants or reply to general appeals.

Applications: In writing to the correspondent at any time. Applications should include: charity title or description of activities; charity commission or tax-exemption status; staff details; contact name, address and telephone number; summary of current work and latest annual report; description of projects/proposals/areas of work for which funding is required, including costs, funds raised and details of any funding promised; indication of the number of beneficiaries likely to benefit and how the work will help them; and evaluation and monitoring procedures to be used.

All applications are acknowledged, and the trust may contact organisations for further details. There is a continuous process of assessment and applicants are advised of any decisions as well as any conditions attached to it.

The trust welcomes written or telephone enquiries from potential applicants requesting further information before applying.

The Van Neste Foundation

Third world, disabled and older people, religion, community and Christian family life, respect for the sanctity and dignity of life

Geographical focus: UK, especially the Bristol area, and overseas

15 Alexandra Road, Bristol BS8 2DD
Tel: 0117 973 5167
Correspondent: Fergus Lyons, Secretary
Trustees: M T M Appleby, Chair;
F J F Lyons; G J Walker.

Total grants: £217,000 (1999/2000)
Grants overseas: £20,000

General: The trustees currently give priority to the following:

- third world
- disabled and older people
- advancement of religion
- community and Christian family life
- respect for the sanctity and dignity of life.

These objectives are reviewed from time to time but applications falling outside them are unlikely to be considered. In 1999/2000 the trust had assets of £5.2 million and an income of £264,000. In all, 29 grants totalling £217,000 were made.

The four grants under the heading 'third world' totalled almost £20,000 and were £6,000 to Franciscan Sisters of the Divine Motherhood to train African sisters, £5,000 each to Familia Trust to secure homes for orphaned children in India and Health Unlimited for a project in Peru, and £3,900 to Abufari Project in Brazil to build and adapt a boat for fishing.

Exclusions: No grants to individuals or to large, well-known charities. Applications are only considered from UK-registered charities.

Applications: Applications should be in the form of a concise letter setting out the clear objectives to be obtained, which must be charitable. Information must be supplied concerning agreed funding from other sources together with a timetable for achieving the objectives of the appeal and a copy of the latest accounts.

The foundation does not normally make grants on a continuing basis. To keep overheads to a minimum only successful applications are acknowledged. Even then it may be a matter of months before any decision can be expected, depending on the dates of the trustees' meetings.

The Scurrah Wainwright Charity

Social reform, root causes of poverty and injustice

Geographical focus: Preference for Yorkshire and South Africa

5 Tower Place, York YO1 9RZ
Tel: 01904 641971
Correspondent: J Reilly
Trustees: R S Wainwright;
J M Wainwright; H A Wainwright;
M S Wainwright; T M Wainwright;
P Wainwright; H Scott; R Bhaskar.

Total grants: £116,000 (1999/2000)
General: The trust supports a wide range of charitable projects with an emphasis on social reform and tackling the root causes of poverty and injustice. Applications from the north of England,

particularly Leeds and Yorkshire, generally will be given strong priority; the trustees also have an interest in Zimbabwe. In exceptional cases, the trust may make a personal award to an individual in recognition of some outstanding personal commitment relevant to the trust's interests; for the period 1999 to 2002 the trust is supporting accessible public art in Leeds as part of the city's regeneration.

Grants have ranged from less than £100 to over £25,000, but there is no minimum or maximum. Support may be given in stages, for example a £30,000 grant over three years via three annual payments of £10,000. The trustees prefer to receive a progress report within a year of making a grant, but this is not a condition of support.

In 1999/2000 the trust had assets of £2.2 million and an income of £110,000. A total of £116,000 was given in 34 grants. Oxfam receives the largest grant each year (£45,000 this year) for its work in South Africa. An annual grant is also given to Zimbabwe Educational Foundation (based in Leeds), which received £10,000 in 1999/2000.

Exclusions: No grants for medical research or animal welfare.

Applications: In writing to the correspondent. Applications are expected to provide background information about themselves and/or their organisation, the work they wish to pursue and their plans for its practical implementation, which will involve an outline budget and details of any other source of finance. The most recent income and expenditure accounts and balance sheets should be included.

The trustees meet in March, July and November. Applications should be received by the first day of the preceding month.

Wallington Missionary Mart and Auctions

Christian mission
Geographical focus: *Worldwide*

99 Woodmansterne Road, Carshalton Beeches, Surrey SM5 4EG
Tel: 020 8643 3616
website: www.wallingtonmissionary.org.uk
Correspondent: B E Chapman, Company Secretary
Trustees: Council of Management: V W W Hedderly, Chair; B E Chapman; Mrs S P Collett; H F Curwood; D C Lewin; Mrs S M Symes; Mrs F L Willey; G C Willey.

Total grants: £208,000 (2000)
General: The purpose of this non-denominational charity is the advancement of Christianity worldwide. It has no permanent endowment but it obtains income from the sale of goods donated through two operating arms, Missionary Mart and Wallington Missionary Auctions. Donors can allocate the net sale proceeds to the Christian charity of their choice. Grants are given to registered UK Christian charities, mostly operating overseas. Grants are also given to individuals embarking on missionary work (although the grants are paid to the organisation involved).

In 2000 grants totalled £208,000. In the previous year, grants to 175 organisations totalled £241,000 with beneficiaries including OMF International (UK) (£19,000), Mission Aviation Fellowship (£18,000), Tearfund (£17,000) and Breadline (£1,300). The majority of grants were for less than £1,000.

Exclusions: Non-Christian outreach and UK appeals are not considered.

Applications: In writing to the correspondent, including an sae. Grants are considered throughout the year.

The Waterside Trust

Christian and welfare purposes
Geographical focus: Worldwide

56 Palmerston Place,
Edinburgh EH12 5AY
Tel: 0131 225 6366; **Fax:** 0131 220 1041
Correspondent: Robert Clark
Trustees: Irvine Bay Trustee Company.

Total grants: £2.1 million (1999)
General: The trust supports Christian causes in the UK and overseas. Grants are made to 'provide adult Christian formation and pastoral care of the young, offer educational and recreational activities for disadvantaged young people, provide care and support for the elderly and deprived families, especially those with young children, engage in community development and the social rehabilitation of the unemployed, the homeless, the mentally ill, ex-offenders, refugees and those with a history of substance abuse'. Grants usually range from £250 to £20,000, although larger grants may be given overseas.

In 1999 there was an extensive list of overseas donations worth over £1 million and going all over the world, although most of this was given to Catholic organisations. The four largest grants were £169,000 to Duchenne Muscular Dystrophy Research Centre in USA, £156,00 to St Stephen's Priory in Israel, £93,000 to Catholic Research Centre in Malaysia and £78,000 to Pontificia Universidade Catholica in Brazil.

Exclusions: No grants to individuals, environmental projects, arts organisations, conservation groups, endowment appeals or major research projects.

Applications: In writing to the correspondent for consideration on an ongoing basis.

The Wates Foundation

General (see below)
Geographical focus: Worldwide, but mostly UK

1260 London Road, Norbury,
London SW16 4EG
Tel: 020 8764 5000; **Fax:** 020 8679 1541
Correspondent: Brian Wheelwright, Director
Trustees: John Wates, Chair; Ann Ritchie; Michael Wates; David Wates; Jane Wates; Revd Jonathan Edwards. (The grants committee also includes other members of the Wates family.)

Total grants: £1.6 million (1999/2000)
Grants overseas: £63,000

General: Grants are given predominately in south London in the areas of homelessness, unemployment, and substance abuse and offending. In 1999/2000 the trust had assets of £36 million and an income of £1.7 million. Grants totalled £1.6 million including £63,000 in 10 grants in the category 'overseas'.

The trust states that overseas grants are not available to new applicants, only to groups which have previously been supported by the trust.

Exclusions: No grants to:
- individuals
- large well-established UK charities
- umbrella organisations
- large building projects
- other grant-making bodies
- medical appeals
- sporting, social or fundraising events
- foreign travel including expeditions
- conferences
- repairs of churches or church appeals
- overseas projects (except those already funded)
- local projects outside Greater London.

Grants are only given to UK-registered organisations.

Applications: On the standardised single application form of the London Funders Group, which is available from the trust. A brief covering letter, accounts, job descriptions of any posts for which funding is sought and a business plan are also required. Applications should also include information on staffing details, management committee and name, address and telephone number of a suitable referee. Please note that applications from local overseas organisations are not considered.

The Mary Webb Trust

General

Geographical focus: *UK and overseas*

Cherry Cottage, Hudnall Common, Little Gaddesden, Berkhamsted, Hertfordshire HP4 1QN
Correspondent: Mrs C M Nash, Trustee
Trustees: Martin Ware; Mrs Jacqueline Fancett; Mrs Cherry Nash.

Total grants: £289,000 (1998/99)
Grants overseas: £29,000

General: The trust has continued its policy of generally supporting smaller charities. In 1998/99 the trust had assets of £1.1 million generating an income of £69,000. Grants, which appear to have been paid from the income and the assets, were given to 135 organisations and totalled £289,000.

The trust broke down its grantgiving as follows (1997/98 figures in brackets):

social services	£94,000	(£98,000)
health	£85,000	(£71,000)
environment	£36,000	(£59,000)
International	£29,000	(£43,000)
culture/recreation	£23,000	(£28,400)
education/research	£14,000	(£15,000)
philanthropic	£5,300	(£16,000)
religion	£2,800	(£200)
development/housing	nil	(£11,000)

Grants ranged from £500 to £20,000. Grants included £2,000 to World in Need and £1,000 to Tools for Self Reliance. Previous recipients have included Africa Now, Ethiopiaid, Intermediate Technology, Fairtrade Foundation, Ugandan Society for Disabled Children and World Vision.

Exclusions: No grants to individuals or non-registered charities.

Applications: The trustees have previously stated that they are 'concerned by the large number of appeals received during the year. They prefer to make their own enquiries and find it difficult to handle the large volume of documents and unsolicited accounts sent to them'.

The trustees meet quarterly in March, May, August and December; applications need to be received by the month prior to the trustees' meetings.

The Westcroft Trust

International understanding, overseas aid, Quaker, Shropshire

Geographical focus: *Asia, Africa, UK*

32 Hampton Road, Oswestry, Shropshire SY11 1SJ
Correspondent: Mary Cadbury, Managing Trustee
Trustees: Dr Edward P Cadbury; Mary C Cadbury; Richard G Cadbury; James E Cadbury; Erica R Cadbury.

Total grants: £94,000 (1998/99)
Grants overseas: £35,000

General: Currently the trustees have five main areas of interest:
- international understanding, including conflict resolution and the material needs of the third world
- religious causes, particularly for social outreach, usually for the Society of

Friends (Quakers) but also of those originating in Shropshire
- development of the voluntary sector in Shropshire
- special needs of those with disabilities, primarily in Shropshire
- development of community groups and reconciliation between different cultures in Northern Ireland.

The trustees favour charities with low administrative overheads and those which pursue clear policies of equal opportunity in meeting need. Printed letters signed by the great and good are wasted on them, as is glossy literature. Few grants are given for capital or endowment. The only support for medical education is for expeditions abroad for pre-clinical students. Medical aid, education and relief work in developing countries is supported, but only through UK agencies. International disasters may be helped in response to public appeals. The core of the trust's programme is regular support for a wide variety of work towards international peace and understanding, social welfare and those with disabilities.

In 1998/99 the trust had assets of £2.2 million and an income of £90,000. Grants totalled £94,000, including 54 grants totalling £35,000 in the 'overseas' category. These were further broken down as follows:

medical aid	18	£9,700
education	15	£8,500
relief work	14	£11,000
international understanding	7	£6,400

Recipients included Bangladesh Floods (£1,500), Budirio Trust for education in South Africa (£1,300) and UNICEF Children's Appeal for disaster relief (£1,000).

Exclusions: No grants to individuals.

Applications: In writing to the correspondent, including the previous year's accounts. Telephone calls and faxes are not welcomed. There are no application forms or set formats. Applicants should state their purpose, financial needs and resources and cover no more than three pages. No acknowledgements are given and unsuccessful applicants will only be notified if an sae is included. Applications are considered six times a year. Some annual grants are made by telepay. If full bank details are given in the application, time and correspondence can be saved later.

The Westminster Foundation for Democracy

Strengthening democracy
Geographical focus: *Worldwide*

2nd Floor, 125 Pall Mall,
London SW1Y 5EA
Tel: 020 7930 0408; **Fax:** 020 7930 0449
e-mail: wfd@wfd.org
website: www.wfd.org
Correspondent: The Chief Executive
Trustees: Ernie Ross, Chair; Georgina Ashworth; Frances D'Souza; Nicola Duckworth; Tim Garton Ash; Nik Gowing; Mary Kaldor; Archie Kirkwood; Gillian Merron; Elizabeth Smith; Richard Spring; Gary Streeter; Ieuan Wyn Jones.

Total grants: £4 million (2000/01)
Grants overseas: £4 million

General: The foundation gives grants, seldom for more than £30,000 and more than two thirds for less than £10,000, for projects to support democracy anywhere in the world. Its work is concentrated in Central and Eastern Europe, in the former Soviet Union and in anglophone Africa.

The foundation receives almost all its money from the Westminster government (which has increased its annual income from £3 million to £4 million a year), but it makes its own decisions about the projects to be supported. It describes its policies as follows:

'The ... foundation may support any project which is aimed at building pluralist democratic institutions abroad. These may include:

- election systems or administration
- parliaments or other representative institutions
- political parties
- independent media
- legal reform
- trades unions
- human rights groups
- women's organisations
- other political non-governmental institutions.

'It will give preference to projects which contain clear action plans, designed to achieve concrete results; those whose effects will be lasting; and to building up organisations which can be self-sustaining, rather than encouraging continuing dependence on outside assistance.

'The foundation concentrates its funding on three priority areas:

- Central and Eastern Europe
- the former Soviet Union
- anglophone Africa.

'It will consider sympathetically applications for projects elsewhere in the world. The foundation seeks to avoid duplication of effort with other governmental and non-governmental agencies and to reinforce their commitment to enhancing participatory democracy. Where possible, it will carry out projects in cooperation with other organisations and foundations. Support for individual political parties is provided through that part of the foundation's budget which is channelled through the UK political parties. Individual parties from overseas seeking ... funding for their programmes must therefore apply to the individual UK party with which they have links.

'Alternatively, the foundation may carry out cross-party projects, where a range of political parties from a country are involved, and these projects are funded directly from the foundation's general resources. The foundation does not seek to foster any particular model of democracy. It seeks to keep administrative costs to a minimum, and will not support the administrative costs of its recipients beyond what is absolutely necessary, nor provide equipment beyond reasonable need.'

In 1999/2000 331 projects were approved from 444 proposals. The main areas of work were as follows:

	No.	Total
political party training and strengthening	135	£1,531,000
building civil society	73	£718,000
strengthening the media	31	£331,000
human rights	30	£297,000
women's political and civil involvement	27	£215,000
parliament	16	£147,000
legal organisations and reform	11	£105,000
trades unions	3	£17,000
cross party	1	£6,000

The value of the projects by area was as follows:

Central and Eastern Europe (EU accession countries)	£183,000
Central and Eastern Europe (other countries)	£1,497,000
CIS and Mongolia	£588,000
anglophone Africa	£662,000
other countries	£497,000

Five projects had a budget of more than £40,000, three being for work in former Yugoslavia: £80,000 funding for the Conservative Party to continue work within its West Balkan Initiative; and two projects funded through the Labour Party to assist the Social Democratic Party of Bosnia-Herzegovina – £64,000 to help purchase necessary equipment and £51,000 to produce materials for the April 2000 municipal elections. The other large awards were for various Eastern European party leaders to attend the Conservative Party conference (£44,000), and £48,000 to support a meeting of the Democratic Union of Africa alliance in Ghana, through the Conservative Party.

Other projects included: £18,000 funding for the Labour Party to assist political awareness training for the Sandinista Front for National Liberation in Nicaragua; £15,000 for a training programme to provide civic education to women in rural Kenya; £10,000 core funding of Deca Press Information Agency in Moldova; £9,000 support for Human Rights in China's website; £6,000 to fund Association Obnovlenie providing legal advice and support to Romany people in Bulgaria; and £5,000 to help the Democratic Left in Slovakia organise a media training workshop.

Exclusions: No grants for conferences, research, educational scholarships, cultural, health or social projects.

Applications: In writing to the correspondent. Applicants are advised first to obtain the trust's pamphlet *Overview*, which includes some guidelines for applications. Project evaluations are part of the conditions of assistance from the foundation. Trustees normally meet in January, April, July and October.

The Wilkins Memorial Trust

General in Nepal

Geographical focus: Nepal

57 Forest Edge, Buckhurst Hill,
Essex IG9 5AE
Tel: 020 8504 9023
Correspondent: Mrs Melanie Hicks, Trustee
Trustees: Roland Randall, Chair; Michael Pipe; Richard Evans; Melanie Hicks.

Total grants: £7,400 (1998/99)
Grants overseas: £7,400

General: This charity stated in its 1998/99 annual report that it made grants in order to 'advance education, relieve poverty, preserve and protect health, conserve, protect and restore the nature resources, beauty and animal life, especially in Nepal.

'The primary aim of the charity is to continue the work of the Wilkins' family who died in the Kathmandu air disaster of 28 September 1992. This is done by aiding in rural community development and conservation projects throughout Nepal, and, especially in memory of the Wilkins children, projects relating to the education and development of the children and young people in Nepal.'

In 1998/99 the trust's assets totalled £78,000 and it had an income of £13,000, of which £8,300 was derived from donations. Grants totalled £7,400 and were recurrent.

Grants vary in size, with amounts tailored to the needs of the organisation with which the trust has established connections. Environmental Camps for Conservation Awareness, which works with secondary school age children and their communities, was the major beneficiary, receiving £4,700. The

Community Based Rehabilitation Project in Pokhara, which works with children who are disabled and their families, seeking to spread awareness of disability issues within the local village communities, is another major beneficiary and is likely to be given greater emphasis during future years.

Educational scholarships have been provided for two girls, but no further scholarships are presently being considered. Sponsorship of the young girl rescued by Mrs Helen Wilkins and subsequently adopted by a Nepali woman is a joint project with the Pitchford & Wilkins Memorial Trust, in honour of the special relationship both families have with this particular young girl. As most of the organisations presently supported will continue to need help for the foreseeable future, the trustees will apply stringent checks to applications from any other organisations seeking help.

Applications: In writing to the correspondent.

The World Trust

Christianity, relief of sickness and distress

Geographical focus: Worldwide

Holly Howe, Copt Hewick, Rippon, North Yorkshire HG4 5BY
Tel: 01765 605508
Correspondent: Susan Goldsbrough, Hon. Secretary

Total grants: £5,100 (1998/99)
Grants overseas: £5,100

General: 'The aims of The World Trust are to promote any charitable purpose throughout the world, in particular the advancement of education, the protection of health and the relief of poverty, disability and sickness and to promote, improve, develop and maintain public education in, and appreciation of, music and the arts.'

The trust gives grants to a wide range of third world organisations. Beneficiaries have included children's groups including Children of Chernobyl, Edendale Hospital in Natal to support abandoned babies, and Hope and Homes for Children and Vila Maninga towards helping orphaned children in Mozambique. Aid agencies to benefit have included Sandy Gall's Afghanistan Appeal to help landmine victims in Afghanistan, Starlight UK for its work with Bosnian refugees and Verona Fathers' Missionaries for relief work in Sudan. Health organisations supported have included ICR to provide medical care in Cambodia, The President of Poland's Charity to help Polish children who are disabled and Sue Ryder Foundation in Tirana to help Albanians with cancer. Development grants have included those to AMREF for water provision in Kenya, Interaid International for educational facilities in Cambodia and San Lorenzo School in Santiago – Chile to help deprived children.

In 1998/99 the trust had assets of £11,000 and an income of £9,600, including £7,700 from a concert. Total expenditure was £11,000, including £5,100 in grants. Beneficiaries included International Care and Relief (£1,500) and CARE International (£750).

Exclusions: While the trust has given grants to children and nurses, it states that grants are not available to individuals and will not be considered.

Applications: In writing to the correspondent. However, please note that this trust has stated that it gets more applications than it can support.

The Matthews Wrightson Charity Trust

Caring and Christian charities
Geographical focus: UK and some overseas

The Farm, Northington, Alresford, Hampshire SO24 9TH
Correspondent: Adam Lee, Secretary and Administrator
Trustees: Miss Priscilla W Wrightson; Anthony H Isaacs; Guy D G Wrightson; Miss Isabelle S White.

Total grants: £96,000 to organisations (2000)
Grants overseas: £5,200

General: The trustees favour smaller charities or projects, e.g. those seeking to raise under £25,000. They do not usually support large UK charities and those seeking to raise in excess of £250,000; however, support may be given to a charity with a turnover greater than £250,000 if it is a previous recipient.

There is a bias towards innovation, Christian work and organisations helping disadvantaged people reintegrate into the community. The standard grant size in 2000 was £400. Grants are generally made from income rather than assets.

The assets in 2000 stood at £2 million and the income for the year was £83,000. The trust gave 193 grants totalling £96,000, of which £9,100 went to individuals. About a quarter of beneficiaries had received grants in the previous year.

The grants were categorised as follows:

	2000	1999
arts causes	£26,000	£14,000
Christian	£12,000	£9,500
disability	£15,000	£13,000
individuals	£6,100	£9,100
medical	£18,000	£6,800
older people	£800	£3,800
rehabilitation	£8,600	£8,300
worldwide	£5,200	£5,800
youth	£22,000	£22,000
miscellaneous	£3,000	£4,000

Beneficiaries included Mongolia Project for Street Children (£1,200), Intermediate Technology (£800), and £400 each to Africa UK, English Language Scholarships for Tibetans, Angels International, Computer Aid International, Child Hope, Lifeline and Tools for Self Reliance.

Exclusions: No support for individuals (other than visitors to the UK from overseas) seeking education or adventure for personal character building. No support for unconnected local churches, village halls, schools or animal charities.

Applications: In writing to the correspondent. No special forms are used, although latest financial accounts are desirable. One or two sheets (usually the covering letter) are circulated monthly to the trustees, who meet every six months only for policy and administrative decisions. Replies are only sent to successful applicants; allow up to three months for an answer. Please include an sae if an answer is required if unsuccessful. Telephone calls are strongly discouraged.

The trust receives over 1,000 applications a year, 'winners have to make the covering letter more attractive than the 90 others received each month'.

Zephyr Charitable Trust

General

Geographical focus: Worldwide

New Guild House, 45 Great Charles Street, Queensway, Birmingham B3 2LX
Tel: 0121 212 2222
Correspondent: R Harriman, Trust Administrator
Trustees: Elizabeth Breeze; Roger Harriman; David Baldock; Donald I Watson.

Total grants: £31,000 (2000)
General: The trust gives grants to a range of organisations working in the UK and overseas. The trust has a list of 15 beneficiaries who regularly receive grants and very little funds are available for unsolicited applications.

In 2000 the trust had assets of £893,000 and an income of £36,000. Grants ranged from £500 to £3,000 and totalled £31,000.

Beneficiaries included DEC Mozambique Floods Appeal and Intermediate Technology (£3,000 each), Pesticide Trust (£2,100), Medical Foundation for the Care of Victims of Torture (£2,000) and Survival International (£1,900).

Exclusions: No grants to individuals.

Applications: In writing to the correspondent, to be considered twice a year. Unsolicited applications are not encouraged as most of the income is given in recurrent grants.

The Zochonis Charitable Trust

General

Geographical focus: Worldwide, particularly Africa, UK and Greater Manchester

Deloitte & Touche, PO Box 500, 201 Deansgate, Manchester M60 2AT
Correspondent: The Secretary
Trustees: John Zochonis; Richard B James; Alan Whittaker.

Total grants: £1.1 million (1999)
General: The trust gives grants to a range of UK and Greater Manchester charities, although most of the larger grants go to local organisations, especially educational or arts institutions. Organisations working in developing countries are also supported. Grants are generally one-off and although they range from £500 to £150,000, the majority of donations are around £5,000.

In 1999 the trust had assets of £14 million and an income of £1 million. Grants totalled £1.1 million, with all the larger grants being given in the UK.

In 1997/98 overseas recipients included VSO (£40,000), with £5,000 each to Royal African Society, Rhodes Foundation Scholarship Trust and Sight Savers International.

Exclusions: Grants are only given to UK-registered charities and not to individuals.

Applications: In writing to the correspondent.

Index

29th May 1961 Charitable Trust 291

A

A B Charitable Trust 291
AAH – *see Action Against Hunger UK*
ABANTU for Development 37
Acacia Charitable Trust 292
Access 4 Trust 292
ACCW – *see Associated Country Women of the World*
ACORD 37
Action Against Hunger UK 38
Action on Disability and Development 39
Action Health 39
Action International Ministries 40
Action Partners Ministries 41
Action for Southern Africa 42
ActionAid 42
Sylvia Adams Charitable Trust 292
ADD – *see Action on Disability and Development*
ADI – *see Alzheimer's Disease International*
AEF – *see Africa Educational Trust*
Afghanaid 44
Africa Book Case 13
Africa Centre 45
Africa Educational Trust 46
Africa Inland Mission 46
AFRICA NOW 47
African Medical and Research Foundation UK 48
AFS – International Youth Development 49
Agency for Cooperation and Research in Development – *see ACORD*
AHRTAG – *see Healthlink Worldwide*
AID – *see Alternative for India Development*
Aid to Russia and the Republics 50
Aid to the Church in Need (UK) 52

AIM – *see Africa Inland Mission*
AIRE Centre 52
Ajahma Charitable Trust 293
ALA – EU budget line – Financial and technical cooperation with Asian developing countries and Financial and technical cooperation with Latin American countries 258
Alchemy Foundation 294
Allachy Trust 295
H B Allen Charitable Trust 295
Alternative for India Development 53
Alzheimer's Disease International 54
Ambika Paul Foundation 295
Amnesty International 55
AMREF UK – *see African Medical and Research Foundation UK*
Anti-Apartheid Movement – *see Action for Southern Africa*
Anti-Slavery International 56
APT Enterprise Development 57
ApTibeT 57
Arid Lands Initiative 58
ARRC – *see Aid to Russia and the Republics*
Article 19 (Global Campaign for Free Expression) 59
AS Charitable Trust 296
Ashden Charitable Trust 296
Ashworth Charitable Trust 297
Associated Country Women of the World 60
Association for the Promotion of Healthcare in the former Soviet Union – *see HealthProm*
ATD Fourth World 61
Richard Attenborough Charitable Trust 298
Avenue Charitable Trust 298

B

Baby Milk Action 63
Scott Bader Commonwealth Ltd 299
Veta Bailey Charitable Trust 299
Cecile Baines Charitable Trust 300
Balcraig Foundation 300
Balmore Trust 301
Baptist Missionary Society – see BMS World Mission
Baring Foundation 301
Barnabas Trust 304
Batchworth Trust 304
BEARR Trust 64
Berkeley Reafforestation Trust 305
BESO 65
BibleLands 66
Miss Jeanne Bisgood's Charitable Trust 305
Bishop Simeon CR Trust 306
BMAC – see Baby Milk Action
BMS World Mission 67
Boltons Trust 306
BOND 68
Book Aid International 70
P G & N J Boulton Trust 307
Bower Trust 307
BNMT – see Britain-Nepal Medical Trust
Britain-Nepal Medical Trust 71
British Leprosy Relief Association 160
British Overseas NGOs for Development – see BOND
British Red Cross 71
Broad Oak Trust 308
Bromley Trust 308
Brooke Hospital for Animals – see Equine Welfare Grants Programme
Burdens Charitable Foundation 309
Clara E Burgess Charity 310
Audrey and Stanley Burton 1960 Charitable Trust 311
Busoga Trust 73
Noel Buxton Trust – see under 'Noel'

C

CADA – see Coalition of Aid & Development Agencies in Northern Ireland
Edward Cadbury Charitable Trust 311
G W Cadbury Charitable Trust 312
William Adlington Cadbury Charitable Trust 312
CAF – see Charities Aid Foundation
CAFOD 73
CAI – see Child Advocacy International
Calpe Trust 313
Cambodia Trust 75
CamFed 75
Canning Trust 313
Care & Relief for the Young 77
CARE International UK 76
Caring and Sharing Association East Sussex 314
Carpenter Charitable Trust 314
Casey Trust 315
Catholic Fund for Overseas Development – see CAFOD
Catholic Institute for International Relations 78
Thomas Sivewright Catto Charitable Settlement 315
CCETSA – see Canon Collins Educational Trust for Southern Africa
CCFGB – see Christian Children's Fund of Great Britain
Centre for International Briefing 79
Centre for World Development Education – see Worldaware
CEWC see Council for Education in World Citizenship
CfBT Education Services 315
Charities Advisory Trust 316
Charities Aid Foundation 79
Charity Know How 317
Charity Projects – see Comic Relief
Chelsea Square 1994 Trust 319
Cheruby Trust 320
Child Advocacy International 82
ChildHope UK 83
Children in Crisis 84
Children in Distress 85

Children of the Andes 86
Children's Aid Direct 86
Christadelphian Samaritan Fund 320
Christian Aid 87
Christian Children's Fund of Great Britain 88
Christian Medical Fellowship 88
Christian Outreach – Relief and Development 90
Christian Response to Eastern Europe 320
Christian Solidarity Worldwide 91
Christians Abroad (including World Service Enquiry) 91
Church Mission Society 92
Church of Scotland Board of World Mission 93
CIIR – *see Catholic Institute for International Relations*
Civicus 10
Civil Society Challenge Fund 275
J A Clark Charitable Trust 321
Cleaford Christian Trust 321
Clothworkers' Foundation 322
CMF – *see Christian Medical fellowship*
CMS – *see Church Mission Society*
Coalition of Aid & Development Agencies in Northern Ireland 10
CODA International Training 94
Dr R J Colley Charitable Trust 323
Canon Collins Educational Trust for Southern Africa 95
George Henry Collins Charity 323
Comic Relief 324
Commonwealth Relations Trust – *see Nuffield Foundation*
Commonwealth Secretariat 10
Commonwealth Society for the Deaf (Sound Seekers) 95
Commonwealth Youth Exchange Council 96
Concern Universal 97
CONCERN Worldwide 98
Conflict & Humanitarian Affairs Department 279
Cooperation with countries of Central and Eastern Europe, the Balkans, the new Independent States and Mongolia – EU budget line 261
Cooperation with developing countries in Asia, Latin America and Southern Africa – EU budget line 258
Cooperation with Mediterranean countries and the Middle East – EU budget line 260
CORD – *see Christian Outreach – Relief and Development*
Council for Education in World Citizenship 99
Council for World Mission 99
Crosslinks 101
CRY – *see Care & Relief for the Young*
CSW – *see Christian Solidarity Worldwide*
Wallace Curzon Charitable Trust 324
Cusichaca Trust 101
CYEC *see Comonwealth Youth Exchange Council*

D

DAA *see Disability Awareness in Action*
Daneford Trust 13
DEA – *see Development Education Association*
Miriam K Dean Refugee Trust Fund 325
DEC – *see Disasters Emergency Committee*
DEP – *see Manchester Development Education Project*
Department of Development Studies 102
Department for International Development 275
Development and Project Planning Centre 103
Development Awareness Fund 278
Development Directorate General 251
Development Education Association 103
Diana, Princess of Wales Memorial Fund 325
Dickon Trust 327
Dinam Charity 327
Disability Awareness in Action 104
Disasters Emergency Committee 105
Donkey Sanctuary 106

Douglas Charitable Trust *328*
DPPC – *see Development and Project Planning Centre*
Duke of Edinburgh's Award International Association *107*
Dulverton Trust *328*

E

Echo International Health Services Ltd *108*
ECT – *see European Children's Trust*
Edinburgh Medical Missionary Society *108*
Education for Development *110*
John Ellerman Foundation *329*
Edith M Ellis 1985 Charitable Trust *330*
Emerging Markets Charity for Children *331*
Emmanuel Hospital Association *13*
Emmanuel International *111*
EMMS – *see Edinburgh Medical Missionary Society*
Enlargement Directorate General *252*
Enterprise Development Department *282*
Enterprise Development Innovation Fund *282*
Equine Welfare Grants Programme – Brooke Hospital for Animals *331*
Ericson Trust *332*
Ethical Trading Initiative *111*
Ethiopiaid *112*
ETI *see Ethical Trading Initiative*
EuropeAid Co-operation Office *251*
European Children's Trust *112*
European Comunity Humanitarian Office *252*
European Development Fund *252*
European Initiative for Democracy and Human Rights – EU budget line *263*
Everest Marathon Fund *333*
Evergreen Trust *113*
External Relations Directorate General *251*

F

Fairtrade Foundation *114*
FARM Africa *115*
Farthing Trust *333*
Feed the Minds *334*
Allan & Nesta Ferguson Charitable Settlement *335*
Find Your Feet (FYF) *116*
Food and Agricultural Research Management *see FARM Africa*
Food for the Hungry UK *117*
Foreign and Commonwealth Office *274*
Donald Forrester Trust *335*
Timothy Franey Charitable Foundation *336*
Jill Franklin Trust *336*
Sydney E Franklin Deceased's New Second Charity *336*
Frays Charitable Trust *337*
Friends of the Gambia Association *13*
Maurice Fry Charitable Trust *337*
Fulmer Charitable Trust *338*
Fund for Human Need *338*
FYF *see Find Your Feet*

G

Gaia Foundation *117*
Angela Gallagher Memorial Fund *339*
GAP Activity Projects *118*
Gatsby Charitable Foundation *339*
Gibbs Charitable Trusts *340*
GOAL (UK) *119*
Anita Goulden Trust *120*
Grace and Compassion Benedictines *120*
Dr Graham's Homes, Kalimpong, India *121*
Grimmitt Trust *341*
Guernsey Overseas Aid Committee *268*
Walter Guinness Charitable Trust *341*

H

H C D Memorial Fund *342*
Habitat for Humanity – Global Village Programme *14*
Hadley Trust *343*
HAI – *see HelpAge International*

Alfred Haines Charitable Trust *343*
Paul Hamlyn Foundation *344*
Beatrice Hankey Foundation Ltd *345*
Lennox Hannay Charitable Trust *345*
Miss K M Harbinson's Charitable Trust *346*
Harvest Help *122*
Dorothy Hay-Bolton Charitable Trust *346*
Charles Hayward Foundation *346*
HCJB–UK *14*
Headley Trust *348*
Health Unlimited *122*
Healthlink Worldwide *123*
HealthProm *125*
Help International *126*
HelpAge International *127*
Henhurst Charitable Trust *349*
Joanna Herbert-Stepney Charitable Settlement – *see Paget Charitable Trust*
Hilden Charitable Fund *349*
L E Hill Memorial Trust *351*
HMD Response *128*
Jane Hodge Foundation *351*
Holy Ghost Fathers *128*
Joe Homan Charitable Trust *129*
Homeless International *129*
Hope Trust *352*
Human Relief Foundation *352*
Human Rights Watch *130*
Humanitarian Aid, Medical Development – *see HMD Response*
Humanitarian Assistance *279*
Humanitarian and food aid – EU budget line *256*
Hunger Project Trust *131*

I

i to i international projects *132*
IBT – *see International Broadcasting Trust*
ICA:UK/The Institute of Cultural Affairs Development Trust *133*
ICR – *see International Care and Relief*
ICW – *see International Community of Women Living with HIV/AIDS*
IHE – *see International Health Exchange*
IIED – *see International Institute for Environment and Development*
IMF – *see International Monetary Fund*
IMPACT Foundation *133*
India Development Group (UK) Limited *14*
INF – *see International Nepal Fellowship*
Innovations Fund for emerging thinking and methodologies *281*
Institute of Development Studies *134*
Institute for War and Peace Reporting *135*
INTERIGHTS *135*
International Aid Trust *136*
International Alert *137*
International Broadcasting Trust *138*
International Care and Relief *138*
International Centre for the Legal Protection of Human Rights – *see* INTERIGHTS
International Childcare Trust *139*
International Children's Trust *140*
International China Concern UK *14*
International Community of Women Living with HIV/AIDS *141*
International Connections Trust *141*
International Family Health *142*
International Fundraising Group – *see Resource Alliance*
International Health Exchange *143*
International HIV/AIDS Alliance *144*
International Institute for Environment and Development *145*
International Monetary Fund *10*
International Nepal Fellowship *146*
International Planned Parenthood Federation *146*
International Records Management Trust *148*
International Service *149*
International Training and NGO Research Centre – *see INTRAC*
International Voluntary Service *150*
INTRAC *151*
IPPF – *see International Planned Parenthood Federation*

IRMT – *see International Records Management Trust*
Islamic Relief Worldwide 152
Isle of Man Overseas Aid Committee 271
ISPA – Instrument for Structural Policies for Pre-Accession – EU budget line 254
ITDG 153
IWPR – *see Institute for War and Peace Reporting*
IVS – *see International Voluntary Service*

J

J J Charitable Trust 353
Jephcott Charitable Trust 353
Jersey Overseas Aid 265
Jerusalem Trust 354
Jerwood Charitable Foundation and The Jerwood Foundation 355
J G Joffe Charitable Trust 357
Elton John Aids Foundation 357
Joint Cooperation Trust Opportunities 14
Jospice International 154
Just World Partners 154

K

Kaloko Trust 155
Karuna Trust/Aid for India 156
Kings World Trust for Children 14
KINGSCARE 156
Ernest Kleinwort Charitable Trust 358
Kulika Charitable Trust 358

L

Lady Tangye Charitable Trust 415
Beatrice Laing Trust 360
Kirby Laing Foundation 361
Maurice Laing Foundation 362
Maurice and Hilda Laing Charitable Trust 363
Landmine Action 157
Latin Link 158
Law Society Charity 364
Learning for Life 158

William Leech Charity 364
Leigh Trust 365
Leonard Cheshire International 159
Leonard Trust 365
Erica Leonard Trust 366
LEPRA 160
Leprosy Mission 161
LFL – *see Learning for Life*
Linbury Trust 366
Enid Linder Foundation 367
Link Africa – *see Link Community Development*
Link Community Development 162
Link Romania – *see Partnership for Growth*
Liverpool School of Tropical Medicine 163
Lloyd's Charitable Trust 367
Lyndhurst Settlement 368
Lyndhurst Trust 368
Lyras Family Charitable Trust 369

M

M N R Charitable Trust 370
MAF – *see Mission Aviation Fellowship*
Manchester Development Education Project 163
MAP – *see Medical Aid for Palestinians*
Mariapolis Limited 370
Marie Stopes International 218
Marr-Munning Trust 371
Marsh Christian Trust 371
Maxco Trust 372
MEDA – Measures to accompany reforms of the economic and social structures in the Mediterranean non-member countries – EU budget line 260
Medact 164
Médecins Sans Frontières 165
Medical Aid for Palestinians 167
Medical Foundation for the Care of Victims of Torture 167
Medical Missionary Association Healthserve 14
Mercury Phoenix Trust 372
Mercy Corps Scotland 168
Mercy Ships UK 169

Merlin *170*
Merstham Aid Project *373*
Methodist Relief and Development Fund *373*
Metropolitan Drinking Foundation and Cattle Trough *374*
Mettyear Charitable Trust *375*
MIA – see Multi International Aid
Millfield Trust *375*
Minority Rights Group *170*
Mission Aviation Fellowship *171*
Modiano Charitable Trust *376*
John Moores Foundation *376*
Morel Charitable Trust *377*
Morris Charitable Trust *377*
Moss Charitable Trust *378*
Motivation *172*
MRG – see Minority Rights Group
MSI – see Marie Stopes International
Multi International Aid *173*
Muslim Aid *173*
Muslim Hands *174*

N

National Centre for Volunteering *15*
NEF – see New Economics Foundation
Nepal Leprosy Trust *174*
Network Foundation *378*
New Economics Foundation *176*
New Frontiers International *177*
Noel Buxton Trust *379*
Novi Most International *177*
Nuffield Foundation and Commonwealth Relations Trust *380*

O

Father O'Mahoney Memorial Trust *381*
Oakdale Trust *382*
Oasis Trust – Global Action Initiative *178*
Ockenden International *179*
ODI – see Overseas Development Institute
OECD – see Organisation for Economic Co-operation and Development
OMF International *179*
Onaway Trust *382*

One World Action *180*
One World Week *181*
OneWorld International Ltd *181*
Open Society Institute *10*
Operation Mobilisation *183*
Operation Sunshine *14*
Opportunity International *184*
ORBIS *185*
Organisation for Economic Co-operation and Development *10*
ORT – see World ORT
OSI – see Open Society Institute
Overseas Development Institute *186*
OWW – see One World Week
Oxfam *187*
Oxford Mission *189*

P

Paget Charitable Trust *383*
Panahpur Charitable Trust *384*
Panos Institute London *190*
Parthenon Trust *384*
Partnership for Growth *191*
Partnership Programme Agreements *277*
Pattaya Orphanage Trust *192*
Peace Brigades International Volunteers *14*
Peace Child International *192*
People in Aid *10*
Pestalozzi Children's Village Trust *193*
Phare – EU budget line *255*
Philanthropic Trust *385*
Hugh Pilkington Charitable Trust *385*
Pilkington Charities Fund *386*
PLAN International UK *194*
Plunkett Foundation *195*
Polden-Puckham Charitable Foundation *387*
Population Concern *196*
POST – see Purley Overseas Trust
POWER – The International Limb Project *196*
PPP Healthcare Medical Trust *388*
Prairie Trust *389*
W L Pratt Charitable Trust *390*
Pre-accession strategy – EU budget line *254*

Prince of Wales's Charitable
    Foundation 390
Prince's Trust 197
Project HOPE UK 198
Project Trust 199
Purley Overseas Trust 391

R

Raleigh International 199
Eleanor Rathbone Charitable Trust 391
Ruben and Elisabeth Rausing Trust 392
RedR International 200
RefAid 202
Relief Fund for Romania 203
Resource Alliance 204
Returned Volunteer Action 15
RFI for Community Mental Health 204
Rhodes Trust Public Purposes Fund 393
Rhododendron Trust 394
Richardson Family Charitable Trust 394
Karim Rida Said Foundation 394
Right Hand Trust 14
Rokpa Trust 205
Romanian Challenge Appeal 205
Romanian Orphanage Trust – see
    European Children's Trust
Mrs L D Rope's Third Charitable
    Settlement 395
Rotary Foundation 396
Rowan Charitable Trust 397
Joseph Rowntree Charitable Trust 398
Royal Commonwealth Society for the
    Blind – see Sight Savers International
Rufford Foundation 399
Russian European Trust 206
Ryder-Cheshire 207
Ryklow Charitable Trust 1992 400

S

Saferworld 207
Karim Rida Said Foundation 394
Alan and Babette Sainsbury
    Charitable Fund 401
St Francis Leprosy Guild 208
St Joseph's Hospice Association – see
    Jospice International
St Mark's Overseas Aid Trust 402

Saranda Charitable Trust 402
Save the Children 209
Schroder Charity Trust 402
SCIAF – see Scottish Catholic International
    Aid Fund
Scottish Catholic International Aid
    Fund 210
Scottish Education and Action for
    Development 210
Scouloudi Foundation 403
SEAD – see Scottish Education and Action
    for Development
SEM Charitable Trust 404
Send a Cow (& StockAid) 211
Sense International 211
Servite Sisters' Charitable Trust Fund 404
Barnett & Sylvia Shine No 1 & No 2
    Charitable Trust 405
Sight Savers International 212
SIL UK 213
SIM International 214
Skillshare Africa 214
Ernest William Slaughter
    Charitable Trust 405
SMB Trust 406
N Smith Charitable Trust 406
SMOAT – see St Mark's Overseas Aid Trust
SOAS – see Department of Development
    Studies
Social Development Department 281
SOS Children's Villages UK 215
SOS Sahel International 216
Sound Seekers – see Commonwealth Society
    for the Deaf
Souter Charitable Trust 407
W F Southall Trust 407
Spear Charitable Trust 408
Spring Harvest Charitable Trust 408
Spurgeon's Child Care 217
Staples Trust 409
Sir Halley Stewart Trust 410
Stobart Newlands Charitable Trust 413
Marie Stopes International 218
Sudan Volunteer Programme 14
Bernard Sunley Charitable
    Foundation 413
Survival 218

T

TACIS – EU budget line *261*
Tadworth and Walton Overseas Aid Trust *415*
TALC – *see Teaching Aids at Low Cost*
Lady Tangye Charitable Trust *415*
C B & H H Taylor Trust *416*
Teaching Aids at Low Cost *219*
Teaching & Projects Abroad *14*
Tearfund *220*
THET – *see Tropical Health and Education Trust*
Three Oaks Trust *417*
Tibet Foundation *221*
Tibet Relief Fund of the UK *222*
Tilda Foundation *417*
Tisbury Telegraph Trust *418*
TLM – *see Leprosy Mission*
Tools for Self Reliance *222*
Tory Family Foundation *418*
Toy Trust *418*
Traidcraft Exchange *223*
TRANSAID Worldwide *224*
Tropical Health and Education Trust *225*
Fred & Pat Tuckman Foundation *419*
TUUT Charitable Trust *419*
Twin *225*
TWOAT – *see Tadworth and Walton Overseas aid Trust*

U

Uganda Society for Disabled Children *226*
UK Foundation for the South Pacific – *see Just World Partners*
UK Working Group on Landmines – *see Landmine Action*
UKJAID – *see United Kingdom Jewish Aid and International Development*
UMN – *see United Mission to Nepal*
UNICEF UK *227*
United Kingdom Jewish Aid and International Development *228*
United Mission to Nepal *228*
USDC – *see Uganda Society for Disabled Children*

V

Bernard Van Leer Foundation (UK) Trust *420*
Van Neste Foundation *421*
Village AiD *229*
Voluntary Service Overseas *229*
VSO – *see Voluntary Service Overseas*

W

Scurrah Wainwright Charity *421*
Wallington Missionary Mart and Auctions *422*
War on Want *231*
WaterAid *232*
Waterside Trust *423*
Wates Foundation *423*
WDM – *see World Development Movement*
Mary Webb Trust *424*
WER – *see World Emergency Relief*
Westcroft Trust *424*
Westminster Foundation for Democracy *425*
Wilkins Memorial Trust *427*
A B Williamson Charitable Trust *400*
WOMANKIND Worldwide *233*
Working for a Charity *15*
World Development Movement *234*
World Emergency Relief *235*
World ORT *235*
World Service Enquiry – *see Christians Abroad*
World Trust *428*
World University Service UK *236*
World Vision UK *237*
Worldaware *239*
WorldShare *240*
WORLDwrite *240*
Matthews Wrightson Charity Trust *429*
WUS – *see World University Service UK*
Wycliffe Bible Translators *241*

Y

Y Care International *242*

Z

Zephyr Charitable Trust *430*
Zochonis Charitable Trust *430*

Further reading and information

The following is a selection of publications available from the Directory of Social Change (DSC). Prices were correct at the time of writing, but may be subject to change. Please also note that new editions of DSC directories are usually published every two years. For up-to-date information and advice, please contact:

Directory of Social Change, 24 Stephenson Way, London NW1 2DP

website: www.dsc.org.uk

Publications tel: 020 7209 5151; fax: 020 7209 5049; e-mail: info@dsc.org.uk

Fundraising directories and CD-ROMs

The following directories give detailed information, including independent commentary, on the largest UK trusts (respectively, the top 300; the next 700; and the next 400 plus major trusts in Northern Ireland, Scotland and Wales):

A Guide to the Major Trusts, volume 1, 8th edition, Luke FitzHerbert and Gavin Richards, DSC 2001, £19.95

A Guide to the Major Trusts, volume 2, 5th edition, Louise Walker and Alan French, DSC 2001, £19.95

A Guide to the Major Trusts, volume 3, Sarah Harland and Louise Walker, DSC 2000, £17.95

Or you can find less detailed information, but on 2,500 trusts, in:

The Directory of Grant Making Trusts 2001–02, 17th edition, Charities Aid Foundation (CAF) 2001, £75

The most comprehensive coverage of all is provided by:

The Grant-making Trusts CD-ROM, CAF/DSC 2001, £129.25 (including VAT)

If you are trying to raise money or other support from the UK corporate sector, you can refer to either a directory or a CD:

The Guide to UK Company Giving, 3rd edition, John Smyth, DSC 2000, £25

The CD-ROM Company Giving Guide, 2nd edition, DSC 2000, £99.88 (including VAT)

Other funding guides

A Guide to Funding from Government Departments & Agencies, 2nd edition, Susan Forrester & Anthony Stenson, DSC 2001, £18.95

Directory of American Grantmakers, Chapel & York 2000, £45

Fundraising from America, Chapel & York 1999, £36.50

Your Way through the Labyrinth: a guide to European Union funding for NGOs, 7th edition, ECAS 2001, £30

Fundraising and other handbooks

A popular title that provides practical advice on all aspects of fundraising for charity is:

The Complete Fundraising Handbook, 4th edition, Nina Botting and Michael Norton, DSC 2001, £16.95

Two other books have been specifically written with voluntary organisations in the developing world in mind:

Getting Started in Fundraising, Michael Norton and Murray Culshaw, Sage Publications (India) 2000, £7

The WorldWide Fundraiser's Handbook, Michael Norton, DSC 1996, £12.95

Other handbooks include:

Building a Fundraising Database Using your PC, 2nd edition, Peter Flory, DSC/CAF 2001, £12.95

The Campaigning Handbook, 2nd edition, Mark Lattimer, DSC 2000, £15.95

Find the Funds, Christopher Carnie, DSC/CAF 2000, £12.95

Fundraising from Grant-making Trusts and Foundations, Karen Gilchrist and Margo Horsley, DSC/CAF 2000, £10.95

Good Ideas for Raising Serious Money, Sarah Passingham, DSC 1995, £9.95

Legacy Fundraising, 2nd edition, ed. Sebastian Wilberforce, CAF/DSC/ICFM 2001, £19.95

Looking after your Donors, Karen Gilchrist, DSC/CAF 2000, £10.95

Organising Local Events, 2nd edition, Sarah Passingham, DSC 1995, £9.95

Organising Special Events for Fundraising and Campaigning, John F. Gray and Stephen Elsden, DSC/CAF 2000, £10.95

Tried and Tested Ideas for Raising Money Locally, 2nd edition, Sarah Passingham, DSC 1997, £9.95

Writing Better Fundraising Applications, 2nd edition, Michael Norton and Mike Eastwood, DSC 1997, £12.95